Parametric Modeling

with UGS NX6

Randy H. Shih
Oregon Institute of Technology

ISBN: 978-1-58503-486-4

SDC PUBLICATIONS
Mission, Kansas

Schroff Development Corporation
P.O. Box 1334
Mission KS 66222
(913) 262-2664
www.SDCpublications.com

Shih, Randy H.
Parametric modeling with UGS NX 6/
Randy H. Shih

ISBN 978-1-58503-486-4

Printed and bound in the United States of America.

Preface

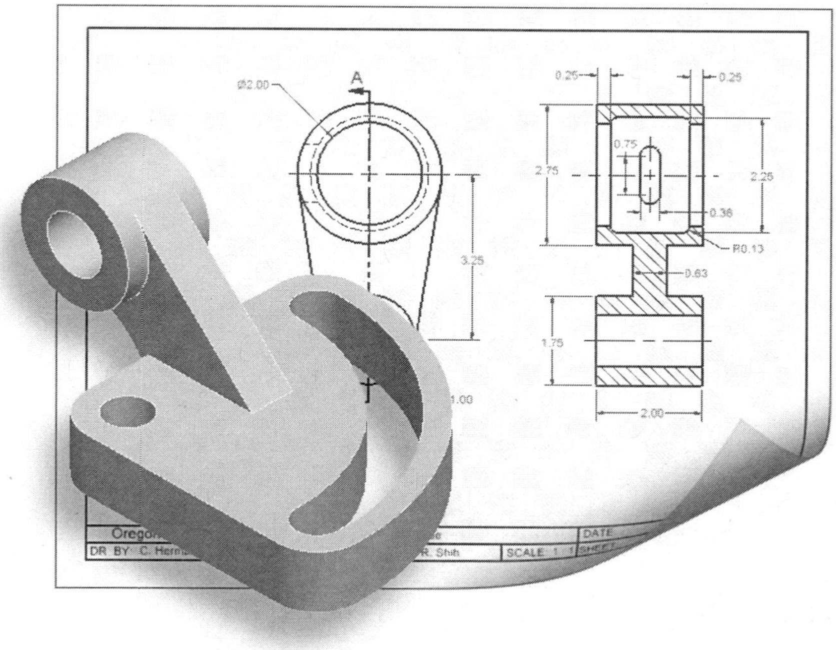

The primary goal of ***Parametric Modeling with UGS NX 6*** is to introduce the aspects of designing with **Solid Modeling** and **Parametric Modeling**. This text is intended to be used as a practical training guide for students and professionals. This text uses *UGS NX 6* as the modeling tool and the chapters proceed in a pedagogical fashion to guide you from constructing basic solid models to building intelligent mechanical designs, creating multi-view drawings and assembly models. This text takes a hands-on, exercise-intensive approach to all the important *Parametric Modeling* techniques and concepts. This textbook contains a series of ten tutorial style lessons designed to introduce beginning CAD users to ***UGS NX***. This text is also helpful to *UGS NX* users upgrading from a previous release of the software. The solid modeling techniques and concepts discussed in this text are also applicable to other parametric feature-based CAD packages. The basic premise of this book is that the more designs you create using *UGS NX*, the better you learn the software. With this in mind, each lesson introduces a new set of commands and concepts, building on previous lessons. This book does not attempt to cover all of *UGS NX*'s features, only to provide an introduction to the software. It is intended to help you establish a good basis for exploring and growing in the exciting field of **Computer Aided Engineering**.

Acknowledgments

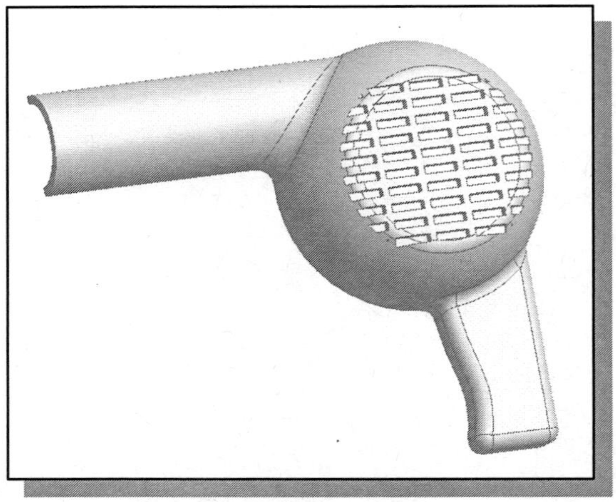

This book would not have been possible without a great deal of support. First, special thanks to two great teachers, Prof. George R. Schade of University of Nebraska-Lincoln and Mr. Denwu Lee, who showed me the fundamentals, the intrigue, and the sheer fun of Computer Aided Engineering.

The effort and support of the editorial and production staff of Schroff Development Corporation is gratefully acknowledged. I would especially like to thank Stephen Schroff and Mary Schmidt for their support and helpful suggestions during this project.

I am grateful that the Mechanical Engineering Technology Department of Oregon Institute of Technology has provided me with an excellent environment in which to pursue my interests in teaching and research. . And I would also like to especially thank Mr. Mark H. Lawry of UGS for his encouragement, suggestions and support.

Finally, truly unbounded thanks are due to my wife Hsiu-Ling and our daughter Casandra for their understanding and encouragement throughout this project.

Randy H. Shih
Klamath Falls, Oregon
Summer, 2008

Table of Contents

Chapter 3
Constructive Solid Geometry Concepts

Chapter 4
Model History Tree

Chapter 5
Parametric Constraints Fundamentals

Chapter 6
Geometric Construction Tools

Chapter 7
Parent/Child Relationships

Chapter 8
Part Drawings and Associative Functionality

Chapter 9
Datum Features and Auxiliary Views

Chapter 10
Symmetrical Features in Designs

Chapter 11
Advanced 3D Construction Tools

Chapter 12
Assembly Modeling - Putting It All Together

Notes:

Chapter 1
Introduction – Getting Started

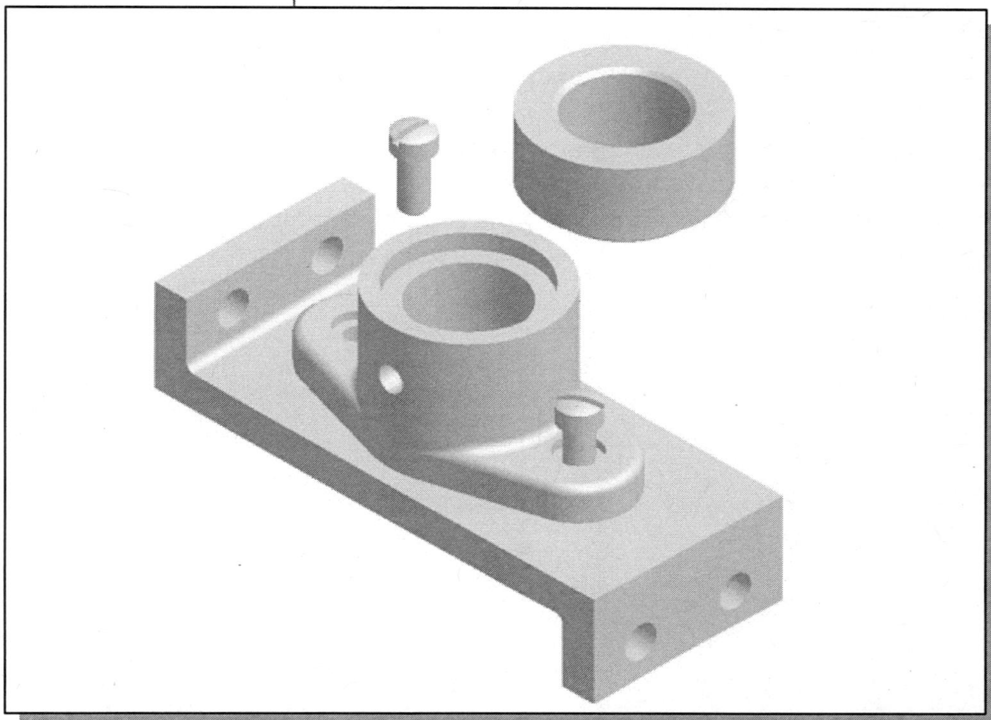

Learning Objectives

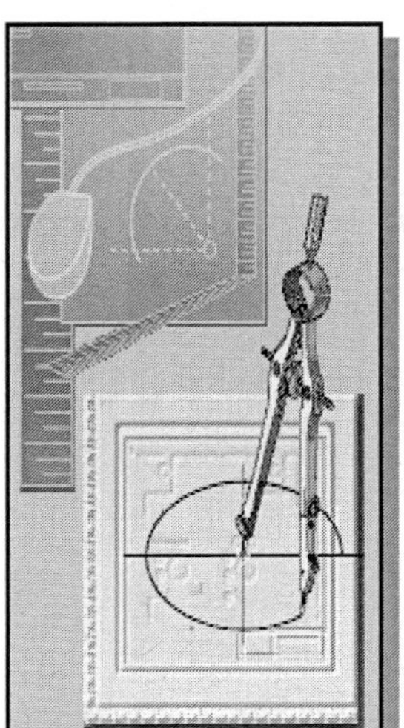

- **Development of Computer Geometric Modeling**
- **Feature-Based Parametric Modeling**
- **Startup Options and Units Setup**
- **UGS NX Screen Layout**
- **User Interface & Mouse Buttons**
- **UGS NX On-Line Help**

Introduction

The rapid changes in the field of **Computer Aided Engineering** (CAE) have brought exciting advances in the engineering community. Recent advances have made the long-sought goal of **concurrent engineering** closer to a reality. CAE has become the core of concurrent engineering and is aimed at reducing design time, producing prototypes faster, and achieving higher product quality. ***UGS NX*** is an integrated package of mechanical computer aided engineering software tools developed by *UGS Corporation*. ***UGS NX*** is a tool that facilitates a concurrent engineering approach to the design and stress-analysis of mechanical engineering products. The computer models can also be used by manufacturing equipment such as machining centers, lathes, mills, or rapid prototyping machines to manufacture the product. In this text, we will be dealing only with the solid modeling modules used for part design and part drawings.

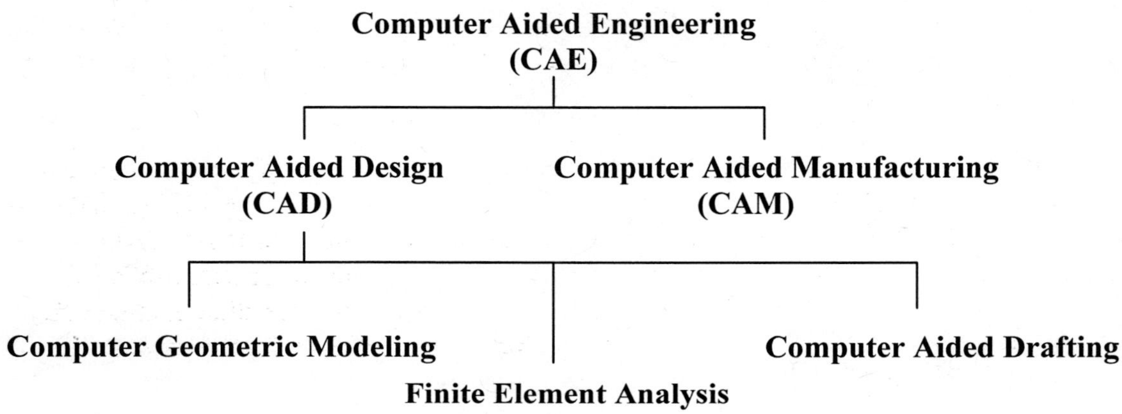

Development of Computer Geometric Modeling

Computer geometric modeling is a relatively new technology, and its rapid expansion in the last fifty years is truly amazing. Computer-modeling technology has advanced along with the development of computer hardware. The first generation CAD programs, developed in the 1950s, were mostly non-interactive; CAD users were required to create program-codes to generate the desired two-dimensional (2D) geometric shapes. Initially, the development of CAD technology occurred mostly in academic research facilities. The Massachusetts Institute of Technology, Carnegie-Mellon University, and Cambridge University were the leading pioneers at that time. The interest in CAD technology spread quickly and several major industry companies, such as General Motors, Lockheed, McDonnell, IBM, and Ford Motor Co., participated in the development of interactive CAD programs in the 1960s. Usage of CAD systems was primarily in the automotive industry, aerospace industry, and government agencies that developed their own programs for their specific needs. The 1960s also marked the beginning of the development of finite element analysis methods for computer stress analysis and computer aided manufacturing for generating machine toolpaths.

The 1970s are generally viewed as the years of the most significant progress in the development of computer hardware, namely the invention and development of **microprocessors**. With the improvement in computing power, new types of 3D CAD programs that were user-friendly and interactive became reality. CAD technology quickly expanded from very simple **computer aided drafting** to very complex **computer aided design**. The use of 2D and 3D wireframe modelers was accepted as the leading edge technology that could increase productivity in industry. The developments of surface modeling and solid modeling technologies were taking shape by the late 1970s, but the high cost of computer hardware and programming slowed the development of such technology. During this period, the available CAD systems all required room-sized mainframe computers that were extremely expensive.

In the 1980s, improvements in computer hardware brought the power of mainframes to the desktop at less cost and with more accessibility to the general public. By the mid-1980s, CAD technology had become the main focus of a variety of manufacturing industries and was very competitive with traditional design/drafting methods. It was during this period of time that 3D solid modeling technology had major advancements, which boosted the usage of CAE technology in industry.

The introduction of the *feature-based parametric solid modeling* approach, at the end of the 1980s, elevated CAD/CAM/CAE technology to a new level. In the 1990s, CAD programs evolved into powerful design/manufacturing/management tools. CAD technology has come a long way, and during these years of development, modeling schemes progressed from two-dimensional (2D) wireframe to three-dimensional (3D) wireframe, to surface modeling, to solid modeling and, finally, to feature-based parametric solid modeling.

The first generation CAD packages were simply 2D **computer aided drafting** programs, basically the electronic equivalents of the drafting board. For typical models, the use of this type of program would require that several to many views of the objects be created individually as they would be on the drafting board. The 3D designs remained in the designer's mind, not in the computer database. Mental translations of 3D objects to 2D views are required throughout the use of these packages. Although such systems have some advantages over traditional board drafting, they are still tedious and labor intensive. The need for the development of 3D modelers came quite naturally, given the limitations of the 2D drafting packages.

The development of three-dimensional modeling schemes started with three-dimensional (3D) wireframes. Wireframe models are models consisting of points and edges, which are straight lines connecting between appropriate points. The edges of wireframe models are used, similar to lines in 2D drawings, to represent transitions of surfaces and features. The use of lines and points is also a very economical way to represent 3D designs.

The development of the 3D wireframe modeler was a major leap in the area of computer geometric modeling. The computer database in the 3D wireframe modeler contains the locations of all the points in space coordinates, and it is typically sufficient to create just one model rather than multiple views of the same model. This single 3D model can then be viewed from any direction as needed. Most 3D wireframe modelers allow the user to create projected lines/edges of 3D wireframe models. In comparison to other types of 3D modelers, the 3D wireframe modelers require very little computing power and generally can be used to achieve reasonably good representations of 3D models. However, because surface definition is not part of a wireframe model, all wireframe images have the inherent problem of ambiguity. Two examples of such ambiguity are illustrated.

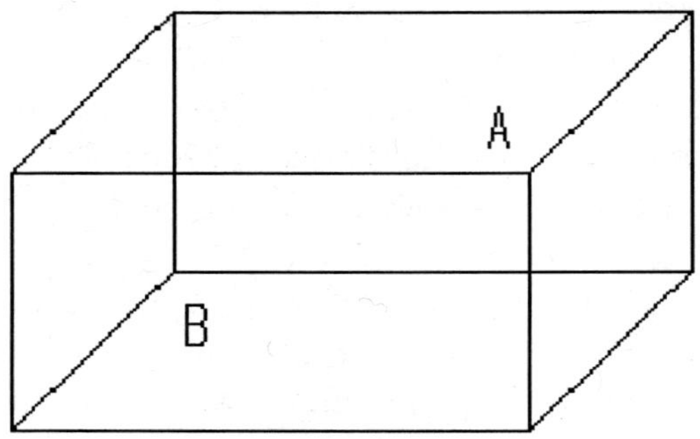

Wireframe Ambiguity: Which corner is in front, A or B?

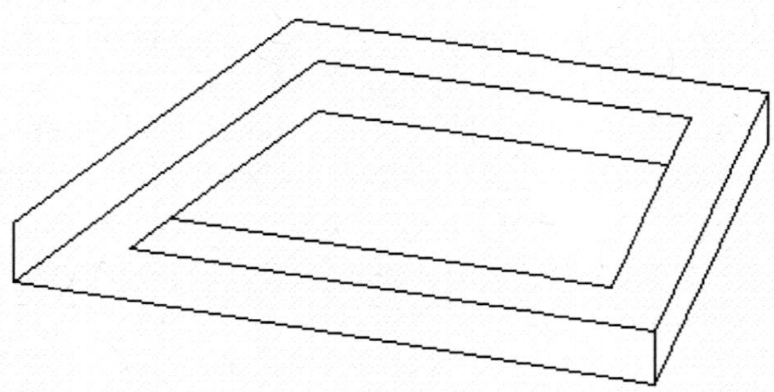

A non-realizable object: Wireframe models contain no surface definitions.

Surface modeling is the logical development in computer geometry modeling to follow the 3D wireframe modeling scheme by organizing and grouping edges that define polygonal surfaces. Surface modeling describes the part's surfaces but not its interiors. Designers are still required to interactively examine surface models to insure that the various surfaces on a model are contiguous throughout. Many of the concepts used in 3D wireframe and surface modelers are incorporated in the solid modeling scheme, but it is solid modeling that offers the most advantages as a design tool.

In the solid modeling presentation scheme, the solid definitions include nodes, edges, and surfaces, and it is a complete and unambiguous mathematical representation of a precisely enclosed and filled volume. Unlike the surface modeling method, solid modelers start with a solid or use topology rules to guarantee that all of the surfaces are stitched together properly. Two predominant methods for representing solid models are **constructive solid geometry** (CSG) representation and **boundary representation** (B-rep).

The CSG representation method can be defined as the combination of 3D solid primitives. What constitutes a "primitive" varies somewhat with the software but typically includes a rectangular prism, a cylinder, a cone, a wedge, and a sphere. Most solid modelers also allow the user to define additional primitives, which are shapes typically formed by the basic shapes. The underlying concept of the CSG representation method is very straightforward; we simply **add** or **subtract** one primitive from another. The CSG approach is also known as the machinist's approach, as it can be used to simulate the manufacturing procedures for creating the 3D object.

In the B-rep representation method, objects are represented in terms of their spatial boundaries. This method defines the points, edges, and surfaces of a volume, and/or issues commands that sweep or rotate a defined face into a third dimension to form a solid. The object is then made up of the unions of these surfaces that completely and precisely enclose a volume.

By the 1980s, a new paradigm called *concurrent engineering* had emerged. With concurrent engineering, designers, design engineers, analysts, manufacturing engineers, and management engineers all work together closely right from the initial stages of the design. In this way, all aspects of the design can be evaluated and any potential problems can be identified right from the start and throughout the design process. Using the principles of concurrent engineering, a new type of computer modeling technique appeared. The technique is known as the *feature-based parametric modeling technique*. The key advantage of the *feature-based parametric modeling technique* is its capability to produce very flexible designs. Changes can be made easily and design alternatives can be evaluated with minimum effort. Various software packages offer different approaches to feature-based parametric modeling, yet the end result is a flexible design defined by its design variables and parametric features.

Feature-Based Parametric Modeling

One of the key elements in the *UGS NX* solid modeling software is its use of the **feature-based parametric modeling technique**. The feature-based parametric modeling approach has elevated solid modeling technology to the level of a very powerful design tool. Parametric modeling automates the design and revision procedures by the use of parametric features. Parametric features control the model geometry by the use of design variables. The word ***parametric*** means that the geometric definitions of the design, such as dimensions, can be varied at any time during the design process. Features are predefined parts or construction tools for which users define the key parameters. A part is described as a sequence of engineering features, which can be modified/changed at any time. The concept of parametric features makes modeling more closely match the actual design-manufacturing process than the mathematics of a solid modeling program. In parametric modeling, models and drawings are updated automatically when the design is refined.

Parametric modeling offers many benefits:

- **We begin with simple, conceptual models with minimal detail; this approach conforms to the design philosophy of "shape before size."**
- **Geometric constraints, dimensional constraints, and relational parametric equations can be used to capture design intent.**
- **The ability to update an entire system, including parts, assemblies and drawings after changing one parameter of complex designs.**
- **We can quickly explore and evaluate different design variations and alternatives to determine the best design.**
- **Existing design data can be reused to create new designs.**
- **Quick design turn-around.**

The feature-based parametric modeling technique enables the designer to incorporate the original **design intent** into the construction of the model, and the individual features control the geometry in the event of a design change. As features are modified, the system updates the entire part by re-linking the individual features of the model.

UGS NX 6 is a digital product development system that is designed to help companies transform the product lifecycle. With the industry's broadest suite of integrated, fully associative CAD/CAM/CAE applications, *UGS NX 6* can be used to cover the full range of development processes in product design, manufacturing and simulation.

UGS NX 6 is the sixth release, with many added features and enhancements, of the original *UGS NX* software produced by UGS Corporation. *UGS* is also considered as the industry leader in product lifecycle management (PLM), which empowers businesses to make unified, information-driven decisions at every stage in the product lifecycle.

Getting Started with *UGS NX*

- *UGS NX* is composed of several application software modules (these modules are called *applications*), all sharing a common database. In this text, the main concentration is placed on the solid modeling modules used for part design. The general procedures required in creating solid models, engineering drawings, and assemblies are illustrated.

  How to start *UGS NX* depends on the type of workstation and the particular software configuration you are using. With most *Windows* systems, you may select **UGS NX** on the *Start* menu or select the **UGS NX** icon on the desktop. Consult your instructor or technical support personnel if you have difficulty starting the software. The program takes a while to load, so be patient.

  The tutorials in this text are based on the assumption that you are using *UGS NX's* default settings. If your system has been customized for other uses, contact your technical support personnel to restore the default software configuration.

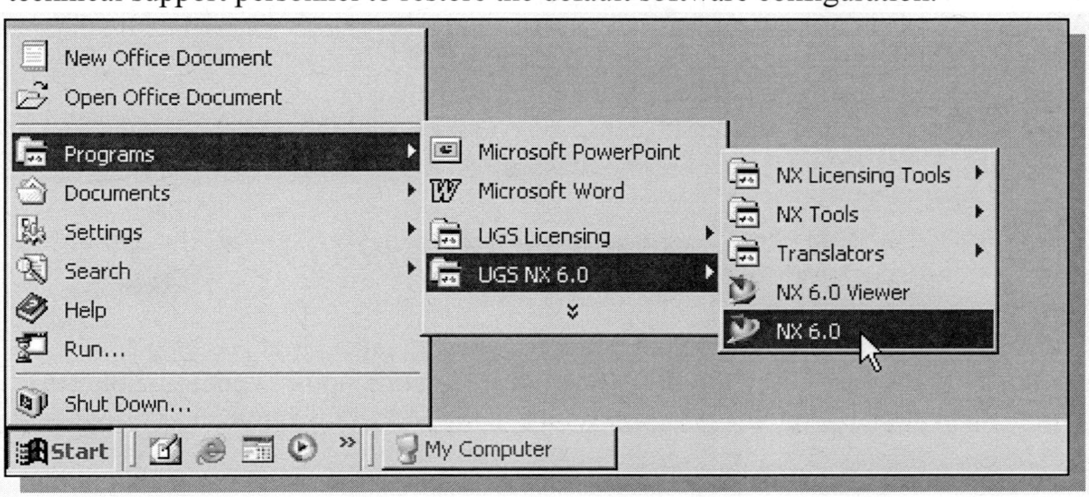

The *UGS NX* Main Window

Once the program is loaded into the memory, the *NX 6 main window* appears at the center of the screen.

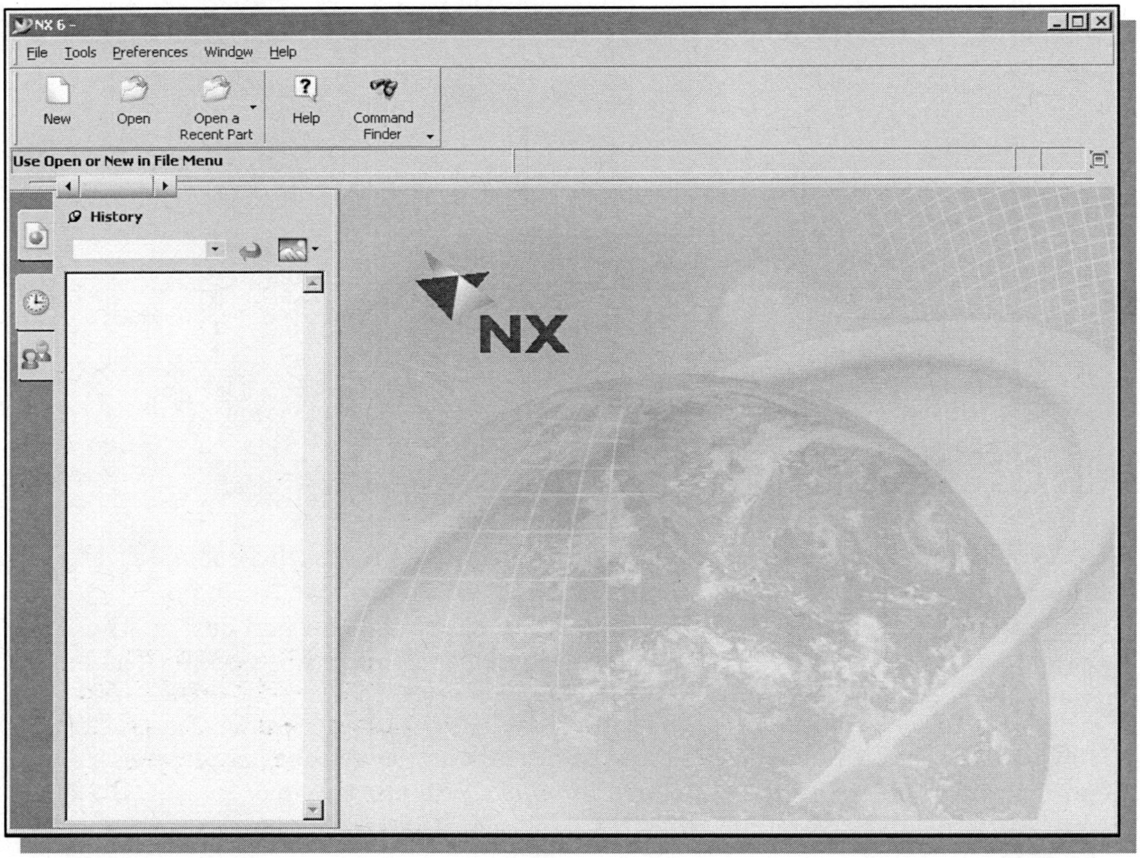

Note that very few options are available in the current state of the main window. This is because *NX* uses three **work area concepts** called the "**No Part**" state, "**Applications**", and "**Task Environments**".

No Part State: When you start *NX*, it opens in a default environment called the "No Part" state. This environment is similar to standing in the lobby of an office building, in the sense that you have entered the building, but you have not yet entered a specific room in the building. From the "No Part" state, you can access all the other rooms in the building or, in this case, all the other applications in *NX*.

Applications: To begin work, first open a part file. Then, you can start the application you want to use, such as Modeling or Drafting.

Task Environments: From some applications, you can enter what is called a Task Environment. For example, from the Modeling application you can enter the Sketcher. When done using the Sketcher, you can return to the Modeling application.

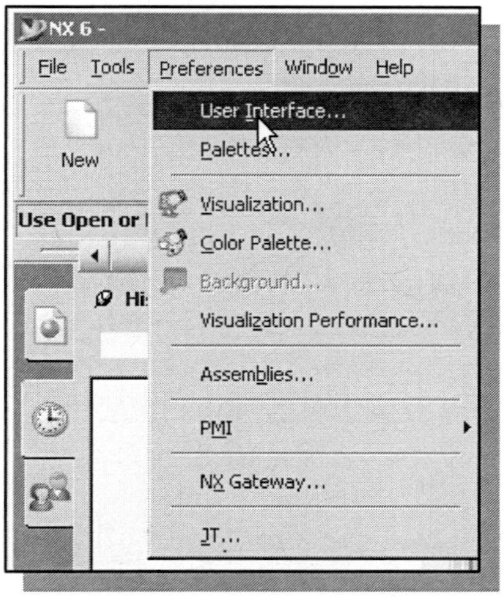

❖ Note that only general setup options are available under the No-Part state.

❖ We will next switch to the *NX* Application work area.

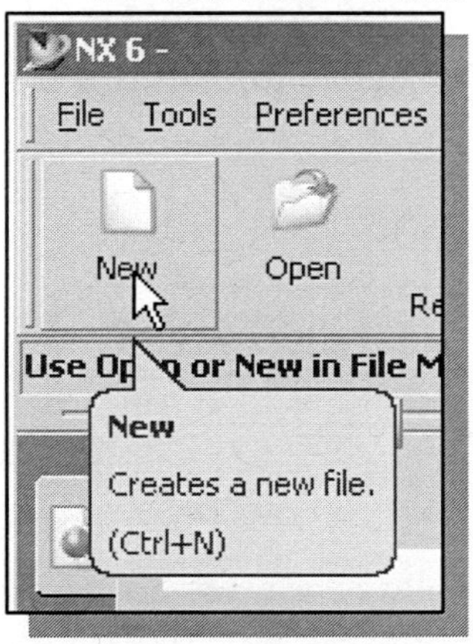

1. Select the **New** icon with a single click of the left-mouse-button in the *What to Do* dialog box.

➢ The ***File New*** dialog box will appear on the screen with three option tabs: **Model**, **Drawing** and **Simulation**. Note that the default is set to Model and we can create a new model using any of the pre-defined templates.

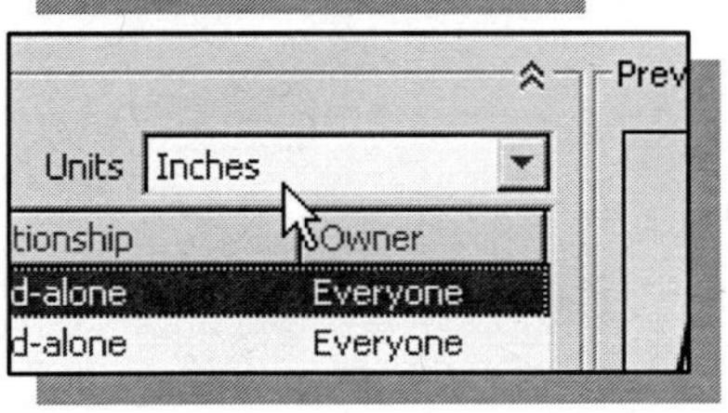

2. Select the **Inches** units as shown in the window. When starting a new CAD file, the first thing we should do is to choose the units we would like to use.

3. Select **Blank** in the *Template list*. Note that the *Blank* template contains no pre-defined settings.

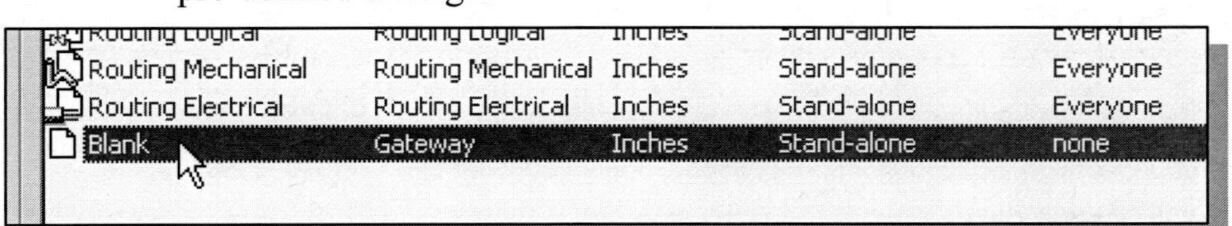

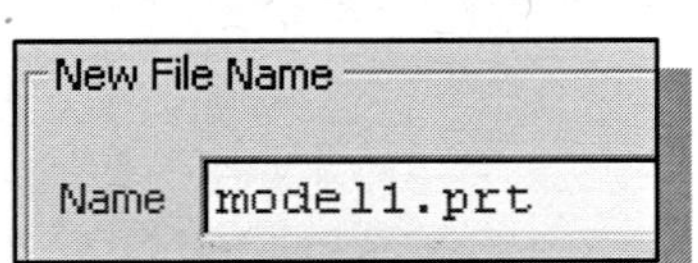

4. In the *New File Name* section, note that **model1.prt** is the default *File Name*.

5. Click **OK** to accept the settings and proceed with the new file command.

UGS NX Screen Layout

Upon opening an existing part or creating a new part in the *NX No Part* state, we now entered the *NX **Gateway*** application. The *NX Gateway* allows us to perform the general functions, such as open existing part files, create new part files, save part files, plot drawings and screen layouts, import and export various types of files, just like in the no part state. It also provides controls to *view display operations*, *screen layout and layer functions*, *WCS manipulation*, *object information and analysis*, and access to online help. Gateway is the gateway to all other interactive applications, and is the first application we enter in *NX*. We can return to *Gateway* at any time from the other applications in *NX* by selecting it from the *Application* pull-down menu.

The default *NX* application screen contains the *pull-down* menus, the *Standard* toolbar, the *View* toolbar, the *Utility* toolbar, the *Graphics* area, the *Selection toolbar*, the *Snap point* toolbar and the *Resource Bars*. A line of quick text appears next to the icon as you move the *mouse cursor* over different icons. You may resize the *UGS NX* window by click and drag at the edges of the window, or relocate the window by click and drag at the window title area.

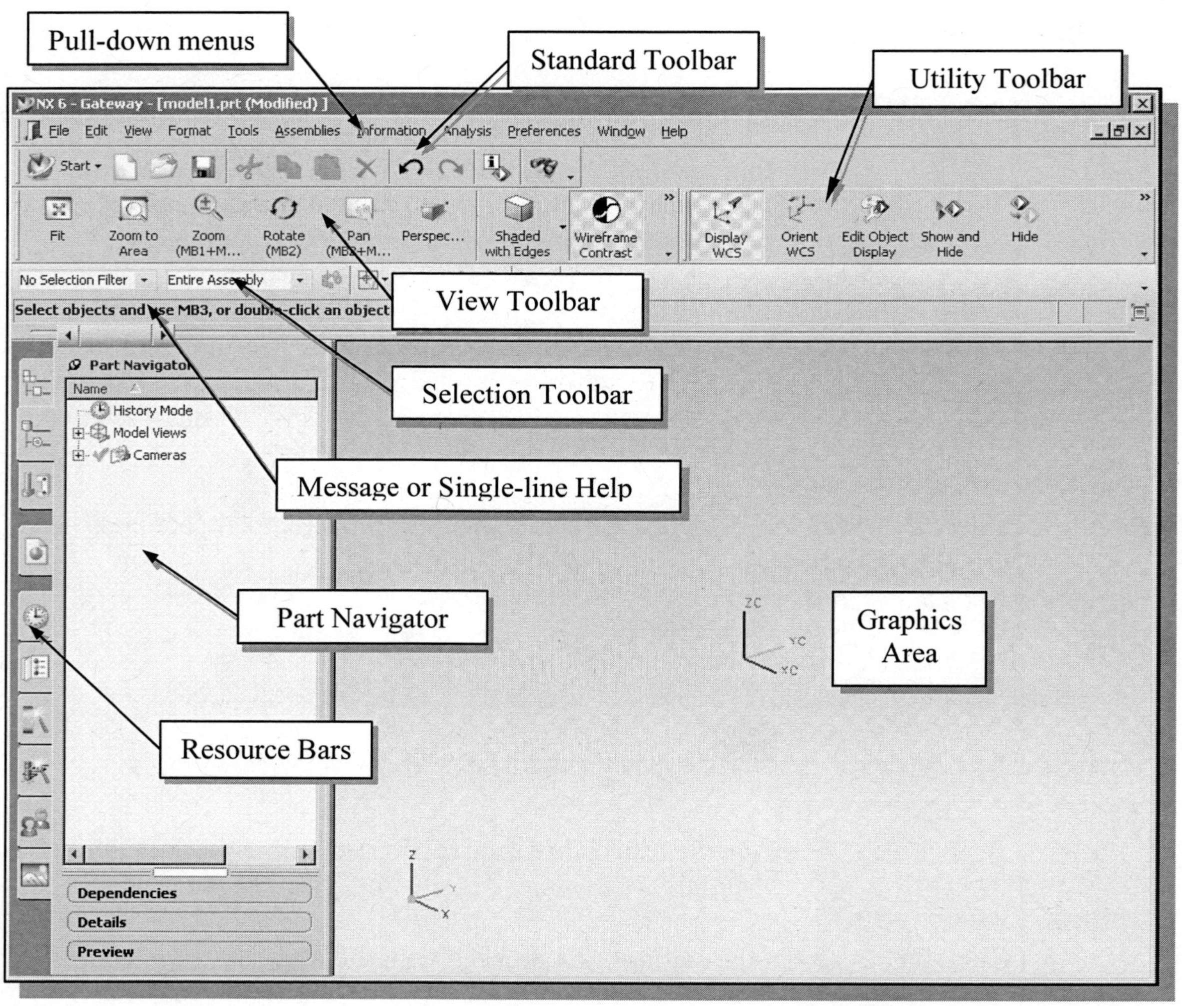

- **Pull-down Menus**

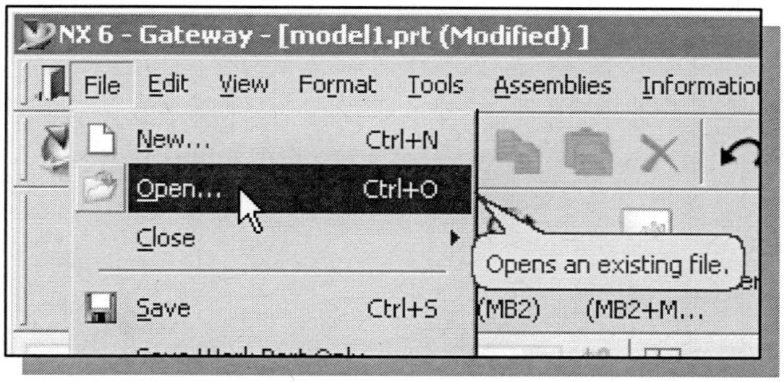

The *pull-down* menus at the top of the main window contain operations that you can use for all modes of the system.

- **Standard Toolbar**

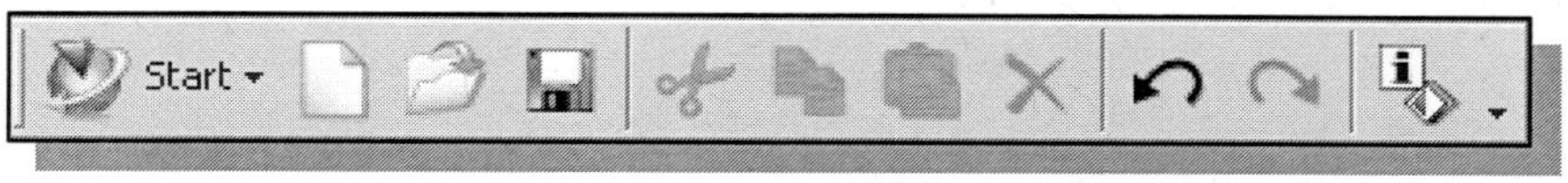

The *Standard* toolbar at the top of the screen window allows us quick access to frequently used commands. For example, the file-related commands, such as Switching Applications, New Part, and Save.

- **View Toolbar**

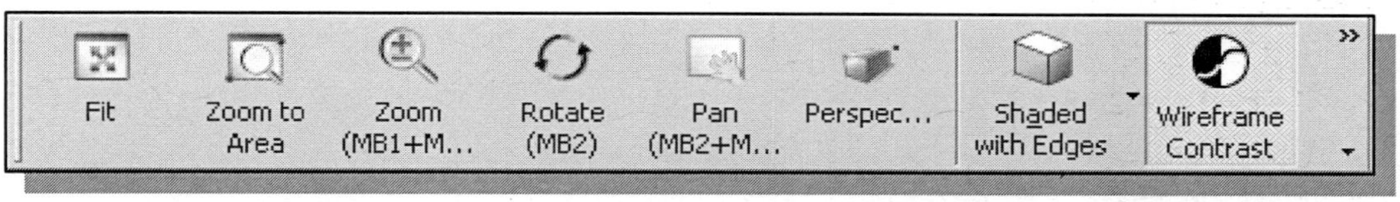

The *View* toolbar allows us quick access to frequently used view-related commands, such as Zoom, Rotate, Creating Section View and Shaded Solids.

- **Utility Toolbar**

The *Utility* toolbar allows us quick access to *WCS manipulation*, such as WCS display, *Move WCS*, and control of the *Object display options*.

- **Additional Tools**

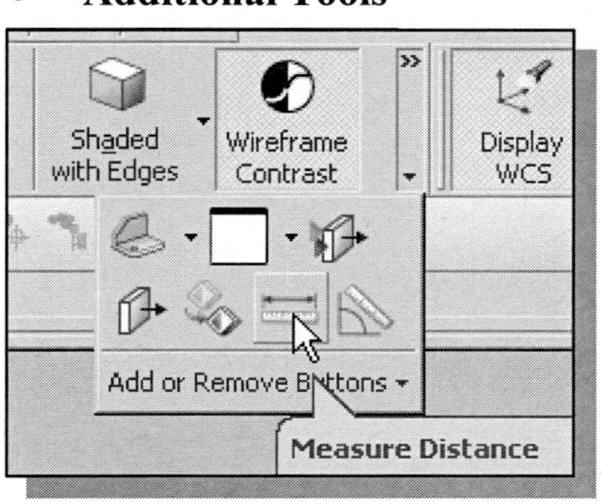

The double-arrow at the end of each toolbar can be used to access the additional tools that are available.

- **Selection Toolbar**

The *Selection* toolbar provides tools for quick selection of 2D/3D features and parts.

- **Message and Status Bar**

The *Message and Status Bar* area shows a single-line help when the cursor is on top of an icon. This area also displays information pertinent to the active operation.

- **Part Navigator**

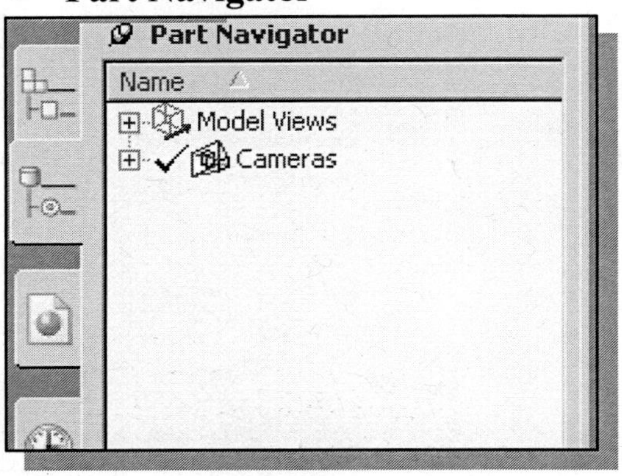

The *Part Navigator* area shows information regarding the current active model. This area is used by the *Resource Bars* options described below.

- **Resource Bars**

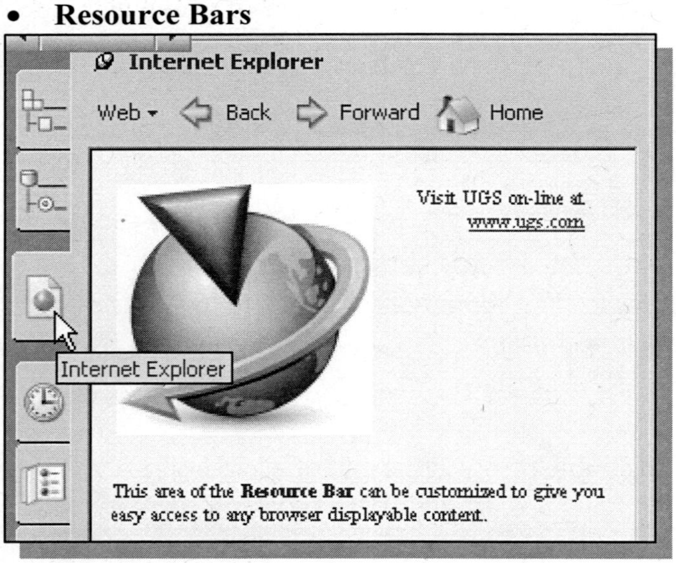

➤ The *Resource Bars* provide three groups of resources, ***Navigators***, ***Explorers*** and ***Palettes***, for multiple functions such as managing access to features and editing, and providing alternate access to functions in the *Context* menu.

➤ On your own, click on the **Internet Explorer** tab and read the general descriptions of the available options for using the *Resource Bars*.

Mouse Buttons

UGS NX utilizes the mouse buttons extensively. In learning *UGS NX*'s interactive environment, it is important to understand the basic functions of the mouse buttons. It is highly recommended that you use a mouse or a tablet with *UGS NX* since the package uses the buttons for various functions.

- **Left mouse button (MB1)**
  The **left-mouse-button** is used for most operations, such as selecting menus and icons, or picking graphic entities. One click of the button is used to select icons, menus and form entries, and to pick graphic items.

- **Middle mouse button/wheel (MB2)**
  The middle-mouse-button/wheel can be used to **Rotate** (hold down the wheel button and drag the mouse) or **Zoom** (rotate the wheel) in realtime.

- **Right mouse button (MB3)**
  The **right-mouse-button** is used to bring up additional available options. The software also utilizes the **right-mouse-button** as the same as the **ENTER** key, and is often used to accept the default setting to a prompt or to end a process.

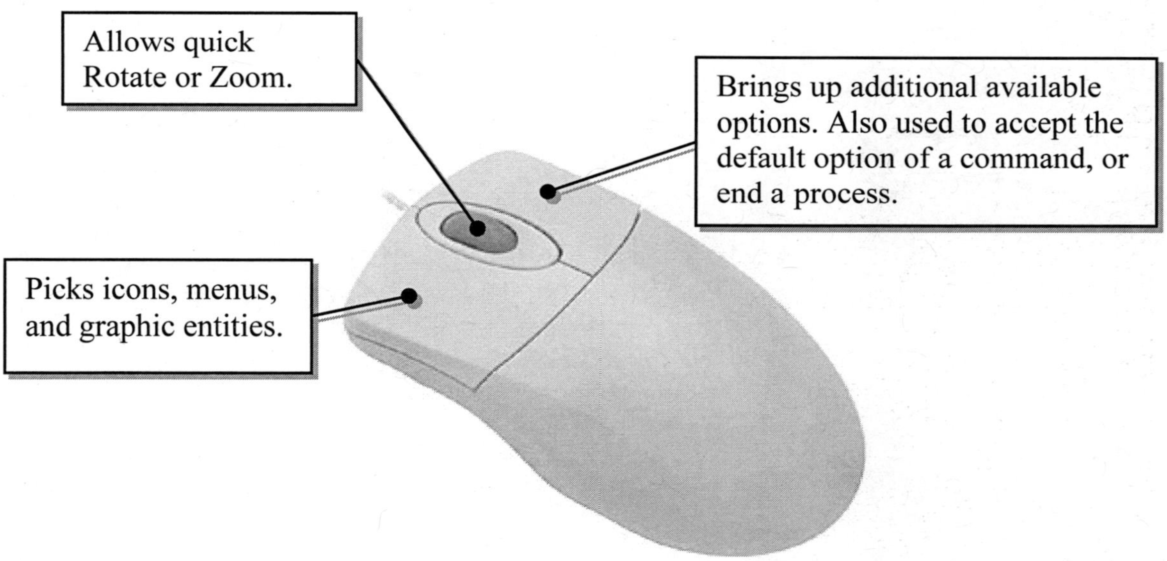

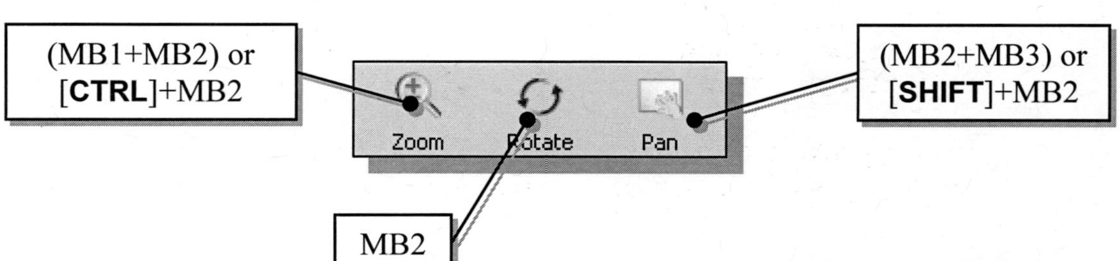

[Esc] – Canceling Commands

The [**Esc**] key is used to cancel a command in *UGS NX*. The [**Esc**] key is located near the top-left corner of the keyboard. Sometimes, it may be necessary to press the [**Esc**] key twice to cancel a command; it depends on where we are in the command sequence. For some commands, the [**Esc**] key is used to exit the command.

On-Line Help

❖ Several types of on-line help are available at any time during an *UGS NX* session. *UGS NX* provides many on-line help functions, such as:

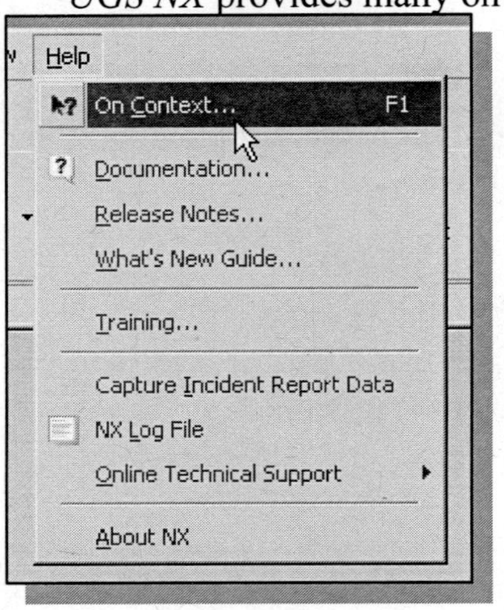

- The **Help** menu: Click on the **Help** option in the pull-down menu to access the *UGS NX* ***Help*** **menu system**.
- Resource Bar: The *Resource Bar* provides quick access to the *Help* menu.
- Help quick key: Press the [**F1**] key to access the ***On-On Context Help*** **system**.

Leaving *UGS NX*

➢ To leave *UGS NX*, use the left-mouse-button and click on **File** at the top of the *UGS NX* screen window, then choose **Exit** from the pull-down menu.

Creating a CAD Files Folder

It is a good practice to create a separate folder to store your CAD files. You should not save your CAD files in the same folder where the *UGS NX* application is located. It is much easier to organize and backup your project files if they are in a separate folder. Making folders within this folder for different types of projects will help you organize your CAD files even further. When creating CAD files in *UGS NX*, it is strongly recommended that you *save* your CAD files on the hard drive.

➢ To create a new folder in the *Windows* environment:

1. In *My Computer*, or start *Windows Explorer* under the *Start* menu, open the folder in which you want to create a new folder.

2. On the **File** menu, point to **New**, and then click **Folder**. The new folder appears with a temporary name.

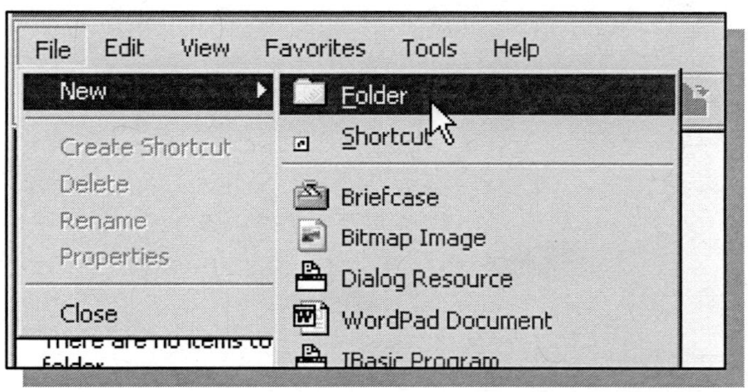

3. Type a name for the new folder, and then press **ENTER**.

Notes:

Chapter 2
Parametric Modeling Fundamentals

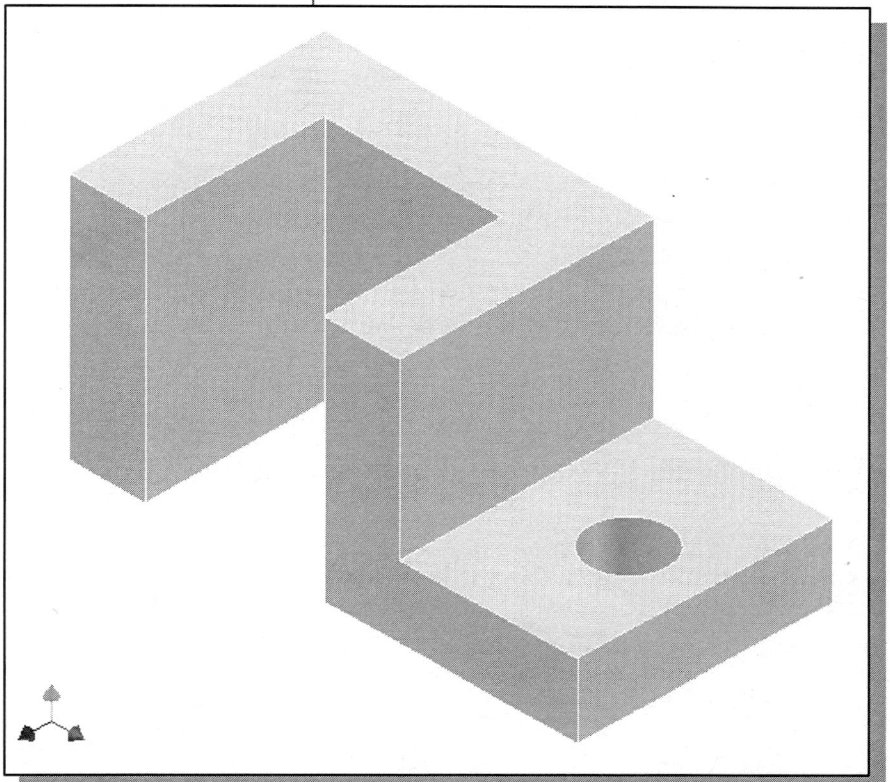

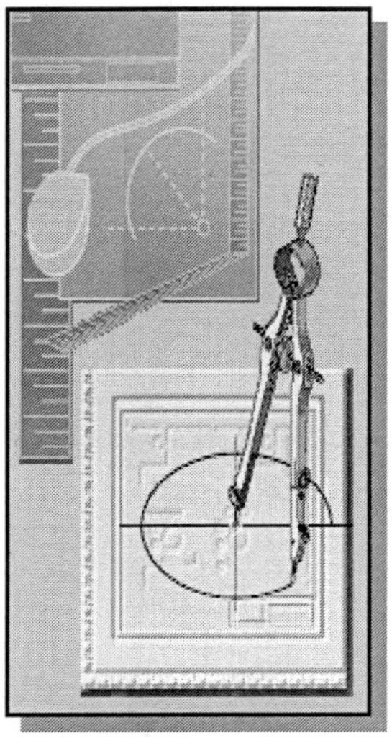

Learning Objectives

- ♦ Create Simple Extruded Solid Models
- ♦ Understand the Basic Parametric Modeling Procedure
- ♦ Create 2-D Sketches
- ♦ Understand the "Shape before Size" Approach
- ♦ Use the Dynamic Viewing Commands
- ♦ Create and Edit Parametric Dimensions

Introduction

The **feature-based parametric modeling** technique enables the designer to incorporate the original **design intent** into the construction of the model. The word ***parametric*** means the geometric definitions of the design, such as dimensions, can be varied at any time in the design process. Parametric modeling is accomplished by identifying and creating the key features of the design with the aid of computer software. The design variables, described in the sketches and described as parametric relations, can then be used to quickly modify/update the design.

In *UGS NX*, the parametric part modeling process involves the following steps:

1. **Set up *Units* and *Part name*.**

2. **Determine the type of the base feature, the first solid feature, of the design. Note that Extrude, Revolve, or Sweep operations are the most common types of base features.**

3. **Create a rough two-dimensional sketch of the basic shape of the base feature of the design.**

4. **Apply/modify constraints and dimensions to the two-dimensional sketch.**

5. **Transform the parametric two-dimensional sketch into a 3D solid.**

6. **Add additional parametric features by identifying feature relations and complete the design.**

7. **Perform analyses/simulations, such as finite element analysis (FEA) or cutter path generation (CNC), on the computer model and refine the design as needed.**

8. **Document the design by creating the desired 2D/3D drawings.**

The approach of creating two-dimensional sketches of the three-dimensional features is an effective way to construct solid models. Many designs are in fact the same shape in one direction. Computer input and output devices we use today are largely two-dimensional in nature, which makes this modeling technique quite practical. This method also conforms to the design process that helps the designer with conceptual design along with the capability to capture the ***design intent***. Most engineers and designers can relate to the experience of making rough sketches on restaurant napkins to convey conceptual design ideas. *UGS NX* provides many powerful modeling and design-tools, and there are many different approaches to accomplishing modeling tasks. The basic principle of **feature-based modeling** is to build models by adding simple features one at a time. In this chapter, the general parametric part modeling procedure is illustrated; a very simple solid model with extruded features is used to introduce the *UGS NX* user interface.

The *Adjuster* design

Step 1. Starting *UGS NX* and Units setup

1. Select the **UGS NX** option on the *Start* menu or select the **UGS NX** icon on the desktop to start *UGS NX*. The *UGS NX* main window will appear on the screen.

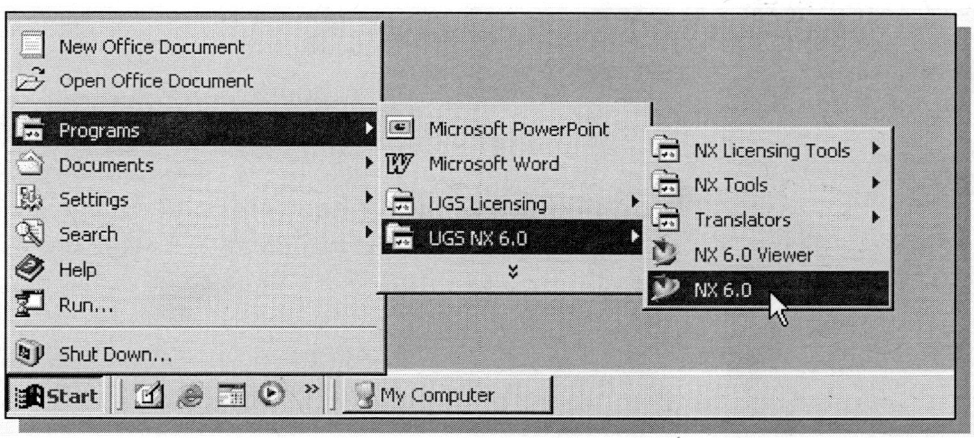

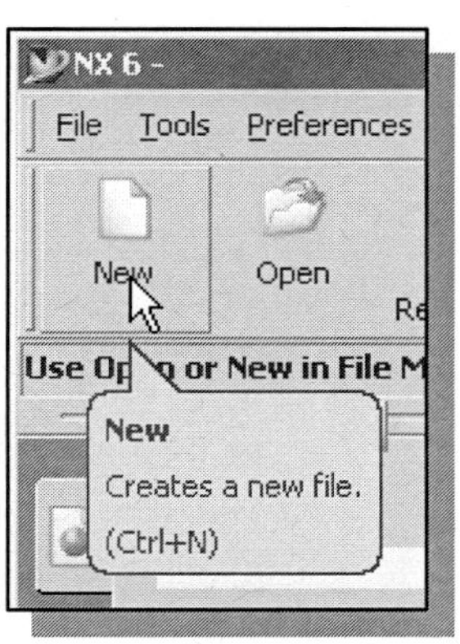

2. Select the **New** icon with a single click of the left-mouse-button (MB1) in the *Standard* toolbar area.

➢ The *File New* dialog box will appear on the screen with three option tabs: **Model**, **Drawing** and **Simulation**. Note that the default is set to Model and we can create a new model using any of the pre-defined templates.

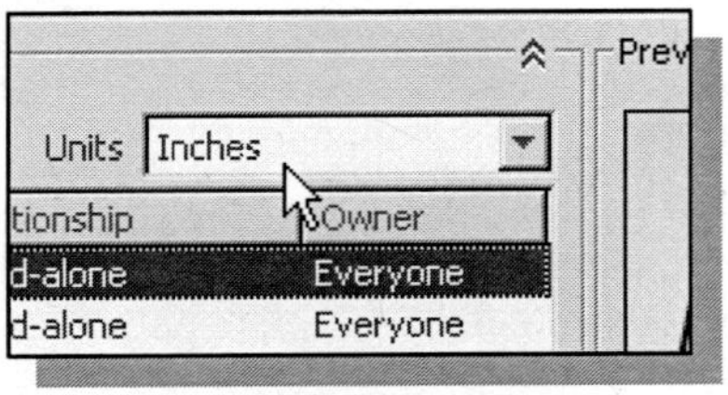

3. Select the **Inches** units as shown in the window. When starting a new CAD file, the first thing we should do is to choose the units we would like to use.

4. Select **Blank** in the *Templates* list. Note that the *Blank* template contains no pre-defined settings.

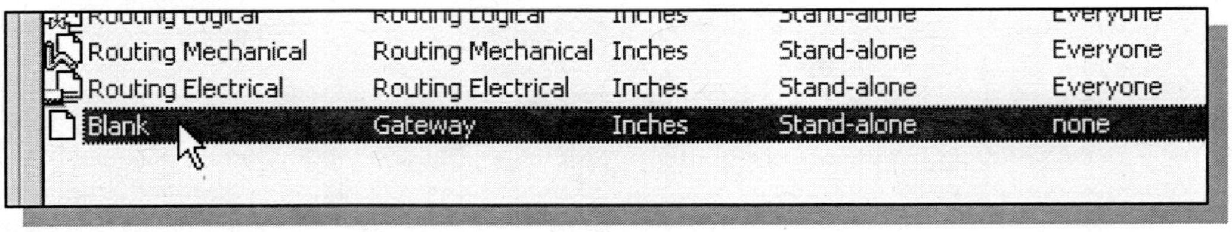

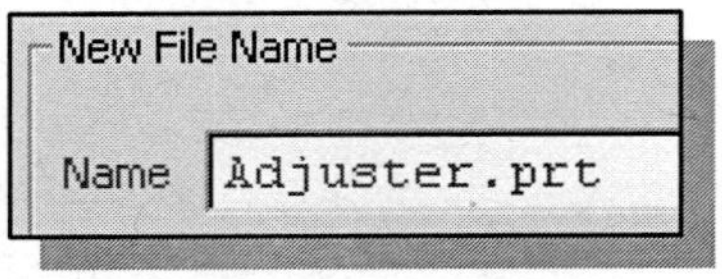

5. In the *New File Name* section, enter **Adjuster.prt** as the file *Name*.

6. Click **OK** to accept the settings and proceed with the New File command.

7. Select the **Start** icon with a single click of the left-mouse-button (MB1) in the *Standard* toolbar.

8. Pick **Modeling** in the pull-down list as shown in the figure.

➢ The above procedure shows the switching of the three *NX* **work areas**, we have gone from the "**No Part**" state to the "**Applications**", and "**Task Environments**" state. In the later chapters, the procedure to use the pre-defined template is also illustrated.

➢ Note that the *NX Modeling* application allows us to perform both the tasks of **parametric modeling** and **3D free-form surface modeling**.

Parametric Modeling
Under the *NX Modeling* application, a variety of tools are available for the creation of 2D and 3D wireframe models, and associative feature-based solid models.

3D Free-Form Surface Modeling
We can also perform more complex-shape modeling tasks, such as the creation of complex surface and solid models. For example, creating *swept features* along 3D curves; *lofted features* using conic methods; and *meshes* of points and curves.

UGS NX Application Screen Layout

➢ The *UGS NX Modeling* screen layout is quite similar to the *NX Gateway* application screen layout (refer to the figure in page 1-12). The new items on the screen include the *Form Feature* toolbar, the *Feature Operation* toolbar, and the *Curve* toolbar.

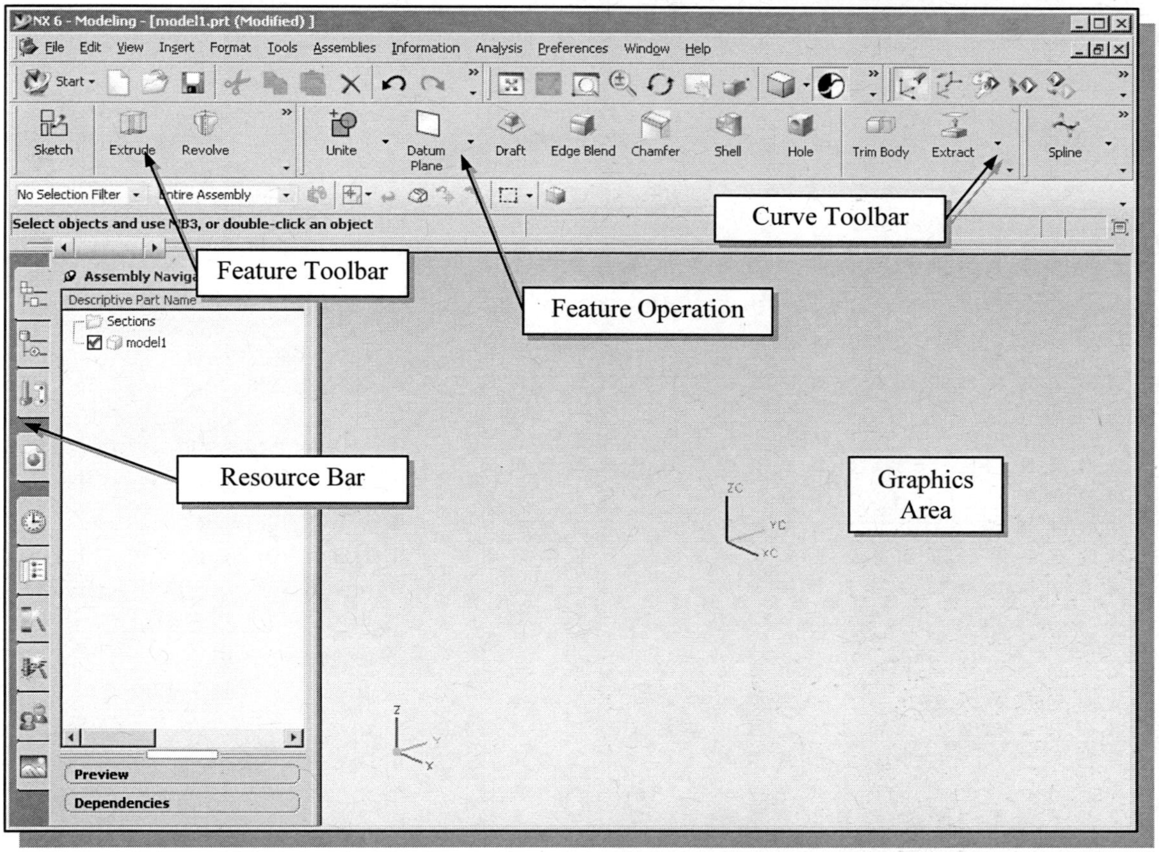

Form Feature Toolbar

This toolbar contains tools that allow us to quickly create 2D sketches and form 3D features.

Feature Operation Toolbar

This toolbar contains tools that allow us to quickly create placed features.

Curve Toolbar

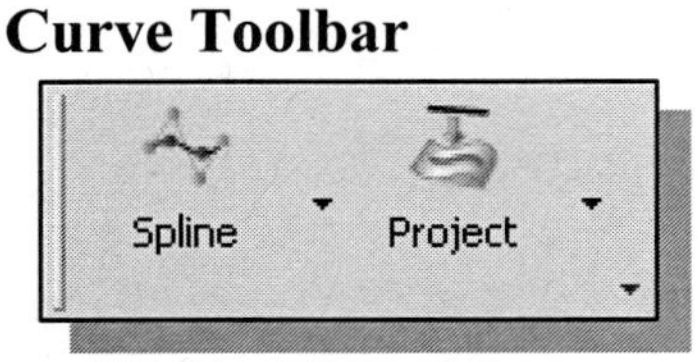

This toolbar contains tools that allow us to quickly access 2D curve options.

Step 2: Define/Set Up the First Solid Feature

- For the *Adjuster* design, we will create an extruded solid as the first feature.

1. In the ***Feature*** toolbars (toolbars aligned to the right edge of the main window), select the **Extrude** icon as shown.

- The ***Extrude Feature Options*** *dialog box*, which contains applicable construction options, is displayed as shown in the figure below.

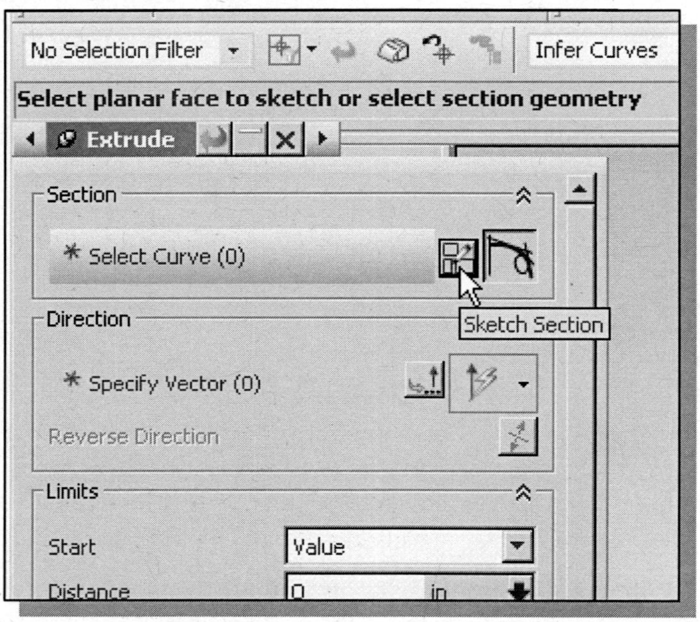

2. On your own, move the cursor over the icons and read the brief descriptions of the different options available. Note that the default *Extrude* option is set to **Select Section**.

3. Click the **Sketch Section** button to begin creating a new 2D sketch.

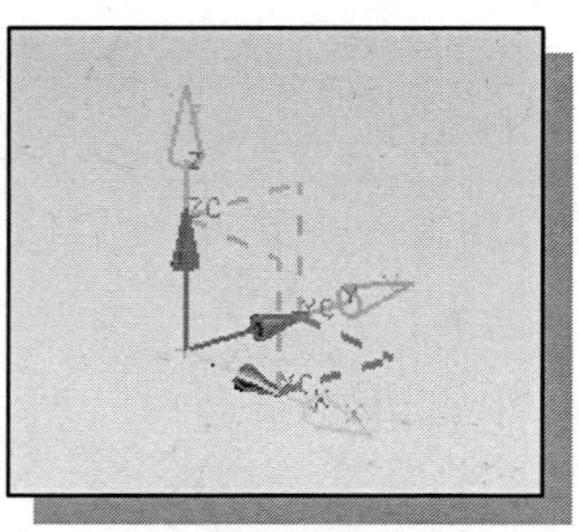

❖ Note the default sketch plane is aligned to the ***XC-YC* plane** of the displayed *work coordinate system.*

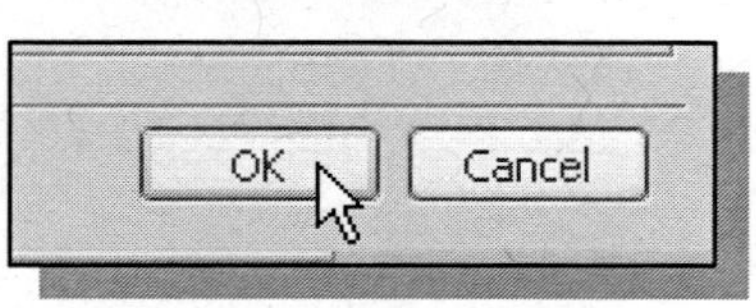

4. Click **OK** to accept the default setting of the *sketch plane*.

Work Plane – It is an XY CRT, but an XYZ World

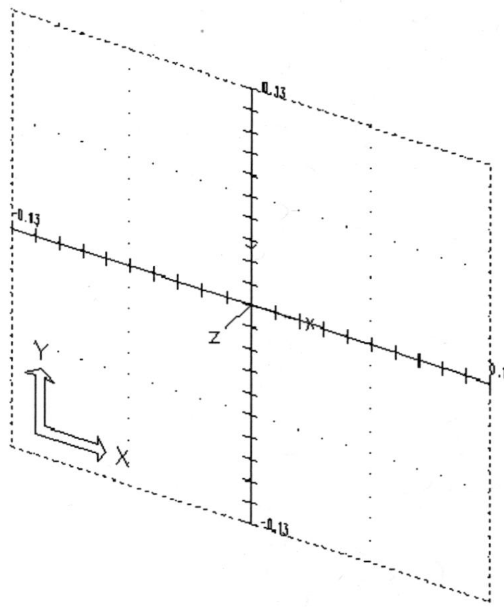

Design modeling software is becoming more powerful and user friendly, yet the system still does only what the user tells it to do. When using a geometric modeler, we therefore need to have a good understanding of what its inherent limitations are. We should also have a good understanding of what we want to do and what to expect, as the results are based on what is available.

In most 3D geometric modelers, 3D objects are located and defined in what is usually called the **absolute space** or **global space**. Although a number of different coordinate systems can be used to create and manipulate objects in a 3D modeling system, the objects are typically defined and stored using the absolute space. The absolute space is usually a **3D Cartesian coordinate system** that the user cannot change or manipulate.

In most engineering designs, models can be very complex, and it would be tedious and confusing if only one coordinate system, the absolute coordinate system, was available. Practical 3D modeling systems allow the user to define **Work Coordinate Systems (WCS)**, also known as **Local Coordinate Systems (LCS)** or **User Coordinate Systems** (**UCS**) relative to the absolute coordinate system. Once a local coordinate system is defined, we can then create geometry in terms of this more convenient system.

The basic concepts of coordinate systems remain the same for most CAD systems, but the actual usage of a particular type of coordinate system may vary greatly from one CAD system to another. *UGS NX* has two primary coordinate systems: the **Absolute Coordinate System** (**ACS**) and the **Work Coordinate System** (**WCS**). The ACS is fixed in space, whereas the WCS is a mobile system to facilitate geometry construction in different orientations. The WCS can be located and oriented anywhere in model space.

Although 3D objects are generally created and stored in 3D space coordinates, most of the 3D geometry entities can be referenced using 2D Cartesian coordinate systems. Typical input devices such as a mouse or digitizers are two-dimensional by nature; the movement of the input device is interpreted by the system in a planar sense. The same limitation is true of common output devices, such as CRT displays and plotters. The modeling software performs a series of three-dimensional to two-dimensional transformations to correctly project 3D objects onto a 2D picture plane.

The *UGS NX* ***sketch plane*** is a special construction tool that enables the planar nature of 2D input devices to be directly mapped into the 3D coordinate systems. The *sketch plane* is part of the *NX* work coordinate system that can be aligned to the absolute coordinate system, an existing face of a part, or a reference plane. By default, the *sketch plane* is aligned to the *XY* plane of the default WCS; note that the default WCS is aligned to the absolute coordinate system (ACS).

Think of a sketch plane as the surface on which we can sketch the 2D sections of the parts. It is similar to a piece of paper, a white board, or a chalkboard that can be attached to any planar surface. The first profile we create is usually drawn on one of the work planes of the work coordinate system (WCS). Subsequent profiles can then be drawn on sketch planes that are defined on **planar faces of a part**, **work planes aligned to part geometry**, or **work planes attached to a coordinate system** (such as the *XY*, *XZ*, and *YZ* planes of WCS).

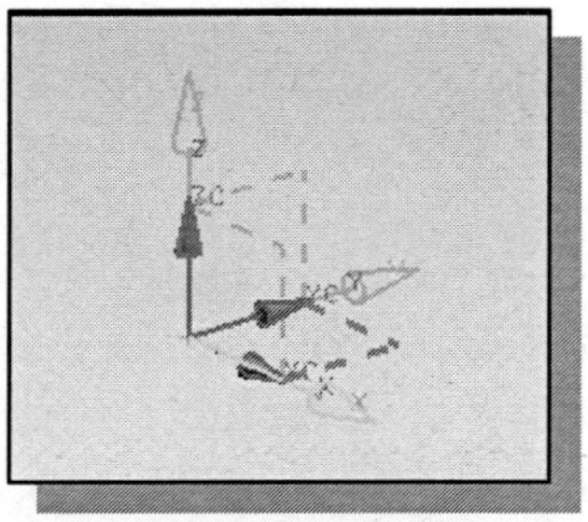

❖ The default sketch plane is aligned to the *XY* plane of the *work coordinate system.*

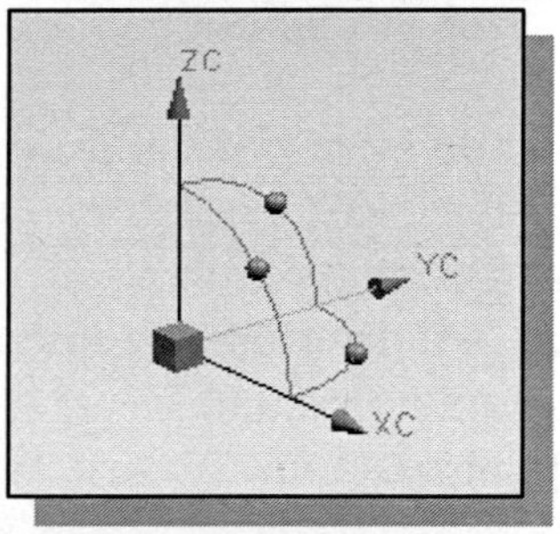

❖ The *work coordinate system* (WCS) is a mobile system to assist geometric construction in different orientations. The WCS can be located and oriented anywhere in model space.

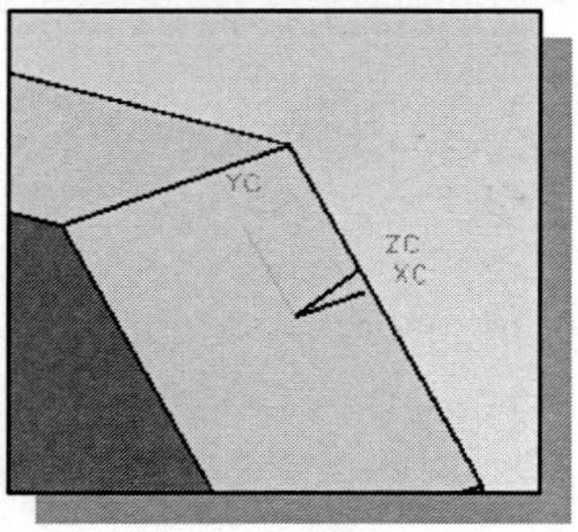

❖ Note that most solid modeling operations do not require manipulation of the WCS. Features are generally added relative to existing geometry of the solid model.

Creating Rough Sketches

Quite often during the early design stage, the shape of a design may not have any precise dimensions. Most conventional CAD systems require the user to input the precise lengths and locations of all geometric entities defining the design, which are not available during the early design stage. With *parametric modeling*, we can use the computer to elaborate and formulate the design idea further during the initial design stage. With *UGS NX*, we can use the computer as an electronic sketchpad to help us concentrate on the formulation of forms and shapes for the design. This approach is the main advantage of *parametric modeling* over conventional solid-modeling techniques.

As the name implies, a ***rough sketch*** is not precise at all. When sketching, we simply sketch the geometry so that it closely resembles the desired shape. Precise scale or lengths are not needed. *UGS NX* provides us with many tools to assist us in finalizing sketches. For example, geometric entities such as horizontal and vertical lines are set automatically. However, if the rough sketches are poor, it will require much more work to generate the desired parametric sketches. Here are some general guidelines for creating sketches in *UGS NX*:

- **Create a sketch that is proportional to the desired shape.** Concentrate on the shapes and forms of the design.

- **Keep the sketches simple.** Leave out small geometry features such as fillets, rounds and chamfers. They can easily be placed using the Fillet and Chamfer commands after the parametric sketches have been established.

- **Exaggerate the geometric features of the desired shape.** For example, if the desired angle is 85 degrees, start by creating an angle that is 50 or 60 degrees (and make adjustment later). Otherwise, *UGS NX* might assume the intended angle to be a 90-degree angle.

- **Draw the geometry so that it does not overlap.** To create a 3D features from a 2D sketch, the 2D geometry used should define a clear boundary. *Self-intersecting* geometry shapes are not allowed, as it cannot be converted into a solid feature.

- **The sketched geometric entities should form a closed region.** To create a solid feature, such as an extruded solid, a closed region is required so that the extruded solid forms a 3D volume.

➢ **Note:** The concepts and principles involved in *parametric modeling* are very different, and sometimes they are totally opposite, to those of conventional computer aided drafting. In order to understand and fully utilize *UGS NX's* functionality, it will be helpful to take a *Zen* approach to learning the topics presented in this text: **Temporarily forget your knowledge and experiences of using conventional Computer Aided Drafting systems.**

Step 3: Creating a Rough 2D Sketch

➢ The *Sketch Curve* toolbar provides tools for creating and editing of the basic 2D geometry, construction tools such as Line and Circle, and editing tools such as Trim and Extend. Notice, by default, the **Profile** tool is activated. The **Profile** tool allows us to create lines and/or arcs that are joined together.

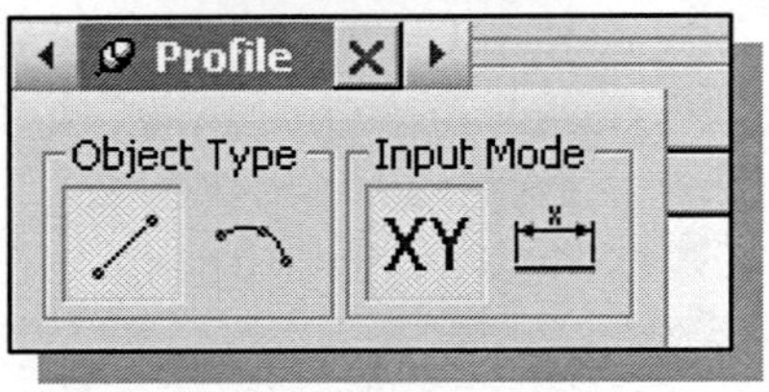

➢ Notice, by default, the **Line** option is activated. The **Line** option allows us to create line segments that are joined together.

1. As you move the cursor, you will see a digital readout next to the cursor. The readout gives you the cursor location relative to the Work Coordinate System. Pick a location that is toward the right side of the WCS as the first point of a line.

2. Move the cursor around and you will notice the readout, next to the cursor, providing the length and angle of the line.

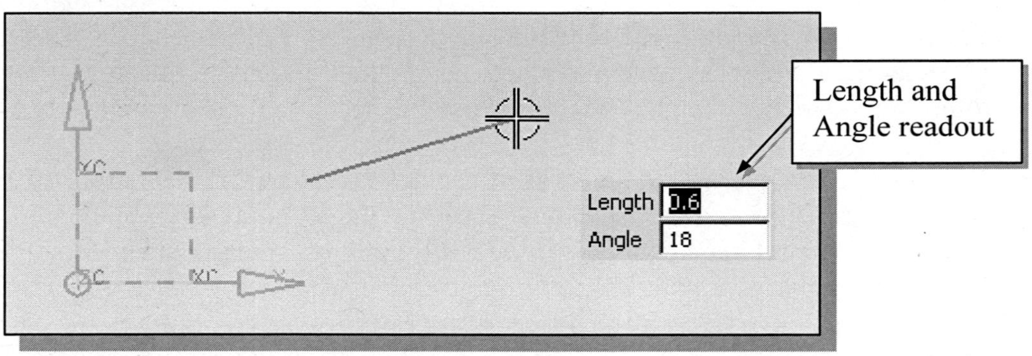

3. Move the graphics cursor directly above the previous point and create a vertical line as shown below (**Point 2**). Notice the geometric constraint symbol displayed.

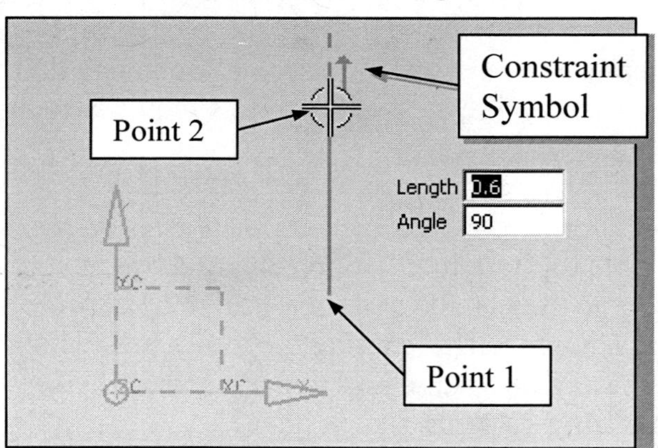

Geometric Constraint Symbols

UGS NX displays different visual clues, or symbols, to show you alignments, perpendicularities, tangencies, etc. These constraints are used to capture the *design intent* by creating constraints where they are recognized. *UGS NX* displays the governing geometric rules as models are built. To prevent constraints from forming, hold down the [**Alt**] key while creating an individual sketch curve. For example, while sketching line segments with the Line command, endpoints are joined with a Coincident constraint, but when the [**Alt**] key is pressed and held, the inferred constraint will not be created.

Symbol	Constraint	Description
	**Vertical**	indicates a line is vertical
	Horizontal	indicates a line is horizontal
	**Dashed line**	indicates the alignment is to the center point or endpoint of an entity
	**Parallel**	indicates a line is parallel to other entities
	**Perpendicular**	indicates a line is perpendicular to other entities
	**Coincident**	indicates the cursor is at the endpoint of an entity
	**Concentric**	indicates the cursor is at the center of an entity
	**Tangent**	indicates the cursor is at tangency points to curves
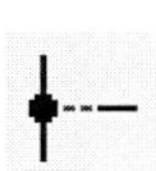	**Midpoint**	indicates the cursor is at the midpoint of an entity
	**Point on Curve**	indicates the cursor is on curves
	Equal Length	indicates the length of a line is equal to another line
	**Equal Radius**	indicates the radius of an arc is equal to another arc

4. Complete the sketch as shown below, creating a closed region ending at the starting point (Point 1.) Do not be overly concerned with the actual size of the sketch. Note that all line segments are sketched horizontally or vertically.

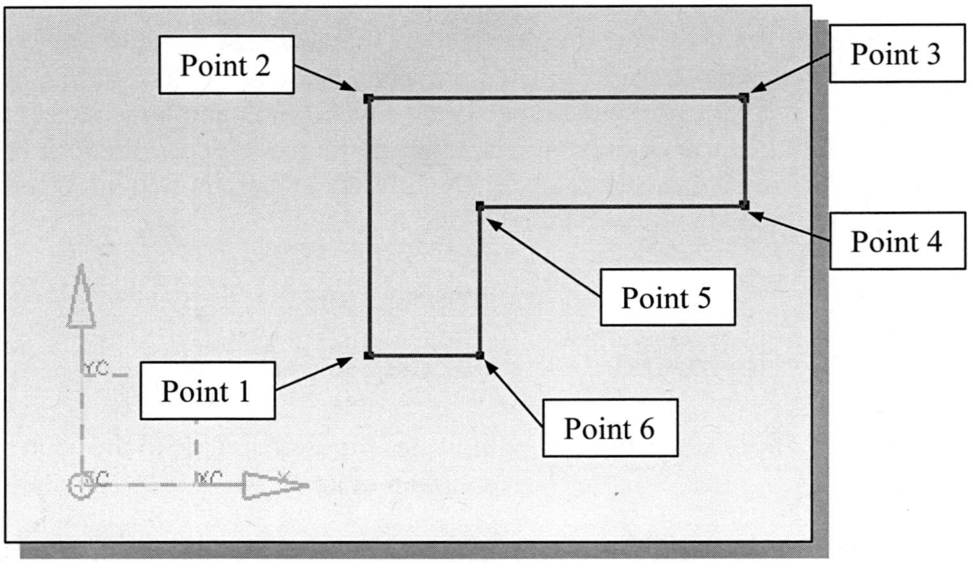

5. Inside the graphics window, click twice with the **middle-mouse-button (MB2),** or press the [**Esc**] key once, to end the Sketch Line command.

Step 4: Apply/Modify Constraints and Dimensions

➢ As the sketch is made, *UGS NX* automatically applies some of the geometric constraints (such as Horizontal, Parallel, and Perpendicular) to the sketched geometry. We can continue to modify the geometry, apply additional constraints, and/or define the size of the existing geometry. In this example, we will illustrate adding dimensions to describe the sketched entities.

1. Move the cursor to the ***Sketch Constraints*** toolbar area, which is located to the right of the *Sketch Curve* toolbar.

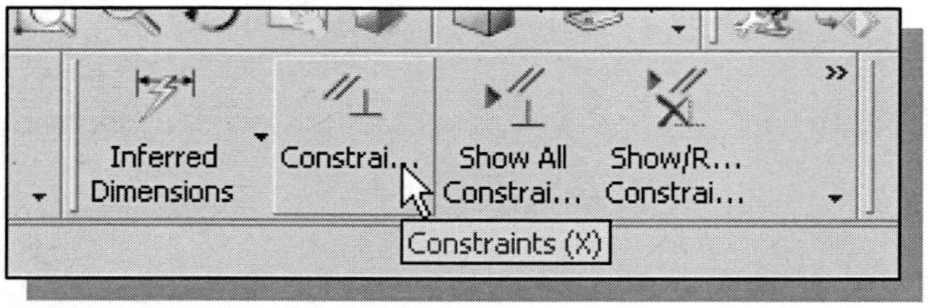

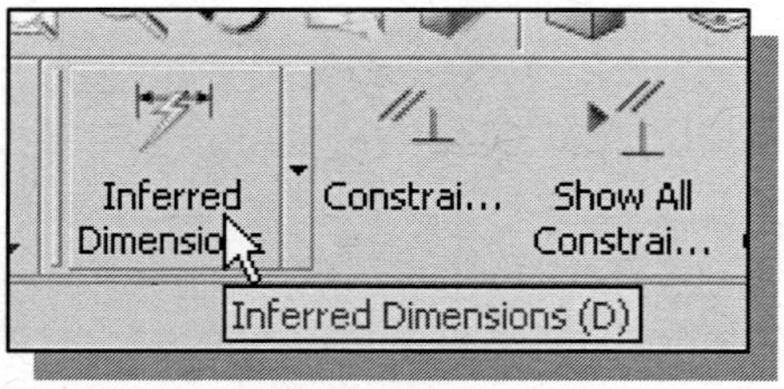

2. Activate the **Inferred Dimensions** command by left-clicking once on the icon as shown. The Inferred Dimensions command allows us to quickly create and modify dimensions.

3. The message "*Select object to Dimension or select dimension to edit*" is displayed in the *Message* area. Select the **top horizontal line** by left-clicking once on the line.

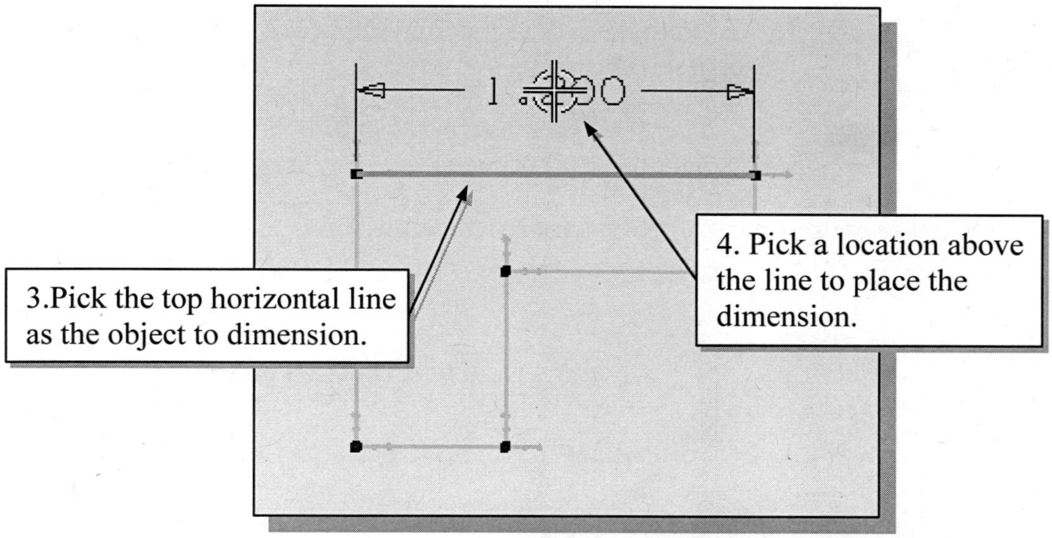

4. Move the graphics cursor above the selected line and left-click to place the dimension. (Note that the value displayed on your screen might be different than what is shown in the figure above.)

❖ The **Inferred Dimension** command will create a length dimension if a single line is selected. The current length of the line is displayed, in the ***edit* box**, next to the dimension as shown in the below figure.

5. Enter **2.5** as the desired length of the line. (Press the **ENTER** key once after you enter the new value.)

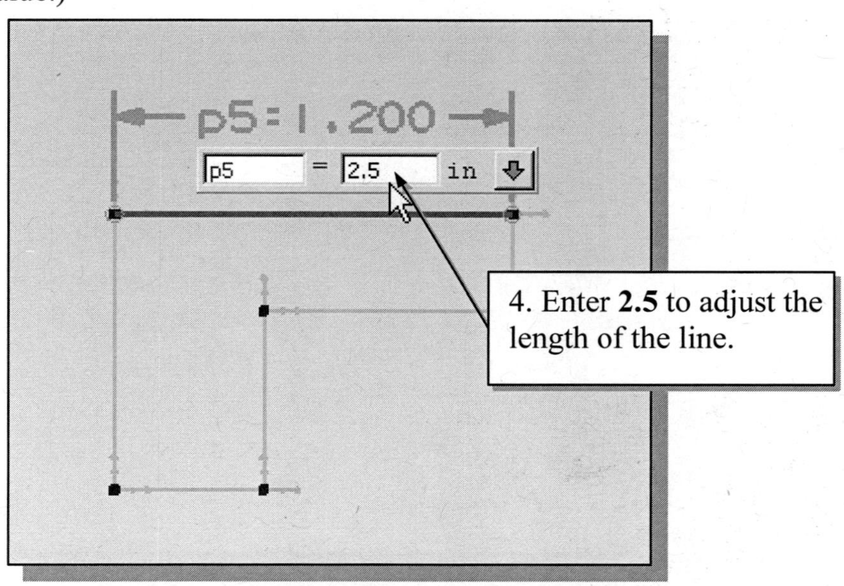

➢ *UGS NX* will now update the profile with the new dimension value. Note that in parametric modeling, dimensions are used as **control variables**.

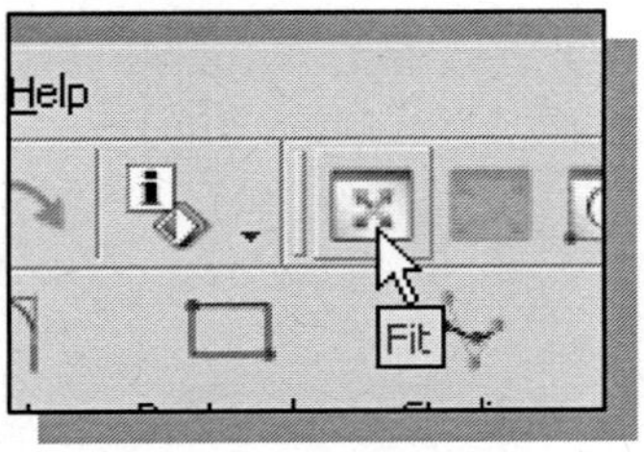

6. Click the **Fit** button to resize the display window.

❖ Note that we are returned to the **Inferred Dimensions** command; the Fit command is executed without interrupting the current active command.

7. The message "*Select object to Dimension or select dimension to edit*" is displayed in the *Message* area. Select the top horizontal line as shown below.

8. Select the bottom-horizontal line as shown below.

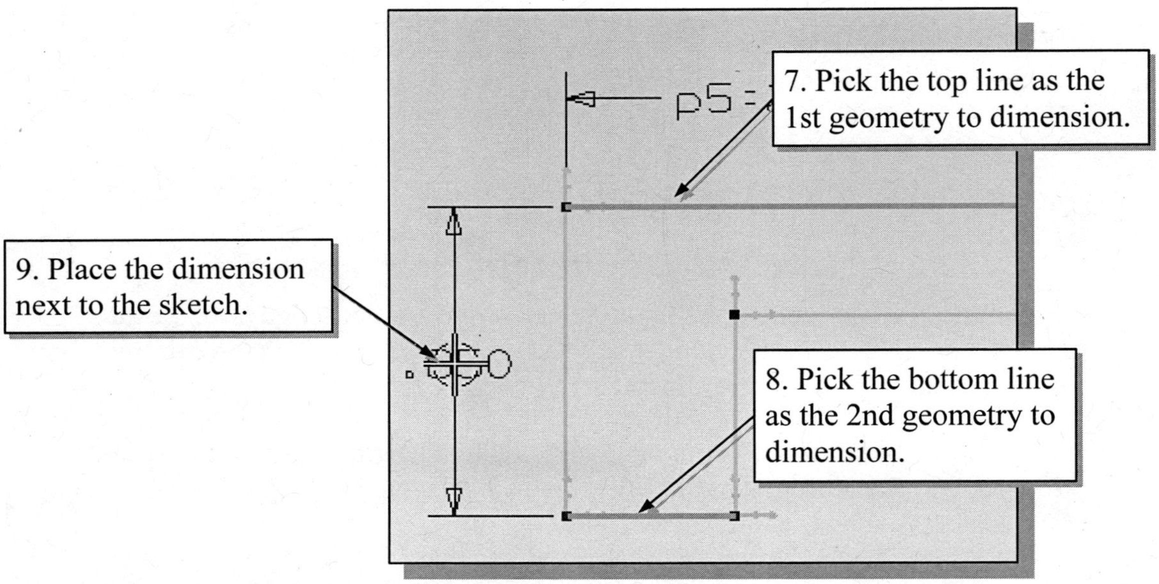

9. Pick a location to the left of the sketch to place the dimension.

10. Enter **2.5** as the desired length of the line.

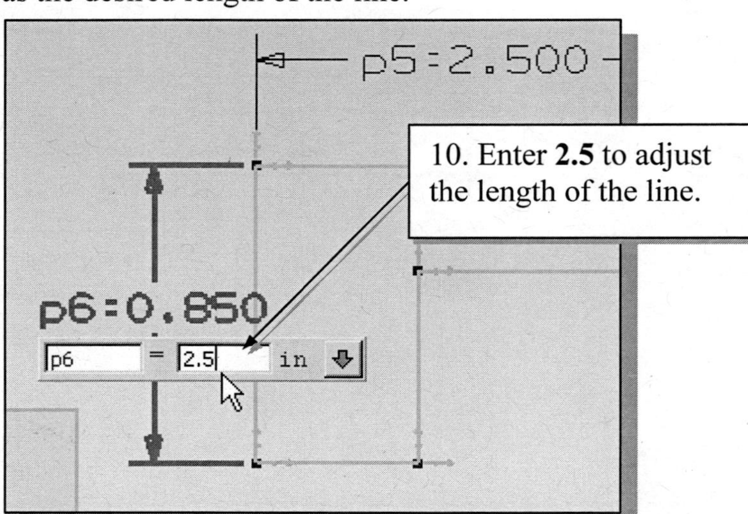

❖ When two parallel lines are selected, the Inferred Dimension command will create a dimension measuring the distance between them.

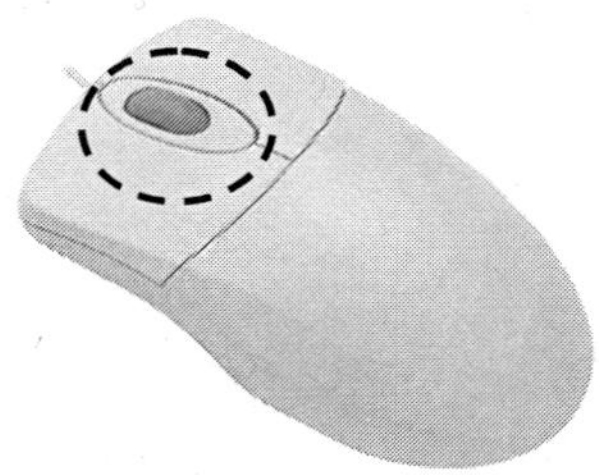

❖ Quick Zoom function by turning the mouse wheel

Turning the **mouse wheel** can adjust the scale of the display. Turning forward will reduce the scale of the display, using the cursor location as the center reference, making the entities display smaller on the screen. Turning backward will magnify the scale of the display.

11. The message "*Select object to dimension or select dimension to edit*" is displayed in the *Message* area. Select the bottom horizontal line as shown below.

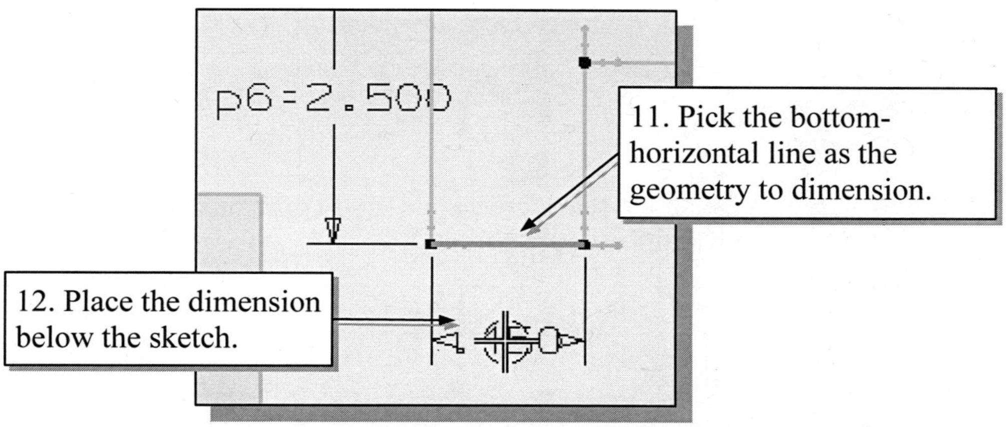

12. Pick a location below the sketch to place the dimension.

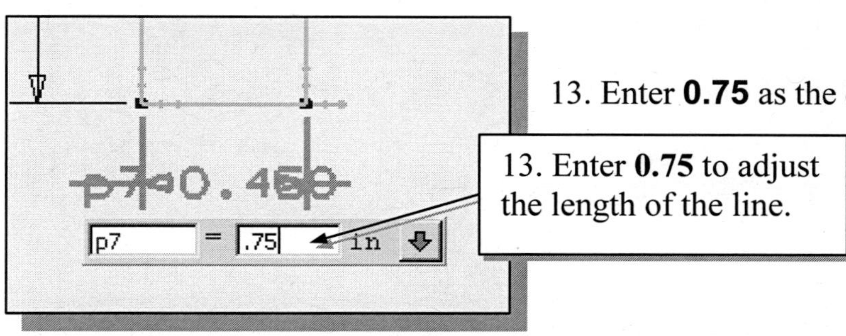

13. Enter **0.75** as the desired length of the line

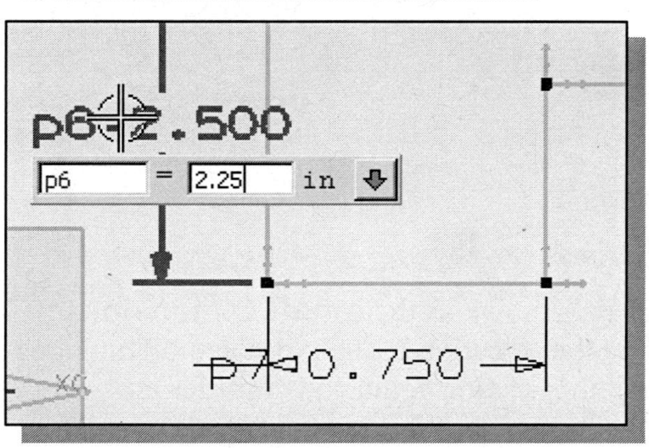

14. Pick the vertical dimension and notice the Inferred Dimensions command can also be used to adjust any existing dimensions.

15. On your own, enter any number and observe the adjustment done by *UGS NX*.

16. Inside the graphics window, click twice with the **middle-mouse-button (MB2),** or hit the [**Esc**] key once, to end the Inferred Dimensions command.

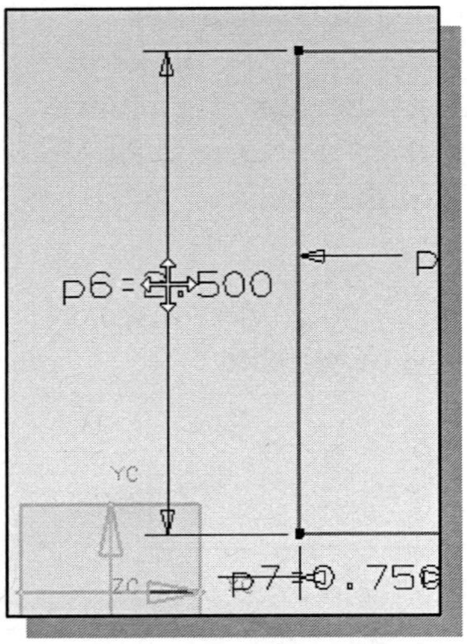

17. To reposition any of the dimensions, simply **press and drag** with the **left-mouse-button (MB1)** on the dimension as shown in the figure.

18. On you own, repeat the above steps, create and modify dimensions so that the sketch appears as shown in the figure below.

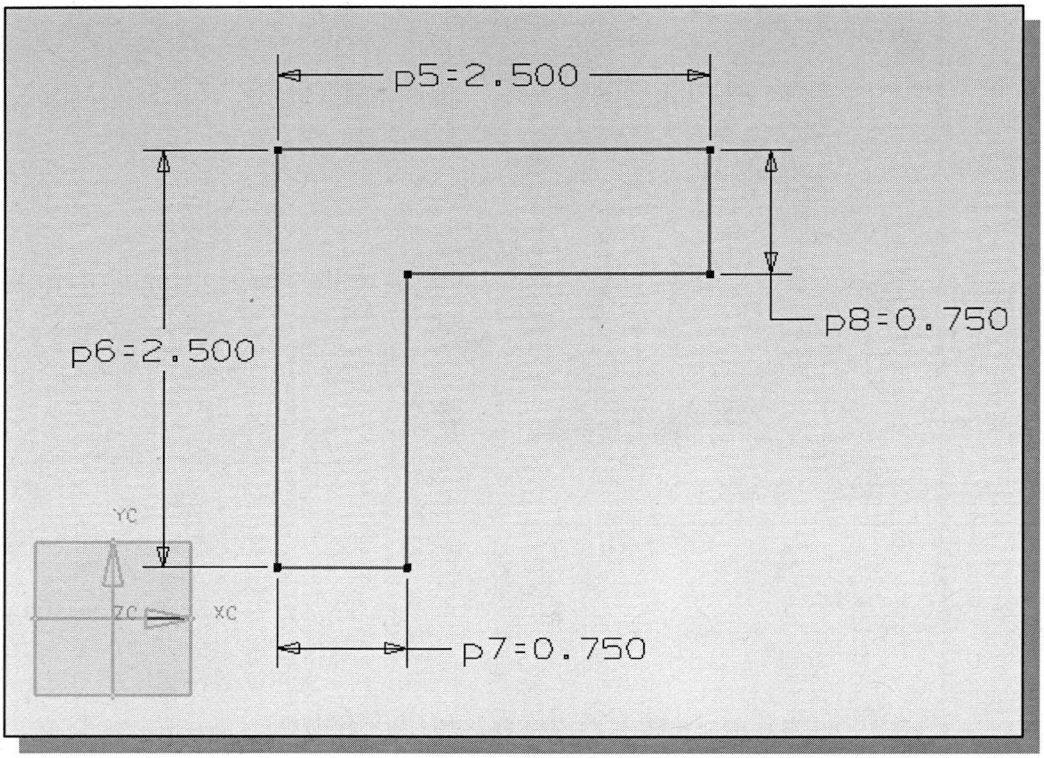

❖ The **Inferred Dimensions** command is also known as the **Smart Dimension** command; dimensions are created based on the selection of the types and orientations of objects. You might want to read through this section again and consider the powerful implication of this command. Also consider this question: How would you create an *angle dimension* using the Inferred Dimensions command?

Dynamic Viewing Functions – *Zoom* and *Pan*

- *UGS NX* provides a special user interface called *Dynamic Viewing* that enables convenient viewing of the entities in the graphics window.

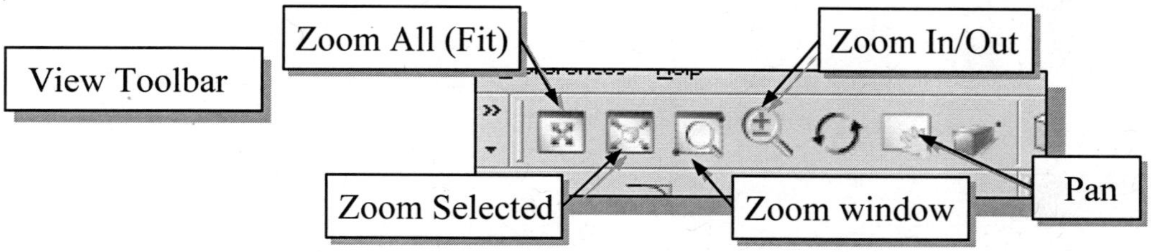

1. Click on the **Zoom In/Out** icon, located in the *Standard* toolbar as shown.

2. Move the cursor near the center of the graphics window.

3. Inside the graphics window, **press and drag with the left-mouse-button**, then move upward to enlarge the current display scale factor.

4. Inside the graphics window, **press and drag with the left-mouse-button**, then move downward to reduce the current display scale factor.

5. Click once with the **middle-mouse-button (MB2),** or press the [**Esc**] key once, to exit the Zoom command.

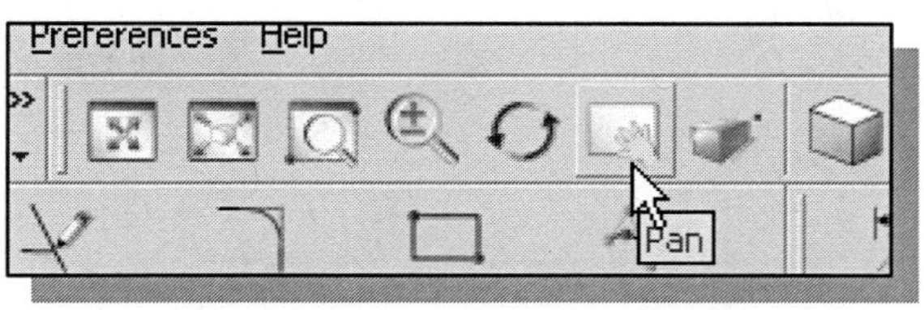

6. Click on the **Pan** icon, located in the *View* toolbar area. The icon is the picture of a hand.

➢ The Pan command enables us to move the view to a different position. This function acts as if you are using a video camera.

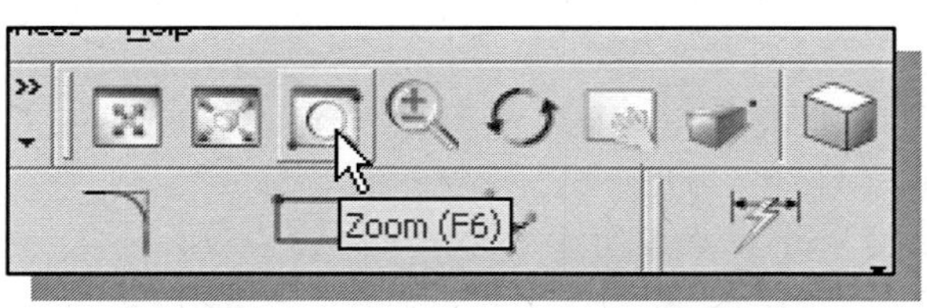

7. Click on the **Zoom Window** icon, located in the *View* toolbar area. (Function key F6 can also be used.)

8. Select two points, forming the two opposite corners of a rectangle, to define the Zoom Window region.

9. The current display is resized/mapped to the selected region.

10. On your own, use the available Zoom and Pan options to reposition the sketch near the center of the screen.

Step 5: Completing the Base Solid Feature

Now that the 2D sketch is completed, we will proceed to the next step: create a 3D part from the 2D section. Extruding a 2D section is one of the common methods that can be used to create 3D parts. We can extrude planar faces along a path. We can also specify a height value and a tapered angle. In *UGS NX*, each face has a positive side and a negative side, the current face we're working on is set as the default positive side. This positive side identifies the positive extrusion direction and it is referred to as the face's ***normal***.

1. Select **Finish Sketch** by clicking once with the left-mouse-button (MB1) on the icon.

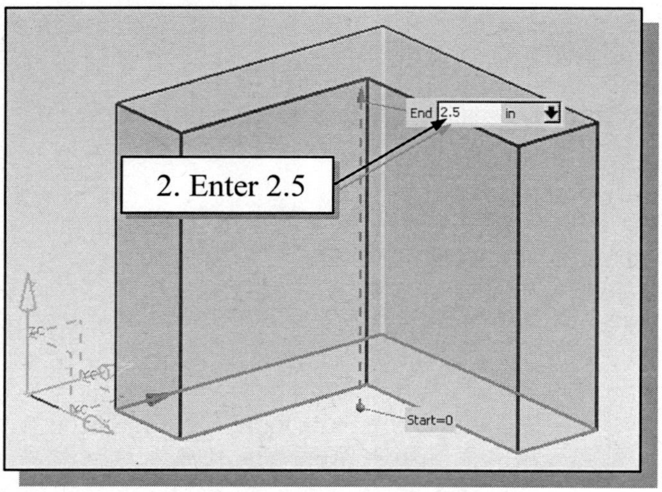

2. In the *Extrude* popup window, enter **2.5** as the extrusion *Distance*. Notice that the sketch region is automatically selected as the extrusion section.

3. Click on the **OK** button to proceed with creating the 3D part.

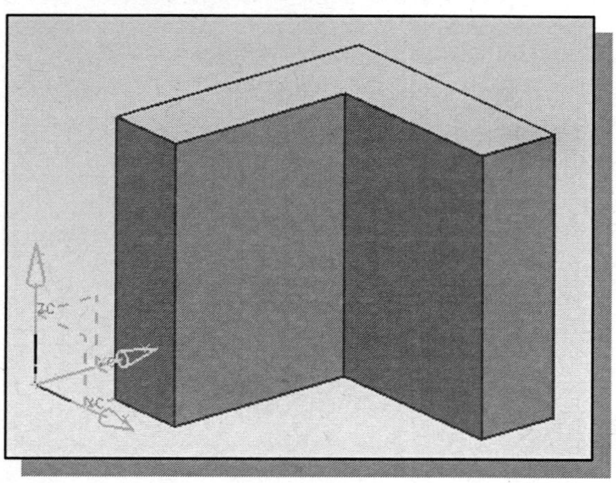

- Note that all dimensions disappeared from the screen. All parametric definitions are stored in the ***UGS NX*** **database** and any of the parametric definitions can be displayed and edited at any time.

Display Orientations

❖ *UGS NX* provides many ways to display views of the three-dimensional design. Several options are available that allow us to quickly view the design to track the overall effect of any changes being made to the model. We will first orient the model to display in the *front view*, by using the *View* toolbar.

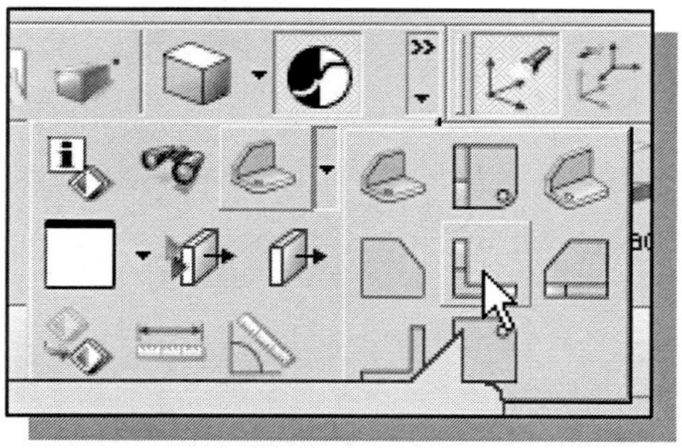

1. Select **Front View** in the *View* toolbar to change the display to the front view. (Note that **[Ctrl+Alt+F]** can also be used to activate this command.)

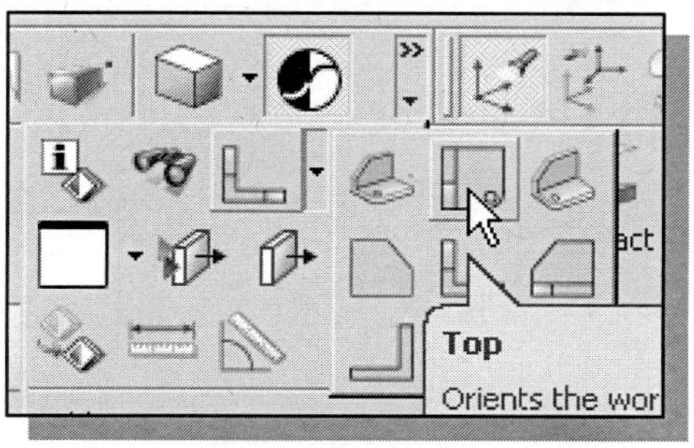

2. Select **Top View** in the *View* toolbar to change the display to the top view. (Note that the **[Ctrl+Alt+T]** keys can also be used to activate this command.)

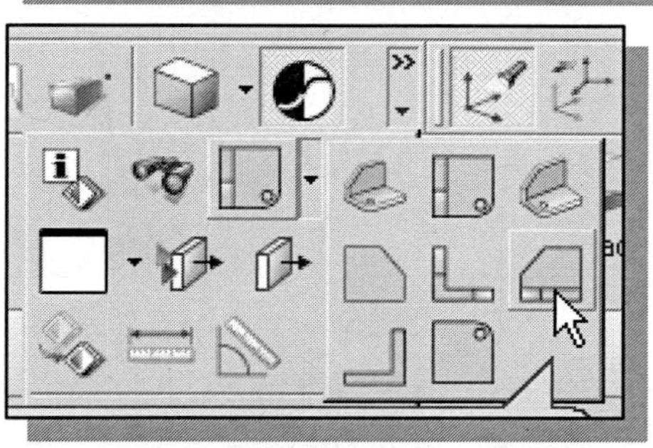

3. Select **Right View** in the *View* toolbar to change the display to the right side view. (Note that the **[Ctrl+Alt+R]** keys can also be used to activate this command.)

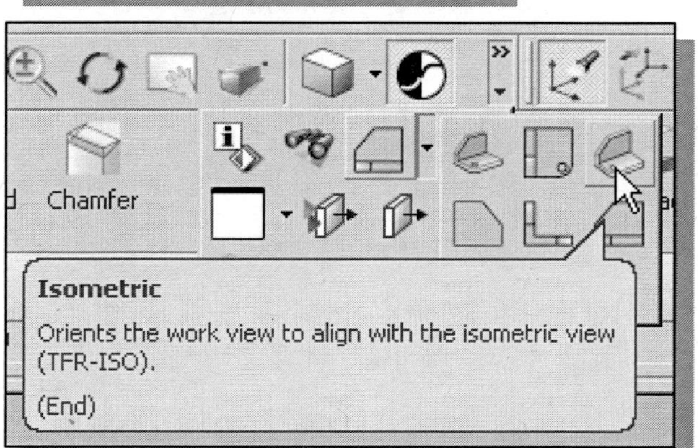

4. Select **Isometric View** in the *View* pull-down menu to change the display to the isometric view. (Note that the **[End]** key can also be used to activate this command.)

❖ Notice the other view-related commands that are available under the *View* toolbar. Most of these commands can be accessible through the toolbar and/or *function keys*.

Dynamic Viewing – Icons, Mouse buttons and Quick keys

➢ The ***3D Rotate*** icon is the icon with two circular arrows in the *View* toolbar. 3D Rotate enables us to manipulate the view of 3D objects by clicking and dragging with the left-mouse-button:

1. Click on the **Rotate** icon in the *View* toolbar.

2. Drag with the left-mouse-button (MB1) for free rotation of the 3D model.

3. Press the [**F7**] key (toggle switch) once to exit the 3D Rotate command.

➢ We can also use the mouse buttons to access the *Dynamic Viewing* functions.

❖ 3D Dynamic Rotation – The Middle-Mouse-Button (MB2)

Hold and drag with the middle-mouse-button to rotate the display interactively.

Dynamic Rotation

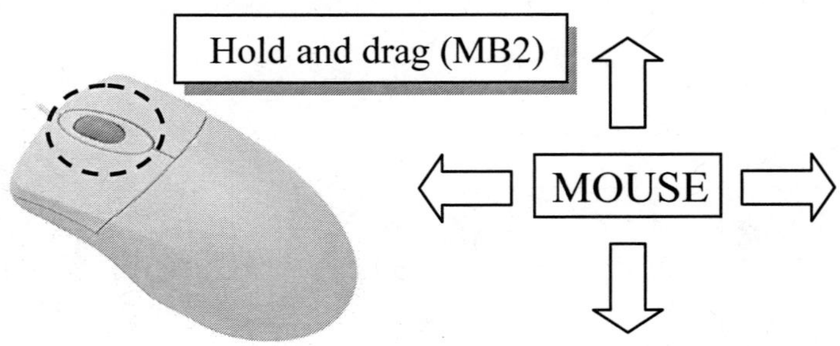

❖ Panning – (1) The Middle and Right Mouse Buttons

Hold and drag with the middle and right mouse buttons (MB2+MB3) to pan the display. This allows you to reposition the display while maintaining the same scale factor of the display.

Pan

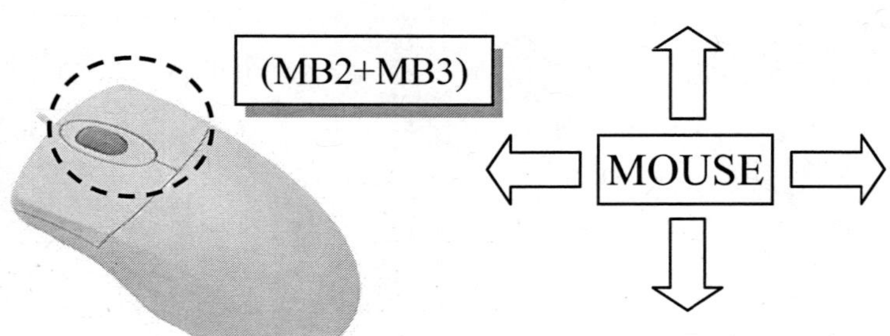

(2) [SHIFT] + [Middle-mouse-button (MB2)]

Hold the [**SHIFT**] key and the [**middle-mouse-button (MB2)**] to Pan the display.

❖ Zooming – The Left and Middle Mouse Buttons

Hold and drag with the left and middle mouse buttons (MB1+MB2) vertically on the screen to adjust the scale of the display. Moving upward will magnify the scale of the display, making the entities display larger on the screen. Moving downward will reduce the scale of the display.

Zoom

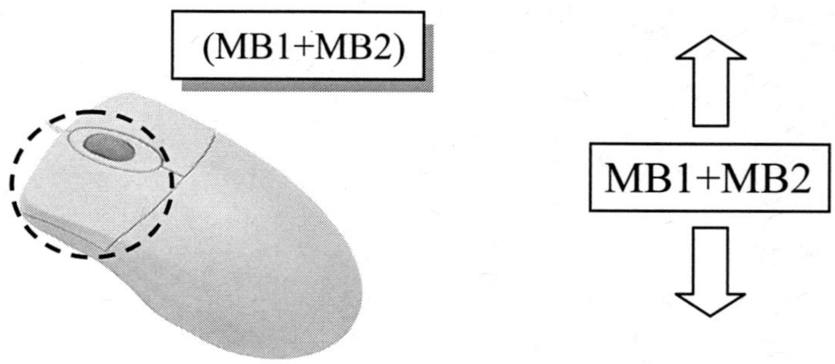

(2) [Ctrl] + [Middle mouse button (MB2)]

Hold the [**Ctrl**] key and the [**middle-mouse-button (MB2)**] to adjust the scale of the display.

Zoom

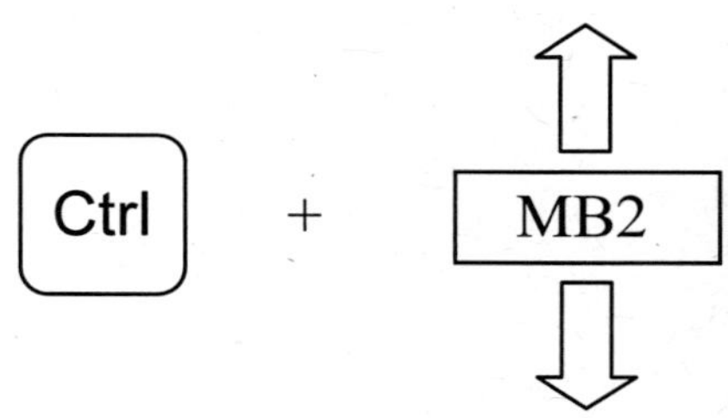

(3) Turning the mouse wheel

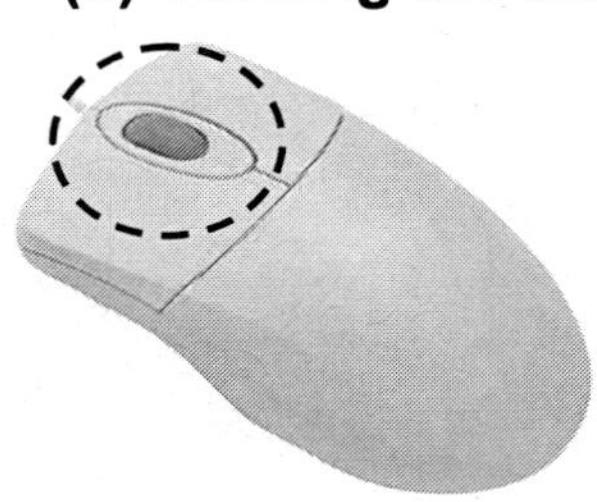

Turning the mouse wheel can also adjust the scale of the display. Turning forward will reduce the scale of the display, making the entities display smaller on the screen. Turning backward will magnify the scale of the display.

➢ Note that the *dynamic viewing* functions are also available through the ***View*** toolbar.

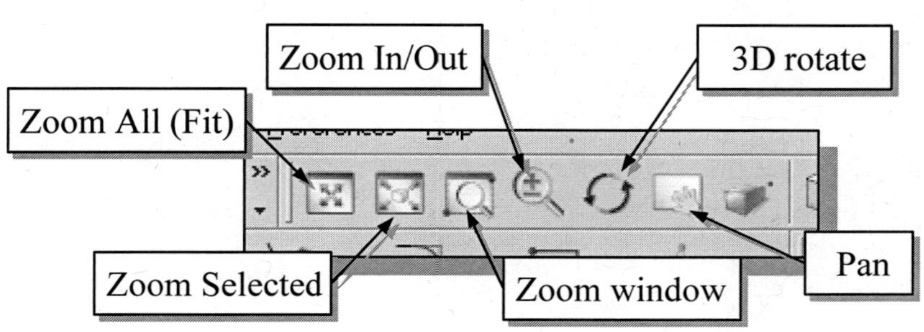

Display Modes

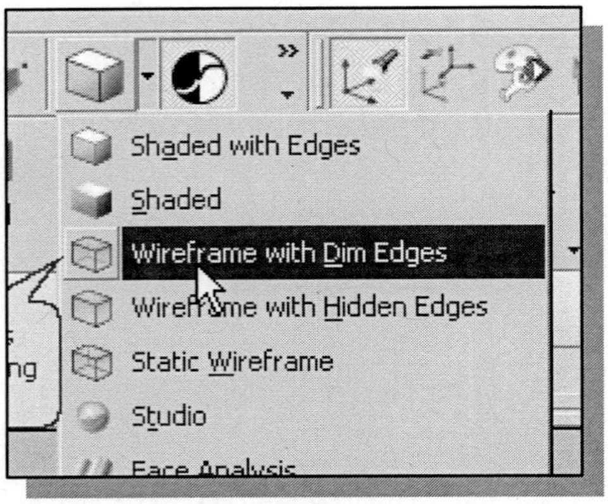

- The display in the graphics window has two basic display modes: wireframe and shaded display. To change the display mode in the active window, click on the triangle icon next to the display mode button on the *View* toolbar, as shown in the figure.

1. Pick the **Wireframe with Dim Edges** option as shown in the figure.

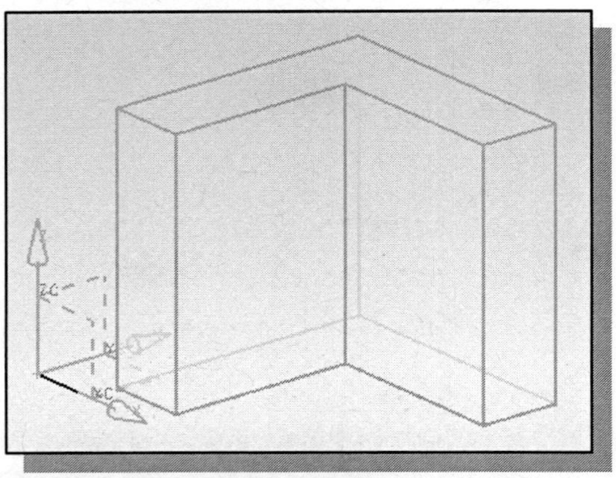

❖ **Wireframe with Dim Edges**

This display mode generates an image of the 3D object with all the back lines shown as lighter edges.

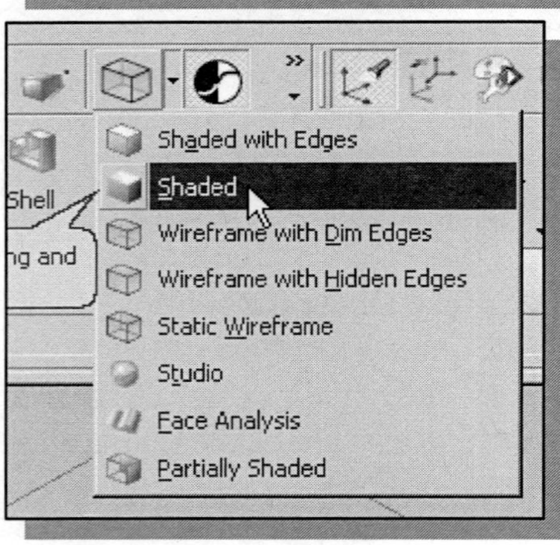

2. Pick the **Shaded** option as shown.

❖ **Shaded Image**

This display mode option generates a shaded image of the 3D object without the edges highlighted.

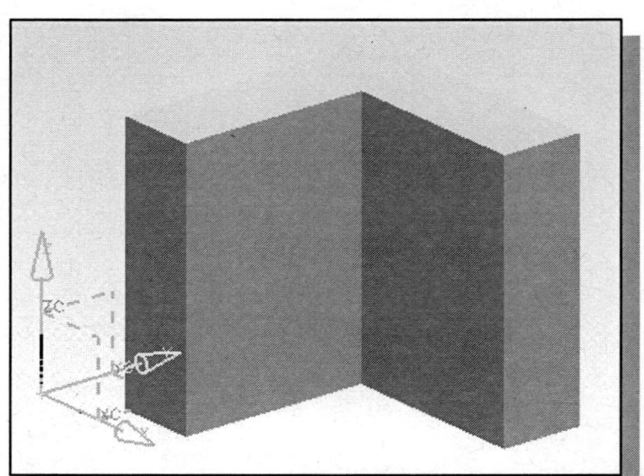

➢ On your own, use the different options to familiarize yourself with the 3D viewing/display commands.

Step 6-1: Adding an Extruded Feature

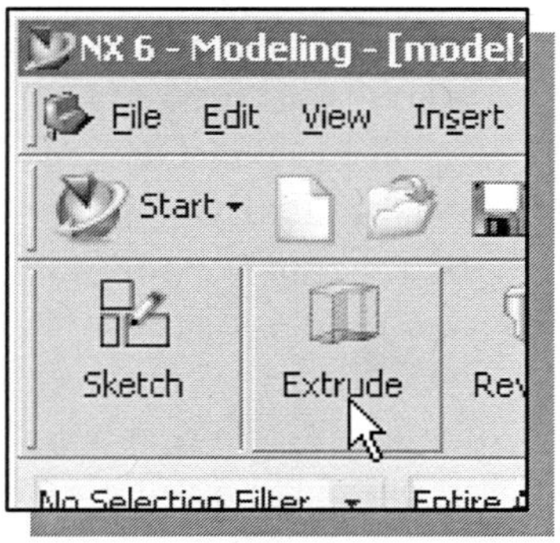

1. In the ***Feature*** toolbars (toolbars aligned to the right edge of the main window), select the **Extrude** icon as shown.

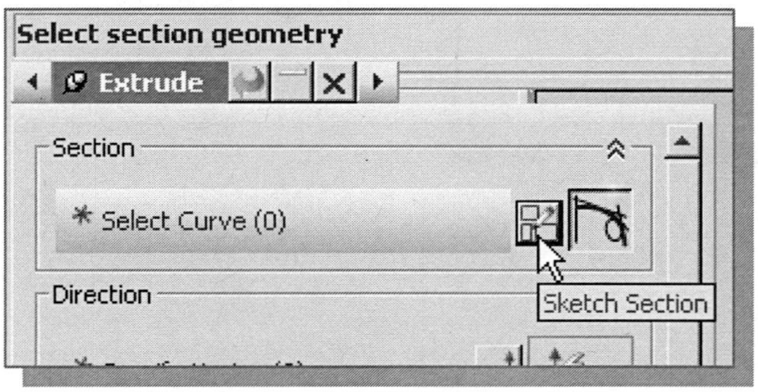

2. Click the **Sketch Section** button to begin creating a new *2D sketch.*

3. In the *Message* area, the message: "*Select planar face to sketch or select section geometry*" is displayed. *UGS NX* expects us to identify a planar surface where the 2D sketch of the next feature is to be created. Move the graphics cursor on the 3D part and notice that *UGS NX* will automatically highlight feasible planes and surfaces as the cursor is on top of the different surfaces. Pick the back vertical face of the 3D solid object, parallel to the ***X-Z* plane**, as shown.

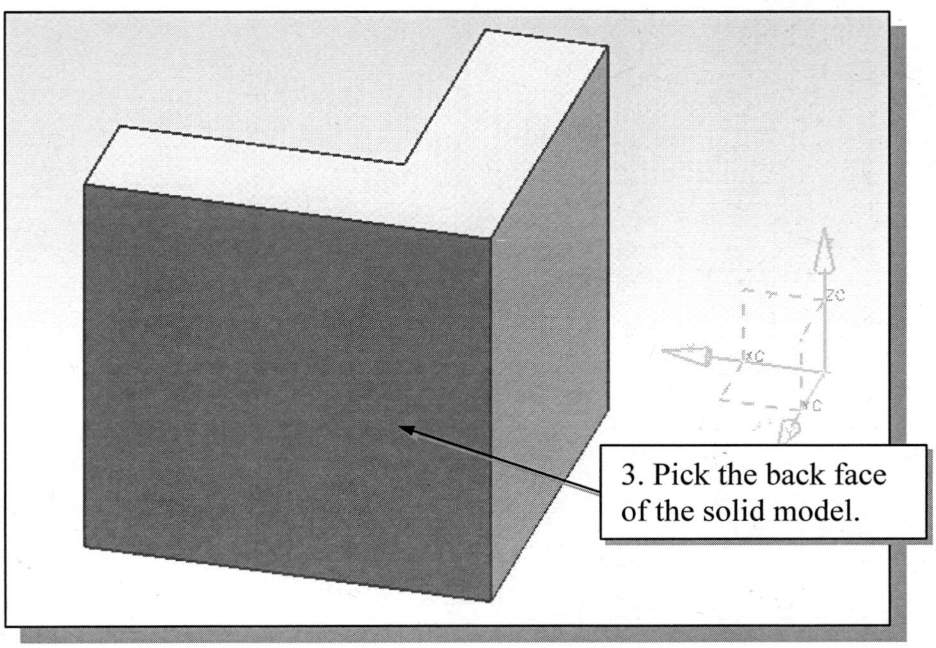

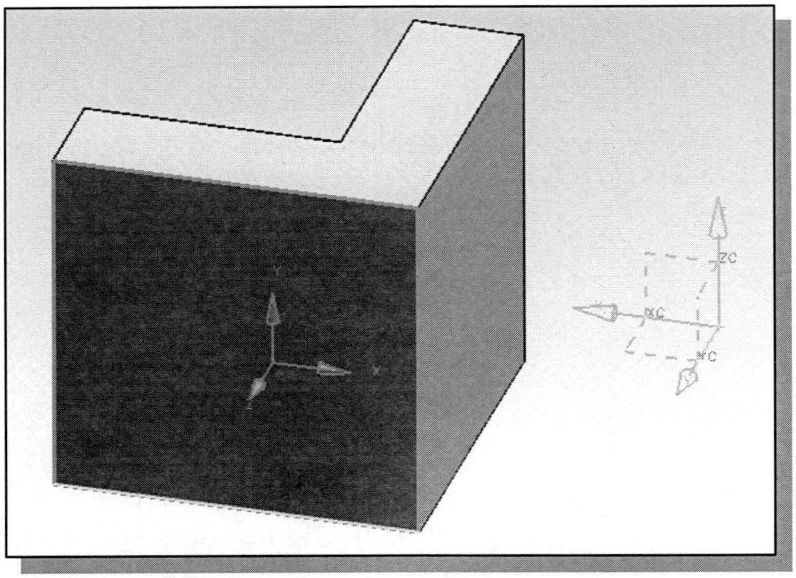

➢ Note that the sketch plane is aligned to the selected face. *UGS NX* automatically establishes a work coordinate system (WCS), and records its location with respect to the part on which it was created.

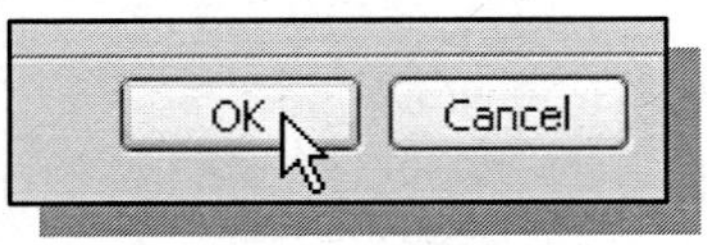

4. Click **OK** to accept the selected face and proceed with the new WCS.

- Next, we will create another 2D sketch, which will be used to create another extrusion feature that will be added to the existing solid object.

5. On your own, create a 2D sketch consisting of horizontal/vertical lines as shown in the figure below. Note that we intentionally do not want to align any of the corners to the 3D model.

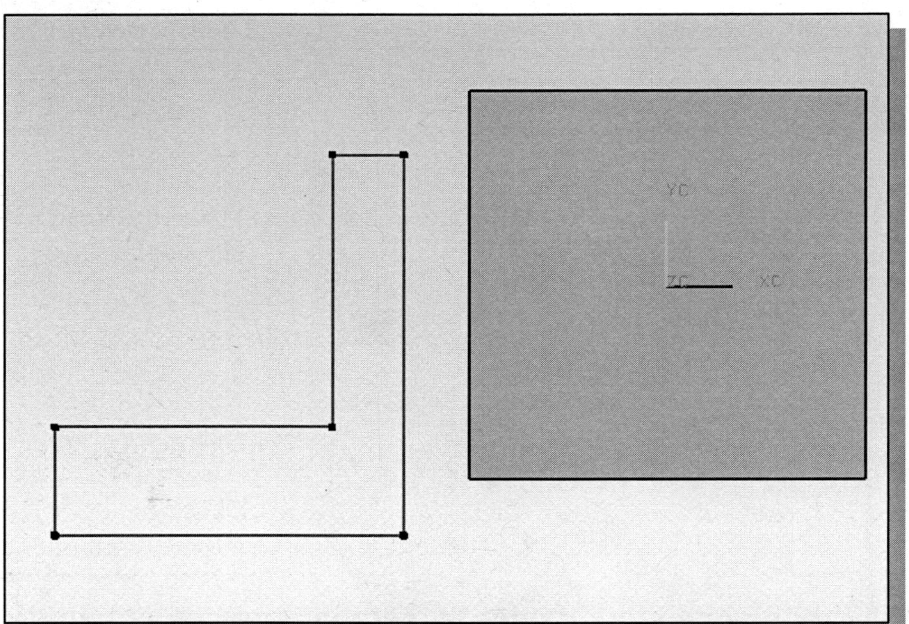

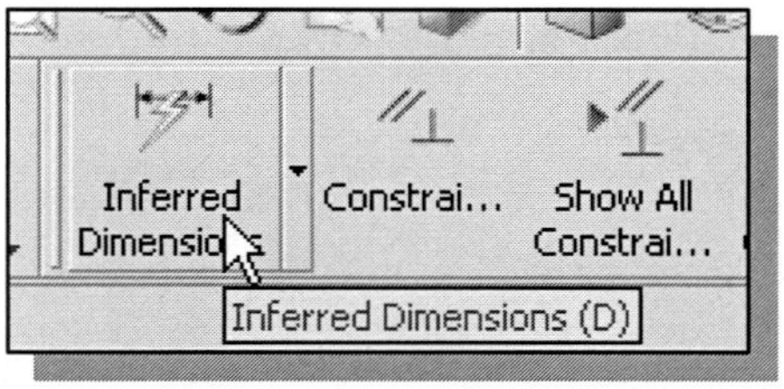

6. Activate the **Inferred Dimensions** command by left-click once on the icon as shown. The Inferred Dimensions command allows us to quickly create and modify dimensions

7. The message "*Select object to dimension or select dimension to edit*" is displayed in the *Message* area, at the bottom of the *UGS NX* window. Create and modify the four dimensions to describe the size of the sketch as shown in the figure.

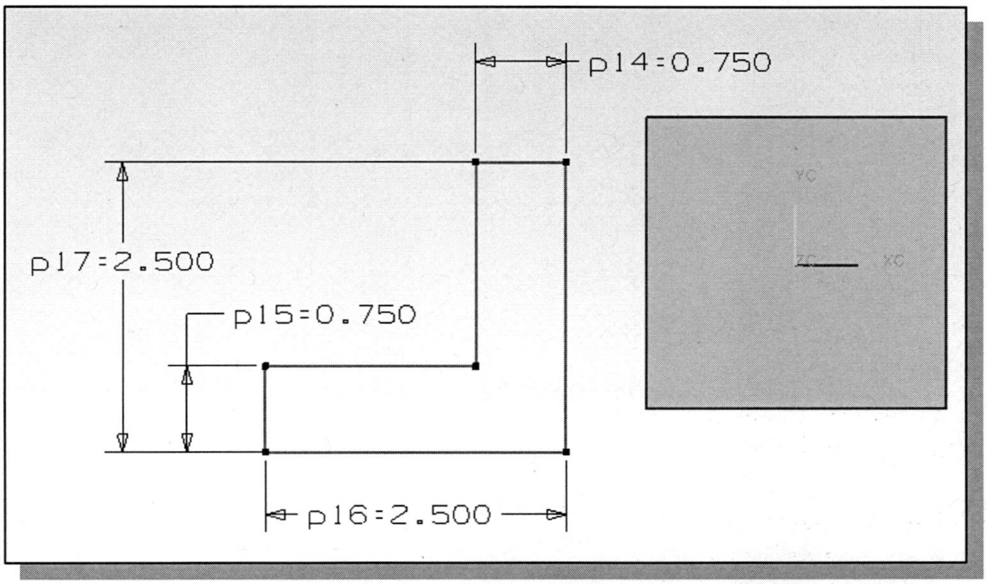

8. Create the two location dimensions to describe the position of the sketch relative to the top corner of the solid model as shown.

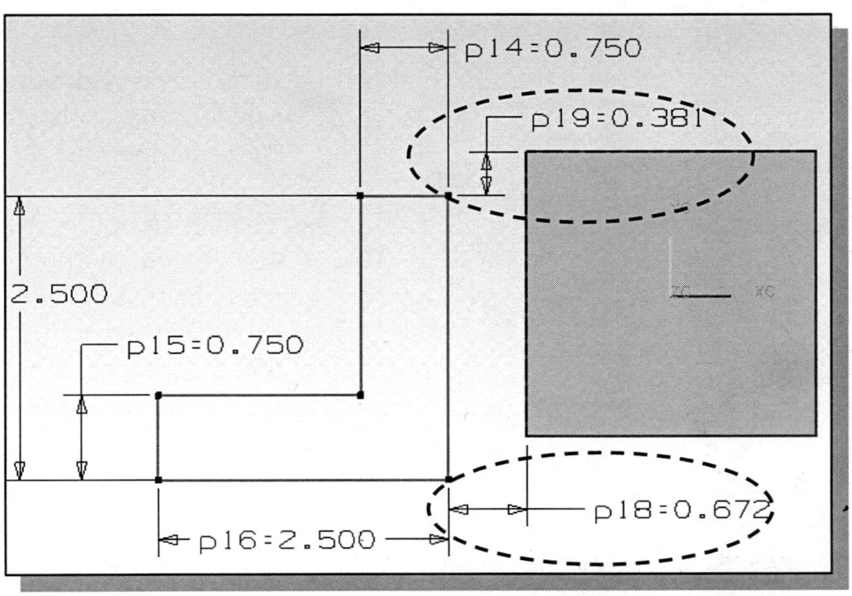

9. On your own, modify the two location dimensions to **0.0** as shown in the figure below.

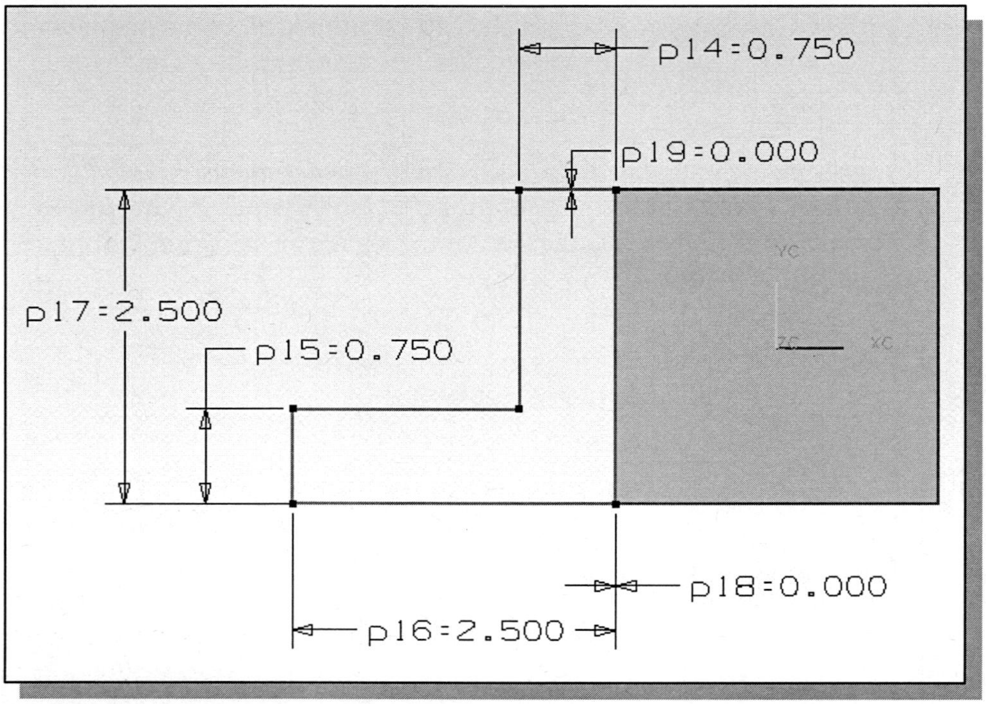

10. Select **Finish Sketch** by clicking once with the left-mouse-button (MB1) on the icon.

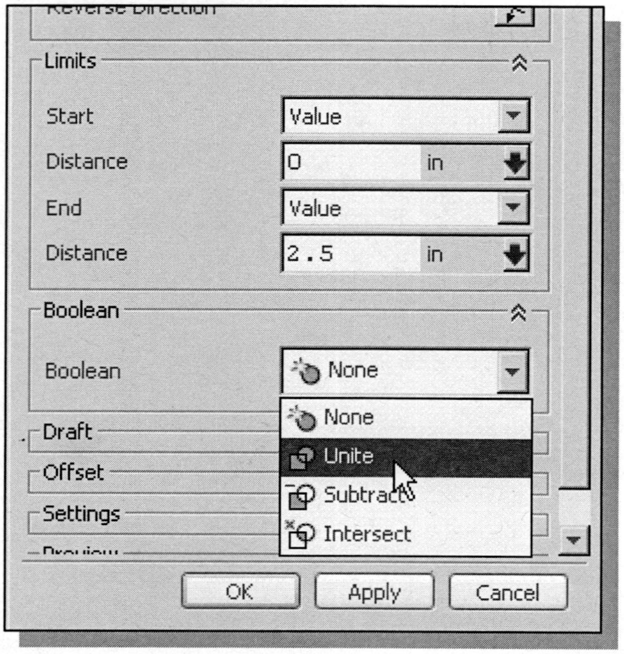

11. In the *Extrude* popup window, select **Unite** as the *Extrude Boolean* option.

➢ The **Unite** option will **add** the new feature to the existing solid. Note that the default option was set to **Create**, which would create a new solid model.

12. In the *Extrude* popup window, enter **2.5** as the extrusion *Distance*.

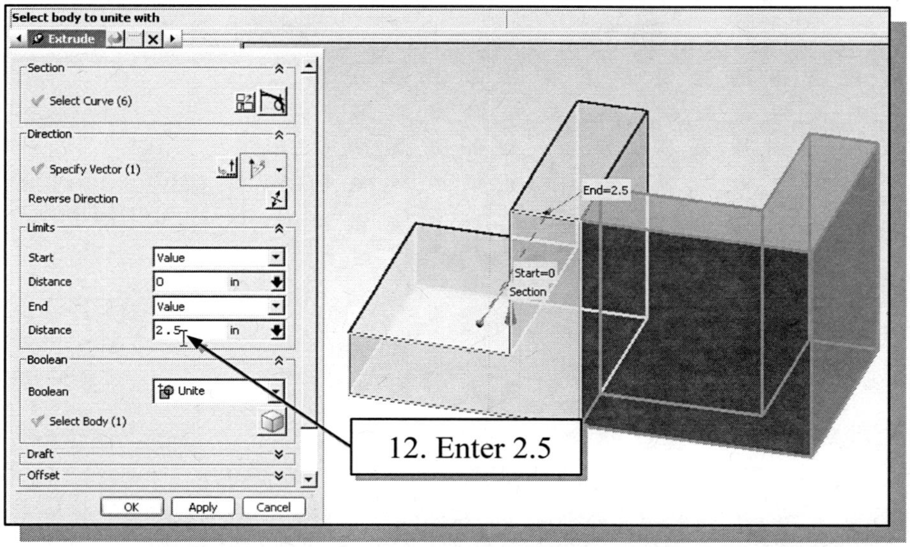

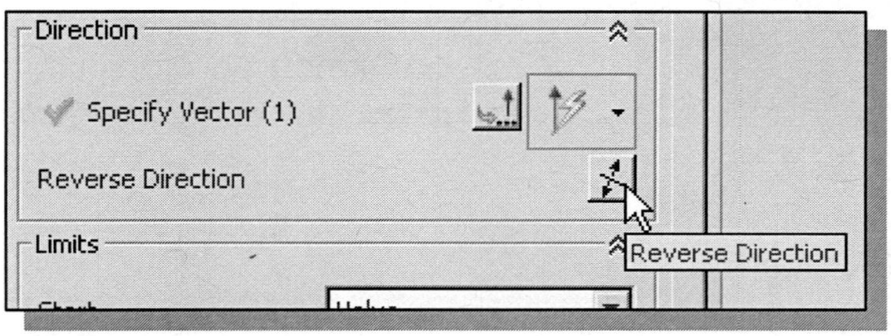

13. Click on the **Reverse Direction** icon to toggle the extrusion direction so that the extrusion appears as shown in the figure above.

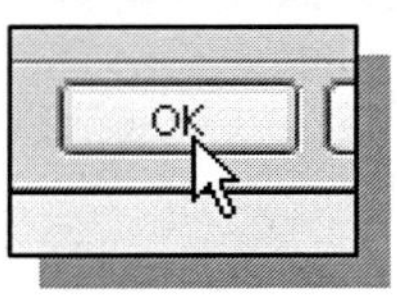

14. Click on the **OK** button to proceed with creating the 3D feature.

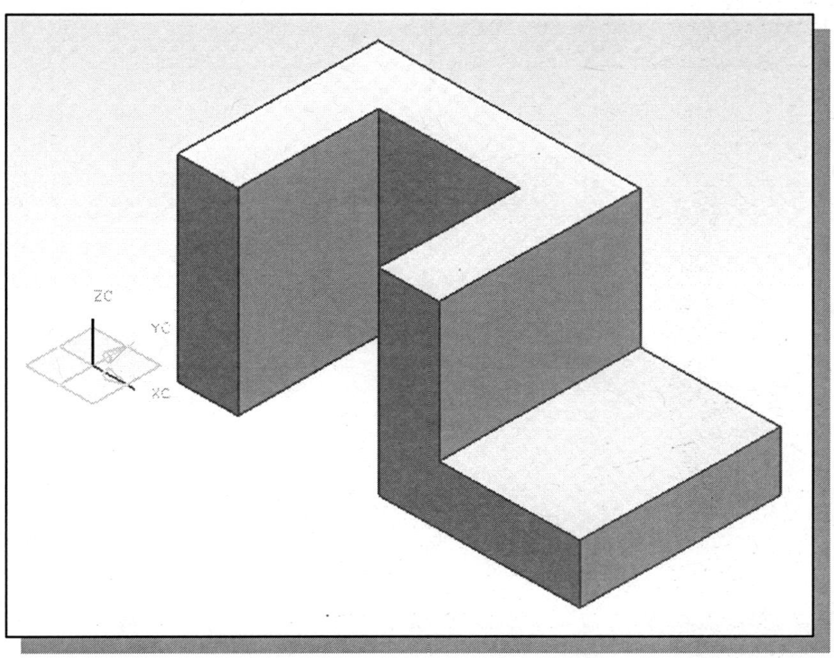

Step 6-2: Adding a Cut Feature

- Next, we will create and profile a circle, which will be used to create a **subtract** feature that will be added to the existing solid object.

1. In the ***Feature*** toolbars (toolbars aligned to the right edge of the main window), select the **Extrude** icon as shown.

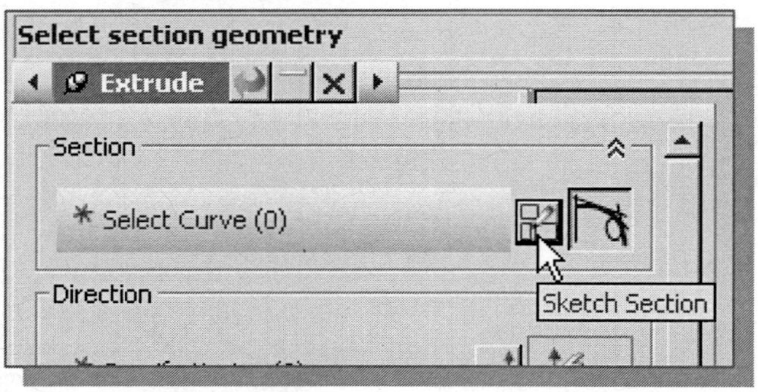

2. Click the **Sketch Section** button to begin creating a new *2D sketch*.

3. In the *Message* area, the message: "*Select planar face to sketch or select section geometry*" is displayed. *UGS NX* expects us to identify a planar surface where the 2D sketch of the next feature is to be created. Move the graphics cursor on the 3D part and notice that *UGS NX* will automatically highlight feasible planes and surfaces as the cursor is on top of the different surfaces. Pick the horizontal face of the 3D solid object as shown.

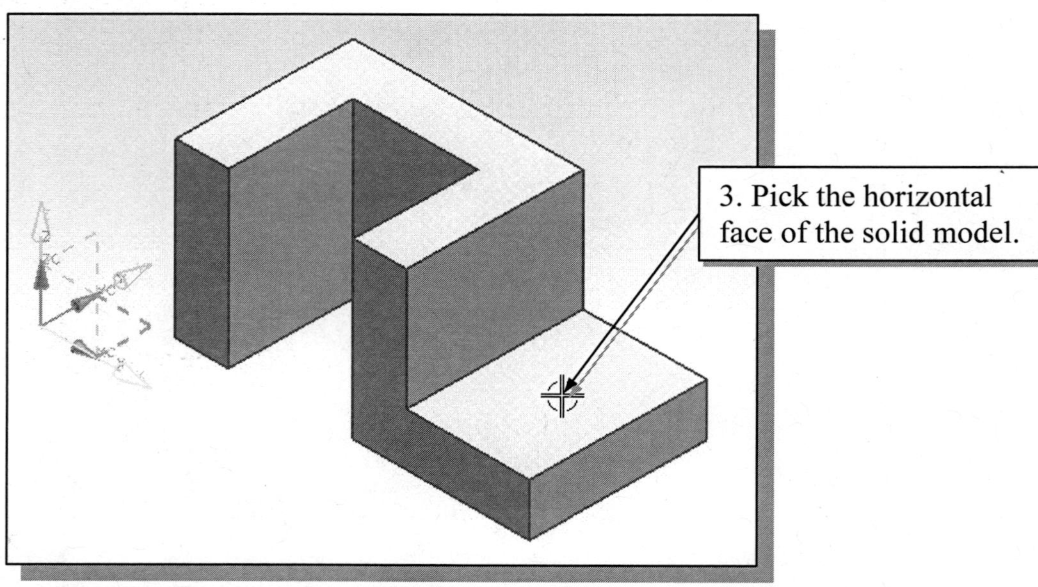

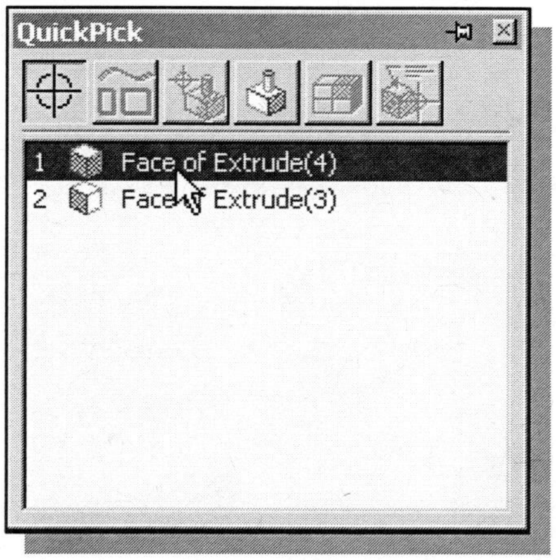

4. Note that if more than one option is feasible for the selection, a ***QuickPick*** dialog box will appear on the screen. Move the cursor over the different items in the displayed list to examine the feasible items. Click on the desired item to select it.

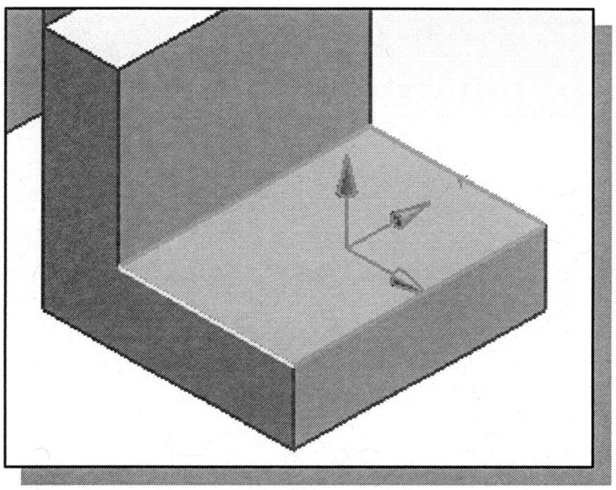

➢ Note that the sketch plane is aligned to the selected face. *UGS NX* automatically establishes a new work coordinate system (WCS), and records its location with respect to the part on which it was created.

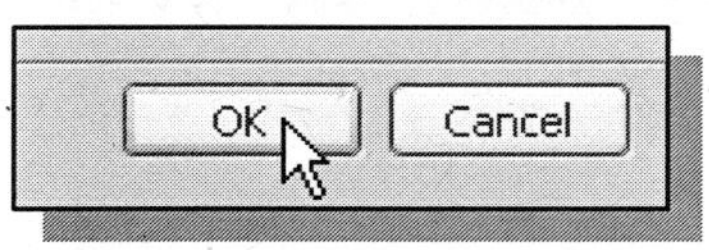

5. Click **OK** to accept the selected face and proceed with the new WCS.

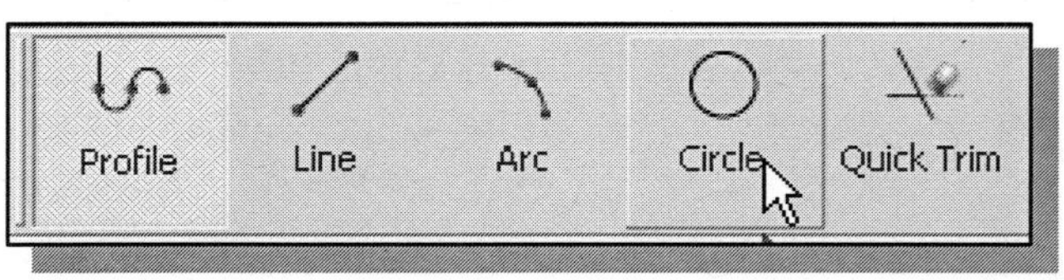

6. Select the **Circle** command by clicking once with the **left-mouse-button (MB1)** on the icon in the *Sketch Curve* toolbar.

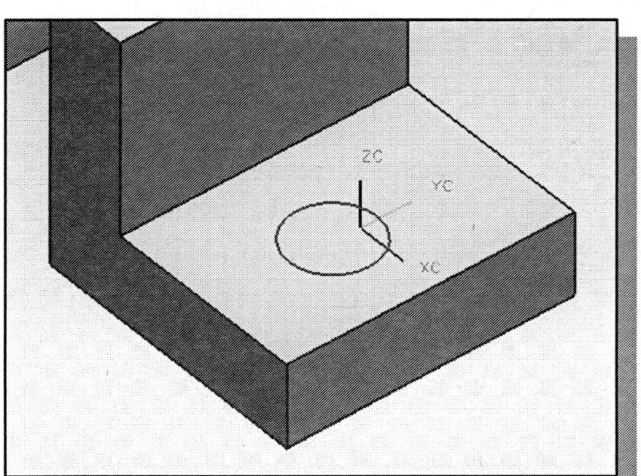

7. Create a circle of arbitrary size on the horizontal face of the solid model as shown.

8. On your own, create and modify the dimensions of the sketch as shown in the figure. (Hint: Use two locational dimensions and one size dimension.)

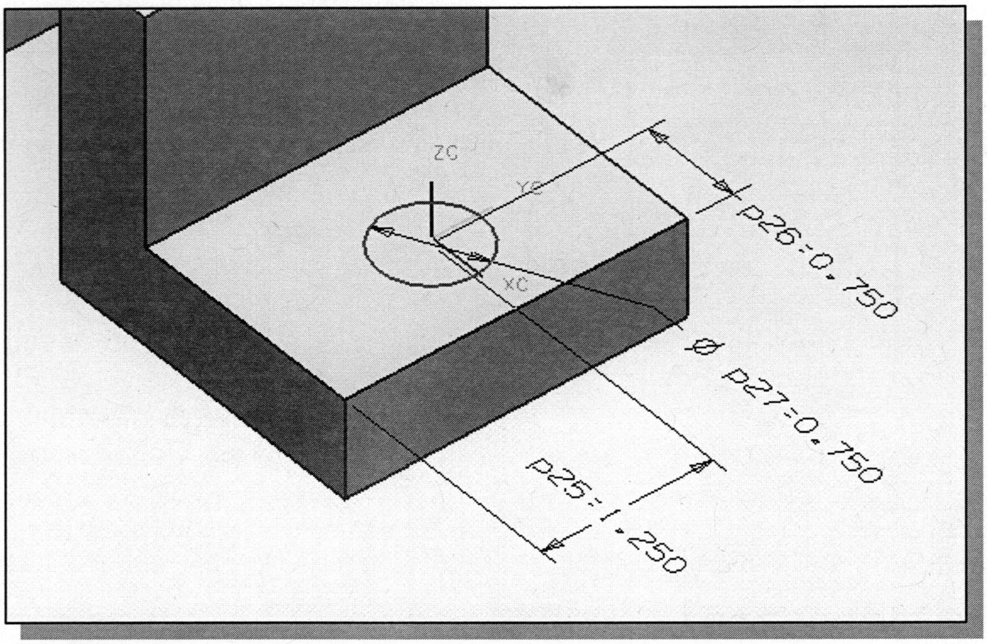

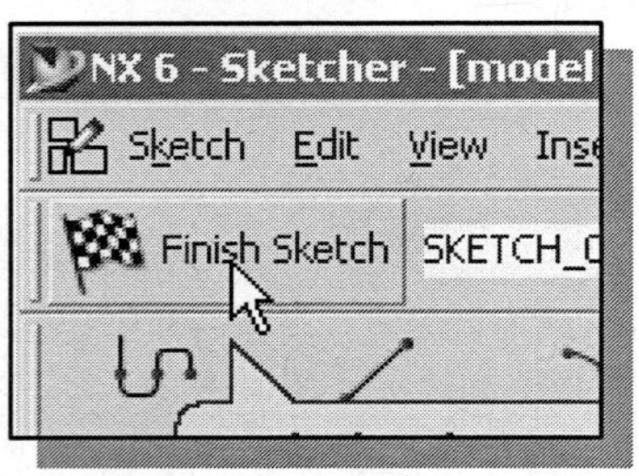

9. Select **Finish Sketch** by clicking once with the left-mouse-button (MB1) on the icon.

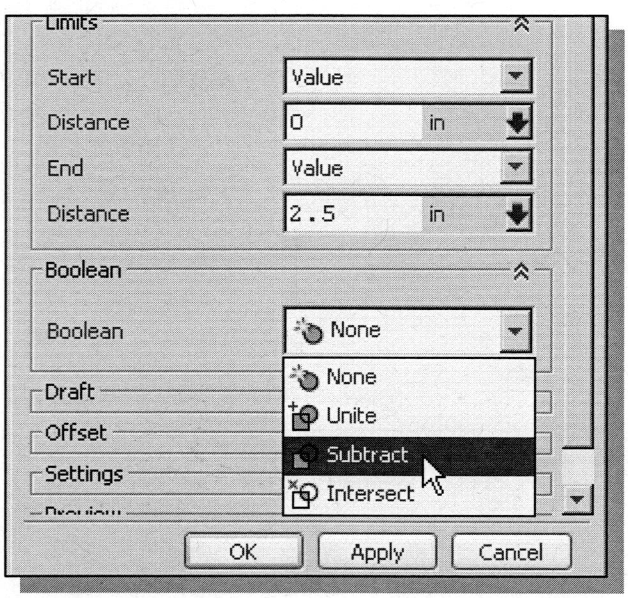

10. In the *Extrude* popup window, select **Subtract** as the *Extrude Boolean* option.

➤ The **Subtract** option will **remove** the volume of the new feature from the existing solid. Note that the default option was set to **Create**, which would create a new solid model.

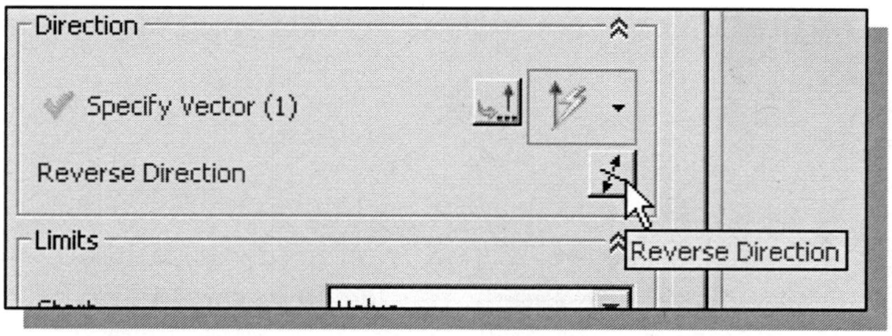

11. Click on the **Reverse Direction** icon to toggle the extrusion *Direction* so that the extrusion appears as shown in the figure.

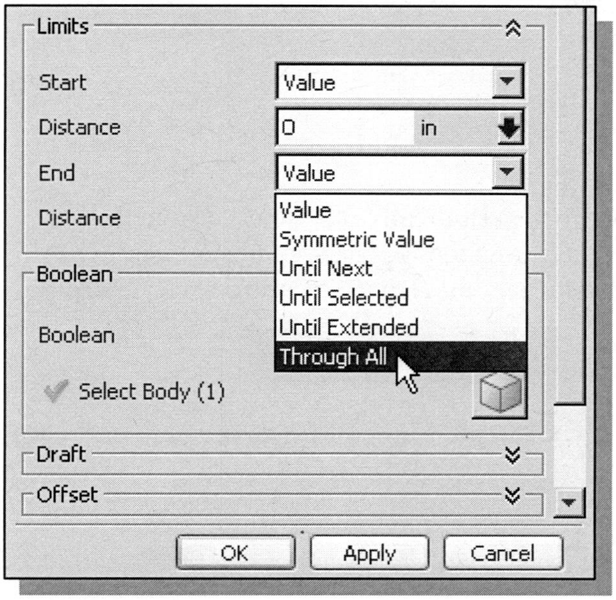

12. In the *Extrude* popup window, choose the **Through All** option to set the *End* extrusion limit.

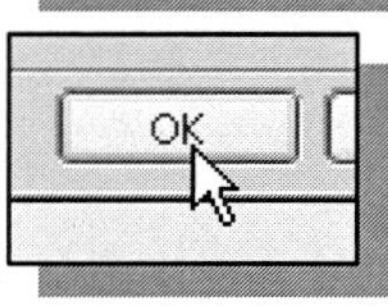

13. Click on the **OK** button to proceed with creating the 3D feature.

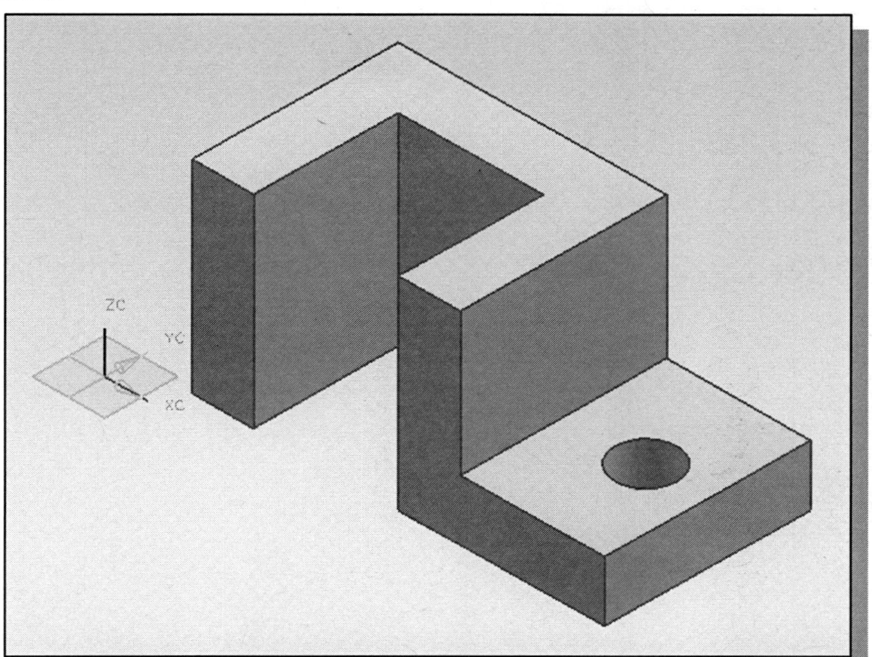

Save the Model and Exit *UGS NX*

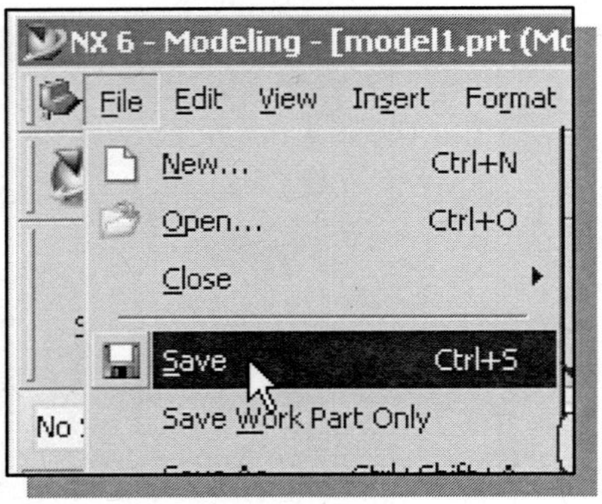

1. Select **Save** in the *File* pull-down menu, or you can also use the "**Ctrl-S**" combination (hold down the "Ctrl" key and hit the "S" key once) to save the part.

❖ You should form a habit of saving your work periodically, just in case something might go wrong while you are working on it. In general, one should save one's work at an interval of every 15 to 20 minutes. One should also save before making any major modifications to the model.

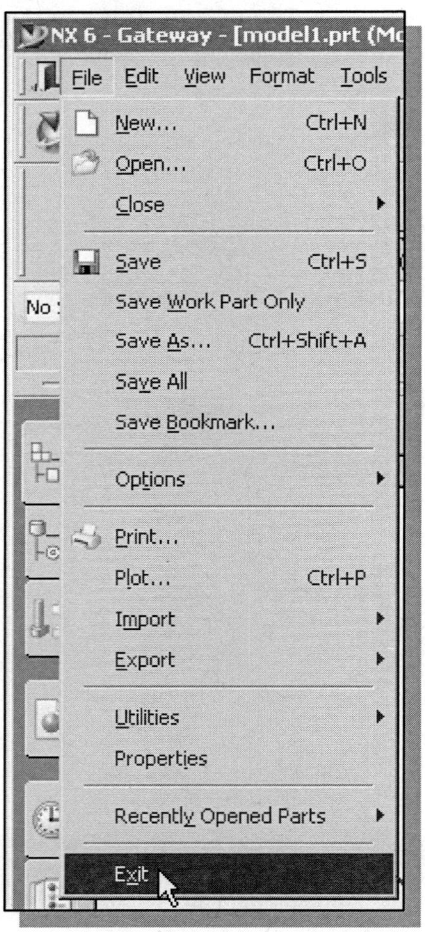

2. Select **Exit** in the *File* pull-down menu to exit *UGS NX.*

Questions:

1. What is the first thing we should set up in *UGS NX* when creating a new model?
2. Describe the general *parametric modeling* procedure.
3. List two of the geometric constraint symbols used by *UGS NX*.
4. What was the first feature we created in this lesson?
5. Describe the steps required to define the orientation of the sketching plane?
6. How do we change the size of 2D geometry in the *2D Sketcher* mode?

Exercises: (All dimensions are in inches.)

1. Plate Thickness: **.25**

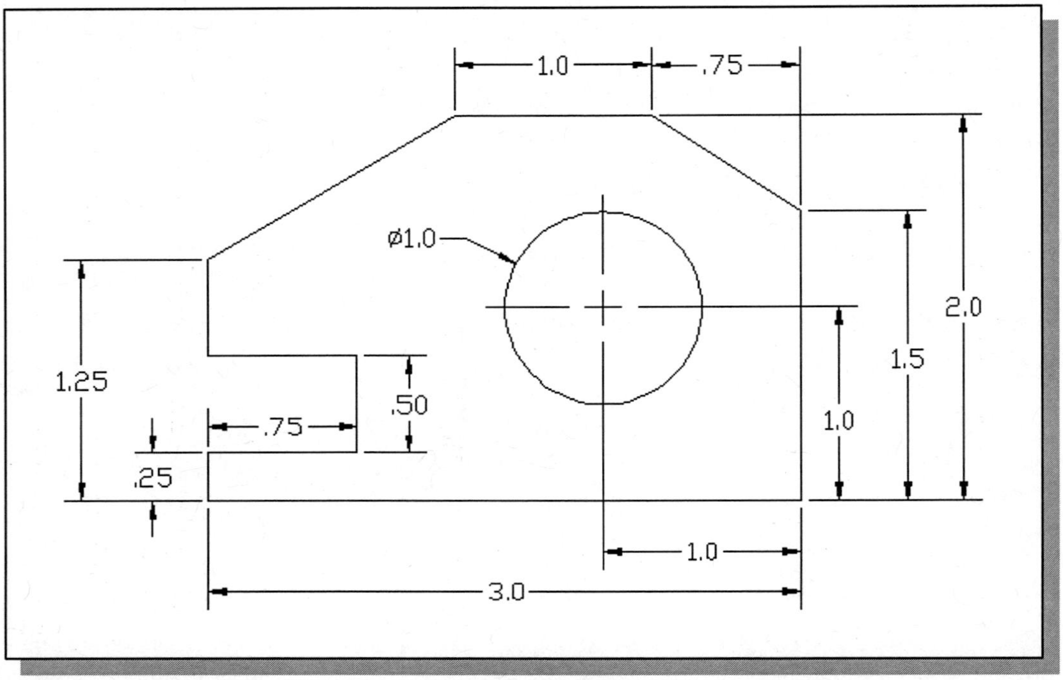

2. Plate Thickness: **.5**

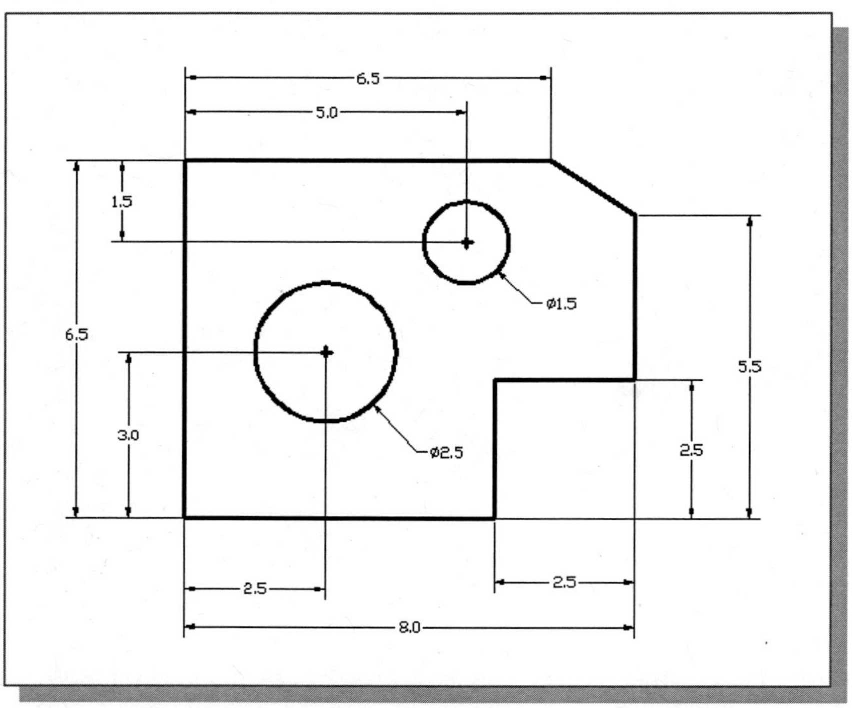

3.

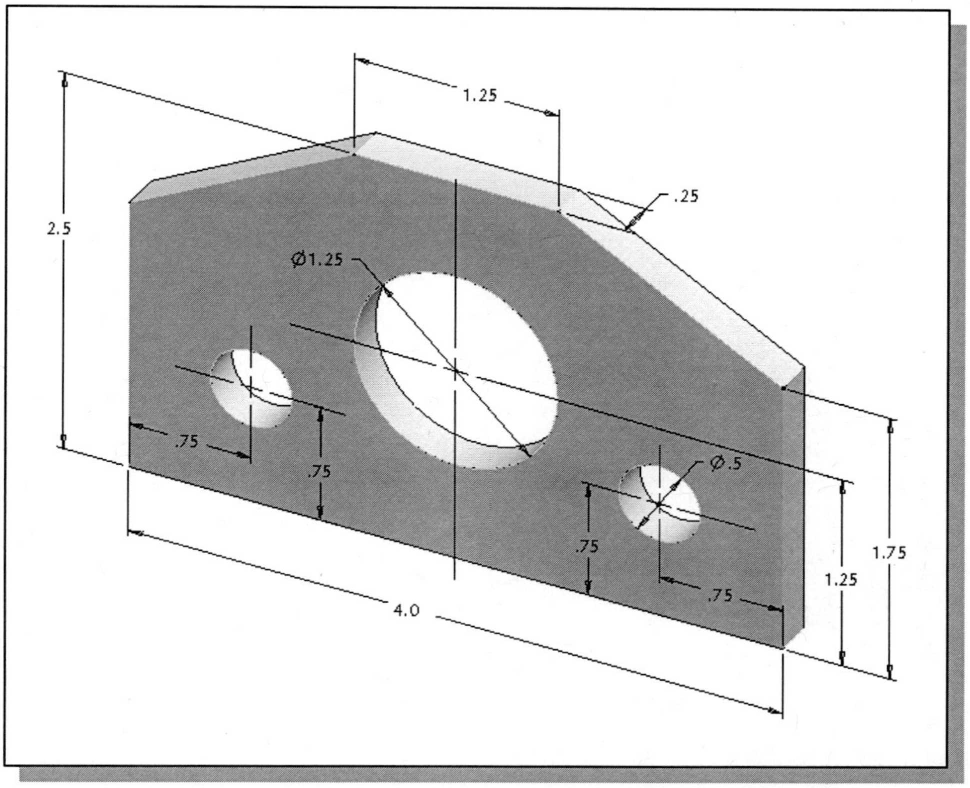
1.25
.25
2.5
Ø1.25
.75
.75
Ø.5
.75
1.75
1.25
.75
4.0

4.

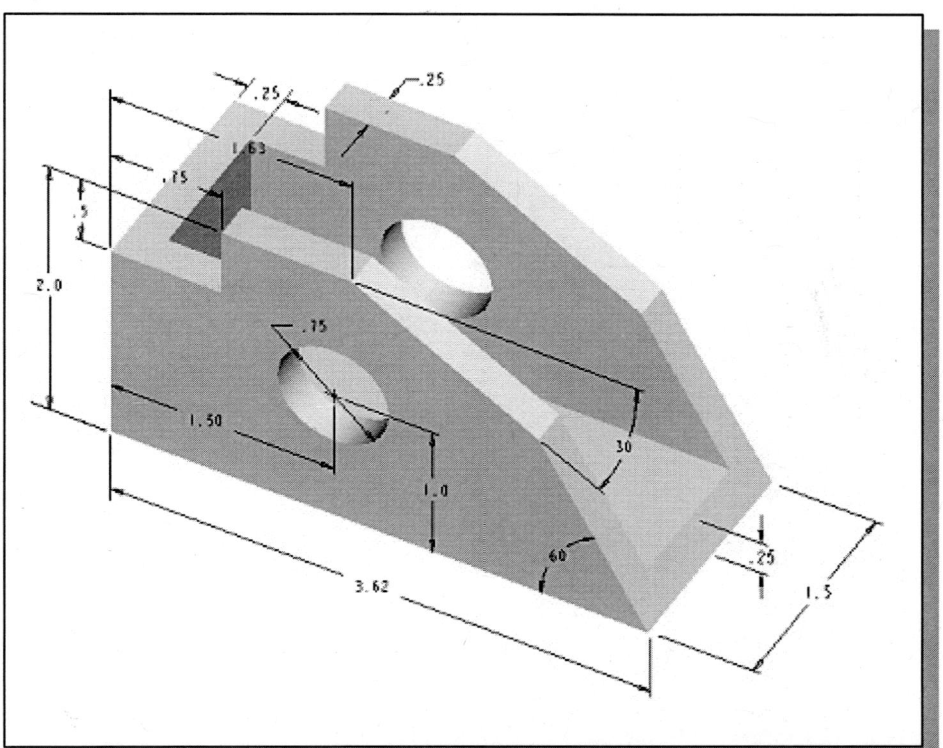
.25
.25
1.63
.75
.5
2.0
.75
1.50
30
1.0
60
.25
3.62
1.5

Notes:

Chapter 3
Constructive Solid Geometry Concepts

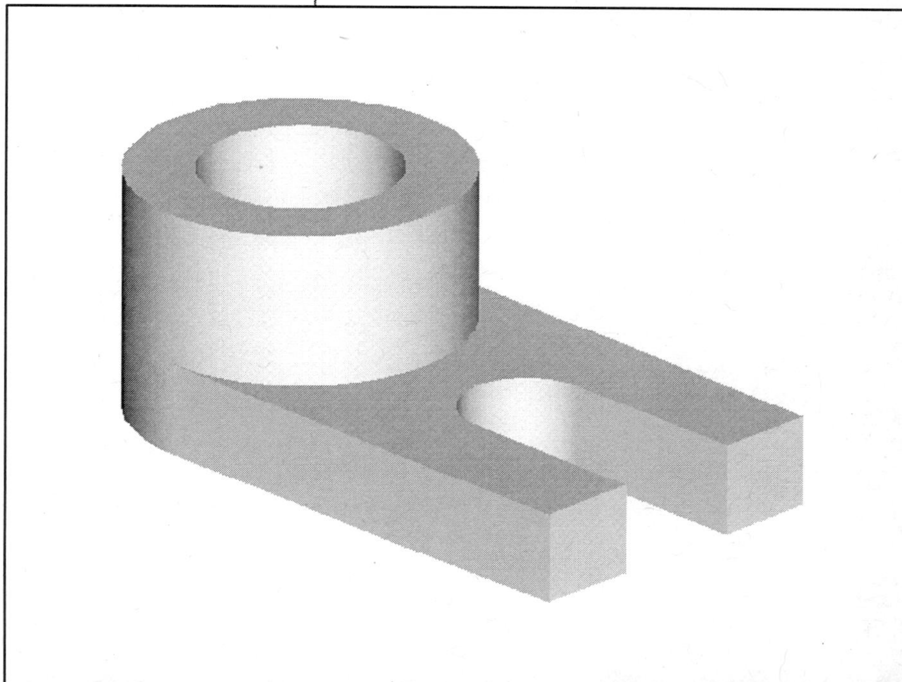

Learning Objectives

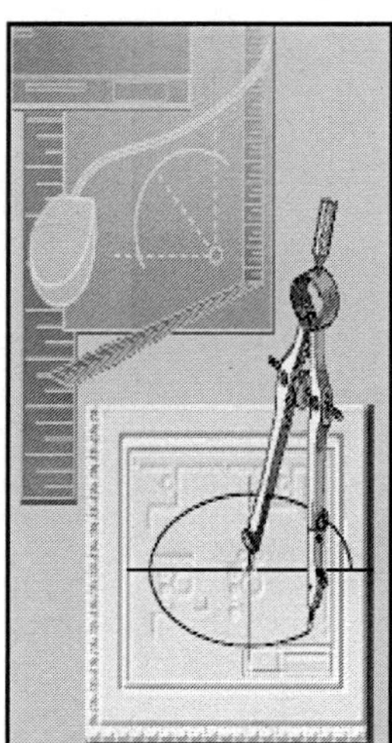

- Understand Constructive Solid Geometry Concepts
- Create a Binary Tree
- Understand the Basic Boolean Operations
- Setup GRID and SNAP Intervals
- Understand the Importance of Order of Features
- Create Placed Features
- Use the Different Extrusion Options

Introduction

In the 1980s, one of the main advancements in **solid modeling** was the development of the **Constructive Solid Geometry** (CSG) method. CSG describes the solid model as combinations of basic three-dimensional shapes (**primitive solids**). The basic primitive solid set typically includes: Rectangular-prism (Block), Cylinder, Cone, Sphere, and Torus (Tube). Two solid objects can be combined into one object in various ways using operations known as **Boolean operations**. There are three basic Boolean operations: **UNITE (Union)**, **SUBTRACT (Difference)**, and **INTERSECT**. The *UNITE* operation combines the two volumes included in the different solids into a single solid. The *SUBTRACT* operation subtracts the volume of one solid object from the other solid object. The *INTERSECT* operation keeps only the volume common to both solid objects. The CSG method is also known as the **Machinist's Approach**, as the method is parallel to machine shop practices.

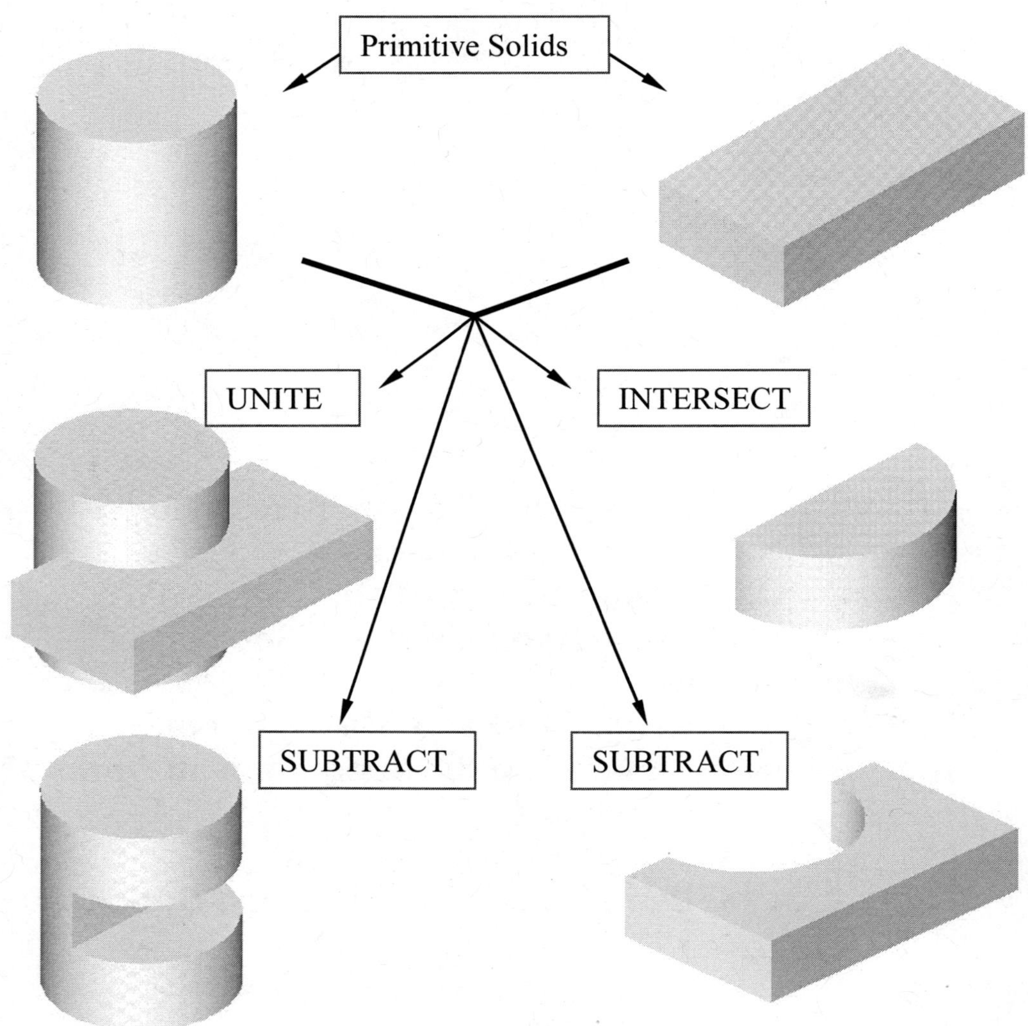

Binary Tree

The CSG is also referred to as the method used to store a solid model in the database. The resulting solid can be easily represented by what is called a **binary tree**. In a binary tree, the terminal branches (leaves) are the various primitives that are linked together to make the final solid object (the root). The binary tree is an effective way to keep track of the *history* of the resulting solid. By keeping track of the history, the solid model can be re-built by re-linking through the binary tree. This provides a convenient way to modify the model. We can make modifications at the appropriate links in the binary tree and re-link the rest of the history tree without building a new model.

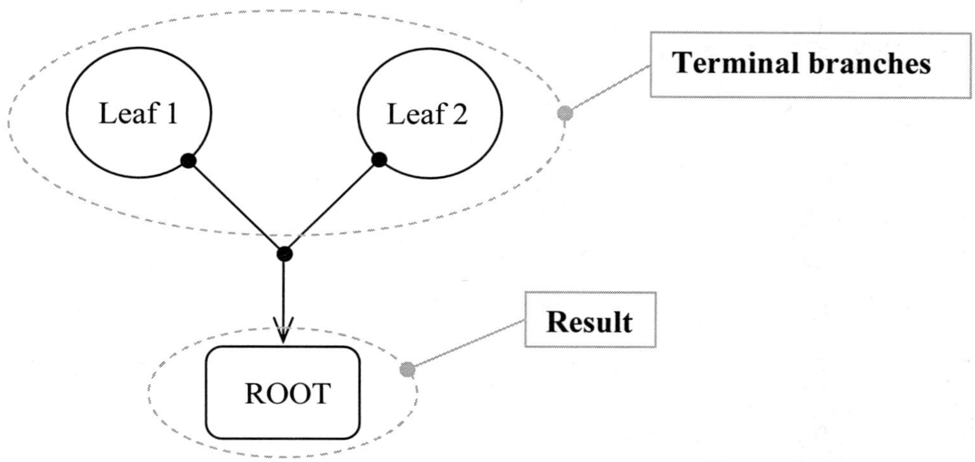

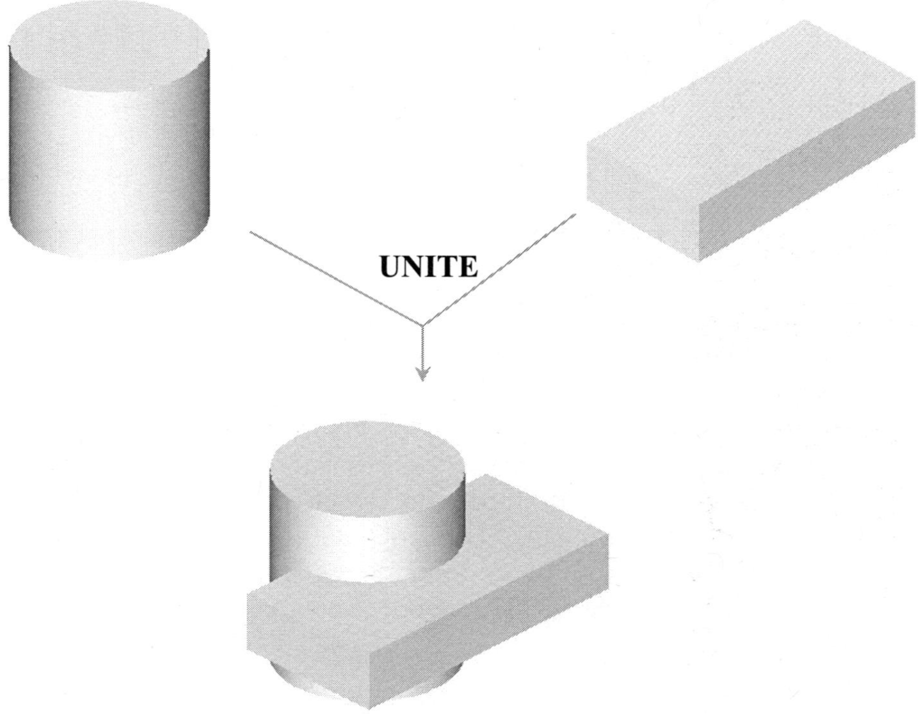

The *Locator* Design

The CSG concept is one of the important building blocks for feature-based modeling. In *UGS NX*, the CSG concept can be used as a planning tool to determine the number of features that are needed to construct the model. It is also a good practice to create features that are parallel to the manufacturing process required for the design. With parametric modeling, we are no longer limited to using only the predefined basic solid shapes. In fact, any solid features we create in *UGS NX* are used as primitive solids; parametric modeling allows us to maintain full control of the design variables that are used to describe the features. In this lesson, a more in-depth look at the parametric modeling procedure is presented. The equivalent CSG operation for each feature is also illustrated.

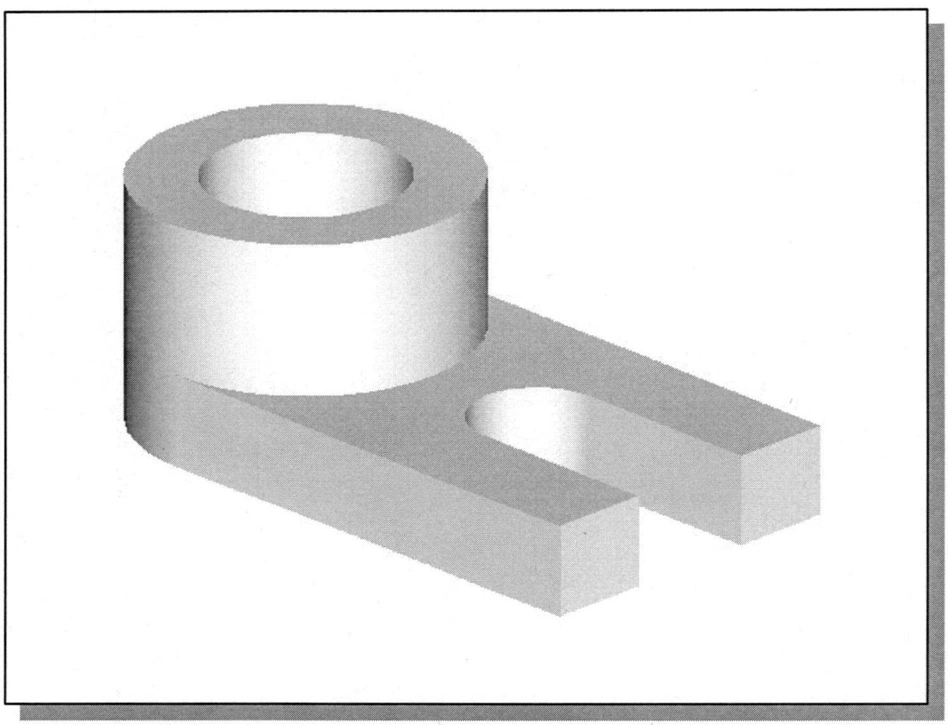

➢ Before going through the tutorial, on your own, make a sketch of a CSG binary tree of the ***Locator*** design using only two basic types of primitive solids: cylinder and rectangular prism. In your sketch, how many *Boolean operations* will be required to create the model? What is your choice of the first primitive solid to use, and why? Take a few minutes to consider these questions and do the preliminary planning by sketching on a piece of paper. Compare the sketch you make to the CSG binary tree steps shown on page 3-5. Note that there are many different possibilities in combining the basic primitive solids to form the solid model. Even for the simplest design, it is possible to take several different approaches to creating the same solid model.

Modeling Strategy - CSG Binary Tree

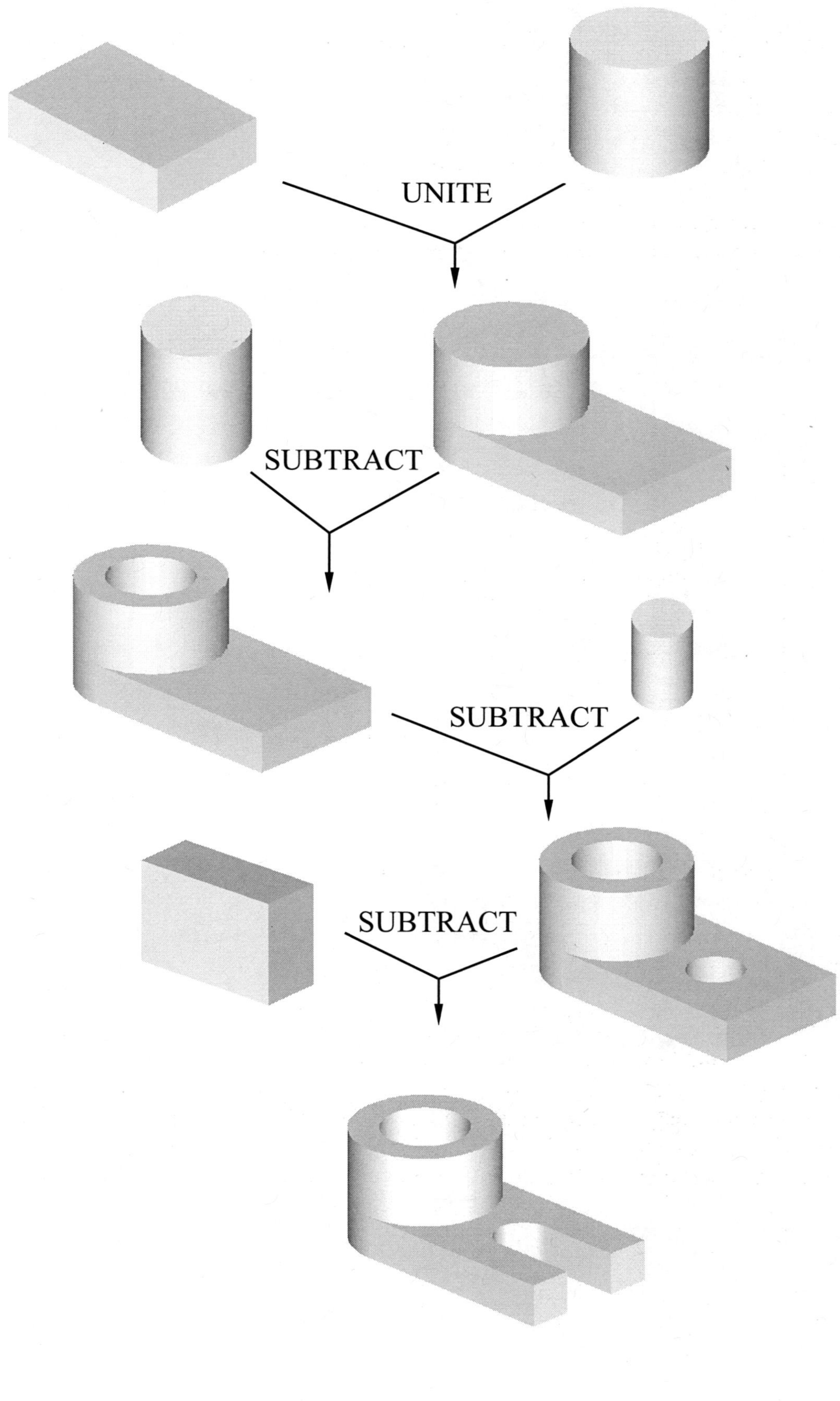

Starting UGS NX

1. Select the **UGS NX** option on the *Start* menu or select the **UGS NX** icon on the desktop to start *UGS NX*. The *UGS NX* main window will appear on the screen.

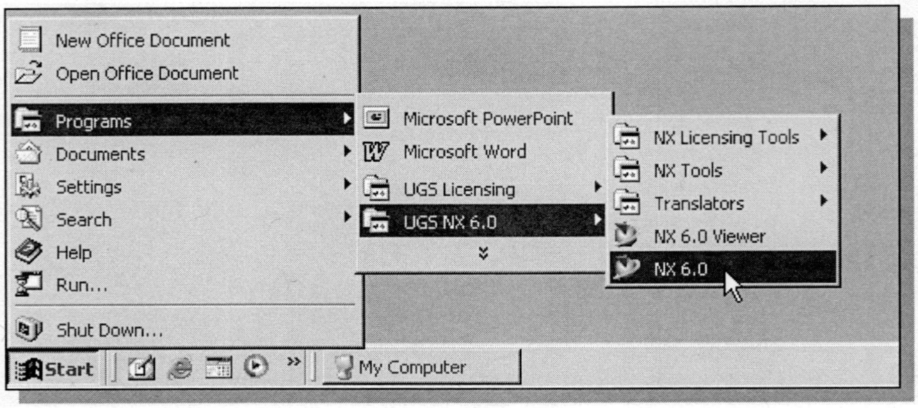

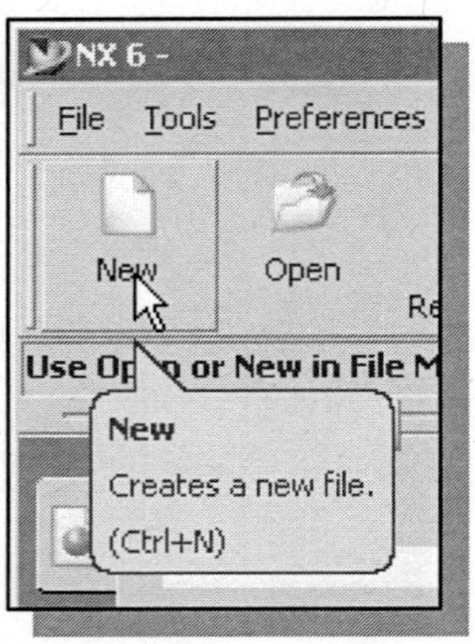

2. Select the **New** icon with a single click of the left-mouse-button (MB1) in the *Standard* toolbar area.

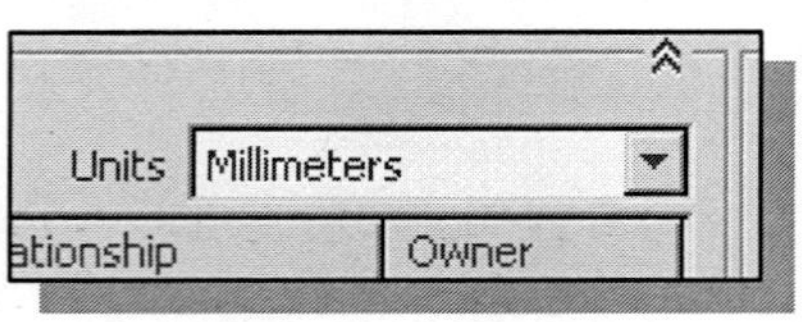

3. In the *New Part* window, confirm the units are set to **Millimeters** as shown in the figure.

4. Select the **Blank** template file as shown.

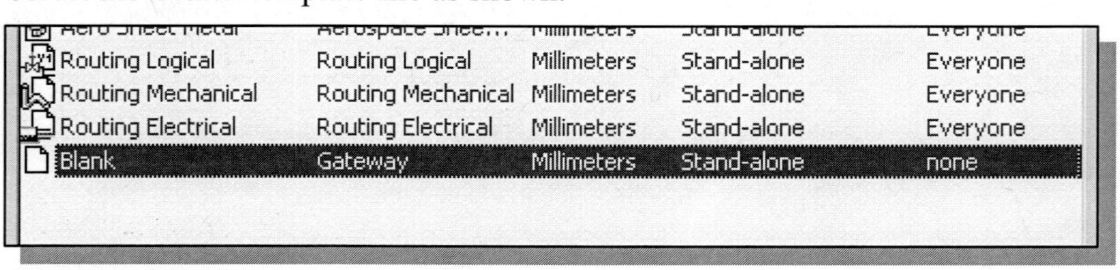

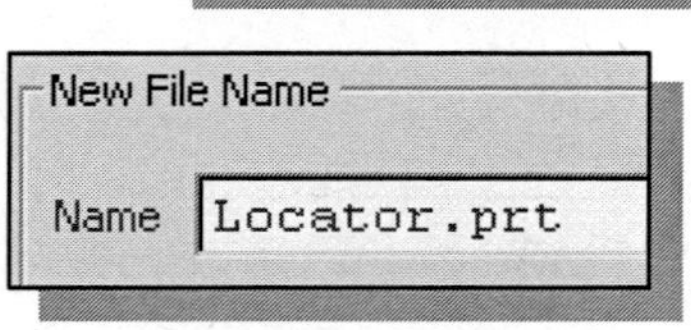

5. Enter **Locator** as the *New File Name*.

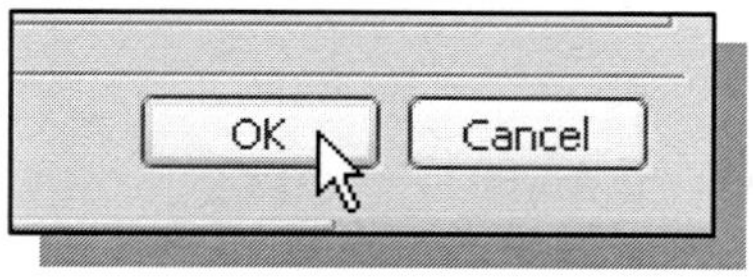

6. Click **OK** to proceed with the **New File** command.

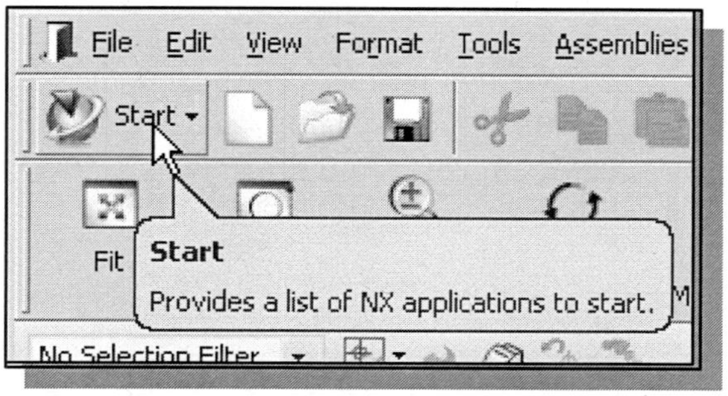

7. Select the **Start** icon with a single click of the left-mouse-button (MB1) in the *Standard* toolbar.

8. Pick **Modeling** in the pull-down list as shown in the figure.

Base Feature

In *parametric modeling*, the first solid feature is called the **base feature,** which usually is the primary shape of the model. Depending upon the design intent, additional features are added to the base feature.

Some of the considerations involved in selecting the base feature are:

- **Design intent** – Determine the functionality of the design; identify the feature that is central to the design.

- **Order of features** – Choose the feature that is the logical base in terms of the order of features in the design.

- **Ease of making modifications** – Select a base feature that is more stable and is less likely to be changed.

➢ A rectangular block will be created first as the base feature of the ***Locator*** design.

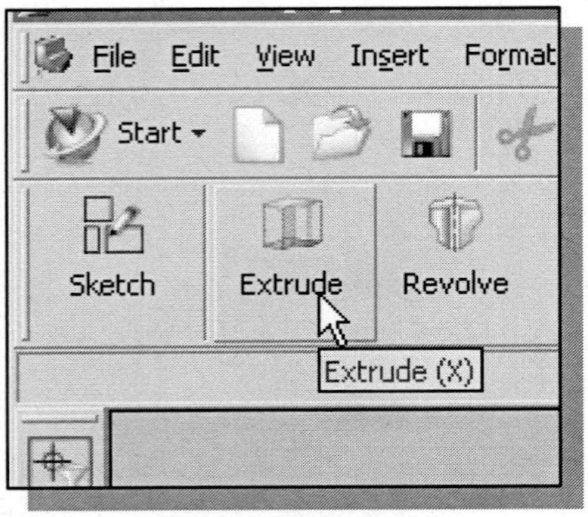

1. In the ***Feature*** toolbars (toolbars aligned to the right edge of the main window), select the **Extrude** icon as shown.

- The ***Extrude*** feature options dialog box, which contains applicable construction options, is displayed as shown in the figure below.

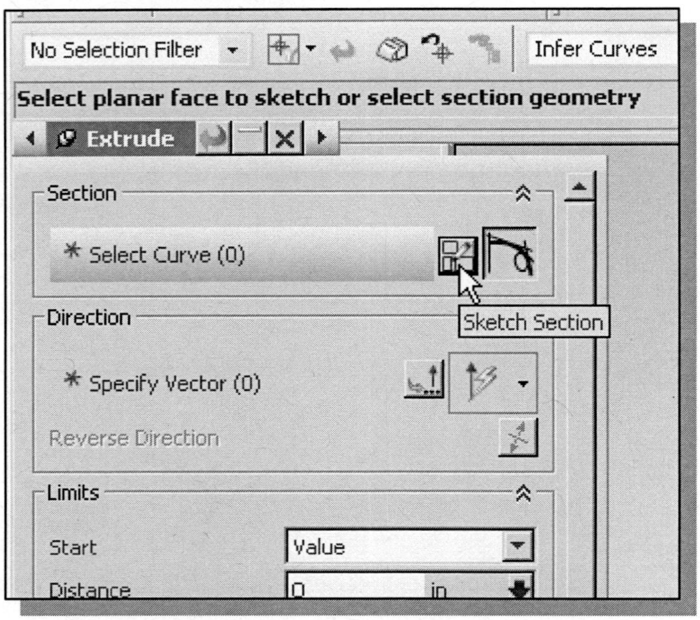

2. On your own, move the cursor over the icons and read the brief descriptions of the different options available.

3. Click the **Sketch Section** button to begin creating a new *2D sketch.*

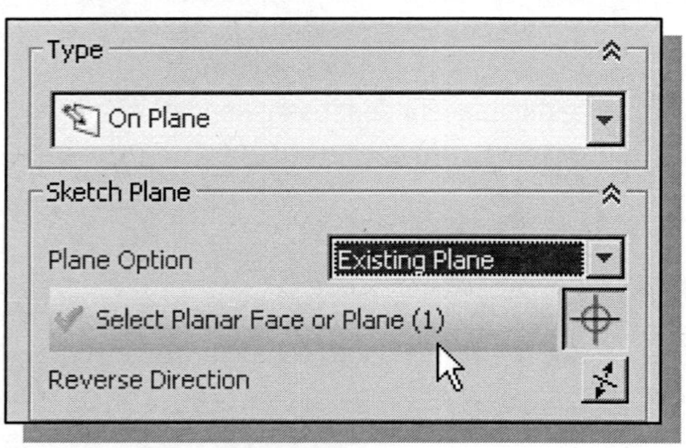

➢ The default sketch plane option is set to sketch on **Existing Plane** and *NX* expects the selection of *Planar Face or Plane.*

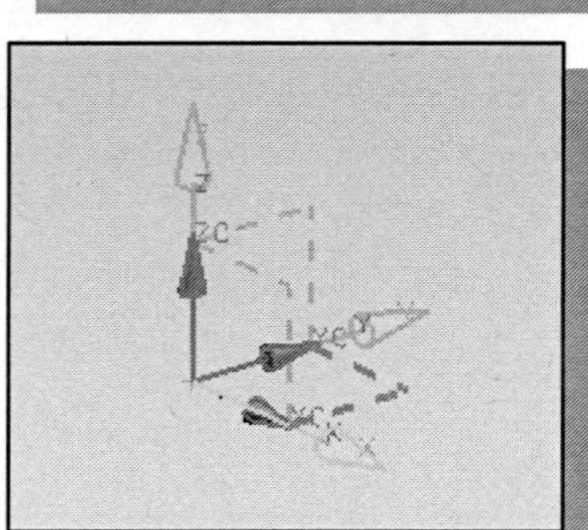

❖ Note the default sketch plane is aligned to the *X-Y* plane of the displayed work coordinate system.

4. Click **OK** to accept the default setting of the sketch plane.

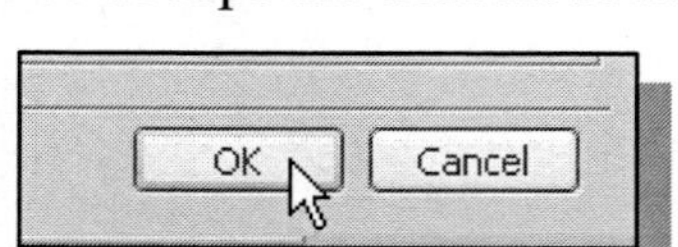

Work plane *GRID* Display Setup

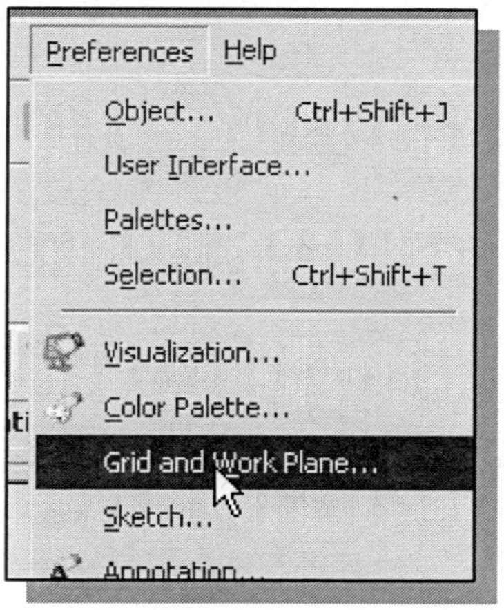

1. In the pull-down menu, select

   [Preferences] → [Grid and Work Plane]

❖ The **Grid Line** option in *UGS NX* can be used to provide visual clues to assist the creations of 2D sketches.

2. In the *Grid and Work Plane Preferences* dialog box, set the *Minor Lines Per Major* to **10**.

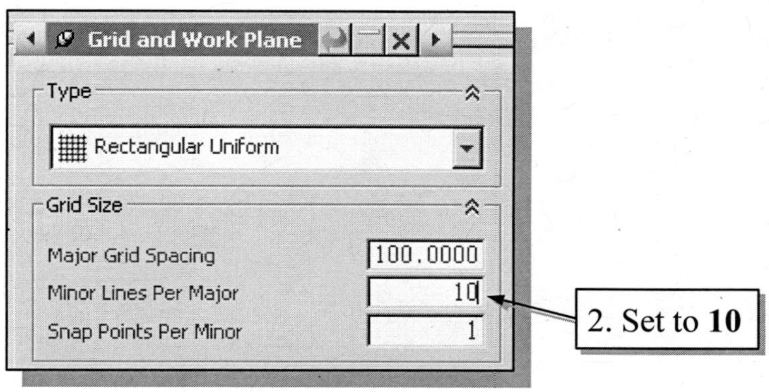

3. Confirm the **Show Grid** option is ***ON*** to display the grid lines on the work plane.

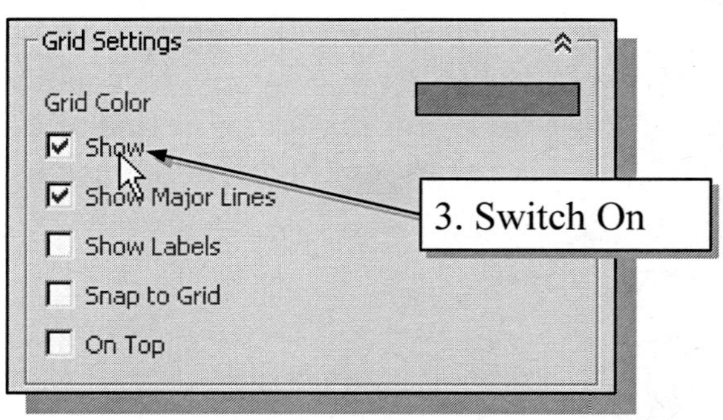

4. Pick **OK** to exit the *Grid and Work Plane Preferences* dialog box.

➢ Note that although the *Snap to Grid* option is also available in *UGS NX*, its usage in parametric modeling is not recommended.

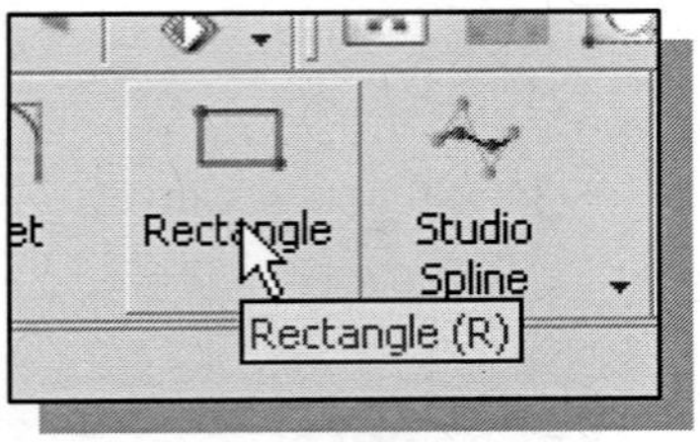

5. Select the **Rectangle** command by clicking once with the **left-mouse-button** on the icon in the *Sketch Curve* toolbar.

6. Create a rectangle of arbitrary size by selecting two locations on the screen as shown below.

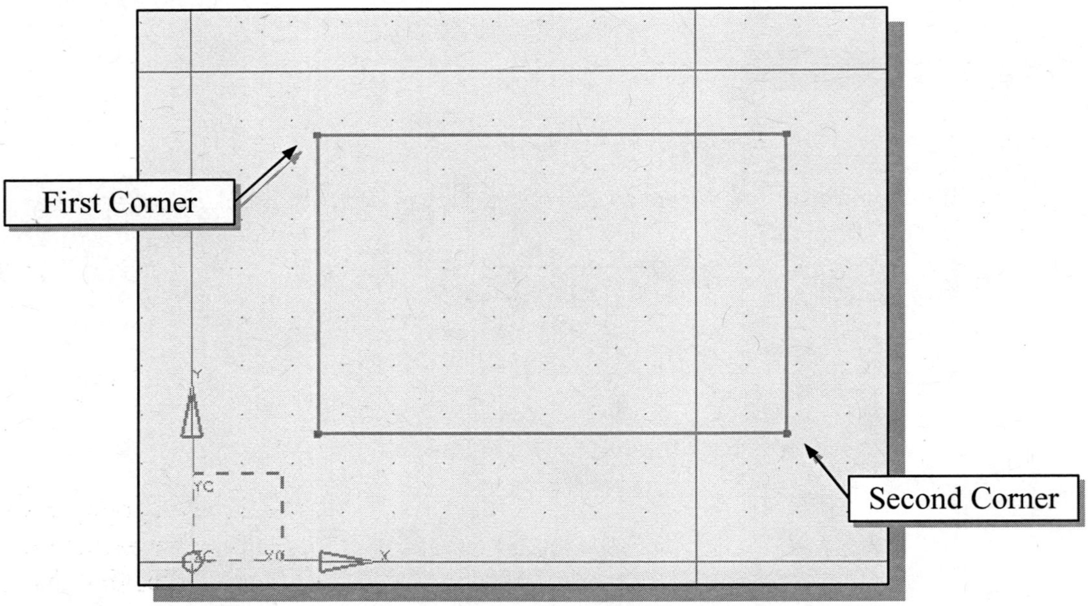

7. Inside the graphics window, click once with the middle-mouse-button (MB2) to end the Rectangle command.

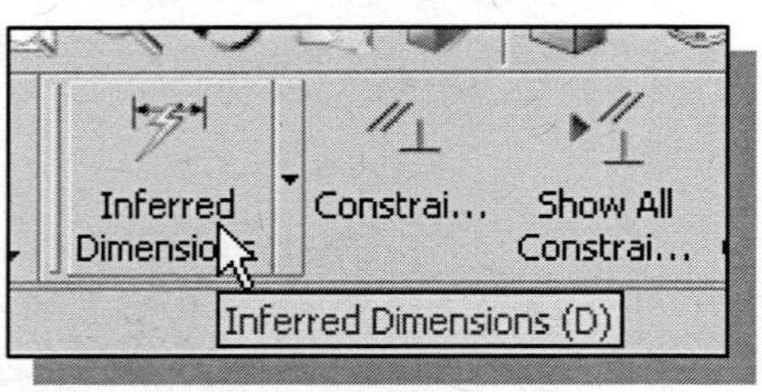

8. Activate the **Inferred Dimensions** command by left-clicking once on the icon as shown. The Inferred Dimensions command allows us to quickly create and modify dimensions.

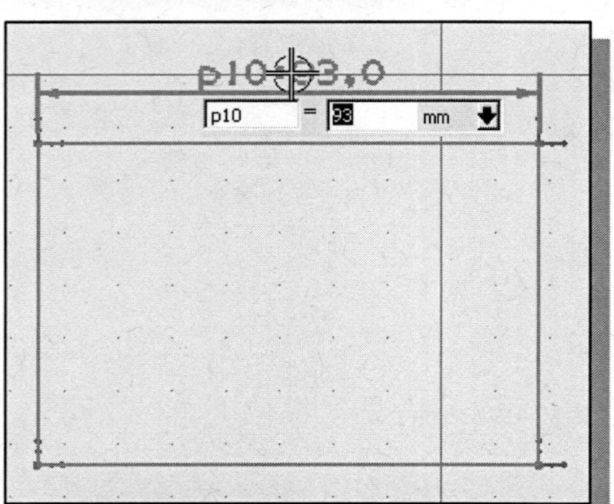

9. The message "*Select object to dimension or select dimension to edit*" is displayed in the *Message* area. Select the **top horizontal line** by left-clicking once on the line.

10. Move the graphics cursor above the selected line and left-click to place the dimension. (Note that the value displayed on your screen might be different than what is shown.)

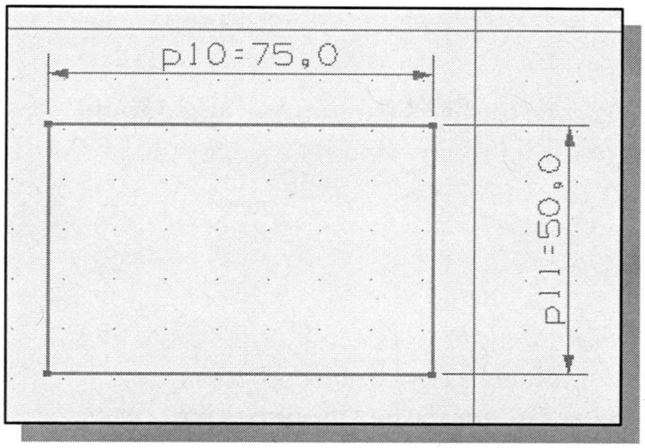

11. On your own, create and modify the dimensions of the sketched rectangle as shown.

Completing the Base Solid Feature

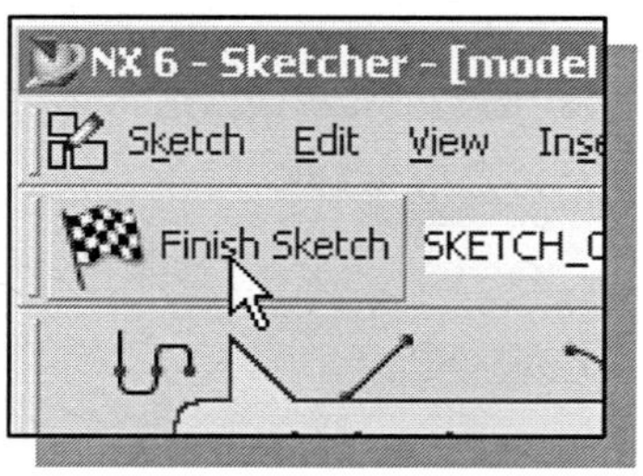

1. Select **Finish Sketch** by clicking once with the left-mouse-button (MB1) on the icon.

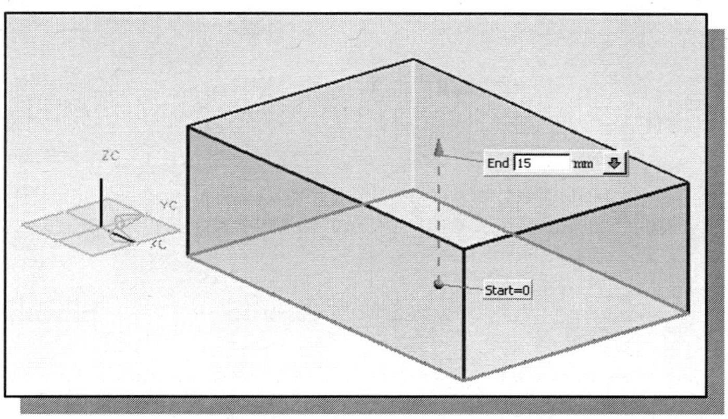

2. In the *Extrude* popup window, enter **15** as the extrusion distance. Notice that the sketch region is automatically selected as the extrusion section.

3. Click on the **OK** button to proceed with creating the 3D part. Use the *Dynamic Viewing* options to view the created part. Change the display to the isometric view as shown before going to the next section.

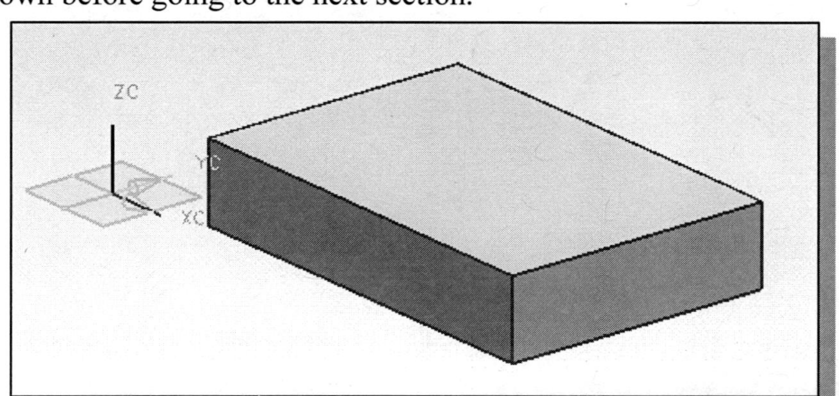

Creating the Next Solid Feature

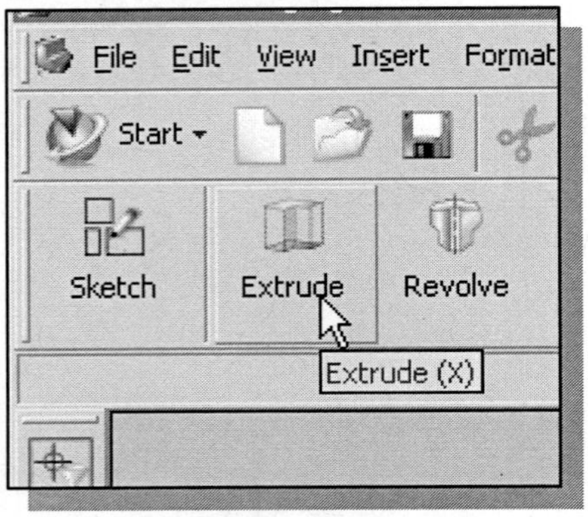

1. In the ***Feature*** toolbars (toolbars aligned to the right edge of the main window), select the **Extrude** icon as shown.

- The ***Extrude*** feature options dialog box, which contains applicable construction options, is displayed as shown in the figure below.

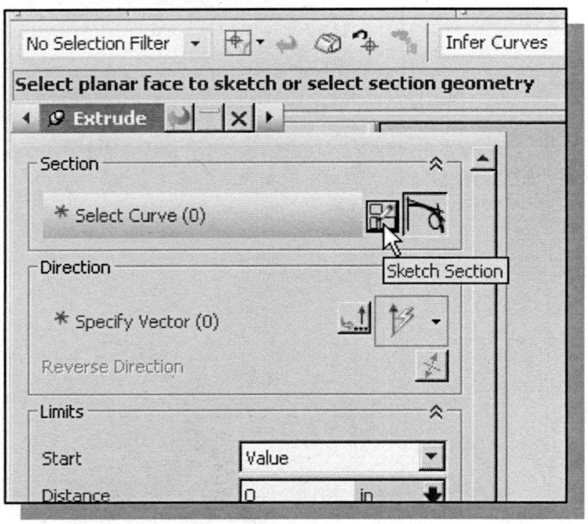

2. On your own, move the cursor over the icons and read the brief descriptions of the different options available.

3. Click the **Sketch Section** button to begin creating a new *2D sketch.*

4. Use the dynamic rotation function to rotate and pick the bottom face as the sketch plane as shown below.

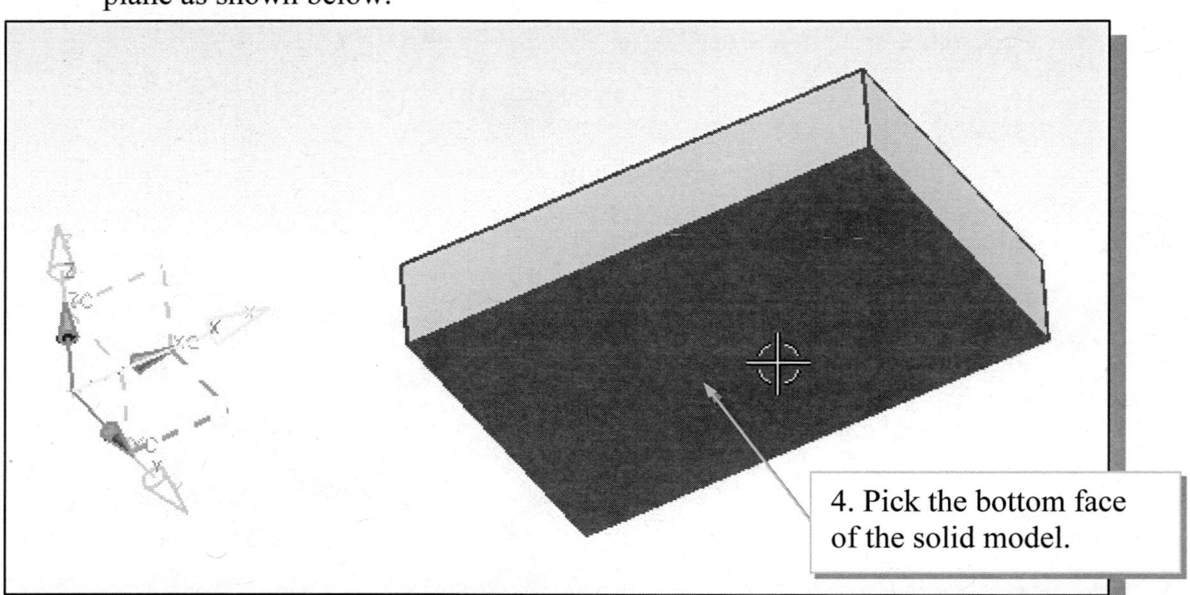

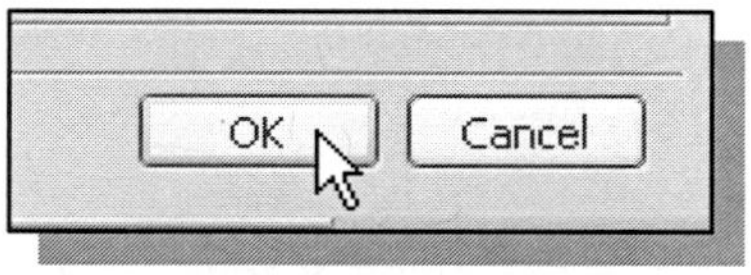

5. Click **OK** to accept the selected face and proceed with the new WCS.

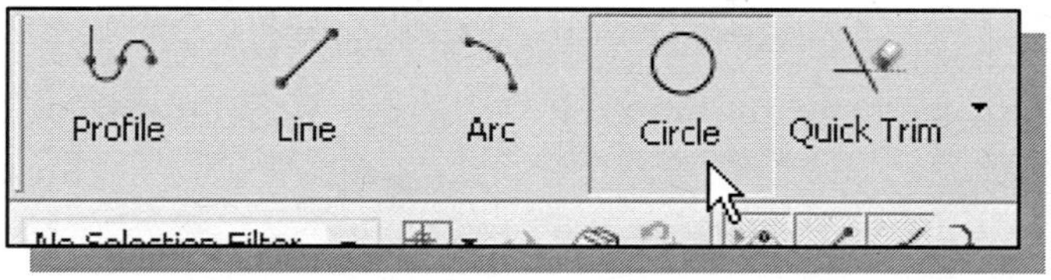

6. Select the **Circle** command by clicking once with the **left-mouse-button (MB1)** on the icon in the *SketchCurve* toolbar.

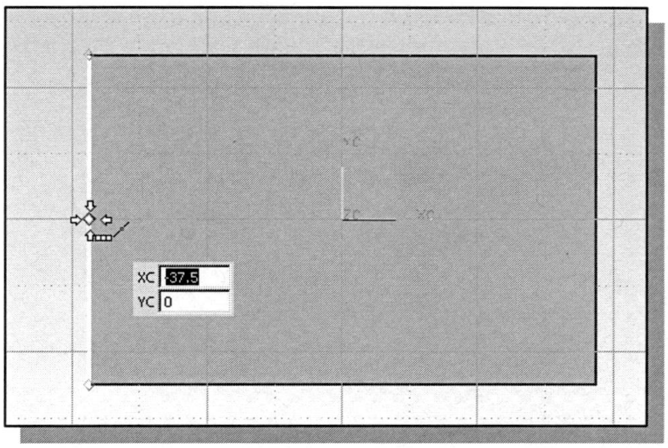

➢ We will align the center of the circle to the midpoint of the base feature.

7. Move the cursor along the shorter edge of the base feature and pick the midpoint of the edge when the midpoint is displayed with the constraint symbol.

8. Select the top corner of the base feature to create a circle as shown below.

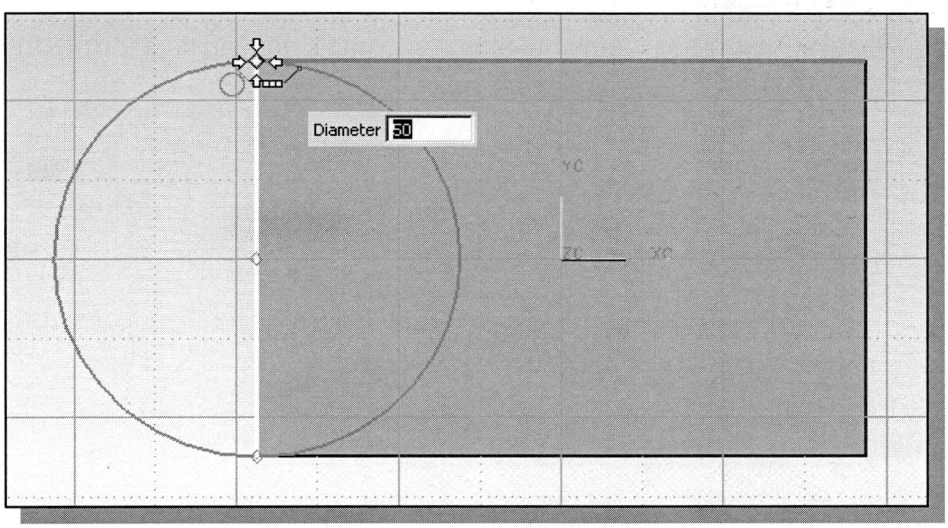

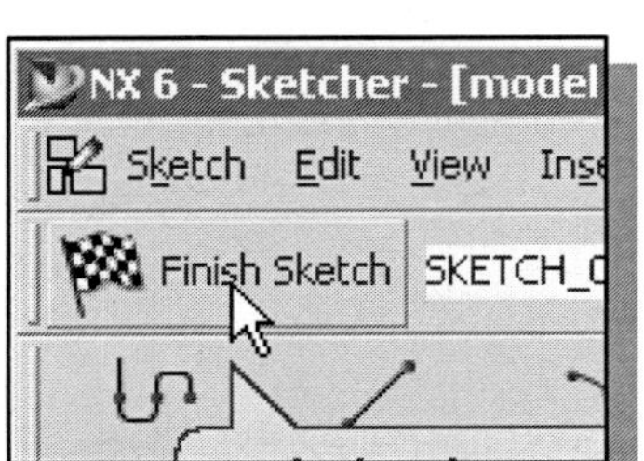

9. Select **Finish Sketch** by clicking once with the left-mouse-button (MB1) on the icon.

10. In the *Extrude* popup window, enter **40** as the extrusion *End* limit and set the Boolean operation option to **Unite.** Click on the **Reverse Direction** button to reverse the direction of extrusion (set upward direction) as shown below.

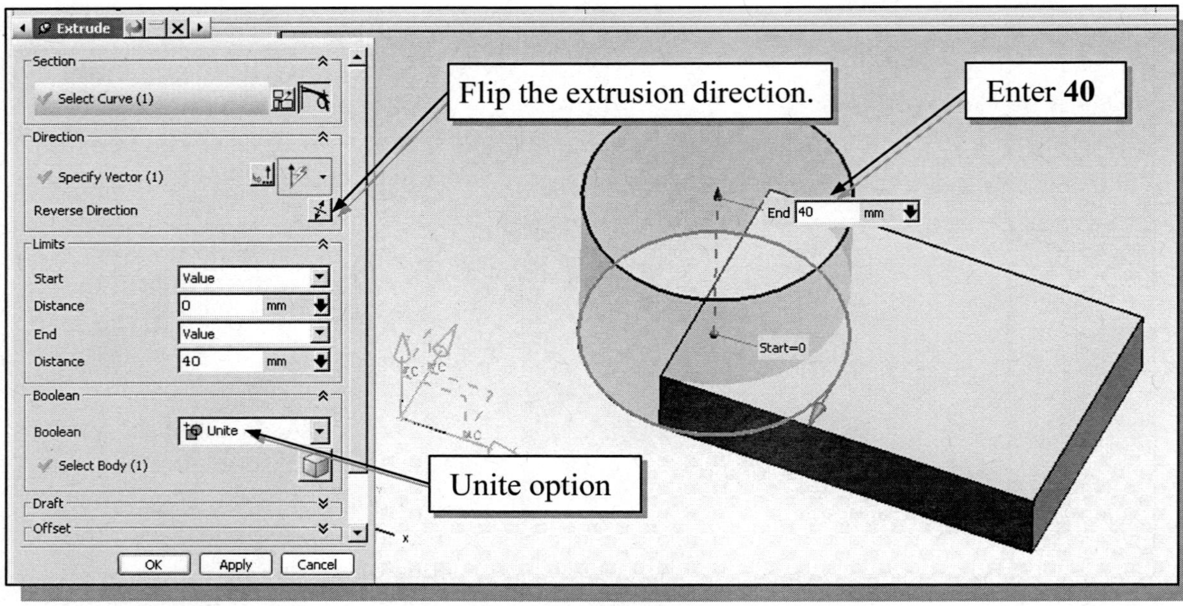

11. Click on the **OK** button to proceed with the **Unite** operation.

- The two features are joined together into one solid part; the *CSG-Unite* operation was performed.

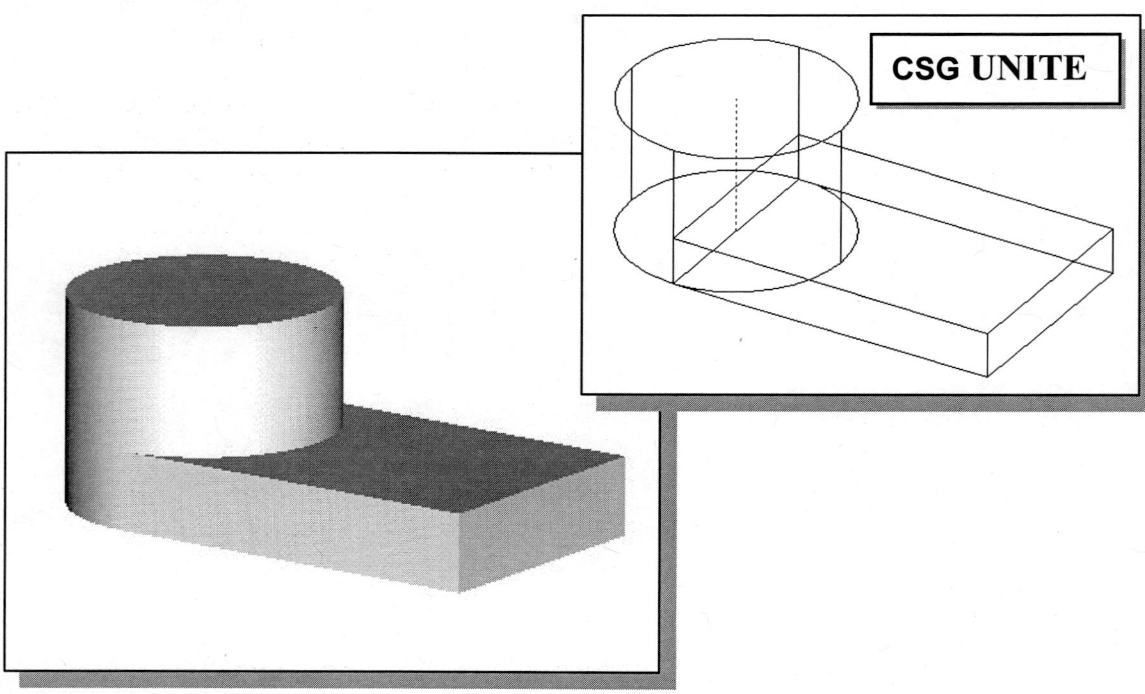

Creating a SUBTRACT Feature

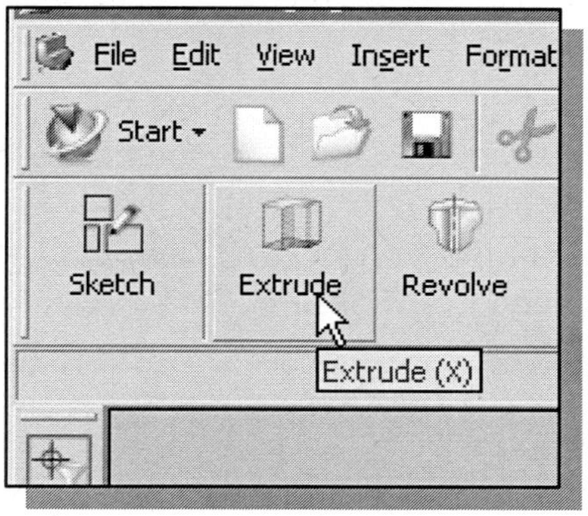

1. In the ***Feature*** toolbars (toolbars aligned to the right edge of the main window), select the **Extrude** icon as shown.

- The ***Extrude*** feature options dialog box, which contains applicable construction options, is displayed as shown in the figure below.

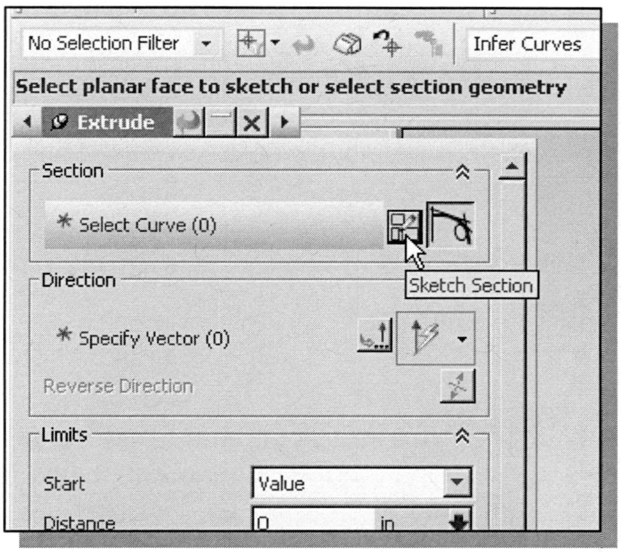

2. On your own, move the cursor over the icons and read the brief descriptions of the different options available.

3. Click the **Sketch Section** button to begin creating a new *2D sketch.*

- We will create a circular subtract feature as the next solid feature of the design. We will align the sketch plane to the top of the last cylinder feature.

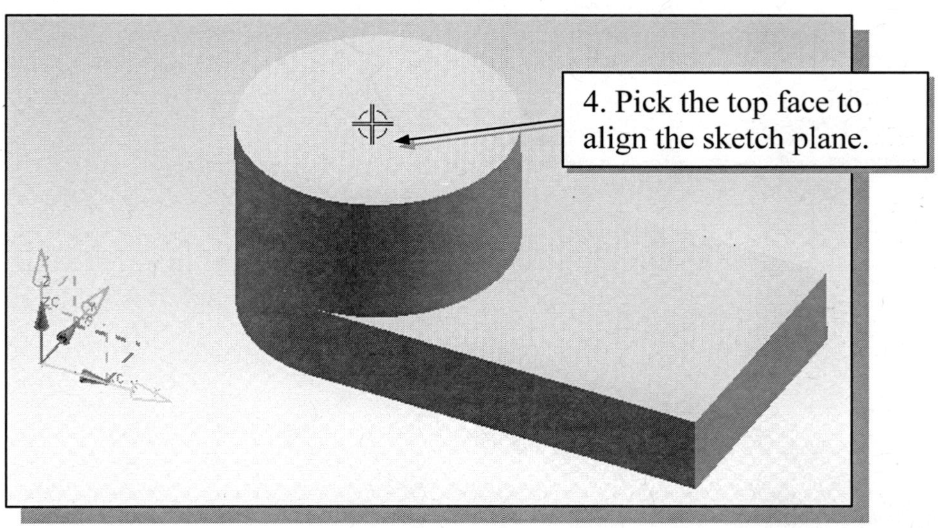

4. Pick the top face of the cylinder as shown.

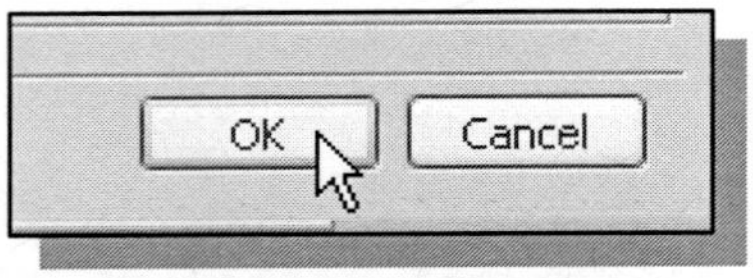

5. Click **OK** to accept the selected face and proceed with the new WCS.

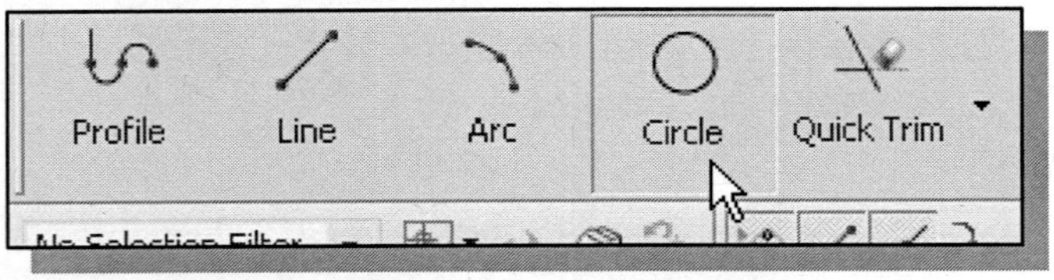

6. Select the **Circle** command by clicking once with the **left-mouse-button (MB1)** on the icon in the *SketchCurve* toolbar.

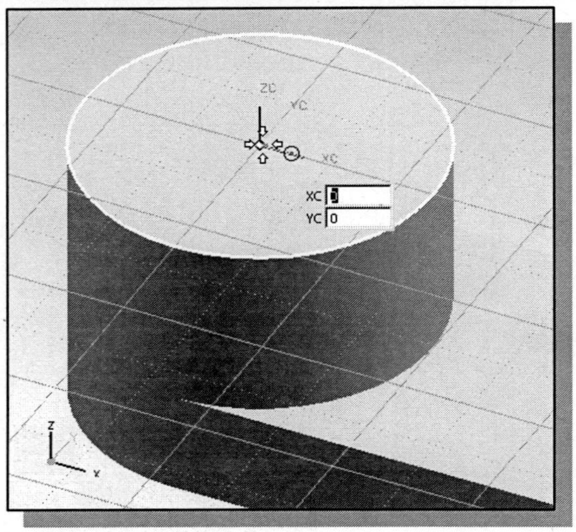

7. Select the **Center** point of the top face of the 3D model by clicking on the circle's centerpoint with the left-mouse-button as shown. (Notice the displayed Concentric constraint symbol.)

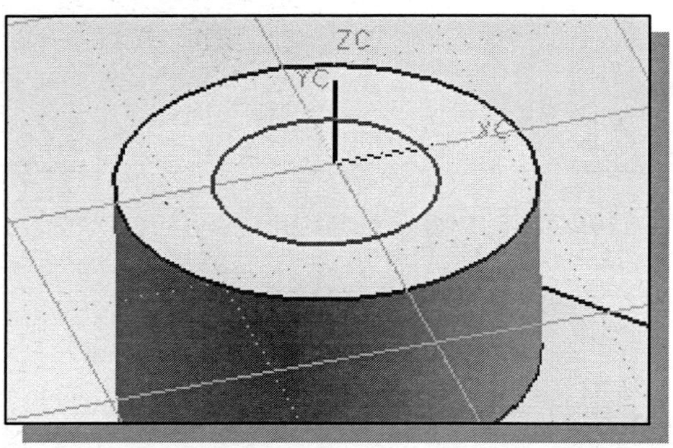

8. Sketch a circle of arbitrary size inside the top face of the cylinder as shown below.

9. Use the middle-mouse-button (MB2) to end the Circle command.

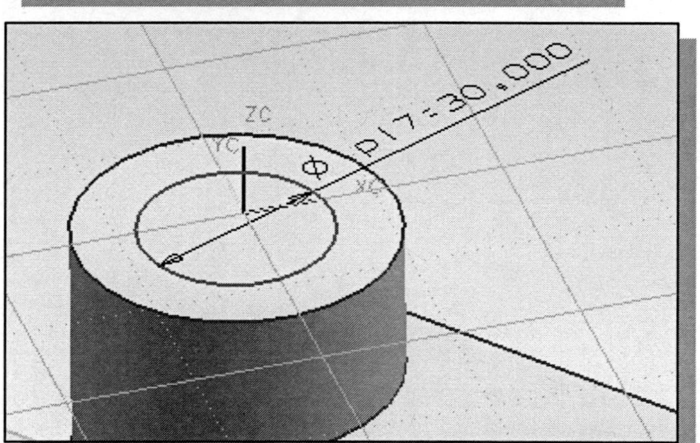

10. Create and modify the size of the circle so that it is set to **30mm**.

11. Select **Finish Sketch** by clicking once with the left-mouse-button (MB1) on the icon.

12. In the *Extrude* popup window, select **Through All** as the *Extrude Limit* and set the Boolean operation option to **Subtract.** Click on the **Reverse Direction** button to reverse the direction of extrusion (set to downward direction) as shown below.

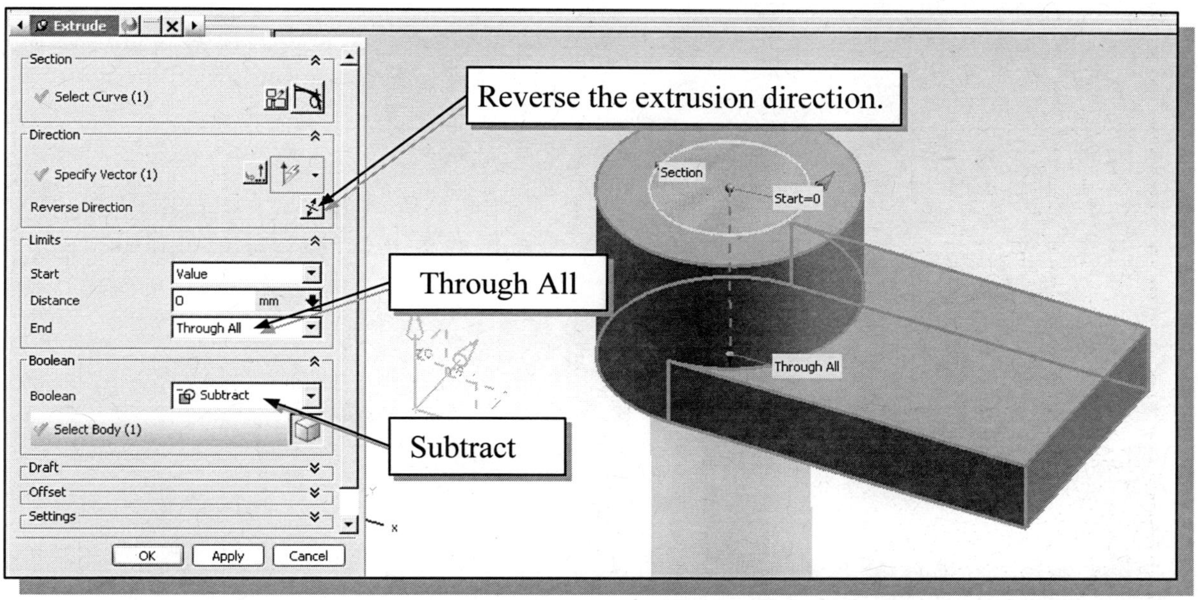

13. Click on the **OK** button to proceed with the ***Subtract*** operation.

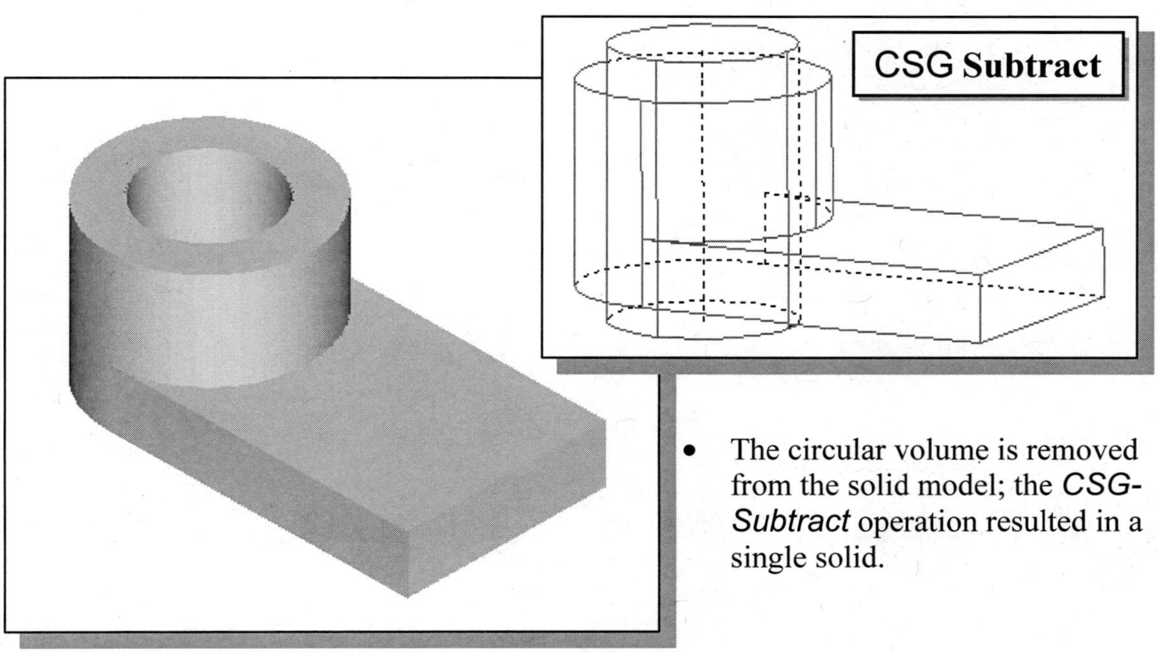

- The circular volume is removed from the solid model; the *CSG-Subtract* operation resulted in a single solid.

Creating a PLACED FEATURE

- In *UGS NX*, there are two basic types of geometric features: **placed features** and **sketched features**. The last subtract feature we created is a *sketched feature*, where we created a rough sketch and performed an extrusion operation. We can also create a hole feature, which is a placed feature. A *placed feature* is a feature that does not need a sketch and can be created automatically. Holes, fillets, chamfers, and shells are all placed features.

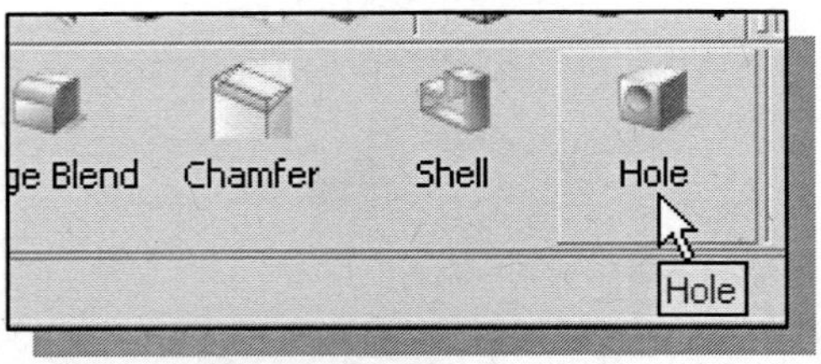

1. In the *Feature Operation* toolbar (the toolbar that is located to the right side of the *Form Feature* toolbar), select the **Hole** command by releasing the left-mouse-button on the icon.

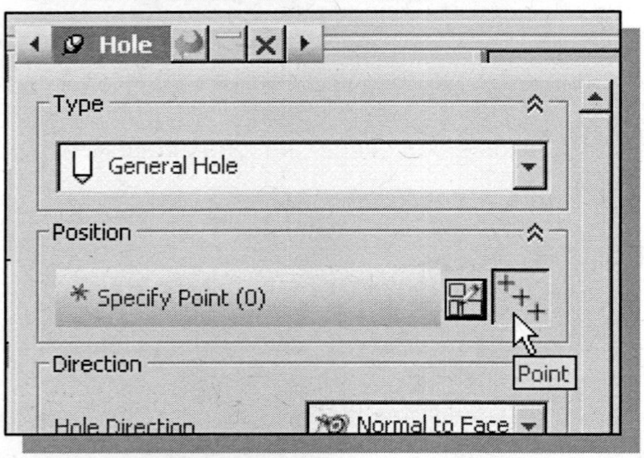

2. In the *Hole* window, notice the default hole *Type* is set to **General Hole** as shown.

❖ Not that by default, the position of the hole is specified using the **Point** command.

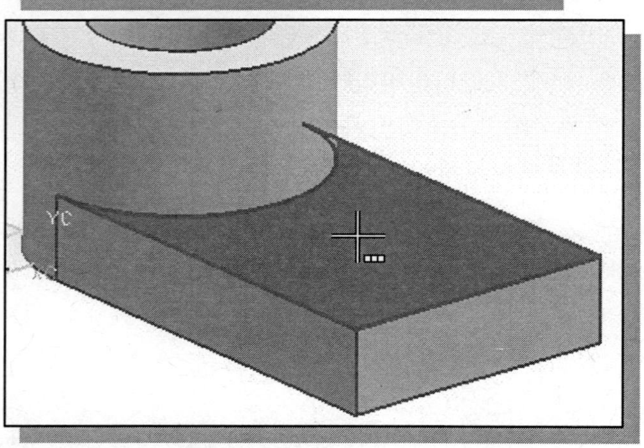

3. Pick a location inside the horizontal surface of the base feature as shown.

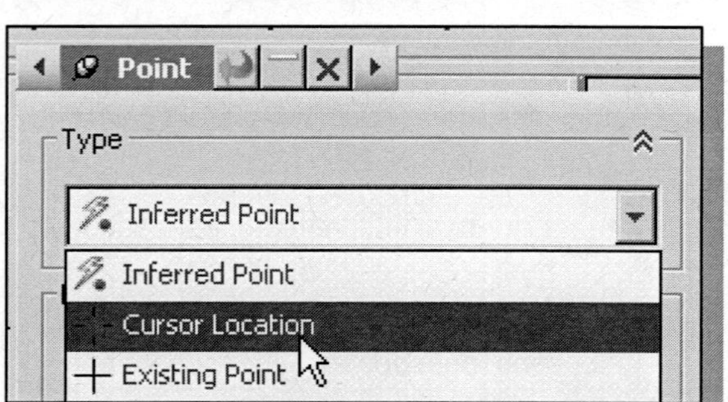

❖ Note the **Point** command is activated automatically once the sketch plane has been selected.

4. In the *Point* dialog box, set the point option to **Cursor Location**, as shown.

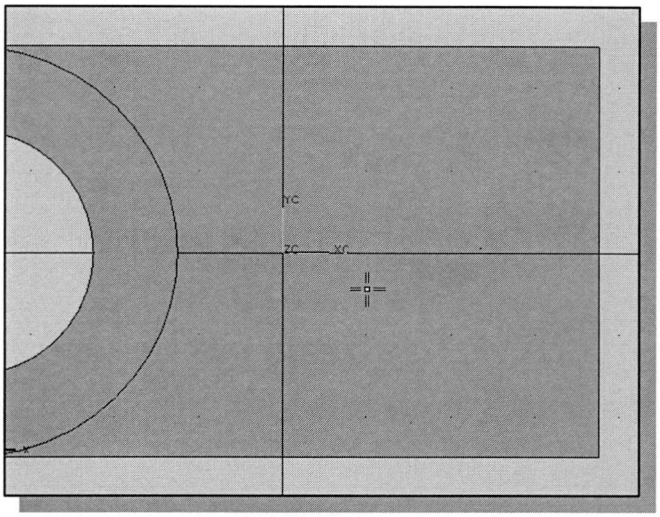

5. Click at a location that is toward the lower right side of the displayed coordinate system to place a point.

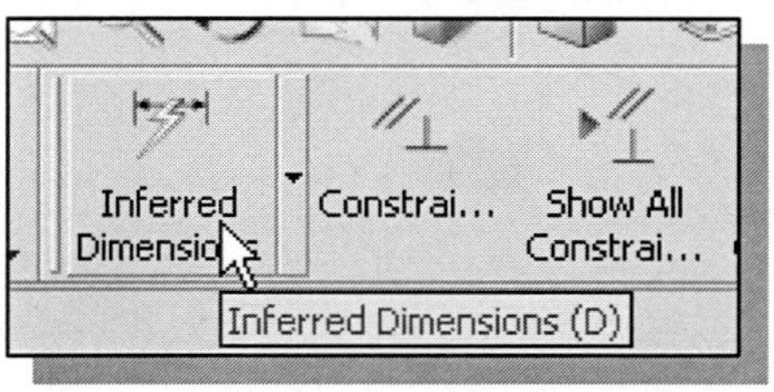

6. Activate the **Inferred Dimensions** command by left-clicking once on the icon as shown. The Inferred Dimensions command allows us to quickly create and modify dimensions.

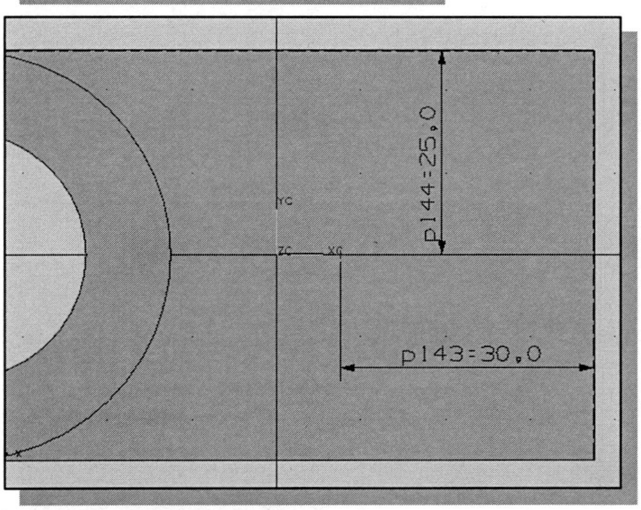

7. On your own, create the two dimensions, **25** and **30**, as shown.

8. Select **Finish Sketch** by clicking once with the left-mouse-button (MB1) on the icon.

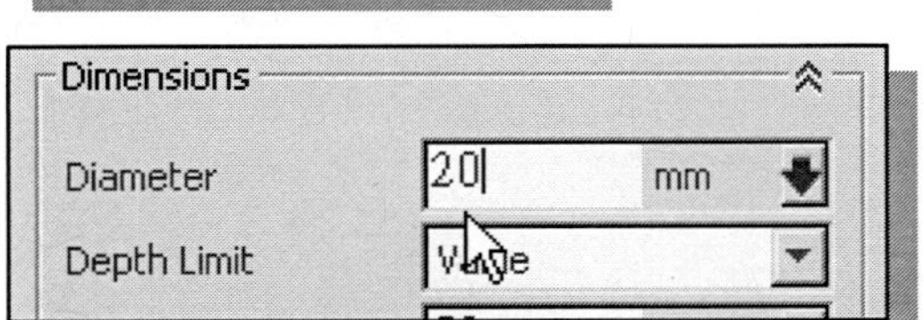

9. Enter **20 mm** as the *Diameter* of the hole as shown in the figure.

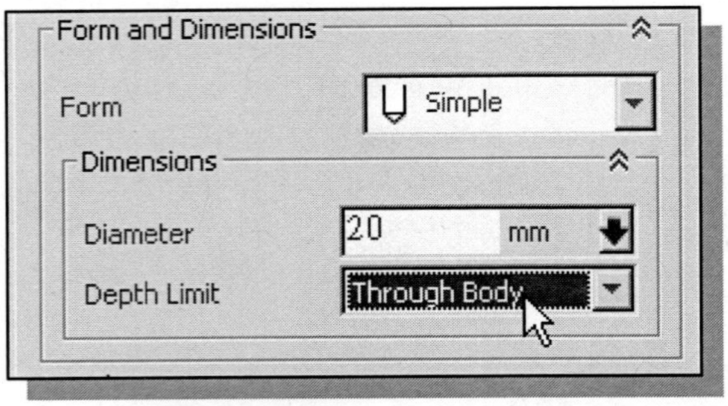

10. In the *Form and Dimensions* options, set the ***Depth Limit*** to **Through Body** as shown in the figure.

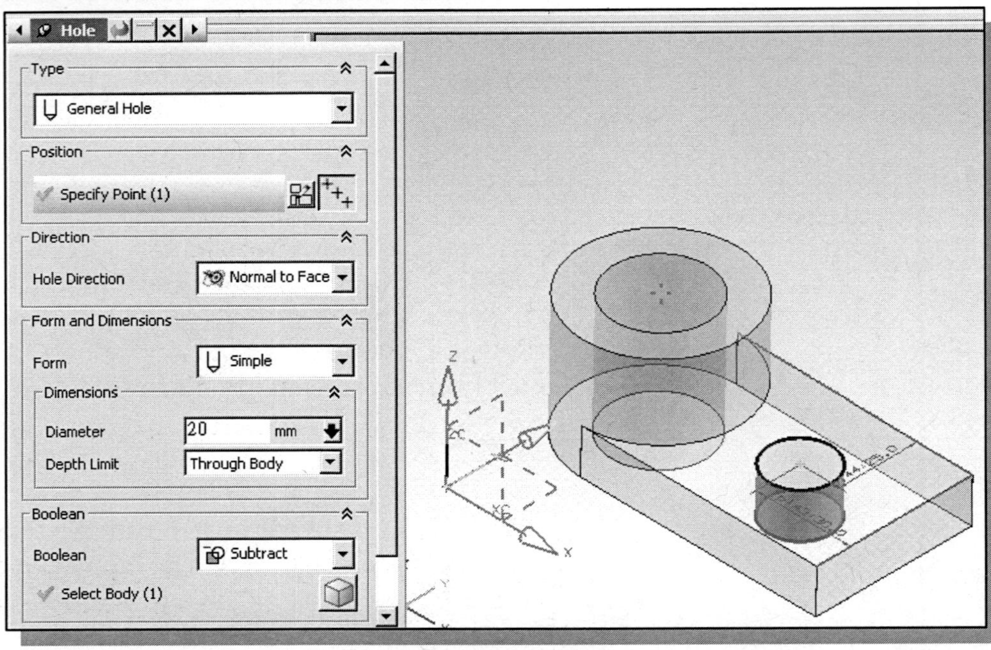

11. Click **OK** to proceed with the creation of the **hole** feature.

- The circular volume is removed from the solid model; the *CSG-Subtract* operation resulted in a single solid.

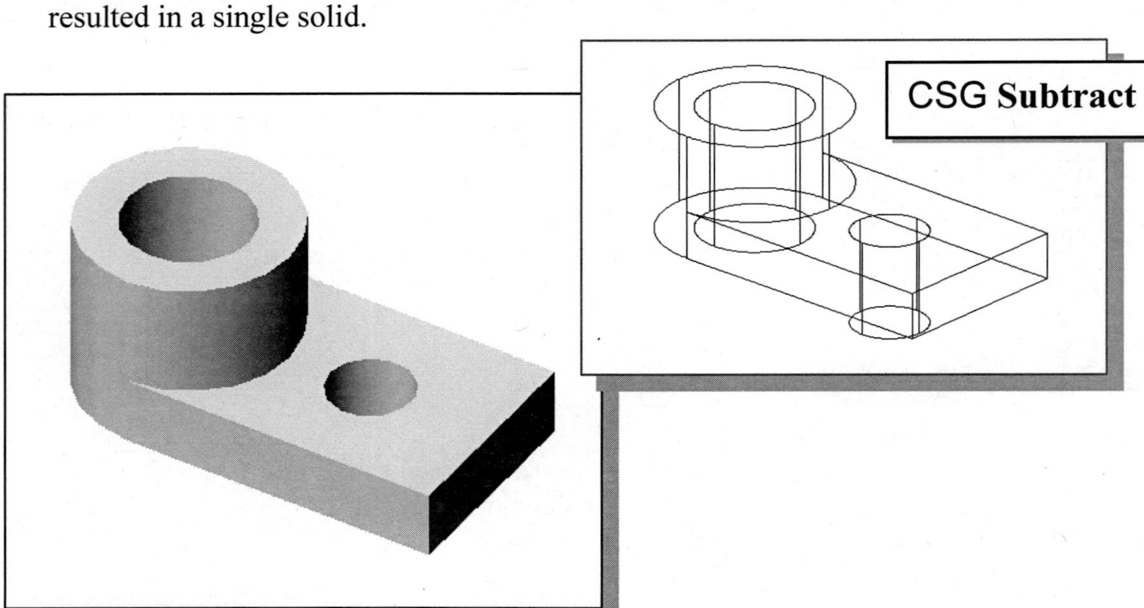

Creating a Rectangular Cut Feature

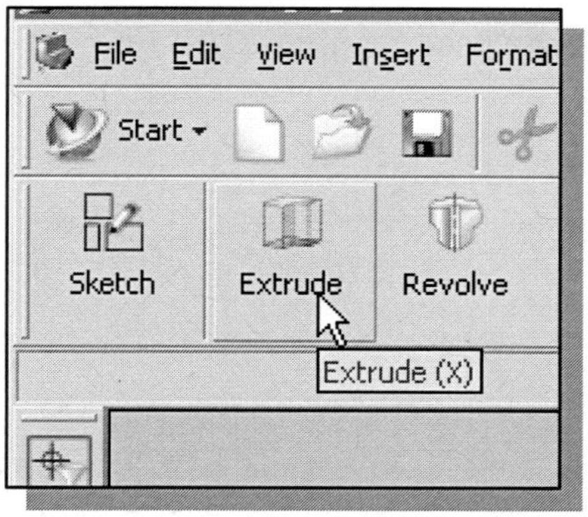

1. In the ***Feature*** toolbars (toolbars aligned to the right edge of the main window), select the **Extrude** icon as shown.

- The ***Extrude*** feature options dialog box, which contains applicable construction options, is displayed as shown in the figure below.

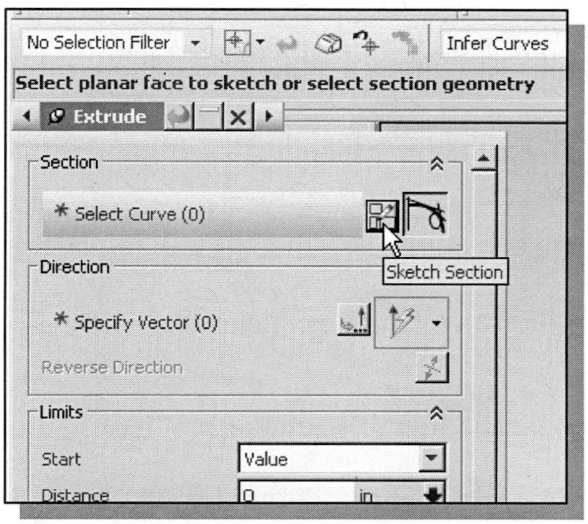

2. On your own, move the cursor over the icons and read the brief descriptions of the different options available. Note that the default extrude option is set to **Select Section**.

3. Click the **Sketch Section** button to begin creating a new *2D sketch*.

- Next create a rectangular subtract feature as the last solid feature of the ***Locator***.

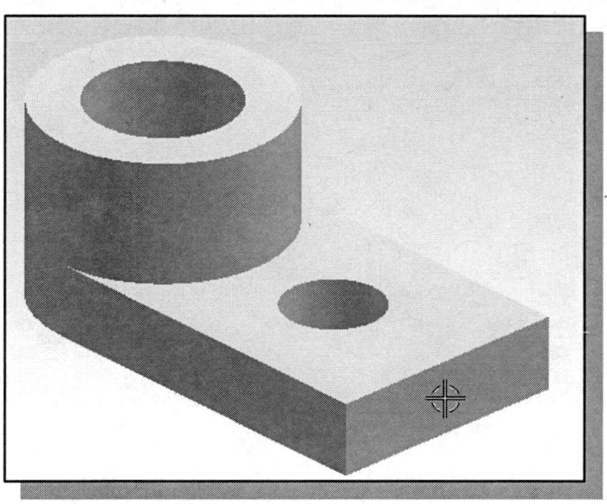

4. Pick the right vertical face of the base feature as shown.

5. Click **OK** to accept the selected face and proceed with the new WCS.

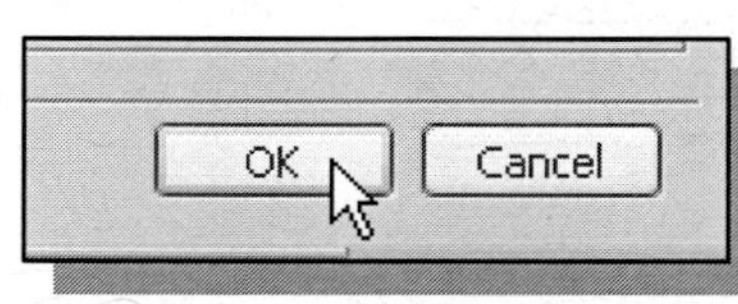

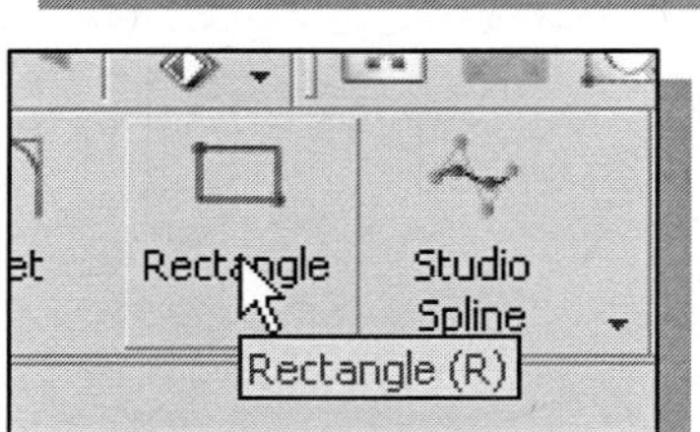

6. Select the **Rectangle** command by clicking once with the **left-mouse-button** on the icon in the *Sketch Curve* toolbar.

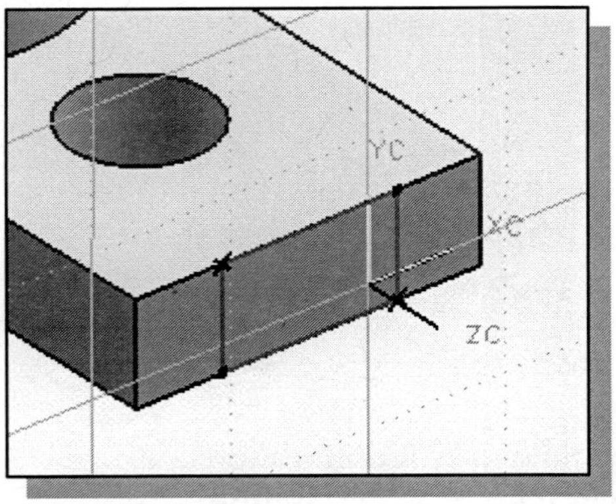

7. Create a rectangle that is aligned to the top and bottom edges of the base feature as shown.

8. On your own, create and modify the two dimensions as shown in the figure below.

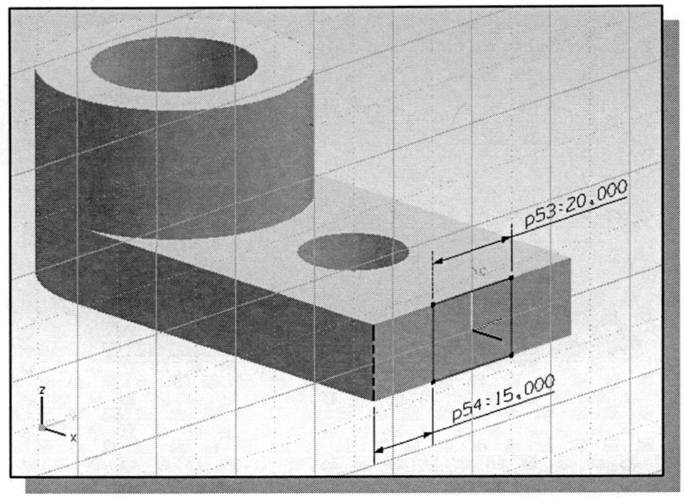

9. Select **Finish Sketch** by clicking once with the left-mouse-button (MB1) on the icon.

10. In the *Extrude* popup window, set the operation option to **Subtract.** Set the *End* option to **Until Next** and set the extrusion direction toward the center of the solid model.

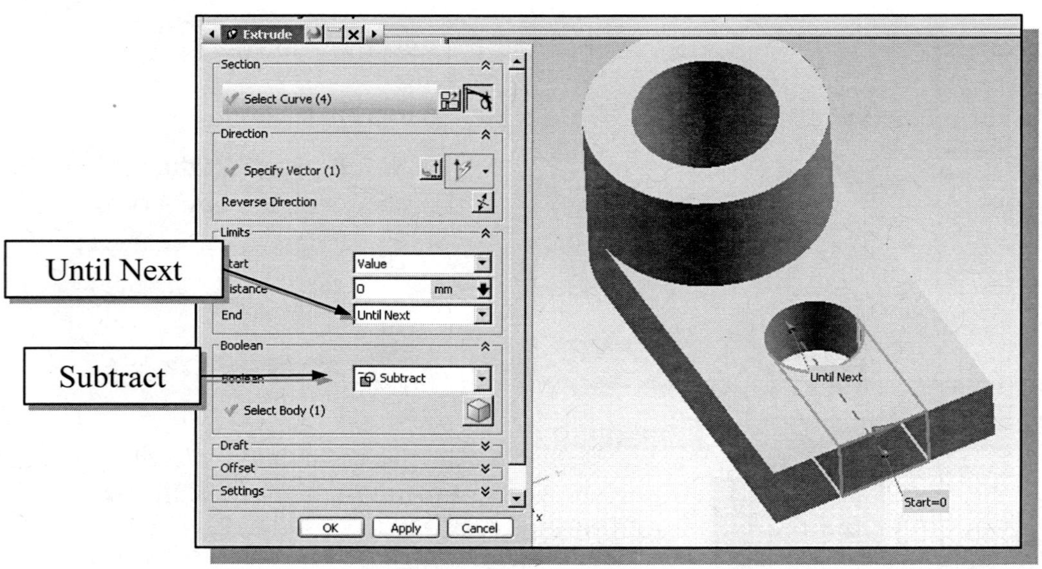

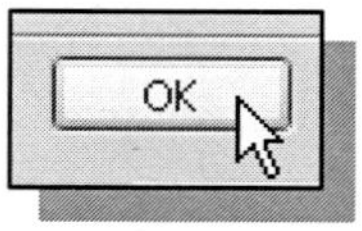

11. Click on the **OK** button to create the subtract feature and complete the design.

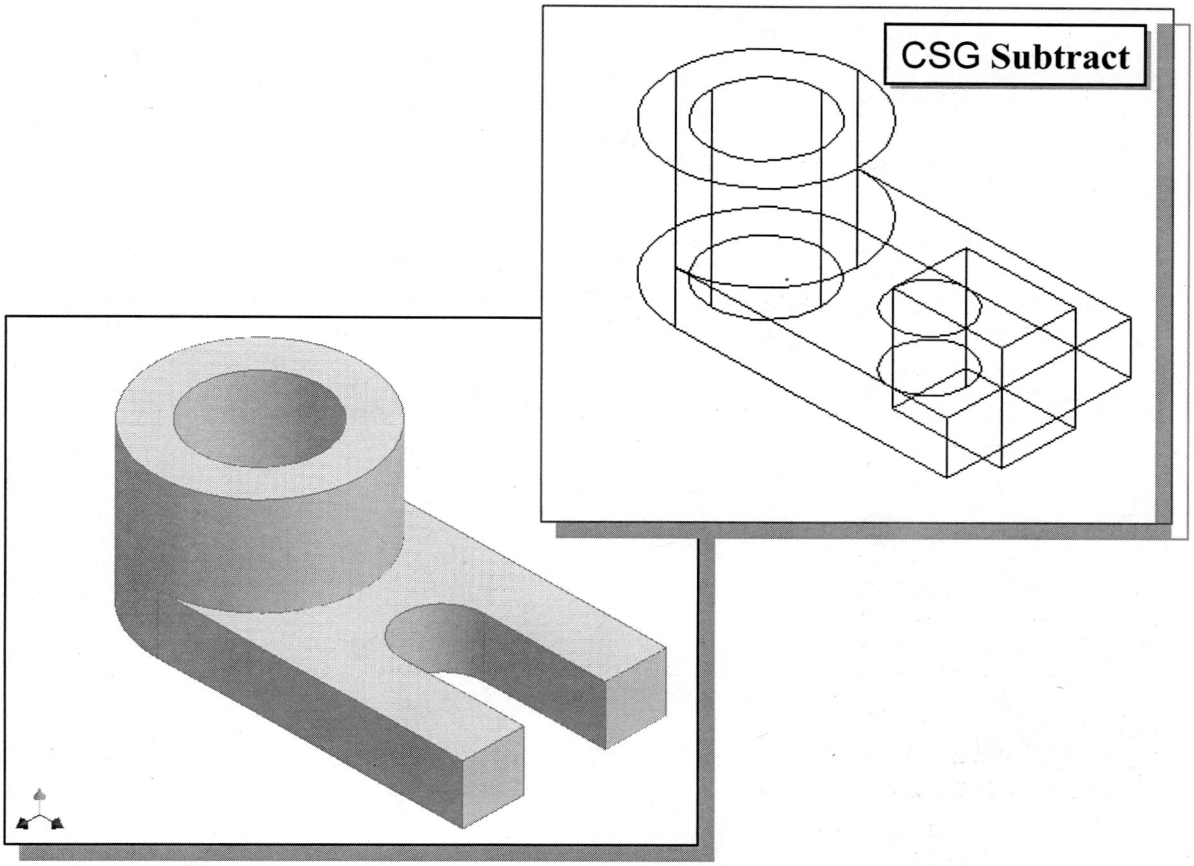

Questions:

1. List and describe three basic *Boolean operations* commonly used in computer geometric modeling software?

2. What is a *primitive solid*?

3. What does *CSG* stand for?

4. Which *Boolean operation* keeps only the volume common to the two solid objects?

5. What is the main difference between a *SUBTRACT* feature and a *HOLE* feature in *UGS NX*?

6. Using the CSG concepts, create *Binary Tree* sketches showing the steps you plan to use to create the two models shown on the next page:

Ex.1)

Ex.2)

Exercises: (All dimensions are in inches.)

1.

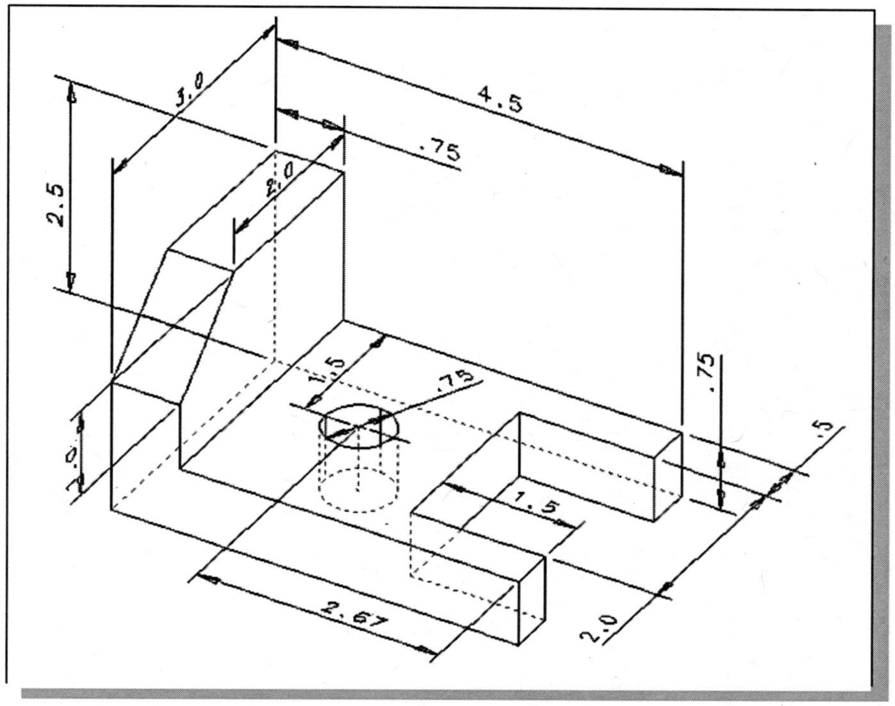

2.

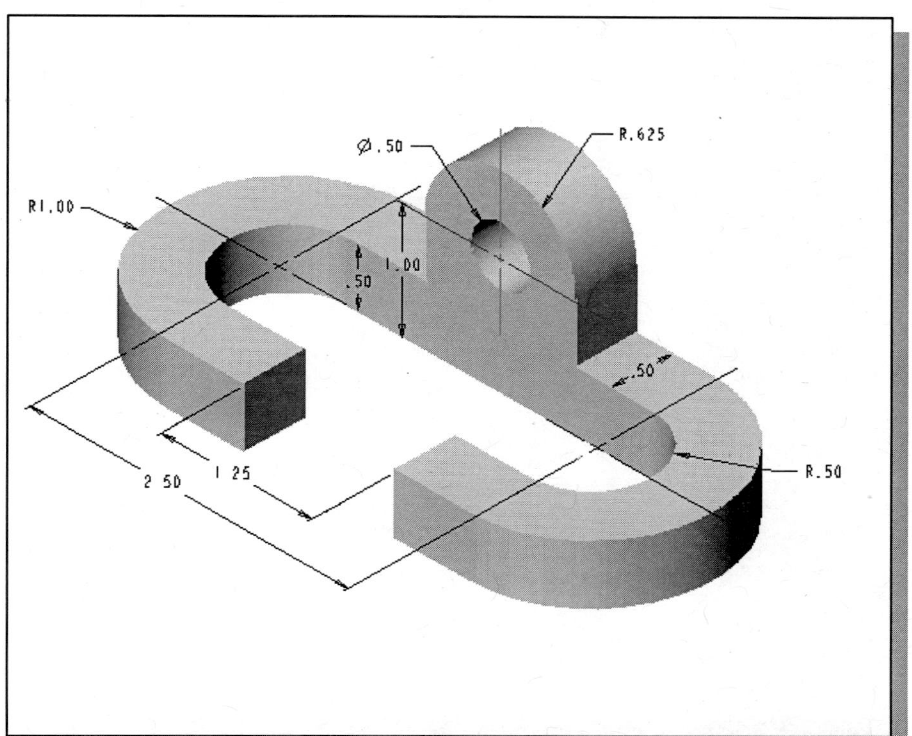

Notes:

Chapter 4
Model History Tree

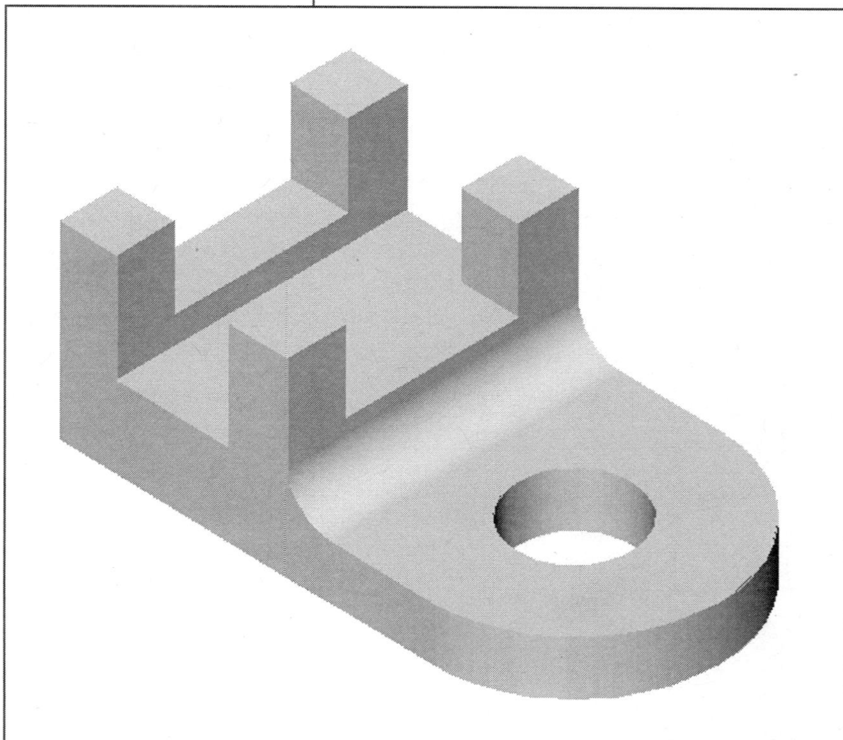

Learning Objectives

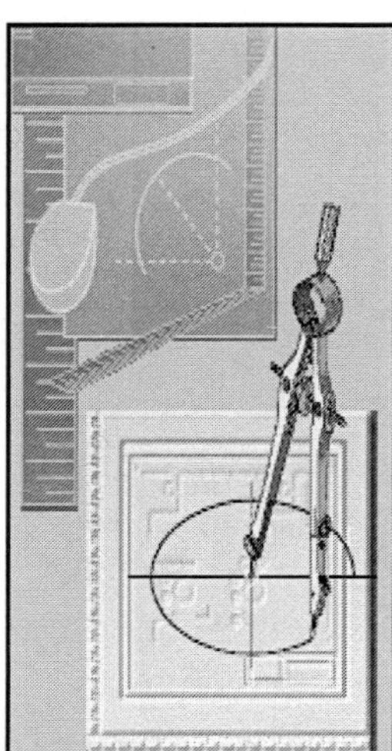

- Understand Feature Interactions
- Use the Part Navigator
- Modify and Update Feature Dimensions
- Perform History-Based Part Modifications
- Change the Names of Created Features
- Implement Basic Design Changes
- Assigning and Calculating the Associated Physical Properties

Introduction

In *UGS NX*, the **design intents** are embedded into features in the **history tree**. The structure of the model history tree resembles that of a **CSG binary tree**. A CSG binary tree contains only *Boolean relations*, while the ***UGS NX* history tree** contains all features, including *Boolean relations*. A history tree is a sequential record of the features used to create the part. This history tree contains the construction steps, plus the rules defining the design intent of each construction operation. In a history tree, each time a new modeling event is created, previously defined features can be used to define information such as size, location, and orientation. It is therefore important to think about your modeling strategy before you start creating anything. It is important, but also difficult, to plan ahead for all possible design changes that might occur. This approach in modeling is a major difference of **FEATURE-BASED CAD SOFTWARE**, such as *UGS NX*, from previous generation CAD systems.

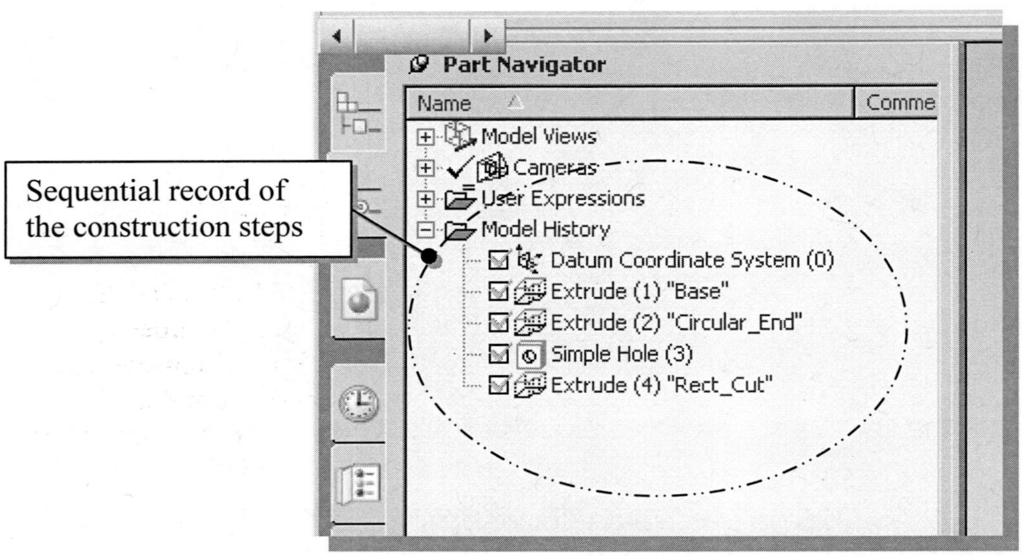

Feature-based parametric modeling is a cumulative process. Every time a new feature is added, a new result is created and the feature is also added to the history tree. The database also includes parameters of features that were used to define them. All of this happens automatically as features are created and manipulated. At this point, it is important to understand that all of this information is retained, and modifications are done based on the same input information.

In *UGS NX*, the history tree gives information about modeling order and other information about the feature. Part modifications can be accomplished by accessing the features in the history tree. It is therefore important to understand and utilize the feature history tree to modify designs. *UGS NX* remembers the history of a part, including all the rules that were used to create it, so that changes can be made to any operation that was performed to create the part. In *UGS NX*, to modify a feature, we access the feature by selecting the feature in the ***Part Navigator*** window.

The *Saddle Bracket* Design

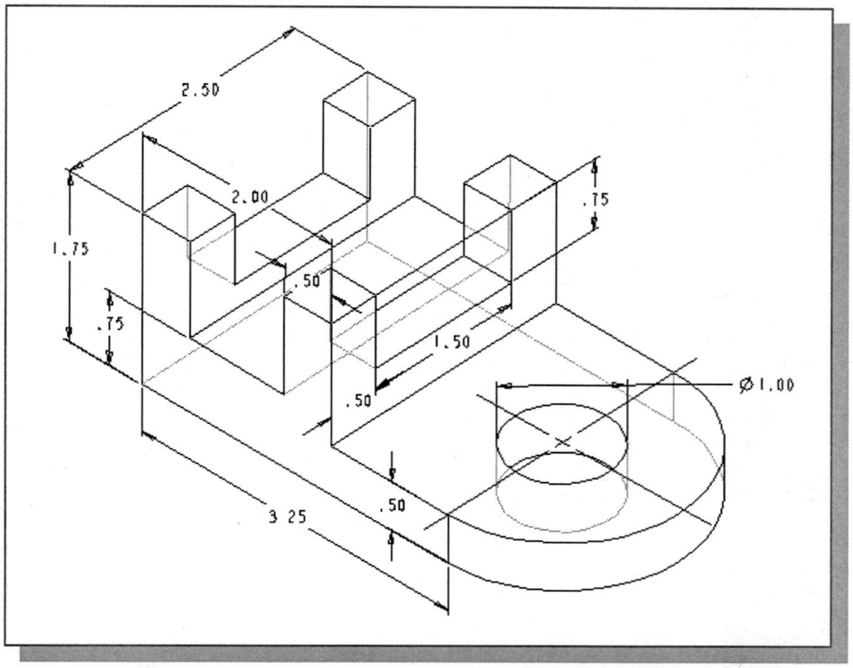

❖ Based on your knowledge of *UGS NX* so far, how many features would you use to create the design? Which feature would you choose as the **BASE FEATURE**, the first solid feature, of the model? What is your choice in arranging the order of the features? Would you organize the features differently if additional fillets were to be added in the design? Take a few minutes to consider these questions and do preliminary planning by sketching on a piece of paper. You are also encouraged to create the model on your own prior to following through the tutorial.

Starting *UGS NX*

1. Select the **UGS NX** option on the *Start* menu or select the **UGS NX** icon on the desktop to start *UGS NX*.

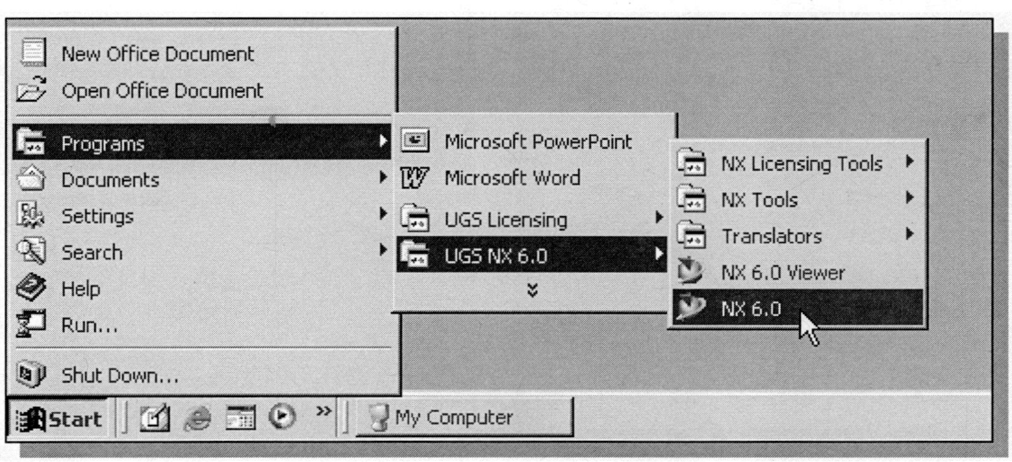

Modeling Strategy

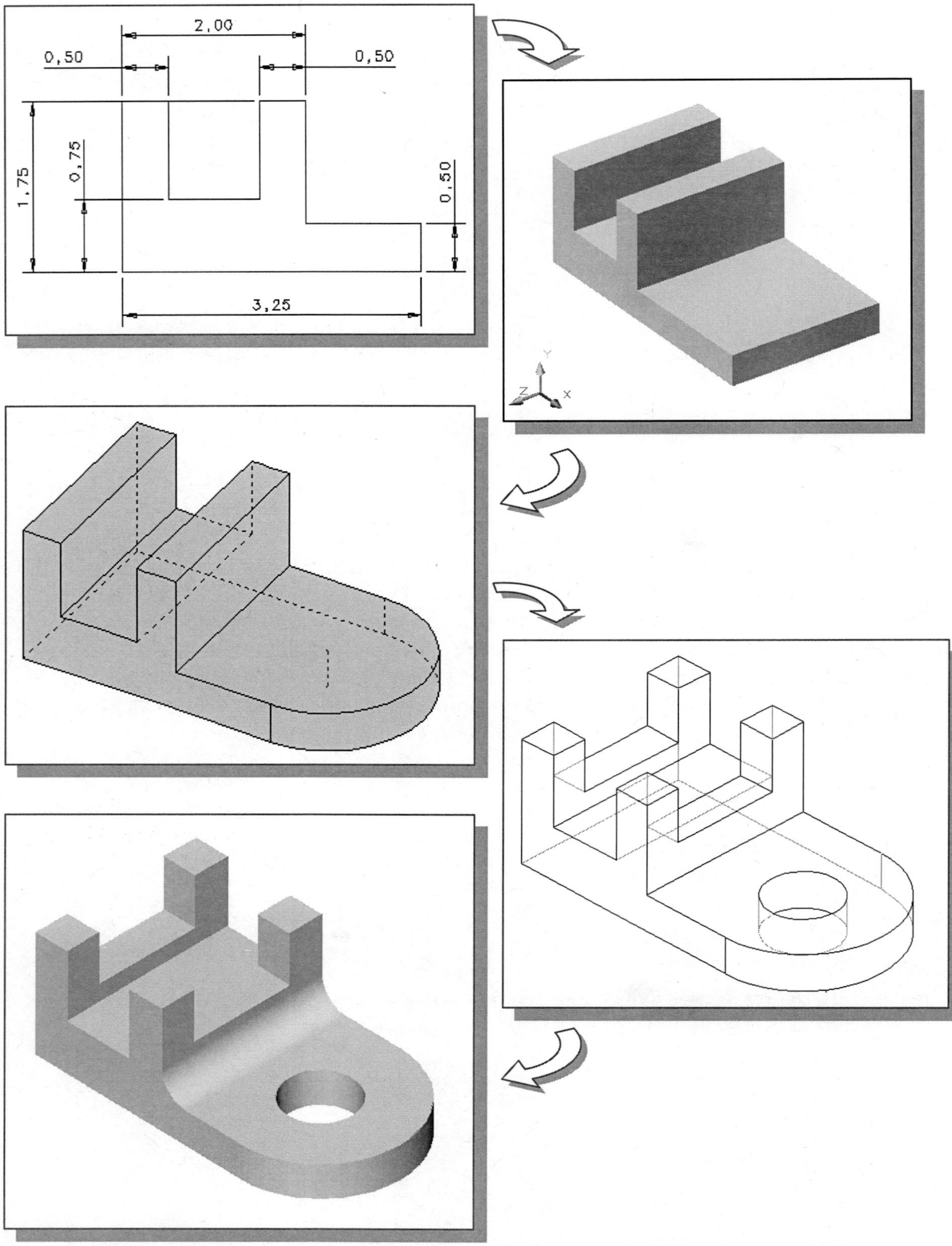

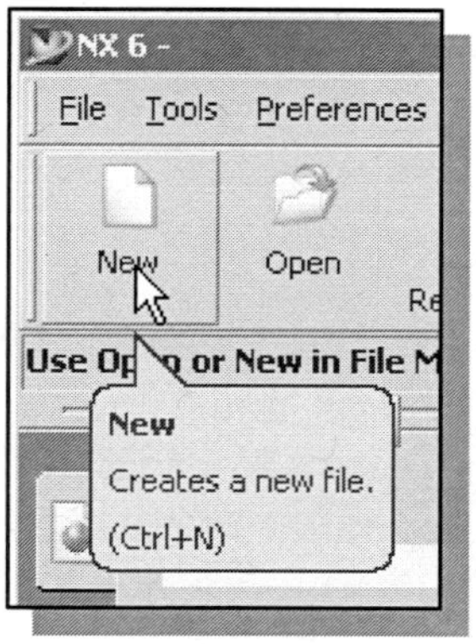

2. Select the **New** icon with a single click of the left-mouse-button (MB1) in the *Standard* toolbar area.

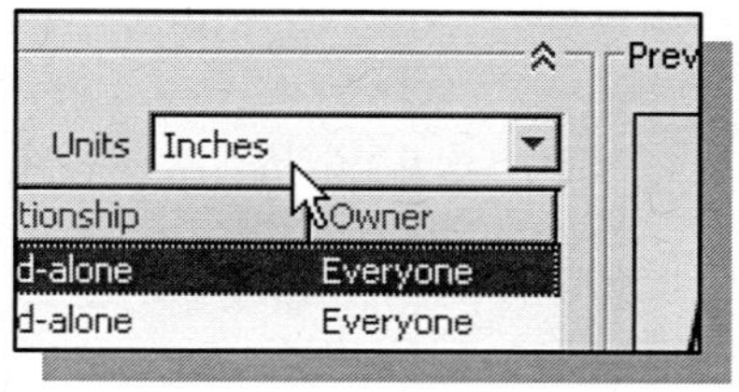

3. In the *New Part File* window, set the units to **Inches** as shown.

4. Select the **Blank** template file as shown.

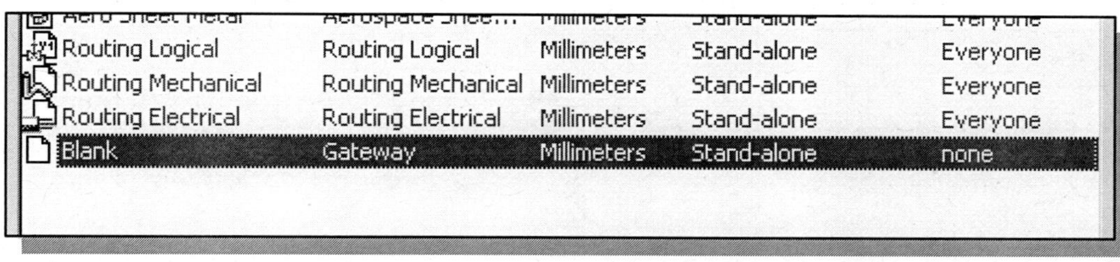

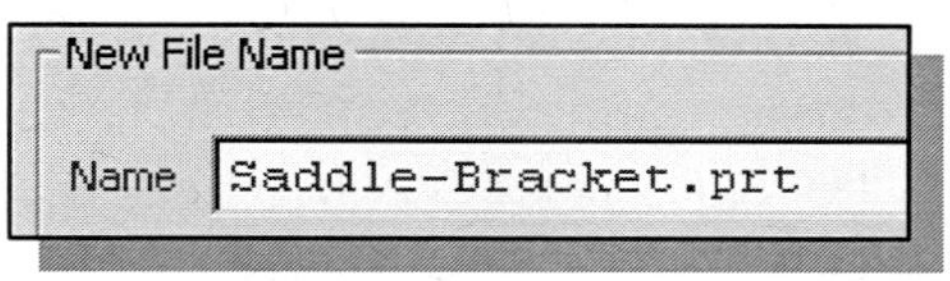

5. In the *New File Name* window, enter **Saddle-Bracket.prt** as the file *Name*.

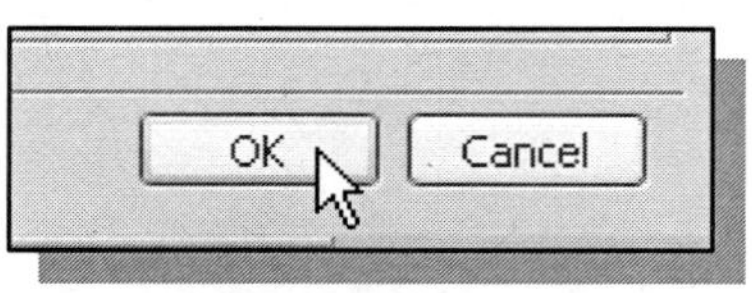

6. Click **OK** to proceed with the New File command.

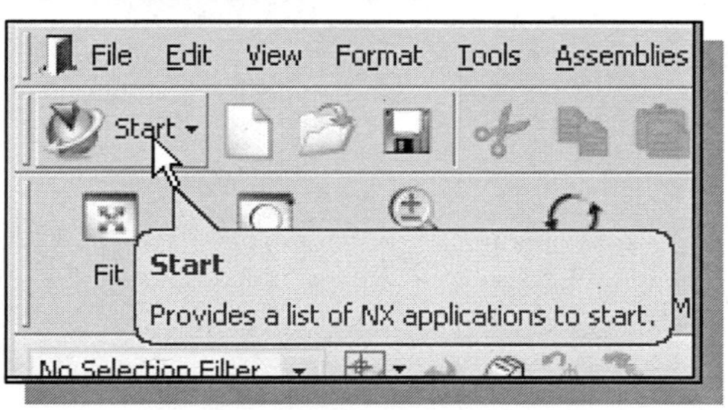

7. Select the **Start** icon with a single click of the left-mouse-button (MB1) in the *Standard* toolbar.

8. Pick **Modeling** in the pull-down list as shown in the figure.

- In the *UGS NX* screen layout, the ***Part Navigator*** is located to the left of the graphics window. The *Part Navigator* window provides a visual structure of the information related to the part.

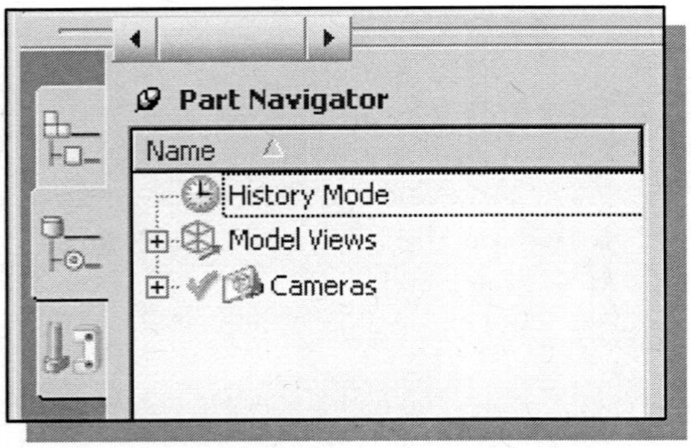

➢ Note that three main items are listed: ***History Mode, Model Views***, and ***Cameras***. There is no **history** information regarding the part, as we have not created anything yet.

9. In the ***Feature*** toolbars (toolbars aligned to the right edge of the main window), select the **Extrude** icon as shown.

- The ***Extrude*** feature options dialog box, which contains applicable construction options, is displayed as shown in the figure below.

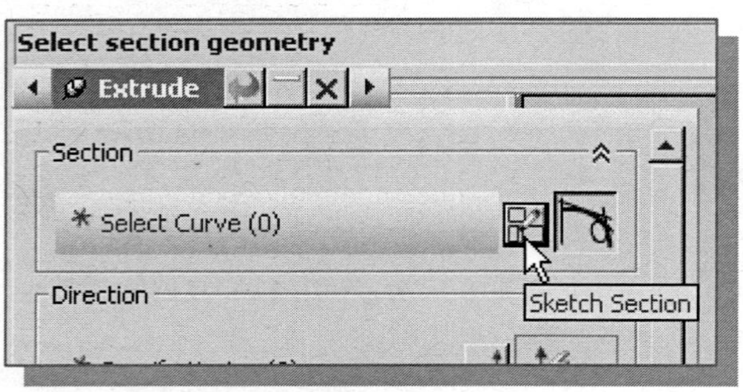

10. Click the **Sketch Section** button to begin creating a new *2D sketch*.

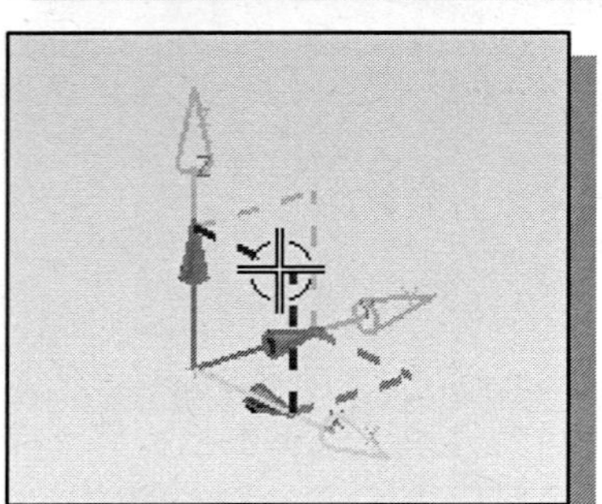

11. Select the ***ZC-XC*** plane of the WCS as the sketch plane of the *base feature*.

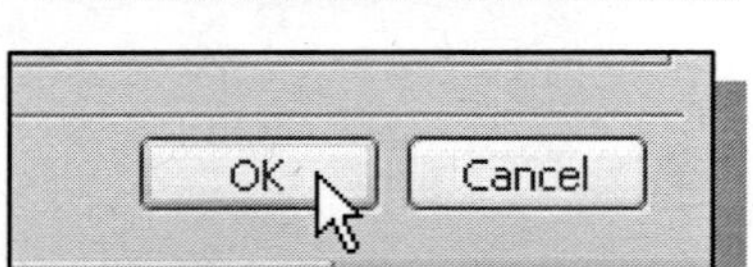

12. Click **OK** to accept the selection of the sketch plane.

13. Create a 2D sketch with line-segments roughly resembling the sketch below.

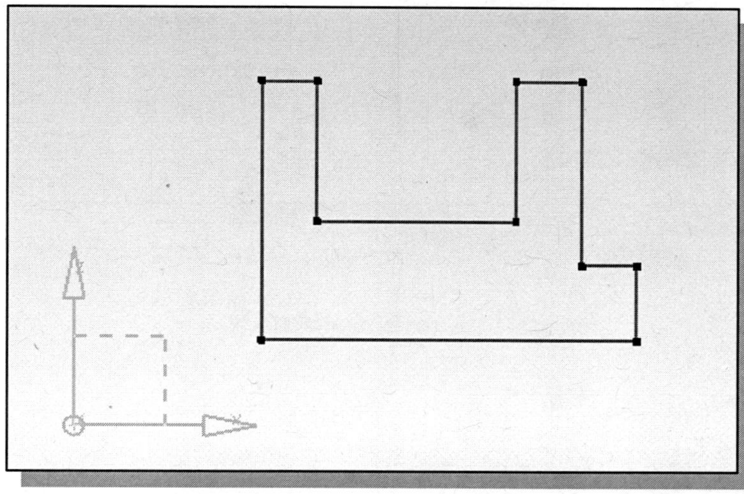

➤ Note that to assure the alignment to a specific location, pause the cursor on top of the alignment point and *NX* will show alignment to that location as shown in the figures below.

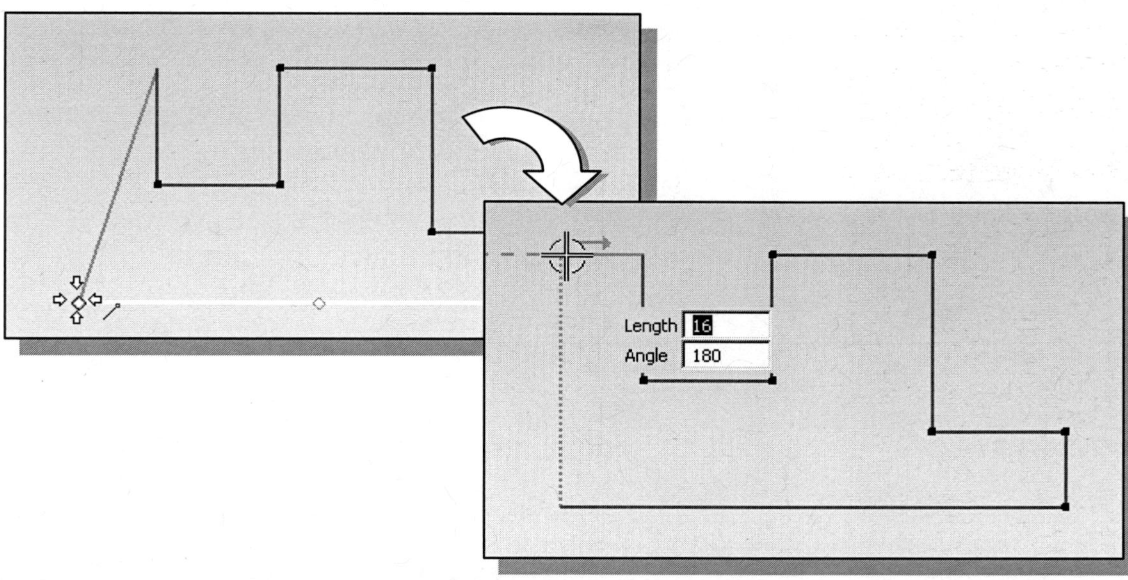

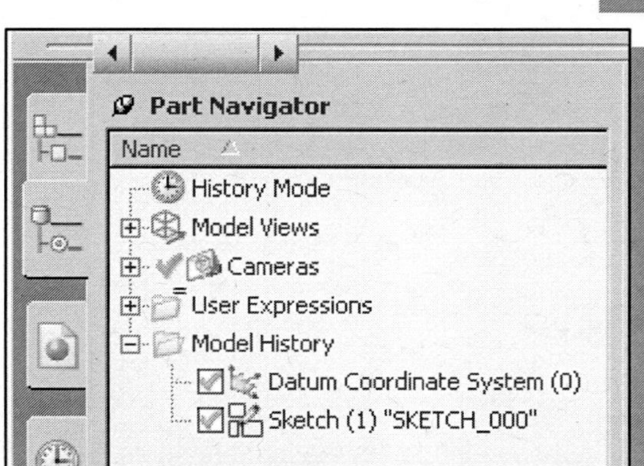

➤ Notice that as we begin to create features, **model history** is added in the ***Part Navigator***: Currently there are two new items: ***Datum Coordinate System***, and ***Sketch***.

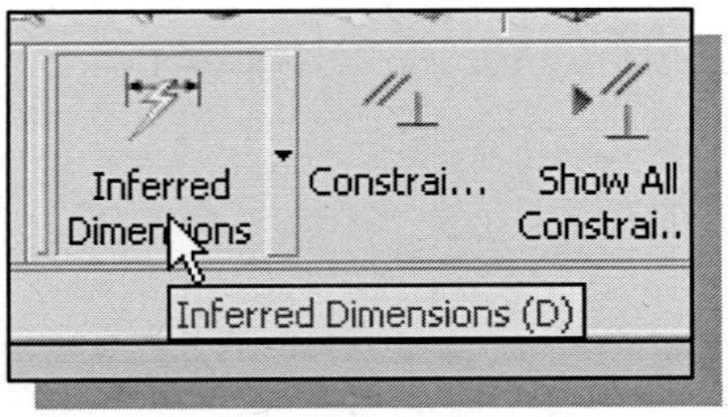

14. On your own, use the **Inferred Dimensions** command to create and adjust the 2D sketch as shown in the figure below.

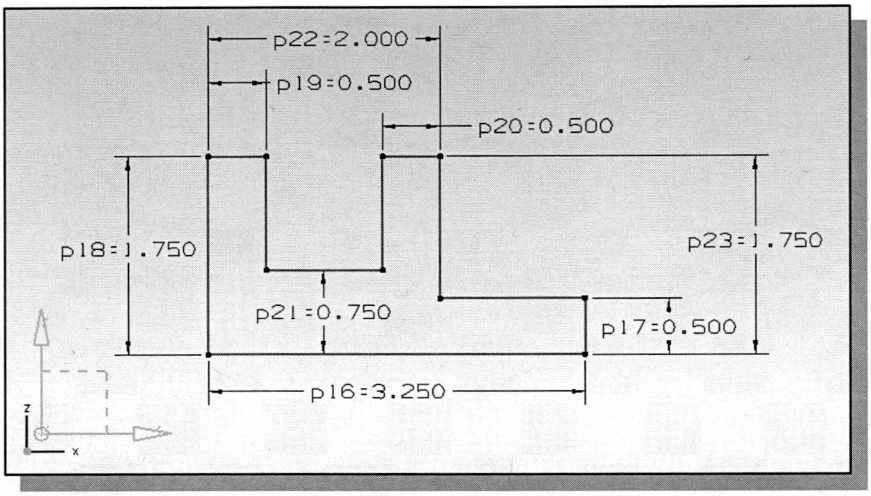

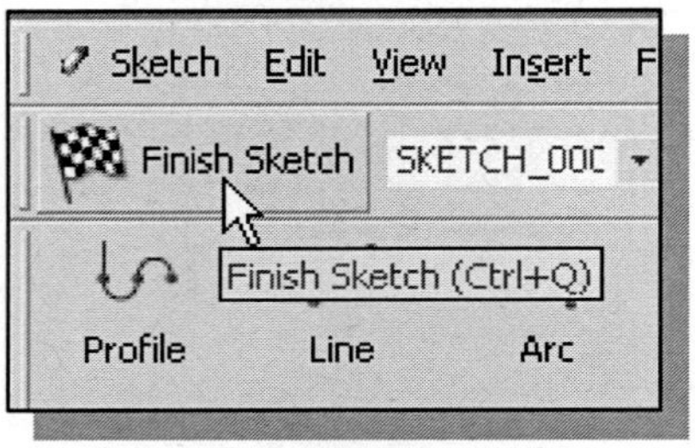

15. Click **Finish Sketch** to exit the *NX Sketcher* mode and return to the *Feature* option dialog window.

16. On your own, complete the **2.5** inch extrusion as shown in the figure below.

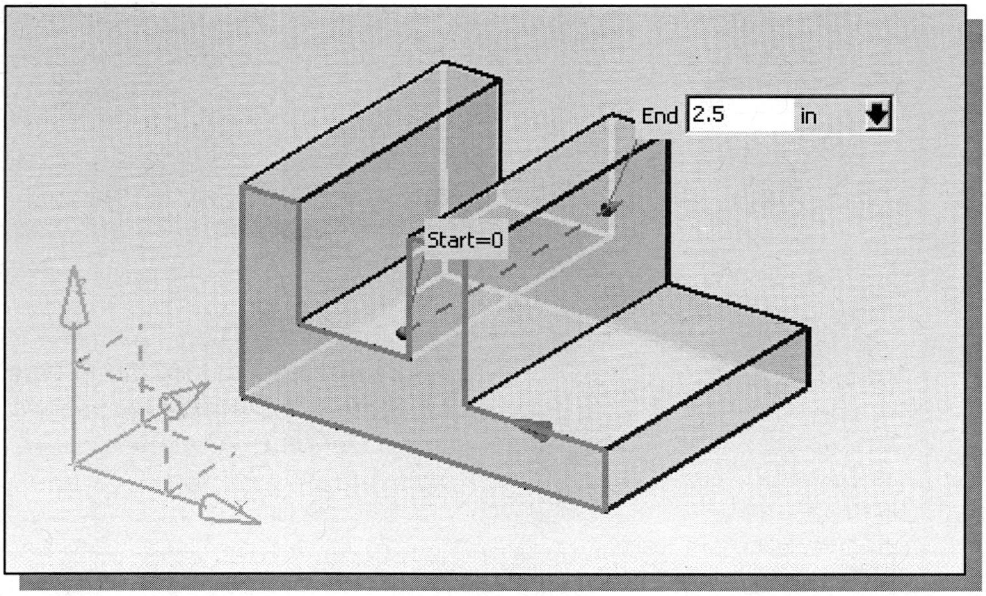

The *UGS NX Part Navigator*

- In the *UGS NX* screen layout, the ***Part Navigator*** is located to the right of the graphics window. *UGS NX* can be used for part modeling, assembly modeling, part drawings, and other CAE functions. The *Part Navigator* window provides a visual structure of the features, constraints, and attributes that are used to create the part, and/or assembly. The *Part Navigator* also provides right-click menu access for tasks associated specifically with the part or feature, and it is the primary focus for executing many of the *UGS NX* commands.

1. Move the cursor on top of the datum coordinate system or the extruded solid and notice the corresponding feature is highlighted in the *NX* ***Part Navigator***.

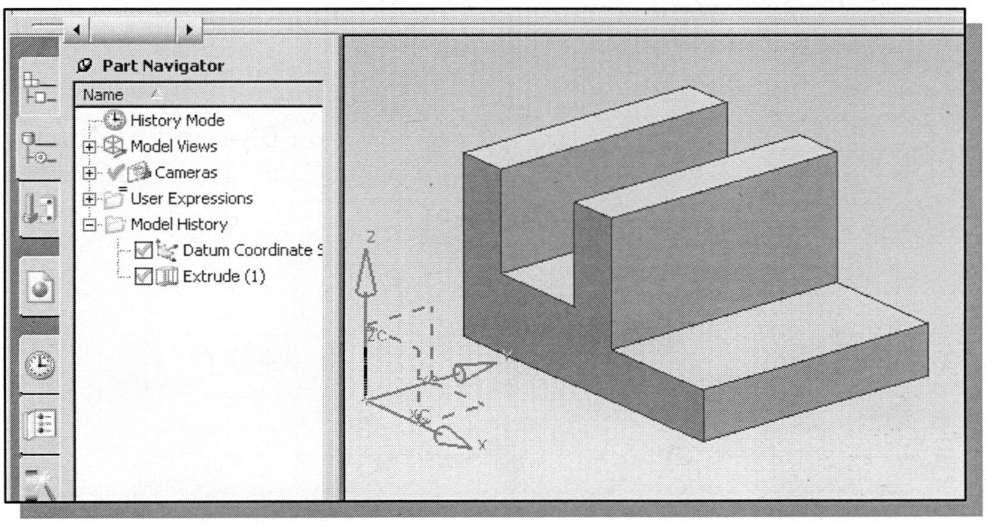

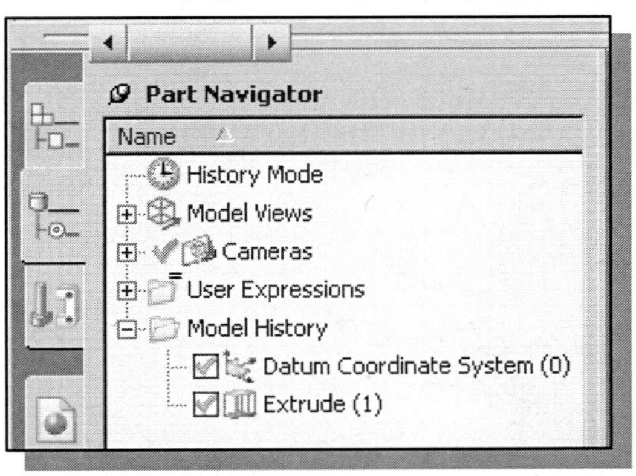

- In the *Part Navigator*, the *model history* item contains the detailed information of the constructed model.

❖ Notice that we have created only one solid body and the solid body contains only one coordinate system and one extruded feature.

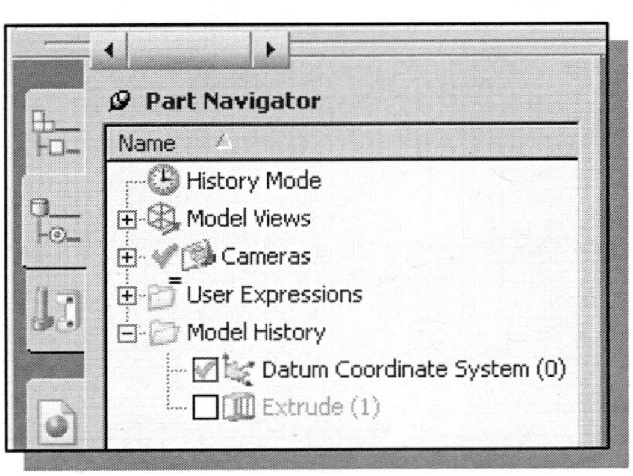

2. Clicking on the check box in front of the ***Extrude*** item to hide the corresponding item on the screen.

3. Redisplay the extruded feature by clicking on the check box again.

Create the Second Solid Feature

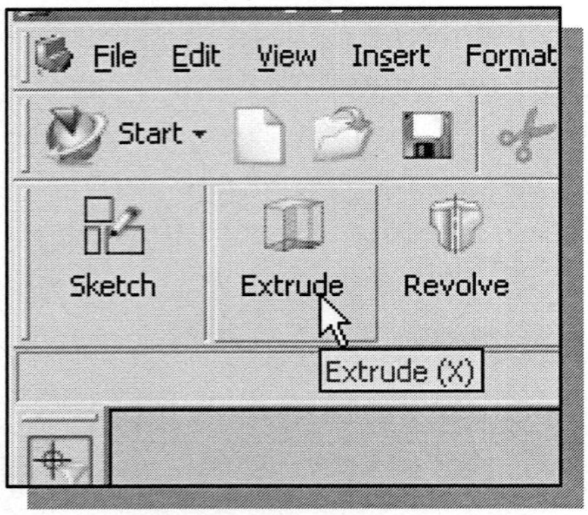

1. In the ***Feature*** toolbars (toolbars aligned to the right edge of the main window), select the **Extrude** icon as shown.

- The ***Extrude*** feature options dialog box, which contains applicable construction options, is displayed as shown in the figure below.

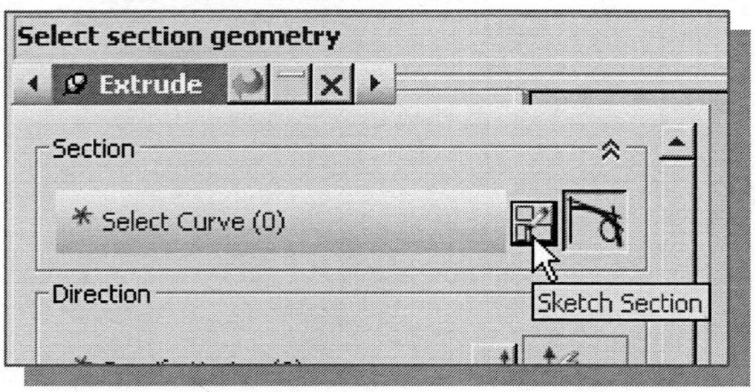

2. Click the **Sketch Section** button to begin creating a new *2D sketch.*

3. Select the **bottom horizontal face of the solid model** to set up the orientation of the sketch plane.

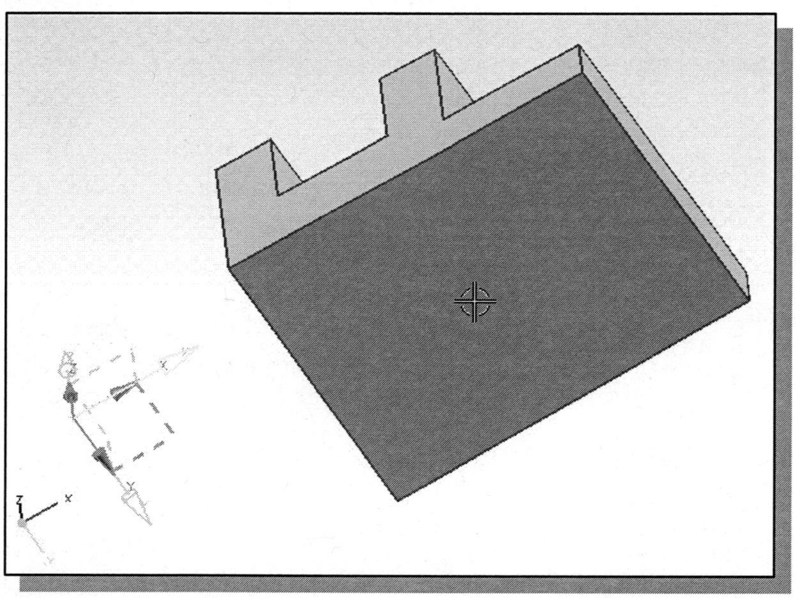

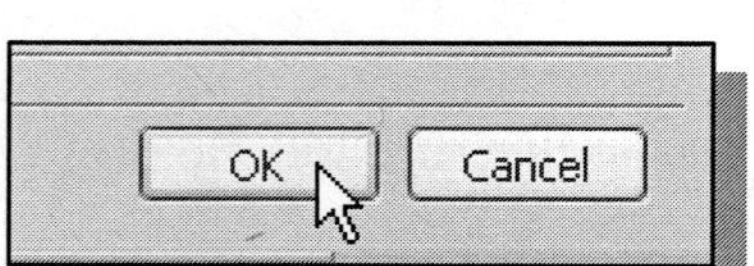

4. Click **OK** to accept the selected face and proceed with the new WCS.

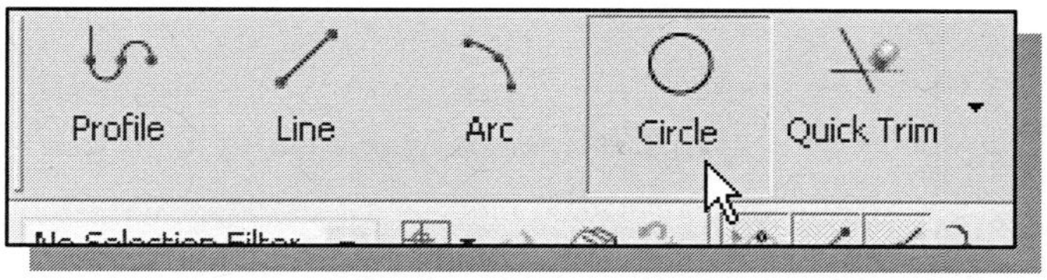

5. Select the **Circle** command by clicking once with the left-mouse-button on the icon in the *Sketch* toolbar.

6. Move the cursor along the shorter edge of the base feature and pick the **midpoint** of the edge when the alignment symbol is displayed as shown.

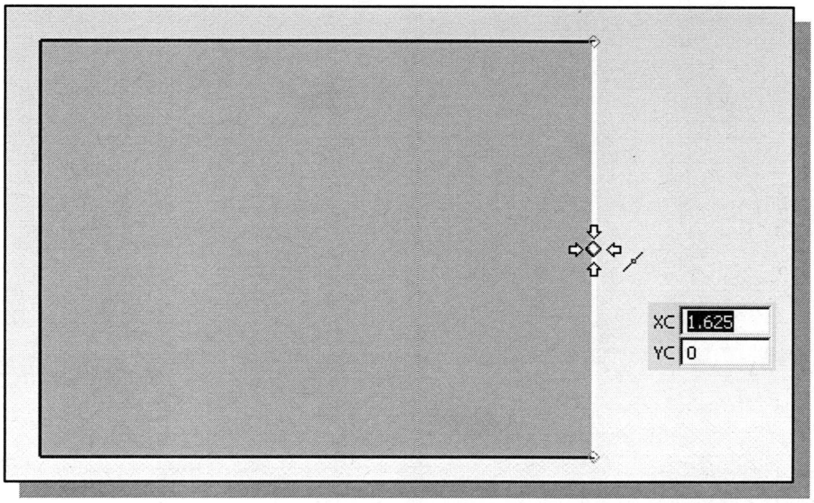

7. Select the top corner of the base feature to create a circle as shown below.

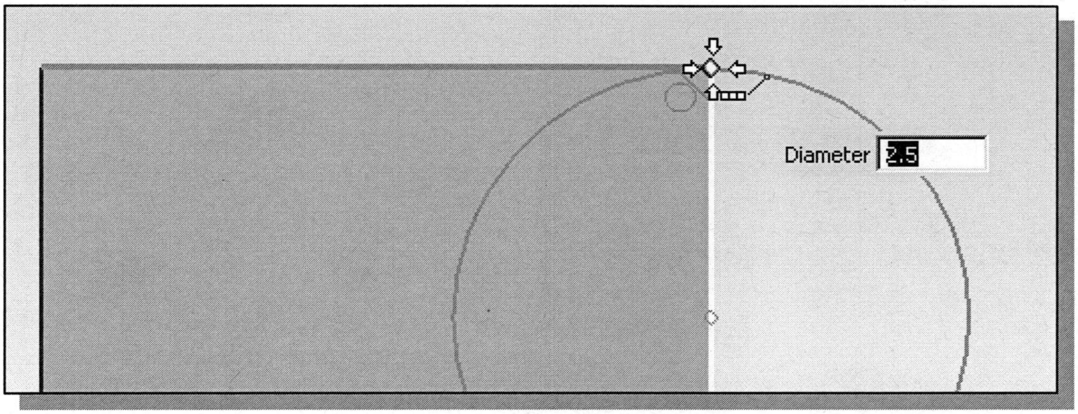

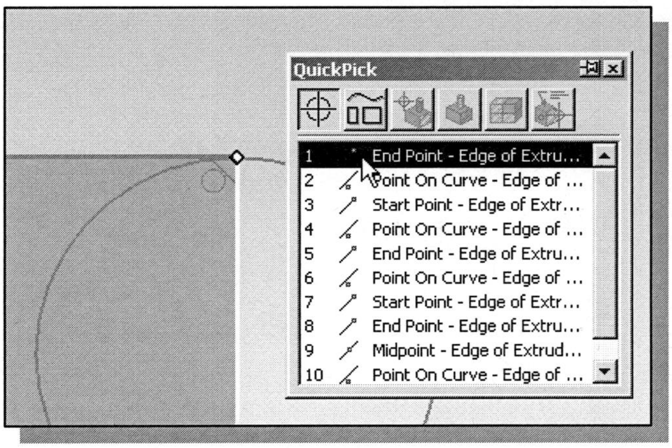

8. If the **QuickPick** dialog box appears on the screen, select one of the ***Endpoint*** options that are listed.

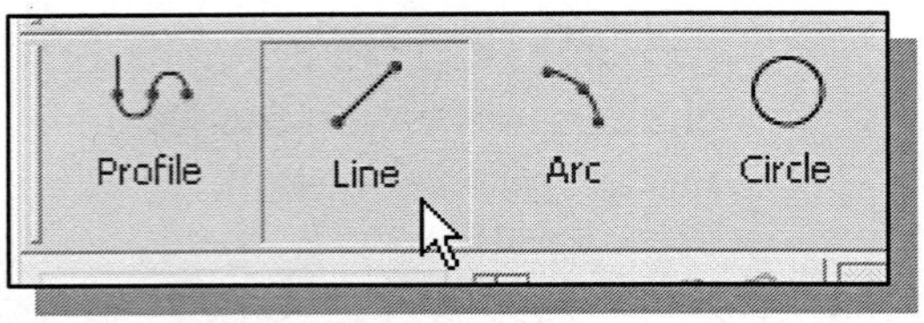

9. Select the **Line** command by clicking once with the left-mouse-button on the icon in the *Sketch* toolbar.

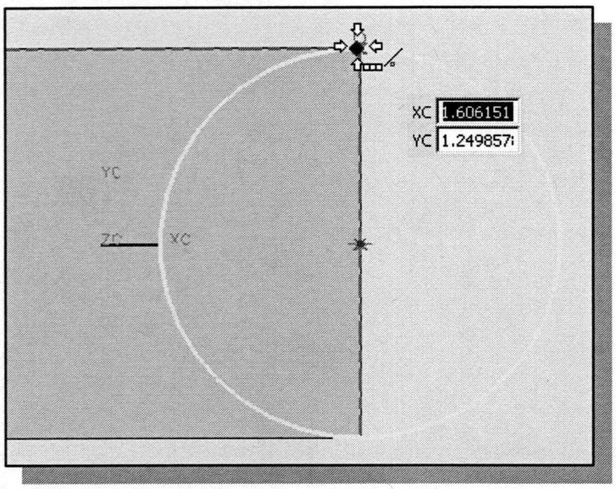

10. Click on the top corner of the solid feature. Notice the different *alignment symbols* displayed on the screen.

11. If the **QuickPick** dialog box appears on the screen, select one of the ***Endpoint*** options that are listed.

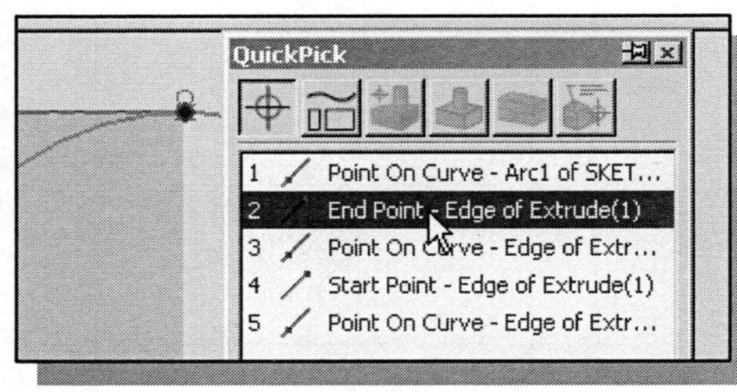

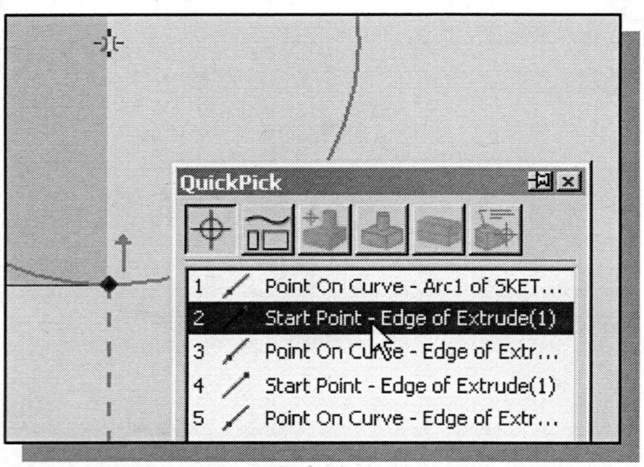

12. Click on the bottom corner of the solid feature and notice the *QuickPick* dialog box appears on the screen.

13. Select one of the ***Edge*** options in the list, if the ***QuickPick*** dialog box appears on the screen.

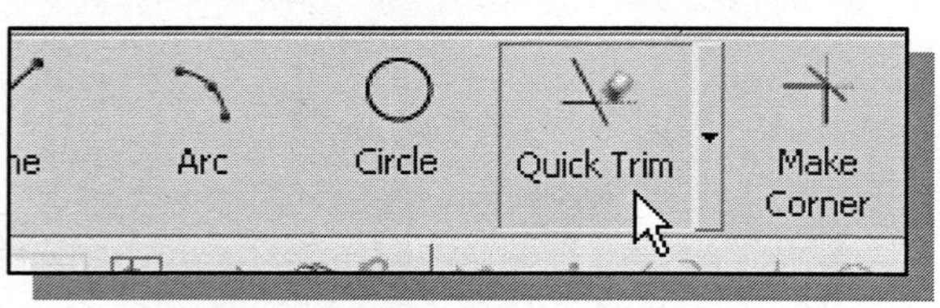

14. Select the **Quick Trim** command by clicking once with the left-mouse-button on the icon in the *Sketch* toolbar.

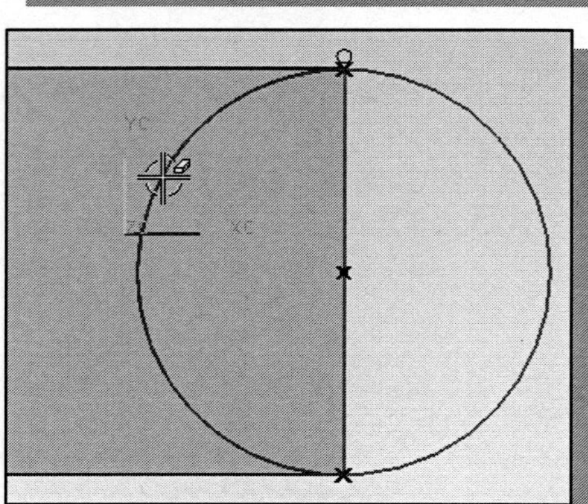

15. Click on the circle that is overlapping with the solid feature; the **Trim** command will remove the selected portion.

16. Click **Close** to end the Trim command.

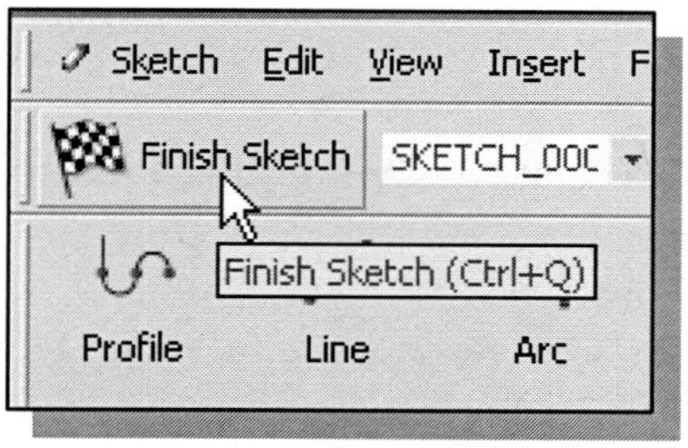

17. Click **Finish Sketch** to exit the *NX Sketcher* mode and return to the *Feature* option dialog window.

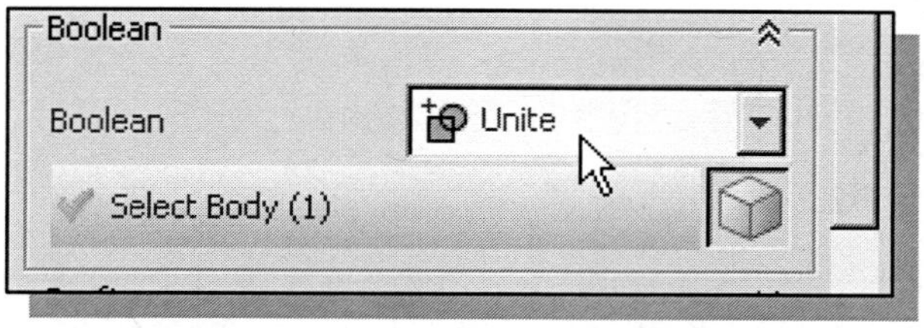

18. In the *Extrude* popup window, set the *Boolean* option to **Unite** as shown.

❖ Notice the solid feature is highlighted when the *Unite* option is set.

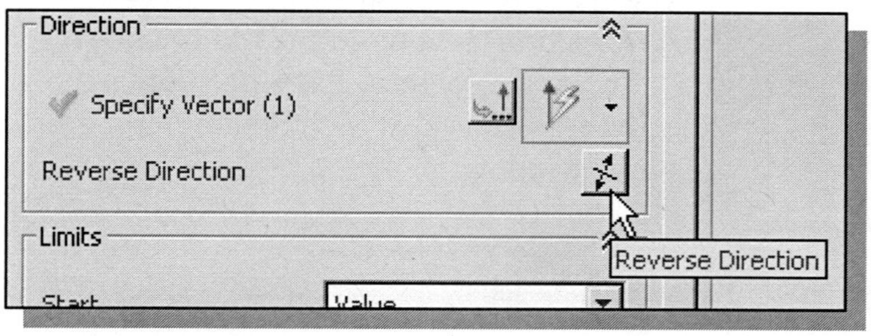

19. Click on the **Reverse Direction** icon to switch the extrusion direction.

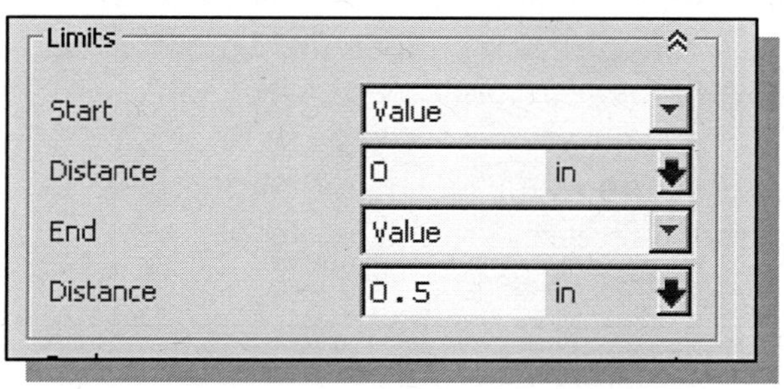

20. Enter **0.5** as the extrusion *Distance* as shown.

21. Click **OK** to create the extrusion feature.

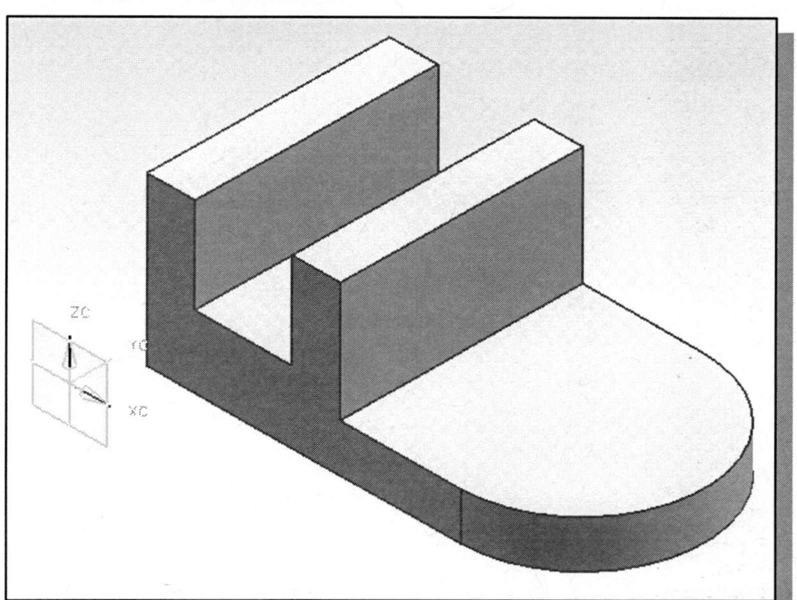

Using More Meaningful Feature Names

- Currently, our model contains two extruded features. The feature is highlighted in the display area when we select the feature in the *Part Navigator* window. Each time a new feature is created, the feature is also added in the *Part Navigator* window. By default, *UGS NX* will use generic names for part features. However, when we begin to deal with parts with a large number of features, it will be much easier to identify the features using more meaningful names. Two methods can be used to rename the features: 1. **Clicking** twice (not double-clicking) on the name of the feature and 2. Using the **Option Menu** by clicking once with the right-mouse-button (MB3).

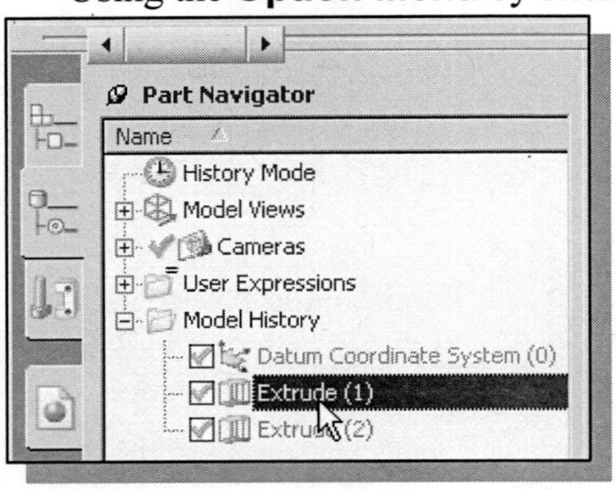

1. Select the first extruded feature in the *Model Part Navigator* area by left-clicking once on the name of the feature, ***Extrude***. Notice the selected feature is also highlighted in the graphics window.

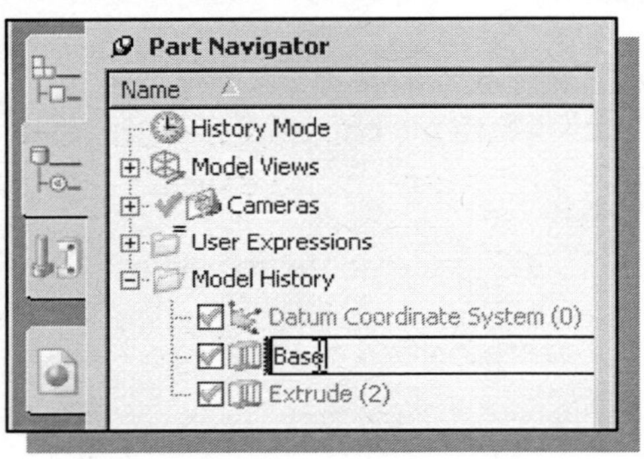

2. Left-mouse-click again, on the feature name, to enter the *Edit* mode as shown.

3. Enter **Base** as the new name for the first extruded feature.

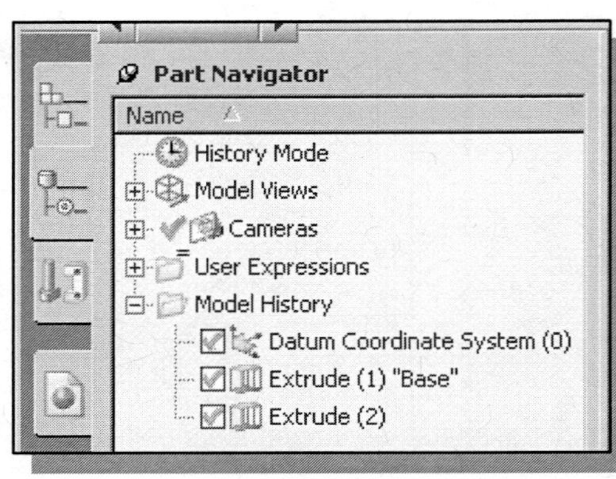

❖ Notice the new name is now shown as part of the extruded feature name.

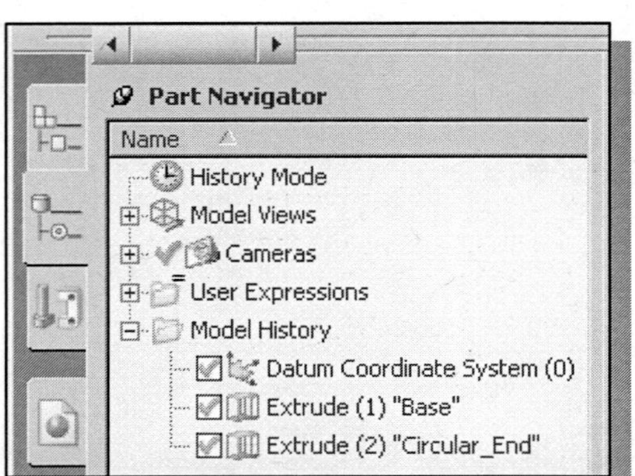

4. On your own, attach ***Circular_End*** to the second extruded feature name.

Adjusting the Width of the Base Feature

❖ One of the main advantages of parametric modeling is the ease of performing part modifications at any time in the design process. Part modifications can be done through accessing the features in the history tree. *UGS NX* remembers the history of a part, including all the rules that were used to create it, so that changes can be made to any operation that was performed to create the part. For our ***Saddle Bracket*** design, we will reduce the extrusion distance from 2.5 to 2.0 inches and the size of the base feature from 3.25 inches to 3.0 inches.

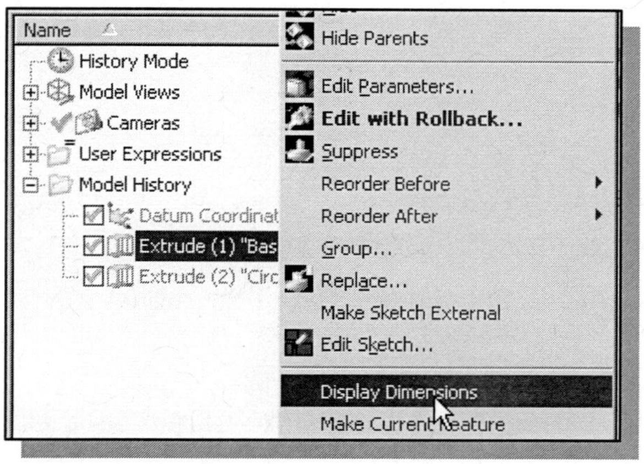

1. Inside the *Part Navigator* area, **right-mouse-click** on the first extruded feature to bring up the option menu and select the **Display Dimensions** option as shown.

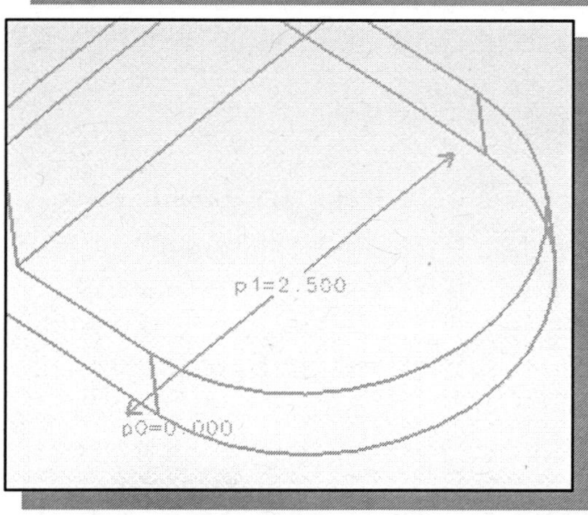

❖ Note the two dimensions shown are the two **extrusion limits** used in the *Extrude* dialog window.

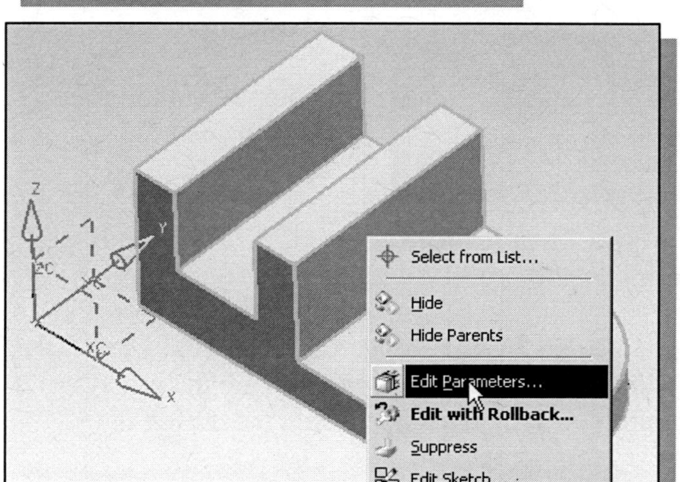

2. Inside the graphics window, right-mouse-click (MB3) on the first extruded feature (*Base*) to bring up the option menu and select the **Edit Parameters...** option in the pop-up menu.

3. Adjust the extrusion distance by changing the *End* limit to **2.0** as shown in the figure.

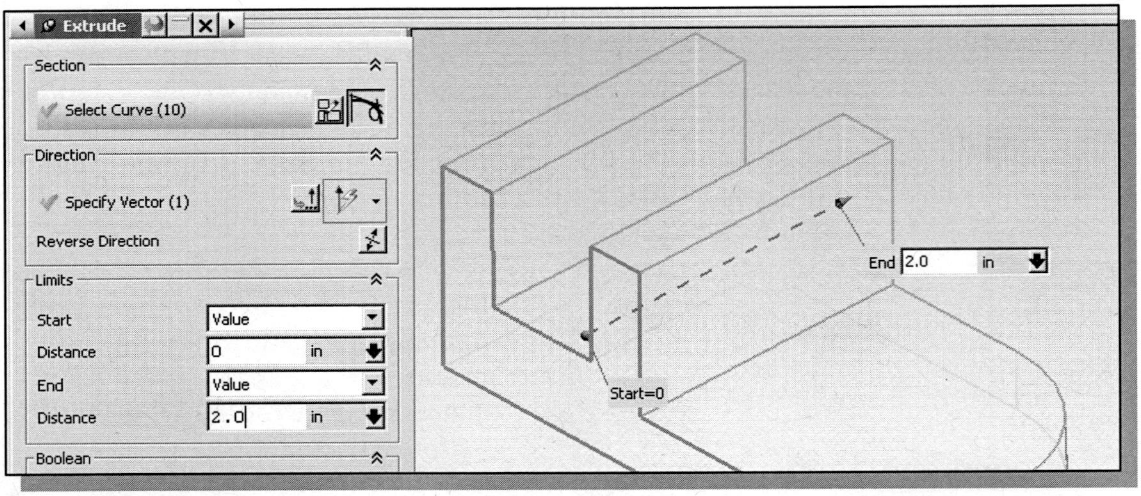

4. Click **OK** to proceed with the adjustment and noticed the size of the model is adjusted accordingly.

5. Inside the *Part Navigator* area, **right-mouse-click** on the first extruded feature to bring up the option menu and select the **Edit Sketch** option in the pop-up menu.

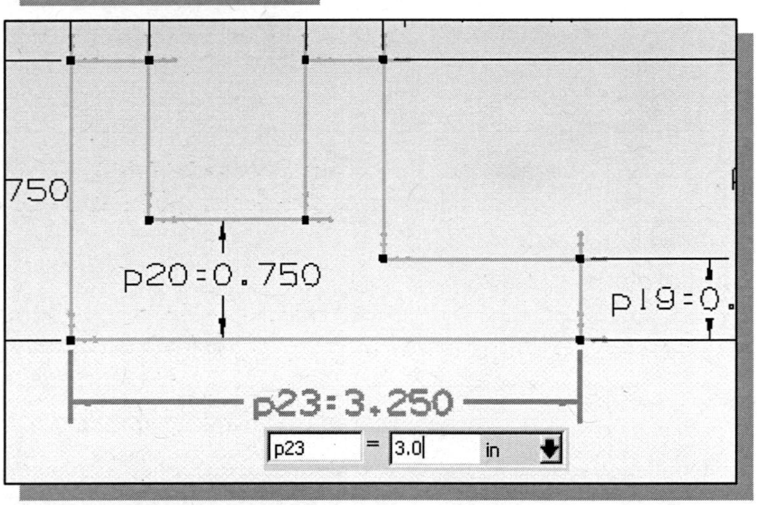

6. The 2D sketch of the *Base* feature now appears on the screen. Select the overall width of the ***Base*** feature, the **3.25** dimension value, by double-clicking on the dimension text as shown.

7. Enter **3.0** in the *Edit Dimension* box.

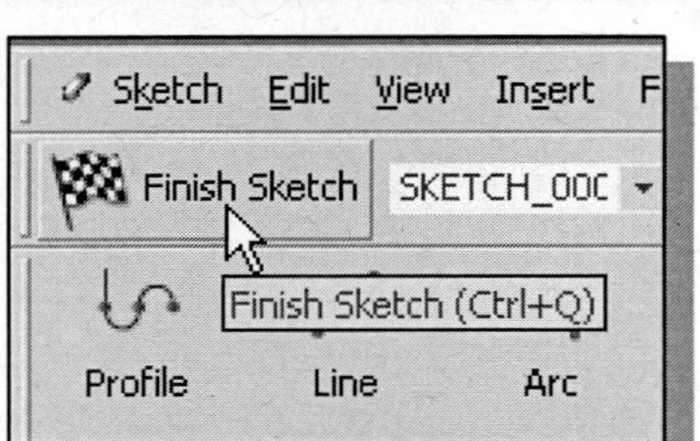

8. Click **Finish Sketch** to exit the *NX Sketcher* mode and proceed with the adjustment.

➢ Note that *UGS NX* updates the model by re-linking all elements used to create the model. Any problems will also be displayed during the updating process.

Adding a Placed Feature

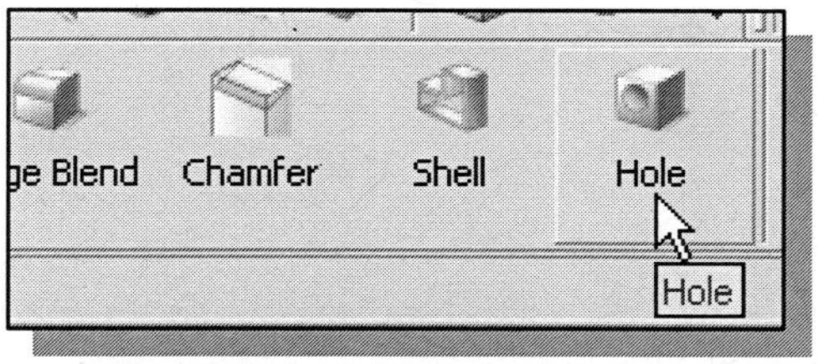

1. In the *Feature Operation* toolbar (the toolbar that is located to the right side of the *Form Feature* toolbar), select the **Hole** command by releasing the left-mouse-button on the icon.

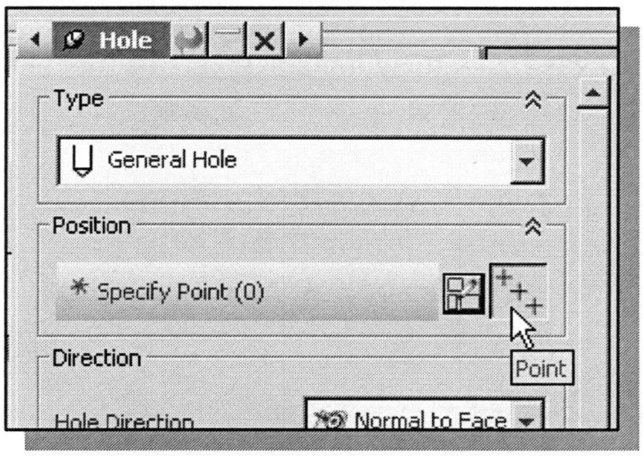

2. In the *Hole* window, notice the default hole *Type* is set to **General Hole** as shown.

❖ Not that by default, the position of the hole is specified using the **Point** command.

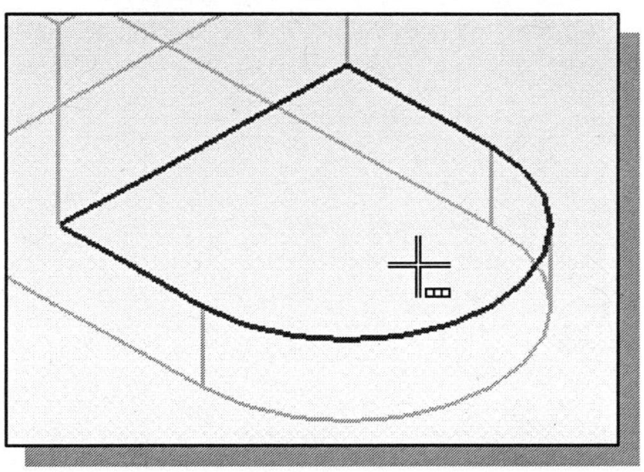

3. Pick a location inside the top horizontal surface of the *Circular_End* feature as shown.

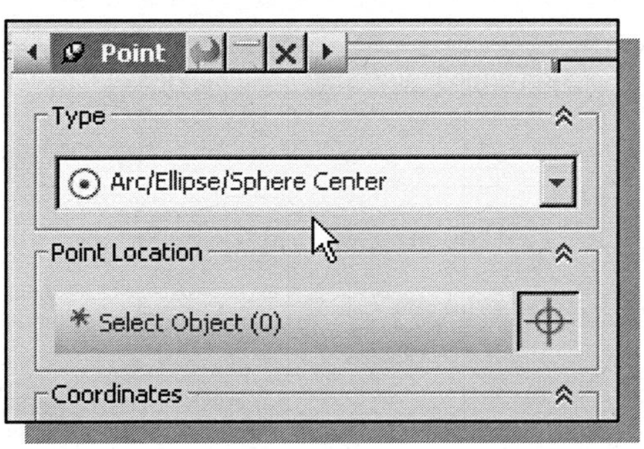

❖ Note the **Point** command is activated automatically once the sketch plane has been selected.

4. In the *Point* dialog box, set the point option to **Aec/Ellipse/Sphere Center**, as shown.

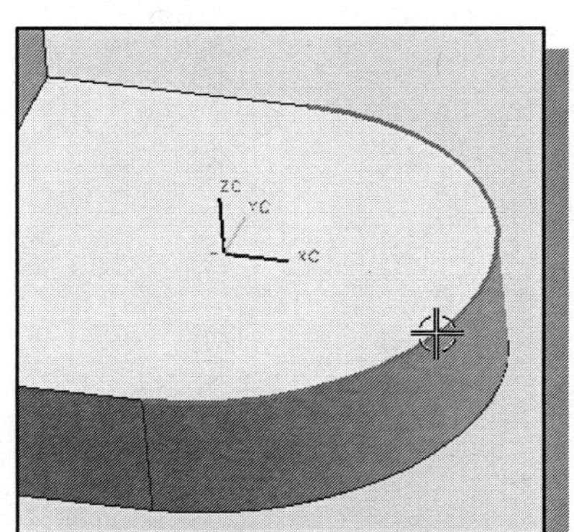

➢ We will align the center of the hole to the center of the large arc.

5. Select the top arc of the *Circular_End* feature as shown in the figure.

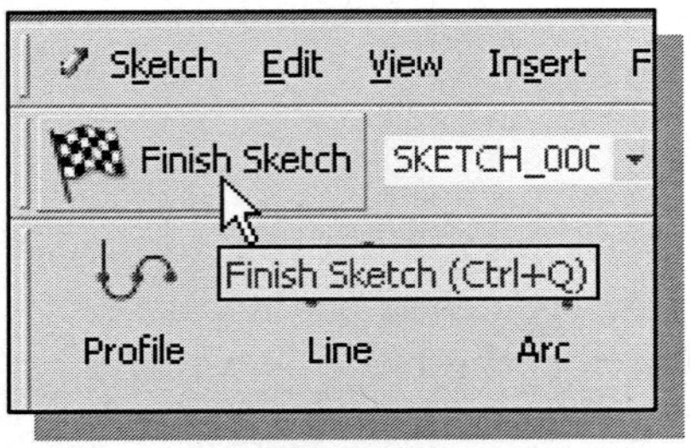

6. Click **Finish Sketch** to exit the *NX Sketcher* mode and return to the *Feature* option dialog window.

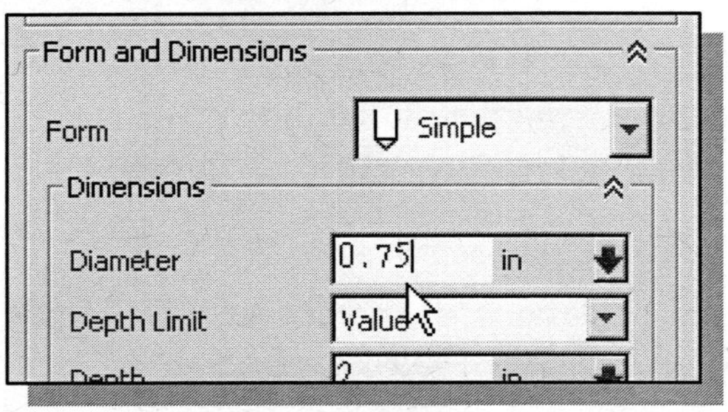

7. Enter **0.75 in** as the *Diameter* of the hole as shown in the figure.

8. In the *Form and Dimensions* options, set the *Depth Limit* to **Through Body** as shown in the figure below.

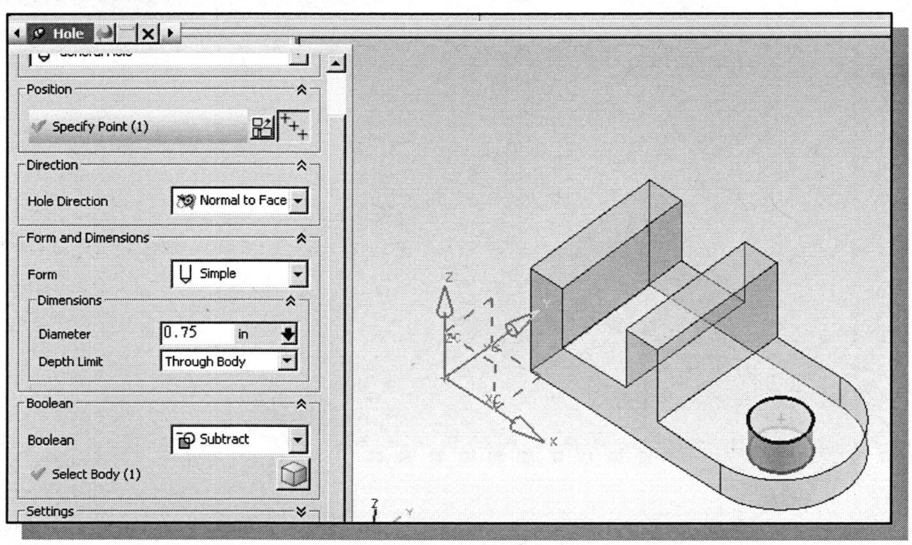

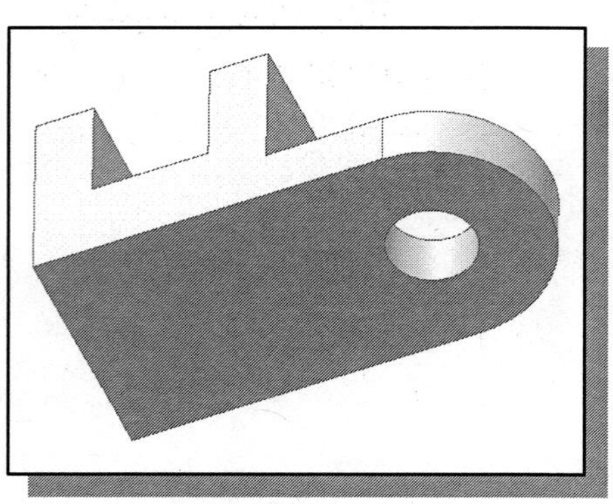

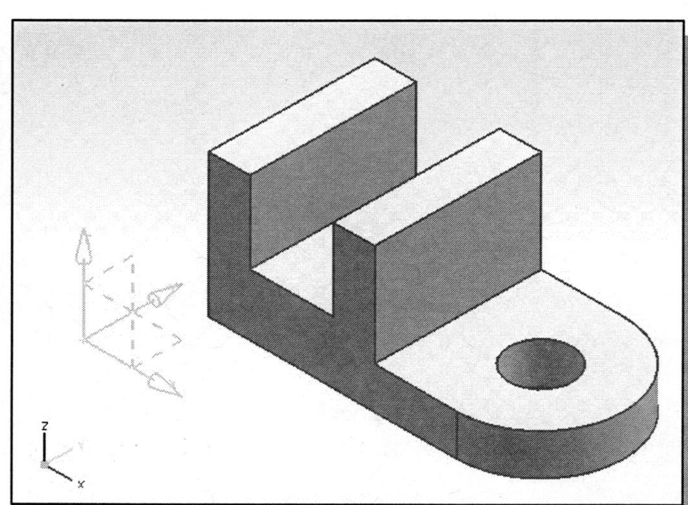

Creating a Rectangular Cut Feature

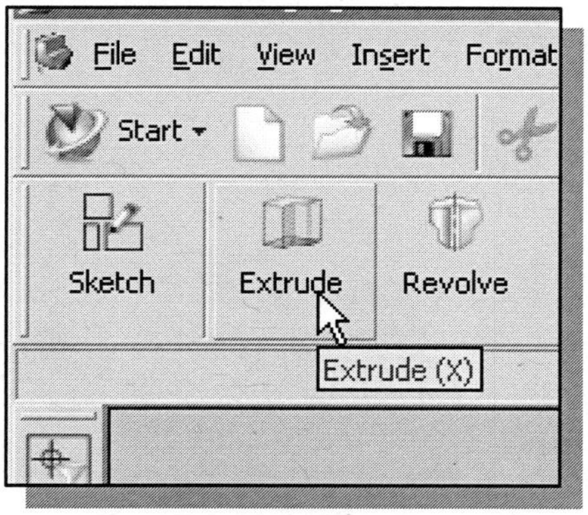

1. In the ***Feature*** toolbars (toolbars aligned to the right edge of the main window), select the **Extrude** icon as shown.

- The ***Extrude*** feature options dialog box, which contains applicable construction options, is displayed as shown in the figure below.

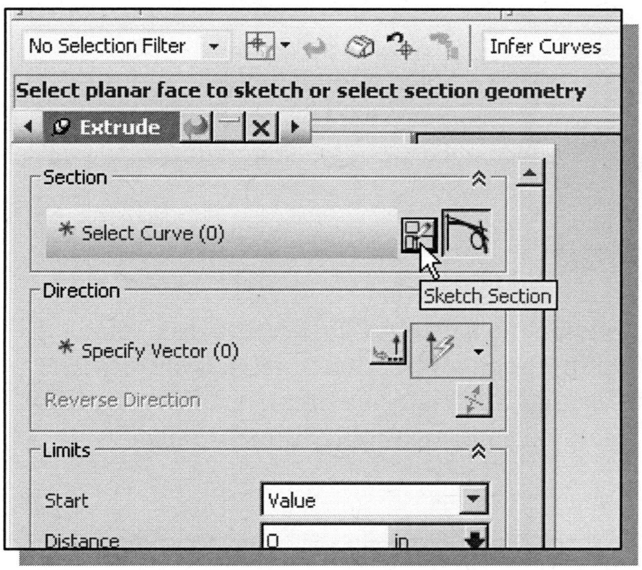

2. On your own, move the cursor over the icons and read the brief descriptions of the different options available. Note that the default extrude option is set to **Select Section**.

3. Click the **Sketch Section** button to begin creating a new *2D sketch*.

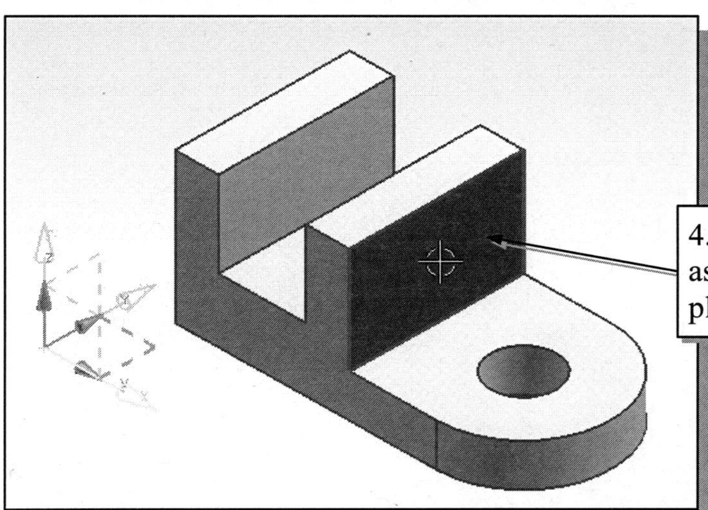

4. Select the **right vertical face** of the base feature to setup the orientation of the sketch plane.

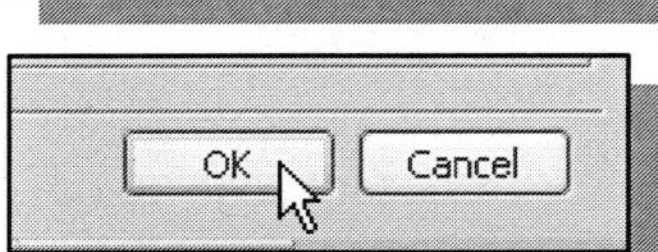

5. Click **OK** to accept the settings of the sketch plane.

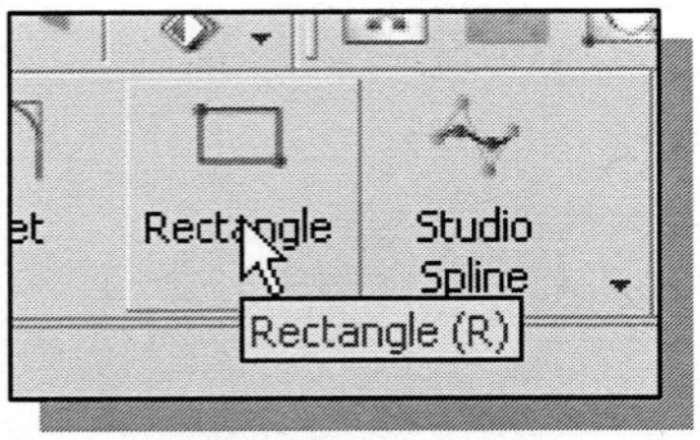

6. Select the **Rectangle** command by clicking once with the left-mouse-button (MB1) on the icon in the *Sketch Curve* toolbar.

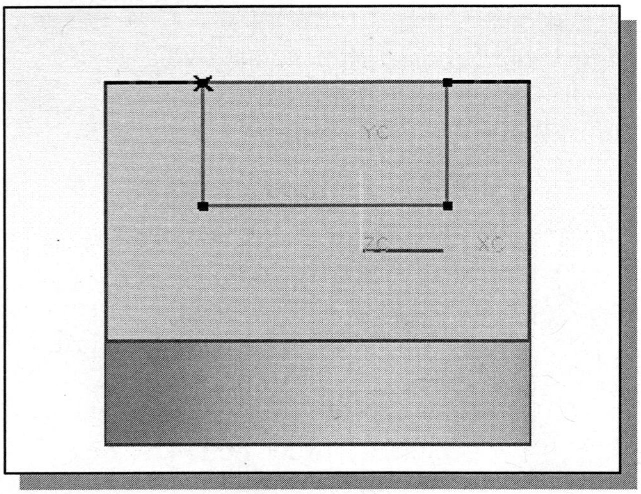

7. Create a rectangle of arbitrary size on the inside of the upper section of the solid model screen as shown. (Note the alignment symbol on top.)

8. Inside the graphics window, click once with the middle-mouse-button (MB2) to end the **Rectangle** command.

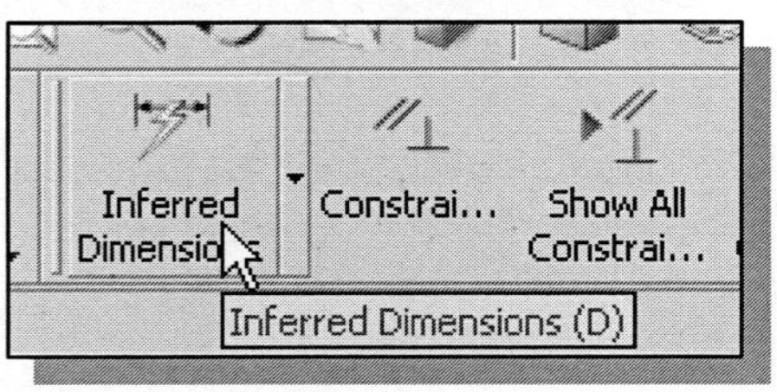

9. Activate the **Inferred Dimensions** command by left-clicking once on the icon as shown. The **Inferred Dimensions** command allows us to quickly create and modify dimensions

10. On your own, create and adjust the three dimensions as shown in the figure below.

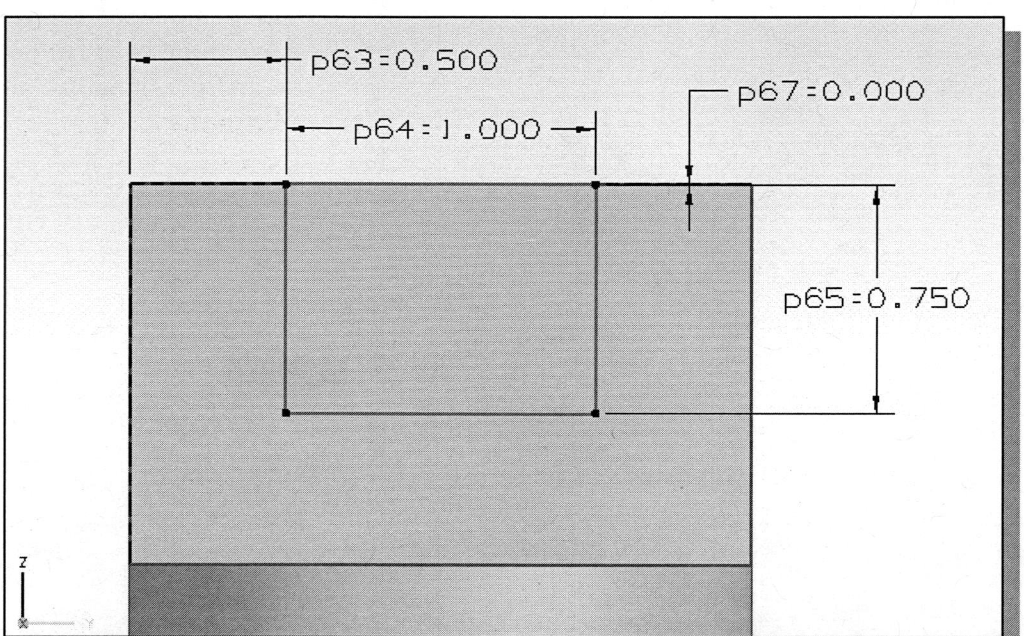

11. Inside the graphics window, click once with the middle-mouse-button (MB2) to end the **Dimension** command.

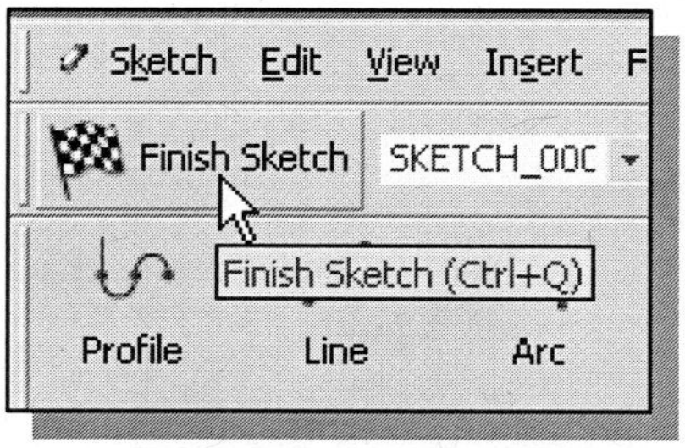

12. Select **Finish Sketch** by clicking once with the left-mouse-button (MB1) on the icon.

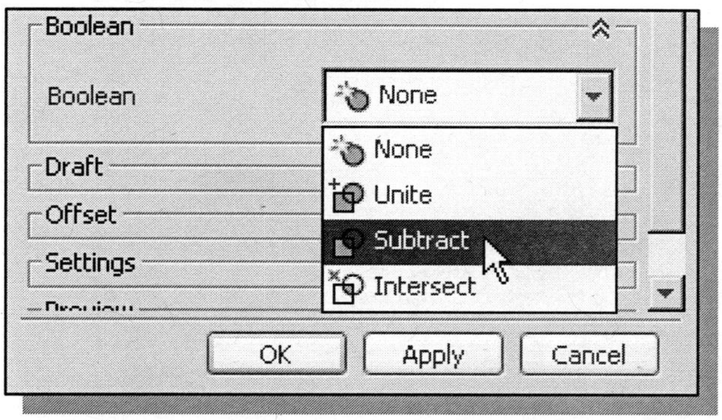

13. In the *Extrude* popup window, set the *Extrude* option to **Subtract** as shown.

❖ Notice the solid feature is highlighted when the *Subtract* option is set.

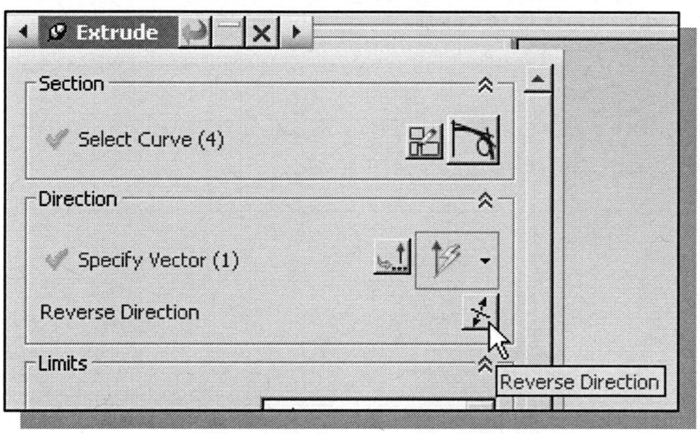

14. Click on the **Reverse Direction** icon to switch the extrusion direction.

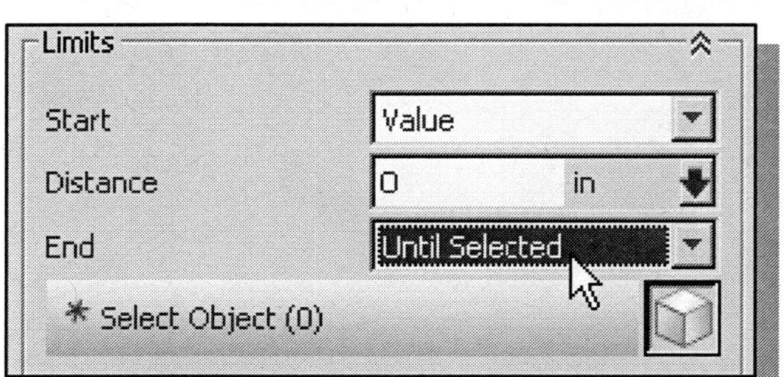

15. Select **Until Selected** as the extrusion distance option as shown.

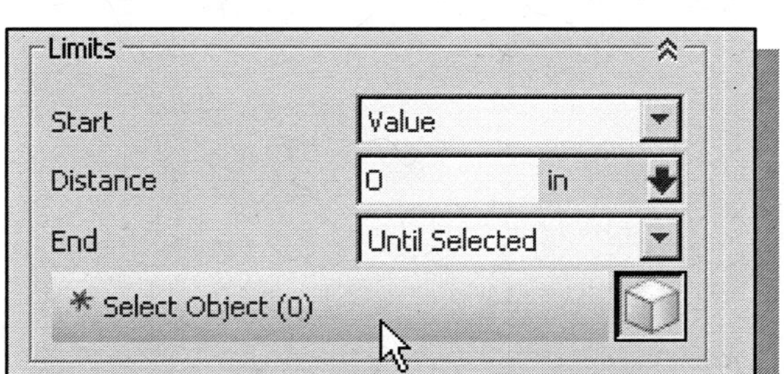

➢ The message in the *Limits* section indicates that no termination geometry has been selected.

16. Select the third vertical face of the upper section of the solid model as shown.

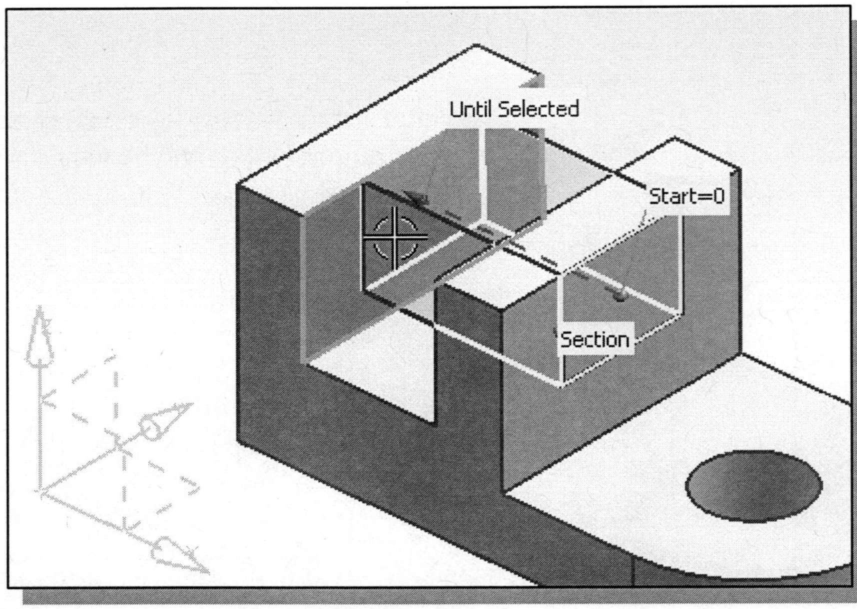

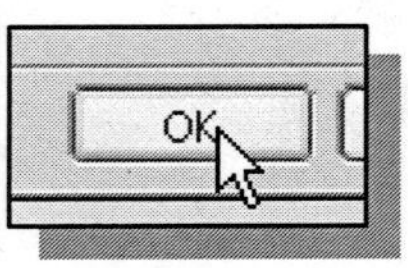

17. Click **OK** to create the extrusion feature.

➢ On your own, rename the rectangular subtract feature to **Rect_Cut** and examine the created solid features by going through the *Part Navigator*.

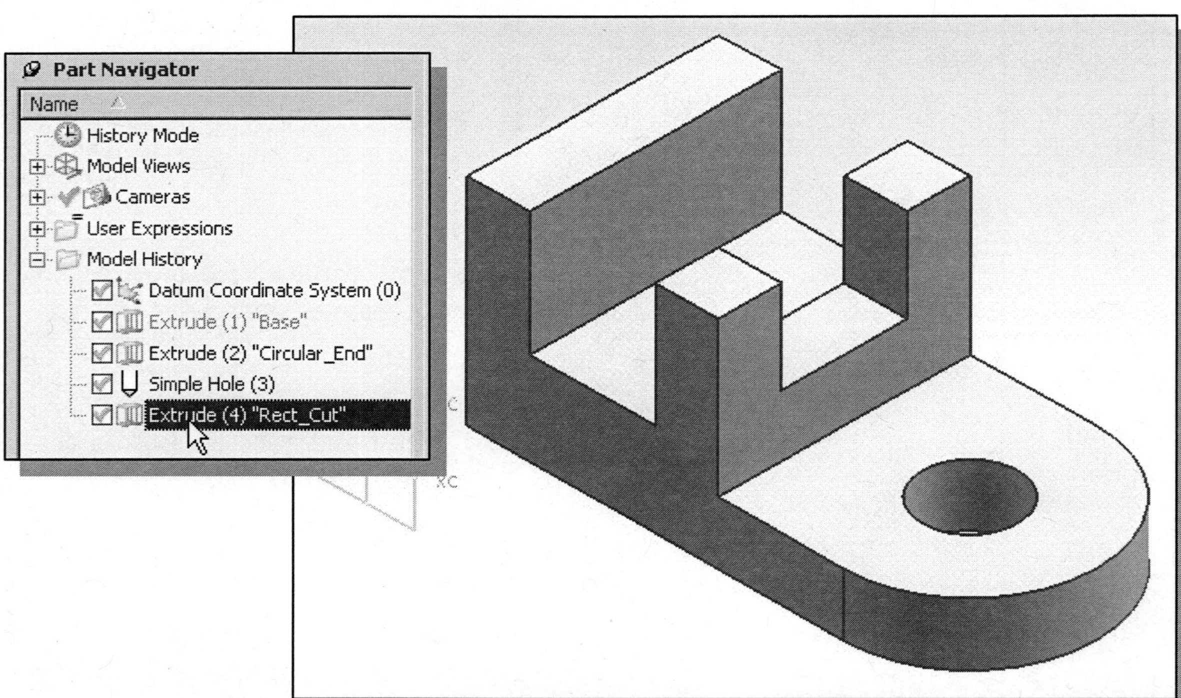

History-based Part Modifications

- *UGS NX* uses the *history-based part modification* approach, which enables us to make modifications to the appropriate features and re-link the rest of the history tree without having to reconstruct the model from scratch. We can think of it as going back in time and modifying some aspects of the modeling steps used to create the part. We can modify any feature that we have created. As an example, we will adjust the depth of the rectangular cutout.

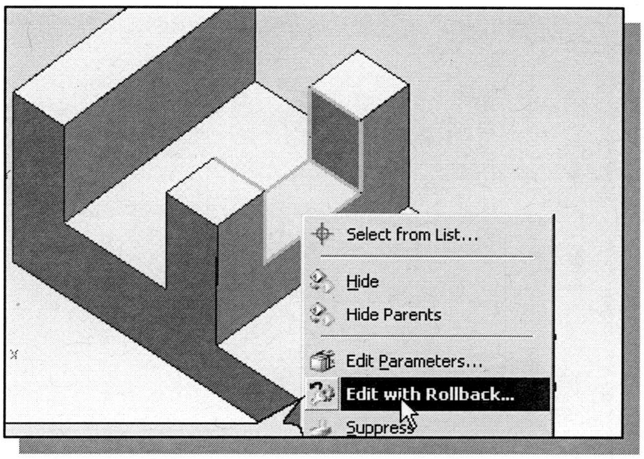

1. Inside the graphics window, right-clicking once on the ***Rect_Cut*** feature and select the **Edit with Rollback...** option.

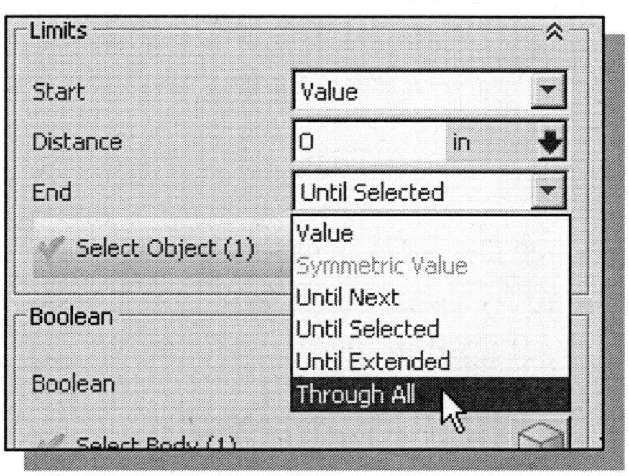

2. In the *Extrude* dialog box, set the termination *Limits* to the **Through All** option.
3. Click on the **OK** button to accept the settings.

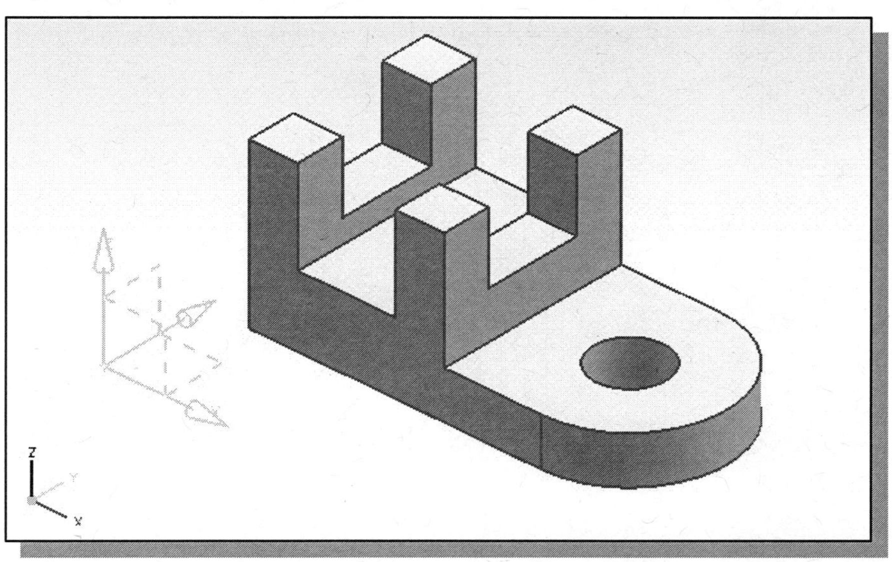

A Design Change

❖ Engineering designs usually go through many revisions and changes. *UGS NX* provides an assortment of tools to handle design changes quickly and effectively. We will demonstrate some of the tools available by changing the ***Base*** feature of the design.

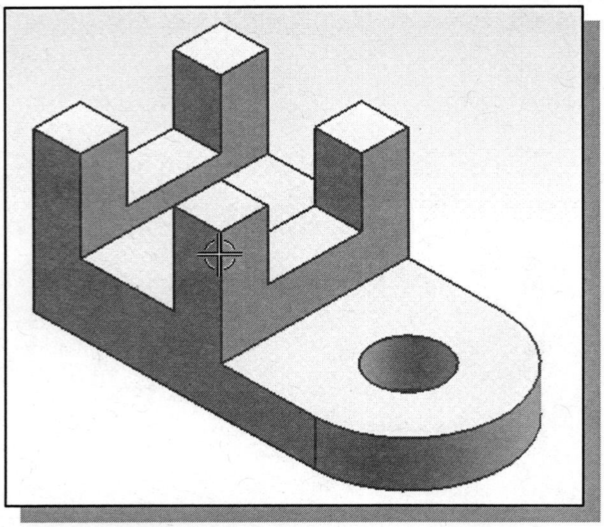

1. Inside the graphics window, double-clicking on the ***Base*** feature.

❖ We have entered the **Edit with Rollback...** option. *UGS NX* provides quite a few options to allow quick modification of the created features.

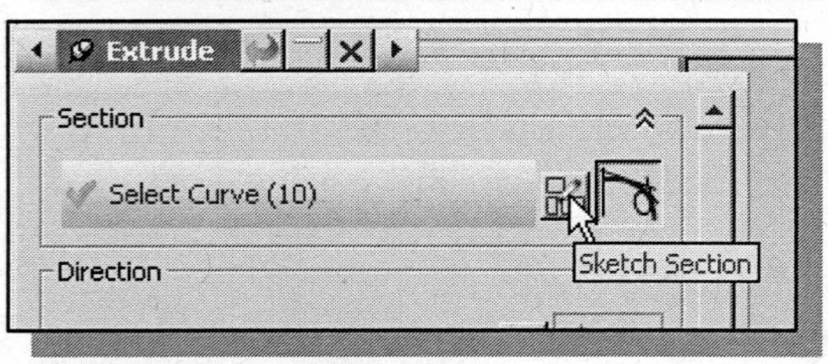

2. In the *Extrude* window, select the **Sketch Section** option by left-clicking once on the icon.

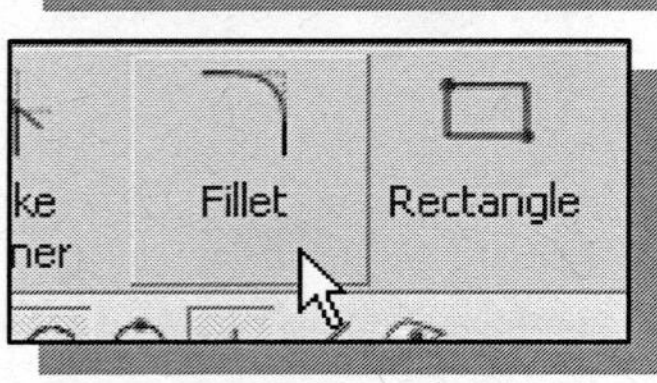

3. Select the **Fillet** command by clicking once with the left-mouse-button (MB1) on the icon in the *Sketch Curve* toolbar.

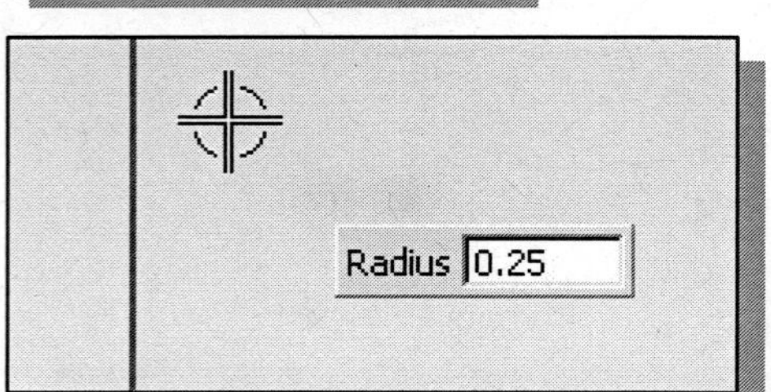

4. Enter **0.25** as the new *Radius* of the fillet.

5. Select the two edges as shown to create the fillet.

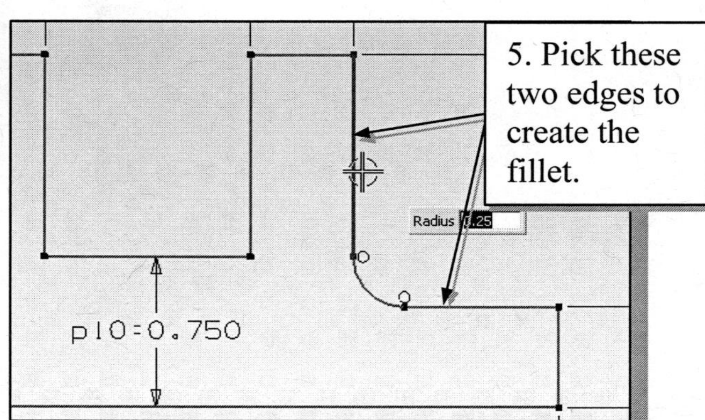

6. Inside the graphics window, click once with the middle-mouse-button (MB2) to end the **Fillet** command.

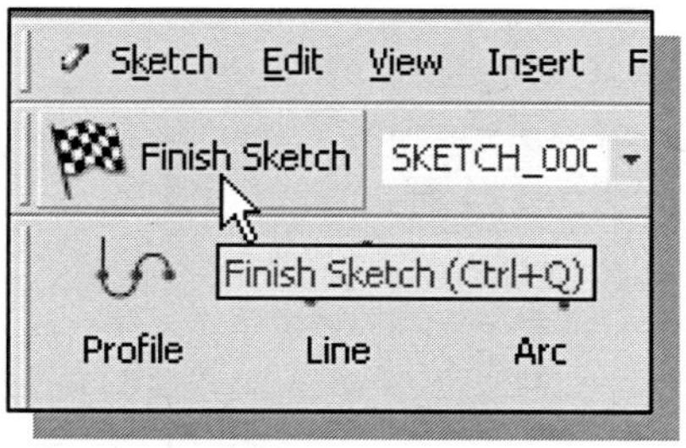

7. Select **Finish Sketch** by clicking once with the left-mouse-button (MB1) on the icon.

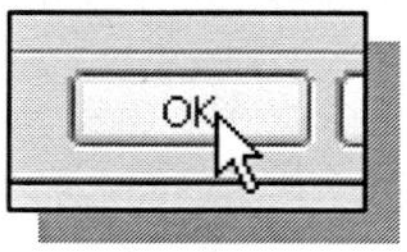

8. Click **OK** to accept the changes to the extrusion feature.

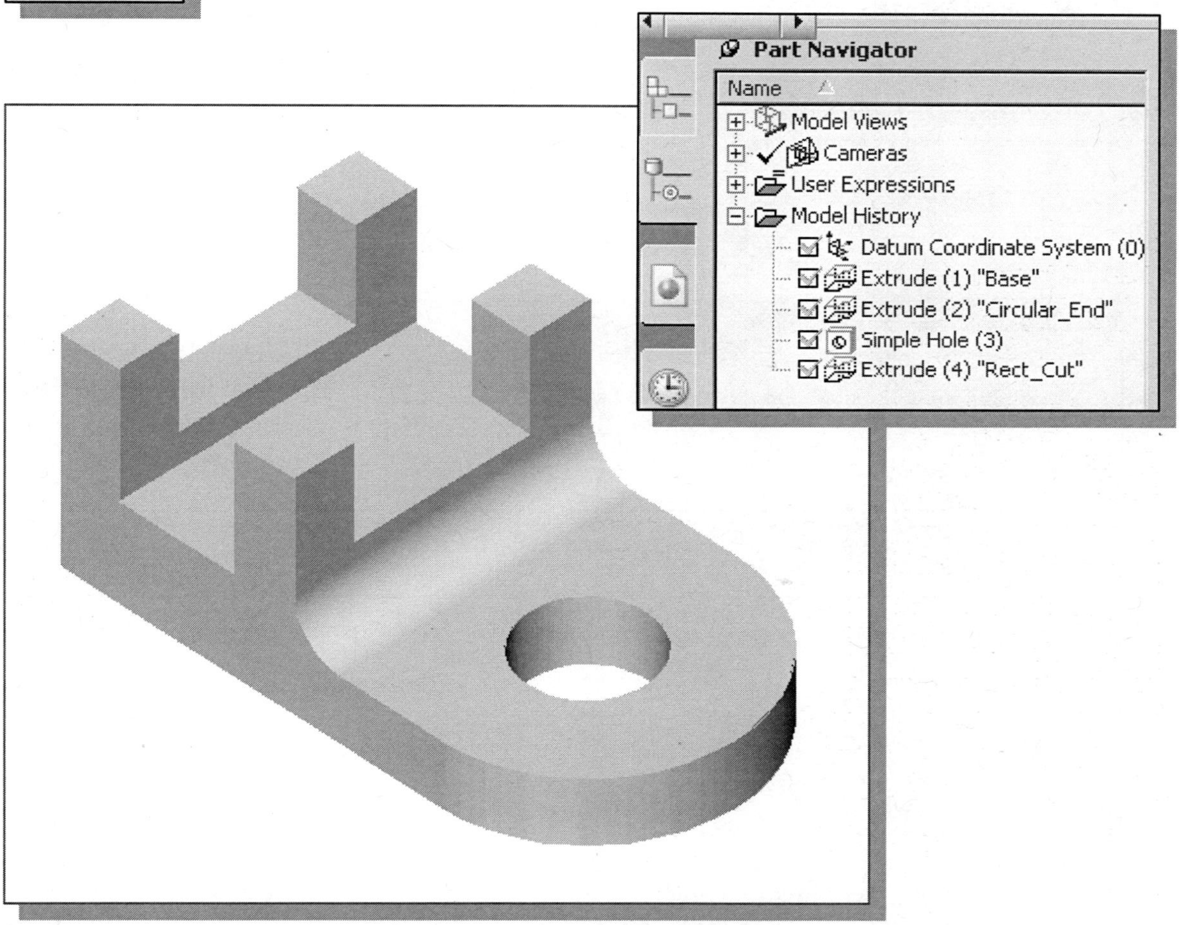

❖ In a typical design process, the initial design will undergo many analyses, testing, and reviews. The *history-based part modification* approach is an extremely powerful tool that enables us to quickly update the design. At the same time, it is quite clear that PLANNING AHEAD is also important in doing feature-based parametric modeling.

Assigning and Calculating the Associated Physical Properties

➢ In parametric modeling, specific material properties can also be assigned to the virtual designs; this allows us to examine the detailed physical information of the model, such as mass, weight, center of gravity and moments of inertia. This information can be used to create bills of materials, prepare for production, and perform further analyses of the designs.

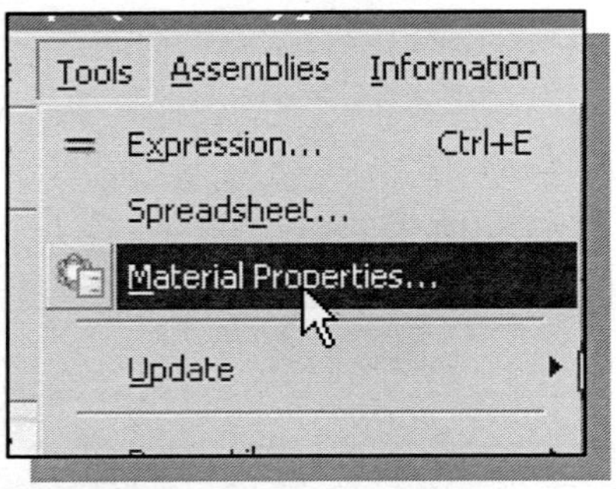

1. In the **Tools** pull-down menu, select **Material Properties...** as shown.

➢ The **Material Properties** option allows us to define material properties and also assign them.

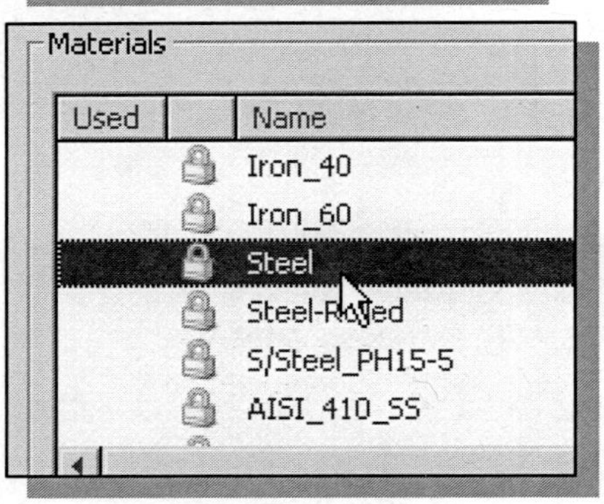

2. Scroll down the *Materials* list and select **Steel** as shown in the figure.

3. Click on the **Display material properties** icon to view the properties of Steel.

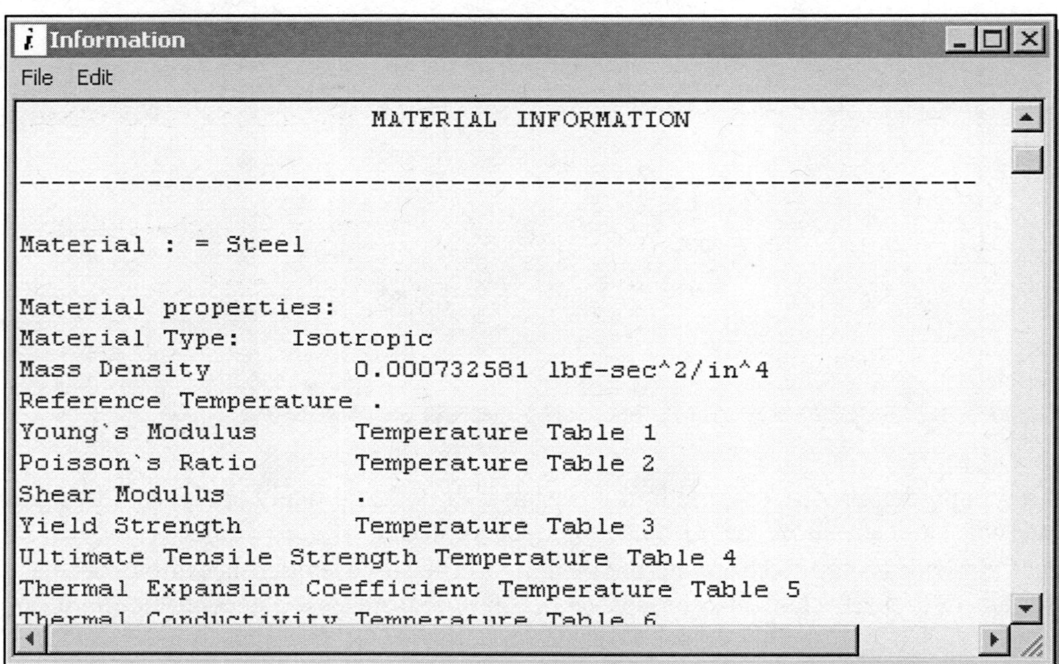

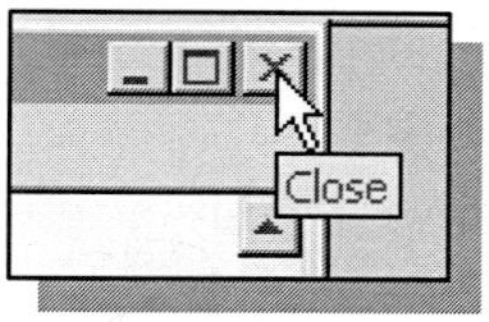

4. On your own, review the associated information. Click on the **Close** icon to close the *Information* window.

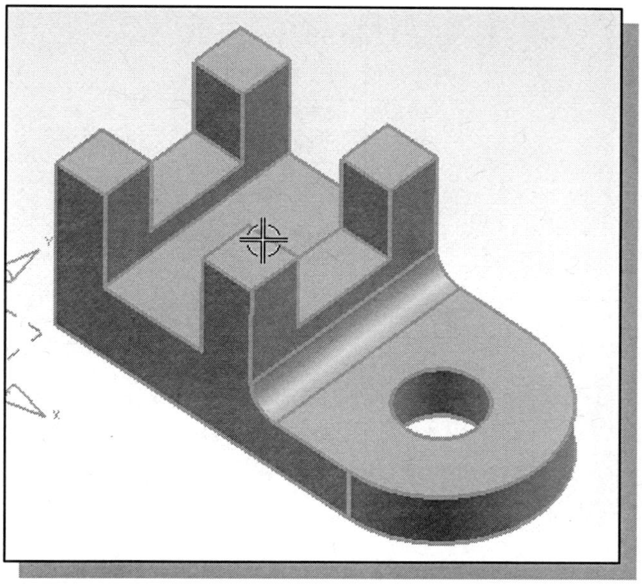

5. Inside the graphics window, select the model by clicking on it with the left-mouse-button.

➢ We will use **Steel** as the material for the model.

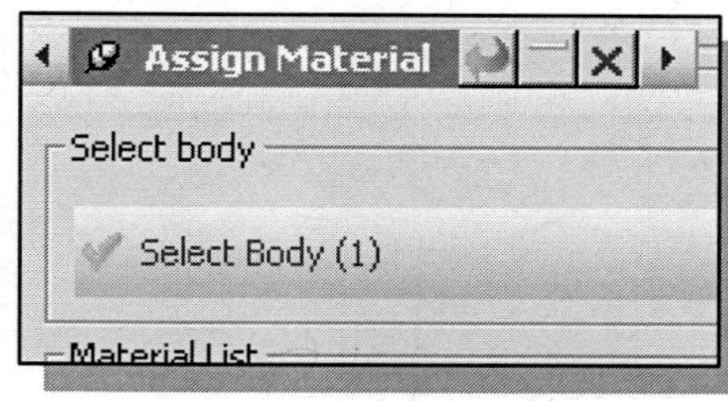

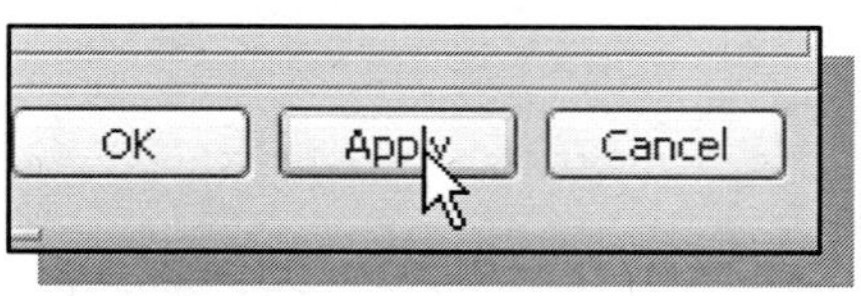

6. Click **Apply** to proceed with assigning the material properties to the selected model.

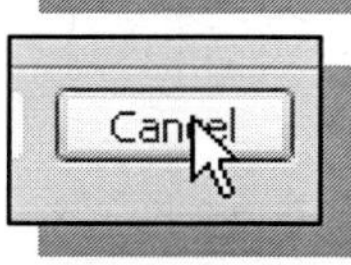

7. Click **Cancel** to exit the **Material Properties** option.

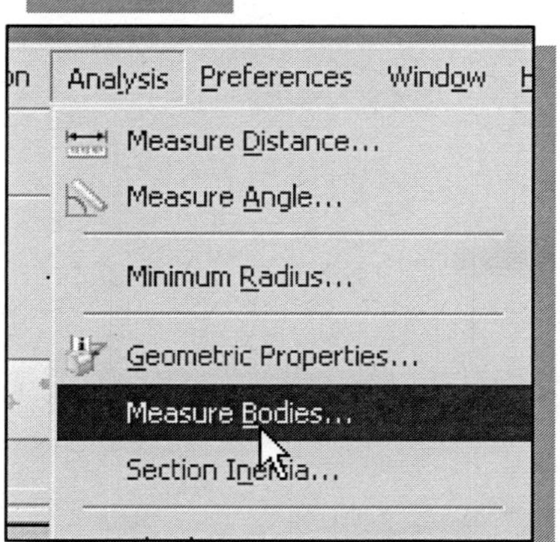

8. In the **Analysis** pull-down menu, select **Measure Bodies...** as shown.

9. Click on the model and note the volume of the model is displayed next to it.

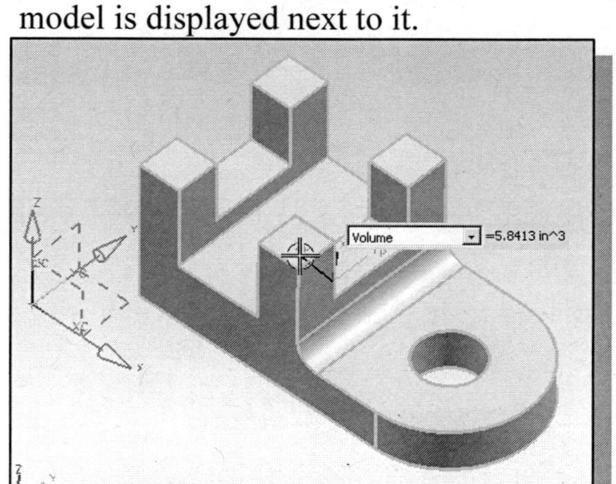

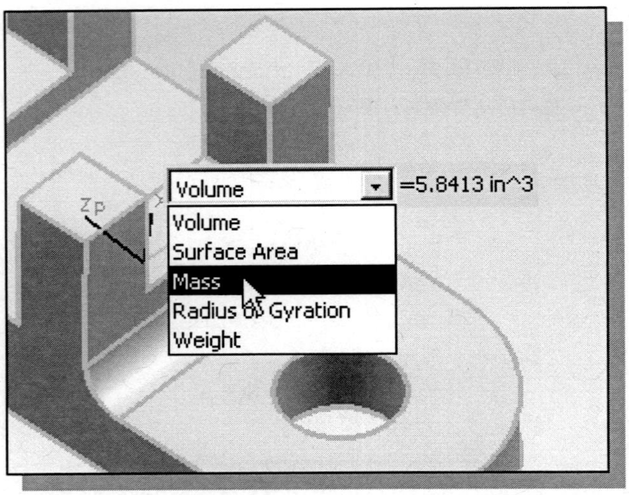

10. Click on the down arrow to display the list of available options as shown.

11. Select **Mass** to see the mass property of the model.

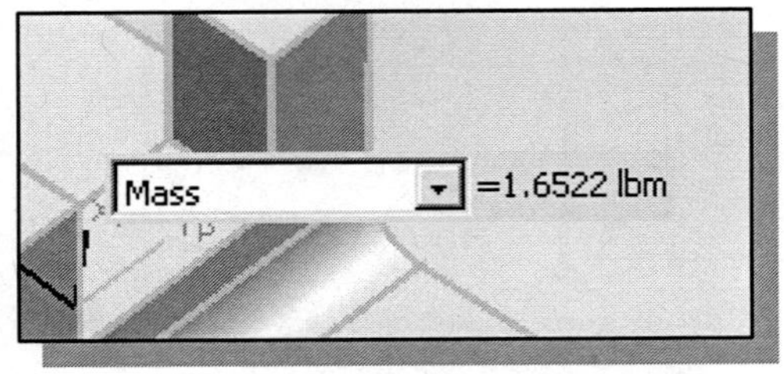

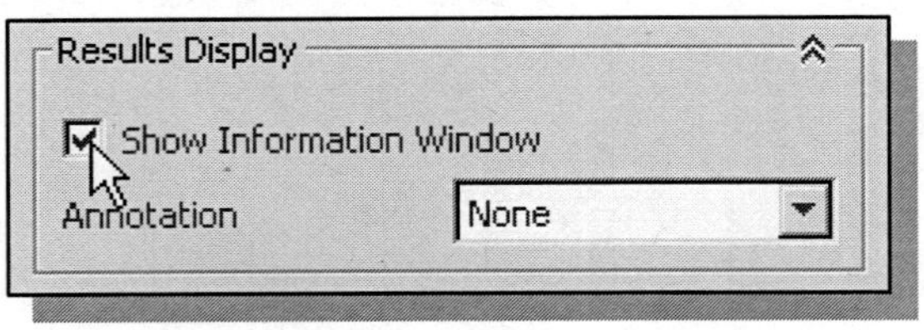

12. In the *Measure Bodies* dialog box, activate the **Show Information Window** option as shown.

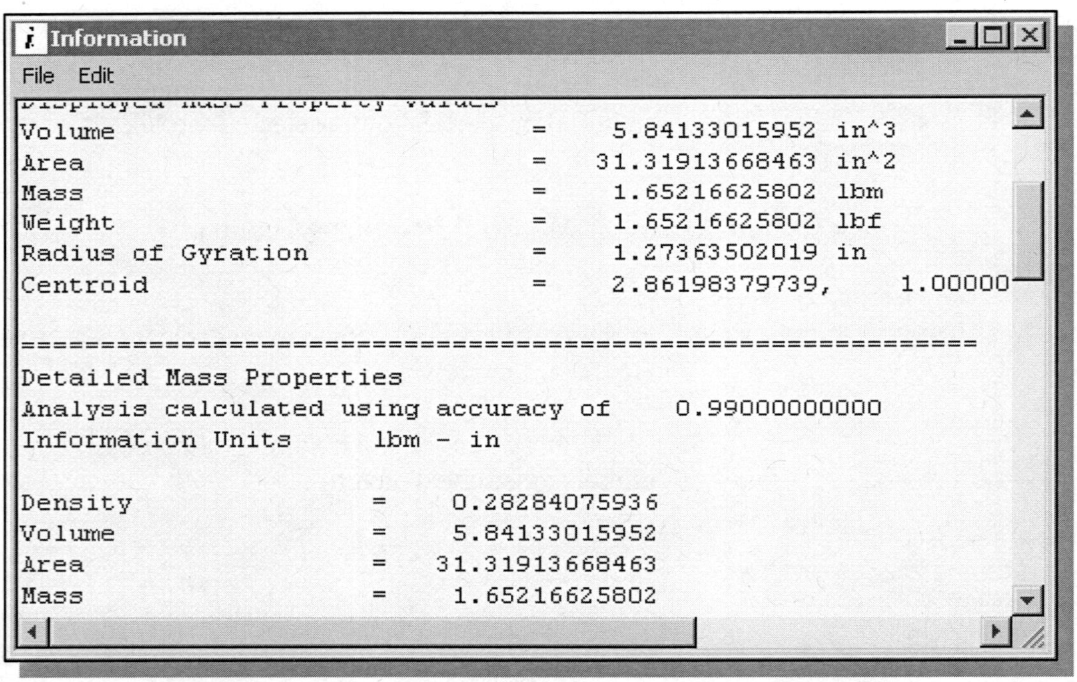

➤ The detailed physical properties of the model, using Steel as the associated material, are displayed inside the information window.

Questions:

1. What are stored in the *UGS NX History Tree*?

2. When extruding, what is the difference between *Value* and *Through All*?

3. Describe the *history-based part modification* approach.

4. Describe two methods available in *UGS NX* to perform the **Edit with Rollback** option of solid features.

5. What are listed in the *Part Navigator* window?

6. Describe two methods available in *UGS NX* to *modify the dimension values* of parametric sketches.

7. Create *History Tree sketches* showing the steps you plan to use to create the two models shown on the next page:

Ex.1)

Ex.2)

Exercises: (Dimensions are in inches.)

1. Plate thickness: **0.25** inches.

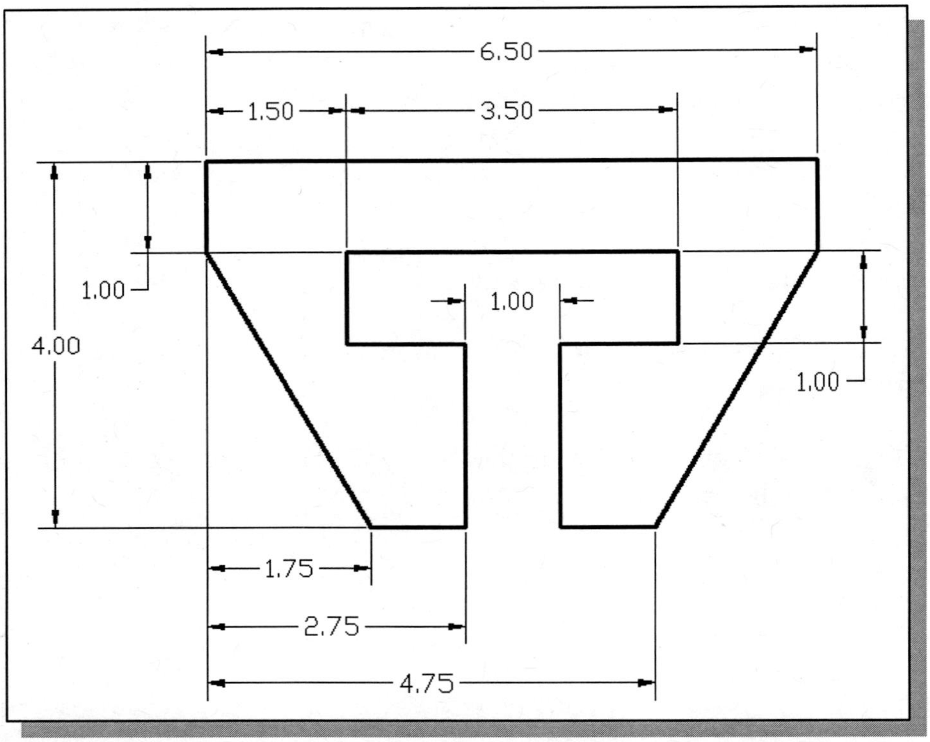

2. Base plate thickness: **0.25** inches. Boss height **0.5** inches.

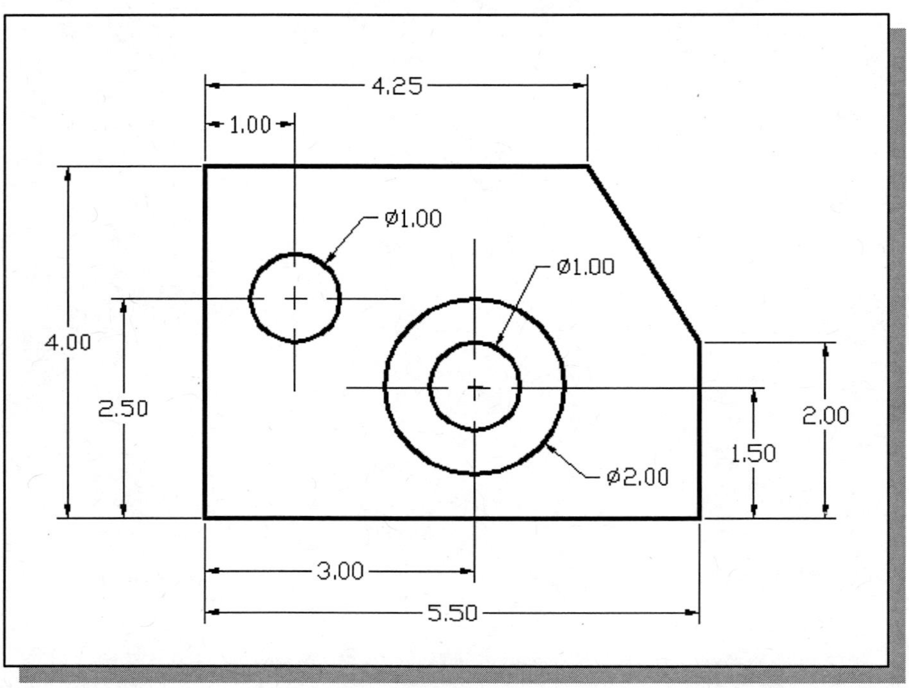

3.

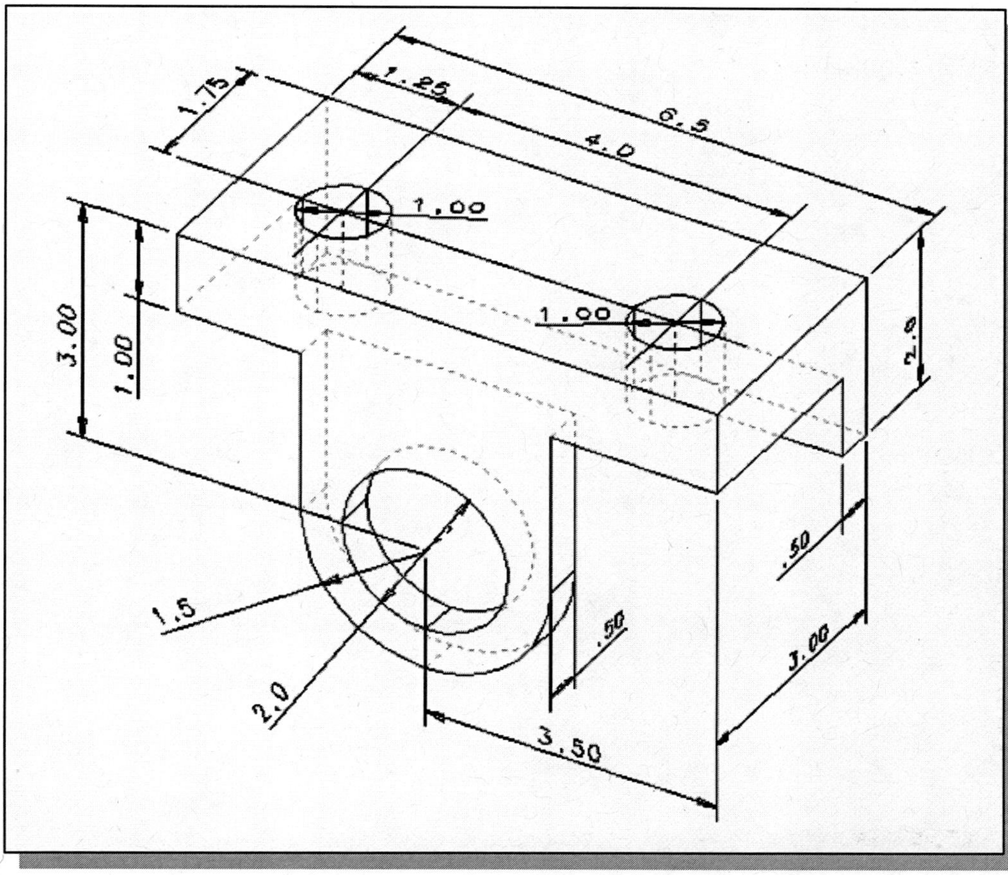

Notes:

Chapter 5

Parametric Constraints Fundamentals

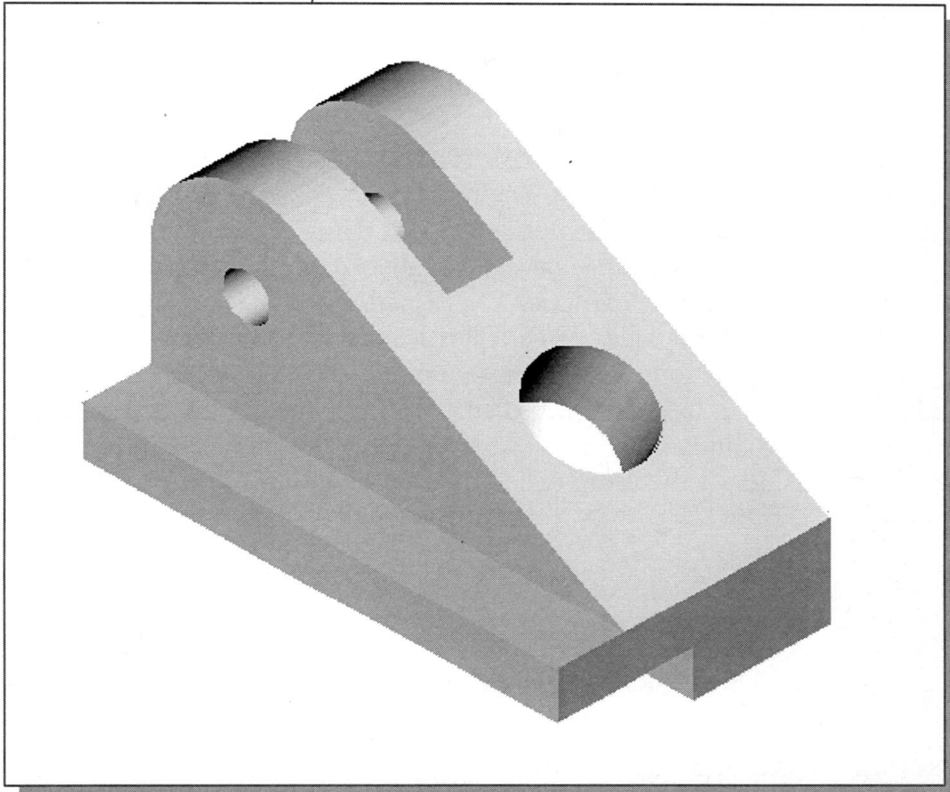

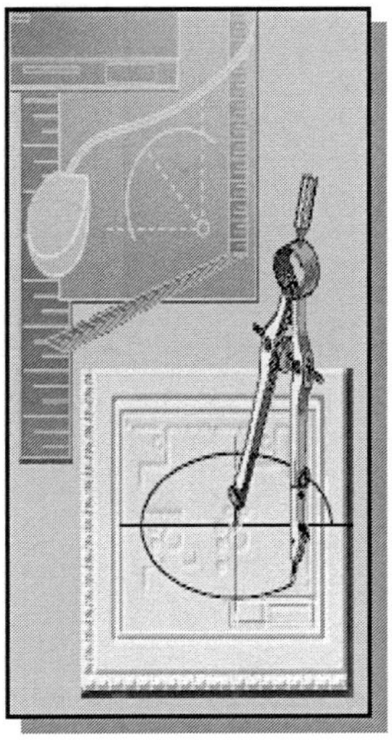

Learning Objectives

- Using the BORN technique
- Create Parametric Relations
- Use Dimensional Variables
- Display, Add, and Delete Geometric Constraints
- Understand and Apply Different Geometric Constraints
- Display and Modify Parametric Relations
- Create Fully Constrained Sketches

The BORN Technique

In the previous chapters, we have concentrated on creating solid models relative to the *first feature* of the solid object. The first solid feature, the *base feature,* is the center of all features and is considered as the key feature of the design. This is a common approach to creating solid models, but this approach places much emphasis on the selection of the *base feature.* All subsequent features, therefore, are built by referencing the first feature, or ***base feature***. In most cases, this approach is quite adequate and proper in creating solid models.

A more advanced technique of creating solid models is what is known as the "**Base Orphan Reference Node**" (**BORN**) technique. The basic concept of the BORN technique is to use a *Cartesian coordinate system* as the first feature prior to creating any solid features. With the *Cartesian coordinate system* established, we then have three mutually perpendicular datum planes (namely the *XY*, *YZ*, and *ZX* planes) available to use as sketching planes. The three datum planes can also be used as references for dimensions and geometric constructions. Using this technique, the first feature in the model isn't a solid feature and it is therefore called an "**orphan**," meaning that it has no history to be replayed. The technique of using a reference geometry, the *Cartesian coordinate system,* in this fashion is therefore called the "Base Orphan Reference Node" (BORN) technique.

UGS NX automatically establishes a set of reference geometry when we start a new part, namely the default WCS, which is a *Cartesian coordinate system* with three reference planes, and three reference axes. All subsequent solid features can then use the coordinate system's reference geometry as sketching planes. The *base feature* is still important, but the *base feature* is no longer the ONLY choice for setting the orientation or selecting the sketching plane for subsequent solid features. In effect, the BORN technique is built-in when creating solid models in *UGS NX.* Note that in *UGS NX*, the default WCS is used to control the location of the solid features in the 3D Global space. This approach provides us with more options while we are creating parametric solid models. More importantly, this approach provides greater flexibility for part modifications and design changes.

CONSTRAINTS and RELATIONS

A primary and essential difference between parametric modeling and previous generation computer modeling is that parametric modeling captures the *design intent.* In the previous lessons, we have seen that the design philosophy of "*shape before size*" is implemented through the use of *UGS NX's Sketcher* and dimensioning commands. In performing geometric constructions, dimensional values are necessary to describe the **SIZE** and **LOCATION** of constructed geometric entities. Besides using dimensions to define the geometry, we can also apply geometric rules to control geometric entities. More importantly, *UGS NX* can capture design intent through the use of **geometric constraints, dimensional constraints**, and **parametric relations.** In *UGS NX*, there are two types of constraints: **geometric constraints** and **dimensional constraints**. For part modeling in *UGS NX*, constraints are applied to *2D sketches*. **Geometric constraints** are **geometric restrictions** that can be applied to geometric entities; for example,

Horizontal, Parallel, Perpendicular, and Tangent are commonly used *geometric constraints* in parametric modeling. **Dimensional constraints** are used to describe the SIZE and LOCATION of individual geometric shapes. One should also realize that, depending upon the way the constraints are applied, the same results can be accomplished by applying different constraints to the geometric entities. In *UGS NX*, **parametric relations** are user-defined mathematical equations composed of dimensional variables and/or *design variables*. In parametric modeling, features are made of geometric entities with both relations and constraints describing individual design intent. In this lesson, we will discuss the fundamentals of parametric relations and geometric constraints.

Fully Constrained Geometry

In *UGS NX*, as we create 2D sketches, geometric constraints such as Horizontal and Parallel are automatically added to the sketched geometry. In most cases, additional constraints and dimensions are needed to fully describe the sketched geometry beyond the geometric constraints added by the system. Although we can use *UGS NX* to build partially constrained or totally unconstrained solid models, the models may behave unpredictably as changes are made. In most cases, it is important to consider the design intent and to add proper constraints to geometric entities. In the following sections, a simple triangular model is used to illustrate the different tools that are available in *UGS NX* to create/modify geometric and dimensional constraints.

Create a *Simple Triangular Plate* Design

➢ In parametric modeling, **geometric properties** such as *horizontal*, *parallel*, *perpendicular*, and *tangent* can be applied to geometric entities automatically or manually. By carefully applying proper **geometric constraints**, very intelligent models can be created. This concept is illustrated by the following example.

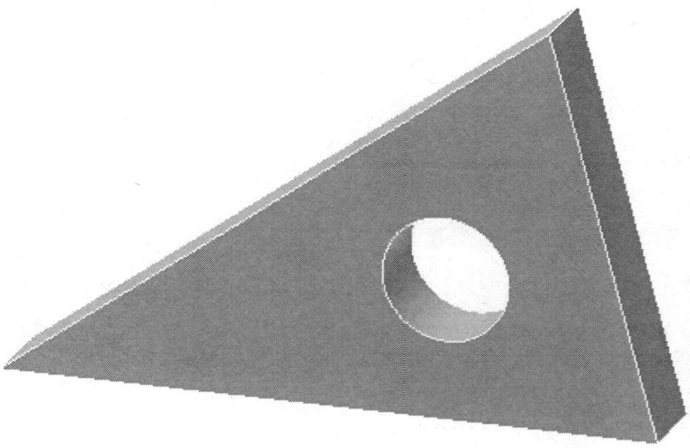

Starting *UGS NX*

1. Select the **UGS NX** option on the *Start* menu or select the **UGS NX** icon on the desktop to start *UGS NX*. The *UGS NX* main window will appear on the screen.

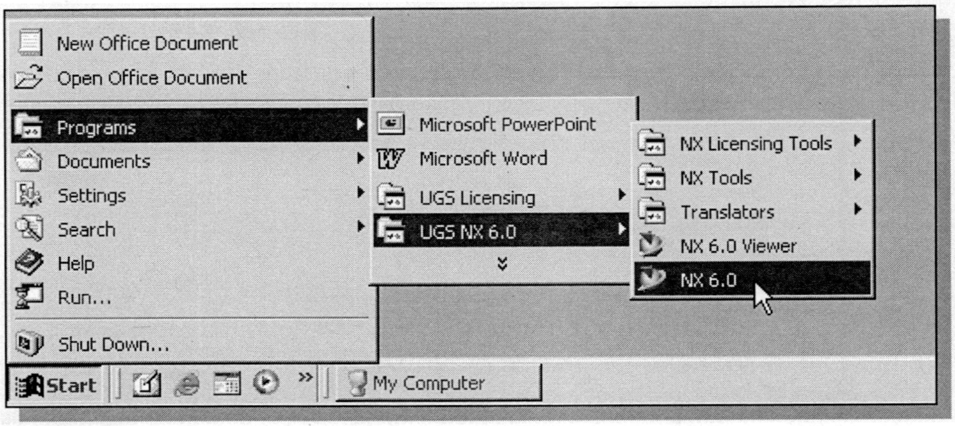

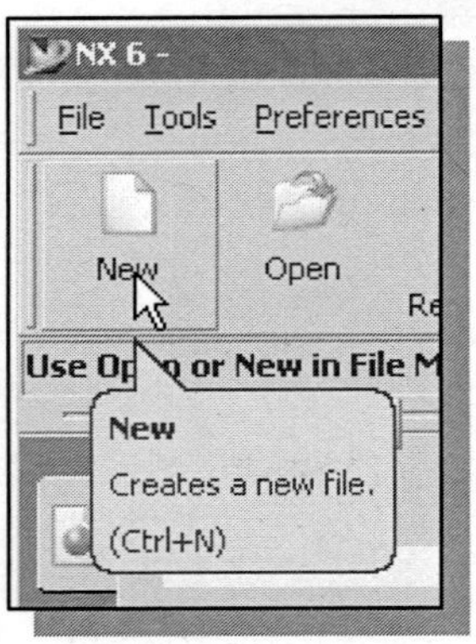

2. Select the **New** icon with a single click of the left-mouse-button (MB1) in the *Standard* toolbar area.

3. Confirm the **Millimeters** units are set as shown in the figure below.

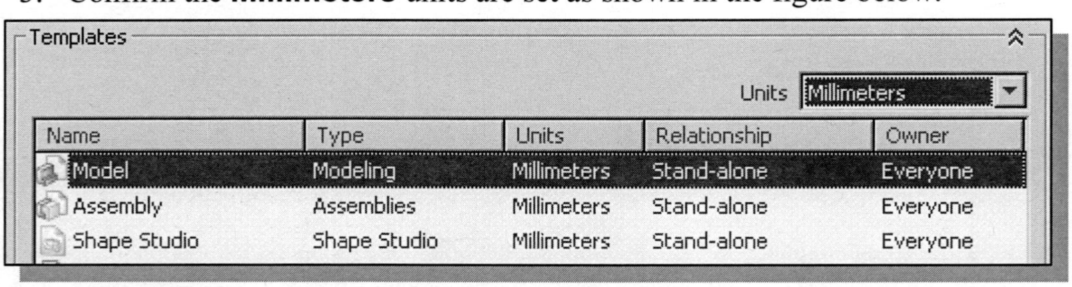

4. Select **Model** in the *Templates* list. Note that the *Model* template will allow us to switch directly into the ***Modeling*** task as indicated in the *Templates* list.

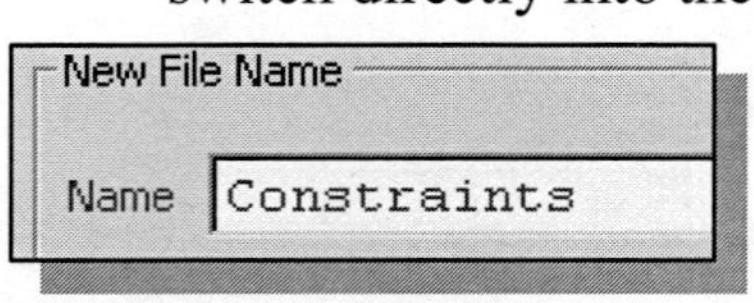

5. In the *New File Name* section, enter **Constraints** as the file *Name*.

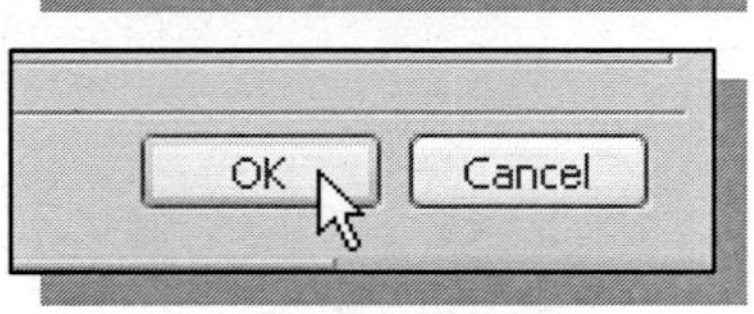

6. Click **OK** to proceed with the New Part File command.

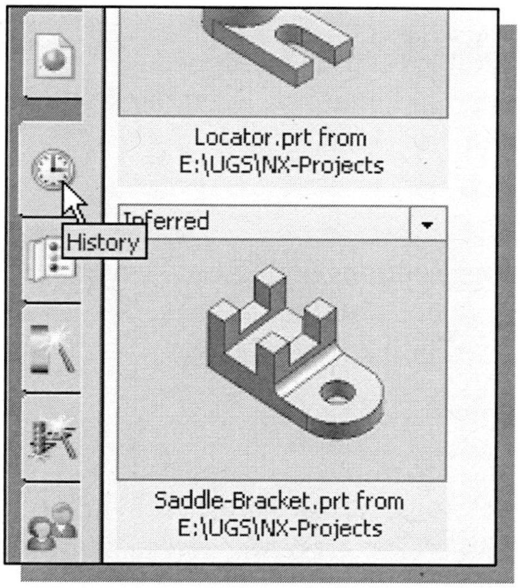

7. In the *Resource Bars* area, click on the **History** option to view the parts that were created recently.

8. Click on the **Part Navigator** tab to switch to the Part Navigator option.

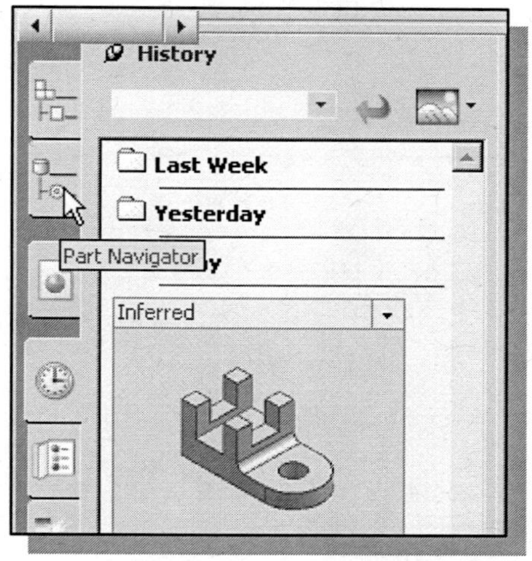

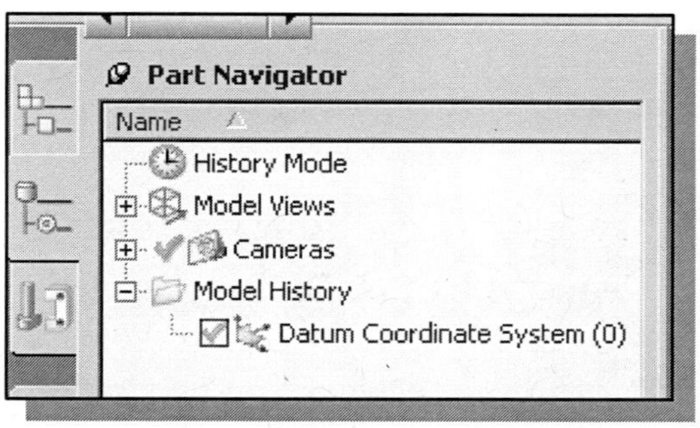

- In the *Part Navigator*, a *Datum Coordinate System* is listed under the *Model History* item. One of the pre-defined settings in the *Model* template is a Cartesian coordinate system, which enables the users to use the BORN technique in creating solid models.

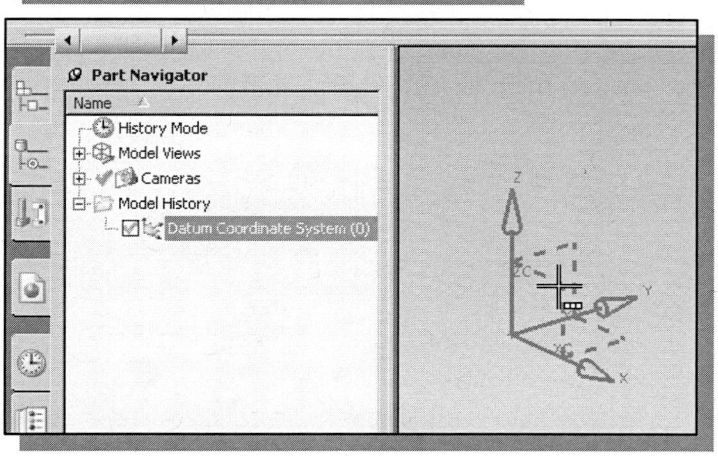

9. Move the cursor on top of the coordinate system in the graphics area and notice the corresponding item is also highlighted in the *Model History* tree as shown in the figure.

- Notice that with the *Model* template file, we have entered the *Modeling* mode with a pre-defined coordinate system. Using a template file also helps to eliminate repetitive steps and make our work much more efficient. Using template files also helps us maintain consistent design and drafting standards. Note that *UGS NX* comes with several templates for both *English* and *Metric* units.

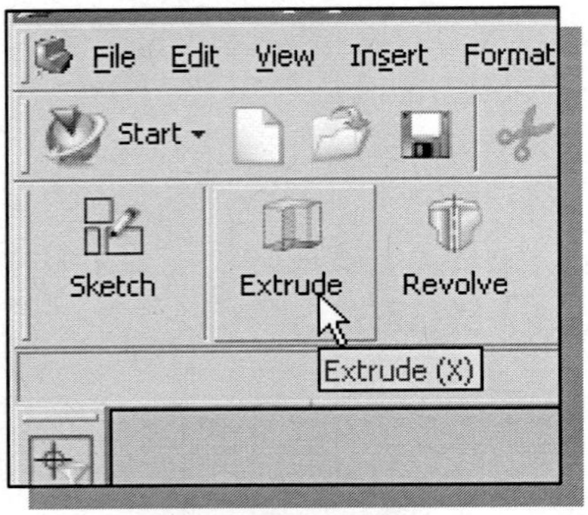

10. In the *Feature* toolbars (toolbars aligned to the right edge of the main window), select the **Extrude** icon as shown.

- The *Extrude* feature options dialog box, which contains applicable construction options, is displayed as shown in the figure below.

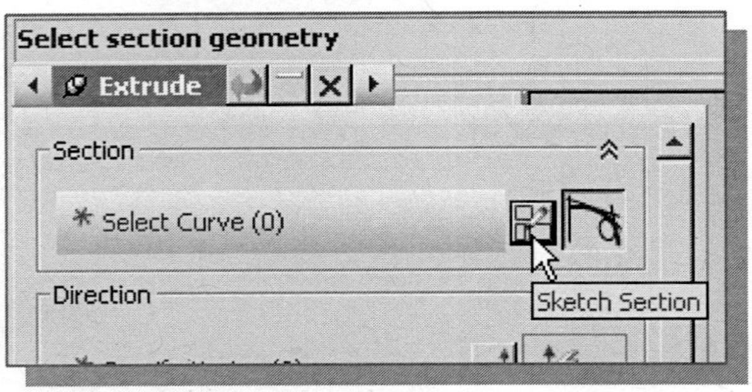

11. Click the **Sketch Section** button to begin creating a new *2D sketch.*

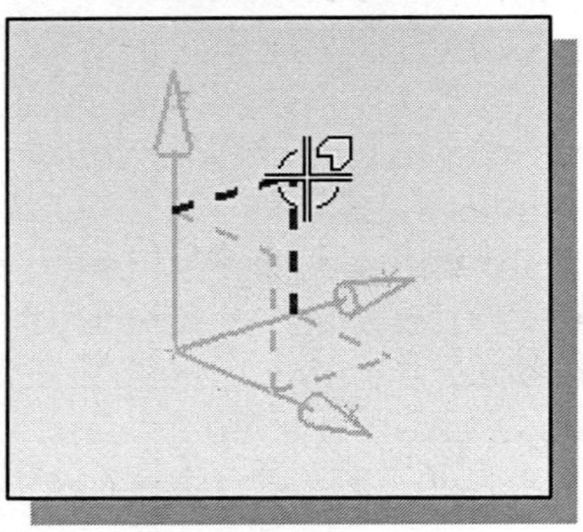

12. Select the ***XC-YC*** plane of the established *Datum Coordinate System* as the sketch plane of the *Base* feature.

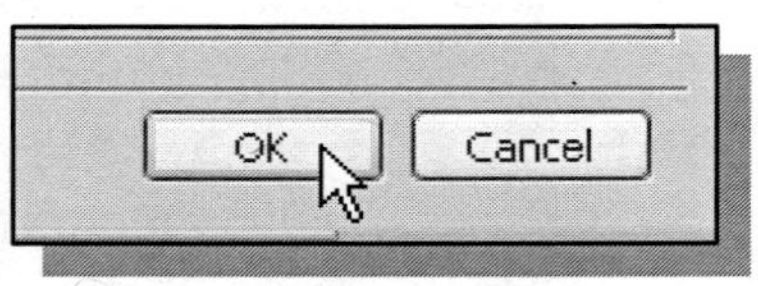

13. Click **OK** to accept the selection of the sketch plane.

14. Create a triangle of arbitrary size positioned near the upper right side of the screen as shown below. (Note that the base of the triangle is horizontal.)

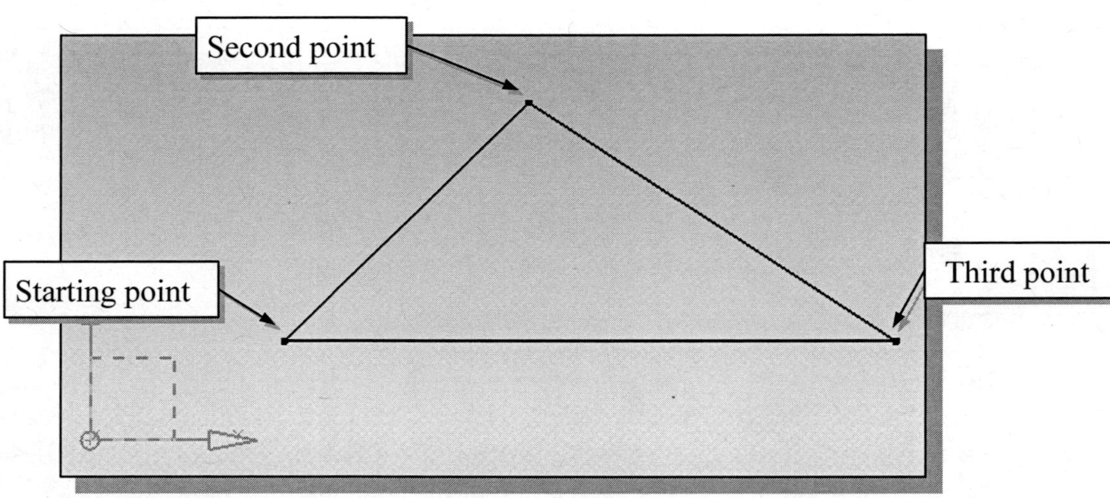

Displaying Existing Constraints

- Two options are available to display the existing constraints that are applied to the 2D sketches.

➢ **Option One:**

1. Select the **Show All Constraints** command in the *Sketch Constraints* toolbar. This icon allows us to display constraints that are already applied to the 2D sketches.

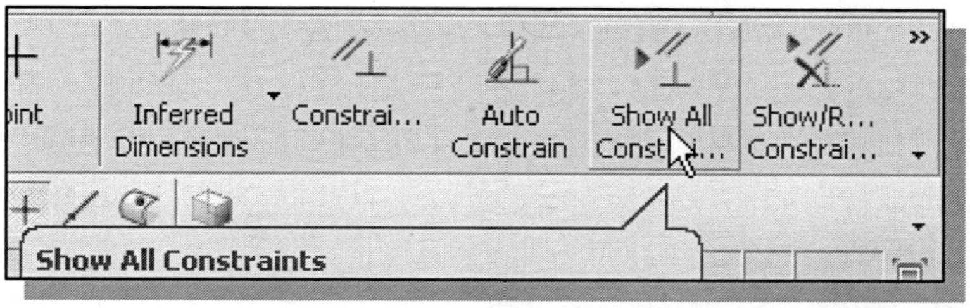

➢ In *UGS NX*, constraints are applied as geometric entities are created. *UGS NX* will attempt to add proper constraints to the geometric entities based on the way the entities were created. Constraints are displayed as symbols next to the entities as they are created. The current sketch consists of three line entities, three straight lines. The horizontal line has one constraint applied to it, a **Horizontal** constraint.

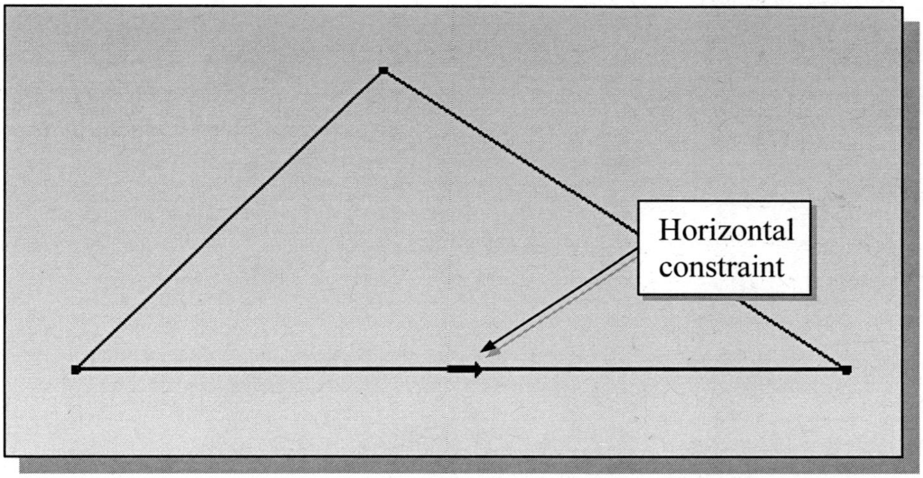

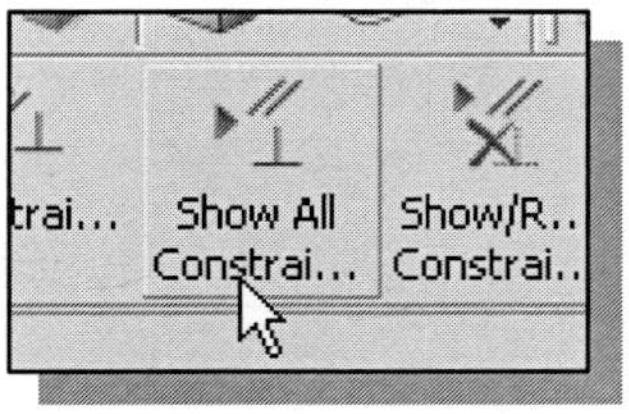

2. Click on the **Show All Constraints** icon again to toggle *OFF* the command.

➢ The **Show All Constraints** command can be used to quickly display the existing constraints. The constraints are displayed as symbols next to the entities. Note that this command can be made active to display constraints at all time.

➤ **Option Two:**

1. Select the **Show/Remove Constraints** command in the *Sketch Constraints* toolbar. This icon allows us to **identify**, and/or **remove**, constraints that are already applied to the 2D sketches.

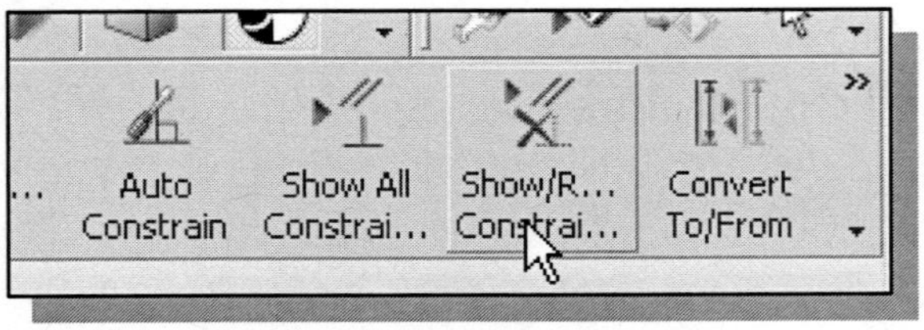

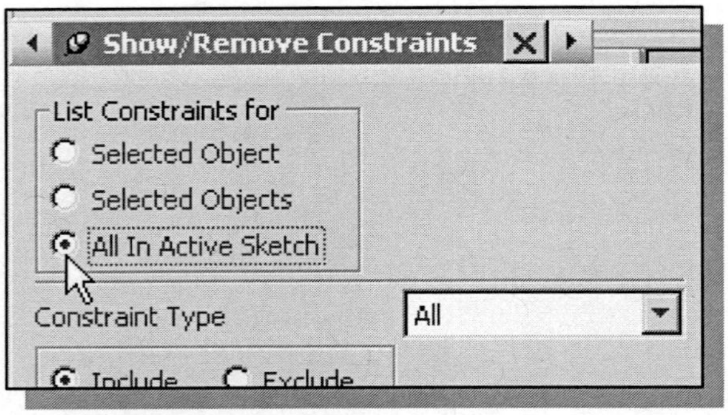

2. Select the **All in active sketch** option, the last option in the *List constraints for* group.

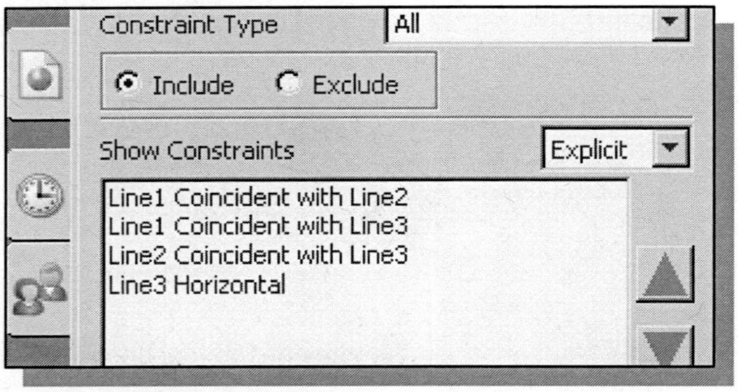

3. *UGS NX* displays the existing constraints in the *Show Constraints* box. Currently several constraints are applied to the active sketch: *Line3* has a **Horizontal** constraint, and three **Coincident** constraints are applied at the three corners.

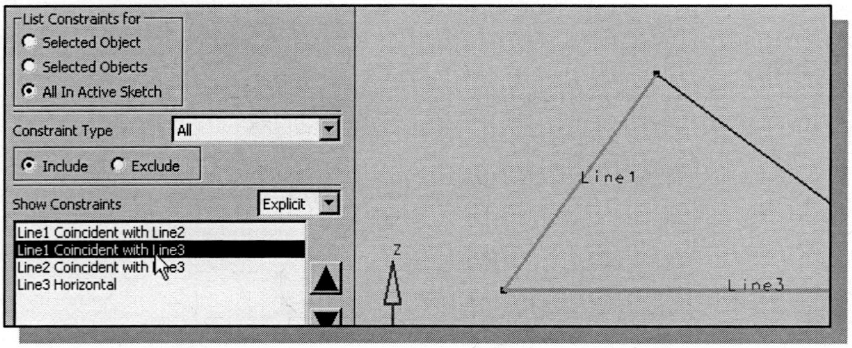

4. Click on one of the displayed constraints and notice the corresponding geometry is highlighted in the graphics window.

5. Click **OK** or **Cancel** to exit the command.

➤ The **Show/Remove Constraints** command can be used to display more detailed information on the existing constraints. The constraints can also be removed with the remove option under this command.

Applying Geometric Constraints Implicitly

- In *UGS NX*, geometric constraints can be applied implicitly (as we create the geometry) or explicitly (apply the constraint individually.)

  UGS NX displays the governing geometric rules as sketches are built. *UGS NX* displays different visual clues, or symbols, to show alignments, perpendicularities, tangencies, etc. These constraints are used to capture the *design intent* by creating constraints where they are recognized. To prevent constraints from forming, hold down the [**Alt**] key while creating an individual sketch curve.

	**Vertical**	indicates a line is vertical
	Horizontal	indicates a line is horizontal
	Dashed line	indicates the alignment is to the center point or endpoint of an entity
	**Parallel**	indicates a line is parallel to other entities
	**Perpendicular**	indicates a line is perpendicular to other entities
	**Coincident**	indicates the cursor is at the endpoint of an entity
	**Concentric**	indicates the cursor is at the center of an entity
	**Tangent**	indicates the cursor is at tangency points to curves
	**Midpoint**	indicates the cursor is at the midpoint of an entity
	**Point on Curve**	indicates the cursor is on curves
	**Equal Length**	indicates the length of a line is equal to another line
	**Equal Radius**	indicates the radius of an arc is equal to another arc

Applying Geometric Constraints Explicitly

- In *UGS NX*, geometric constraints can be applied explicitly, by first selecting the geometry and then the type of constraint desired.

1. Select the **Constraints** command in the *Sketch Constraint* toolbar. This command allows us to apply the desired constraints individually.

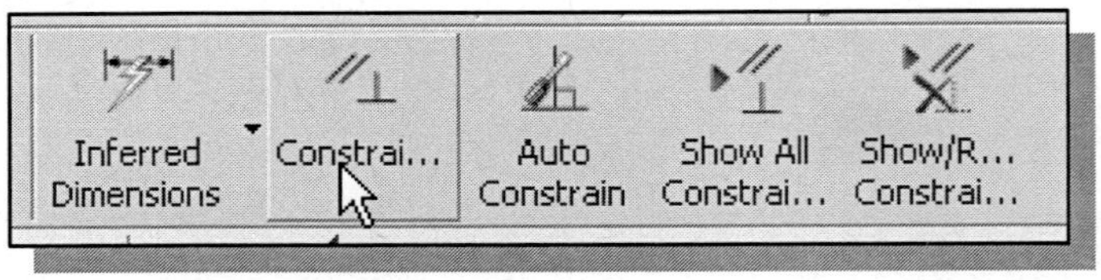

2. Select the two inclined lines and notice the display of applicable constraints near the upper left corner of the graphics window.

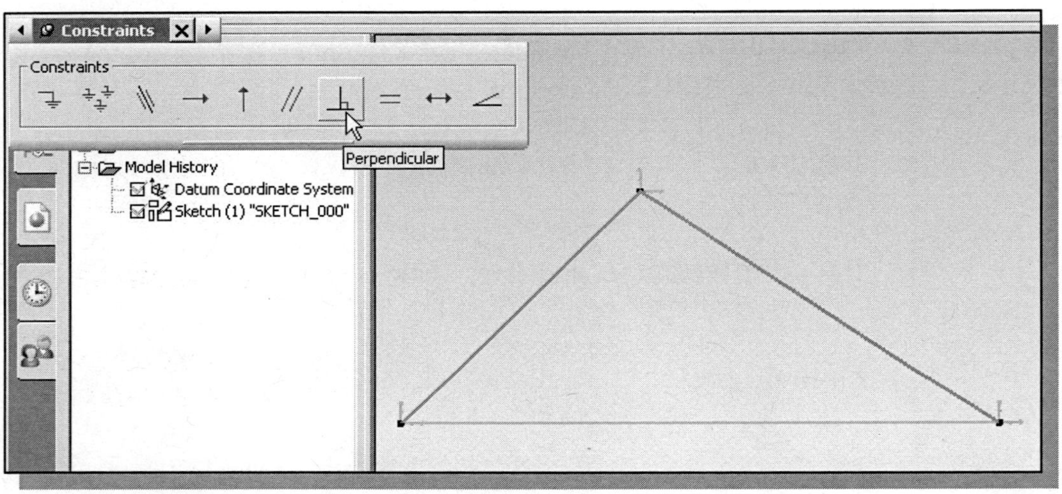

3. Select the **Perpendicular constraint** as shown in the above figure.

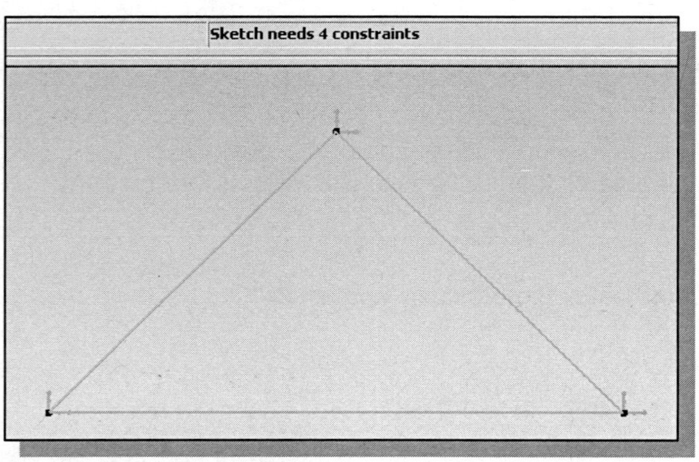

4. The geometry is quickly adjusted so that the two selected lines are now perpendicular to each other. Also, notice *UGS NX* indicates that **four** more constraints are needed to *fully constrain* the current sketch.

5. Inside the graphics window, click twice with the middle-mouse-button (MB2), or press the [**Esc**] key once, to end the **Constraint** command.

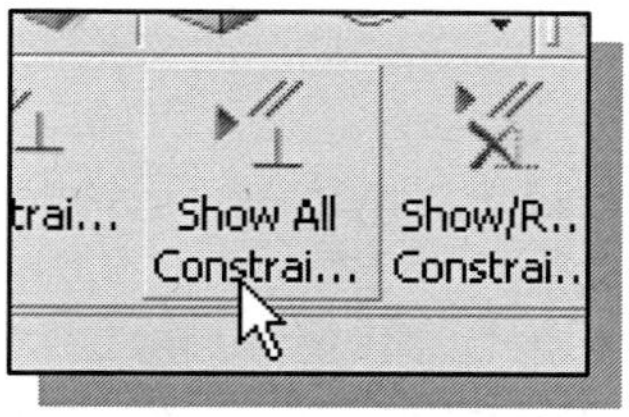

6. Select the **Show All Constraints** command in the *Sketch Constraints* toolbar. This icon allows us to display constraints that are already applied to the 2D sketches.

- Five constraints were applied to the 2D sketch, four were done implicitly and the other explicitly.

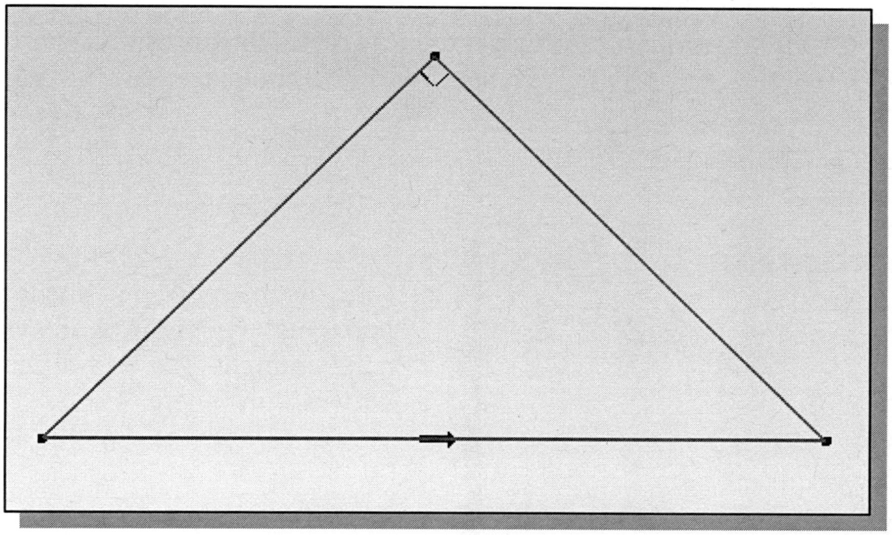

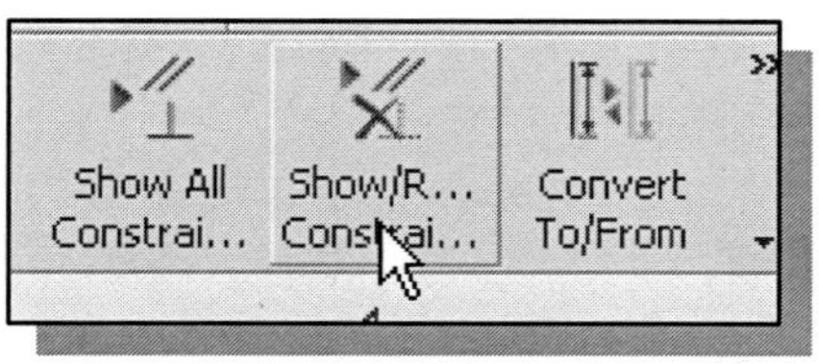

7. Select the **Show/Remove Constraints** command in the *Sketch Constraints* toolbar.

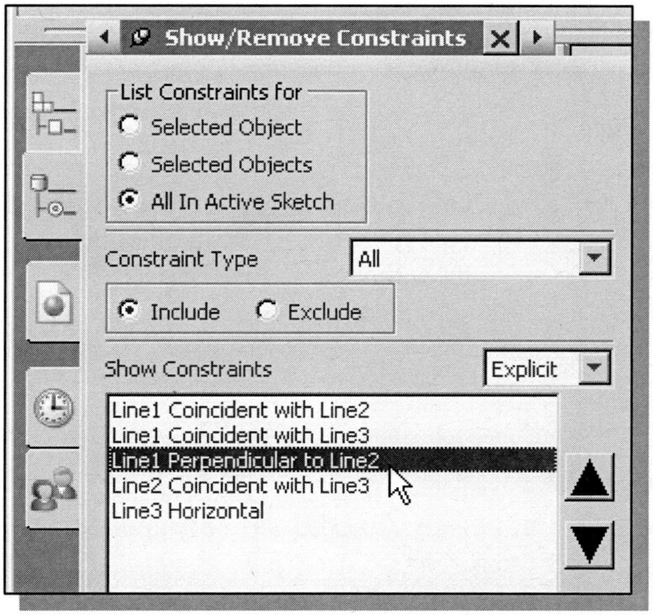

8. Select the **All in active sketch** option, the last option in the *List constraints for* group.

- The five constraints are listed in the *Show Constraints* box as shown.

9. Click **OK** or **Cancel** to exit the command..

Adding Dimensional Constraints

- In *parametric modeling*, **geometric constraints** and **dimensional constraints** are interchangeable. For example, the Perpendicular constraint we applied in the previous section can also be achieved by applying an angular dimension set to 90°. It is more important to consider the functionality of the design and embed the *design intent* through the use of proper geometric constraints and dimensional constraints.

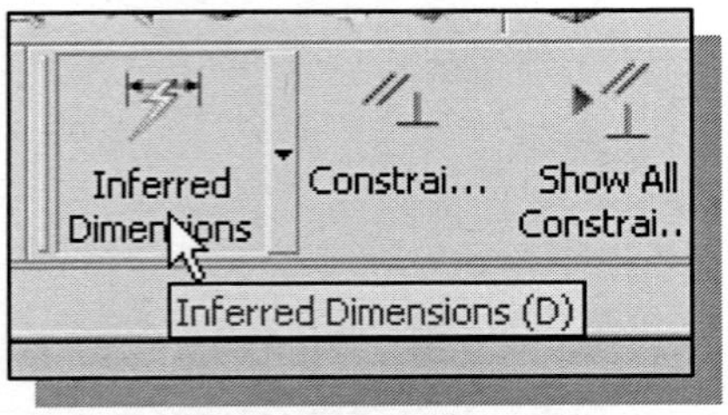

1. Select the **Inferred Dimensions** command in the *Sketch Constraints* toolbar as shown.

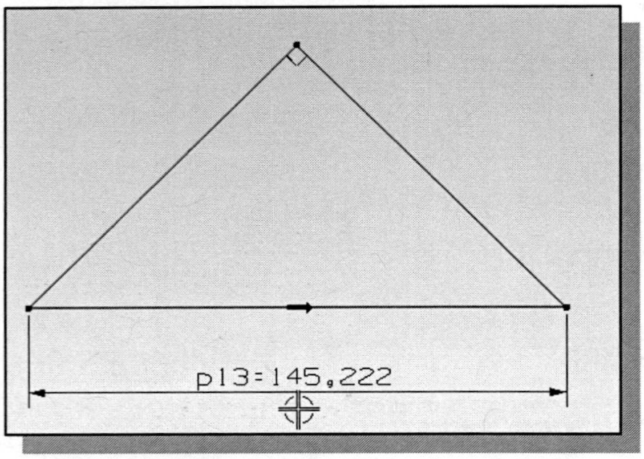

2. Click on the horizontal line to create a horizontal dimension as shown. Your number might look very different than what is shown here.

❖ Before continuing to the next step, consider this: What if we want to adjust the length of the line so that it is roughly 5 mm longer? Yes, we can simply change the dimension by adding 5 mm to the current displayed number. Now comes the more difficult question: In which direction will the line be lengthened? To the left? To the right? Or maybe in both directions?

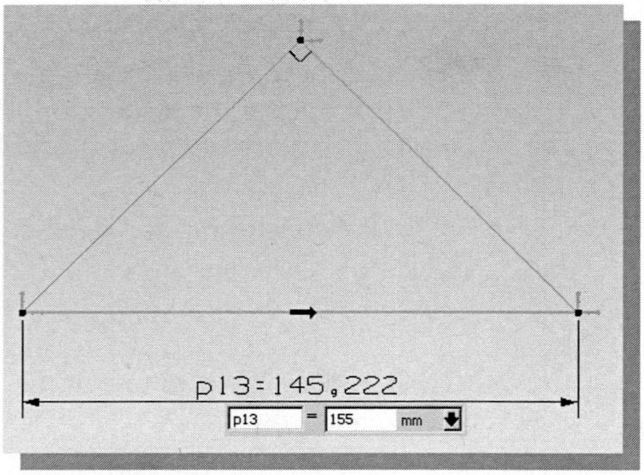

3. On your own, increase the displayed value by about 10 mm and observe the adjustment done by *UGS NX.*

❖ The adjustment will be made based on several factors, but the currently applied geometric constraints will definitely affect the results.

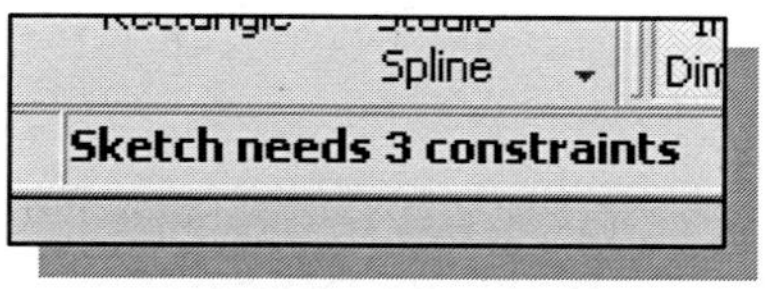

❖ Also notice the message "*Sketch needs 3 constraints*" is displayed in the message area. Can you identify the three constraints needed to fully constrain the sketch?

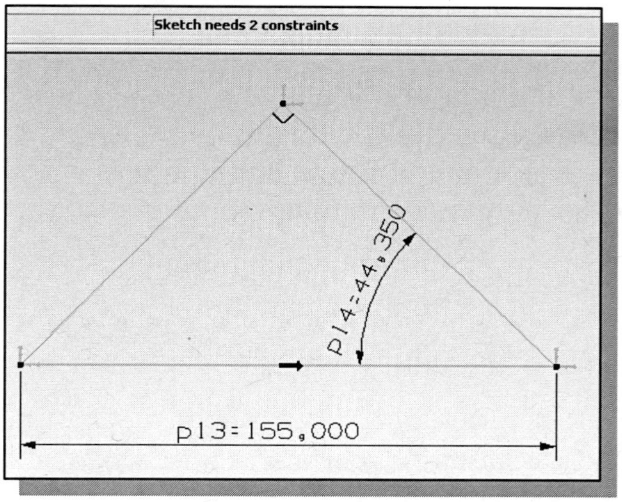

4. On your own, create the angular dimension between the inclined line on the right and the horizontal line as shown. Again, the actual value displayed on your screen may look very different.

❖ Also notice the message "*Sketch needs 2 constraints*" is displayed in the message area. The triangle seems to be fully defined, what are missing here?

➢ Notice, in the above drawing, the three corners have little arrows showing; this indicates the triangle can still be repositioned. One option for identifying the missing constraints is to perform a **drag and drop** with the left-mouse-button on the constructed geometry.

5. Use the middle-mouse-button (MB2), or click **OK** to exit the Inferred Dimensions command.

6. Click and drag with the left-mouse-button (MB1) on one of the inclined lines and noticed that the triangle can be moved to a new location. This is an indication that the triangle is probably fully defined, but its **LOCATION** relative to the 3D environment is not fully defined.

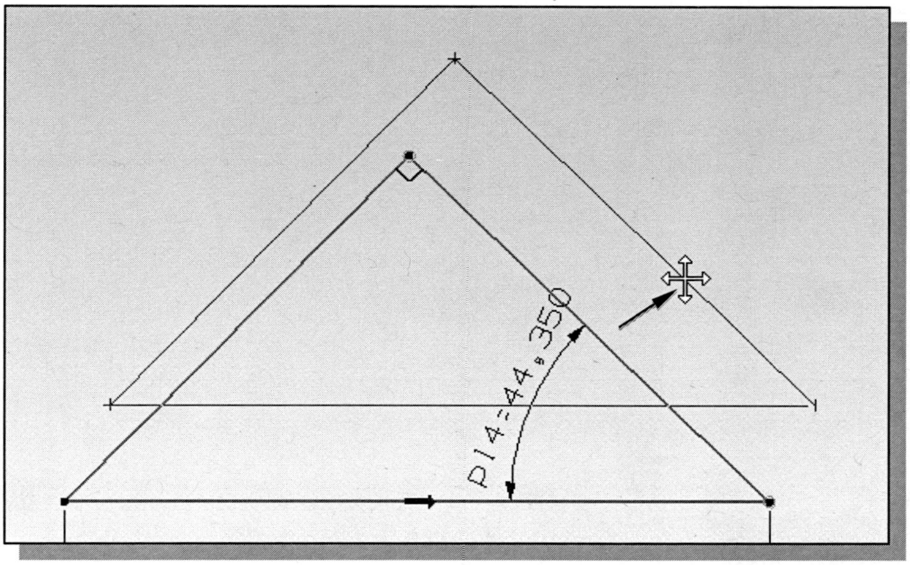

A Fully Constrained Sketch

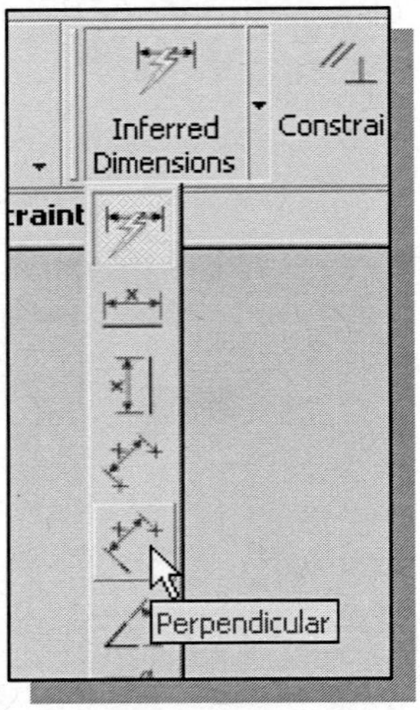

1. Click on the little triangle next to the **Inferred Dimensions** command, in the *Sketch Constraints* toolbar, to expand the icon list and select **Perpendicular** as shown.

➢ Note the different dimensioning options available in the list. The Inferred Dimensions command is the most flexible command, but we can choose a specific dimensioning command to assure the proper dimensions are created.

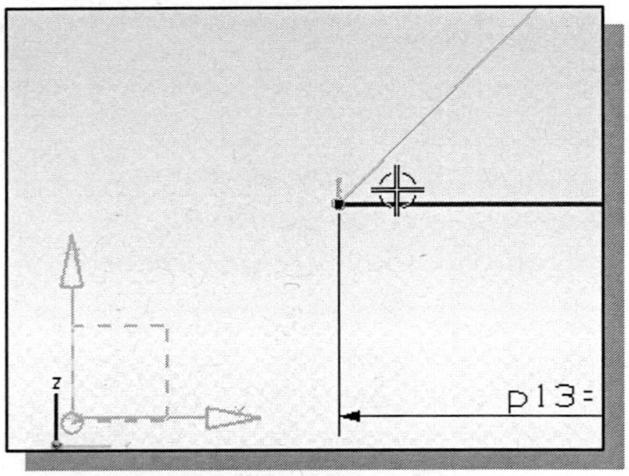

2. Select **Line3** by clicking near the left endpoint of the line as shown.

   (If the *QuickPick* window appears on the screen, choose **Line3** in the displayed list.)

3. Select the ***YC* axis** and place the perpendicular dimension to the left of the triangle between the endpoint and the *YC* axis as shown in the figure.

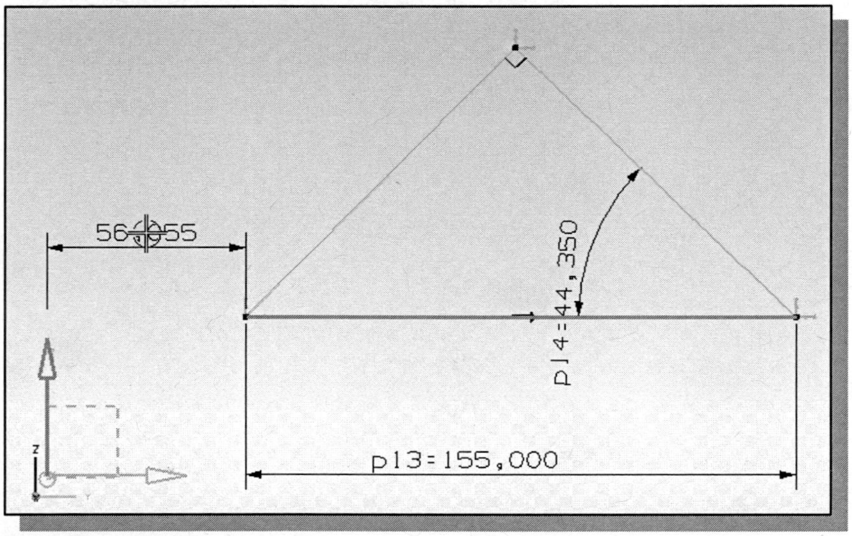

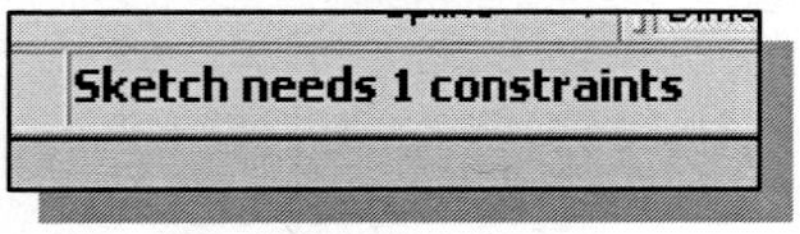

➢ Only one more constraint is needed to fully constrain the 2D sketch.

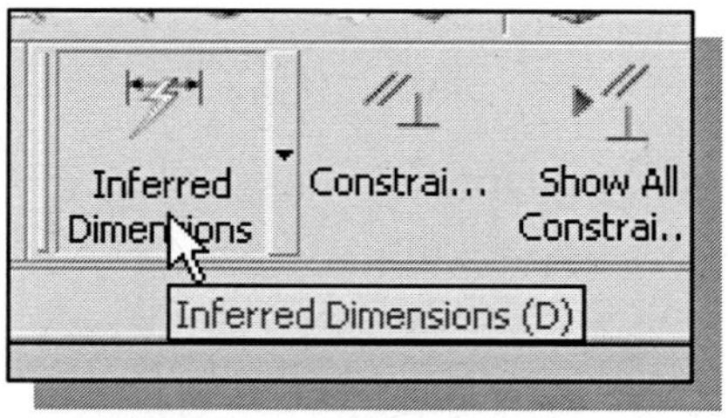

4. Select the **Inferred Dimensions** command in the *Sketch Constraints* toolbar as shown.

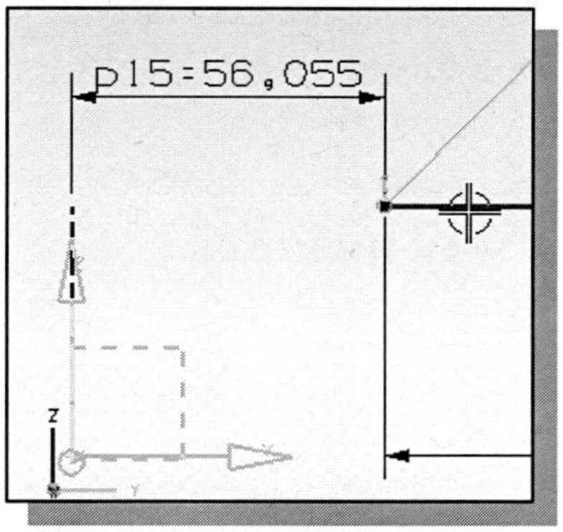

5. Select the horizontal line, **Line3**, as shown in the figure.

6. Select the ***XC* axis** as the second entity to create a parallel dimension as shown in the figure.

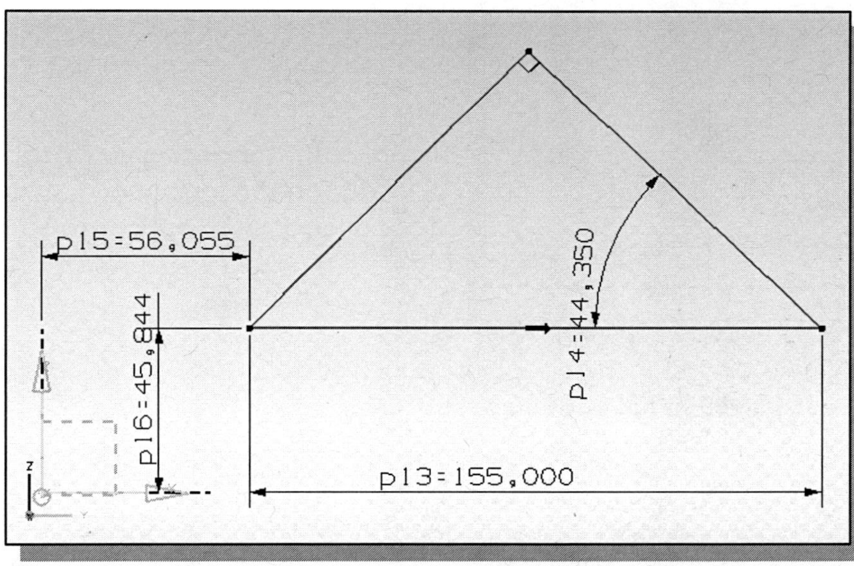

➢ Notice the color of the sketch turned **black**; we now have a fully constrained 2D sketch.

❖ A fully constrained 2D sketch is desirable as it means that we have full control of the 2D sketch and we know exactly what will happen as changes are made. For example, in the current design we have a horizontal dimension to control the length of the horizontal line. If the length of this line is modified to a greater value, *UGS NX* can only lengthen the line toward the right side. This is due to the fact that the location of the left endpoint is governed by the two location dimensions we just added. On your own, lengthen the horizontal line by another 10 mm and confirm the adjustment is done exactly as expected.

Over Constraining 2D Sketches

- We can use *UGS NX* to build partially constrained or totally unconstrained solid models. In most cases, these types of models may behave unpredictably as changes are made. On the other hand, *UGS NX* will also let us over constrain a sketch, but with warnings. It is best not to create over constrained sketches; only create extra dimensions as references, if necessary. These additional dimensions are generally called ***reference dimensions***. *Reference dimensions* do not constrain the sketch; they only reflect the values of the dimensioned geometry.

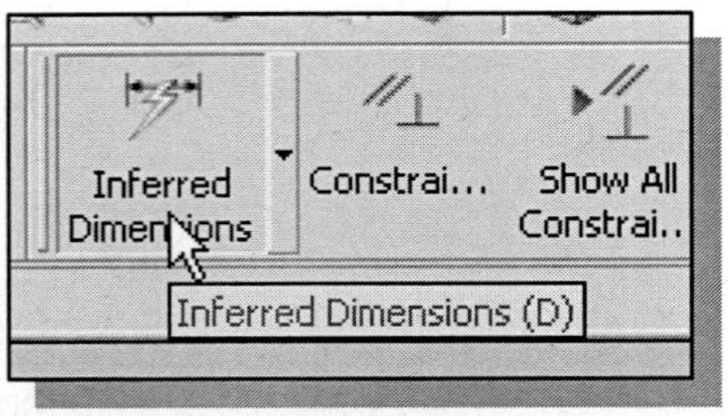

1. Select the **Inferred Dimensions** command in the *Sketch Constraints* toolbar as shown.

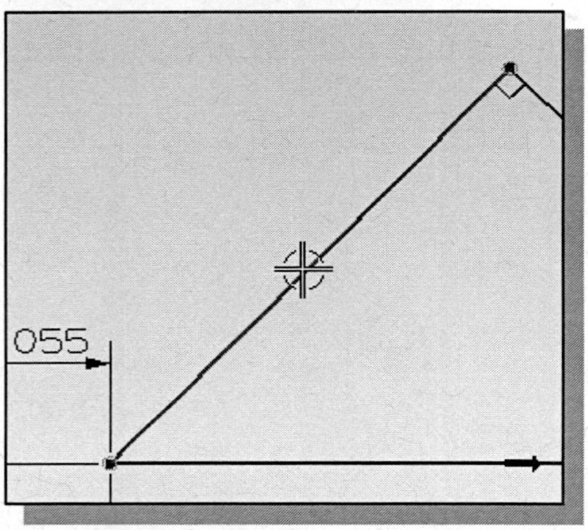

2. Select the **left inclined line** of the triangle as shown.

3. Place the dimension above the line; note the **Edit Dimension** option is automatically activated.

4. Notice a warning message indicating that we have over constrained the 2D sketch is displayed in the message area.

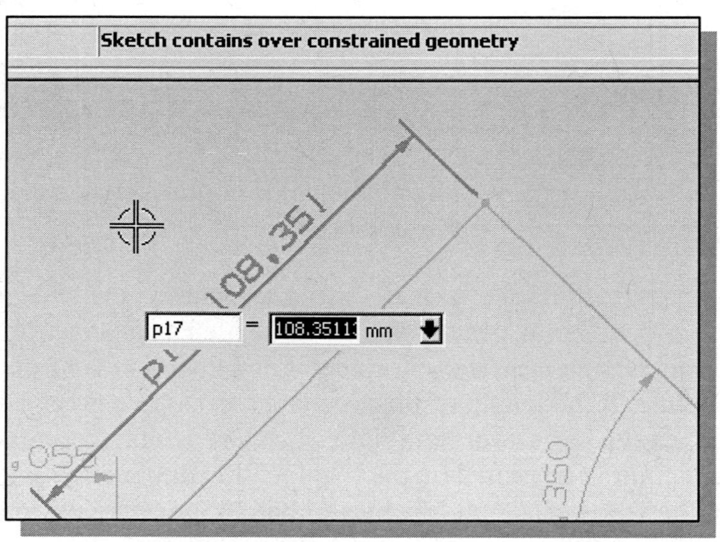

5. Click **Undo**, or use **[Ctrl+Z]**, to remove the dimension we just added.

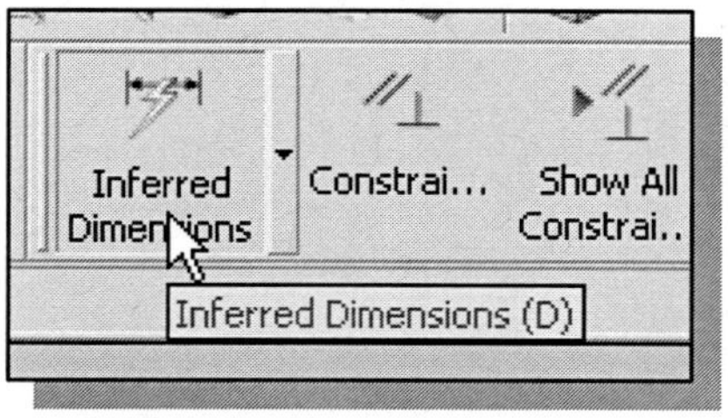

6. Select the **Inferred Dimensions** command in the *Sketch Constraints* toolbar as shown.

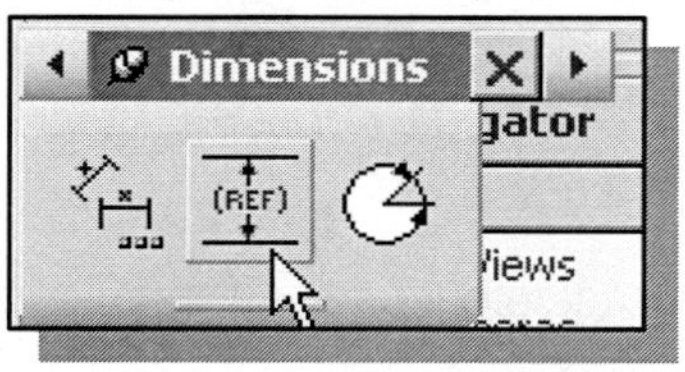

7. Choose the **Create Reference Dimension** option in the *Dimensions* option box near the left hand corner of the graphics window as shown.

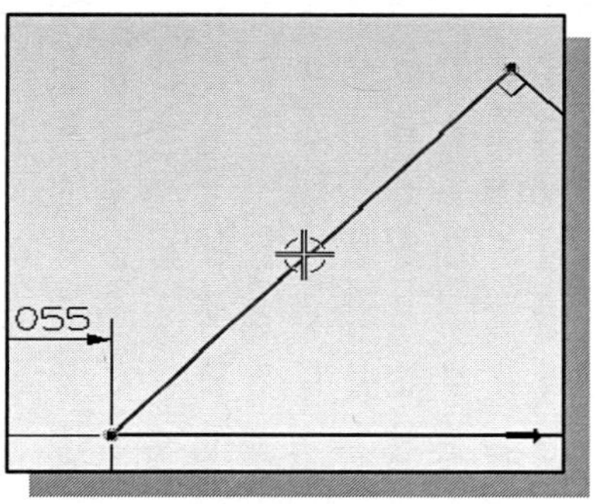

8. Select the **left inclined line** of the triangle as shown.

9. Place the dimension above the line; note the reference dimension is displayed as a single numerical value. Note that a reference dimension cannot be edited.

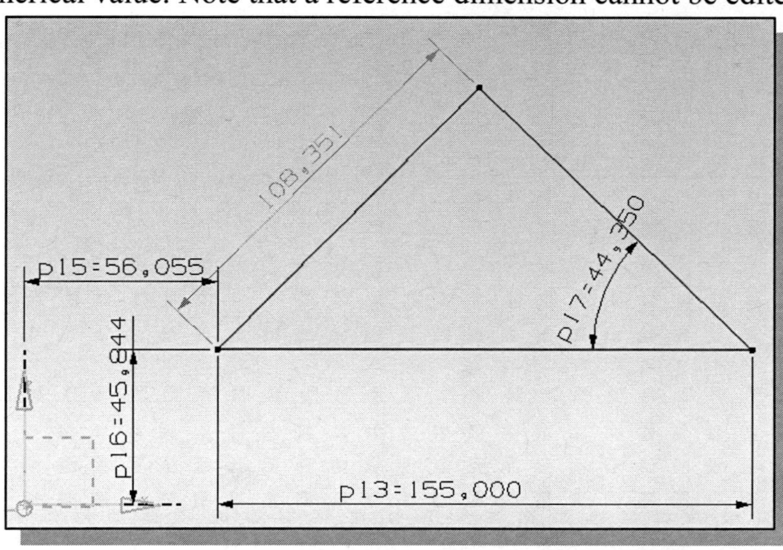

❖ Again, it is best not to create over constrained 2D sketches, only create extra dimensions as reference dimensions.

Deleting Existing Dimensions and Constraints

1. On your own, pre-select the **reference dimension** and the **angle dimension** by clicking on the entities with the left-mouse-button (MB1).

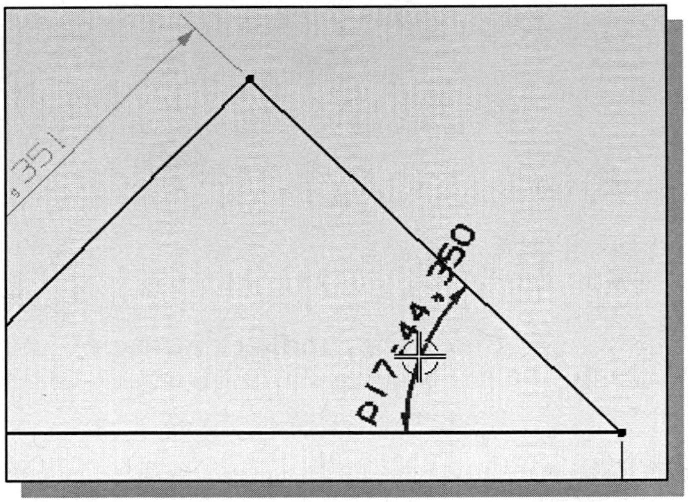

2. Hit the **Delete** key once to remove the pre-selected dimensions.

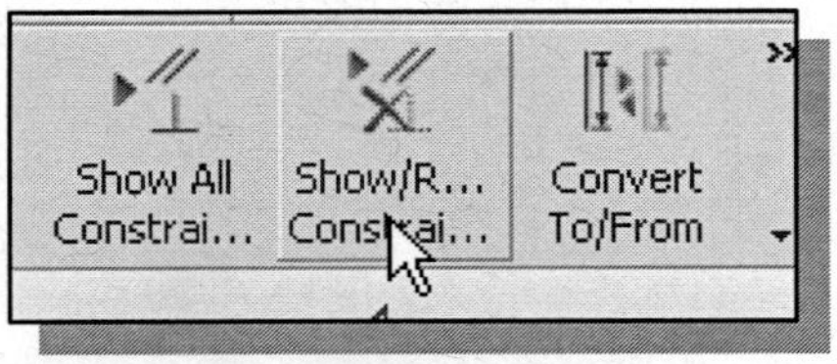

3. Select the **Show/Remove Constraints** command in the *Sketch Constraints* toolbar.

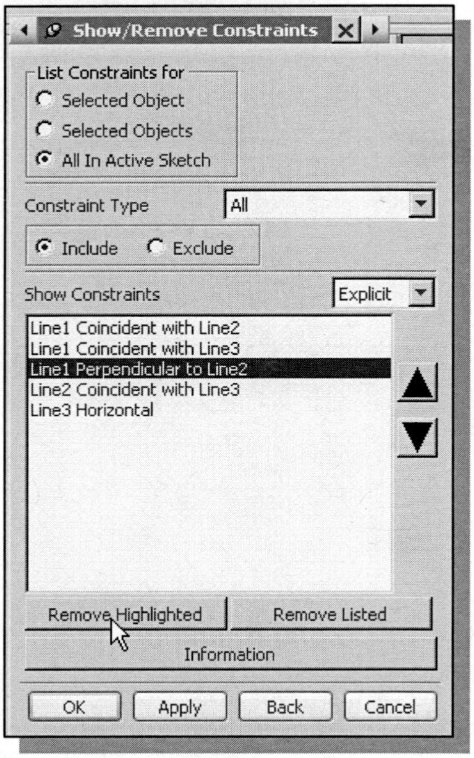

4. Select the **All in active sketch** option, the last option in the *List constraints for* group.

5. Select the **Line1 Perpendicular to Line2** constraint in the *Show Constraints* list as shown..

6. Click **Remove Highlighted** to remove the selected constraint.

7. Click **OK** to exit the **Show/Remove Constraints** command.

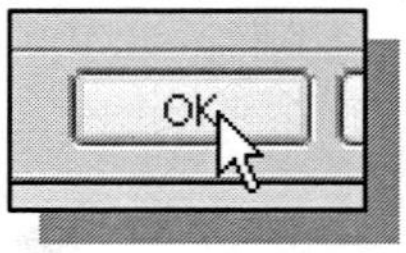

8. Click and drag with the left-mouse-button (MB1) on one of the inclined lines and noticed that we can adjust the upper portion of the triangle but the horizontal line of the triangle remains fixed.

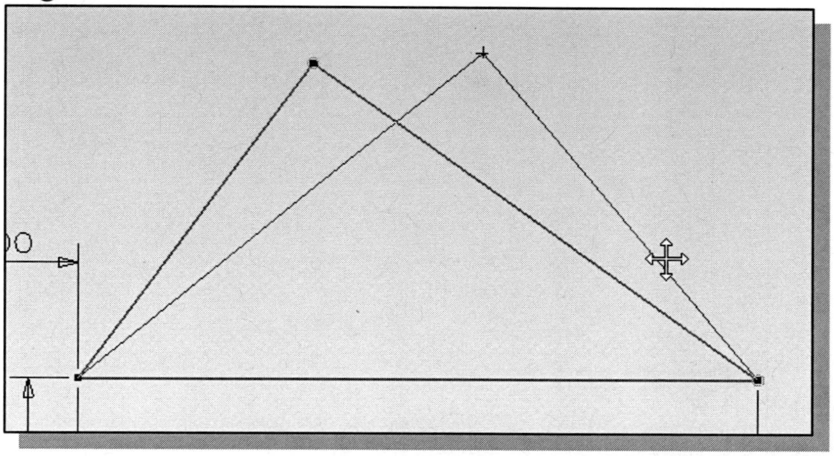

9. Pre-select the **right inclined line** by clicking once with the left-mouse-button (MB1).

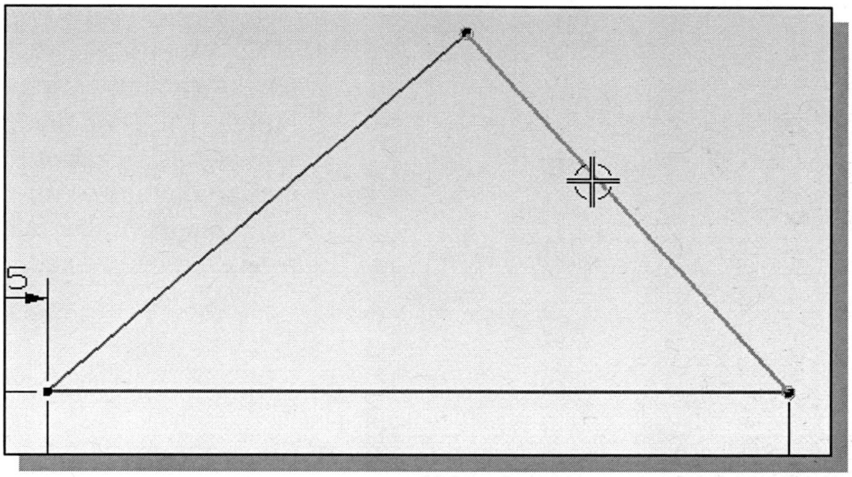

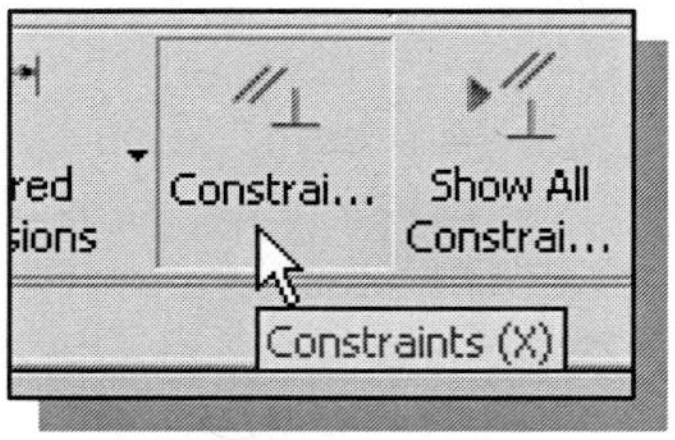

10. Select the **Constraints** command in the *Sketch Constraints* toolbar.

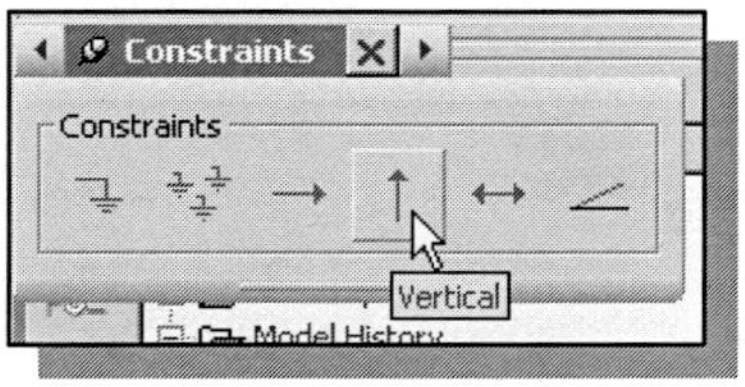

11. Choose the **Vertical** option as shown.

❖ Note that *UGS NX* displays only options that are feasible for the current selected objects. This is known as the context-sensitive approach, which makes the selection much easier.

❖ Currently two geometric constraints and three dimensions are applied to the sketch. How many more constraints are needed to make the sketch fully constrained?

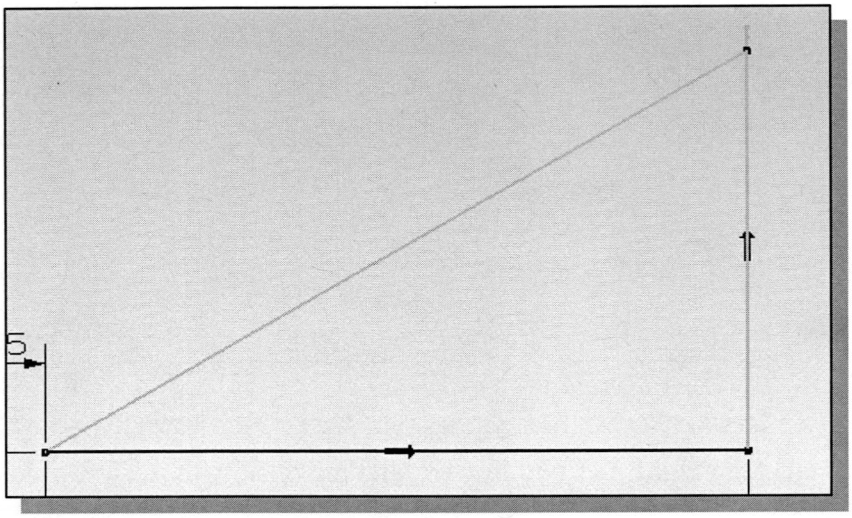

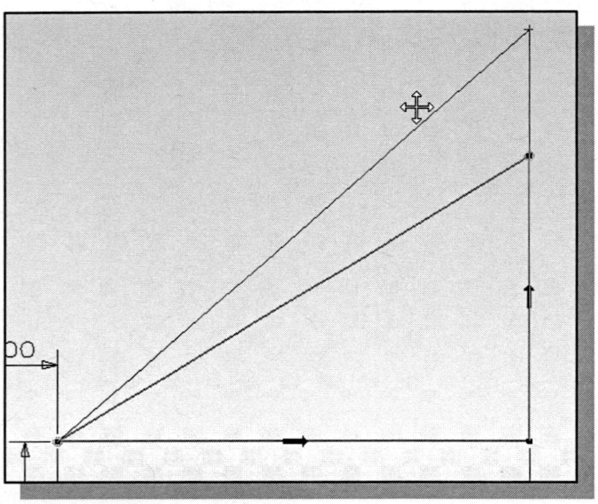

12. Click and drag with the left-mouse-button (MB1) on the inclined line and notice that we can still adjust the upper corner aligning to the right vertical line, but the lower two corners of the triangle remain fixed.

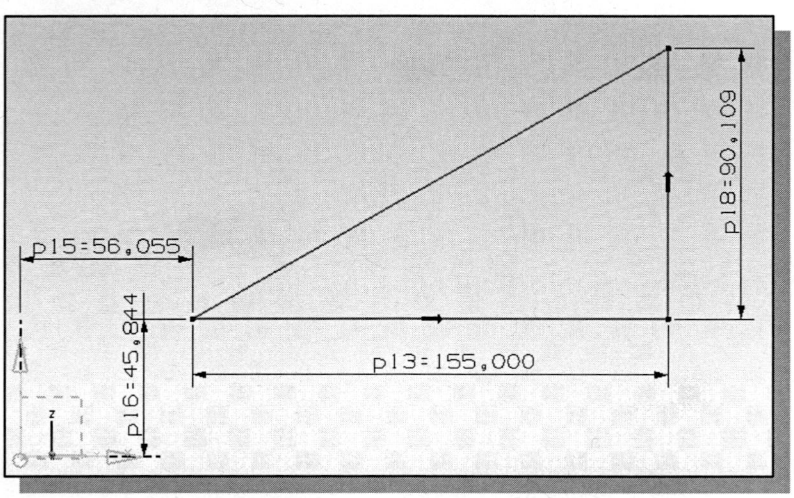

10. On your own, add a vertical dimension as shown. (Remember to un-check the *Reference* option.)

❖ Note that the sketch is now fully constrained. Consider what other constraints can be applied to the triangles while achieving the same results.

2D Sketches with Multiple Loops

❖ In *parametric modeling*, one option for combining multiple features into one feature is to create multiple loops within a 2D sketch. For example, if we need to create a hole in a triangular plate, one option is to create the triangular plate first and then create a hole feature. This approach will require two steps of solid features to complete. We can simplify the construction by creating two loops in one sketch. The outside loop (the triangle) will form the boundary of the material, and the inside loop (the circle) indicates a region of material that will be removed. The use of multiple loops can greatly simplify the content in the feature history tree.

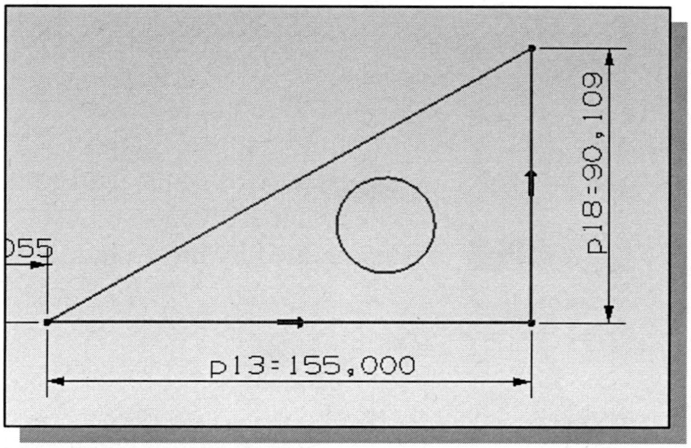

1. On your own, create a circle of arbitrary size inside the triangle as shown in the figure.

2. Pre-select the circle by left-mouse-clicking once on the geometry.

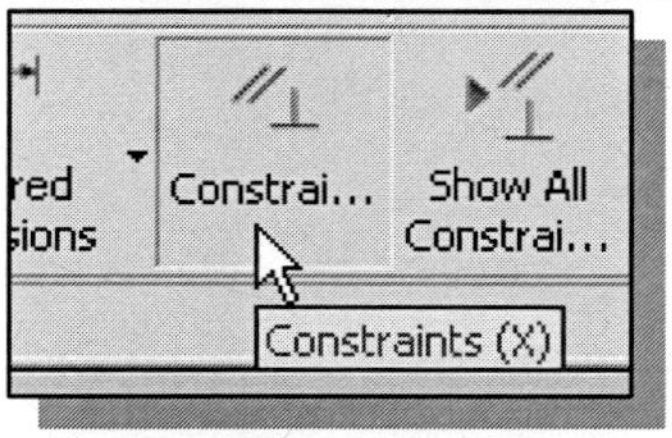

3. Select the **Constraints** command in the *Sketch Constraints* toolbar.

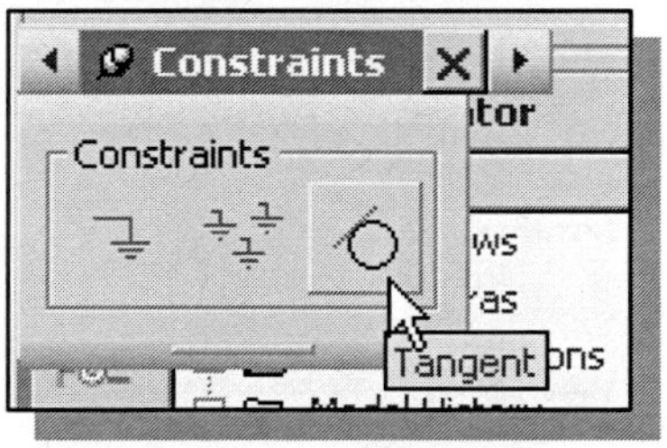

4. Pick the inclined line.

5. Click on the **Tangent** constraint icon in the *Sketch Constraints* toolbar. The sketched geometry is adjusted.

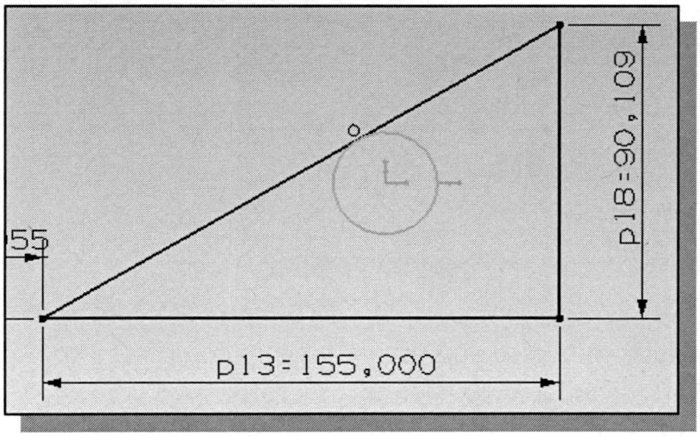

6. Use the middle-mouse-button (MB2) to exit the **Constraints** command.

- How many more constraints or dimensions do you think will be necessary to fully constrain the circle? Which constraints or dimensions would you use to fully constrain the geometry?

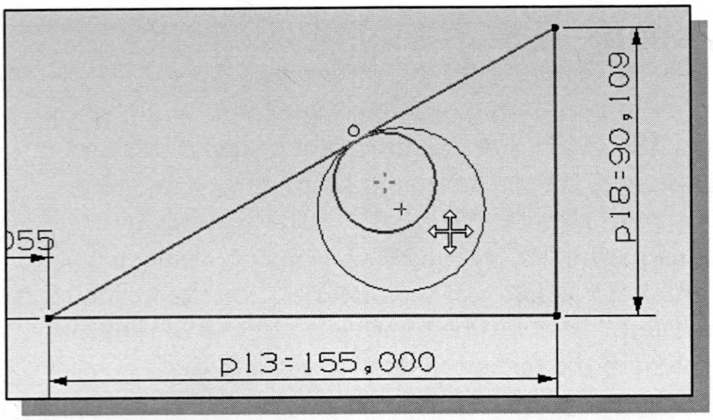

7. Move the cursor on top of the right side of the circle, and then drag the circle toward the right edge of the graphics window. Notice the size of the circle is adjusted while the system maintains the **Tangent** constraint.

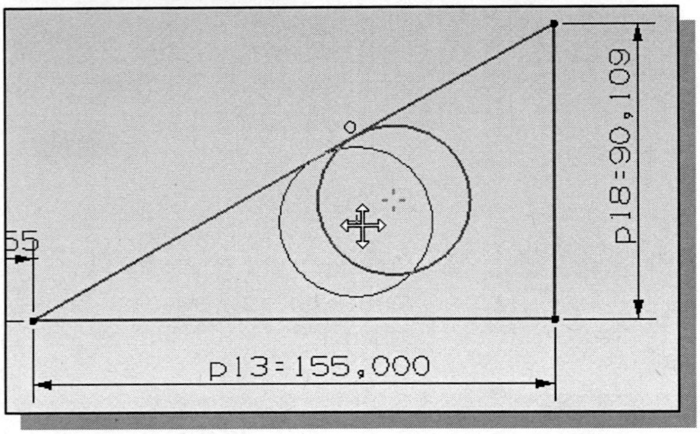

8. Drag the center of the circle toward the upper right direction. Notice the **Tangent** constraint is always maintained by the system.

➢ On your own, experiment with adding additional constraints and/or dimensions to fully constrain the sketched geometry.

❖ One possible option is to have two tangency constraints and an alignment constraint as shown in the figure below (circle center aligned to the mid-point of the vertical line).

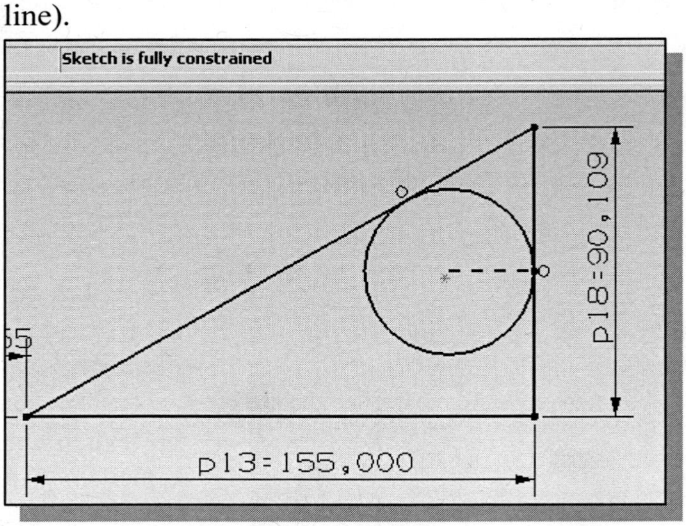

❖ The application of different constraints affects the geometry differently. The design intent is maintained in the CAD model's database and thus allows us to create very intelligent CAD models that can be modified and revised fairly easily.

9. On your own, modify the 2D sketch as shown below.

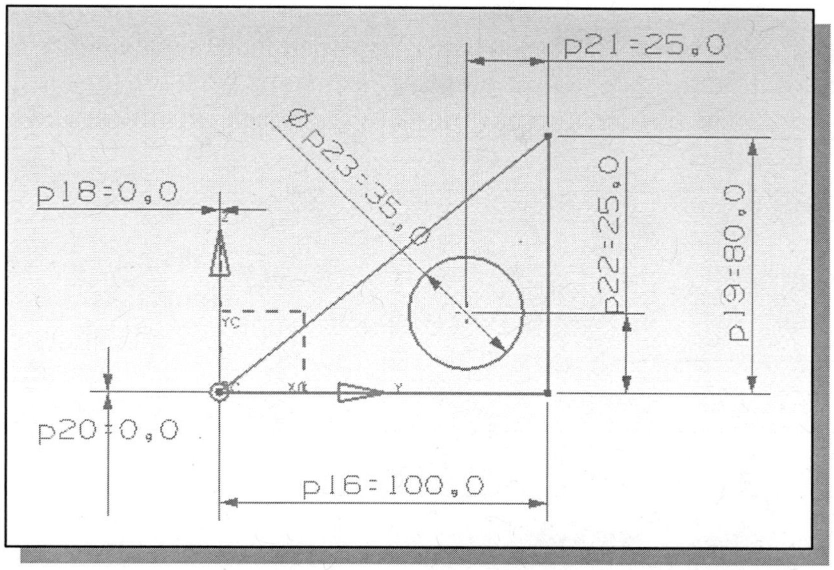

➢ On your own, complete the **Extrude** command and create a 3D solid model with a plate thickness of **40mm**.

Inferred Constraint Settings

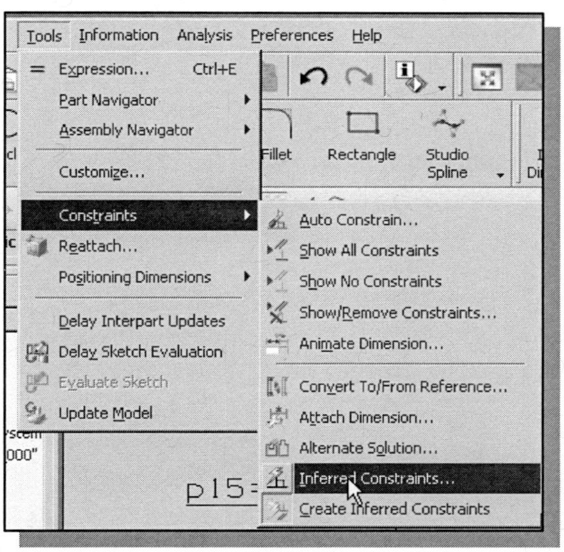

➢ Select **Tools→ Constraints → Inferred Constraints** in the *pull-down* menu.

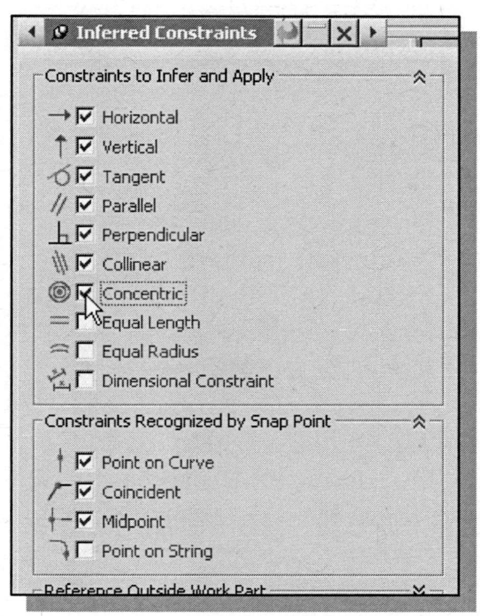

❖ In the **Inferred Constraint Settings** window, we can determine which constraints are recognizable and can be applied by the system.

➢ On your own, adjust the settings and experiment with the effects of the different settings. Especially note the **Dimensional Constraints** option.

Parametric Relations

- In parametric modeling, dimensions are design parameters that are used to control the sizes and locations of geometric features. Dimensions are more than just values; they can also be used as feature control variables. This concept is illustrated by the following example.

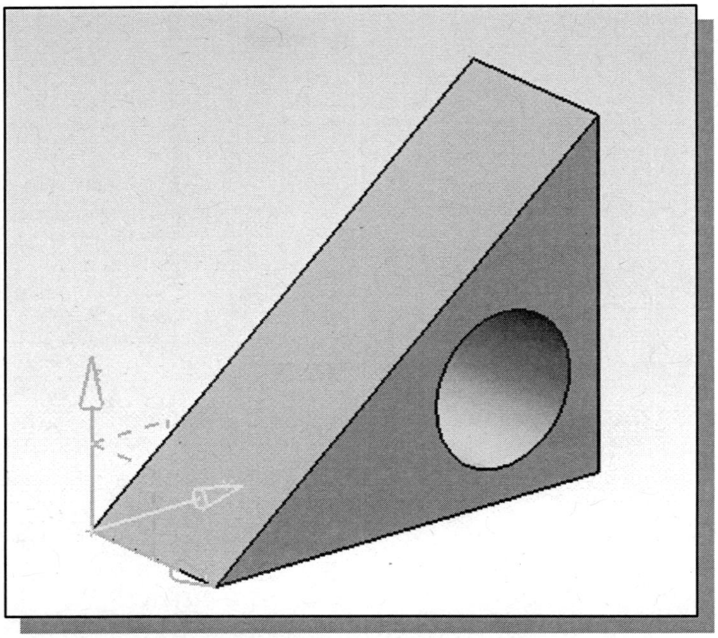

1. Double-click on the solid model to enter the **Edit with Rollback** option.

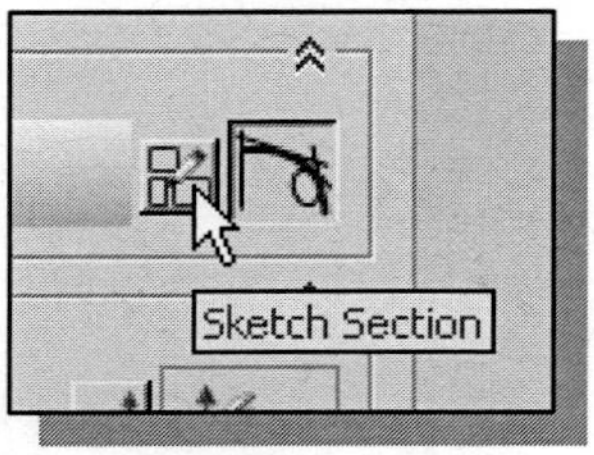

2. Click on the **Sketch Section** icon to enter the *2D Sketcher* mode.

- On your own, change the overall width of the triangle to **150** and the overall height of the rectangle to **100** and observe the location of the circle in relation to the edges of the triangle. Adjust the dimensions back to those shown in the figure before continuing to the next page.

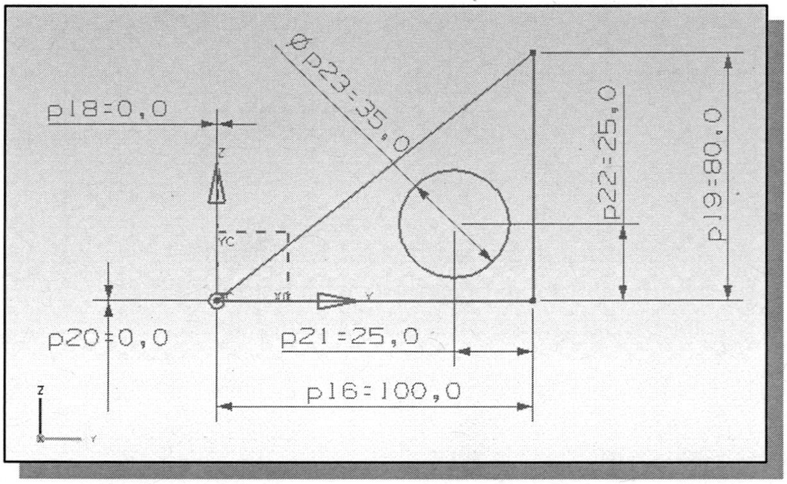

Dimensional Values and Dimensional Variables

Initially in *UGS NX*, values are used to create different geometric entities. The text created by the **Dimension** command also reflects the actual location or size of the entity. **Dimensional constraints** are used to describe the SIZE and LOCATION of individual geometric shapes. Each dimension is also assigned a name that allows the dimension to be used as a control variable. The default format is "pxx," where the "xx" is a number that *UGS NX* increments automatically each time a new dimension is added.

Let us look at our current design, which represents a triangular plate with a hole. The dimensional values describe the size and/or location of the plate and the hole. If a modification is required to change the width of the plate, the location of the hole will remain the same as described by the two location dimensional values. This is okay if that is the design intent. On the other hand, the *design intent* may require (1) keeping the location of the hole at a specific proportion to the length of the edges and (2) maintaining the size of the hole to always be one-third of the height of the plate. We will establish a set of parametric relations using the dimensional variables to capture the design intent described in statements (1) and (2) above.

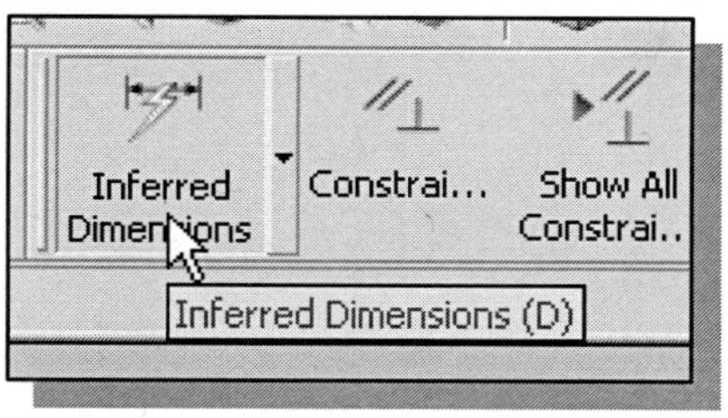

1. Select the **Inferred Dimensions** command in the *Sketch Constraints* toolbar as shown.

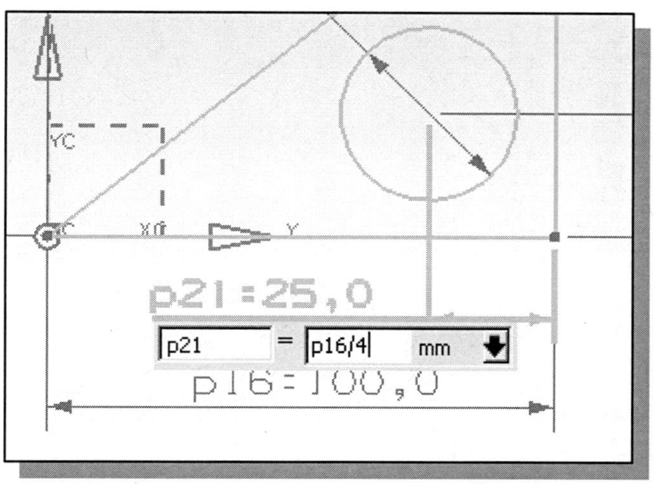

2. Select the horizontal location dimension of the circle and enter **p16/4** as shown. (The ***p16*** variable name is the overall width of the triangle; note the variable name may be different for your triangle.)

3. Click on the vertical location dimension of the circle and enter **p19/3** to make the dimension always equal to one third of the height of the overall height of the triangle. (Again, use the corresponding variable name for your equation.)

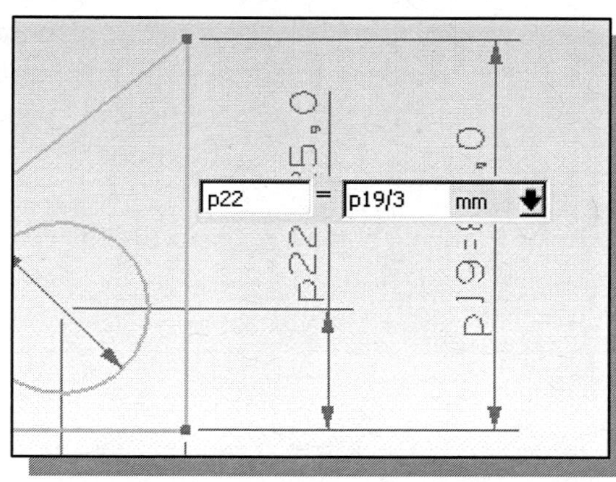

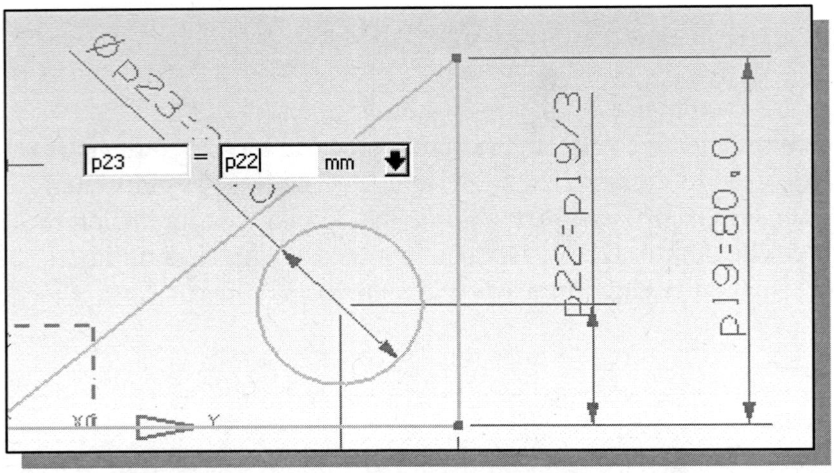

4. On your own, adjust the size dimension of the circle to be one third of the overall height of the triangle.

5. On your own, change the dimensions of the rectangle to **150 x 100** and observe the changes to the location and size of the circle.

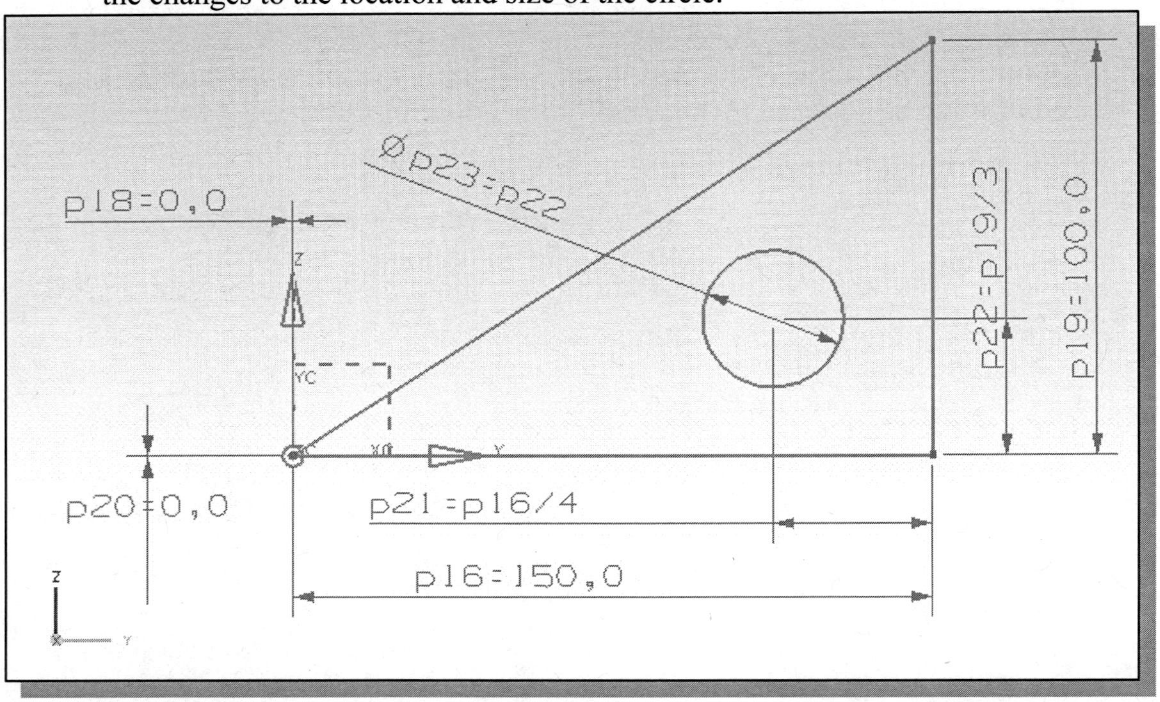

❖ *UGS NX* automatically adjusts the dimensions of the design, and the parametric relations we entered are also applied and maintained. The dimensional constraints are used to control the size and location of the hole. The design intent, previously expressed by statements (1) and (2) at the beginning of this section, is now embedded into the model.

➢ On your own, experiment with establishing and modifying additional parametric relations in the model.

Questions:

1. Seacribe the basic concepts of the BORN technique.

2. What is the difference between *dimensional* constraints and *geometric* constraints?

3. How can we confirm a sketch is fully constrained?

4. How do we create derived dimensions ?

5. Describe the procedure to Display/Edit user-defined equations.

6. How do we show and remove constraints?

7. List and describe three different geometric constraints available in *UGS NX*.

8. Does *UGS NX* allow us to build partially constrained or totally unconstrained solid models? What are the advantages and disadvantages of building these types of models?

9. How do we confirm the 2D sketch is fully constrained?

10. Create sketches showing the steps you plan to use to create the model shown on the next page:

Exercises:

(Create and establish three parametric relations for each of the following designs.)

1. Dimensions are in millimeters. (Base thickness: 10 mm., Boss height: 20 mm.)

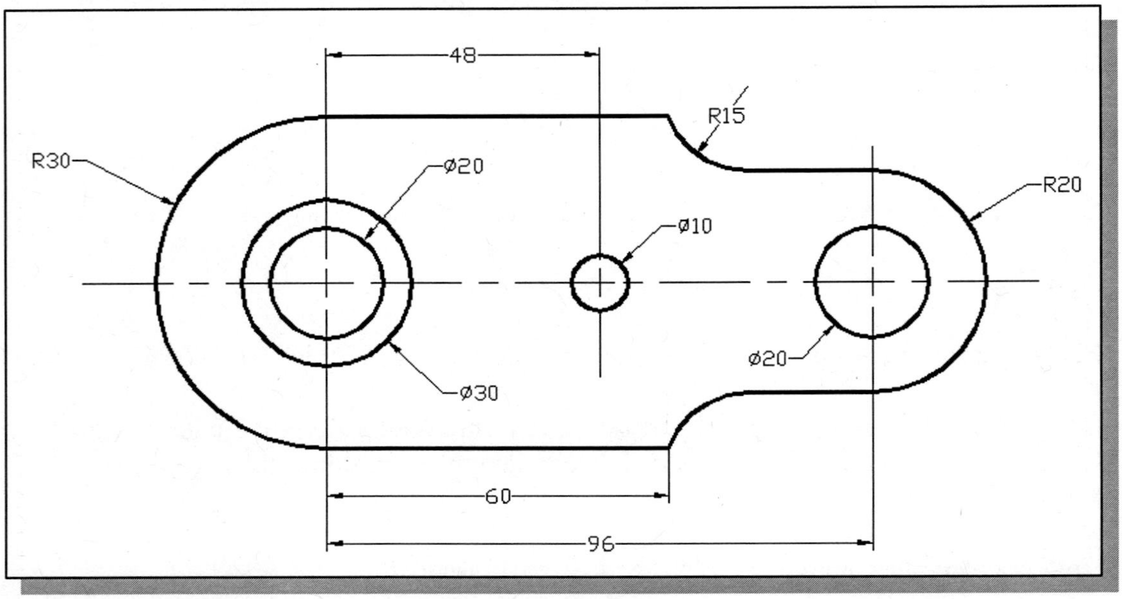

2. Dimensions are in inches. Plate thickness: 0.25 inches.

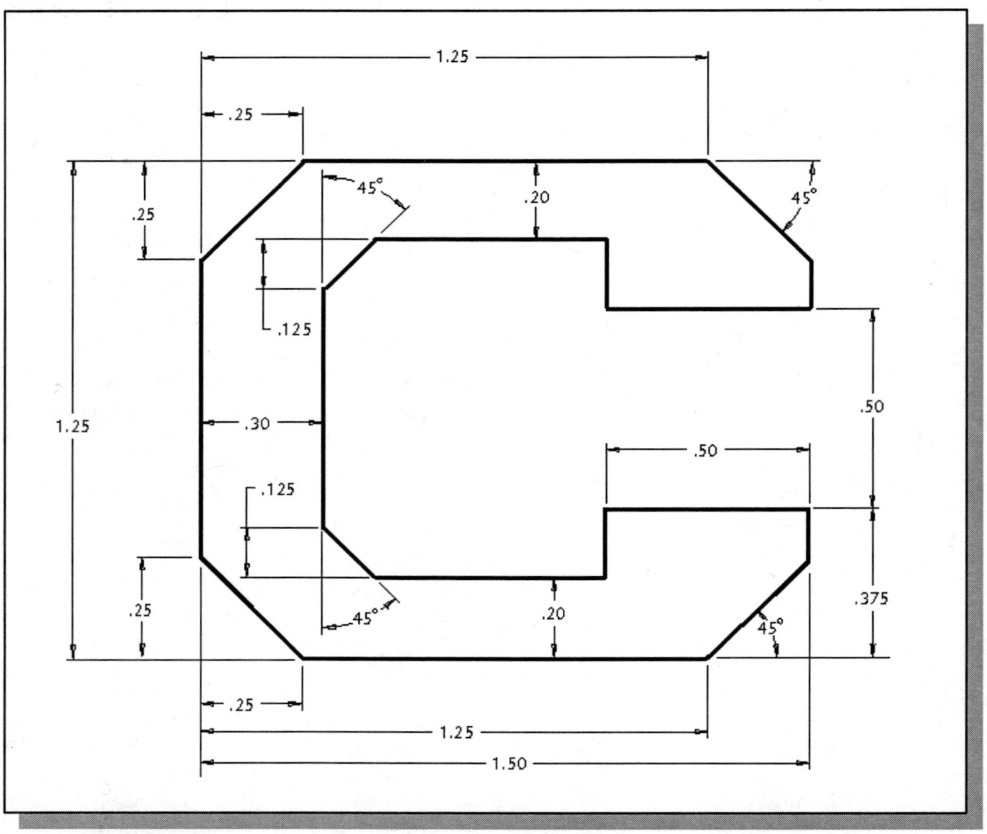

3. Dimensions are in inches

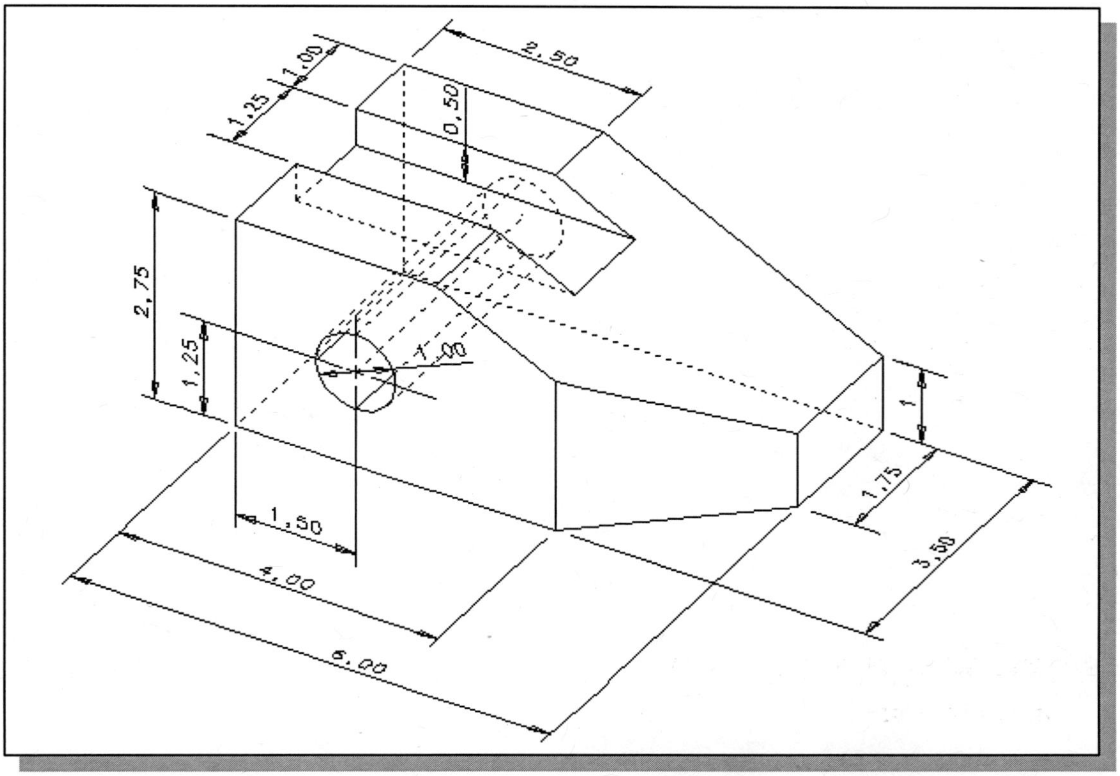

4. Dimensions are in inches.

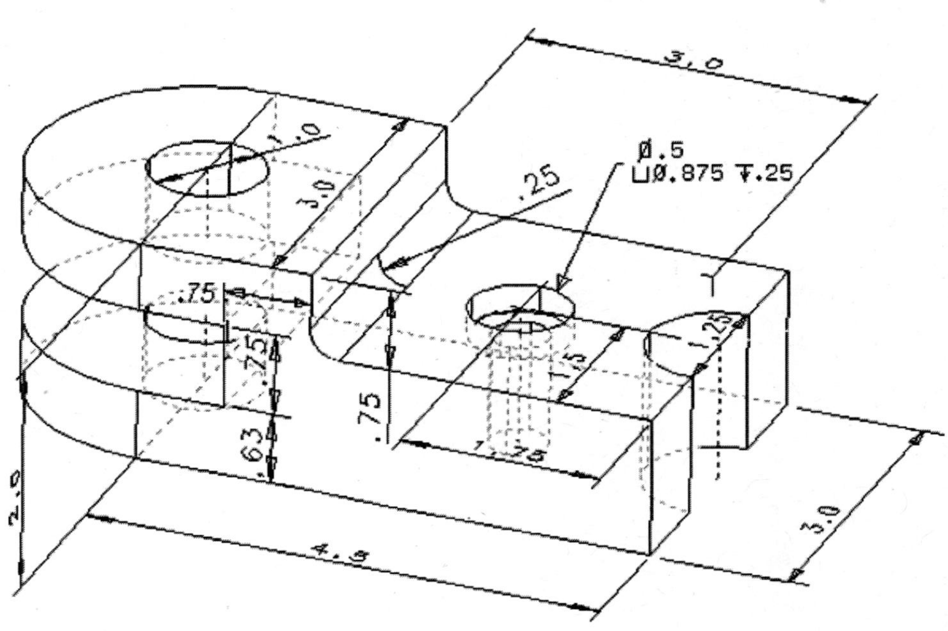

Notes:

Chapter 6
Geometric Construction Tools

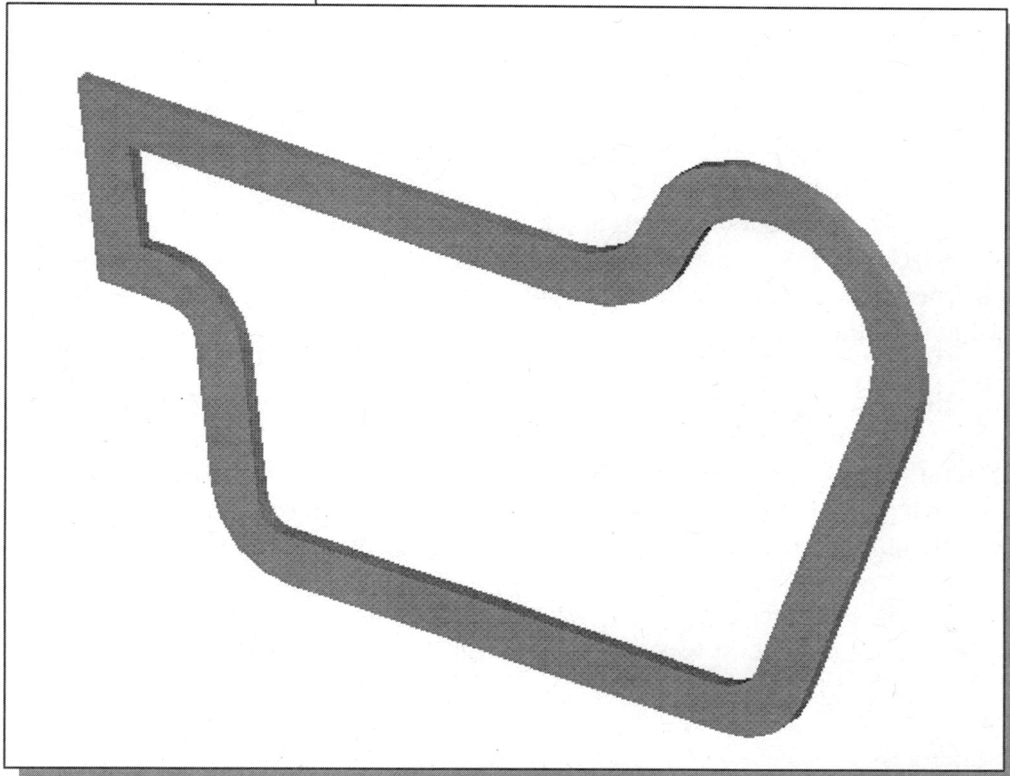

Learning Objectives

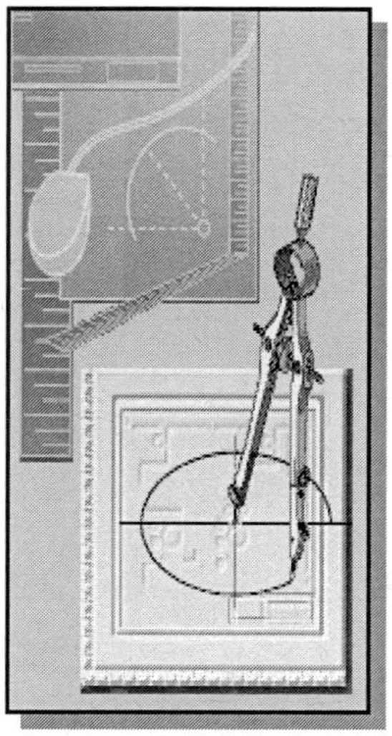

- ♦ Apply Geometry Constraints
- ♦ Use the Trim/Extend Command
- ♦ Use the Offset Command
- ♦ Understand the Haystacking Approach
- ♦ Create Projected Geometry
- ♦ Edit with Click and Drag

Introduction

The main characteristics of solid modeling are the accuracy and completeness of the geometric database of the three-dimensional objects. However, working in three-dimensional space using input and output devices that are largely two-dimensional in nature is potentially tedious and confusing. *UGS NX* provides an assortment of two-dimensional construction tools to make the creation of wireframe geometry easier and more efficient. *UGS NX* includes two types of wireframe geometry: ***curves*** and ***sections***. Curves are basic geometric entities such as lines, arcs, etc. Sections are a group of curves used to define a boundary. A *section* is a closed region and can contain other closed regions. Sections are commonly used to create extruded and revolved features. An *invalid section* consists of self-intersecting curves or open regions. In this lesson, the basic geometric construction tools, such as **Trim** and **Extend**, are used to create sections. *UGS NX's* ***haystacking*** approach to creating sections is also introduced. Mastering the geometric construction tools along with the application of proper constraints and parametric relations is the true essence of *parametric modeling*.

In *UGS NX*, **sections** are closed regions that are defined from sketches. Sections are used as cross sections to create solid features. For example, **Extrude**, **Revolve**, and **Sweep** operations all require the definition of at least a single section. The sketches used to define a section can contain additional geometry since the additional geometric entities are consumed when the feature is created. To create a section we can create single or multiple closed regions, or we can select existing solid edges to form closed regions. A section cannot contain self-intersecting geometry; regions selected in a single operation form a single section. As a general rule, we should dimension and constrain sections to prevent them from unpredictable size and shape changes. *UGS NX* does allow us to create under-constrained or non-constrained sections; the dimensions and/or constraints can be added/edited later.

The *Gasket* Design

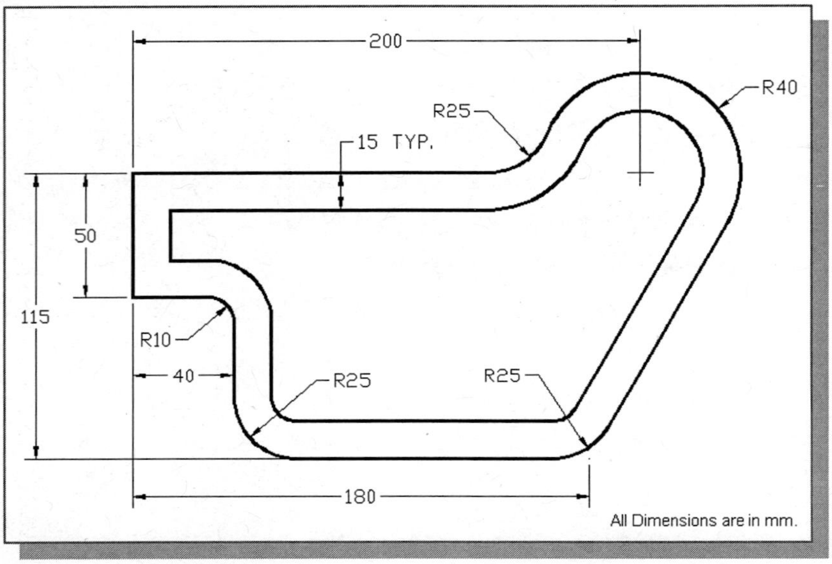

❖ Based on your knowledge of *UGS NX* so far, how would you create this design? What are the more difficult geometry involved in the design? You are encouraged to create the design on your own prior to following through the tutorial.

Modeling Strategy

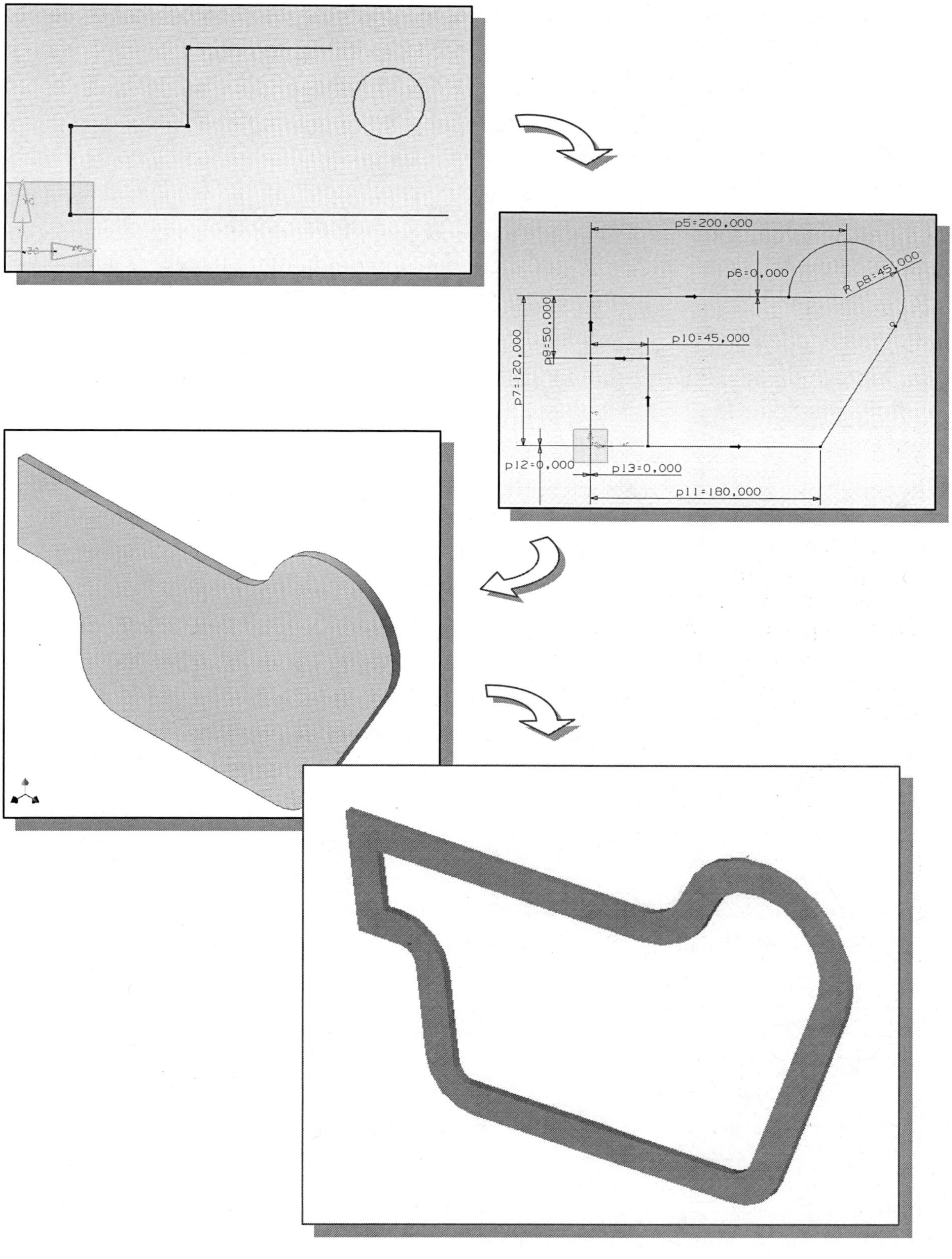

Starting *UGS NX*

1. Select the **UGS NX** option on the *Start* menu or select the **UGS NX** icon on the desktop to start *UGS NX*. The *UGS NX* main window will appear on the screen.

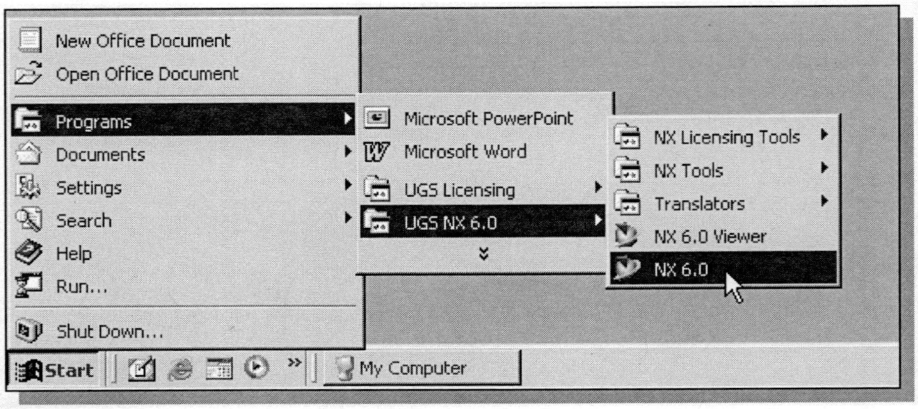

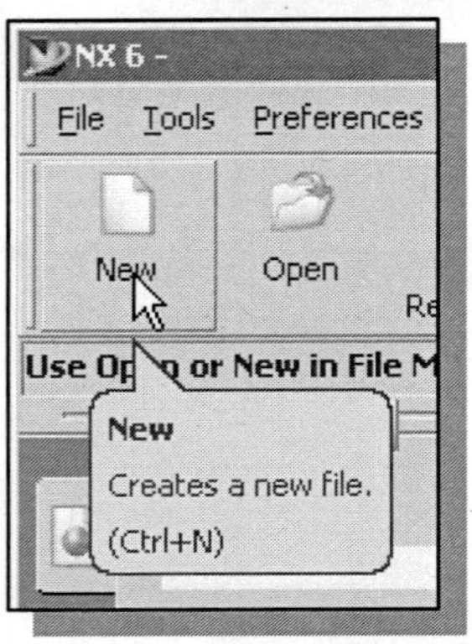

2. Select the **New** icon with a single click of the left-mouse-button (MB1) in the *Standard* toolbar area.

3. Confirm the **Millimeters** units are set as shown in the figure below.

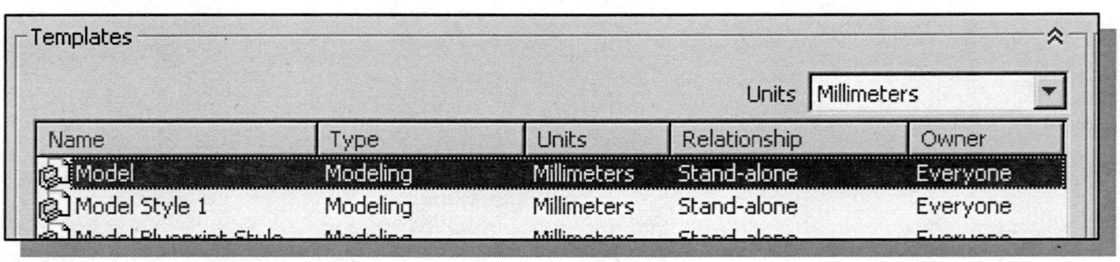

4. Select **Model** in the *Templates* list. Note that the *Model* template will allow us to switch directly into the *Modeling* task as indicated in the *Templates* list.

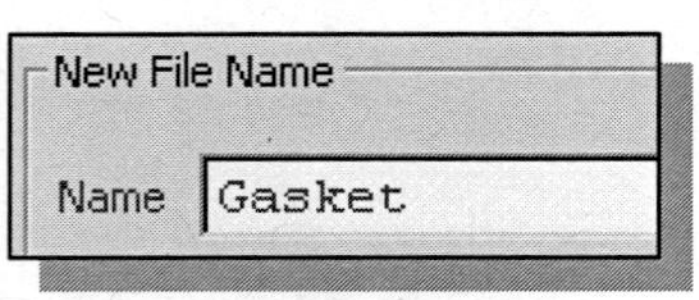

5. In the *New File Name* section, enter **Gasket** as the file *Name*.

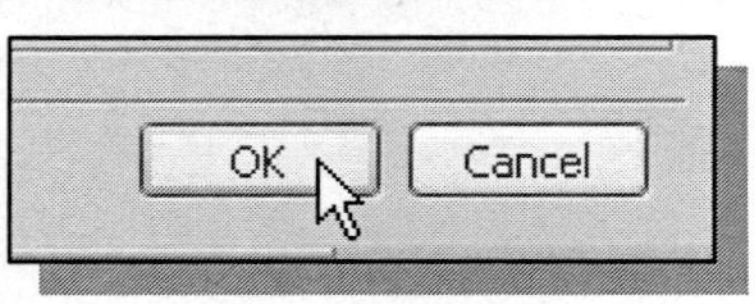

6. Click **OK** to proceed with the New Part File command.

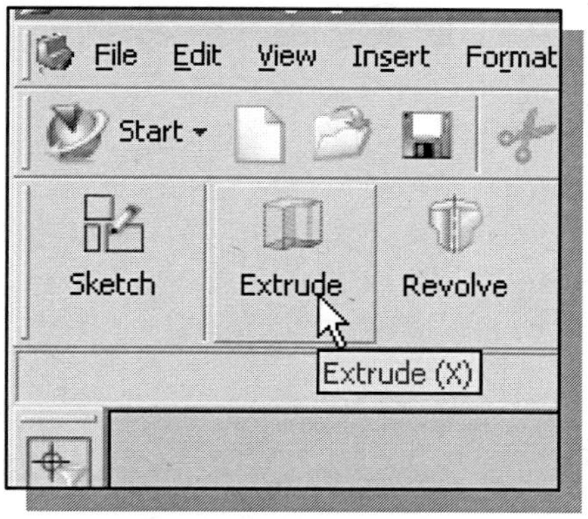

7. In the *Form Feature* toolbars (toolbars aligned to the right edge of the main window), select the **Extrude** icon as shown.

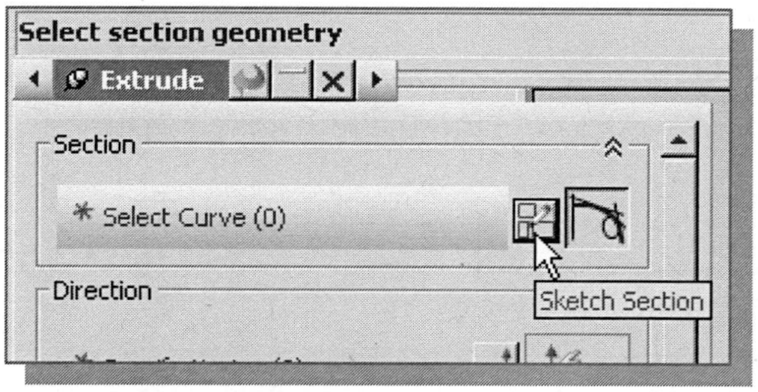

8. Click the **Sketch Section** button to begin creating a new *2D sketch.*

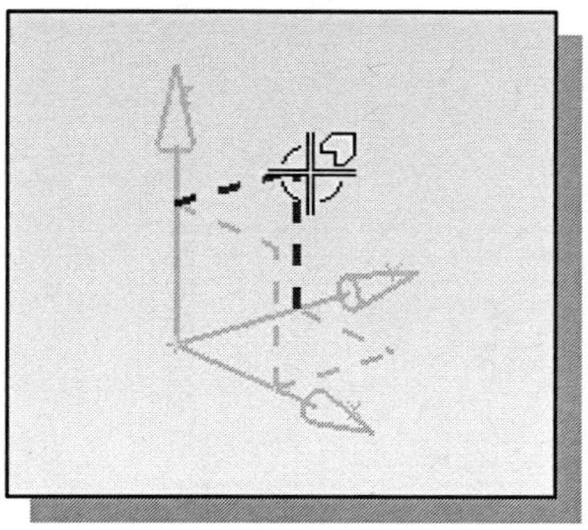

9. Select the ***Y-Z* plane** of the established datum coordinate system as the sketch plane of the *base feature*.

10. Create a sketch as shown in the figure below. Start the sketch from the top right corner. The line segments are all parallel and/or perpendicular to each other. We will intentionally make the line segments of arbitrary length, as it is quite common during the initial design stage that not all of the values are determined.

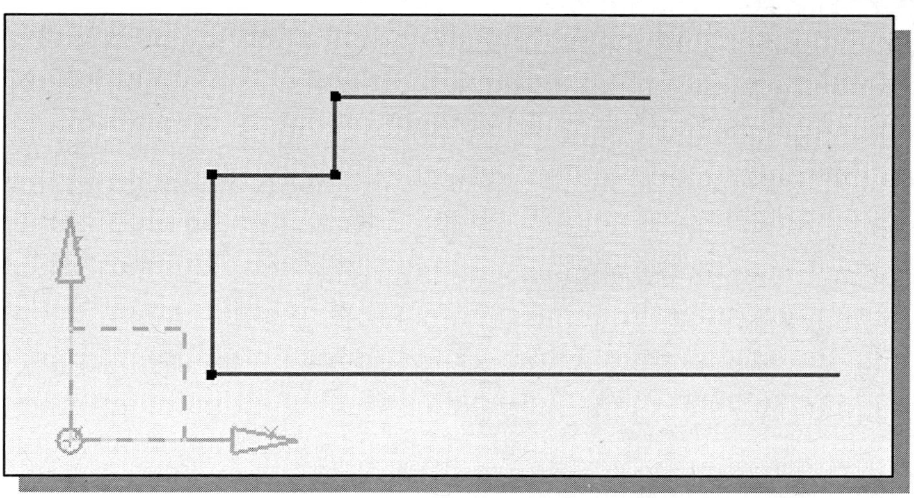

11. Inside the graphics window, middle-mouse-click (MB2) once to end the **Profile** command.

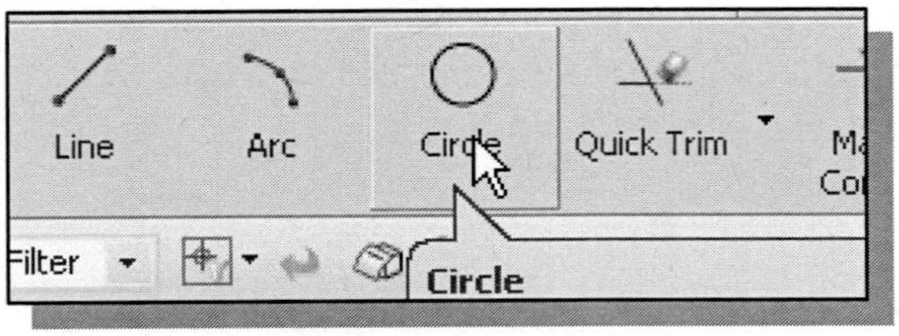

12. Select the **Circle** command by clicking once with the left-mouse-button (MB1) on the icon in the *Sketch Curve* toolbar.

13. Pick a location that is above the bottom horizontal line as the center location of the circle.

14. Move the cursor toward the right and create a circle of arbitrary size and not aligned to any of the existing geometry. by clicking with the left-mouse-button.

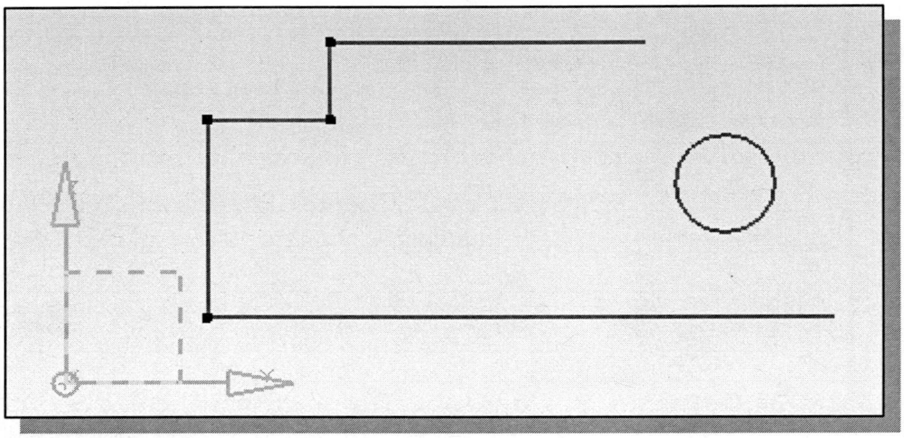

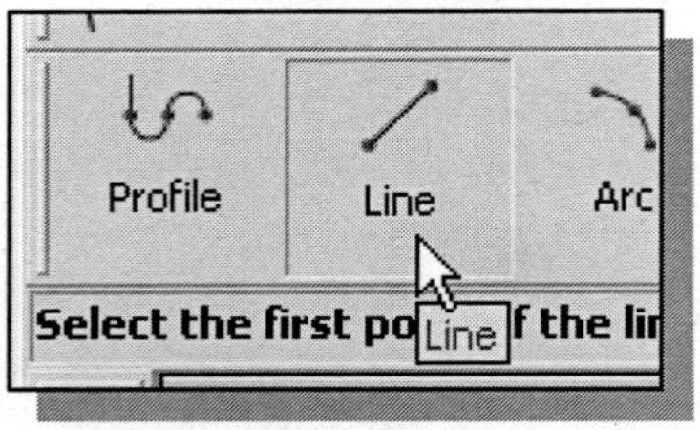

15. Click on the **Line** icon in the *2D Sketch Panel*.

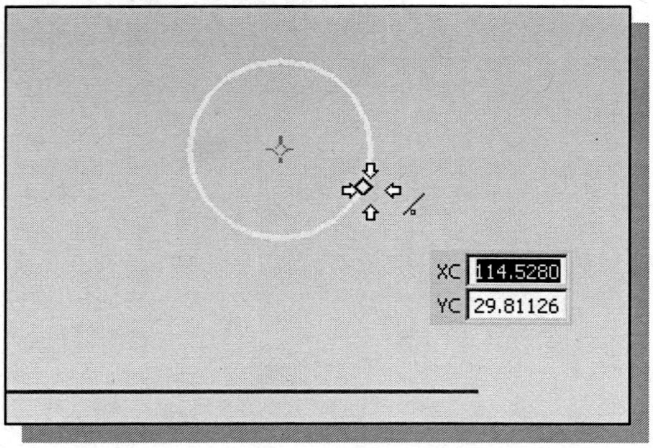

16. Move the cursor near the upper portion of the circle and pick a location on the circle when the **Tangent** constraint symbol is displayed.

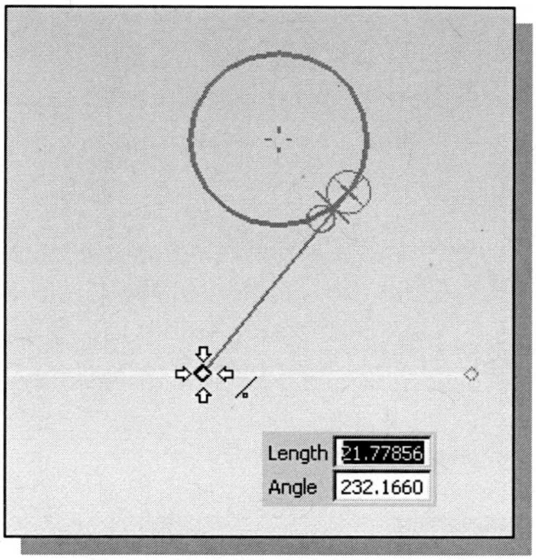

17. For the other end of the line, select a location that is on the lower horizontal line and about one-third from the right endpoint. Notice the **Coincident** constraint symbol is displayed when the cursor is on the horizontal line.

18. Inside the graphics window, middle-mouse-click (MB2) twice to end the **Line** command.

Editing the Sketch by Dragging the Entities

❖ In *UGS NX*, we can click and drag any under-constrained curve or point in the sketch to change the size or shape of the sketched section. As illustrated in the previous chapter, this option can be used to identify under-constrained entities. This *editing by dragging* method is also an effective visual approach that allows designers to quickly make changes.

1. Move the cursor on the lower left vertical edge of the sketch. Click and drag the edge to a new location that is toward the right side of the sketch.

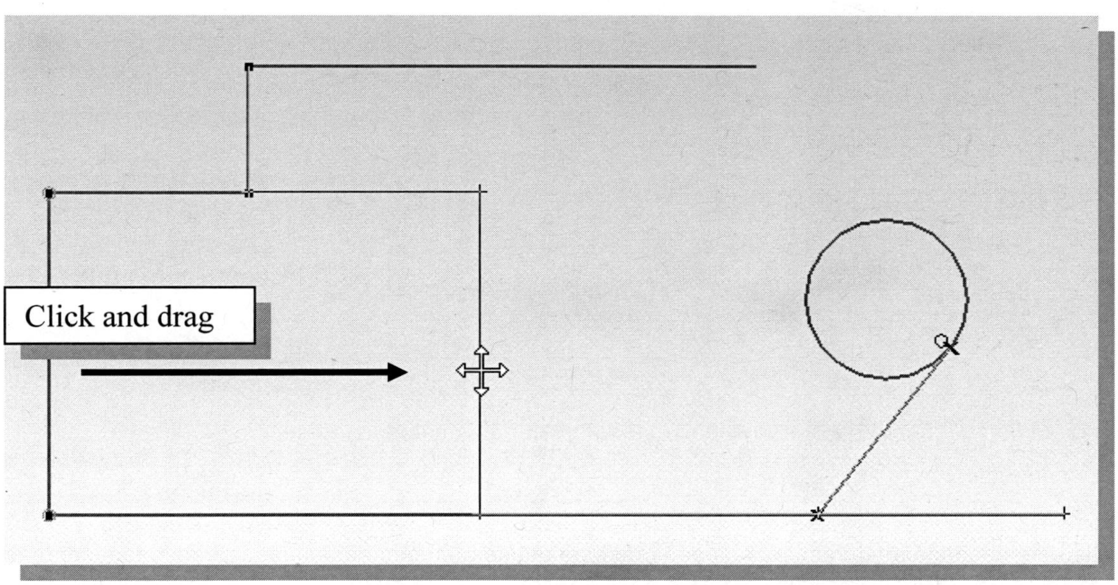

❖ Note that we can only drag the vertical edge horizontally; the connections to the two horizontal lines are maintained while we are moving the geometry.

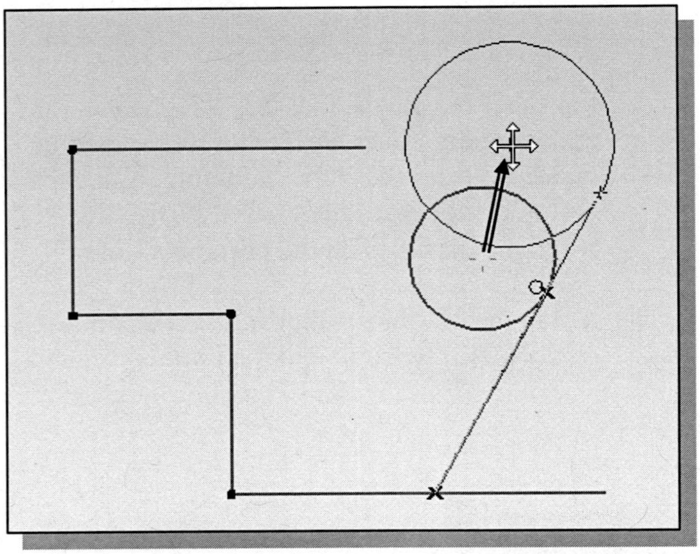

2. Click and drag the center point of the circle to a new location.

❖ Note that as we adjust the size and the location of the circle, the connection to the inclined line is maintained.

3. Click and drag the inclined line to a new location.

❖ Note that as we adjust the location of the inclined line the location of the circle and the size of the bottom horizontal edge are also adjusted.

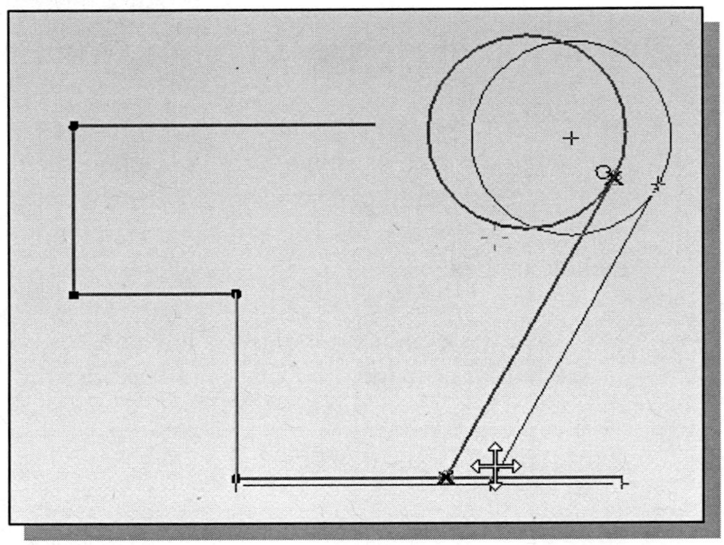

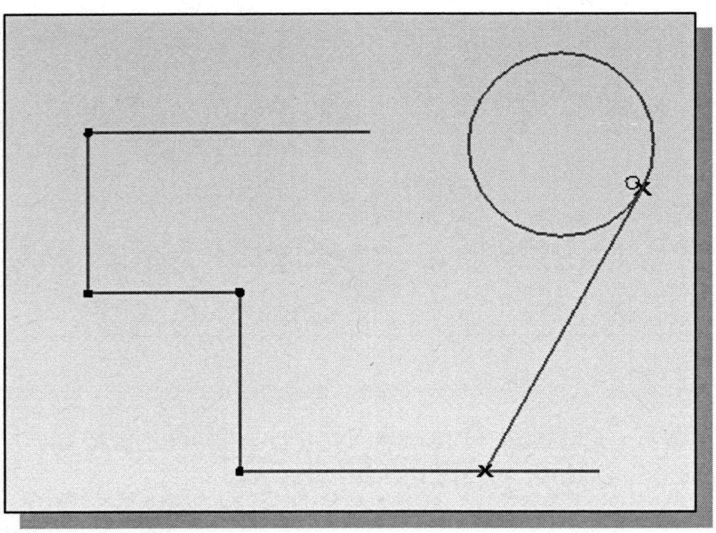

4. On your own, adjust the sketch so that the shape of the sketch appears roughly as shown.

❖ The *Editing by Dragging* method is an effective approach that allows designers to explore and experiment with different design concepts.

Adding Additional Constraints

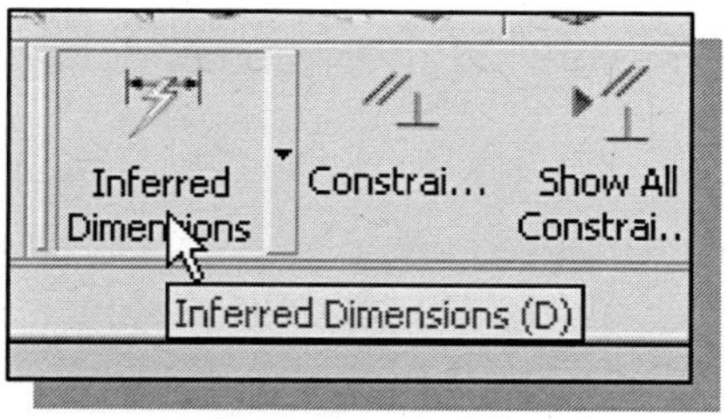

1. Select the **Inferred Dimensions** command in the *Sketch Constraints* toolbar as shown.

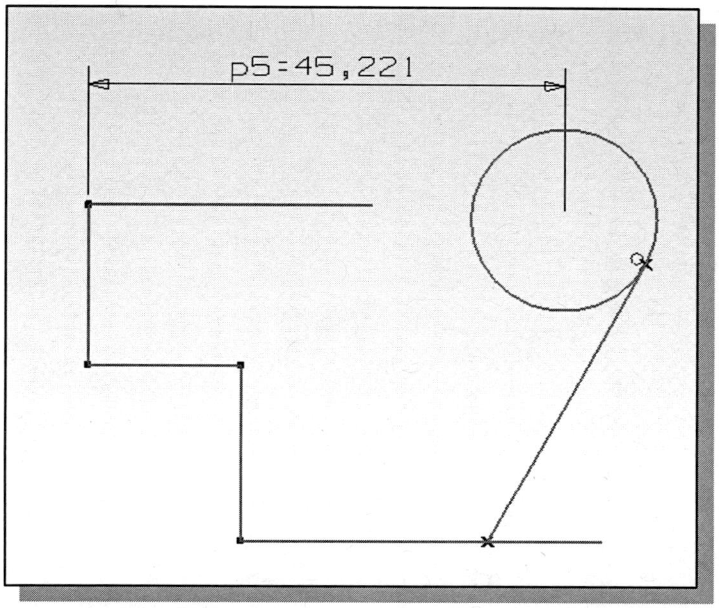

2. Add the horizontal location dimension, from the top left vertical edge to the center of the circle as shown. (Do not be overly concerned with the dimensional value; we are still working on creating a *rough sketch.*)

3. Inside the graphics window, middle-mouse-click (MB2) twice to end the Dimension command.

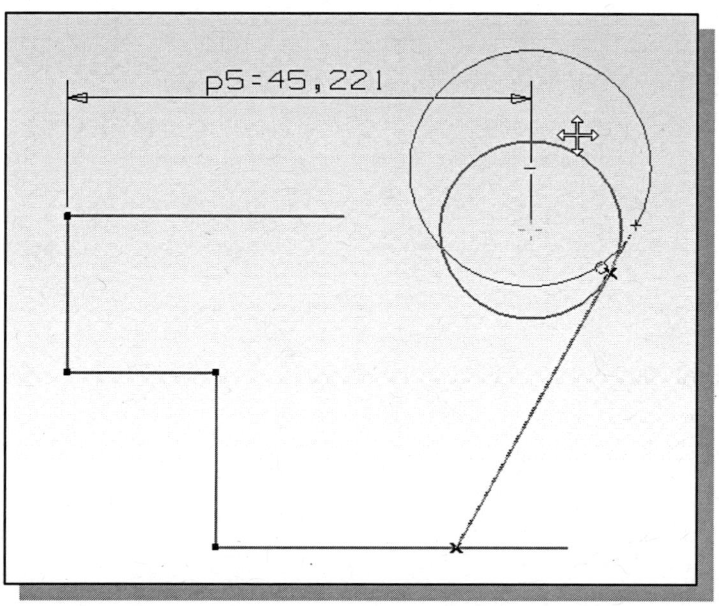

4. Click and drag the circle to a new location.

❖ Notice that the dimension we added now restricts the horizontal movement of the center of the circle. The tangent relation to the inclined line is also maintained.

First Construction Method – Trim/Extend

➢ In the following sections, we will illustrate using the Trim and Extend commands to complete the desired 2D sketch.

❖ The **Trim** and **Extend** commands can be used to shorten/lengthen an object so that it ends precisely at a boundary. As a general rule, *UGS NX* will try to clean up sketches by forming a closed region sketch.

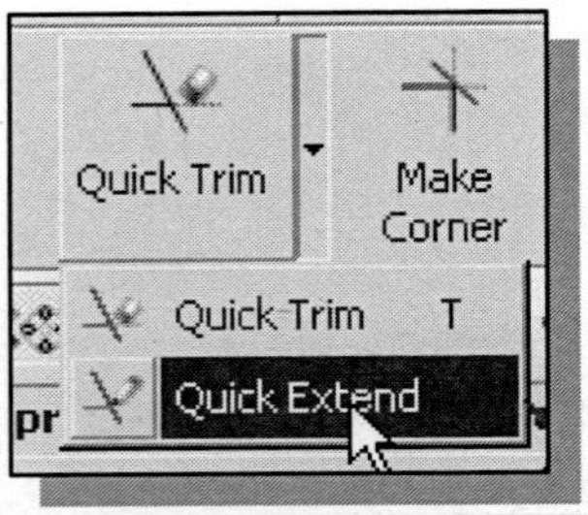

1. Choose **Quick Extend** in the *Sketch Curve* toolbar.

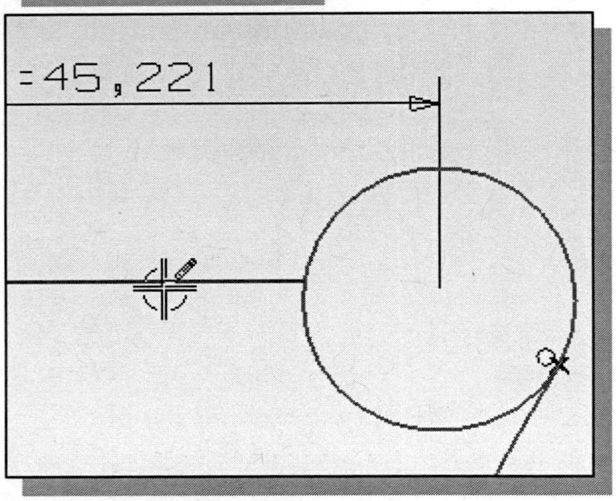

2. We will first extend the top horizontal line to the circle. Move the cursor near the right hand endpoint of the top horizontal line. *UGS NX* will automatically display the possible result of the selection.

3. Click the left-mouse-button (MB1) to accept the selection and extend the selected line.

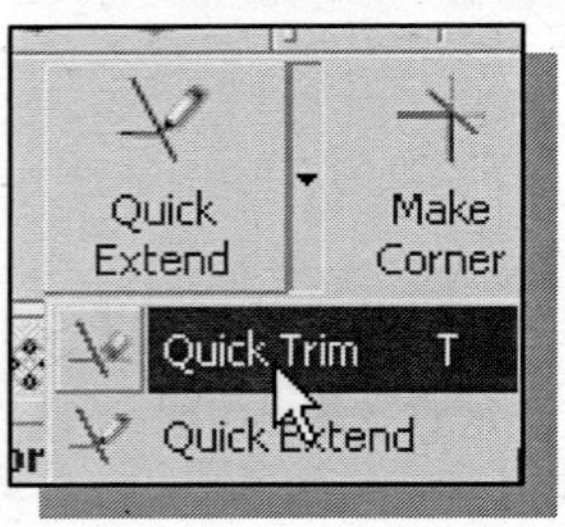

4. Choose **Quick Trim** in the *Sketch Curve* toolbar.

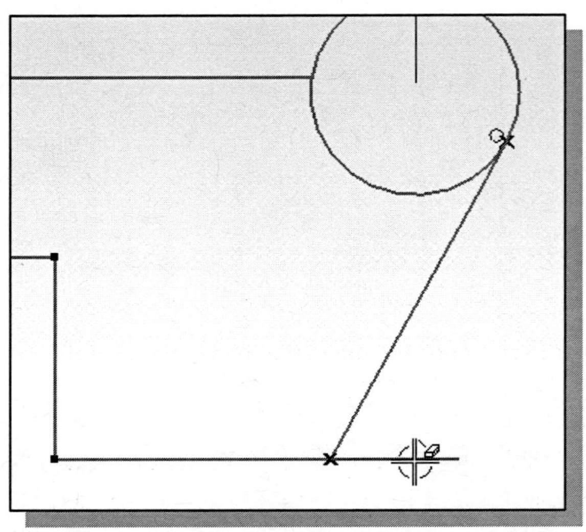

5. We will next trim the bottom horizontal line to the inclined line. Move the cursor near the right hand endpoint of the bottom horizontal line. *UGS NX* will highlight the portion of the line that will be trimmed.

6. Left-mouse-click once on the line to perform the Trim operation.

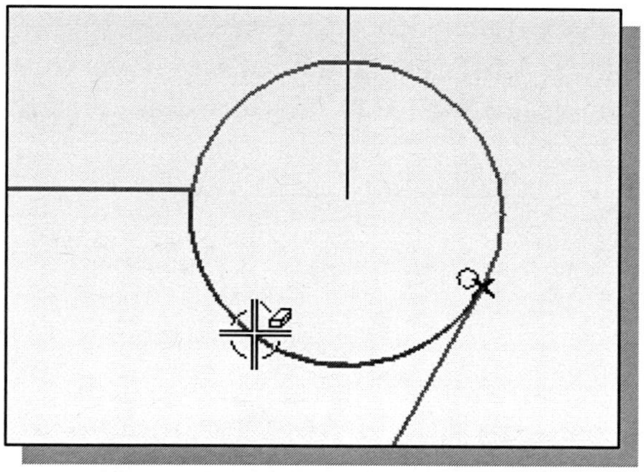

7. Left-mouse-click once on the lower portion of the circle to perform the **Trim** operation on it.

8. Inside the graphics window, middle-mouse-click (MB2) twice to end the **Trim** command.

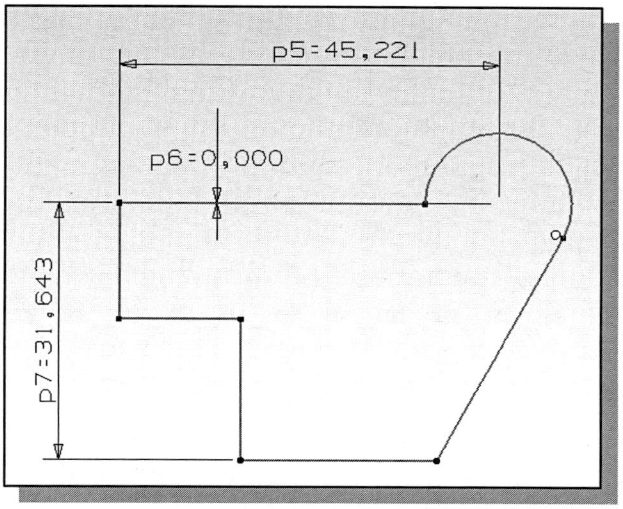

9. On your own, create the vertical location dimension of the center of the arc as shown below.

10. Adjust the dimension to **0.0** so that the horizontal line and the center of the circle are aligned horizontally.

11. On your own, create the **height dimension** to the left and use the **Show Constraints** command to examine the applied constraints. Confirm that **proper constraints** are applied to the horizontal and vertical lines as shown.

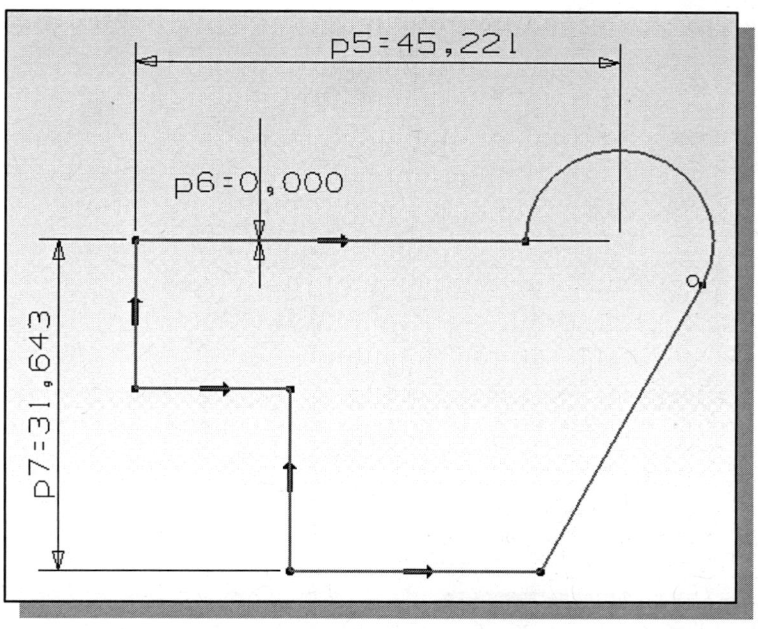

12. On your own, create the additional length/size dimension as shown. Again, the values displayed on your screen may look very different than what are shown in the figure below. How many more constraints are needed to fully constrain the 2D sketch?

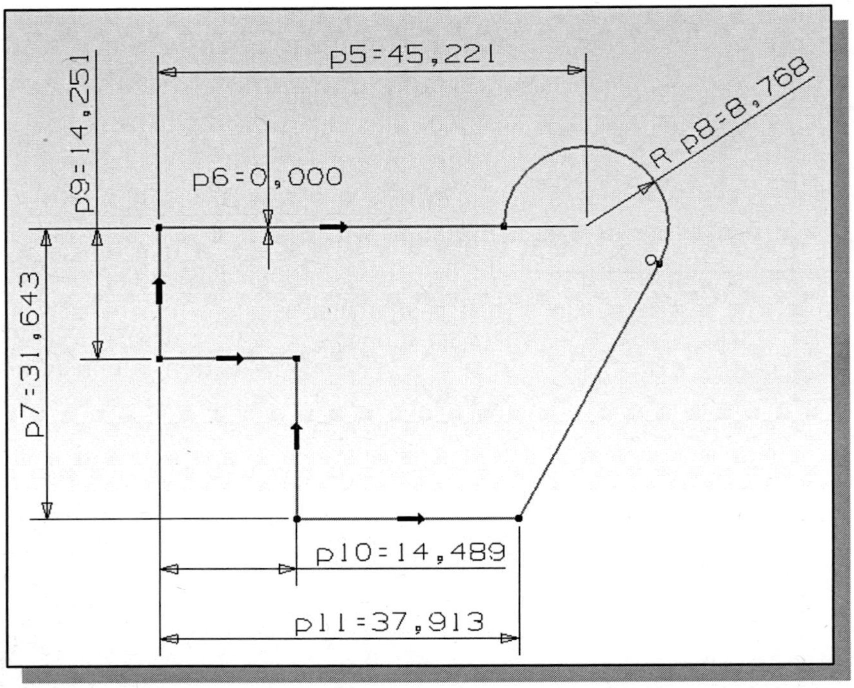

13. On your own, create the two locational dimensions to align the sketch to the origin of the WCS as shown in the figure. Also, adjust the dimensions to those shown in the figure. The 2D sketch is now fully constrained.

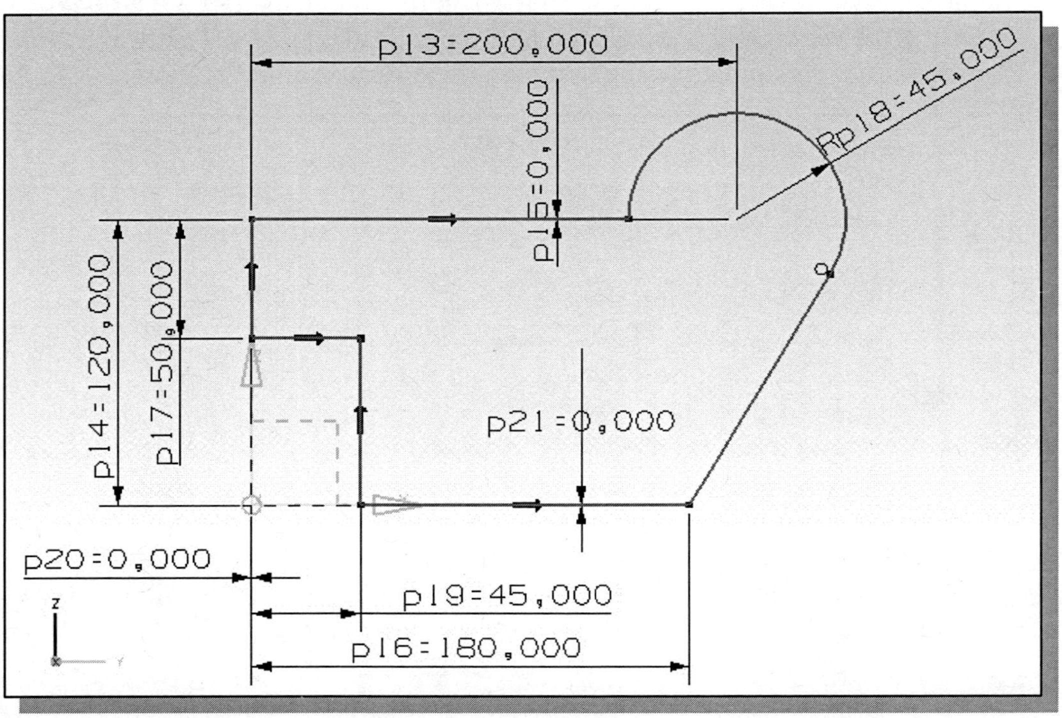

Creating Fillets and Completing the Sketch

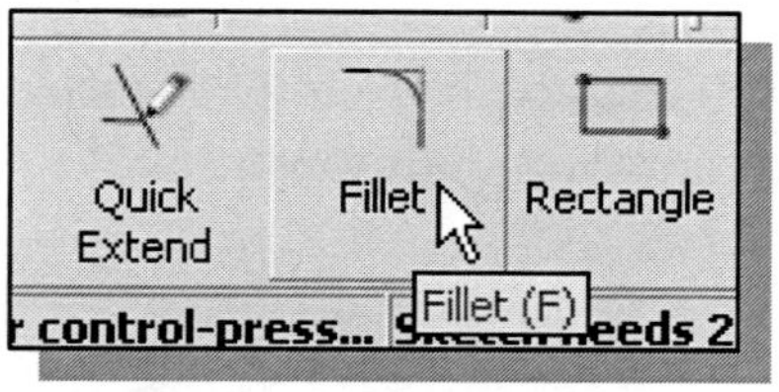

1. Select the **Fillet** command by clicking once with the left-mouse-button (MB1) on the icon in the *Sketch Curve* toolbar.

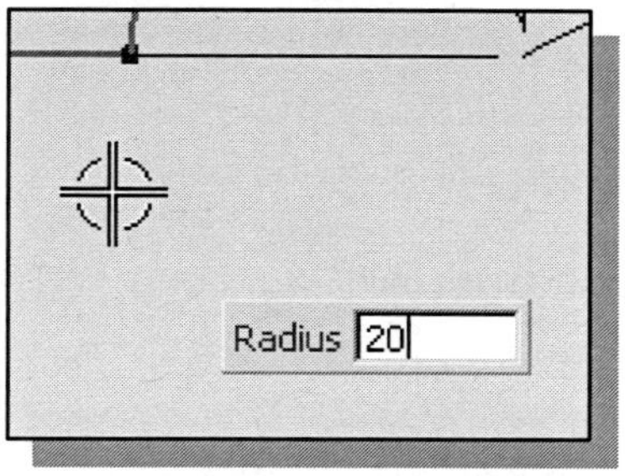

2. Enter **20** as the new radius of the fillet.

3. On your own, create the four additional fillets as shown in the figure below. Note that the same radius value is used on all rounds and fillets. Also, note that all of the rounds and fillets are created with the proper constraints.

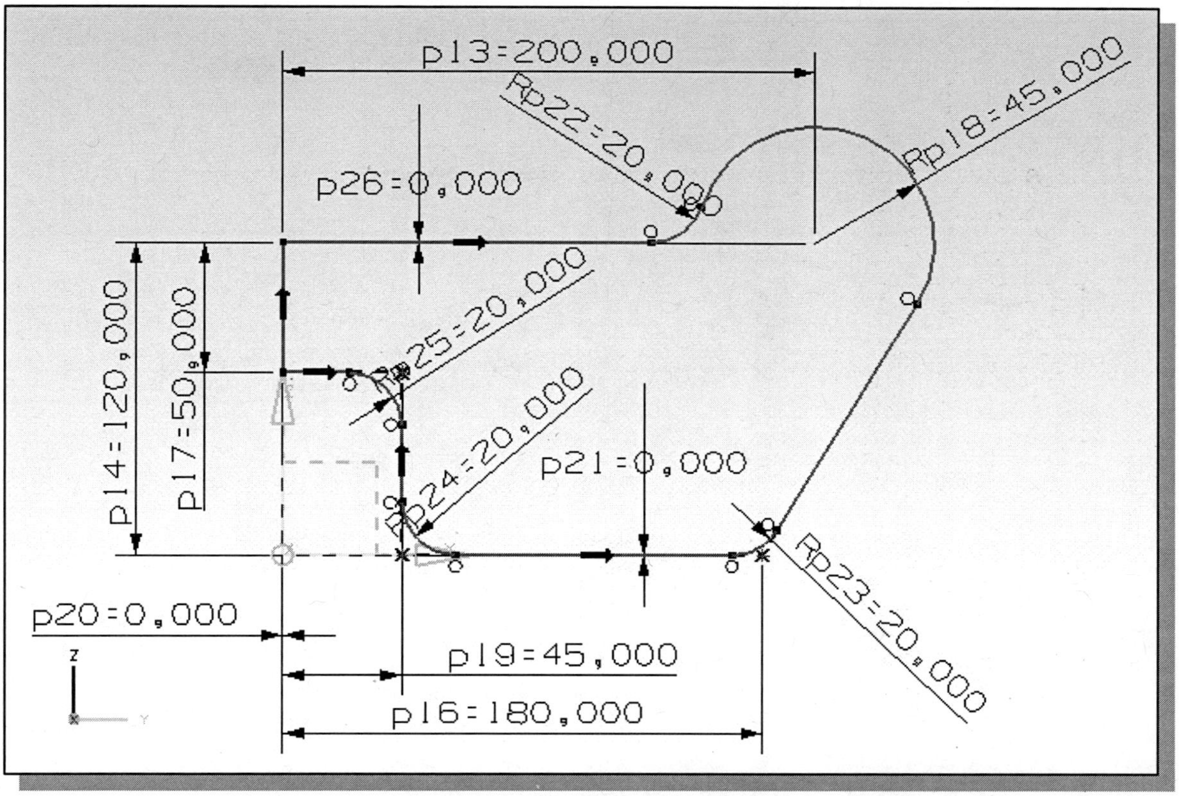

❖ On your own, use the **Inferred Dimension** command to confirm the 2D sketch is still fully constrained. (Also use the drag and drop option and read the associated message.)

Completing the Extrusion Feature

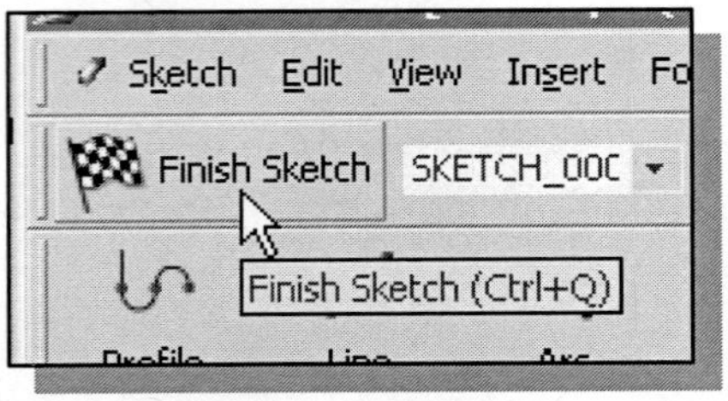

1. Click **Finish Sketch** to exit the *NX Sketcher* mode and return to the *Feature* option dialog window.

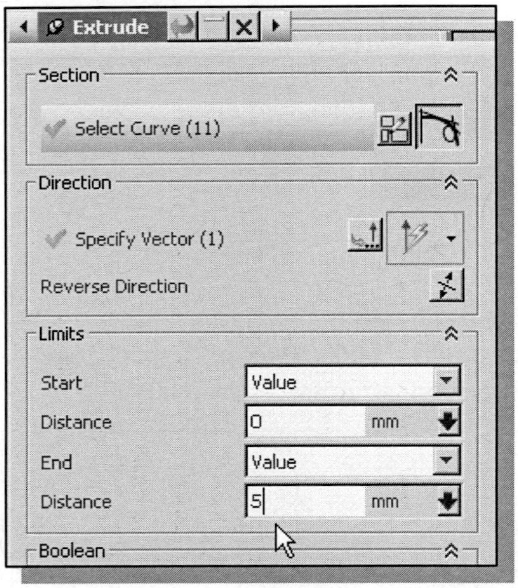

2. Enter **5** mm as the extrusion *Distance* as shown.

3. Click **OK** to create the extrusion feature.

❖ Note that all the sketched geometric entities and dimensions are consumed and have disappeared from the screen after the feature is created.

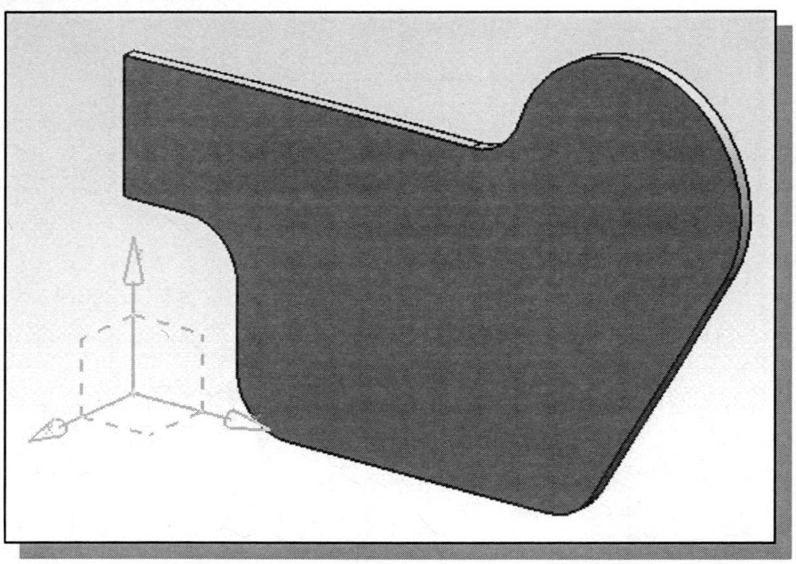

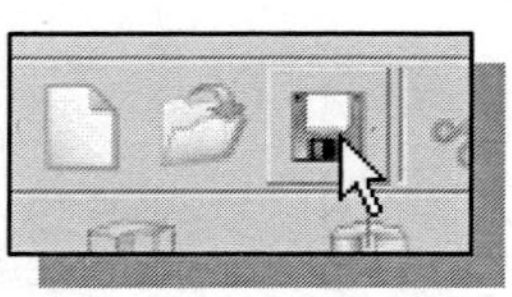

4. Click **Save** to save the *Gasket* design.

❖ The above procedure illustrated the *trim/extend* approach to create the design. We will next look at the *haystacking* approach to create the same design.

Second Construction Method – Haystacking Geometry

Haystacking is a grouping mechanism that allows us to select only the wireframe entities that we wish to include in the section. *Haystacking* is a tool that helps maintain design intent by reducing the amount of trimming necessary to build a section. Note that in *UGS NX*, the *haystacking* approach is done through the selection option.

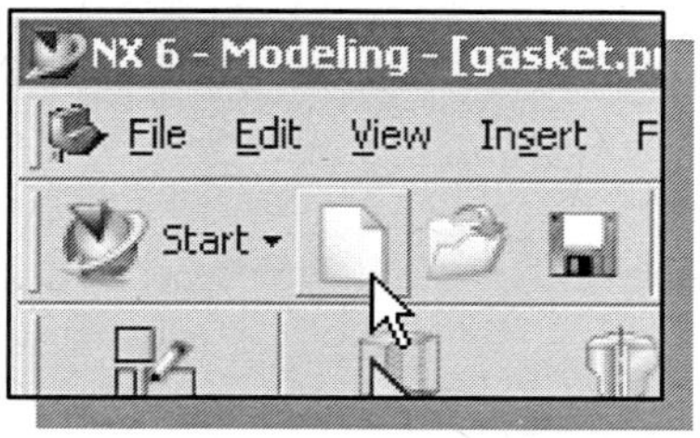

1. Select the **New** icon with a single click of the left-mouse-button (MB1) in the *Standard* toolbar area.

2. Confirm the **Millimeters** units are set as shown in the figure below.

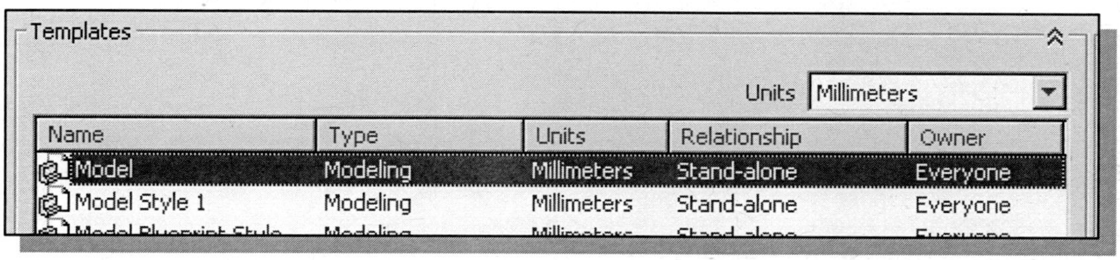

3. Select **Model** in the *Templates* list. Note that the *Model* template will allow us to switch directly into the *Modeling* task as indicated in the *Templates* list.

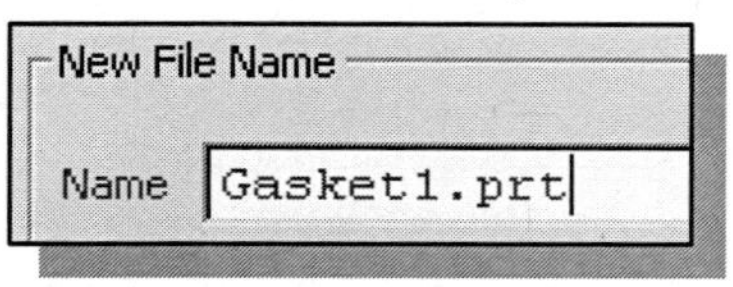

4. In the *New Part File* window, enter **Gasket1** as the file *Name.*

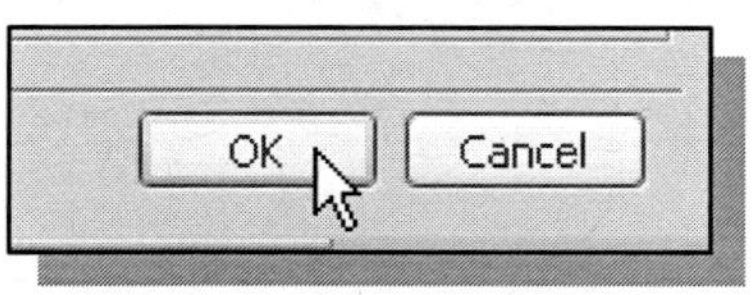

5. Click **OK** to proceed with the **New Part File** command.

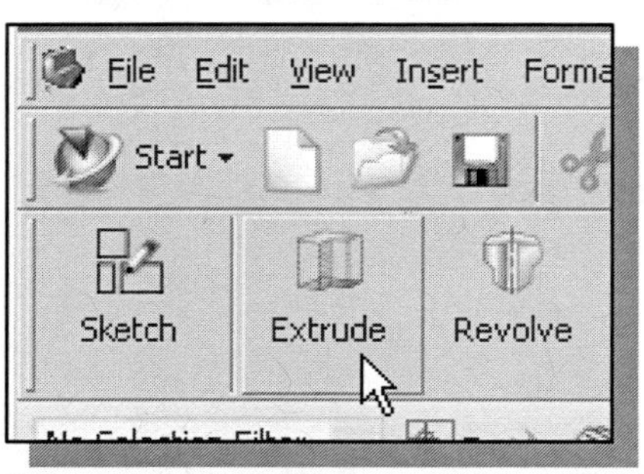

6. In the *Form Feature* toolbars (toolbars aligned to the right edge of the main window), click the **Extrude** button as shown.

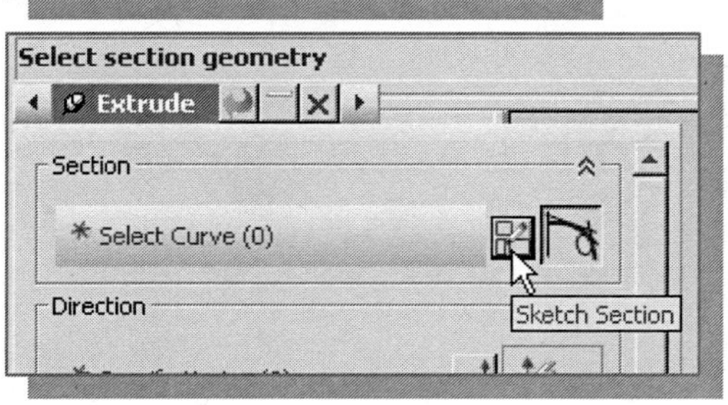

7. Click the **Sketch Section** button to begin creating a new *2D sketch.*

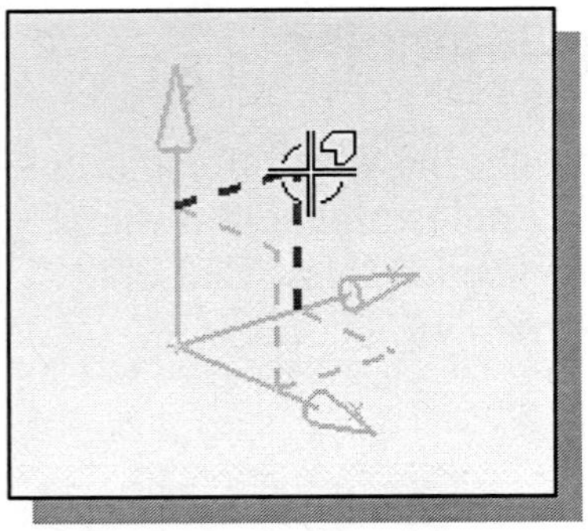

8. Select the ***XC-YC* plane** of the established datum coordinate system as the *sketch plane* of the *base feature.*

9. Click **OK** to accept the selection of the *sketch plane*.

10. Create a sketch using the steps shown in the figures below. Start the sketch from the top right corner. Place the circle at the right-endpoint of the top horizontal line and apply the proper constraints to the inclined line.

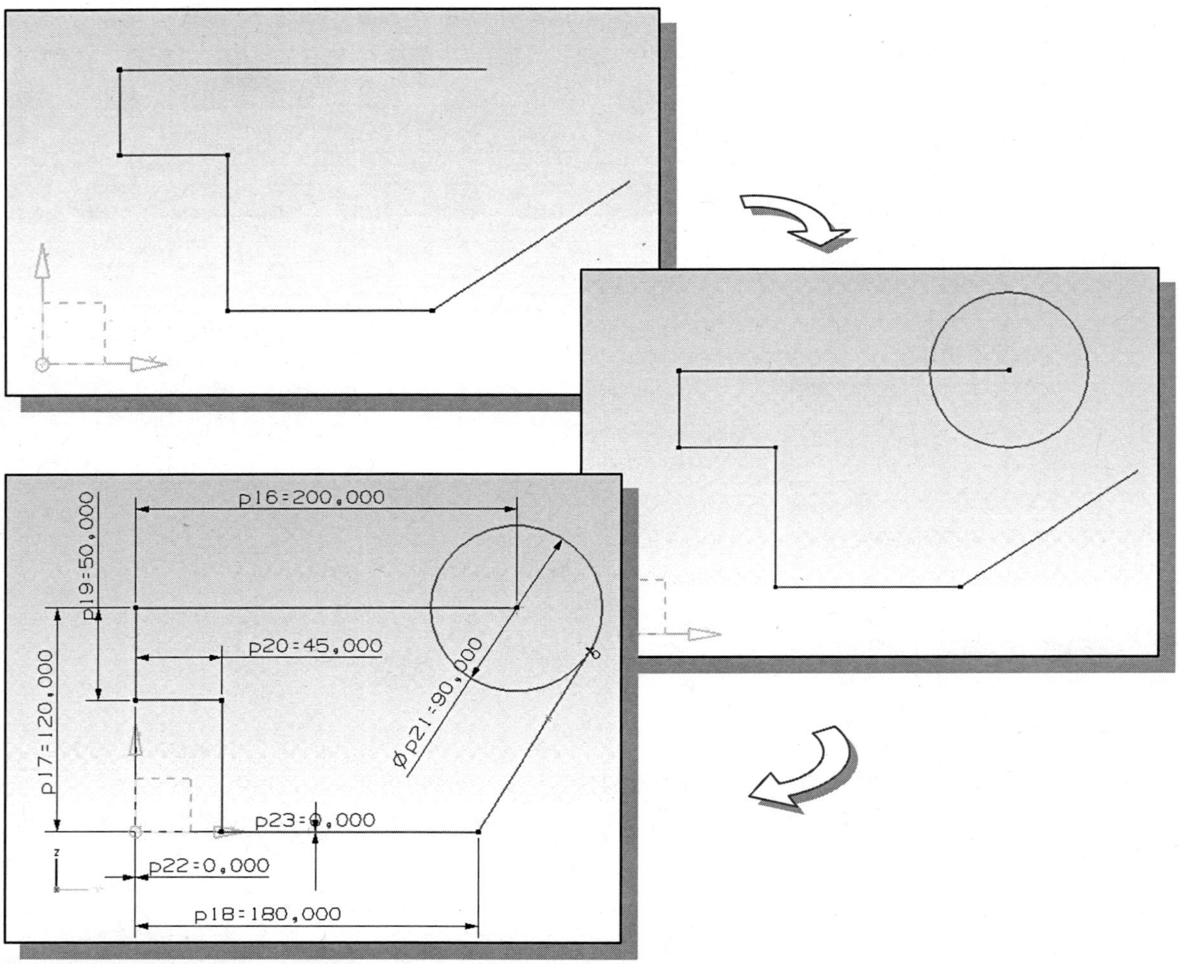

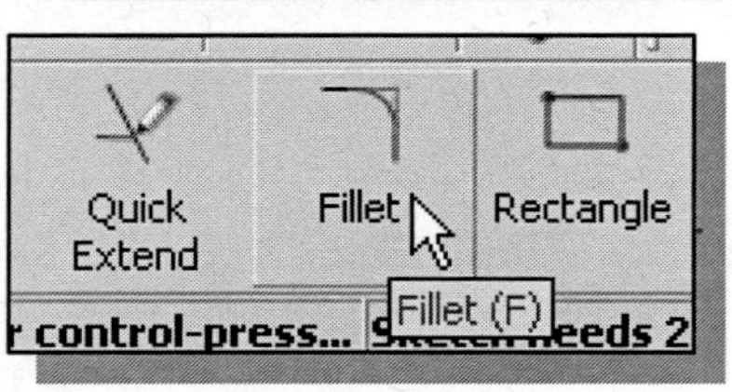

11. Select the **Fillet** command by clicking once with the left-mouse-button (MB1) on the icon in the *Sketch Curve* toolbar.

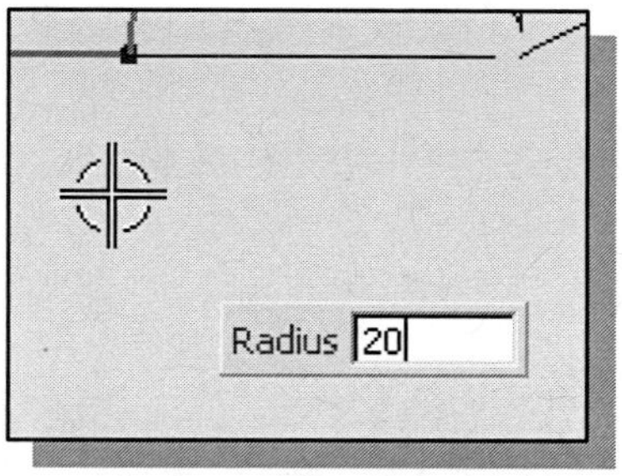

12. Enter **20** as the new radius of the fillet.

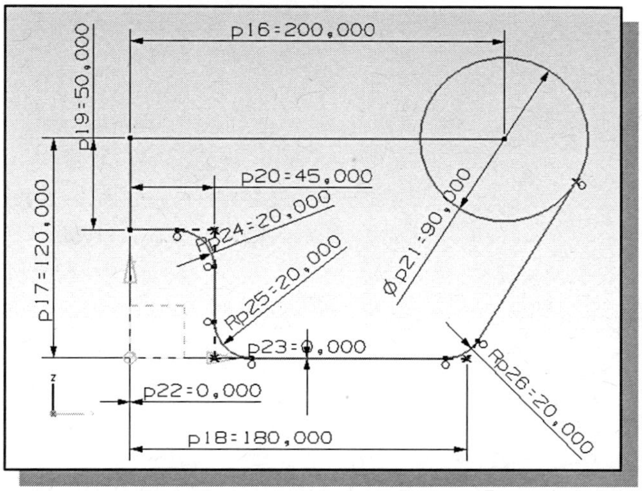

13. On your own, create the three additional fillets as shown in the figure. Note that the same radius value is used on all rounds and fillets. Also note that all of the rounds and fillets are created with the proper constraints.

14. Complete the sketch by adding a circle tangent to both the large circle and the top horizontal line as shown.

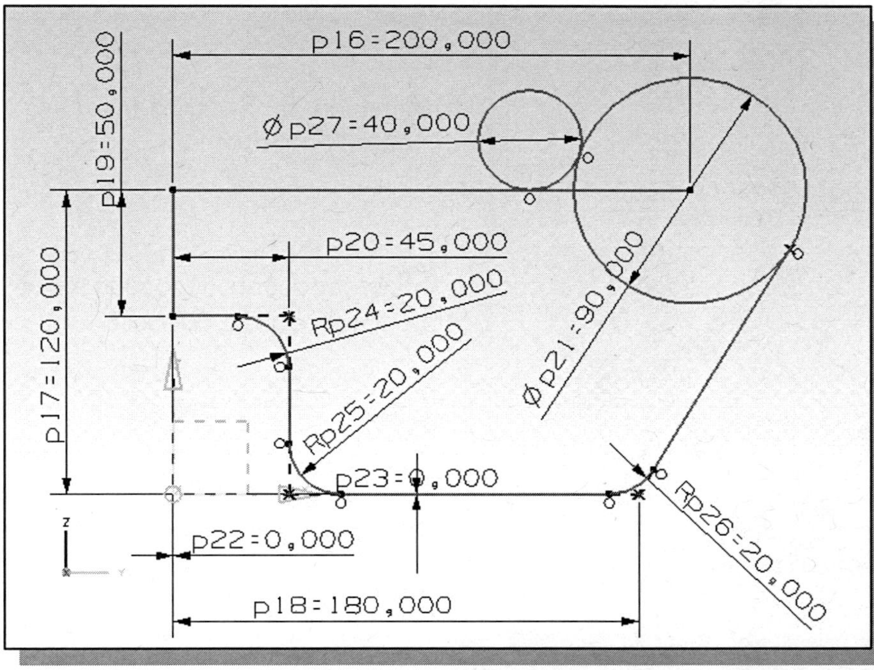

❖ On your own, examine the constraints and confirm the 2D sketch is fully constrained.

Using the *UGS NX* Selection Intent option

❖ To complete the extrusion, we will select only the segments we need by using the selection option.

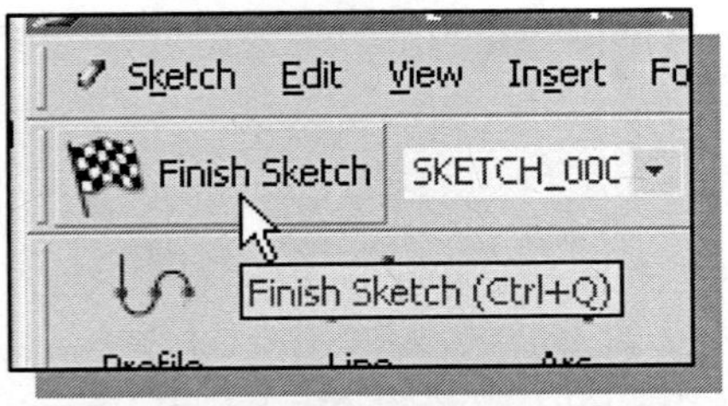

1. Click **Finish Sketch** to exit the *NX Sketcher* mode and return to the *Feature* option dialog window.

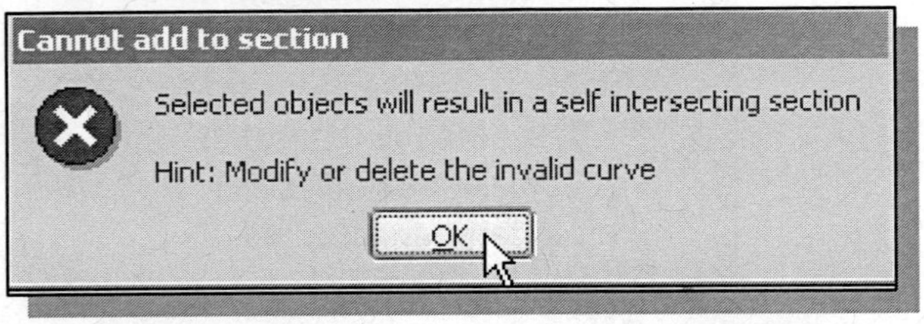

❖ An error message is displayed on the screen indicating the **Auto-Select** option found more than one loop for the section.

2. Click **OK** to continue.

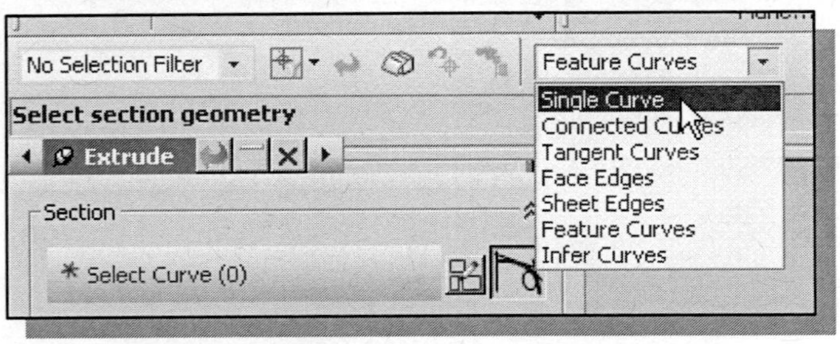

3. In the *Selection Filter* option area, select **Single Curve** option as shown.

4. Click on the **Stop at Intersection** button as shown.

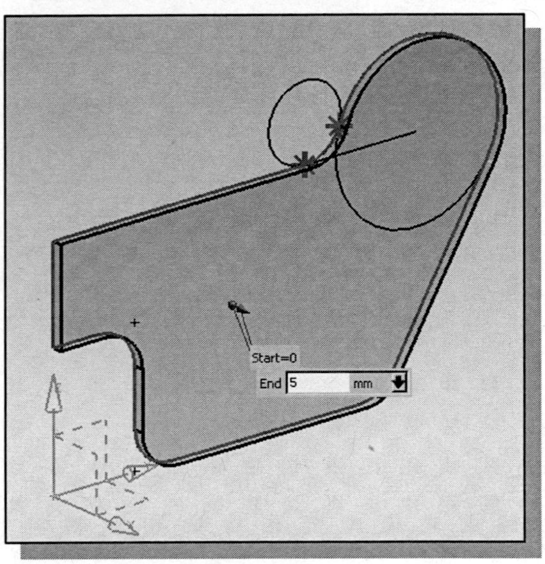

5. Select the segments, one at a time, to form the outline of the *Gasket* design.

6. In the *Extrude* popup window, confirm the *Extrude* option is set to **Create**.

7. Enter **5** mm as the extrusion *Distance* as shown.

8. Click **OK** to create the extrusion feature.

❖ Note the haystacking approach is a very flexible and fast method to create 2D sections.

Create an Associative OFFSET Subtract Feature

➢ To complete the design, we will create a cutout feature by using the **Offset Curve** command. In order to make the *offset curve* associative to the existing solid model, we will first create a projected sketch.

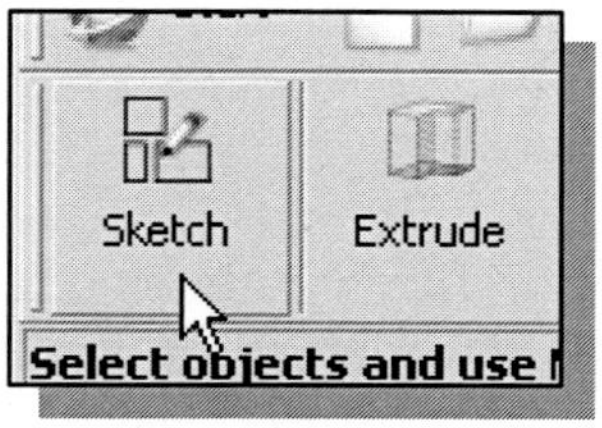

1. In the *Form Feature* toolbar select the **Sketch** command by left-clicking once on the icon.

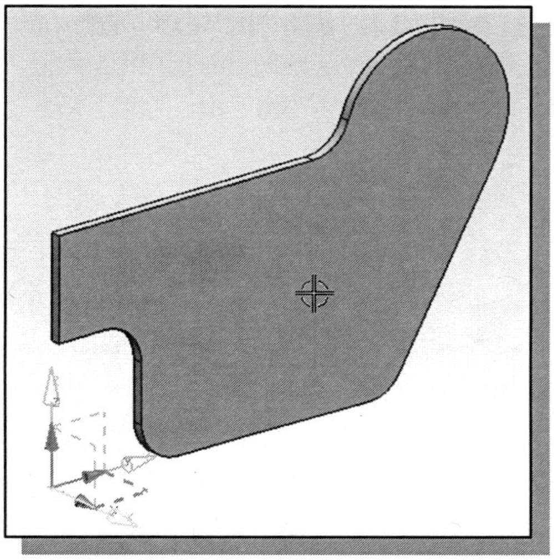

2. Select the front face of the 3D model in the graphics window.

3. Click **OK** to accept the new setting of the *sketch plane*.

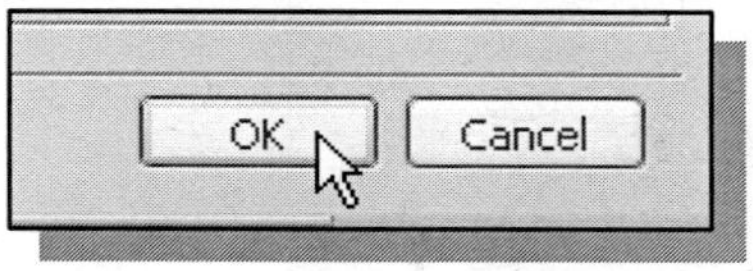

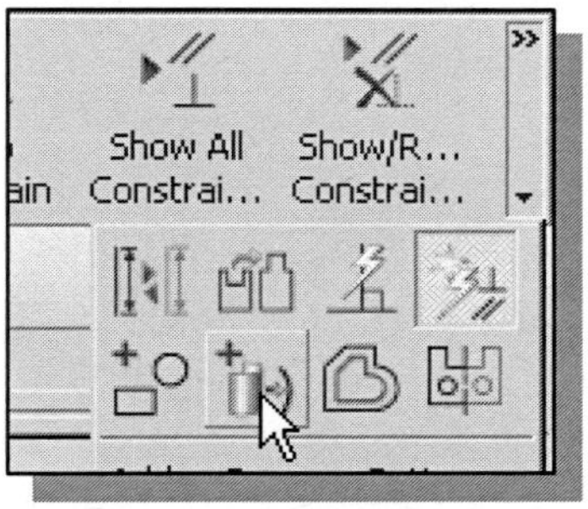

4. Select the **Project Curve** command by clicking once with the left-mouse-button on the icon in the *Sketch* toolbar. (Click on the little triangle icon to the right to display additional icons, if the *project curve* icon is not visible on the screen.)

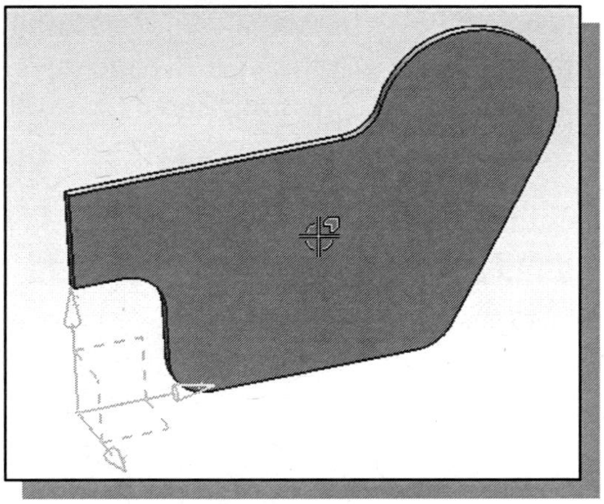

5. Select the front face of the 3D model. *UGS NX* will automatically select the connecting edges of the selected surface.

6. Click **OK** to accept the selection.

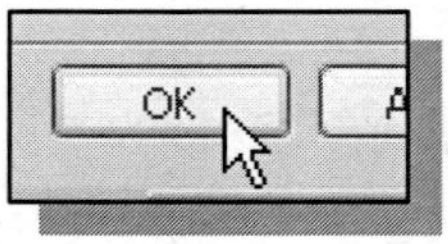

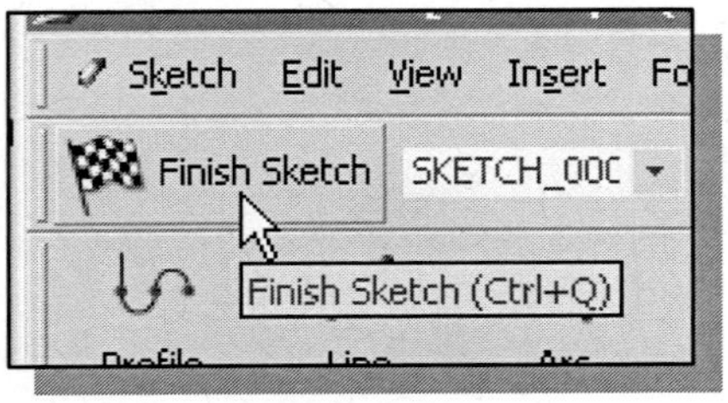

7. Click **Finish Sketch** to exit the *NX Sketcher* mode and return to the *Modeling* window.

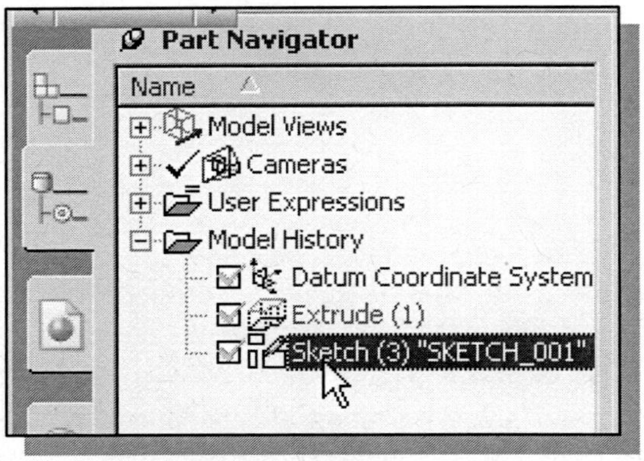

8. Switch on the *Part Navigator* by clicking on the navigator in the *Resource Bars* area.

9. Click on the last item in the *Model History*, *SKETCH_001*, and notice the highlighted curve in the graphics area.

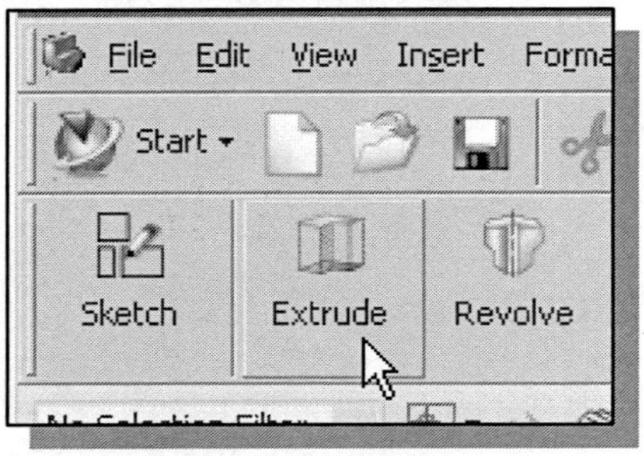

10. In the *Form Feature* toolbars, select the **Extrude** icon as shown.

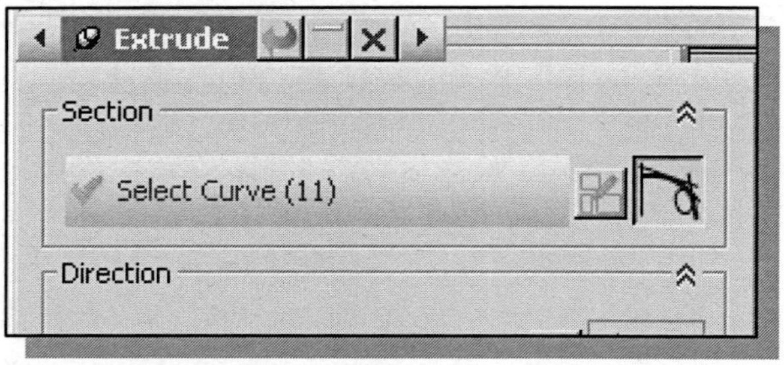

11. Confirm the pre-selected curves are highlighted and the message ***Select Curve (11)*** is displayed as shown.

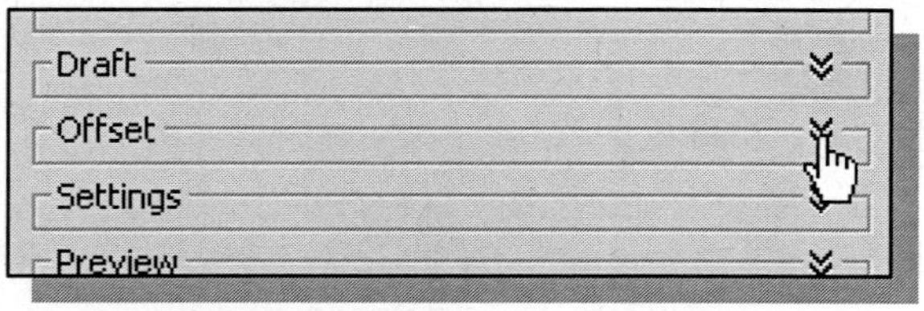

12. Click on the downward arrowhead next to the **Offset** option as shown.

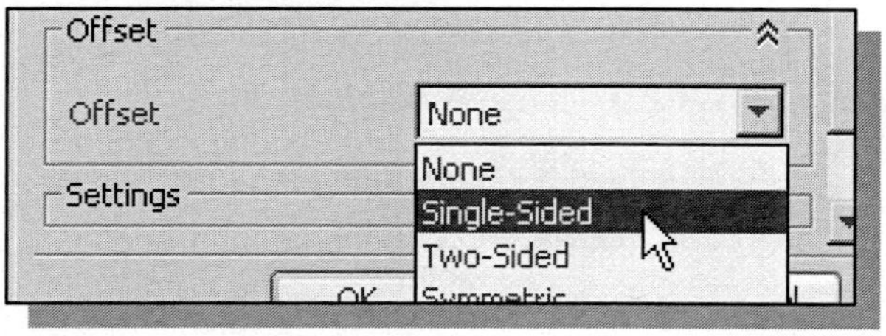

13. Choose **Single-Sided** as the offset option as shown.

14. Enter **-15** mm in the offset distance input box as shown. (The negative value indicates the offset is toward the inside of the sketch.)

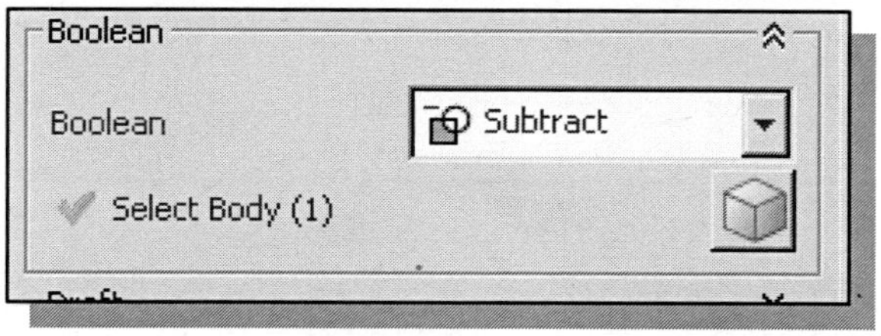

15. Set the *Boolean* option to **Subtract** as shown.

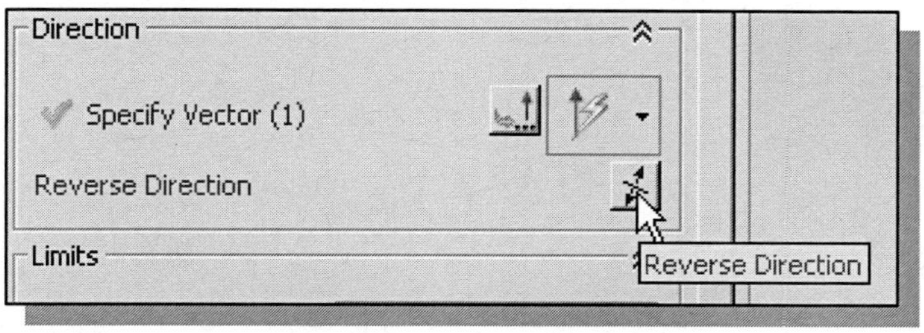

16. Confirm the extrusion will be cutting through the existing solid; hit the Reverse Direction button if necessary.

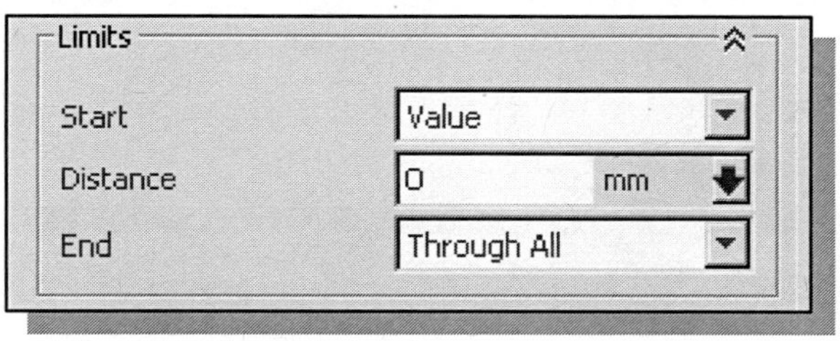

17. In the *Extrude* dialog box, set the termination *End Limit* to the **Through All** option.

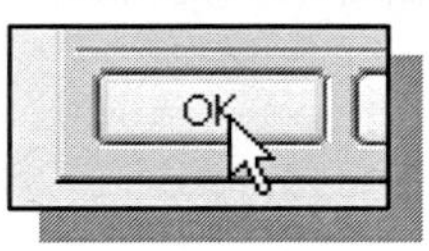

18. Click on the **OK** button to accept the settings and complete the design.

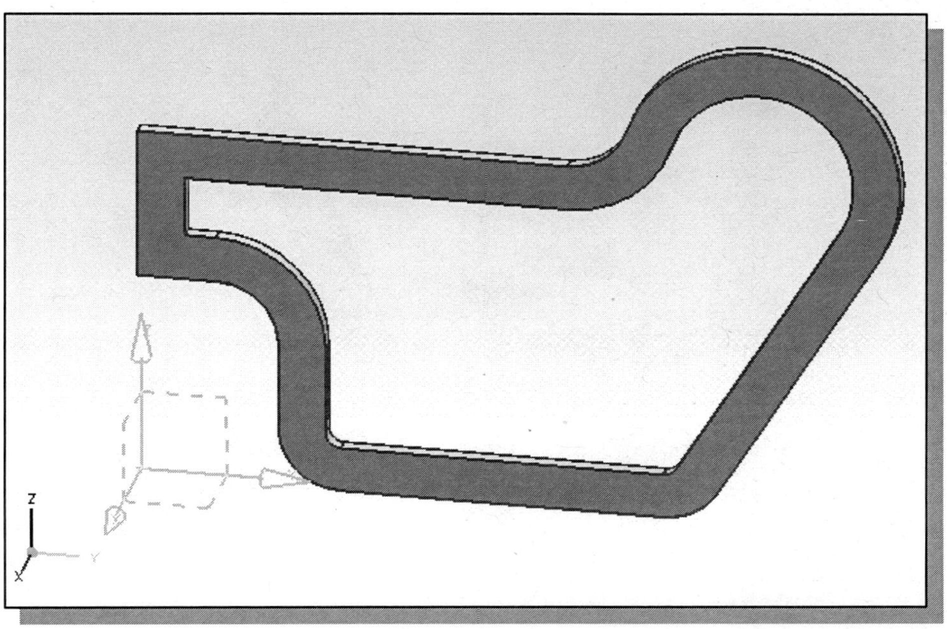

➢ The offset geometry is associated with the original geometry. On your own, adjust the overall height of the design to **150 millimeters** and confirm that the entire model, including the offset geometry, is adjusted accordingly.

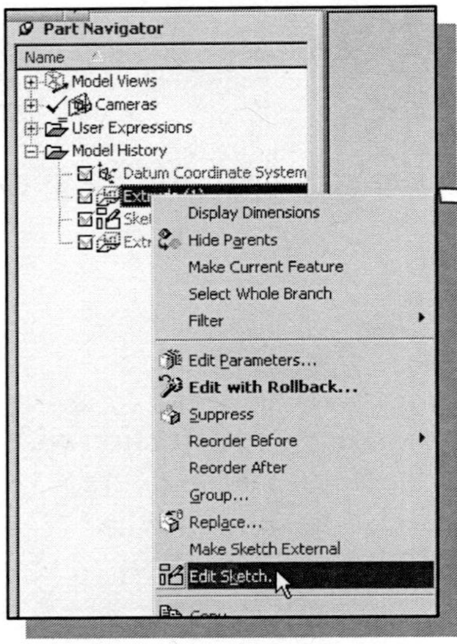

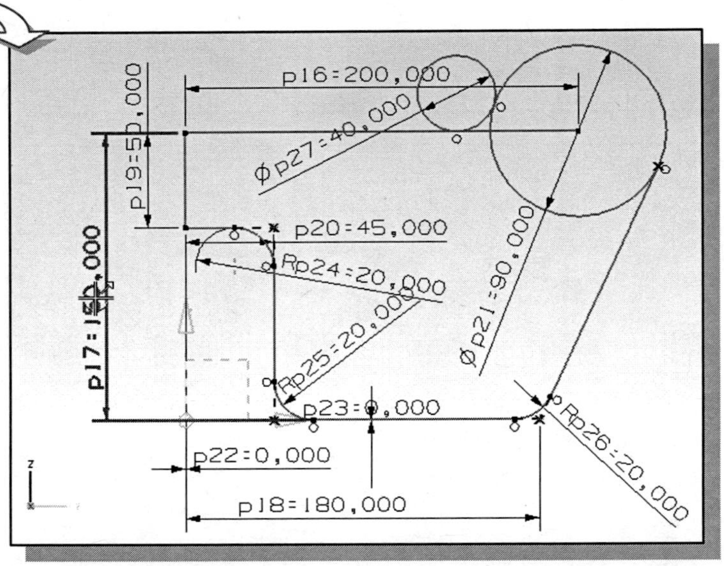

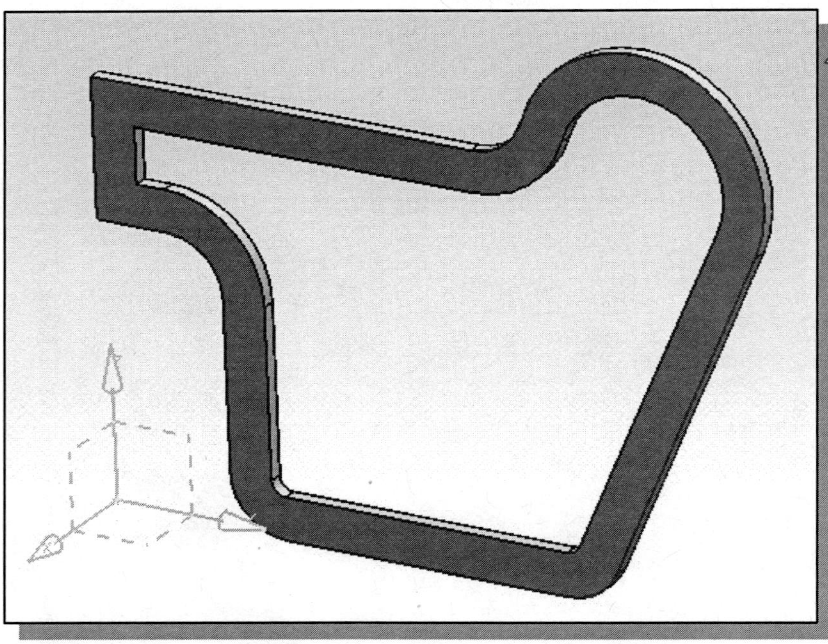

Questions:

1. What are the two types of wireframe geometry available in *UGS NX*?
2. Can we create a section with extra 2D geometry entities?
3. How do we access the *UGS NX's* **Edit Sketch** option?
4. How do we create a *haystacking section* in *UGS NX*?
5. Can we build a section that consists of self-intersecting curves?
6. Describe the general procedure to create an associative *offset curve*.
7. Can we remove a portion of an existing 2D curve? How is this done?
8. What is the main advantage of using the *haystacking section* approach?
9. Create sketches showing the steps you plan to use to create the model shown on the next page:

Exercises:

1. Dimensions are in inches. Plate Thickness: 0.25

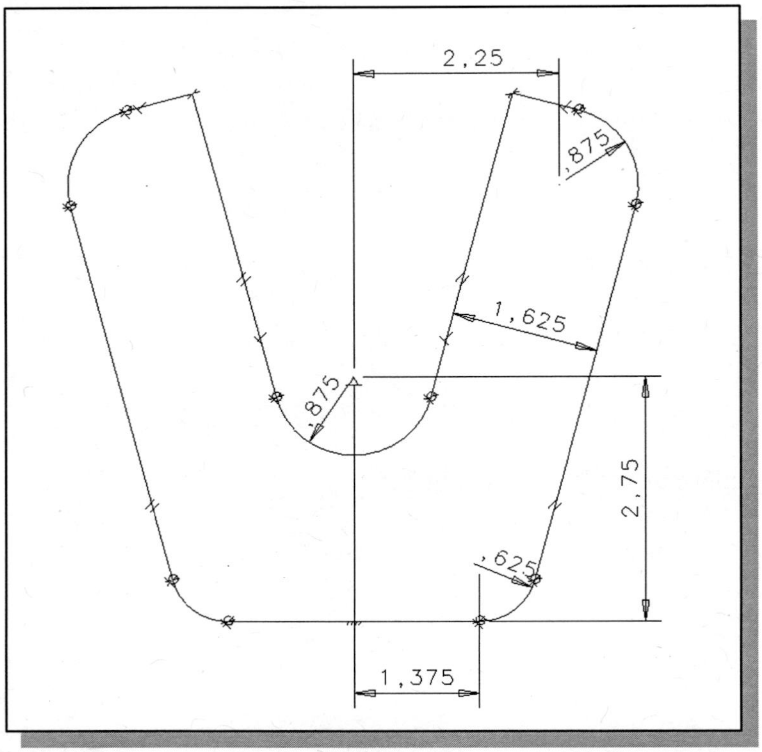

2. Dimensions are in millimeters.

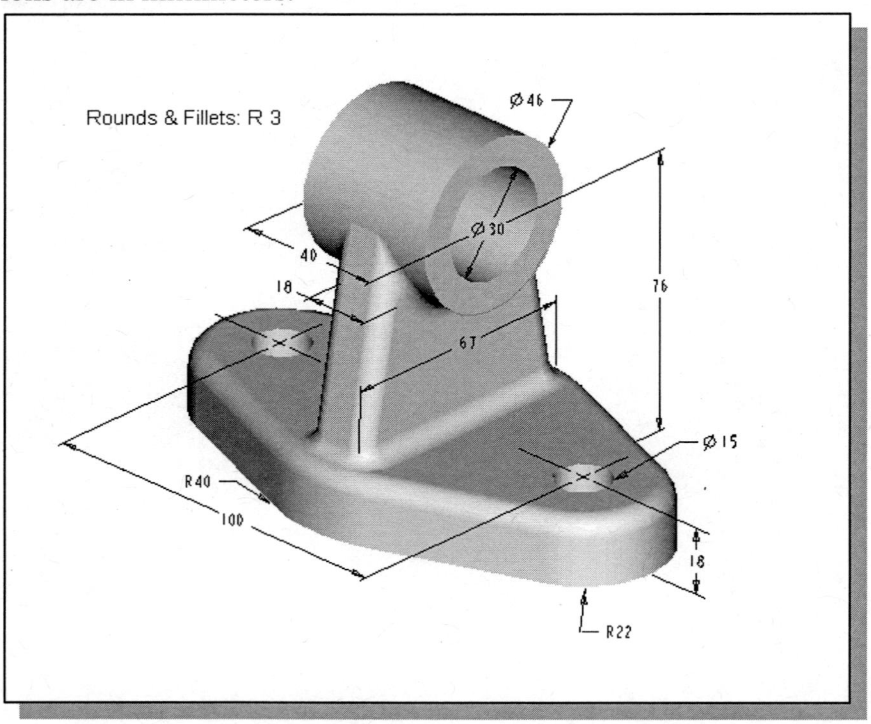

3. Dimensions are in inches.

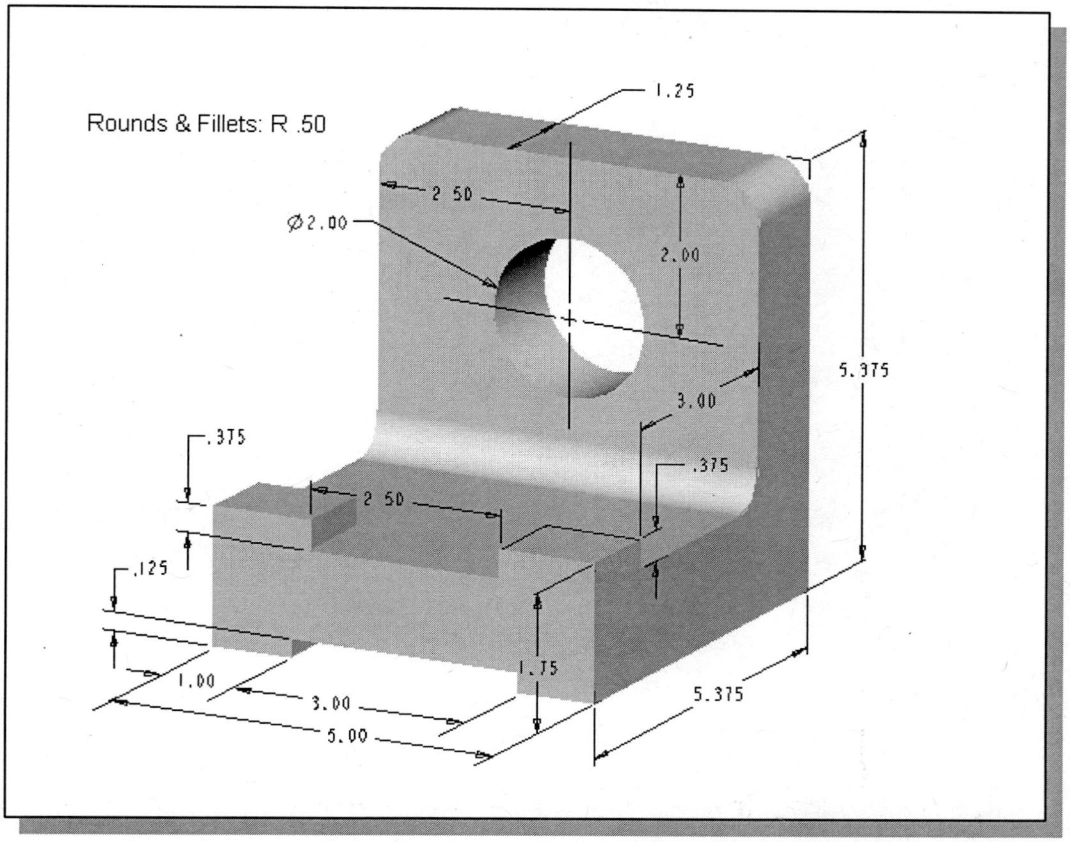

Notes:

Chapter 7
Parent/Child Relationships

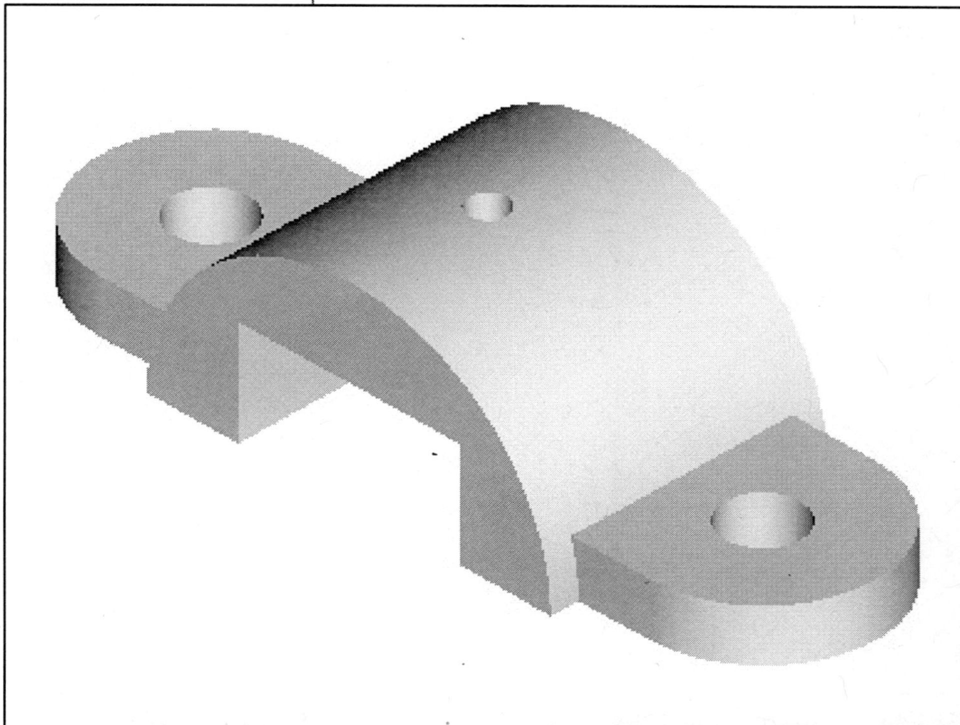

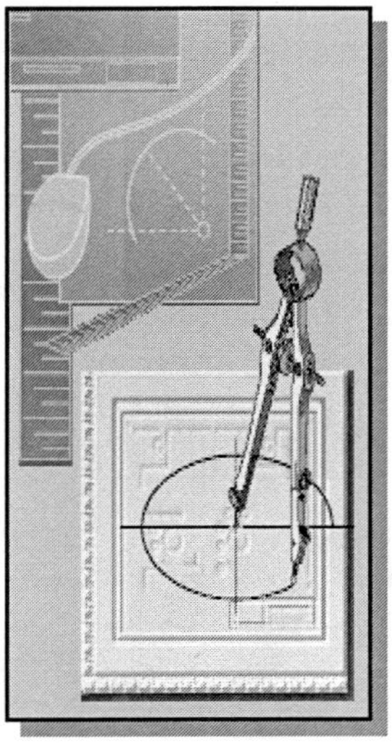

Learning Objectives

- Understand the Importance of Parent/Child Relations in Features
- Use the Suppress Feature Option
- Resolve Undesired Feature Interactions
- Apply the BORN Technique to create Flexible Designs

Introduction

The parent/child relationship is one of the most powerful aspects of ***parametric modeling***. In *UGS NX*, each time a new modeling event is created previously defined features can be used to define information such as size, location, and orientation. The referenced features become **PARENT** features to the new feature, and the new feature is called the **CHILD** feature. The parent/child relationships determine how a model reacts when other features in the model change, thus capturing design intent. It is crucial to keep track of these parent/child relations. Any modification to a parent feature can change one or more of its children.

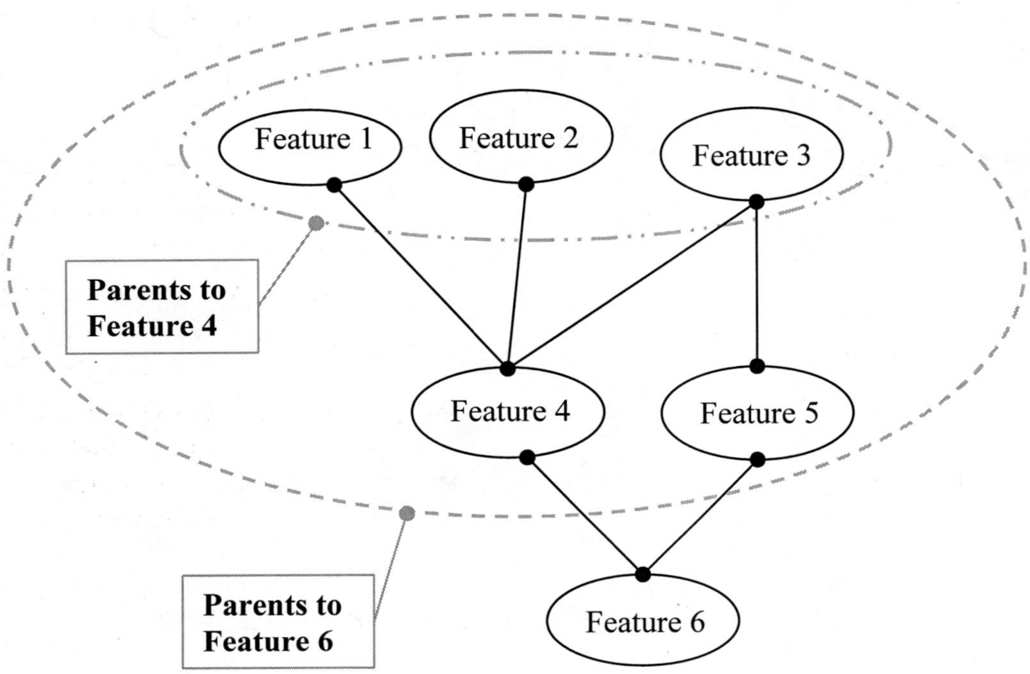

Parent/child relationships can be created *implicitly* or *explicitly*; implicit relationships are implied by the feature creation method and explicit relationships are entered manually by the user. In the previous chapters, we first select a sketching plane before creating a 2D profile. The selected surface becomes the parent of the new feature. If the sketching plane is moved, the child feature will move with it. As one might expect, parent/child relationships can become quite complicated when the features begin to accumulate. It is therefore important to think about modeling strategy before we start to create anything. The main consideration is to try to plan ahead for possible design changes that might occur which would be affected by the existing parent/child relationships. Parametric modeling software, such as *UGS NX*, also allows us to adjust feature properties so that any feature conflicts can be quickly resolved. In this chapter, we will concentrate the discussion on parent/child relationships and also look at some of the tools that are available to handle design changes quickly and effectively.

The *U-Bracket* Design

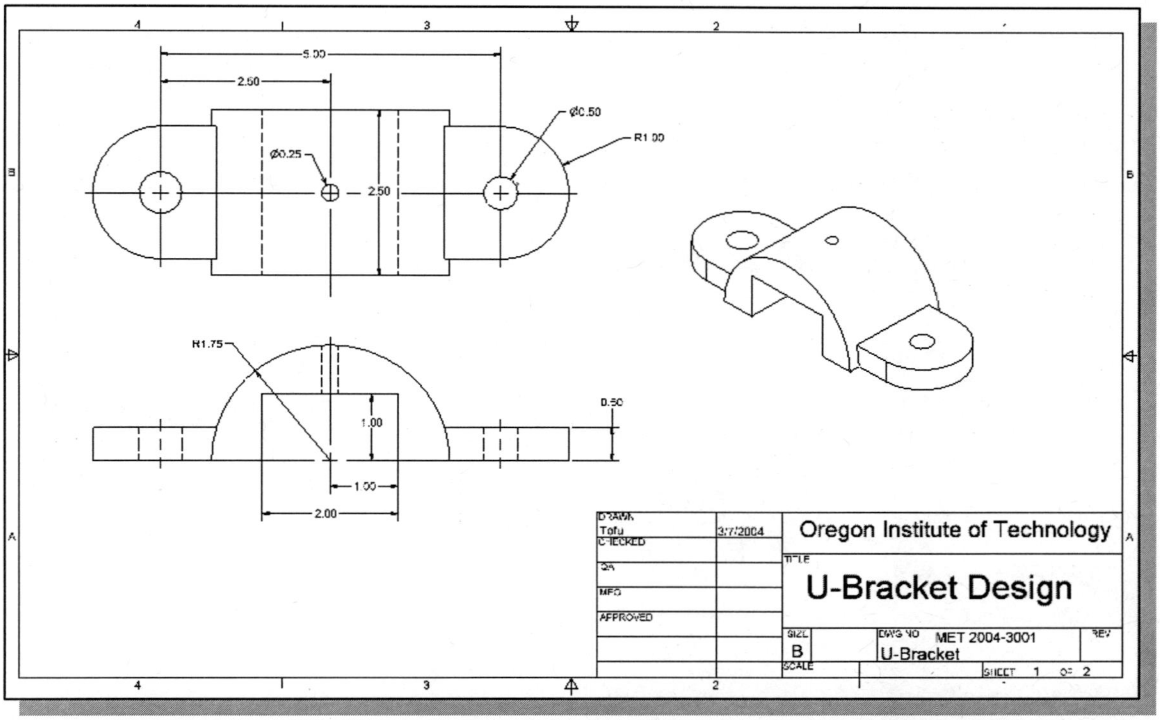

➢ Based on your knowledge of *UGS NX* so far, how many features would you use to create the model? Which feature would you choose as the **base feature**? What is your choice for arranging the order of the features? Would you organize the features differently if the rectangular cutout at the center is changed to a circular shape?

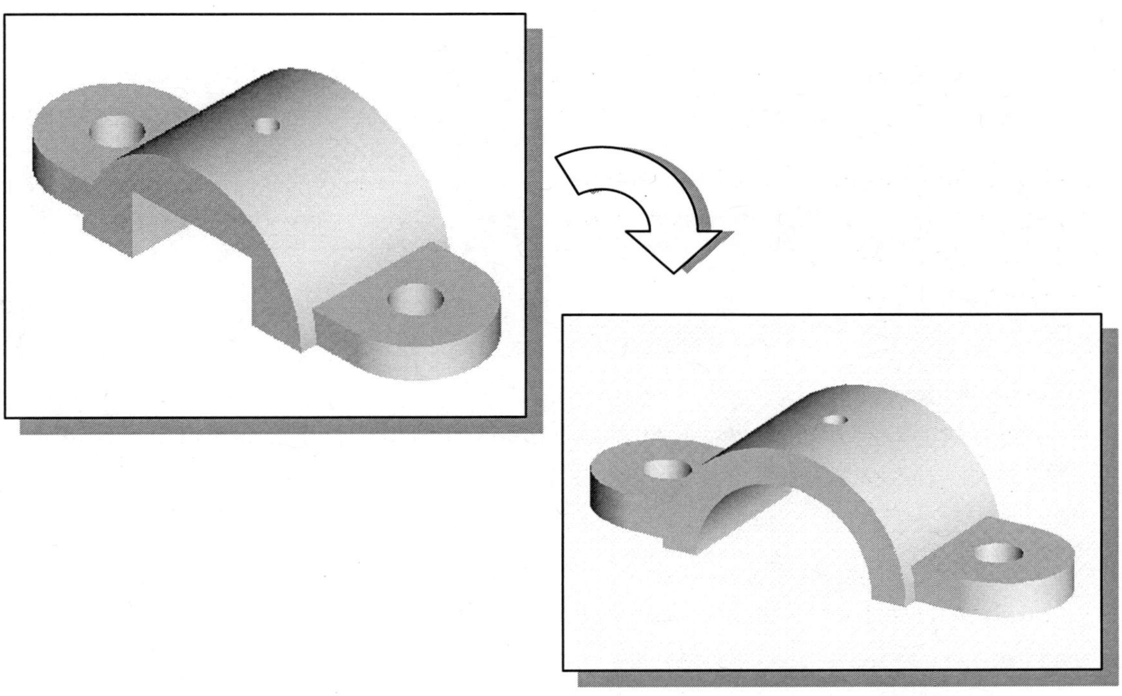

Creating the Base Feature

1. Select the **UGS NX** option on the *Start* menu or select the **UGS NX** icon on the desktop to start *UGS NX*. The *UGS NX* main window will appear on the screen.

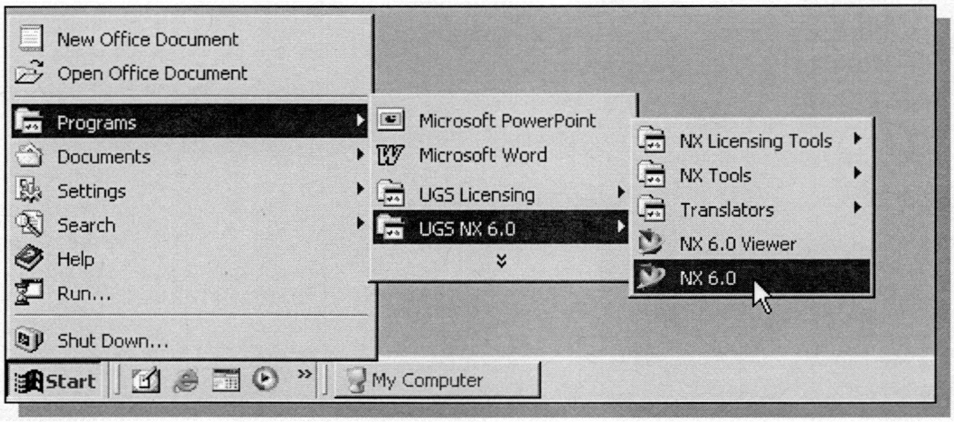

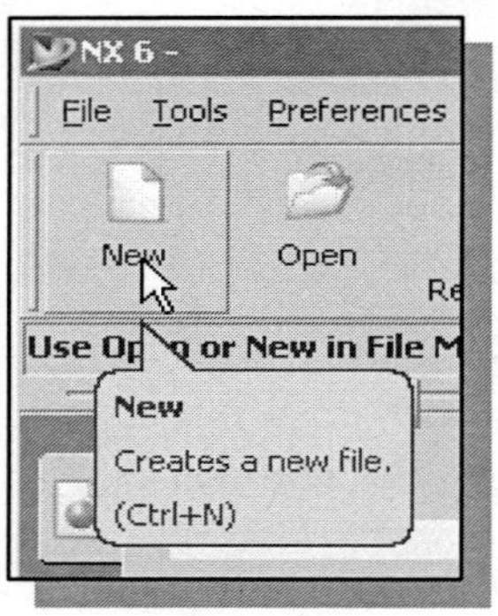

2. Select the **New** icon with a single click of the left-mouse-button (MB1) in the *Standard* toolbar area.

3. Select the **Inches** units as shown in the figure below.

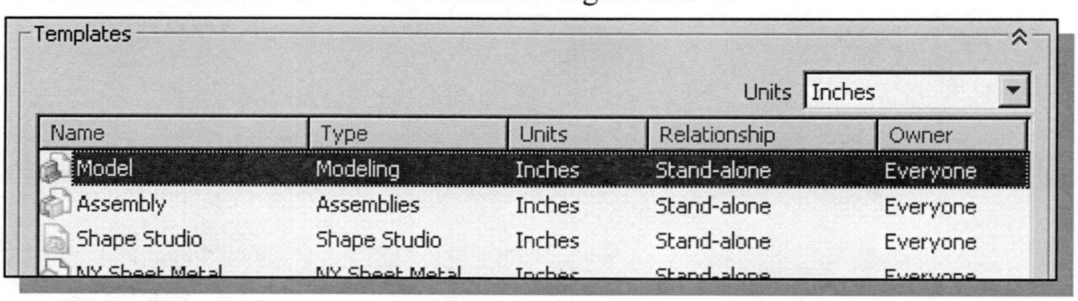

4. Select **Model** in the *Templates* list. Note that the *Model* template will allow us to switch directly into the *Modeling* task as indicated in the *Templates* list.

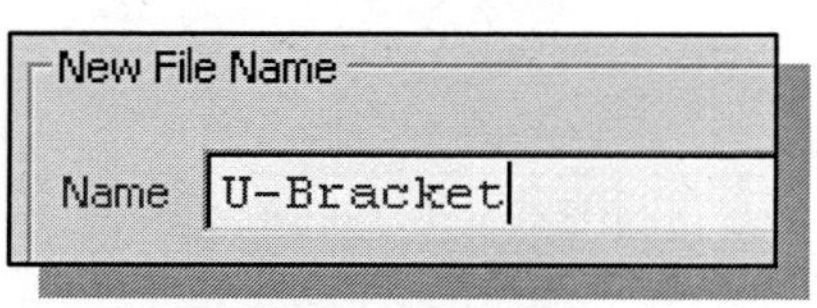

5. In the *New File Name* section, enter **U-Bracket** as the file *Name*.

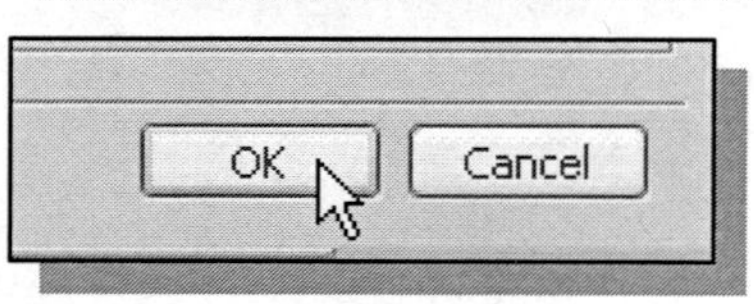

6. Click **OK** to proceed with the New File command.

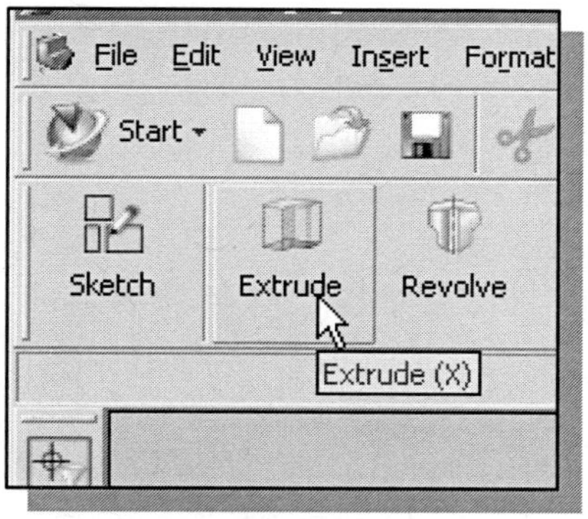

7. In the *Form Feature* toolbars (toolbars aligned to the right edge of the main window), select the **Extrude** icon as shown.

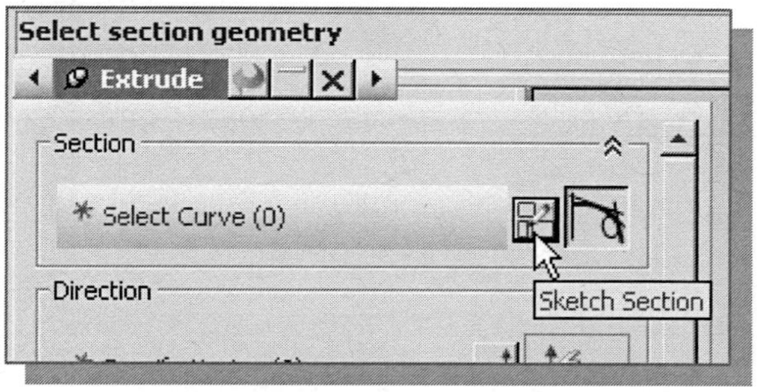

8. Click the **Sketch Section** button to begin creating a new *2D sketch.*

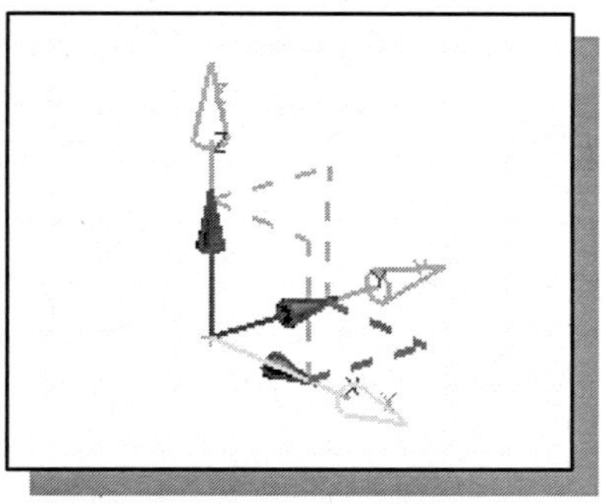

➢ Note that the ***X-Y*** plane is the pre-selected as the default sketch plane.

9. Click **OK** to accept the default setting of the *sketch plane.*

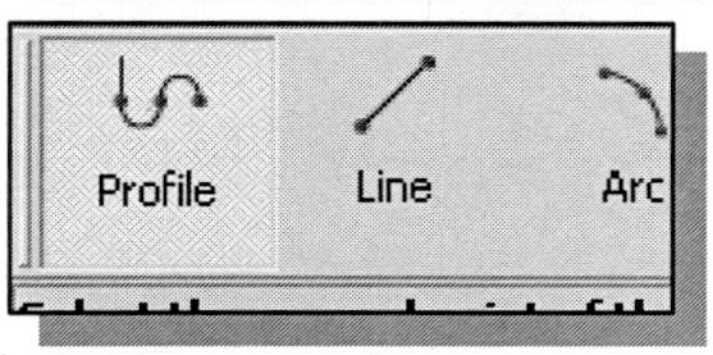

❖ Note that we can create both lines and arcs with the default **Profile** command.

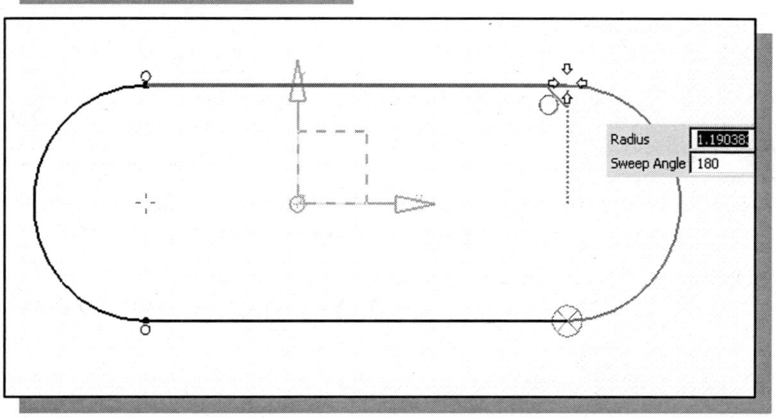

10. On your own, create the 2D sketch with two horizontal lines and two tangent arcs as shown. (Hint: Drag the MB1 to switch to the **Arc** option while sketching.)

11. Click twice with the middle-mouse-button (MB2) to end the **Profile** command.

12. On your own, create and adjust the dimensions as shown in the figure below.

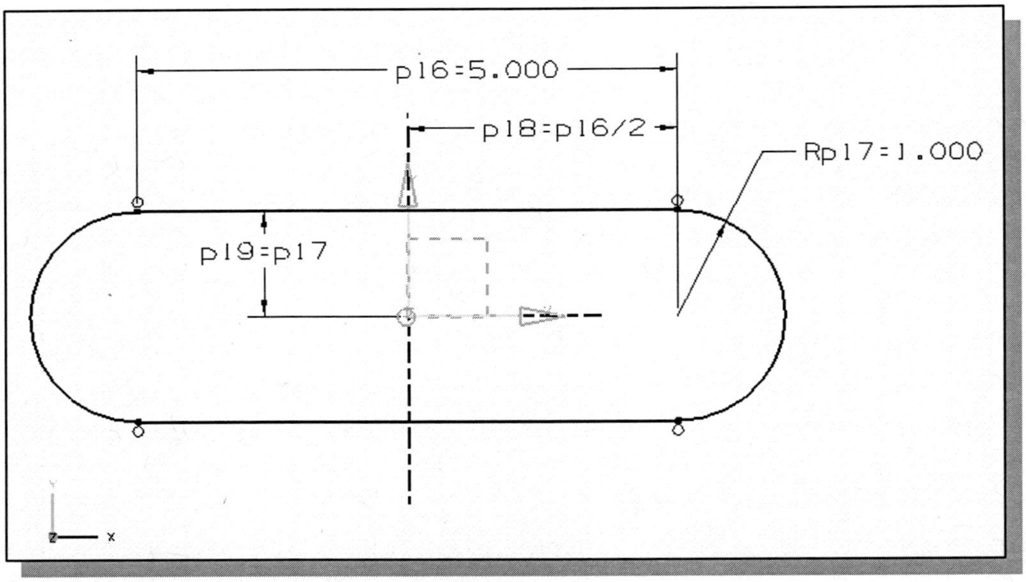

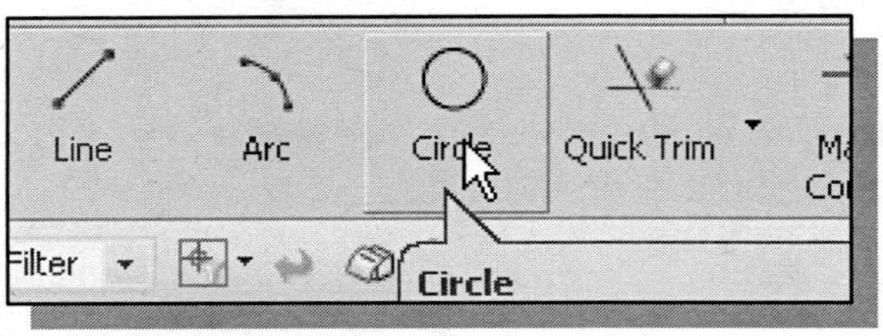

13. Select the **Circle** command by clicking once with the left-mouse-button (MB1) on the icon in the *Sketch Curve* toolbar.

14. Create two circles aligned to the centers of the two large arcs as shown.

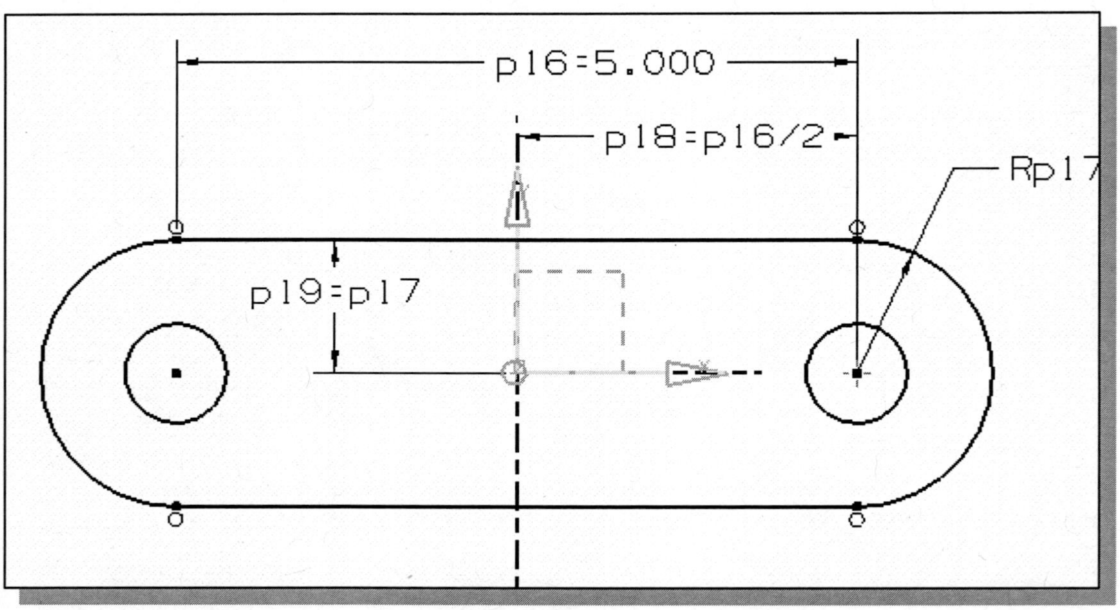

➢ How many more dimension/constraints are needed to make the sketch fully constrained?

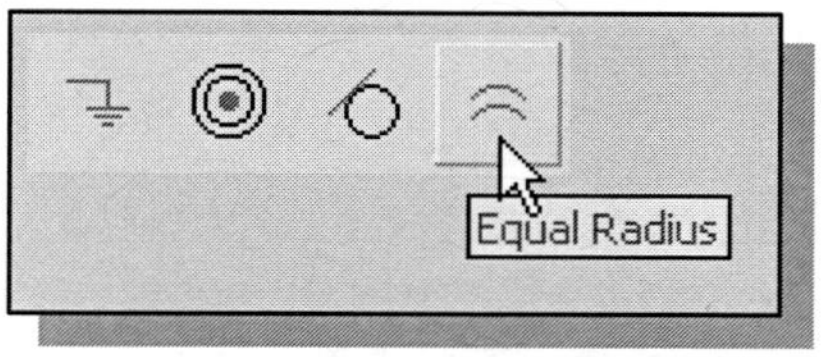

15. Create the necessary constraints and dimensions to make the sketch fully constrained as shown in the figure. (Hint: Try the **Equal Radius** constraint.)

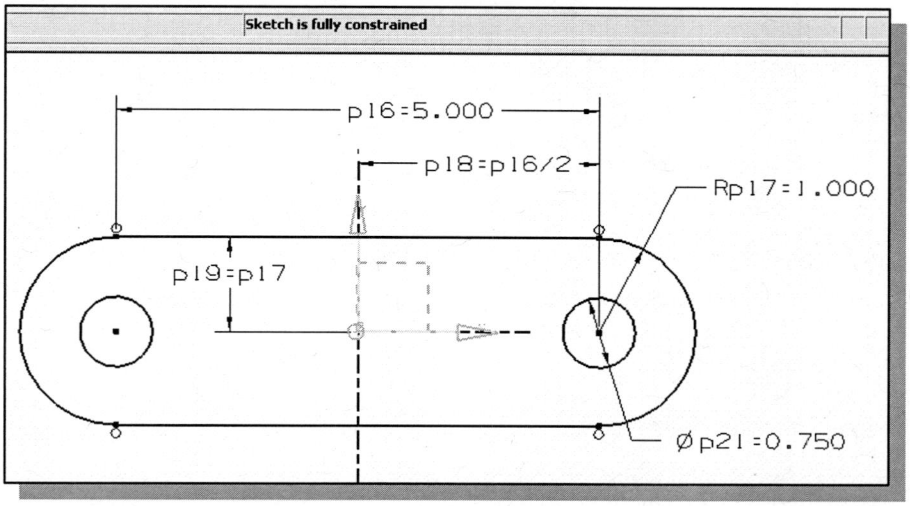

Complete the Base Feature

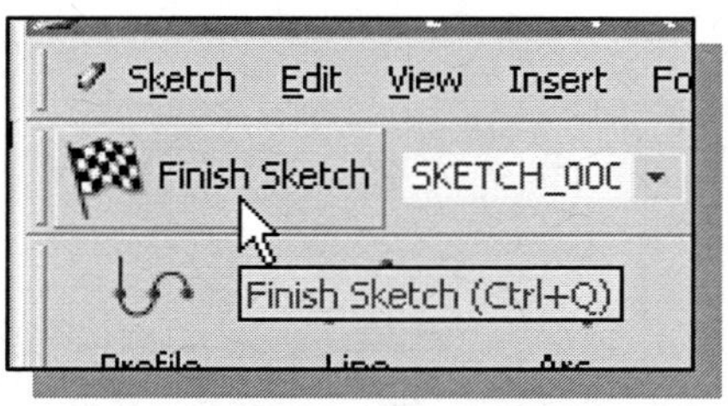

1. Click **Finish Sketch** to exit the *NX Sketcher* mode and return to the *Feature* option dialog window.

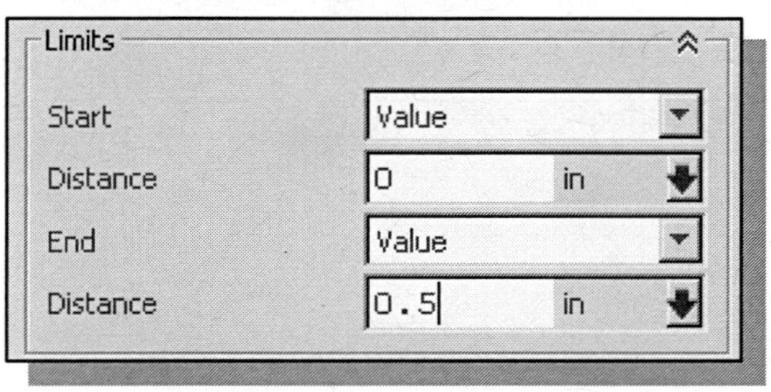

2. Enter **0.5** in as the extrusion *Distance* as shown.

3. Click **OK** to create the extrusion feature.

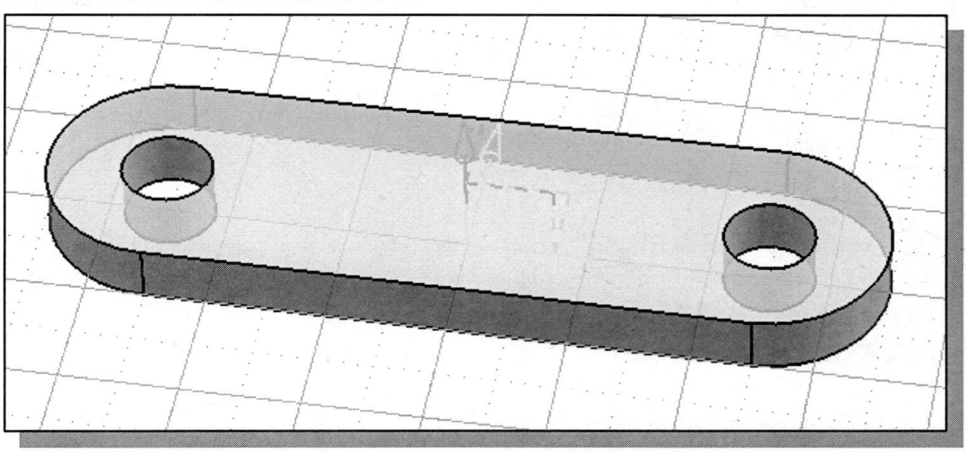

The Implied Parent/Child Relationships

- As we build solid features, *UGS NX* records the individual steps and the parent/child relationships. Currently, several parent/child relationships have been established implicitly: the *X-Y* plane was selected as the sketch plane and the *X* and *Y* axes were used as references to position the 2D sketch in the 3D environment.

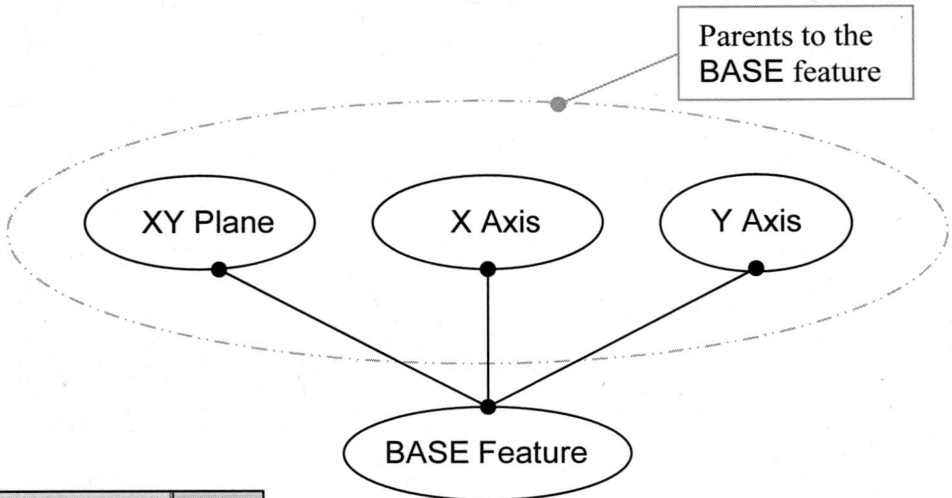

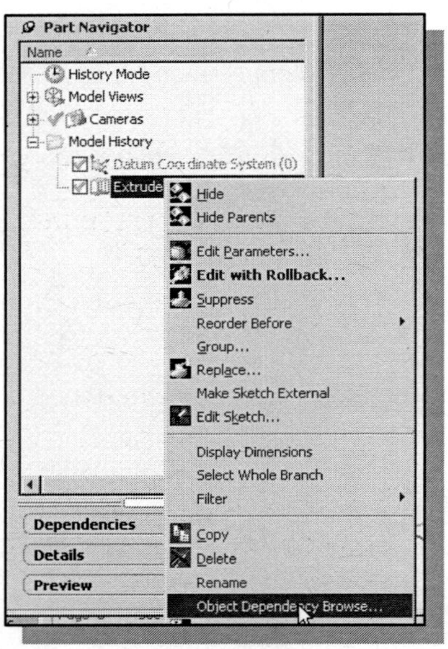

1. Open the *Part Navigator* and right-mouse-click (MB3) on the ***Extrude*** feature to bring up the option list.

2. Select the **Object Dependency Browser** option as shown.

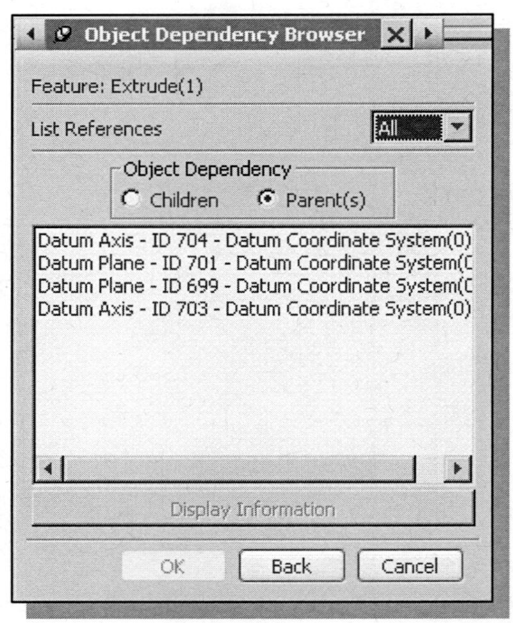

3. Select the **Parent(s)** option in the *Object Dependency Browser* window.

❖ Note the four items listed as the **parents feature** of the base feature (two datum planes and two datum axes) are just as expected.

Creating the Second Solid Feature

- For the next solid feature, we will create the top section of the design. Note that the center of the base feature is aligned to the *origin* of the established datum coordinate system. This was done intentionally so that additional solid features can be created referencing the same location. For the second solid feature, the *X-Z* plane will be used as the *sketch plane*.

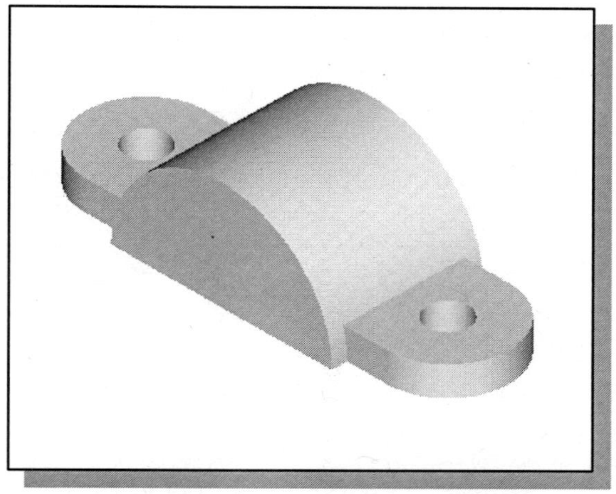

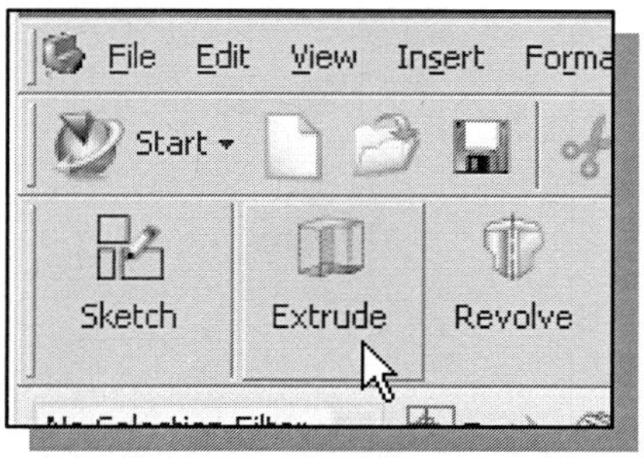

1. In the *Form Feature* toolbars select the **Extrude** icon as shown.

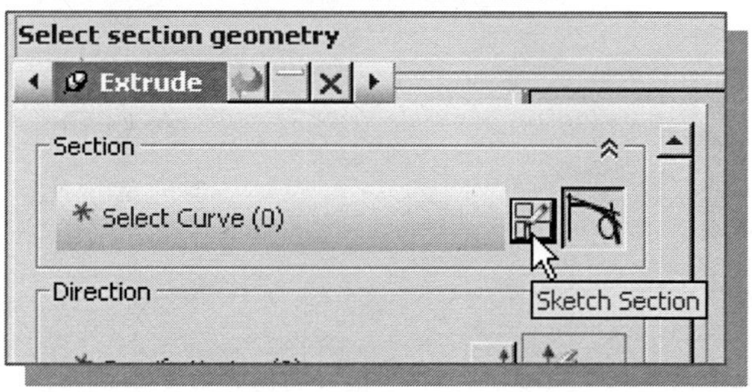

2. Click the **Sketch Section** button to begin creating a new *2D sketch.*

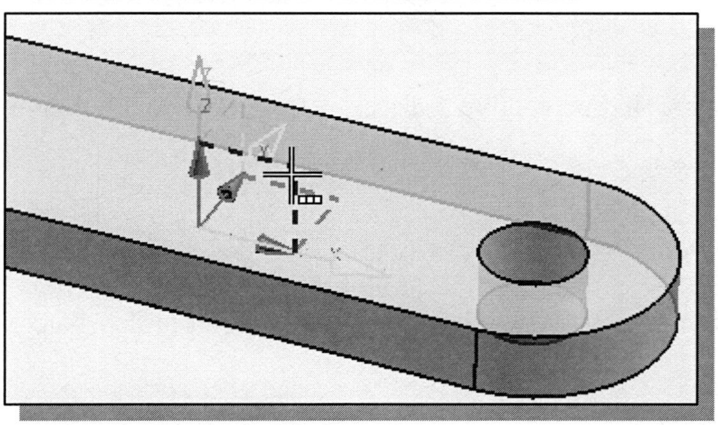

3. Select the ***Z-X*** plane of the datum coordinate system as the *sketch plane* of the second solid feature.

4. Click **OK** to accept the selection of the *sketch plane*.

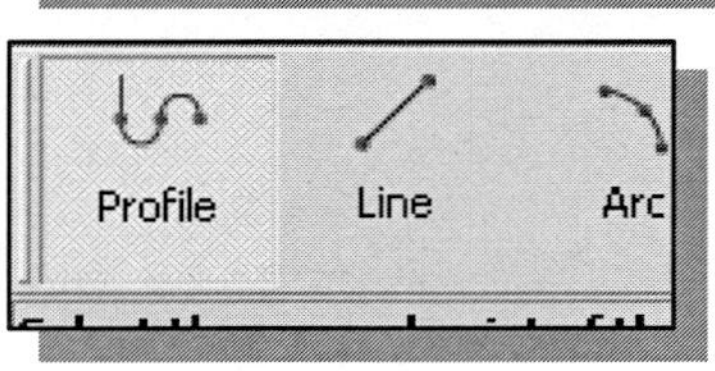

❖ Note that we can create both lines and arcs with the **Profile** command.

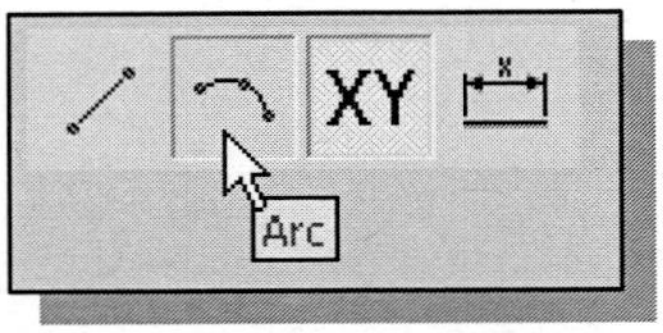

5. Activate the **Arc** option by clicking the icon in the option list near the upper left corner of the screen.

6. Click on the bottom edge of the base feature as shown in the figure below. Select the 1st point on curve option in the *QuickPick* window if necessary.

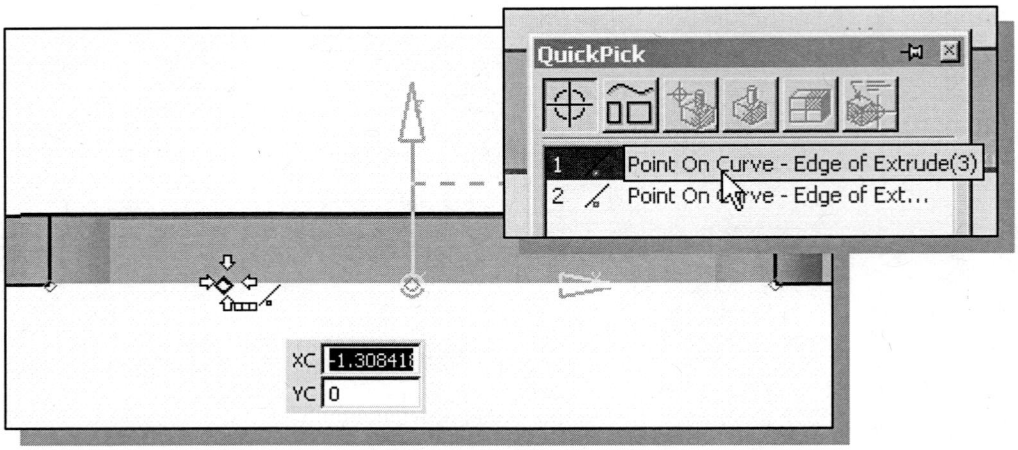

7. Move the cursor along the bottom edge of the base feature to the right and place the second endpoint of the arc also on the edge. (Select the 1st point on the **Curve** constraint if necessary.)

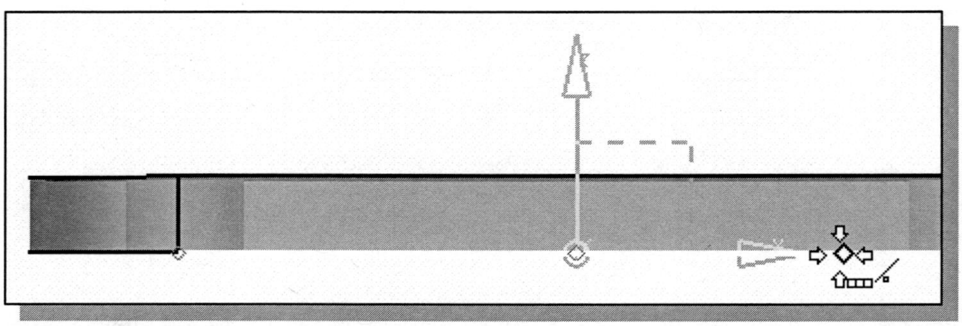

8. Click on any location of the arc, in the positive *Y* direction, to proceed with the **Profile** command.

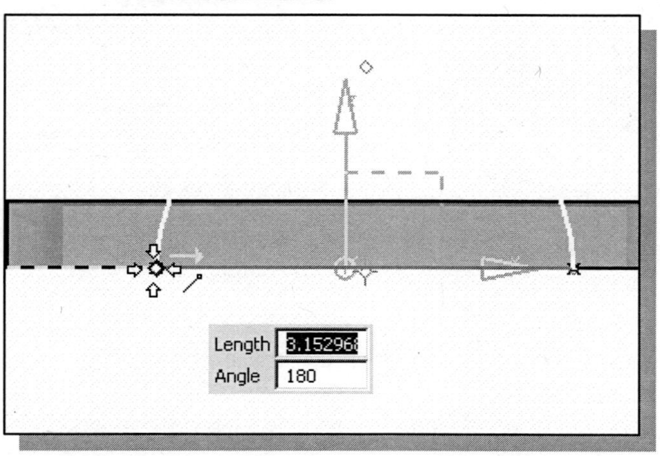

9. Complete the sketch by adding a straight line segment connecting to the starting point of the sketch.

Fully Constraining the Sketch

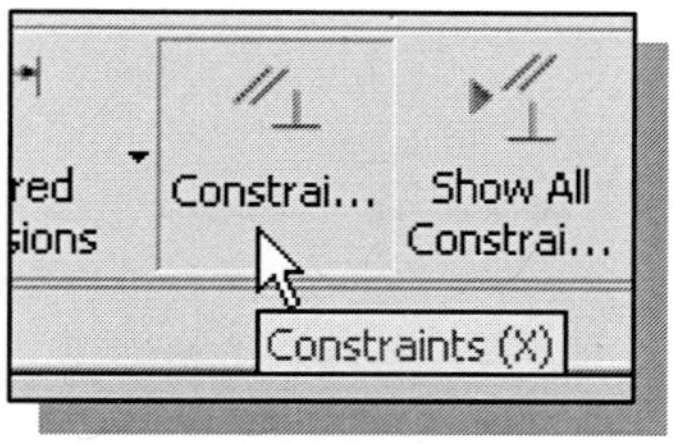

1. Select the **Constraints** command in the *Sketch Constraints* toolbar.

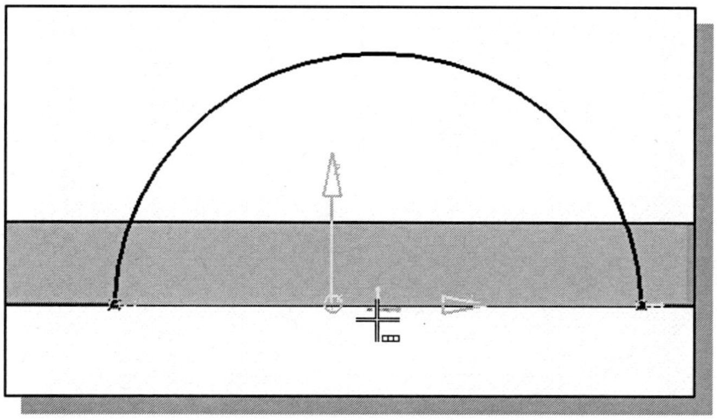

2. Select the center of the arc as shown. (Hint: Observe the color of the arc as you move near the center of the arc.)

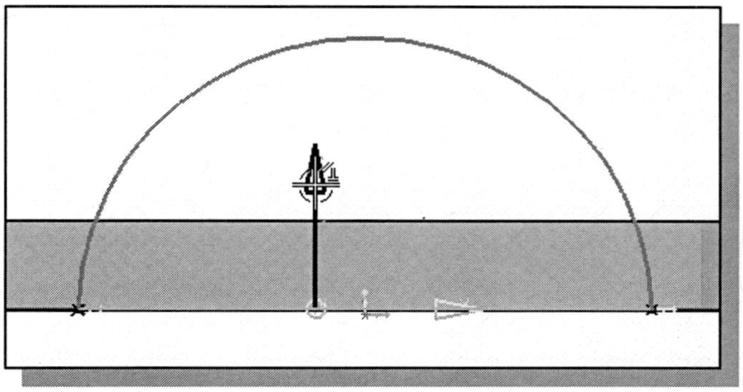

3. Select the *Z* axis.

4. Choose the **Point On Curve** option as shown.

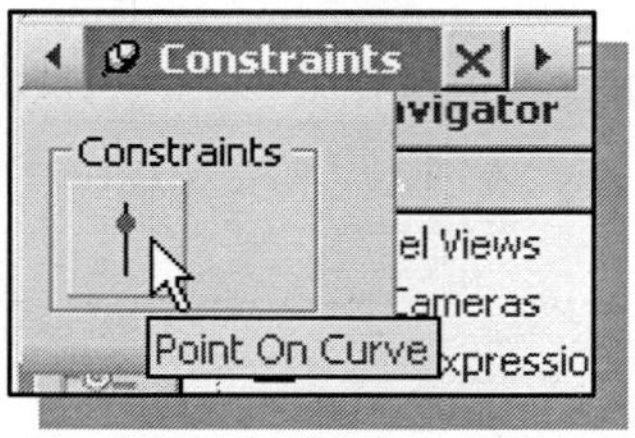

5. Repeat the above steps and align the center point to the *X* axis as shown.

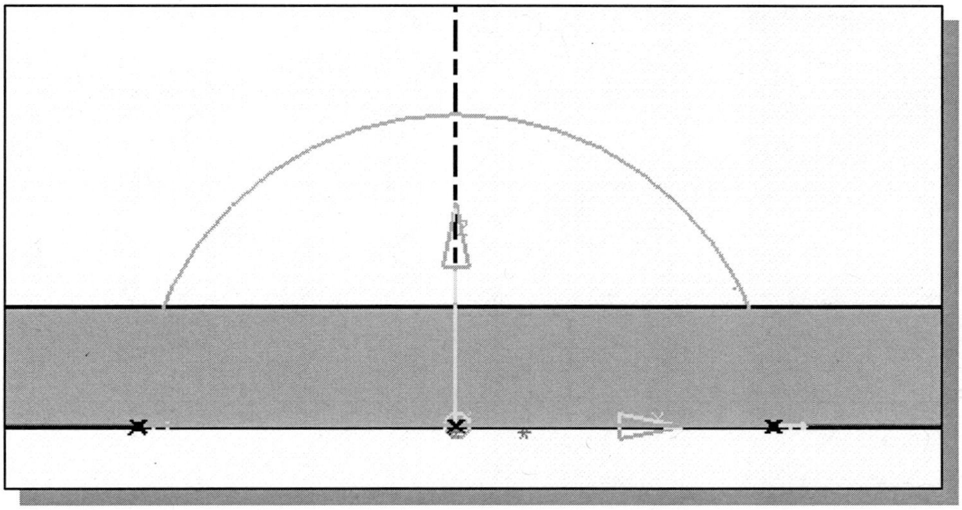

6. On your own, add the radius dimension and confirm the 2D sketch is fully constrained.

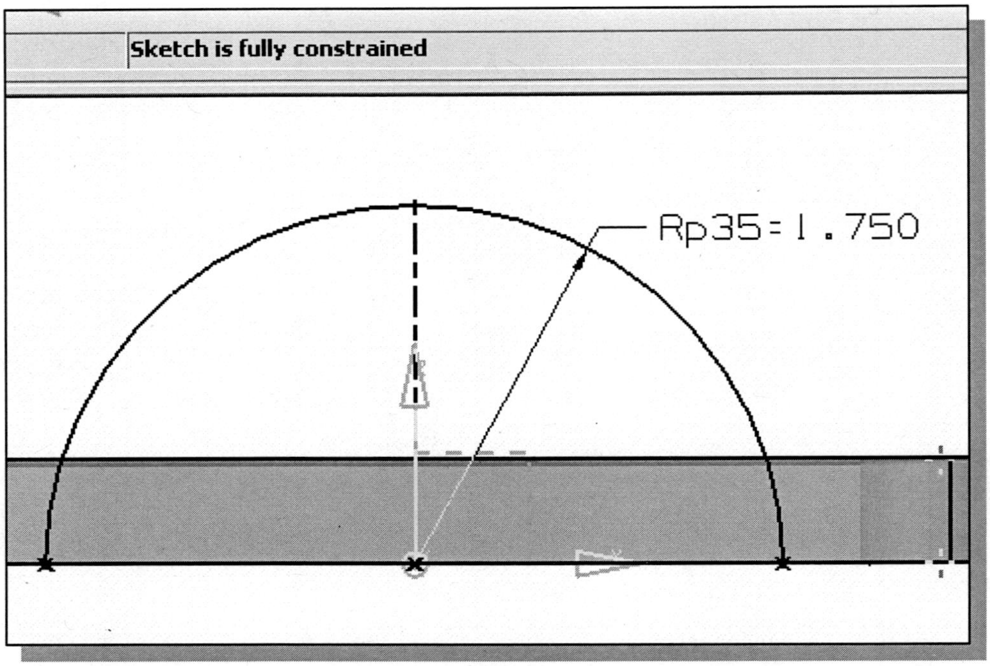

❖ In the above example, we used two constraints and one dimension to fully constrain the sketch. What other combinations can you think of that will produce the same result?

7. On your own, rotate the solid model and notice the new sketch is located at the center of the part, aligned to the *Z-X* plane of the datum coordinate system.

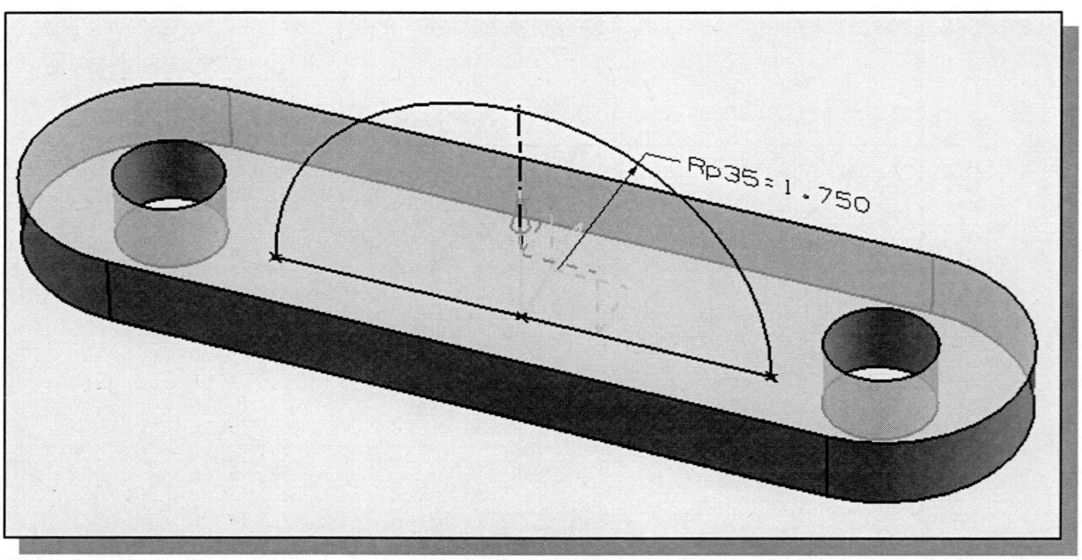

Completing the Extrude Feature

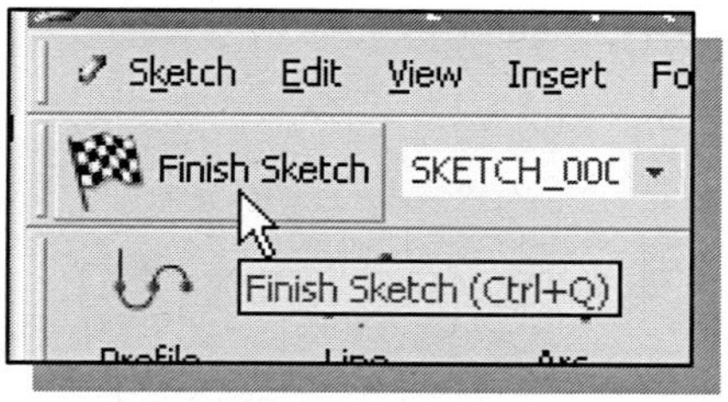

1. Click **Finish Sketch** to exit the *NX Sketcher* mode and return to the *Feature* option dialog window.

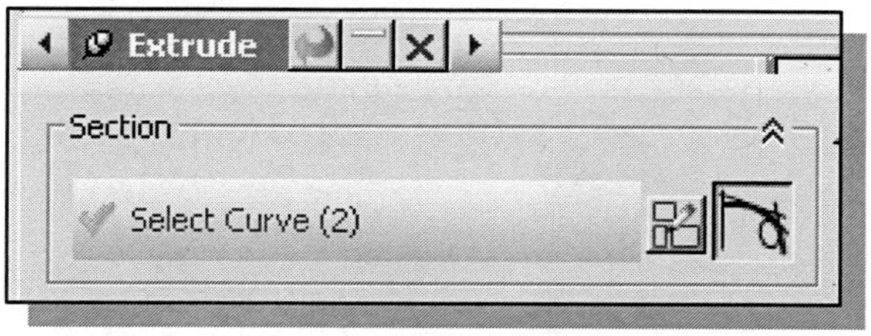

2. Note that two curves are currently selected: one arc and one line.

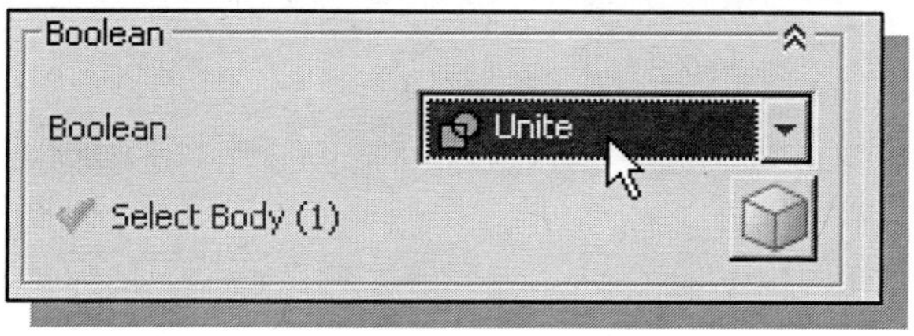

3. In the *Extrude* popup window, select **Unite** as the *Extrude* option as shown.

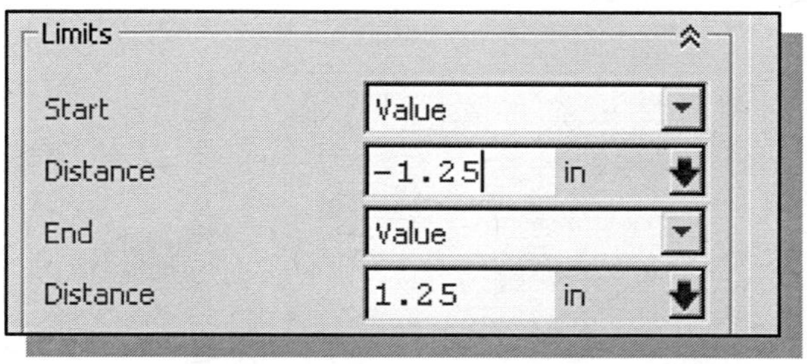

4. Enter **-1.25** in as the extrusion *Start* location, and **1.25** as the *End* location as shown.

5. Click **OK** to create the extrusion feature.

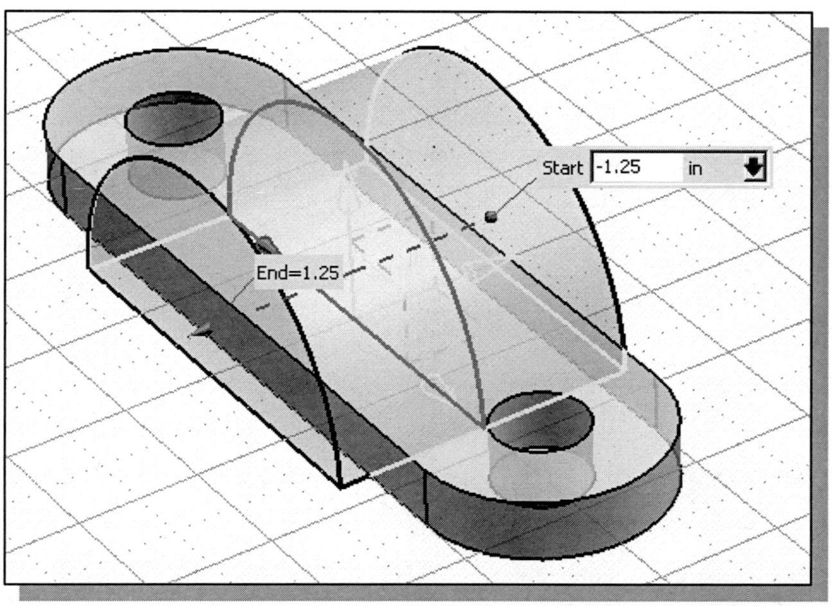

Creating a Subtract Feature

- A rectangular subtract feature will be created as the next solid feature.

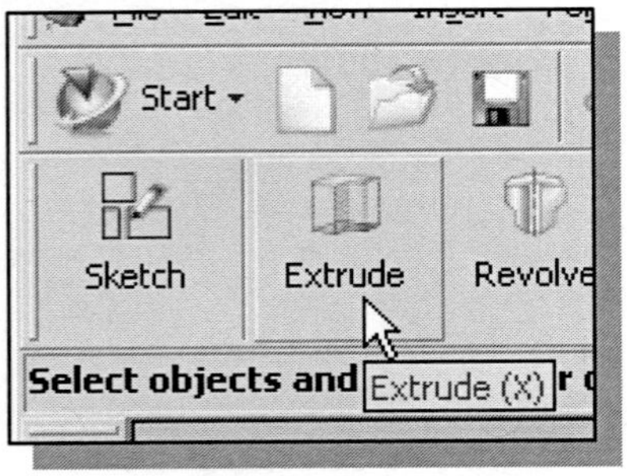

1. In the *Form Feature* toolbar select the **Extrude** command by left-clicking once on the icon.

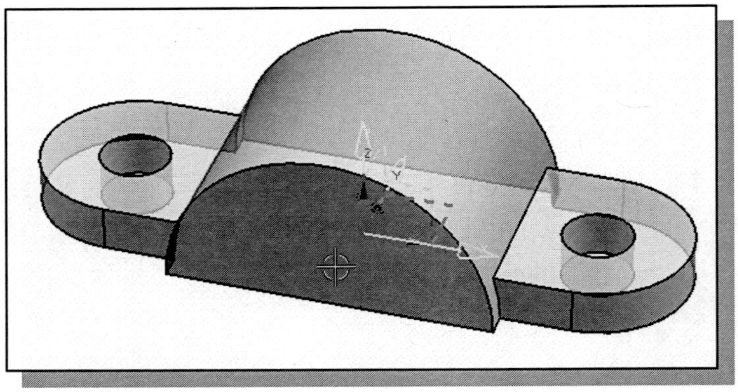

2. On your own, use the front vertical face as the *sketch plane* as shown.

3. On your own, create a rectangle and apply the dimensions as shown below.

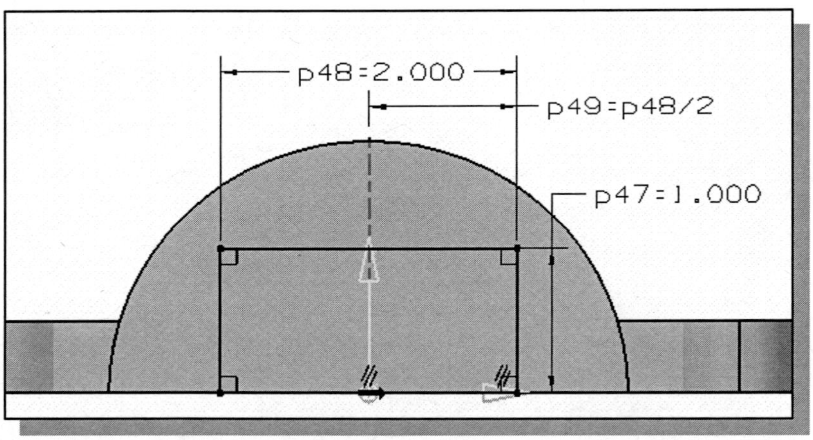

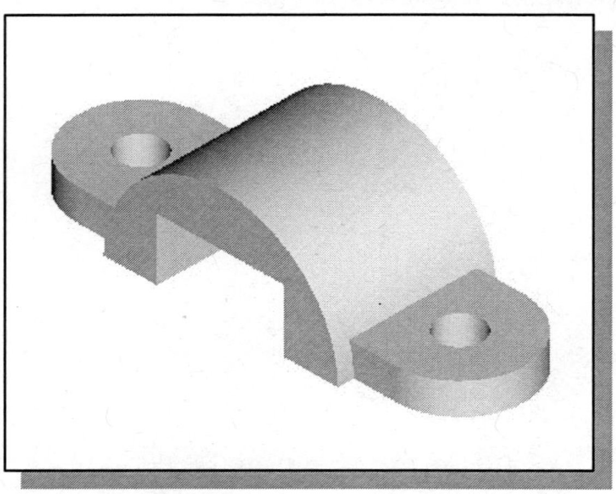

4. On your own, use the **Subtract – Through All** options and create a cutout that cuts through the entire 3D solid model as shown.

Another Subtract Feature

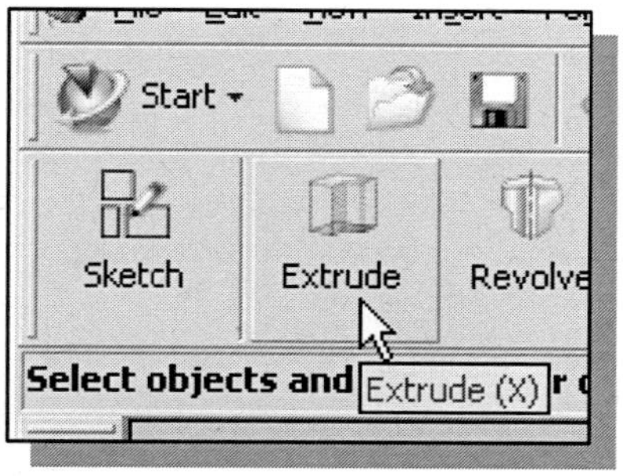

1. In the *Form Feature* toolbar select the **Extrude** command by left-clicking once on the icon.

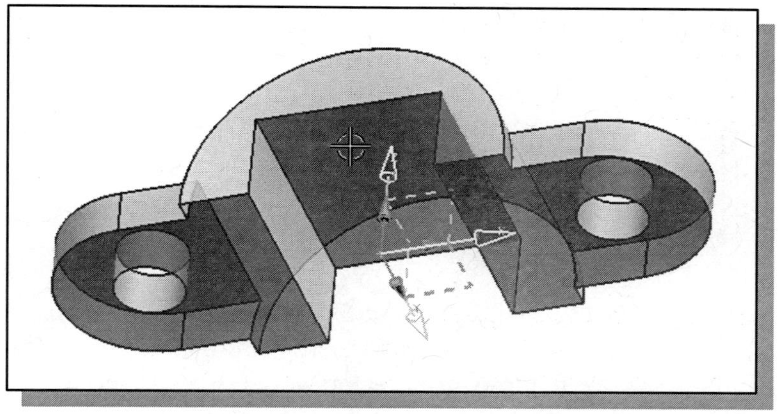

2. On your own, setup the horizontal face of the last subtract feature as the *sketching plane*.

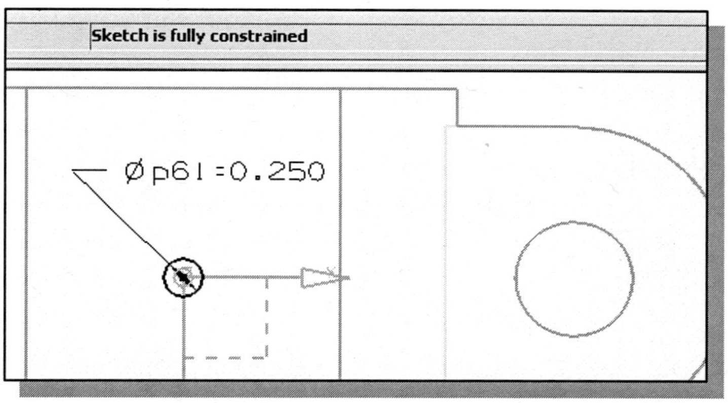

3. On your own, create a **circle** of size **0.25** in and with the center point aligned to the **horizontal** and **vertical axes** of the datum coordinate system.

4. On your own, use the **Subtract – Through All** options and create a cutout that cuts through the entire 3D solid model as shown.

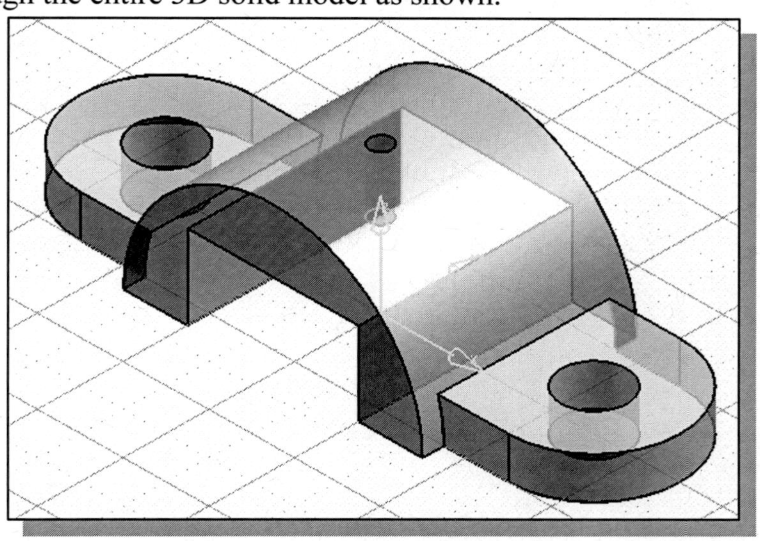

Examining the Parent/Child Relationships

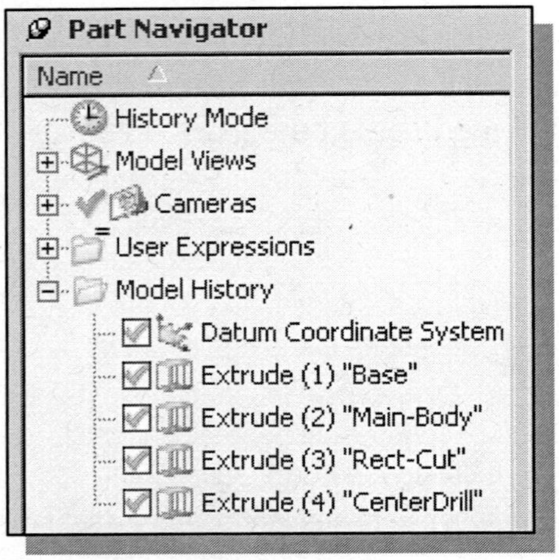

1. On your own, rename the feature names to: ***Base***, ***Main-Body***, ***Rect-Cut*** and ***CenterDrill*** as shown in the figure.

❖ The *Part Navigator* window now contains the four extruded features. All of the parent/child relationships were established implicitly as we created the solid features. As more features are created, it becomes much more difficult to make a sketch showing all the parent/child relationships involved in the model. On the other hand, it is not really necessary to have a detailed picture showing all the relationships among the features. In using a feature-based modeler, the main emphasis is to consider the interactions that exist between the **immediate features**. Treat each feature as a unit by itself, and be clear on the parent/child relationships for each feature. Thinking in terms of *features* is what distinguishes *feature-based modeling* and the previous generation solid modeling techniques. Let us take a look at the last feature we created, the ***CenterDrill*** feature. What are the parent/child relationships associated with this feature? (1) Since this is the last feature we created, it is not a parent feature to any other features. (2) Since we used one of the surfaces of the rectangular cutout as the sketching plane, the ***Rect-Cut*** feature is a parent feature to the ***CenterDrill*** feature. (3) We also used the ***Datum Axes*** as references to align the location of the *CenterDrill*; therefore, the ***Datum Axes*** are also a parent to the ***CenterDrill*** feature.

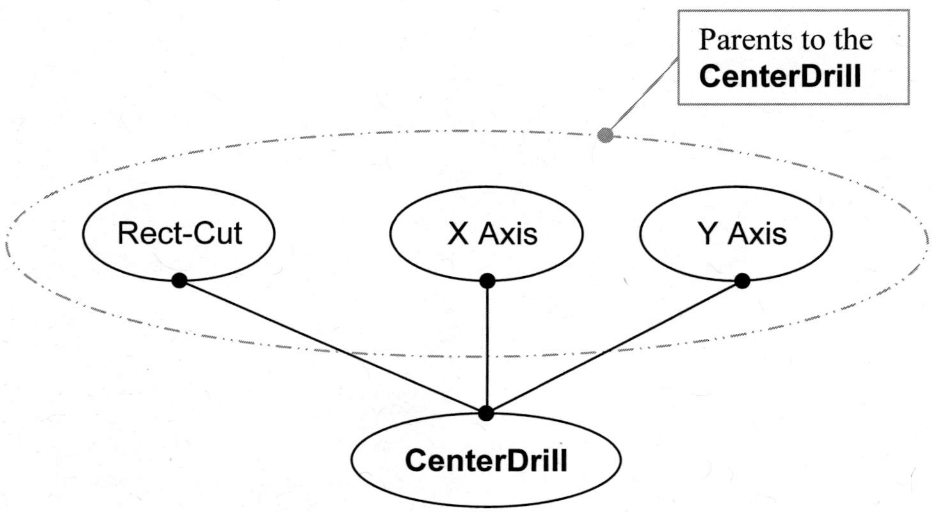

A Design Change

➤ Engineering designs usually go through many revisions and changes. For example, a design change may call for a circular cutout instead of the current rectangular cutout feature in our model. *UGS NX* provides an assortment of tools to handle design changes quickly and effectively. In the following sections, we will demonstrate some of the more advanced tools available in *UGS NX*, which allow us to perform the modification of changing the rectangular cutout (2.0 × 1.0 inch) to a circular cutout (radius: 1.25 inch).

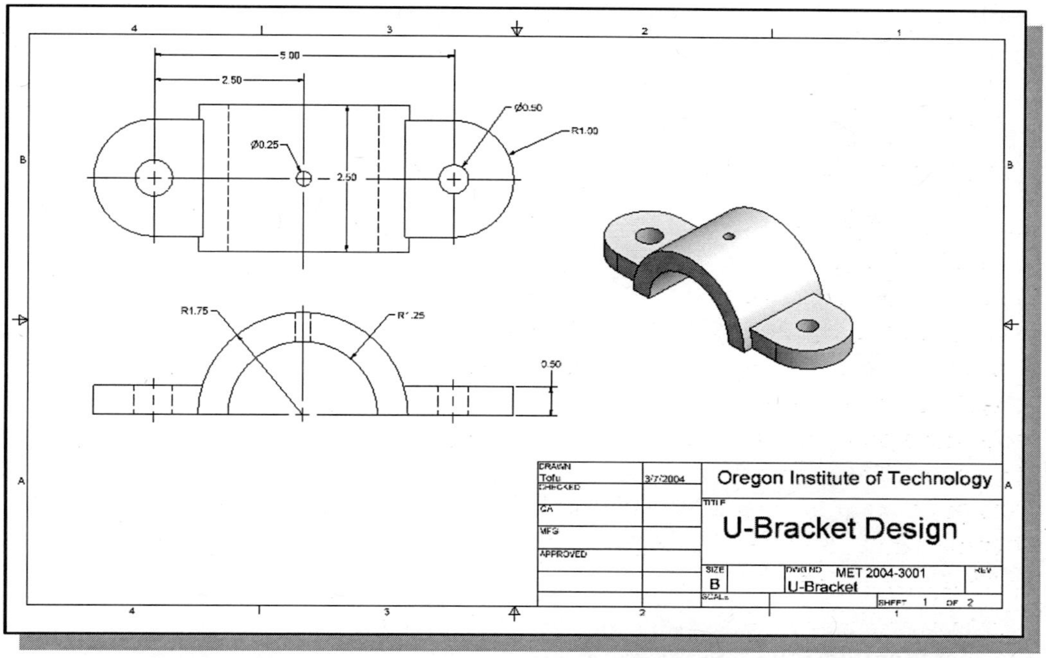

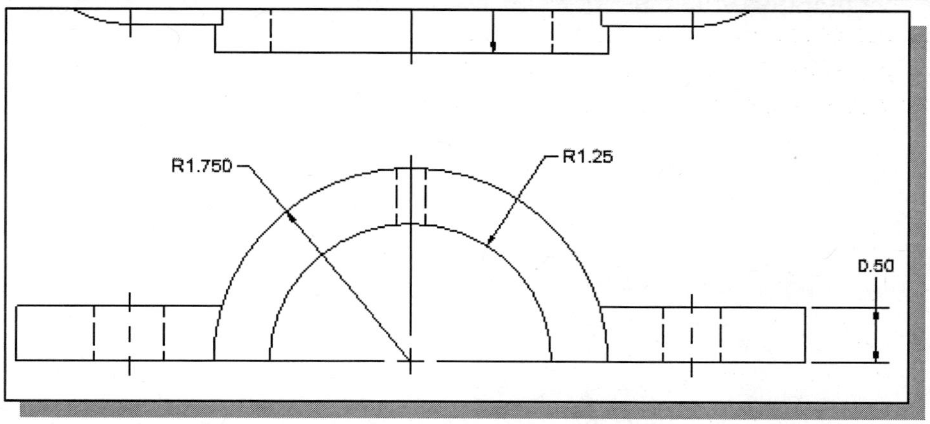

❖ Based on your knowledge of *UGS NX* so far, how would you accomplish this modification? What other approaches can you think of that are also feasible? Of the approaches you came up with, which one is the easiest to do and which is the most flexible? If this design change were anticipated right at the beginning of the design process, what would be your choice in arranging the order of the features? You are encouraged to perform the modifications prior to following through the rest of the tutorial.

Feature Suppression

❖ With *UGS NX*, we can take several different approaches to accomplish this modification. We could (1) create a new model, or (2) change the shape of the existing cutout feature using the **Edit with Rollback** command, or (3) perform **feature suppression** on the rectangular cutout feature and add a circular cutout feature. The third approach offers the most flexibility and requires the least amount of editing to the existing geometry. **Feature suppression** is a method that enables us to disable a feature while retaining the complete feature information; the feature can be reactivated at any time. Prior to adding the new cutout feature, we will first suppress the rectangular cutout feature.

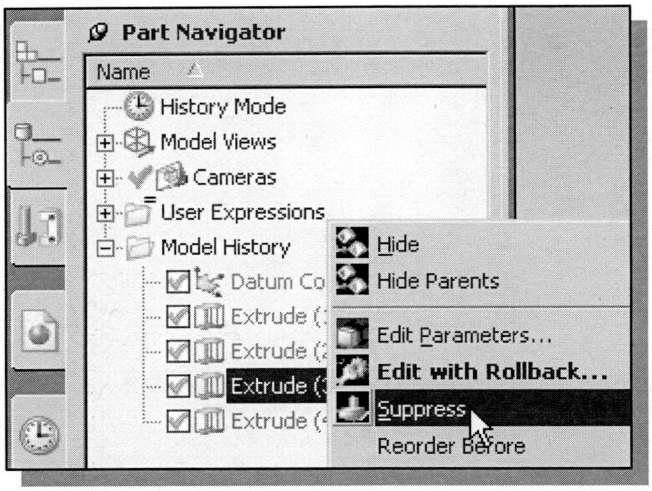

1. Open the *Part Navigator* window; click once with the right-mouse-button on top of ***Rect-Cut*** to bring up the option menu.

2. Pick **Suppress** in the pop-up menu.

❖ We have literally ***gone back in time***. The *Rect-Cut* and *Center_Drill* features have disappeared in the display area. The child feature cannot exist without its parent(s), and any modification to the parent *(Rect-Cut)* may influence the child *(CenterDrill)*.

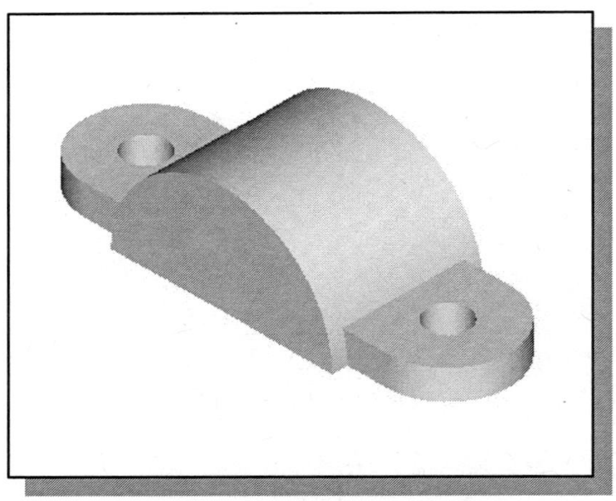

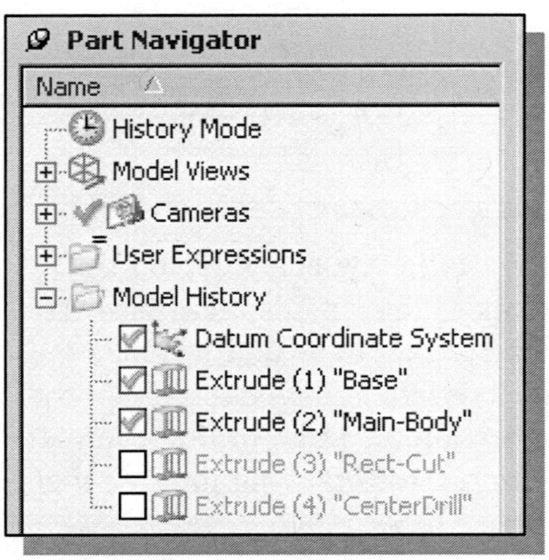

❖ In the *Part Navigator* window, the boxes in front of the suppressed features are un-checked, indicating those features are disabled.

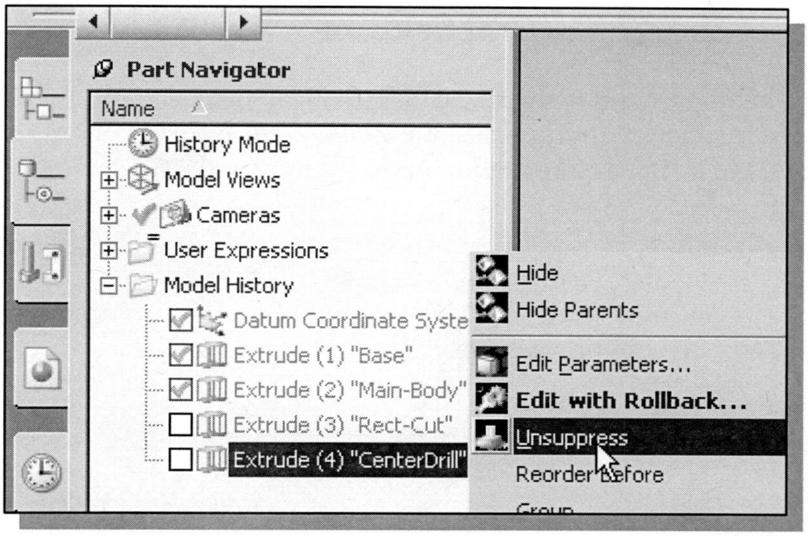

3. Open the *Part Navigator* window; click once with the right-mouse-button on top of *CenterDrill* to bring up the option menu.

4. Pick **Unsuppress** in the pop-up menu.

➢ In the graphics area and the *Part Navigator* window, both the ***Rect-Cut*** feature and the ***CenterDrill*** feature have been re-activated. The child feature cannot exist without its parent(s); the parent *(Rect-Cut)* must be activated to enable the child *(CenterDrill)*.

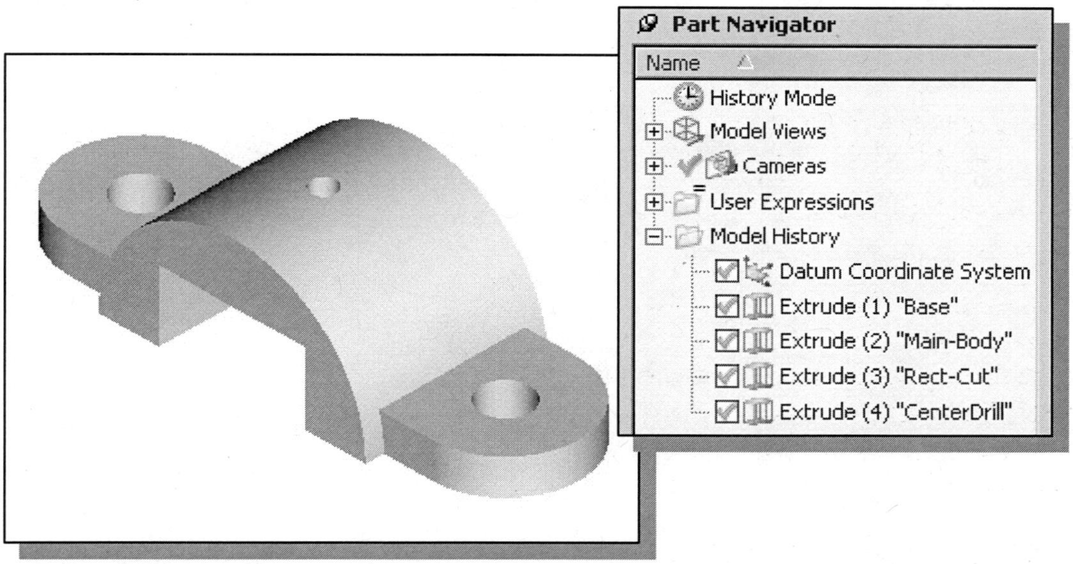

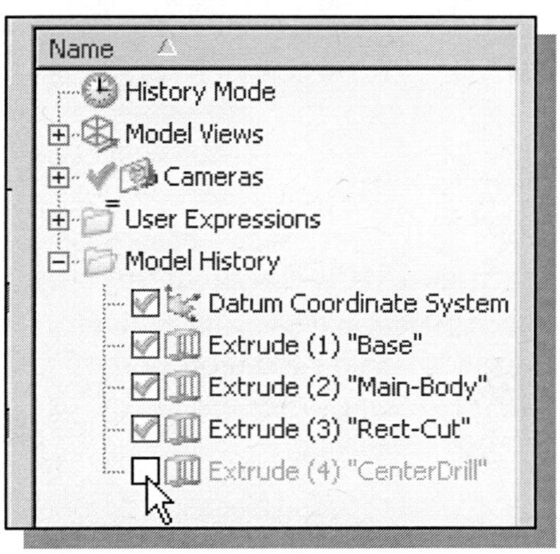

❖ Note that we can also simply click on the check-box in front of the features, with the left-mouse-button (MB1) to quickly **Suppress** and/or **Unsuppress** features.

A Different Approach to the *CenterDrill* Feature

❖ The main advantage of using the BORN technique is to provide greater flexibility for part modifications and design changes. In this case, the *CenterDrill* feature can be placed on the *X-Y* datum plane and therefore not be linked directly to the *Rect-Cut* feature.

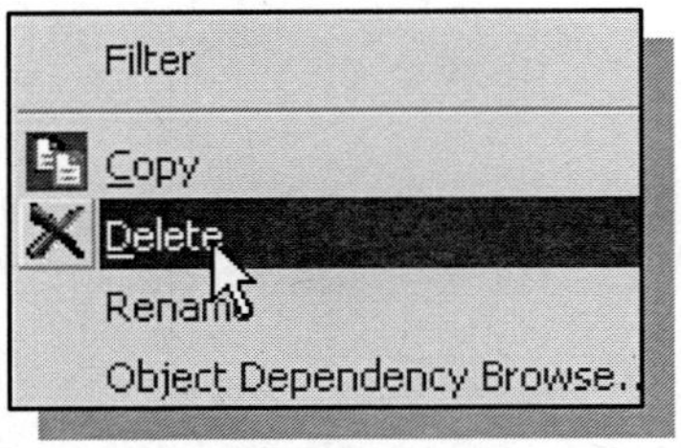

1. Open the *Part Navigator* window; click once with the right-mouse-button (MB3) on top of ***CenterDrill*** to bring up the option menu.

2. Pick **Delete** in the pop-up menu.

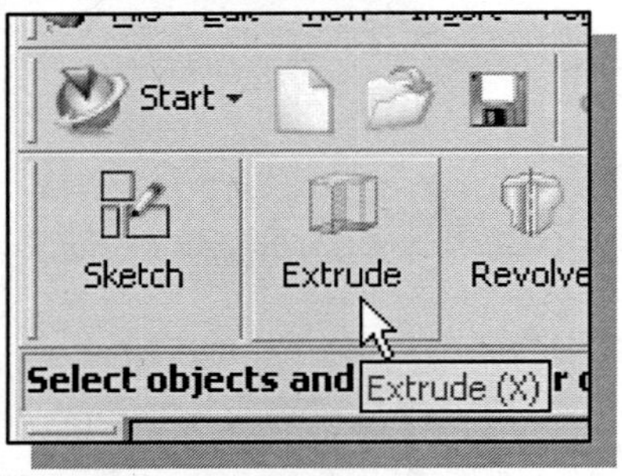

3. In the ***Feature*** toolbars (toolbars aligned to the right edge of the main window), select the **Extrude** icon as shown.

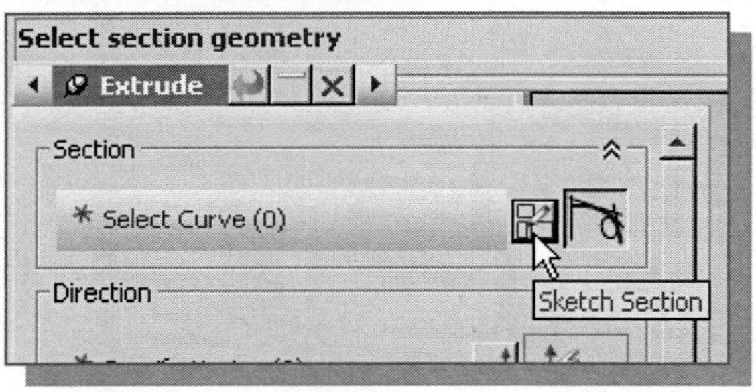

4. Click the **Sketch Section** button to enter the *2D Sketcher* mode and begin creating a new *2D sketch.*

❖ Note the default sketch plane is aligned to the *X-Y* plane of the displayed datum coordinate system.

5. Click **OK** to accept the default setting of the *sketch plane.*

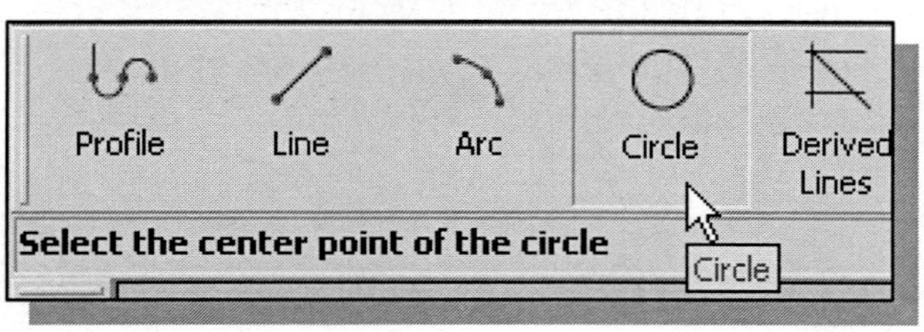

6. Select the **Circle** command by clicking once with the left-mouse-button (MB1) on the icon in the *Sketch Curve* toolbar.

7. Select the **Static Wireframe** display mode in the *Standard* toolbar as shown.

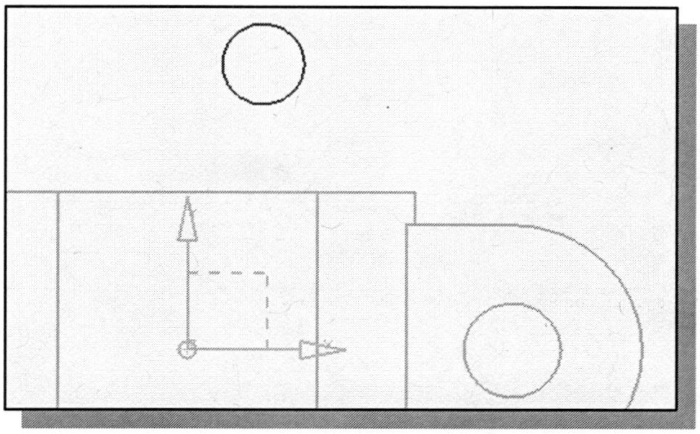

8. Create a circle of arbitrary size that is to the upper-right side of the screen.

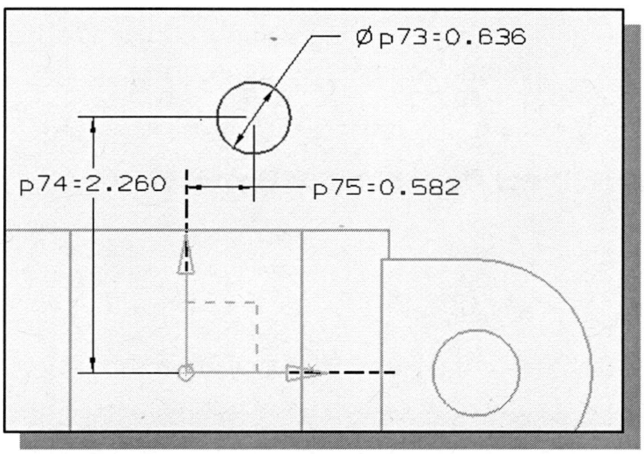

9. On your own, add the size and locational dimensions of the circle as shown.

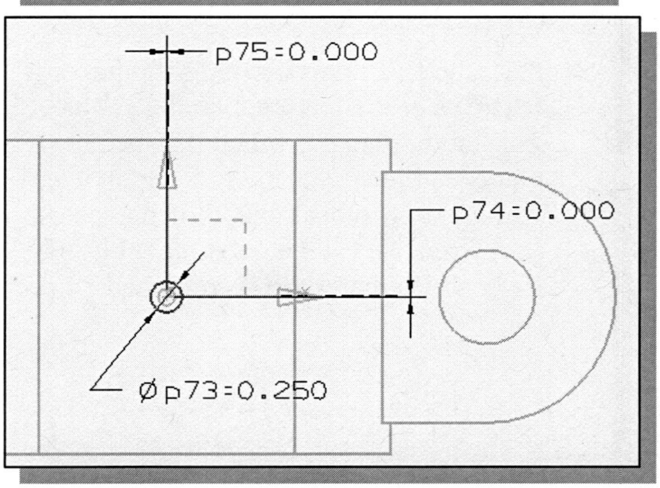

10. Set the size dimension to **0.25** and locational dimensions to **0.0** as shown.

❖ Note that the circle is fully constrained by using three dimensions. How did we constrain the circle feature last time?

11. On your own, complete the *Extrude* subtract feature.

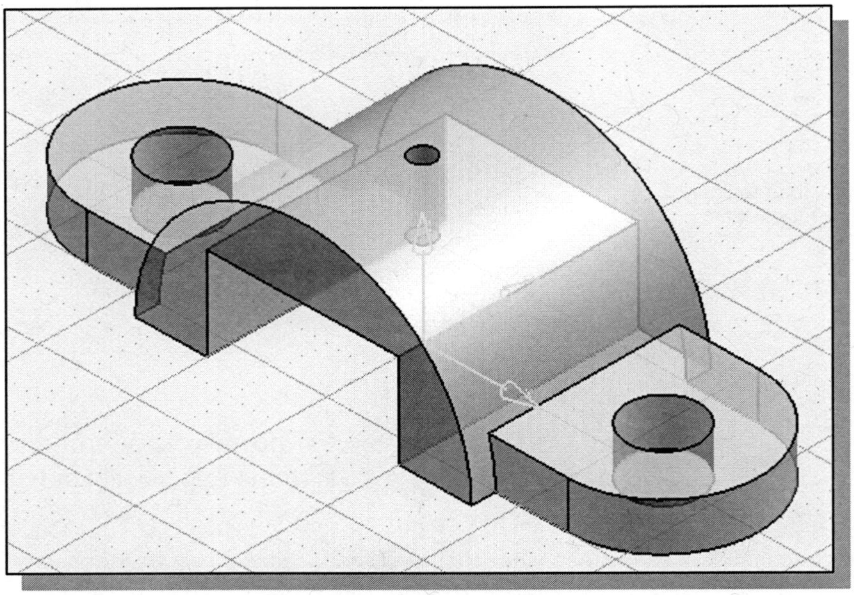

Examining the Parent/Child Relationships

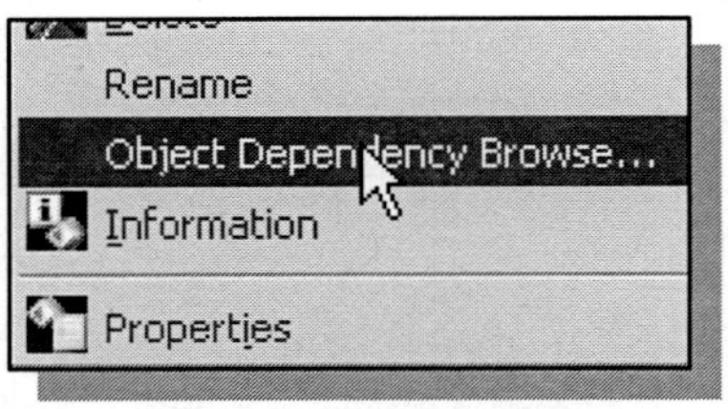

1. Open the *Part Navigator* and right-mouse-click (MB3) on the newly created ***Extrude*** feature to bring up the option list.

2. Select the **Object Dependency Browse** option as shown.

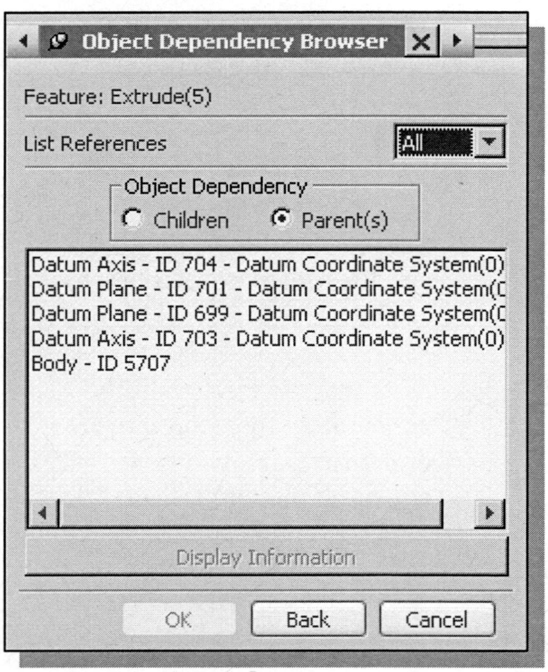

3. Select the **Parent(s)** option in the *Object Dependency Browser* window.

❖ Note the five items listed, as the **parents features** of the feature include: (1) the *X-Y* datum plane to which the sketch plane is aligned; (2) the two datum axes which the two locational dimensions use as references; (3) the solid model itself, from which material was removed.

Suppress the *Rect-Cut* Feature

❖ Now the ***CenterDrill*** feature is no longer a child of the ***Rect-Cut*** feature; any changes to the ***Rect-Cut*** feature will no longer affect the ***CenterDrill*** feature.

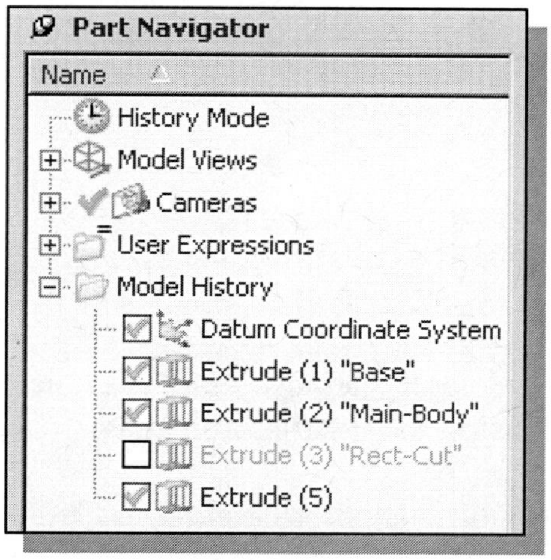

1. Open the *Part Navigator* and uncheck the ***Rect-Cut*** feature by clicking once with the left-mouse-button (MB1) on the check-box in front.

❖ The ***Rect-Cut*** feature is now disabled without affecting the **new *Center_Drill*** feature.

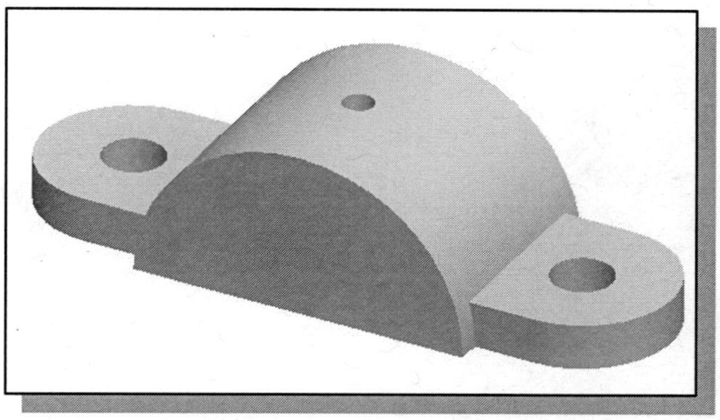

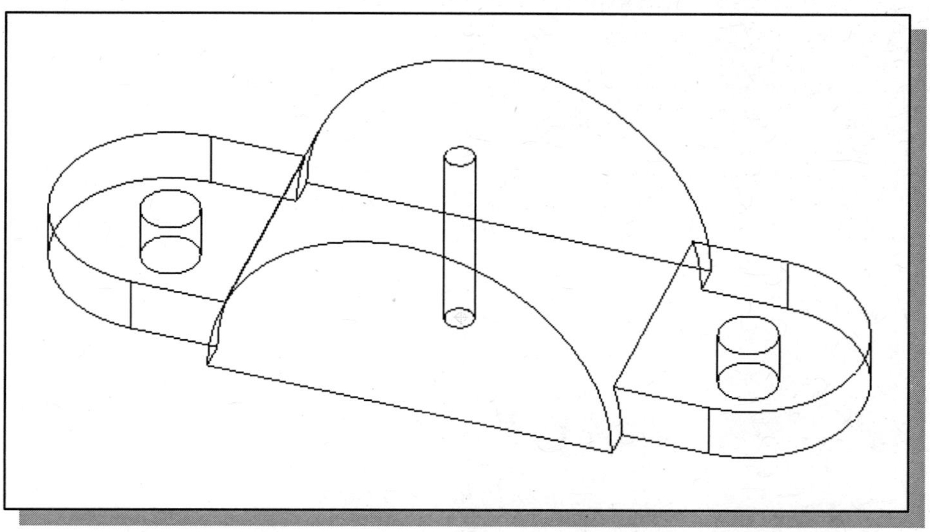

Creating a Hole Feature

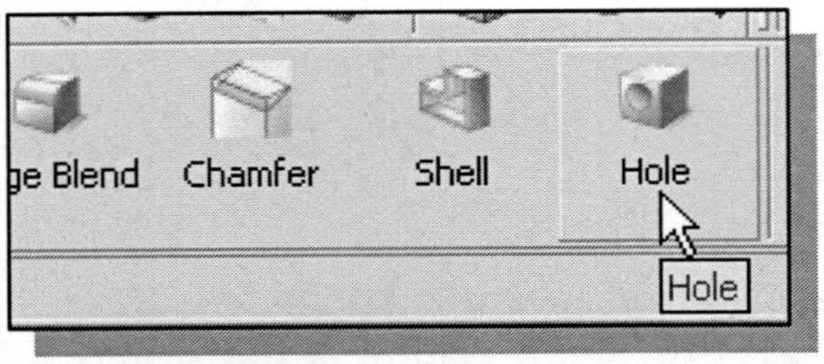

1. In the *Feature Operation* toolbar (the toolbar that is located to the right side of the *Form Feature* toolbar), select the **Hole** command by releasing the left-mouse-button on the icon.

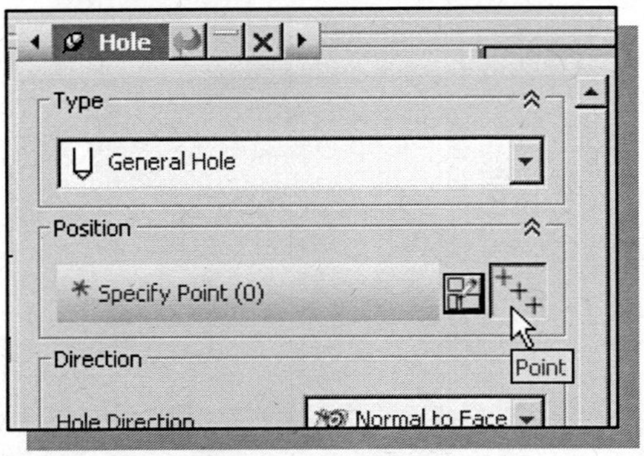

2. In the *Hole* window, notice the default hole *Type* is set to **General Hole** as shown.

❖ Note that by default, the position of the hole is specified using the **Point** command.

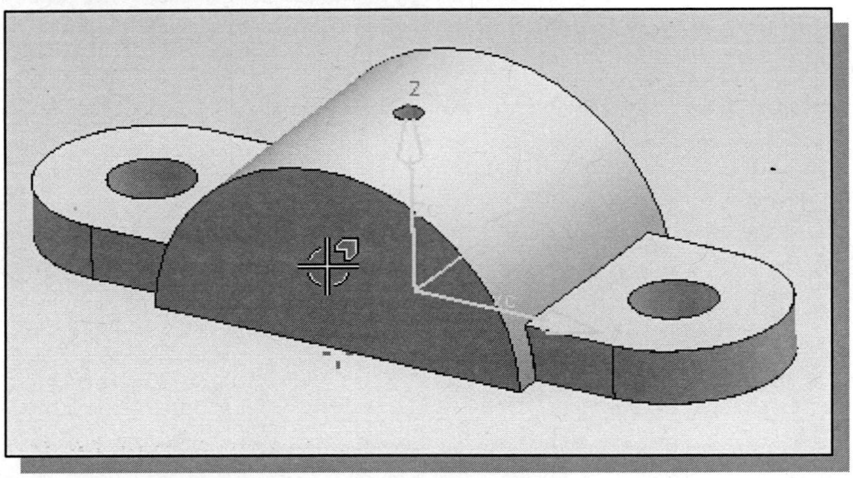

3. Pick a location inside the front horizontal surface of the *Main_Body* feature as shown.

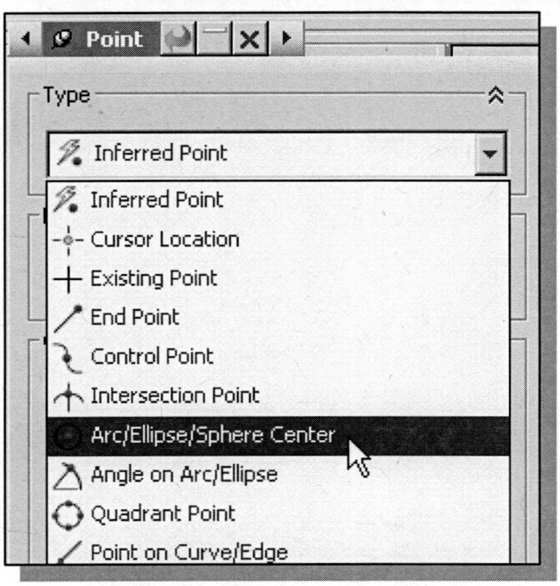

❖ Note the **Point** command is activated automatically once the sketch plane has been selected.

4. In the *Point* dialog box, set the point option to **Aec/Ellipse/Sphere Center**, as shown.

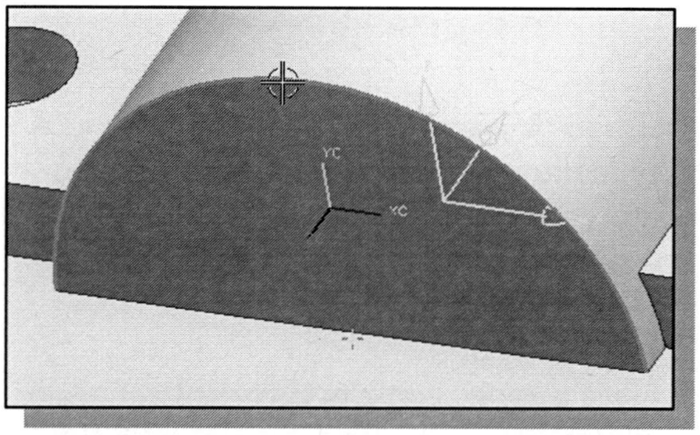

5. Select the front arc of the *Main_Body* feature as shown in the figure.

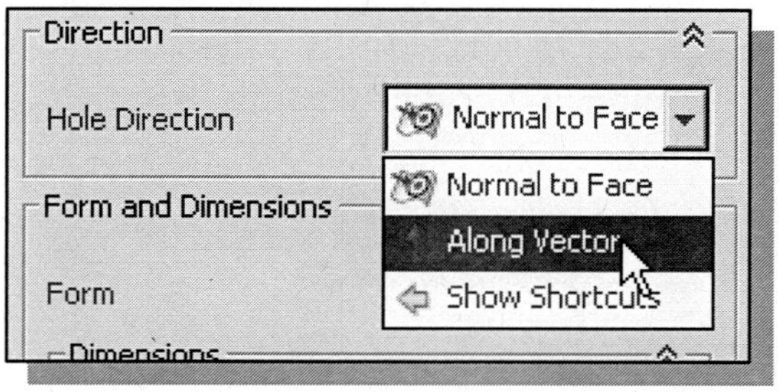

6. Set the hole *Direction* to **Along Vector** as shown.

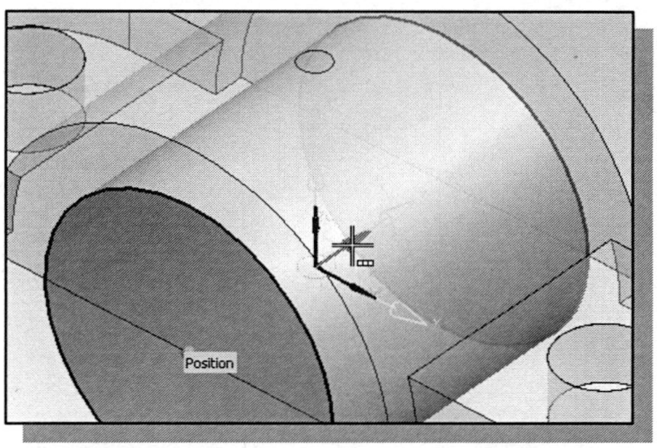

7. Select the *Y-C* axis to set the vector direction as shown.

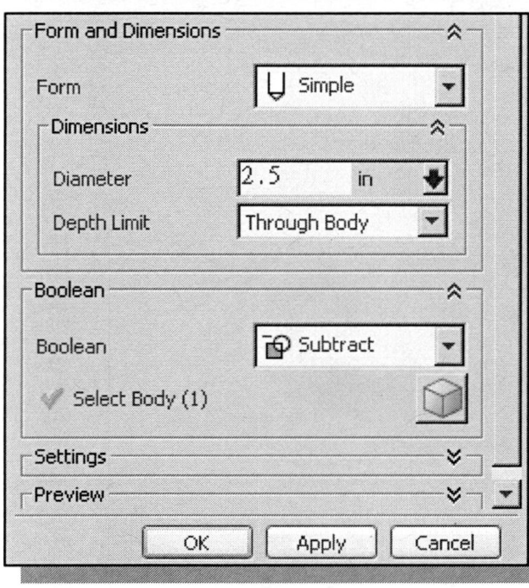

8. Set the ***Diameter*** to **2.5 in** and *Depth Limit* to **Through Body** as shown.

9. Confirm the *Boolean* option is set to **Subtract** and click **OK** to create the feature.

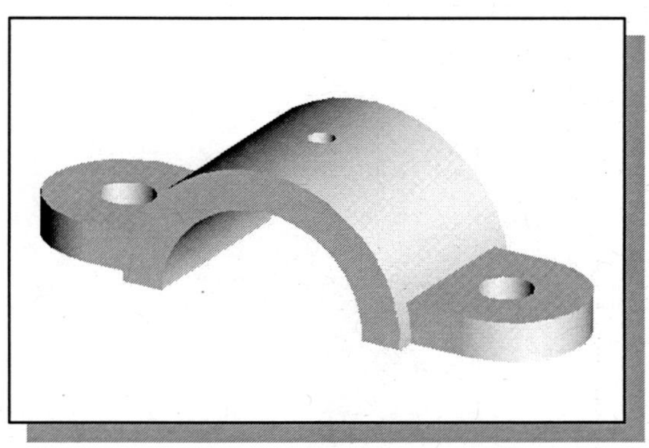

➤ Save the ***U-Bracket*** model; this model will be used again in the next chapter.

A Flexible Design Approach

In a typical design process, the initial design will undergo many analyses, testing, reviews and revisions. *UGS NX* allows the users to quickly make changes and explore different options of the initial design throughout the design process.

The model we constructed in this chapter contains two distinct design options. The *feature-based parametric modeling* approach enables us to quickly explore design alternatives and we can include different design ideas into the same model. With parametric modeling, designers can concentrate on improving the design and the design process to be much more quickly and effortlessly. The key to successfully using parametric modeling as a design tool lies in understanding and properly controlling the interactions of features, especially the parent/child relations.

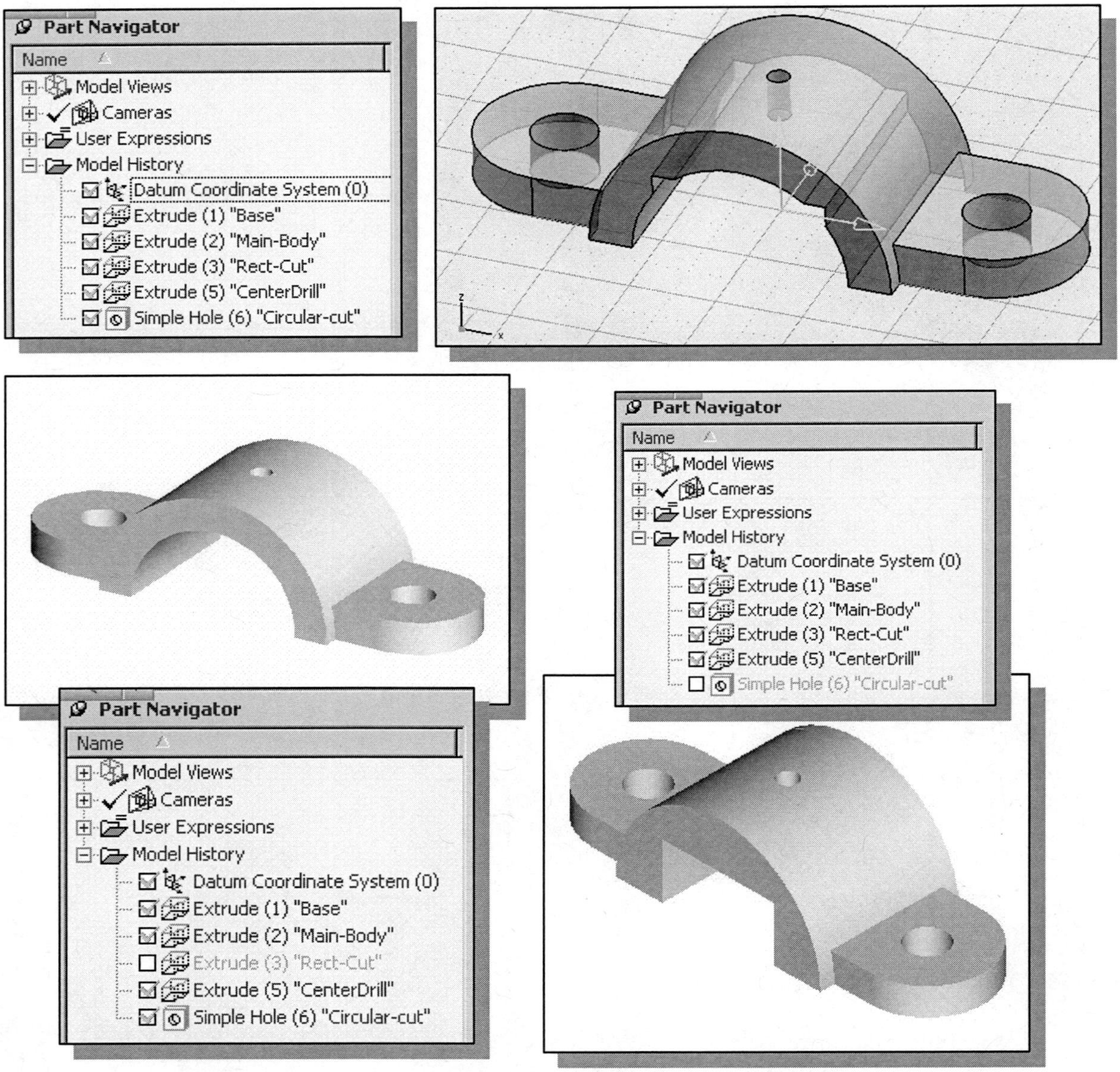

Questions:

1. Why is it important to consider the parent/child relationships in between features?
2. Describe the procedure to **Suppress** a *feature.*
3. What is the basic concept of the BORN technique?
4. What happen to a feature when it is suppressed?
5. How do you **Unsuppress** a suppressed feature in a model?
6. Describe the advantages of parametric modeling in creating alternate designs over traditional CAD systems.
7. Create sketches showing the steps you plan to use to create the models shown on the next page:

Exercises: (Dimensions are in inches)

1.

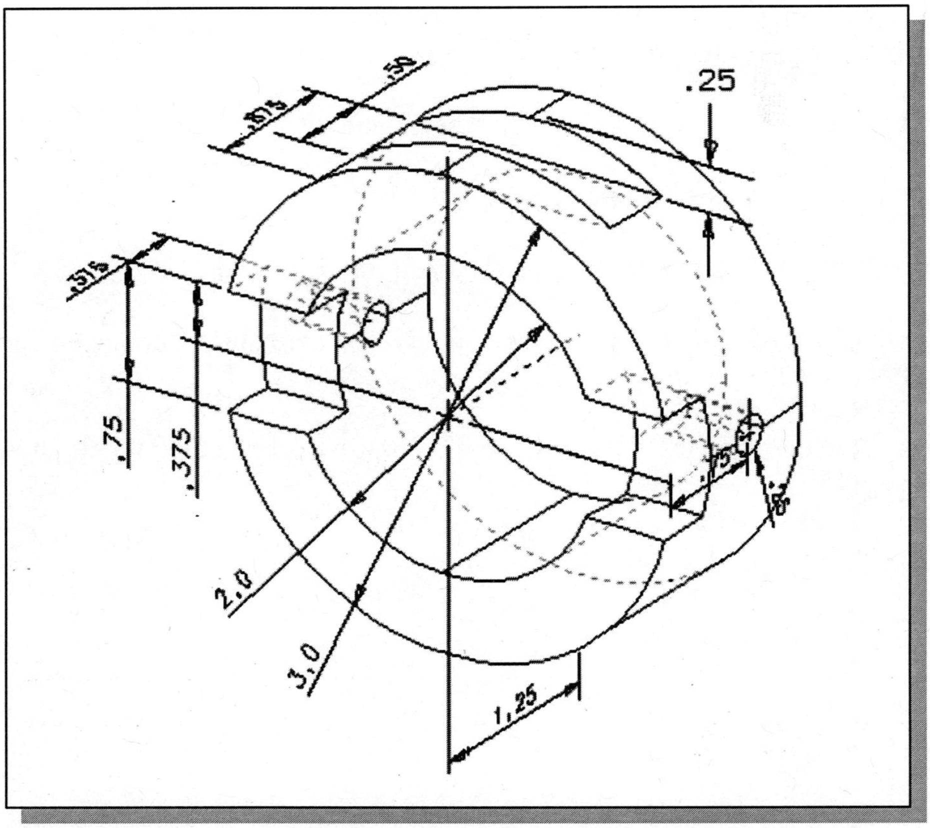

2.

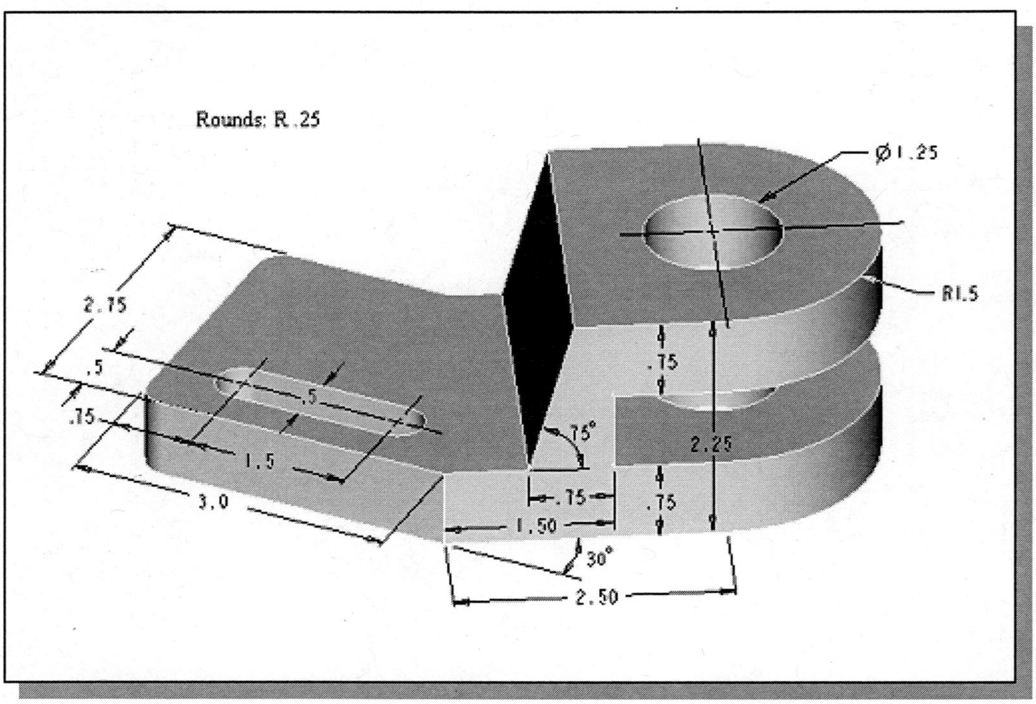

3.

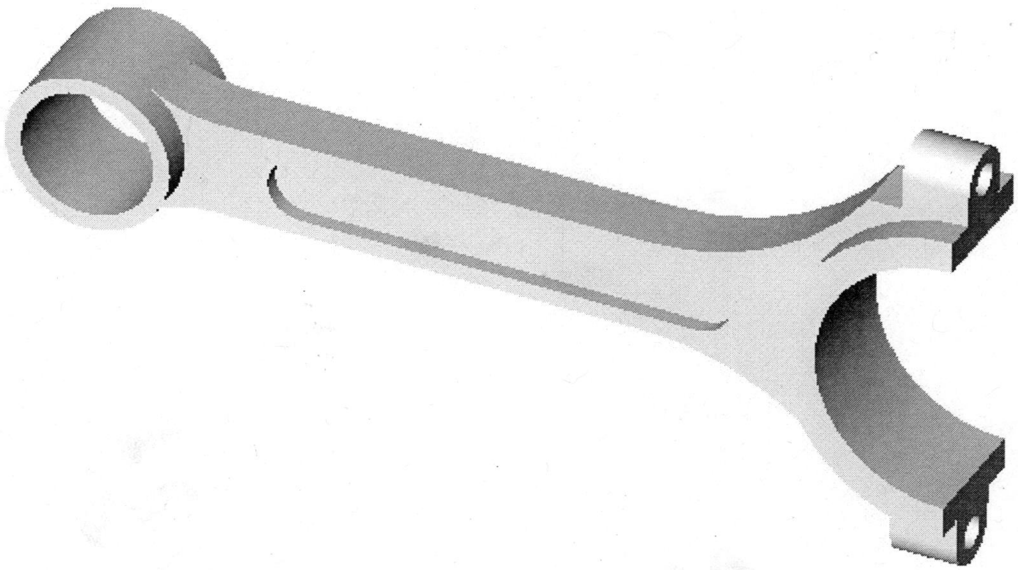

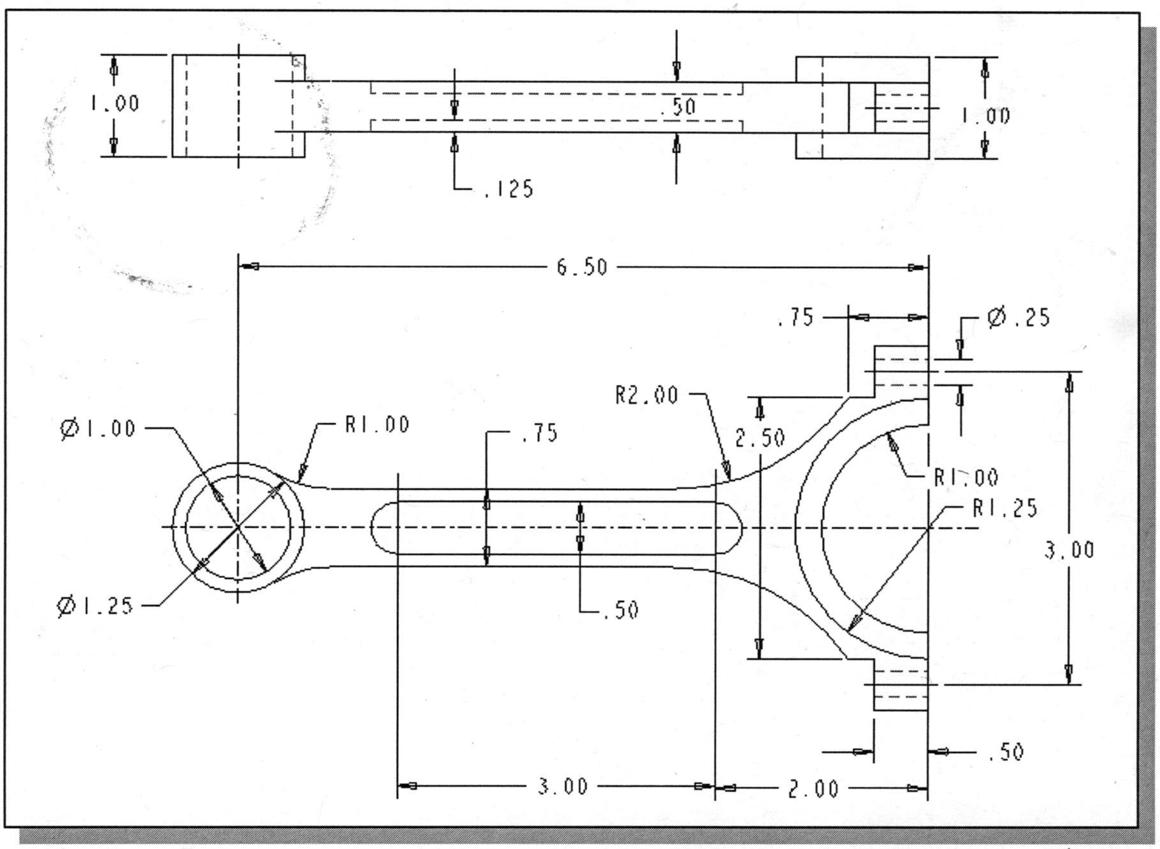
1.00
.50
1.00
.125
6.50
.75
Ø.25
R2.00
Ø1.00
R1.00
.75
2.50
R1.00
R1.25
3.00
Ø1.25
.50
.50
3.00
2.00

Notes:

Chapter 8
Part Drawings and Associative Functionality

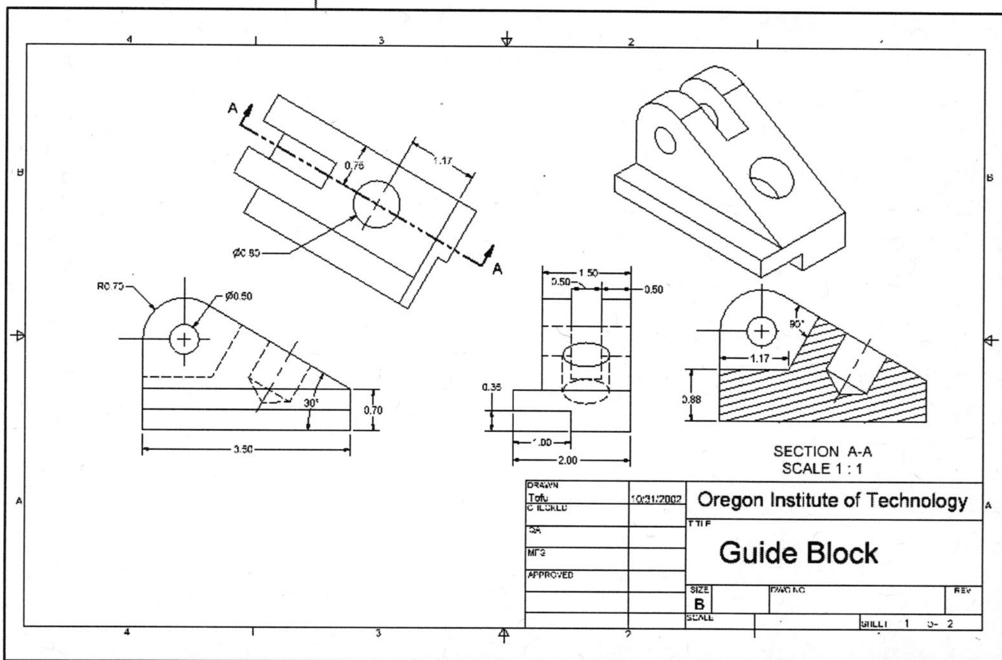

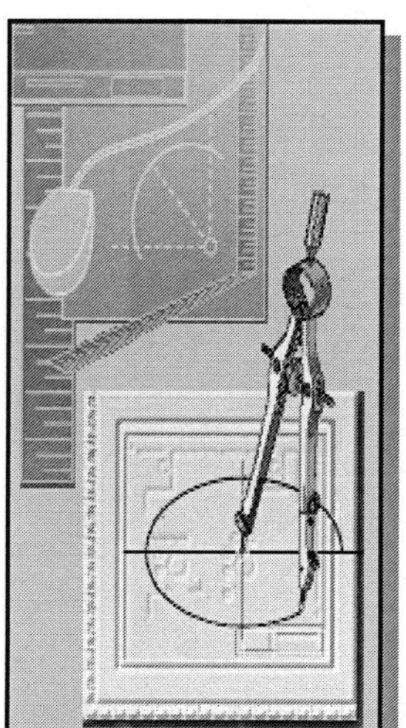

Learning Objectives

- ♦ **Create Drawing Layouts from Solid Models**
- ♦ **Understand Associative Functionality**
- ♦ **Use the default Borders and Title Block in the Layout Mode**
- ♦ **Arrange and Manage 2D Views in Drafting mode**
- ♦ **Display and Hide Feature Dimensions**
- ♦ **Create Reference Dimensions**

Drawings from Parts and Associative Functionality

With the software/hardware improvements in solid modeling, the importance of two-dimensional drawings is decreasing. Drafting is considered one of the downstream applications of using solid models. In many production facilities, solid models are used to generate machine tool paths for *computer numerical control* (CNC) machines. Solid models are also used in *rapid prototyping* to create 3D physical models out of plastic resins, powdered metal, etc. Ideally, the solid model database should be used directly to generate the final product. However, the majority of applications in most production facilities still require the use of two-dimensional drawings. Using the solid model as the starting point for a design, solid modeling tools can easily create all the necessary two-dimensional views. In this sense, solid modeling tools are making the process of creating two-dimensional drawings more efficient and effective.

UGS NX provides associative functionality in the different *UGS NX* modes. This functionality allows us to change the design at any level, and the system reflects it at all levels automatically. For example, a solid model can be modified in the *Part Modeling* mode and the system automatically reflects that change in the *Drafting* mode. And we can also modify a feature dimension in the *Drafting* mode, and the system automatically updates the solid model in all modes.

In this lesson, the general procedure of creating multi-view drawings is illustrated. The *U_Bracket* design from last chapter is used to demonstrate the associative functionality between the model and drawing views.

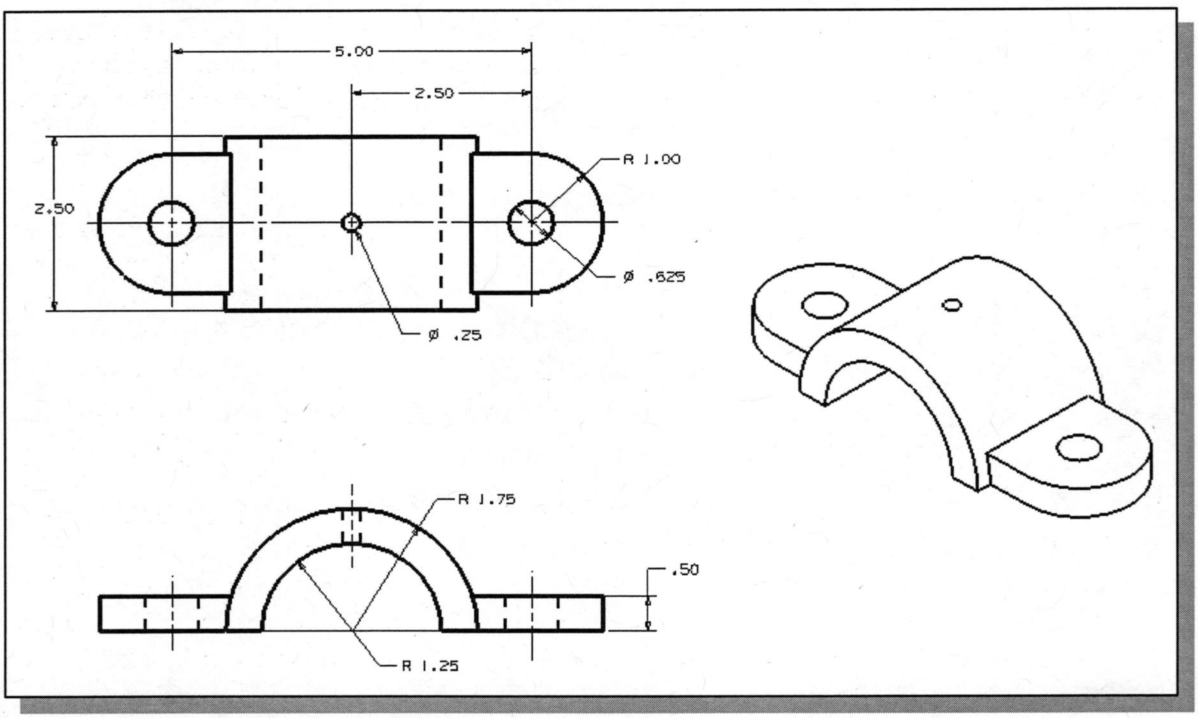

Starting *UGS NX*

1. Select the **UGS NX** option on the *Start* menu or select the **UGS NX** icon on the desktop to start *UGS NX*. The *UGS NX* main window will appear on the screen.

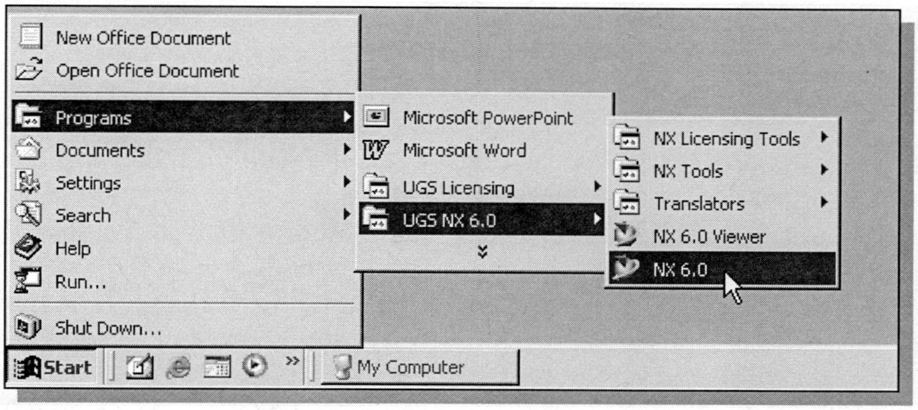

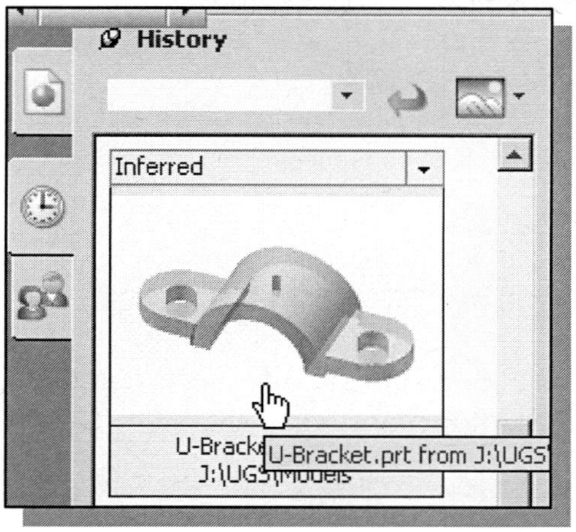

2. Select the ***U-Bracket.prt*** file in the displayed *History Palette* with a single click of the left-mouse-button.

➤ The ***History Palette*** of the *Resource Bar* provides a quick way to retrieve recently worked on parts.

➤ For organizations using the *Academic Partner License*, confirm the *ACD* license has been activated before continuing to the next section.

Drafting mode – 2D Paper Space

➤ *UGS NX* allows us to generate 2D engineering drawings from solid models so that we can plot the drawings to any exact scale on paper. An engineering drawing is a tool that can be used to communicate engineering ideas/designs to manufacturing, purchasing, service, and other departments. Until now we have been working in ***model space*** to create our design in ***full size***. We can arrange our design on a two-dimensional sheet of paper so that the plotted hardcopy is exactly what we want. This two-dimensional sheet of paper is generally known as ***paper space***. We can place borders and title blocks in the *paper space*. In general, each company uses a set of standards for drawing content, based on the type of product and also on established internal processes. The appearance of an engineering drawing varies depending on when, where, and for what purpose it is produced. However, the general procedure for creating an engineering drawing from a solid model is fairly well defined. In *UGS NX*, creation of 2D engineering drawings from solid models consists of four basic steps: drawing sheet formatting, creating/positioning views, annotations, and printing/plotting.

UGS NX Drafting Mode

1. Click on the **Start** icon in the *Standard* toolbar area to display the available options.

2. Select **Drafting** from the option list.

❖ In the *Sheet* dialog box, *UGS NX* displays different settings for the drawing sheet that will be used.

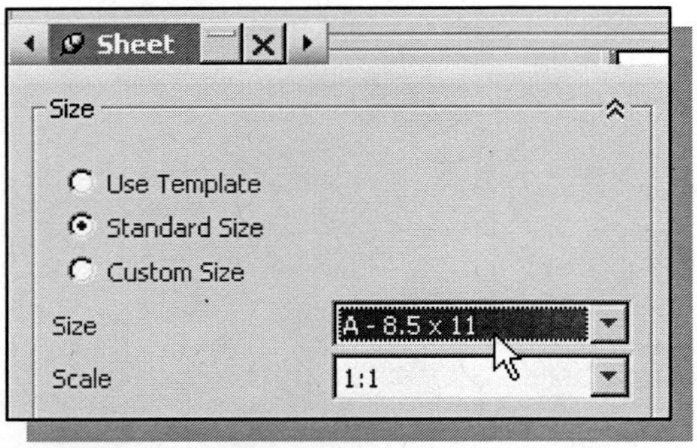

3. Select **A-8.5x11** from the sheet *Size* list.

4. Confirm the *Scale* is set to **1:1**, which is ***full scale***.

➢ Note that ***Sheet 1*** is the default drawing sheet name that is displayed in the *drawing sheet name* area.

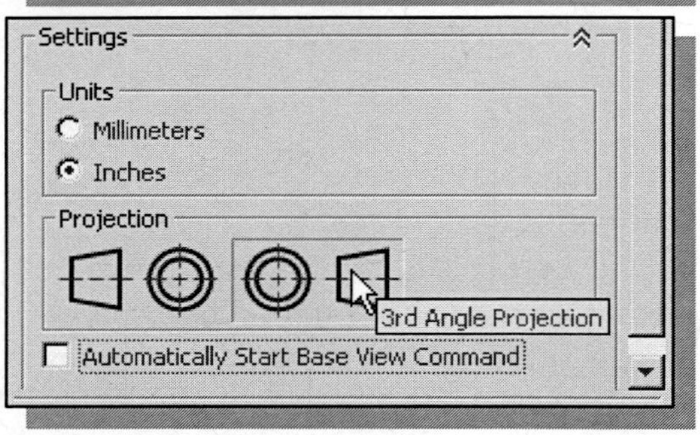

5. In the *Settings* area, confirm the *Units* are set to **Inches** and the *Projection* type is set to **3rd Angle Projection** as shown.

6. **Uncheck** the Automatically Start Base View Command option as shown.

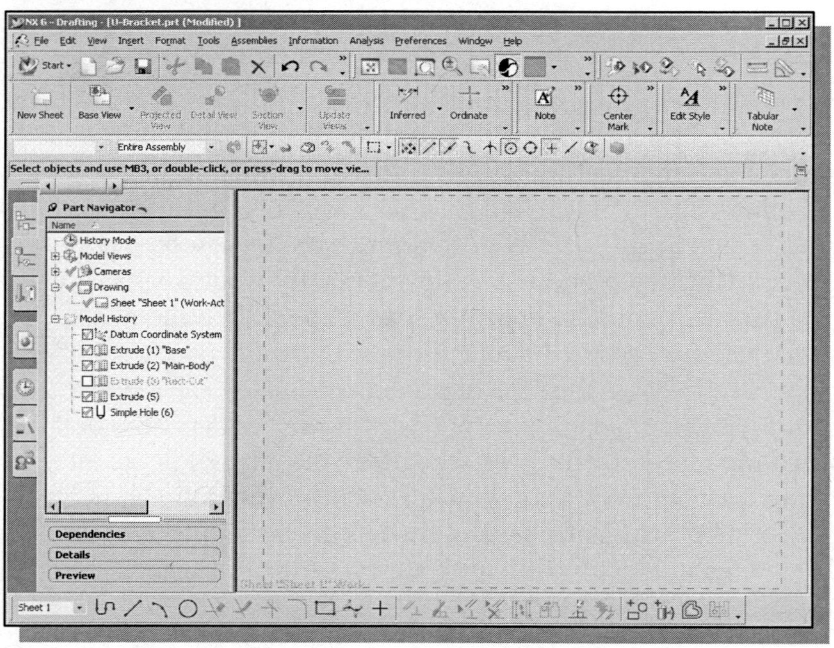

7. Click **OK** to accept the settings and proceed with the creation of the drawing sheet.

➢ Note that a new graphics window appears on the screen. The dashed rectangle indicates the size of the current active drawing sheet.

Adding a Base View

❖ In *UGS NX Drafting* mode, the first drawing view we create is called a ***base view***. A *base* view is the primary view in a drawing; other views can be derived from this view. When creating a *base* view, *UGS NX* allows us to specify one of the principle views to be shown. By default, *UGS NX* will treat the *world X-Z* plane as the *front* view of the solid model.

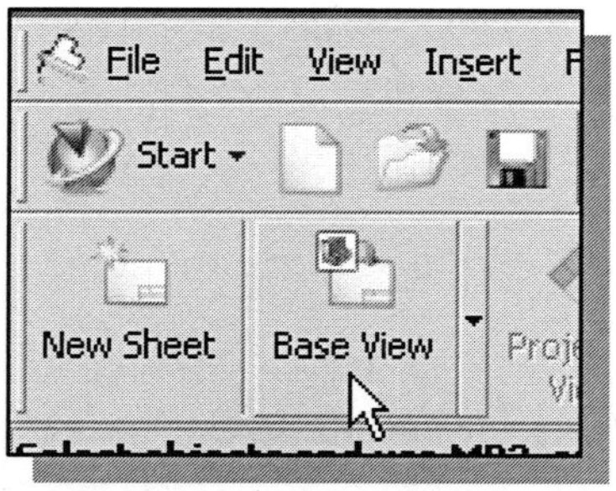

1. Click on the **Base View** icon in the *Drawing Layout* toolbar to create a new *base* view.

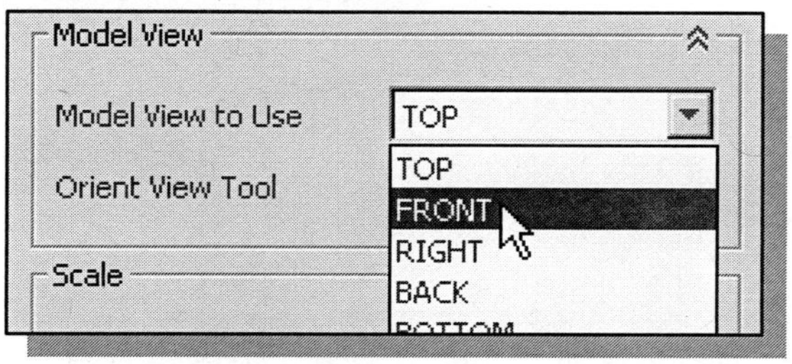

2. In the *Model View* option area, set the view option to **Front** as shown.

3. In the *View Style* option area, click the **View Style** icon as shown.

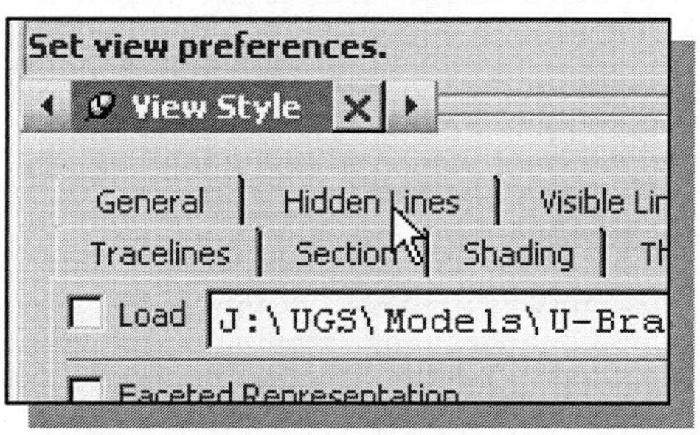

4. In the *View Style* window, click the **Hidden Lines** tab as shown.

➢ The *View Style* window contains the different settings for the *base* view.

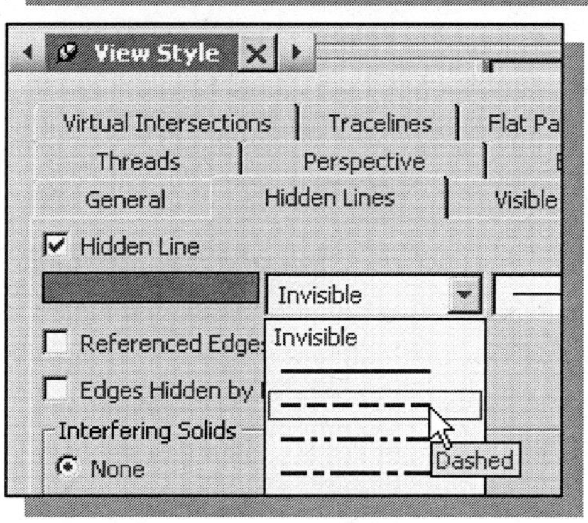

5. Choose **Dashed** as the linetype to be used for hidden lines in the *base* view.

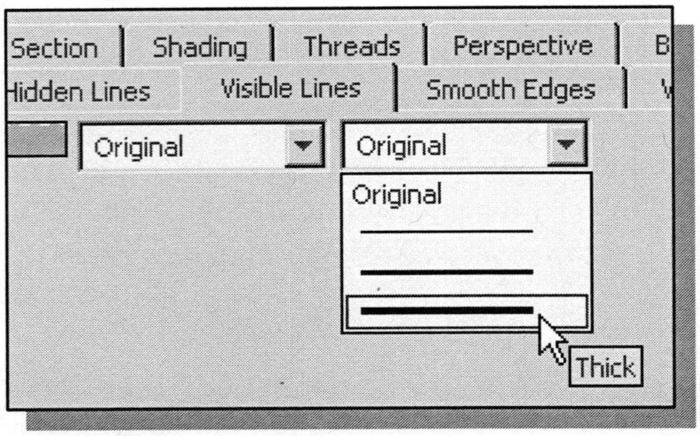

6. Click on the **Visible Lines** tab and select **Thick** as the linetype for the *base* view.

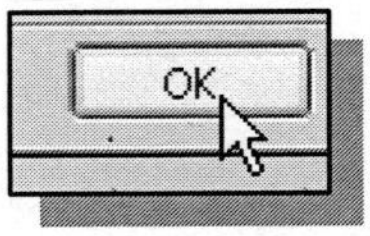

7. Click **OK** to accept the settings and exit the **View Style** command.

8. Place the ***base* view**, the *front* view of the *U-Bracket* model, near the lower half of the drawing sheet as shown.

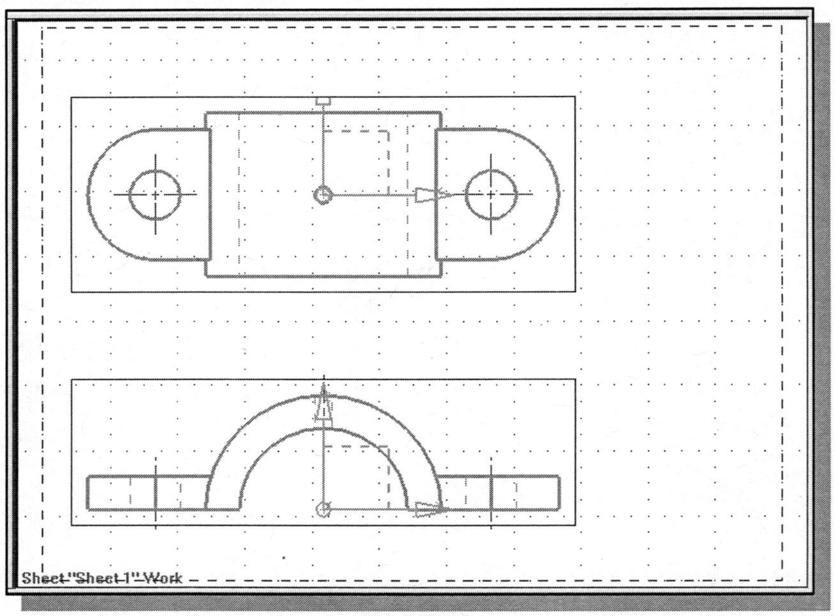

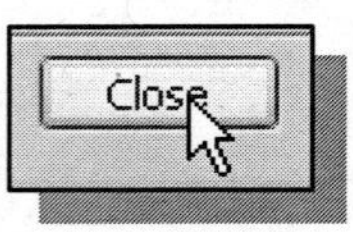

9. Move the cursor above the *front* view and place the ***top* view**; close the *Projected View* dialog box. Note the projection is done automatically, relative to the established *base* view.

❖ In *UGS NX Drafting mode*, ***projected* views** can be created with a first-angle or third-angle projection, depending on the drafting standard used for the drawing. We must have a ***base* view** before a *projected* view can be created. In *UGS NX*, the *base* view can be a 2D principal view, or an isometric or trimetric view. Also, *projected views* are done using orthographic projections; orthographic projections are always aligned to the *base* view and inherit the *base* view's scale and display settings. We will also add an *isometric* view in the following sections. Before adding the *isometric* view, we will first make two adjustments to the current drawing sheet: (1) change the drafting display to monochrome, and (2) change to a B-Size drawing sheet for more space.

Drawing Display Option

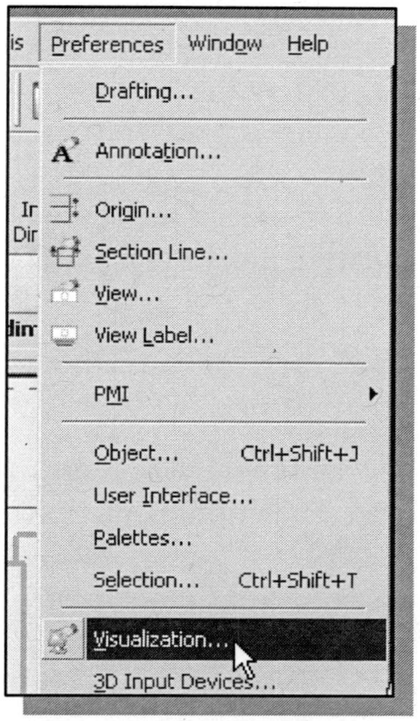

1. Select **Visualization** in the *Preferences* pull-down menu as shown.

2. Click on the **Color Settings** tab as shown.

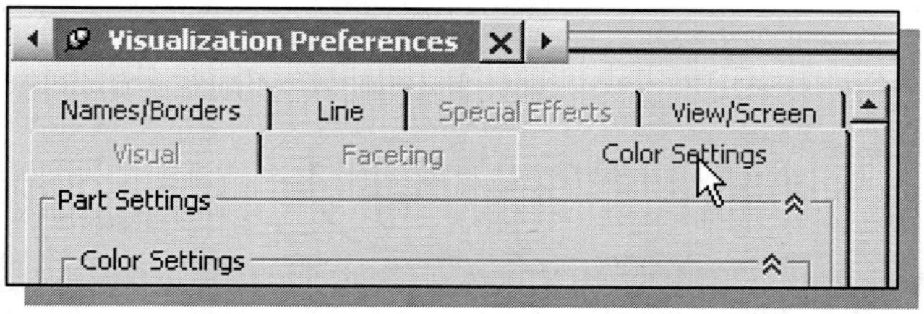

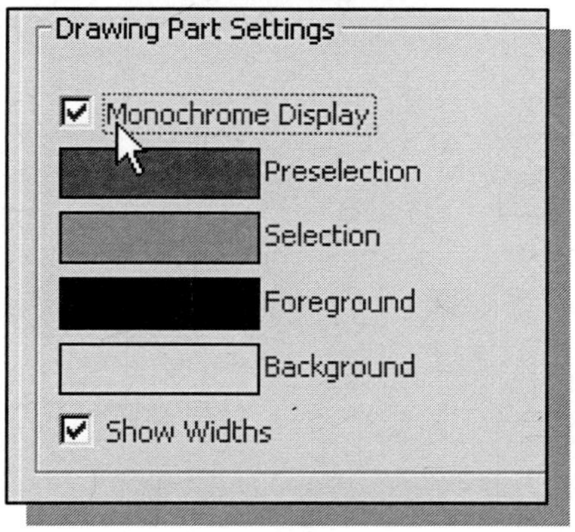

3. Activate the **Monochrome Display** and the **Show Widths** options as shown.

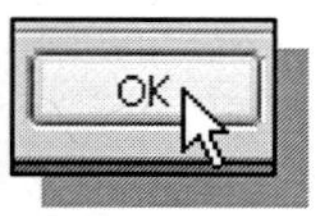

4. Click **OK** to accept the settings and exit the *Visualization Preferences* window.

Changing the Size of the Drawing Sheet

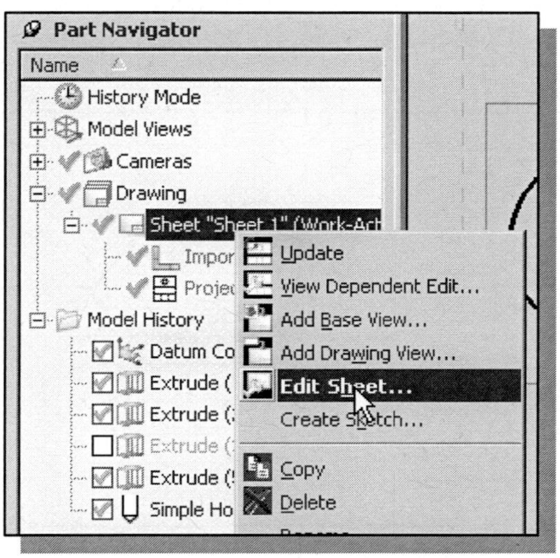

1. Open the *Part Navigator* and right-mouse-click (MB3) on ***Sheet "SH1"*** to bring up the options list.

2. Select **Edit Sheet** in the option menu.

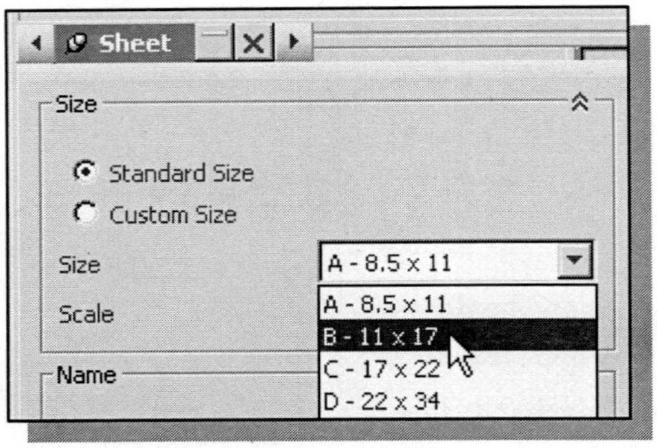

3. Inside the *Edit Sheet* dialog box, set the sheet *Size* to **B-11X17** as shown in the figure.

4. Click on the **OK** button to accept the settings and proceed with updating the drawing views.

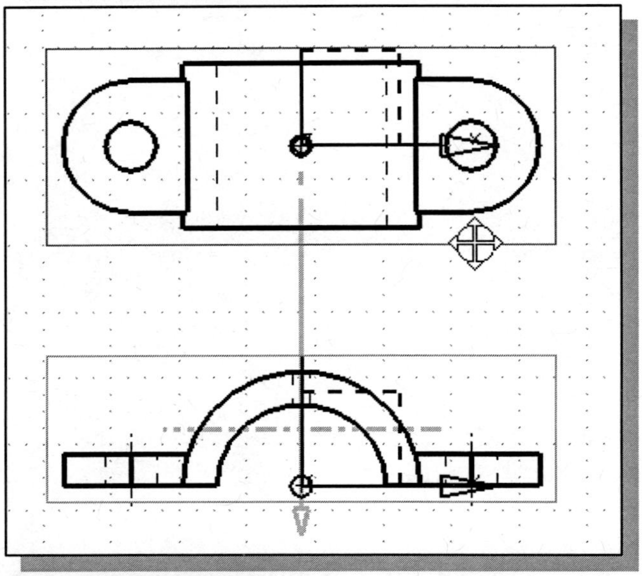

5. Click and drag the view borders of the views to reposition them.

➢ Note the dashed lines indicating alignments between the views.

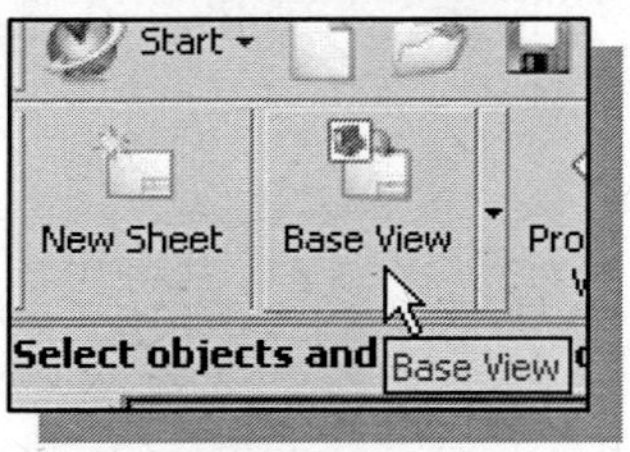

6. Click on **Base View** in the *Drawing Layout* toolbar to create a new *base* view.

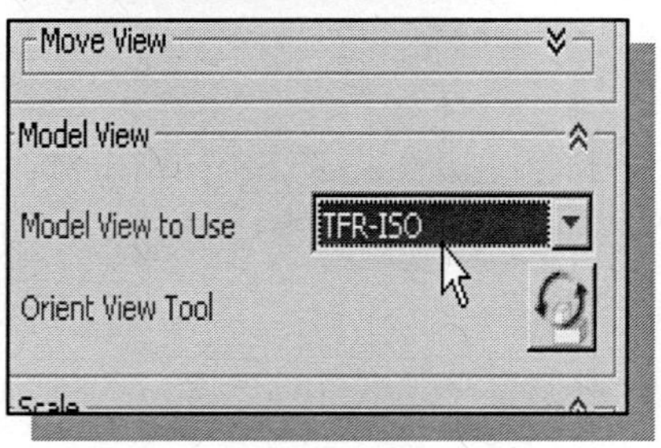

7. Select **TFR-ISO** in the view list, and place an *isometric* view to the right side of the drawing sheet as shown.

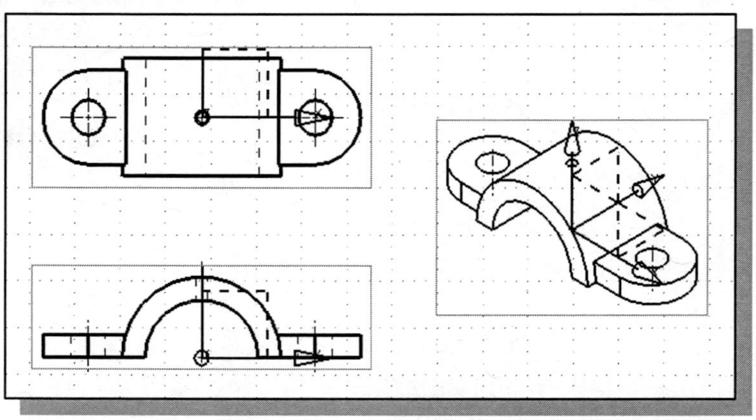

Turning Off the Datum Planes and WCS

➢ The display of the datum planes and/or WCS can be turned off in *Drafting* mode or in *Modeling* mode. To illustrate the relations between the different modules, we will perform this operation in the *Modeling* mode.

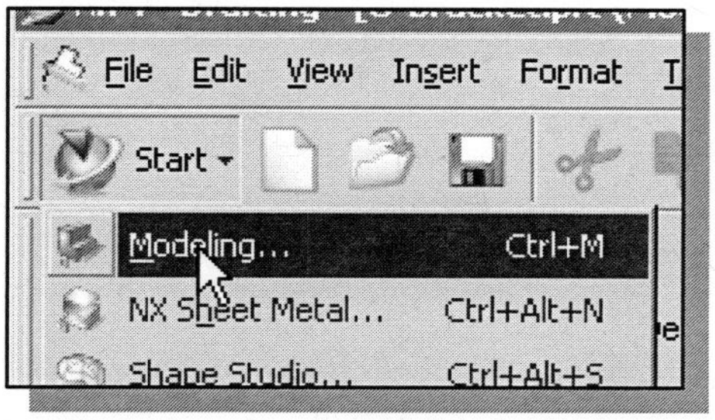

1. Switch back to the *Modeling* module by selecting **Modeling** in the *Start* list as shown.

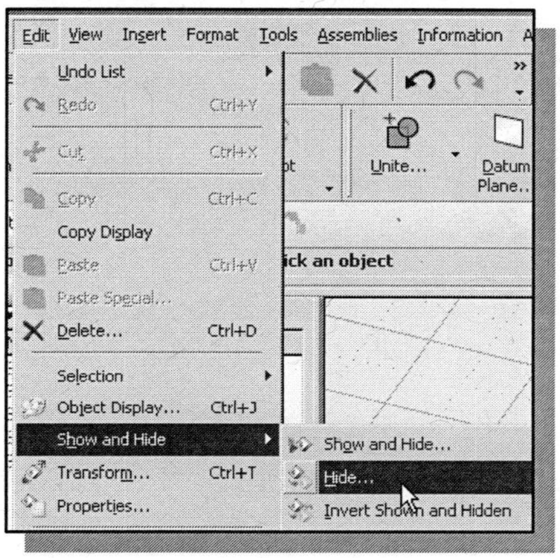

2. Select the **Hide** command through the *Edit* pull-down menu:

   [Edit] → [Show and Hide] → [Hide]

➢ The **Hide** command can be used to temporarily turn *OFF* the display of objects.

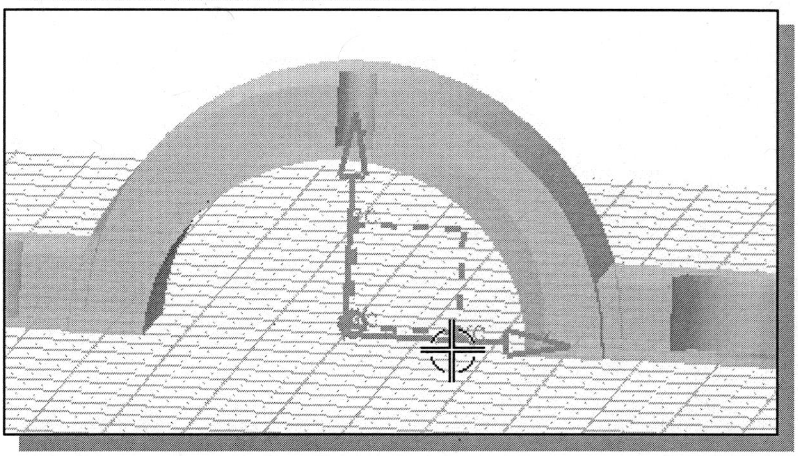

3. On your own, select the datum features near the center of the solid model as shown. (Hint: Use the dynamic rotation function to assist the selection of objects.)

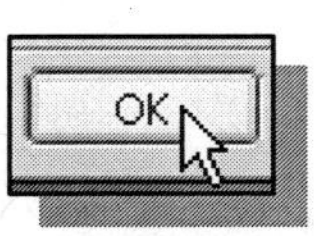

4. Click **OK** to accept the selections.

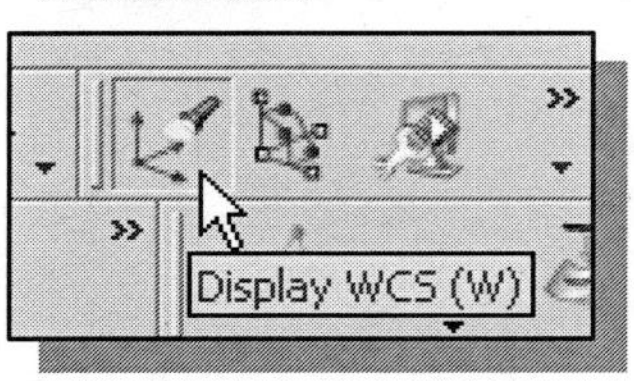

5. Click on the **Display WCS** icon to toggle *OFF* the display of the WCS as shown.

❖ Turning *OFF* the *datum features* and *WCS* does not affect the solid features in any way; all of the information is preserved correctly in the *Model History*.

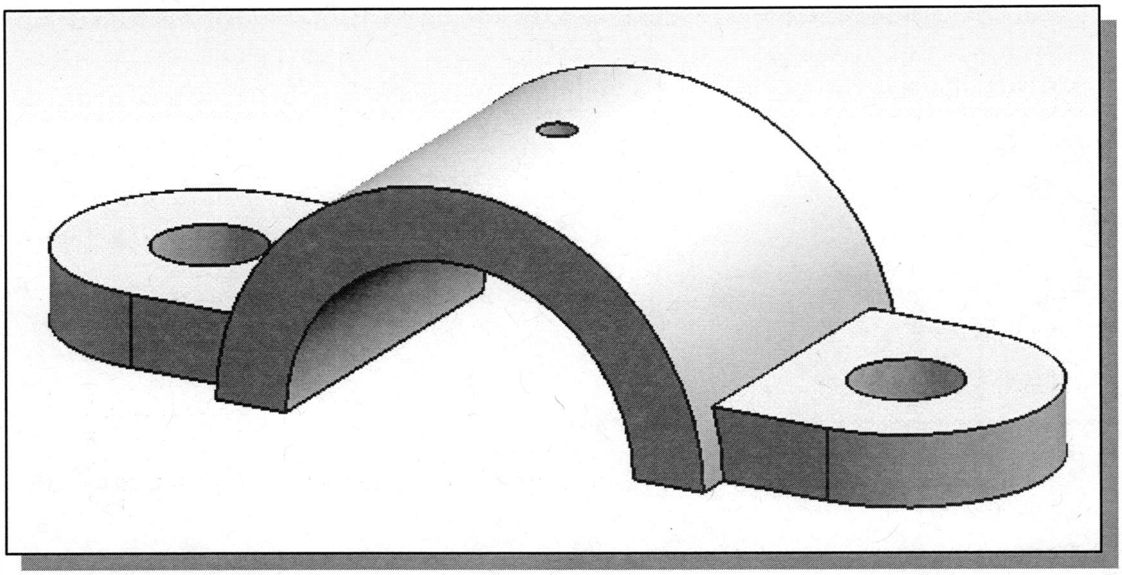

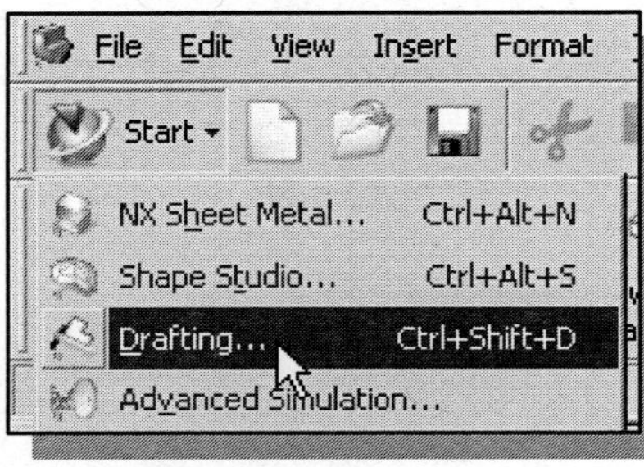

6. Click on the **Start** icon in the *Standard* toolbar area to display the available options.

7. Select **Drafting** from the option list.

❖ With *parametric modeling*, all modules use the same database; any changes made in the *Modeling* module are reflected in the *Drafting* module, as shown in the figure.

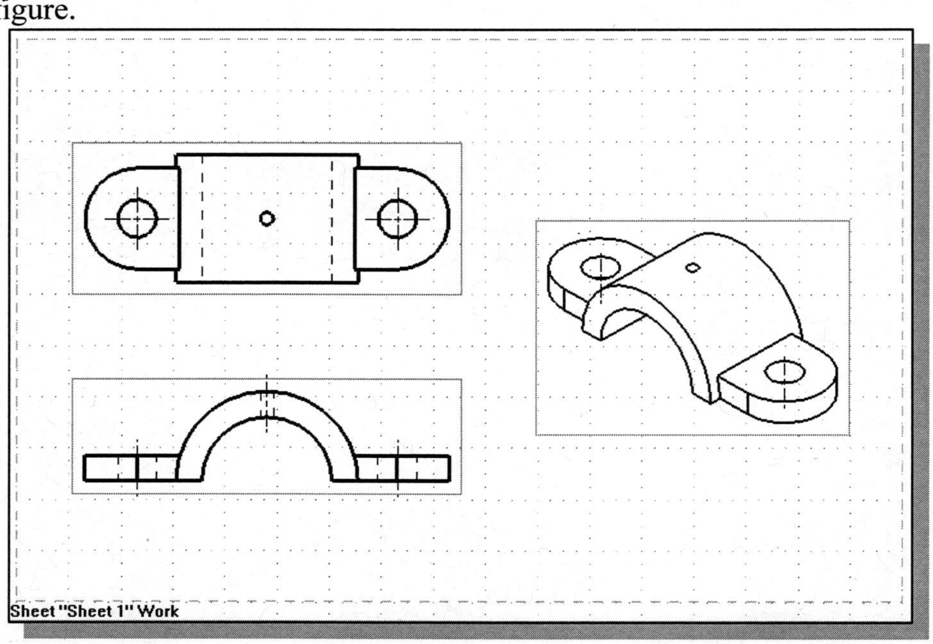

Displaying Feature Dimensions

- Feature dimensions (parameters) can be displayed in 2D views in *UGS NX*. We have the option of selecting which feature parameters to display in which views.

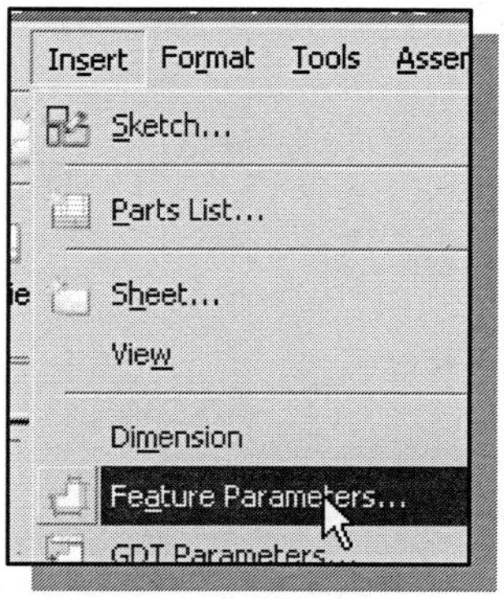

1. Select **Feature Parameters** in the **Insert** pull-down list as shown.

2. In the *Feature Parameters* window, notice the **ansi** standard is used for the dimension settings.

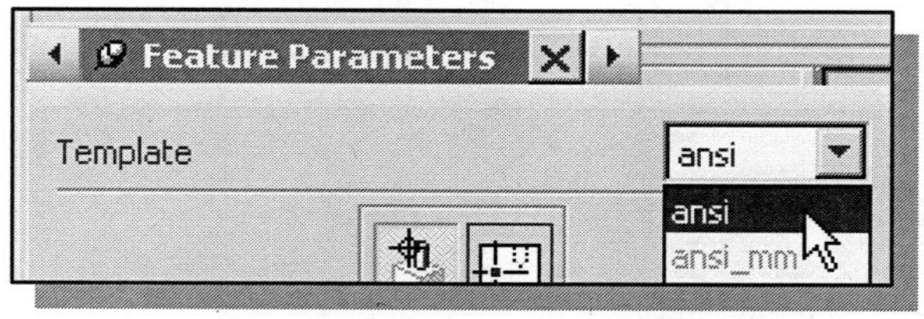

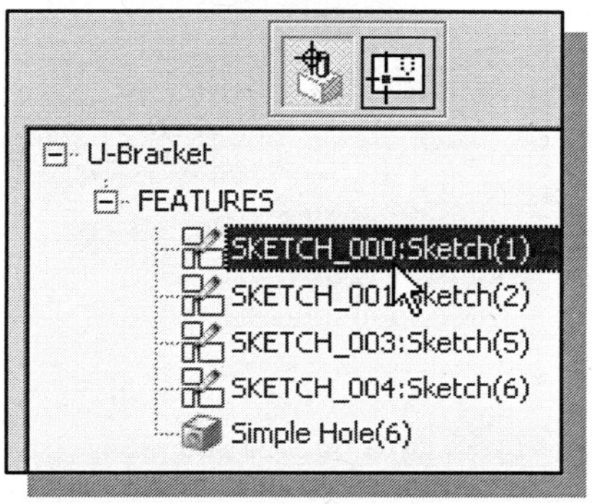

❖ Two steps are required: (1) select the feature used; and (2) select the view to place the dimensions.

3. Expand the *FEATURES* list and choose the first sketch, which is related to the ***base*** feature *(Sketch(1))*, as shown in the figure.

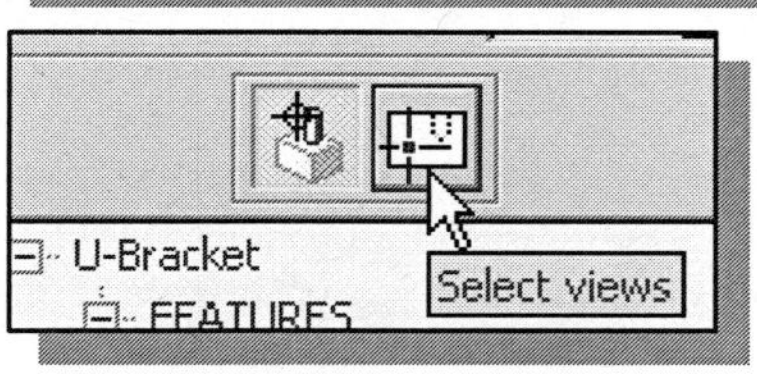

4. Click the **Select views** icon to proceed to the next step.

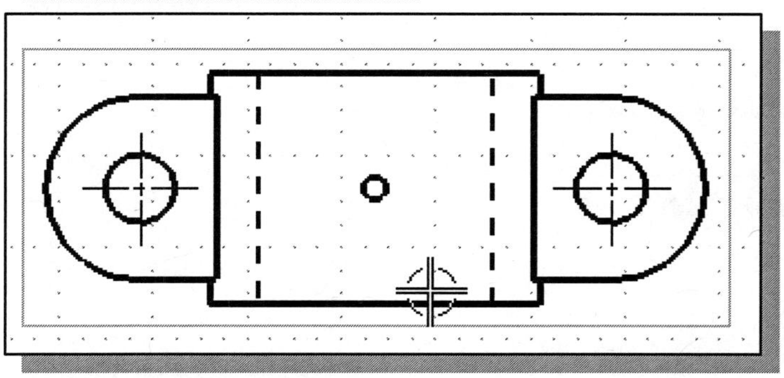

5. Inside the graphics window, select the ***top* view** by clicking once with the left-mouse-button (MB1) as shown.

❖ Note that the corresponding view name is highlighted as soon as we click on a view in the graphics window.

6. Click **Apply** to accept the settings.

❖ The feature dimensions that were used to create the *base* feature have now been retrieved and placed in the *top* view.

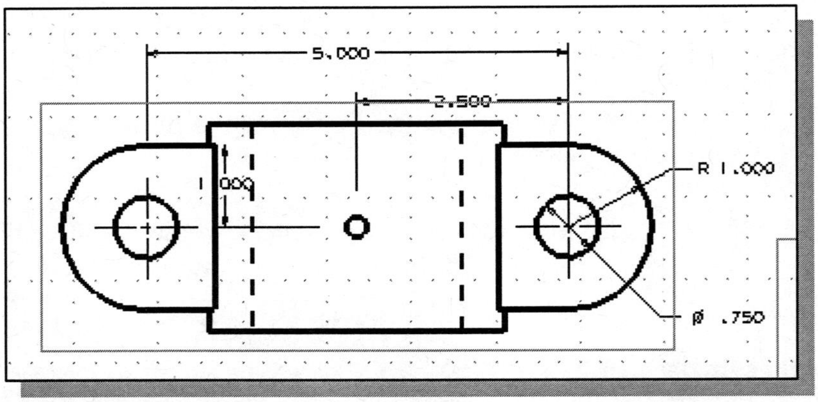

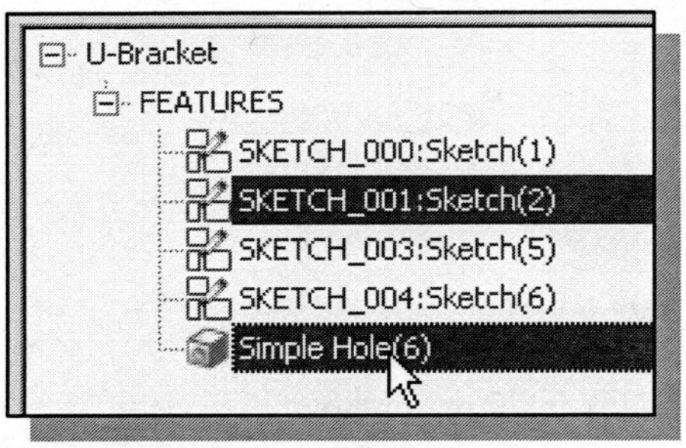

7. Hold down the [**Ctrl**] key and select both the sketches related to the ***Main-Body (Sketch 2)*** and ***Circular_Cut (6)*** features in the *FEATURES* list as shown.

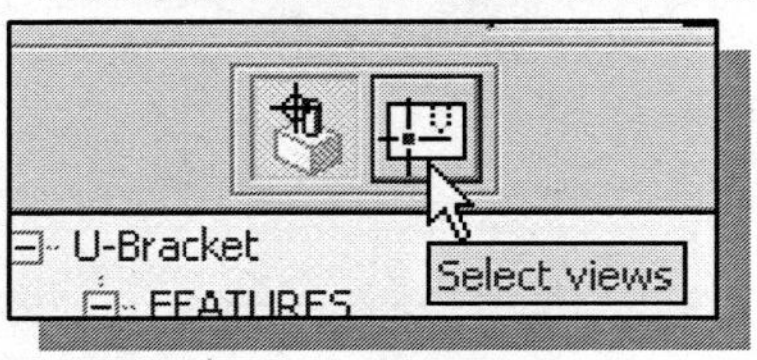

8. Click the **Select views** icon to proceed to the next step.

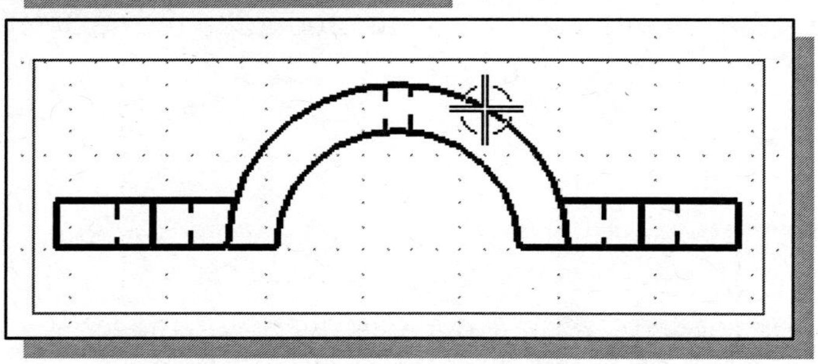

9. Inside the graphics window, select the ***front* view** as shown.

10. Click **Apply** to accept the settings.

❖ Note that more than one feature can be selected when placing feature dimensions with the **Feature Parameters** command.

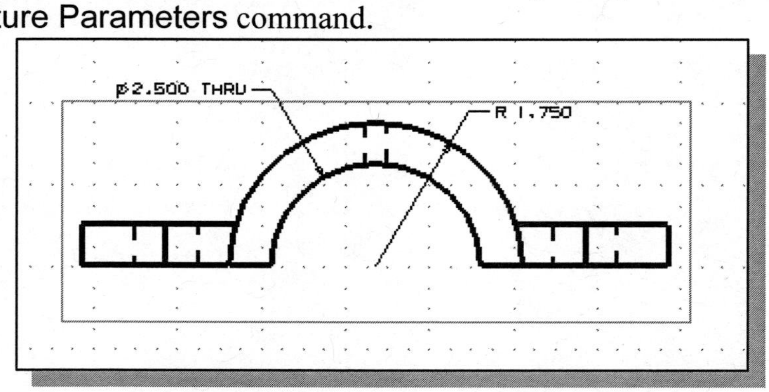

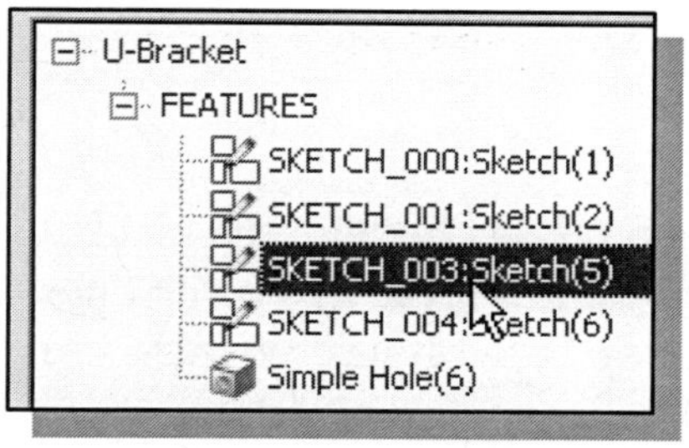

11. On your own, repeat the above process and retrieve the feature dimensions of the *CenterDrill (5)* feature and place them in the ***top* view** as shown in the figure below.

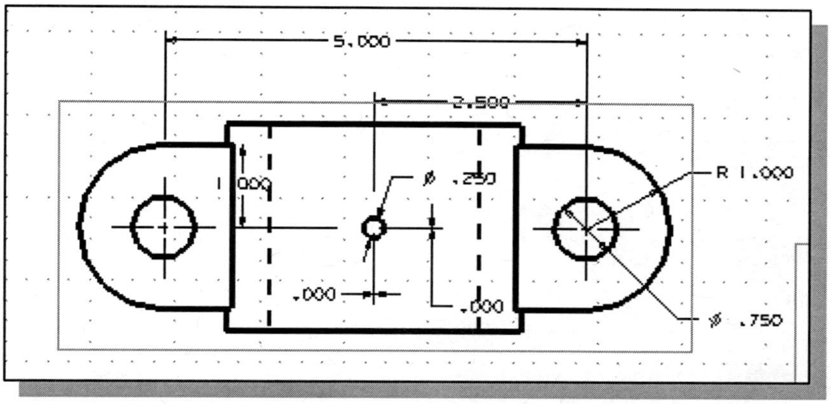

12. Click **Cancel** to end the **Feature Parameters** command.

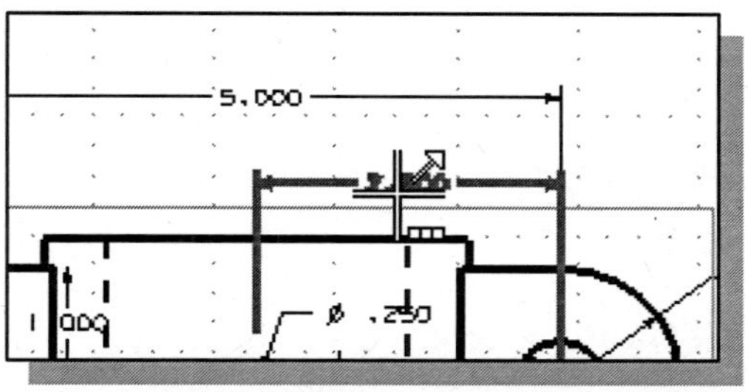

13. On your own, reposition the dimensions by **click and drag** with the left-mouse-button on the individual dimension.

❖ Your screen should appear as shown in the figure below.

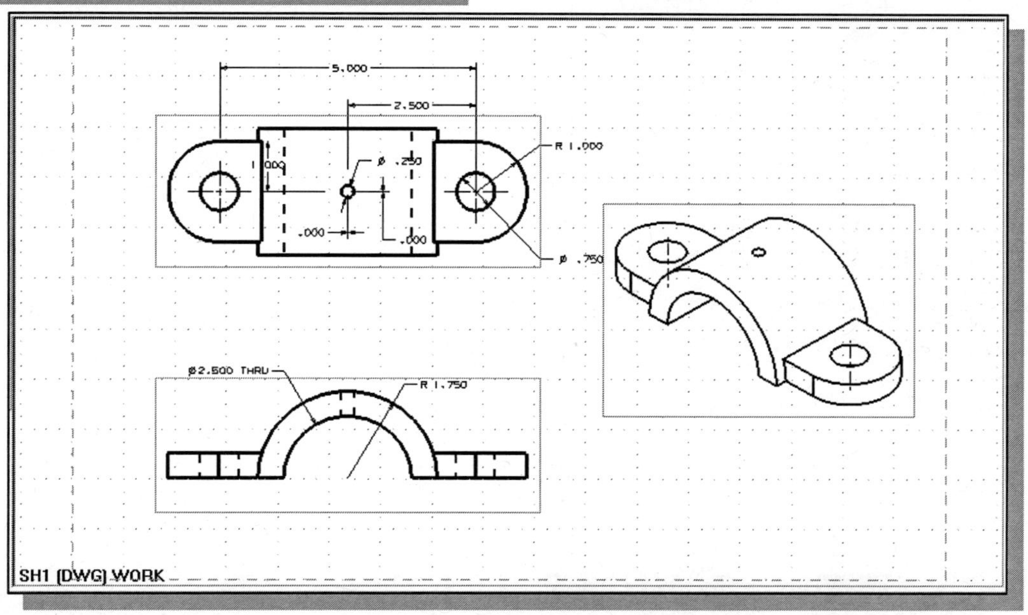

➢ Several commonly used drafting standards, such as *ISO* and *DIN* can be loaded through the **Tools → Drafting Standard** option.

Adjusting the Display of Tangency Edges

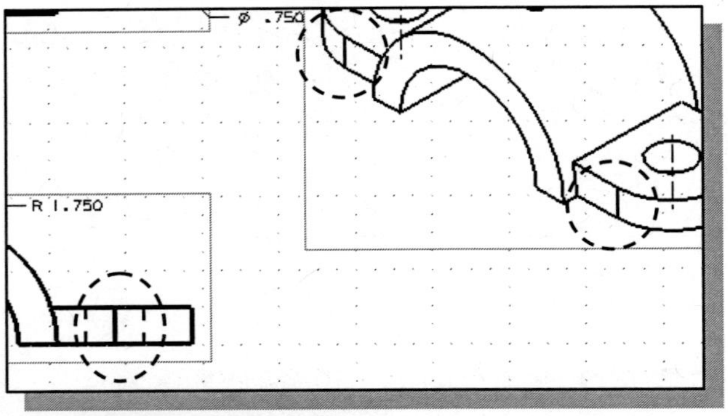

- In *UGS NX*, by default, the tangency edges are displayed as visible lines as shown in the figure. We can turn off the display through the **View Style** command.

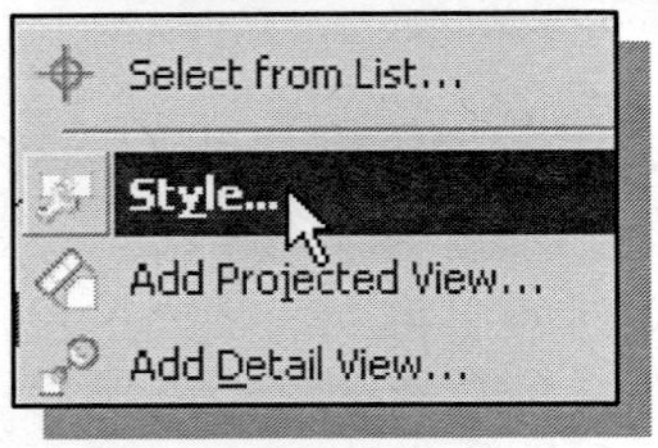

1. Right-mouse-click once on the view border of the *isometric* view to bring up the options list.

2. Select the **Style** option as shown.

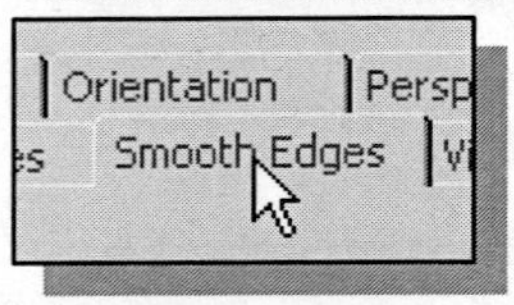

3. Left-mouse-click (MB1) the **Smooth Edges** tab as shown.

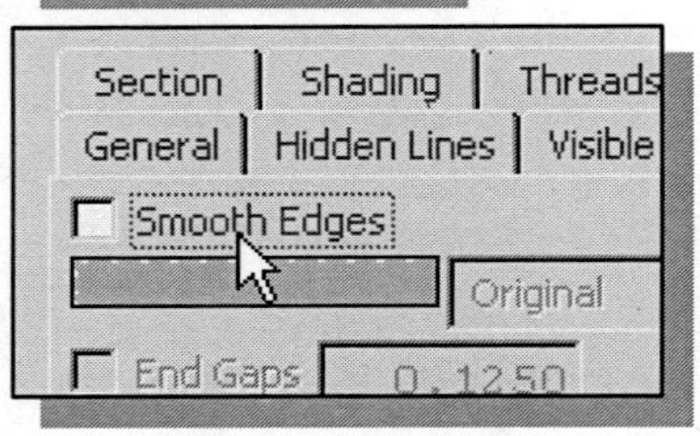

4. Turn *OFF* the **Smooth Edges** option as shown.

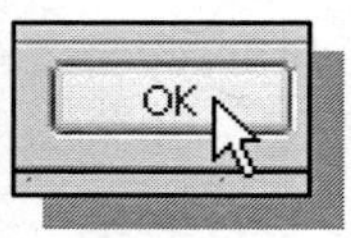

5. Click **OK** to accept the settings.

➢ Note the tangency edges are turned off as shown in the figure below.

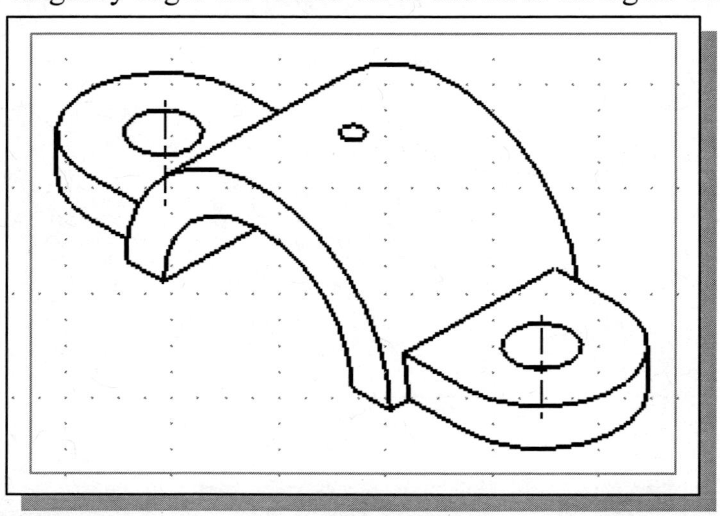

➢ On your own, repeat the above steps to turn off the edges in the *front* view.

Hiding Feature Dimensions

❖ In *UGS NX*, two options are available to remove any of the displayed feature dimensions: (1) the **Delete** command, or (2) the **Hide** command. Using the Delete command, removed feature dimensions can be redisplayed by using the Feature Parameters command, which is a more intuitive approach. The Hide command is more of a general Hide command, and the Show command is required to redisplay any of the hidden items.

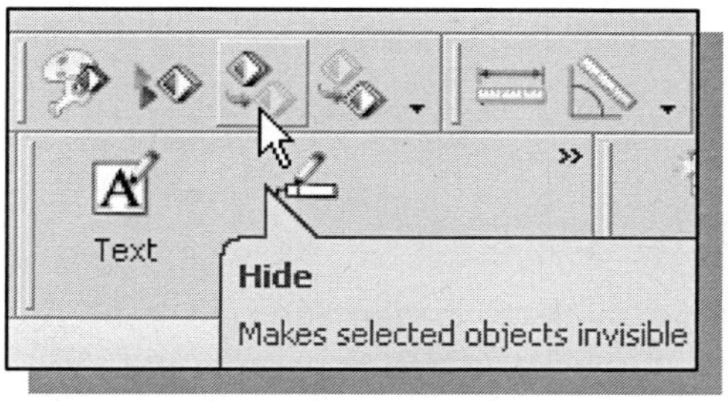

1. Select the **Hide** command in the *Utility* toolbar as shown.

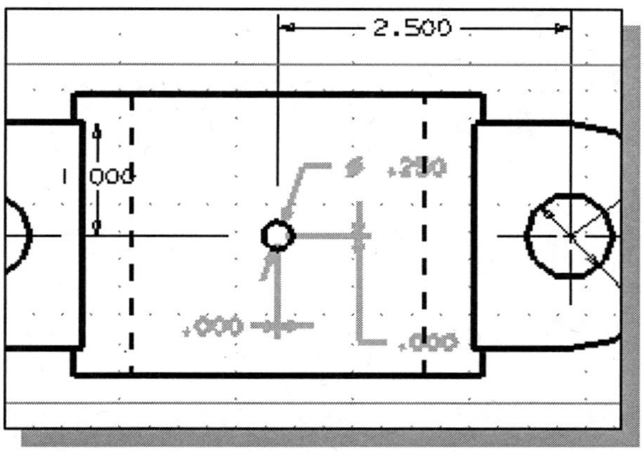

2. Select the three dimensions associated with the *CenterDrill* feature in the *top* view as shown.

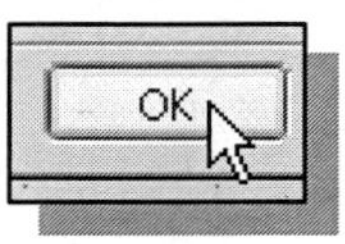

3. Click **OK** to accept the selections.

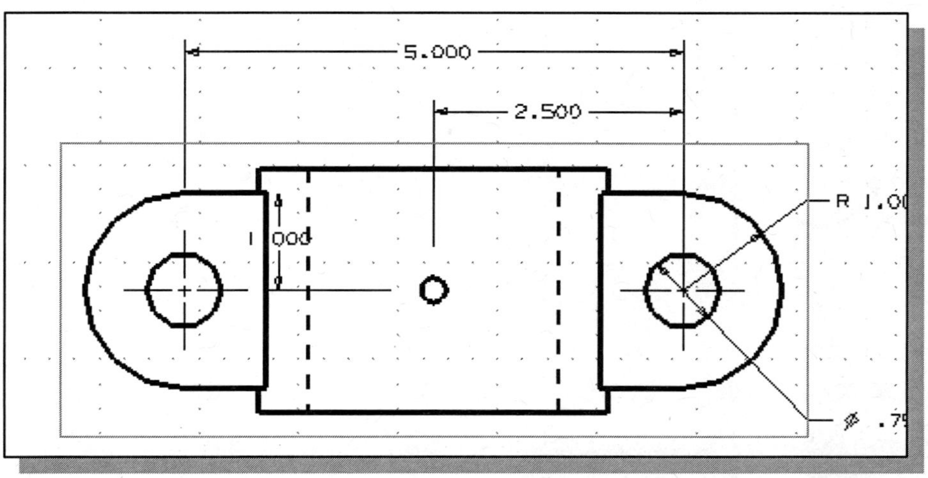

Unhide the Hidden Dimensions

❖ The **Show** command is required to redisplay any of the objects that were turned off using the **Hide** command.

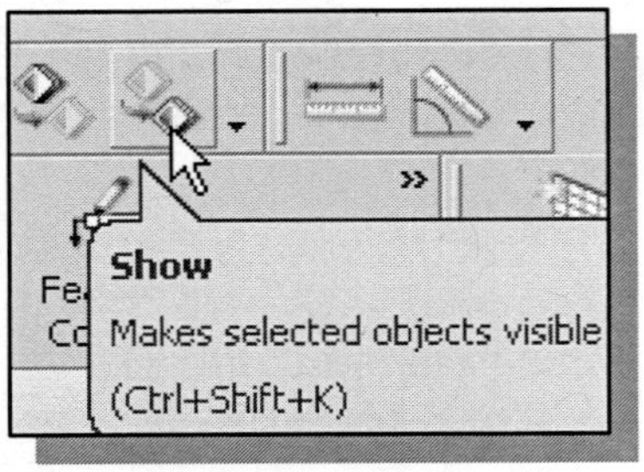

1. Select the **Show** command in the *Utility* toolbar as shown.

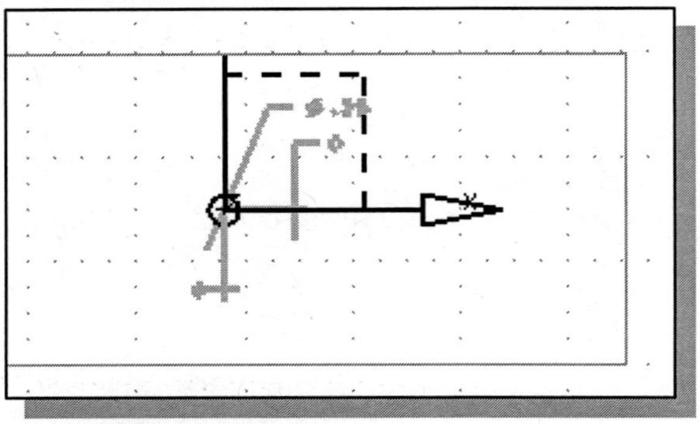

2. Select the three dimensions associated with the *CenterDrill* feature in the top view as shown.

❖ Note the datum features are also available to be redisplayed.

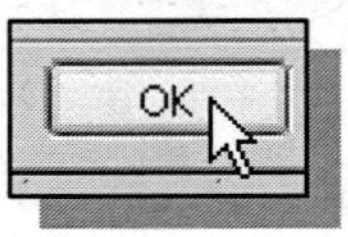

3. Click **OK** to accept the selections.

❖ The dimensions that were removed from the display are redisplayed on the screen as shown in the figure below.

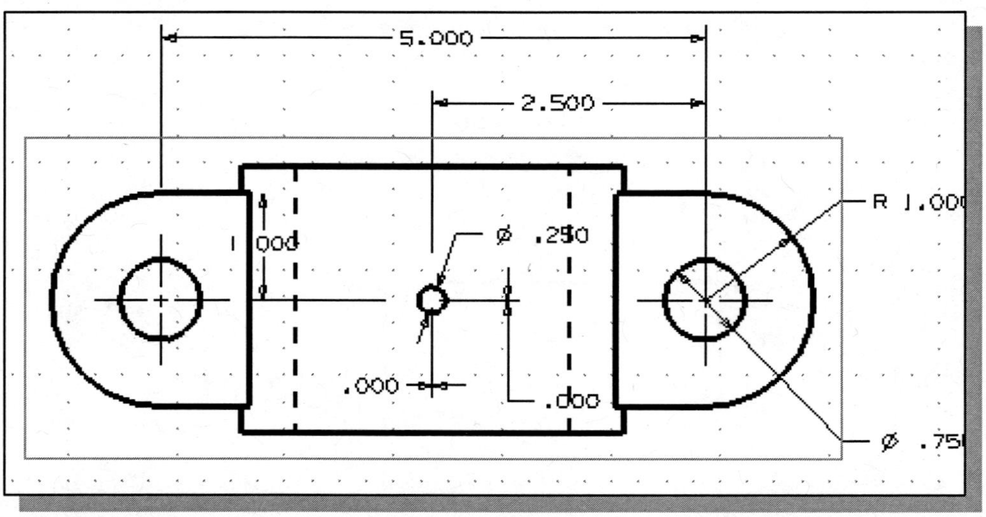

Deleting Feature Dimensions

❖ The **Delete** command is a more intuitive approach for removing feature dimensions. The removed features are not stored in a temporary location, as they are with the Hide command. To redisplay any deleted feature dimensions, use the Feature Parameters command (page 8-11), which is what is expected.

1. Select the **Delete** command through the *Edit* pull-down menu:

   [Edit] → [Delete]

➢ The Delete command can also be activated using the key combination [**Ctrl+D**].

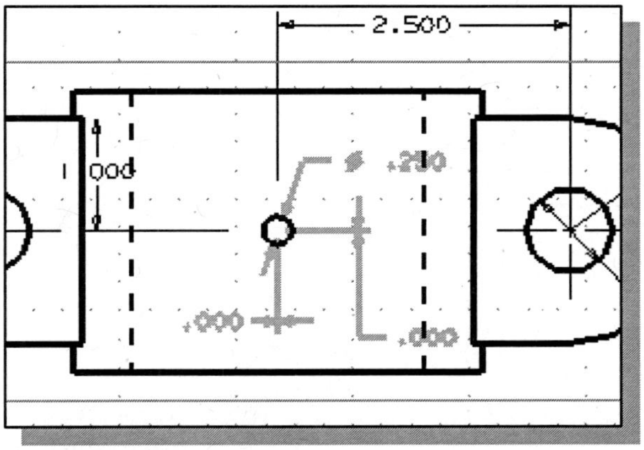

2. Select the three **dimensions** associated with the *CenterDrill* feature in the top view as shown.

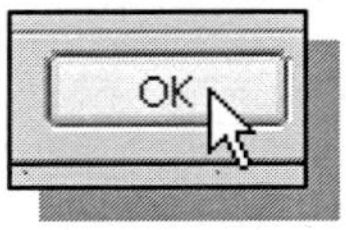

3. Click **OK** to accept the selections.

4. On your own, confirm the deleted dimensions cannot be redisplayed using the Show command.

❖ Also, note another quick way to delete objects is to use the ***pre-selection*** option. Pre-select the objects before issuing a command, then hit the [**Delete**] key on the keypad.

Adding Center Marks

1. Select the **Center Mark** command through the *Dimension* toolbar.

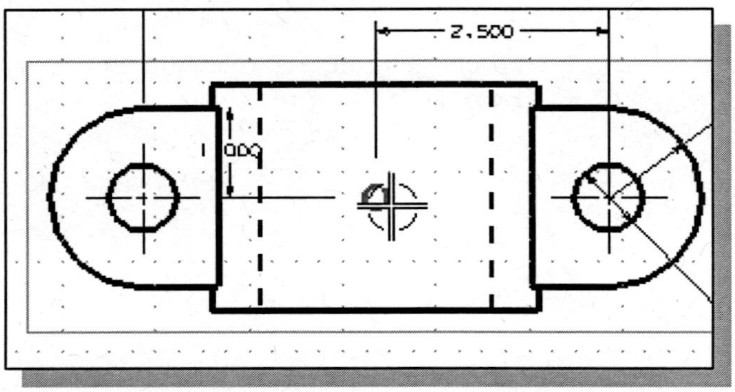

2. Click once, with the left-mouse-button (MB1), on the small circle in the *top* view as shown.

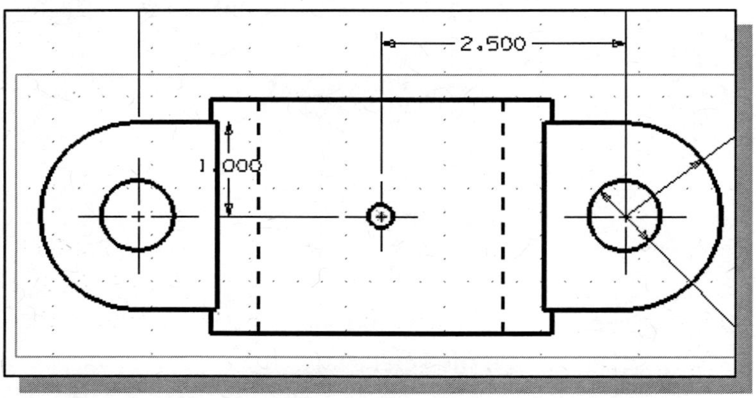

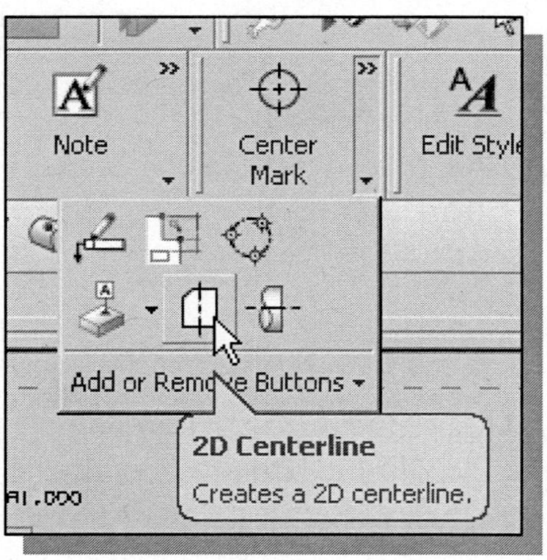

➢ Note that the **Center Mark** command is used to create centermarks on circular views of cylindrical features. For edge views of cylindrical features, we can use the **2D Centerline** command. Note other centerline options are also available.

Adding Additional Dimensions – Reference Dimensions

- Besides displaying the **feature dimensions**, dimensions used to create the features, we can also add additional **reference dimensions** in the drawing. *Feature* dimensions are used to control the geometry, whereas *reference* dimensions are controlled by the existing geometry. In the drawing layout, therefore, we can ***add*** or ***delete*** *reference* dimensions, but we can only ***hide*** the *feature dimensions.* One should try to use as many *feature* dimensions as possible and add *reference* dimensions only if necessary. It is also more effective to use *feature* dimensions in the drawing layout since they are created when the model was built. Note that additional *Drafting* mode entities, such as lines and arcs, can be added to drawing views. Before *Drafting* mode entities can be used in a reference dimension, they must be associated to a *drawing view.*

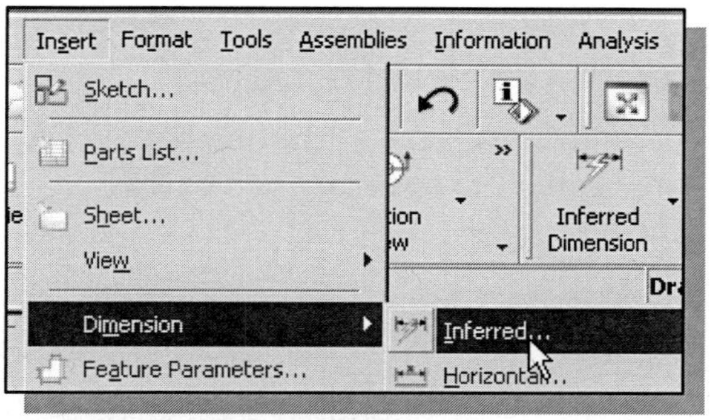

1. Select the **Inferred Dimension** command through the *Insert* pull-down menu:

   [Insert] → [Dimension] → [Inferred]

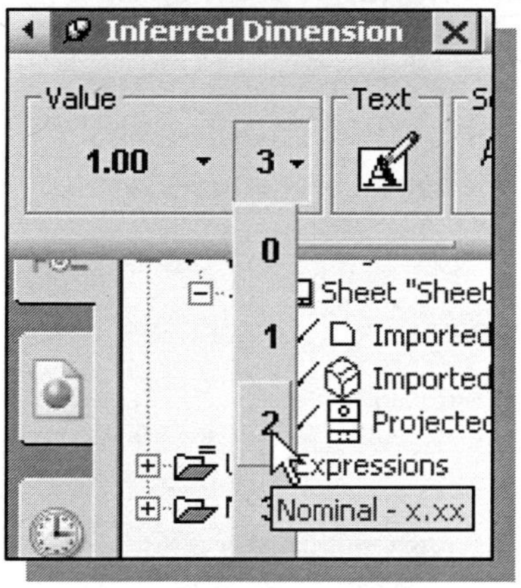

- ➢ Note the different settings available near the upper left corner of the graphics window.

2. On your own, set the display of the number of digits after the decimal point to **2** as shown.

3. In the prompt area, the message "*Select first object for inferred Dimension or double click to edit*" is displayed. Select the **small circle** in the top view.

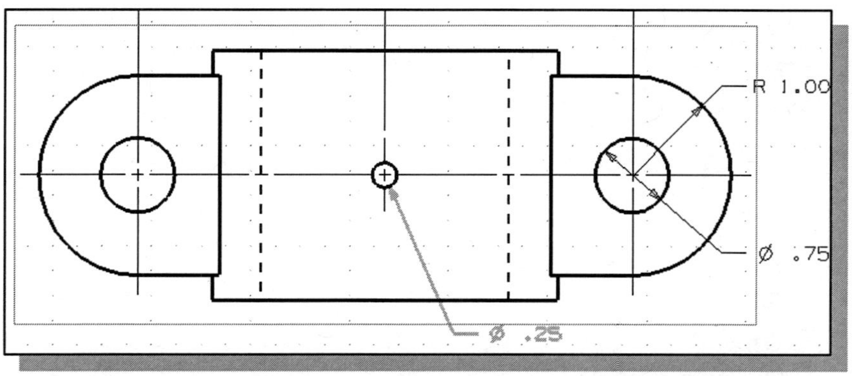

4. Place the dimension text below the *top* view as shown.

5. Click once with the middle-mouse-button (MB2) to end the Dimension command.

Changing the Dimension Appearance

1. Edit the length dimension ***5.000***, by **double-clicking** on the dimension with the left-mouse-button.

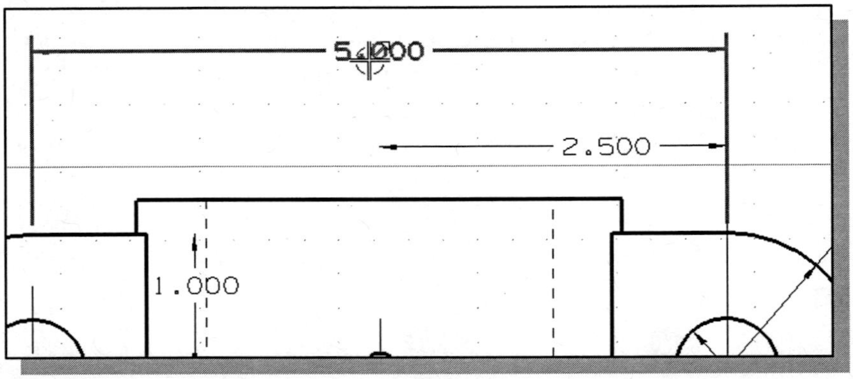

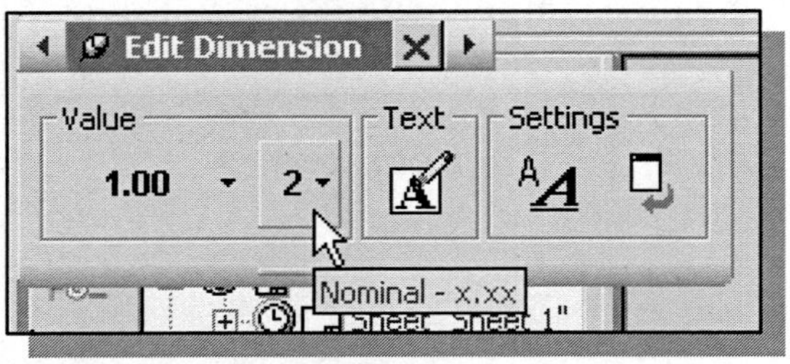

2. Change the display of the number of digits after the decimal point to **2** as shown.

3. Click once with the middle-mouse-button (MB2) to accept the settings and proceed with the **Edit Dimension** command.

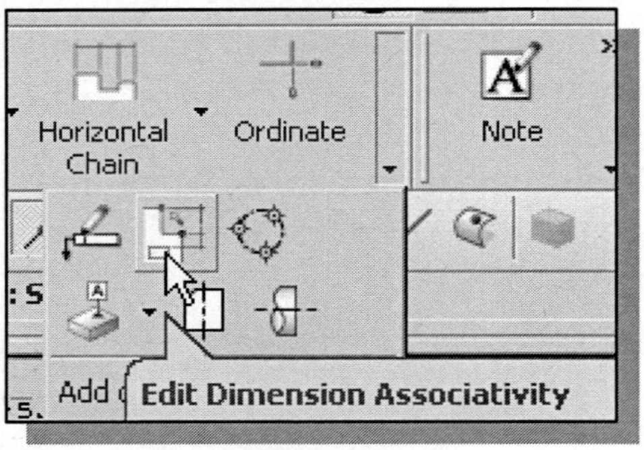

4. Click the **Edit Dimension Associativity** icon in the *Dimension* toolbar as shown.

5. Select the ***5.00*** dimension with the left-mouse button.

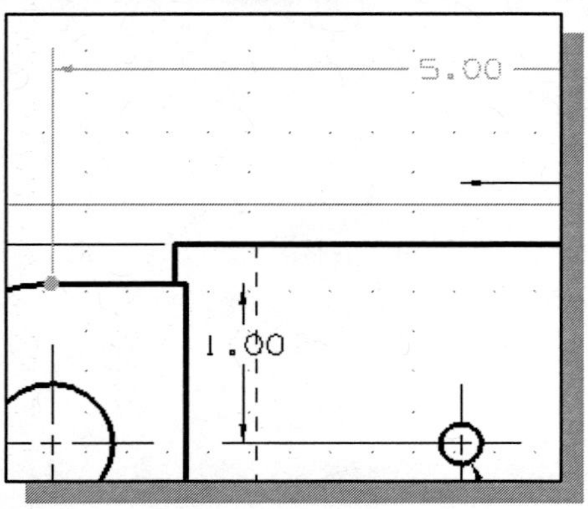

6. Notice that a little dot on one side of the dimension indicating the dimension is attached to the end of the arc as shown.

7. Also note the selection option is activated in the dialog box as shown.

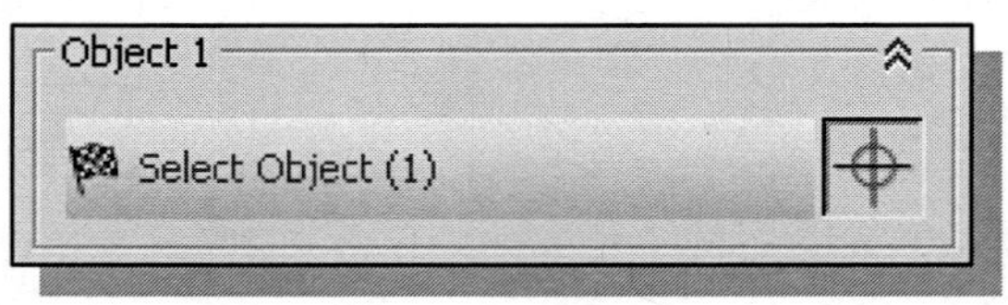

8. Select the small circle, directly below its current position. Click the circle when its **Centerpoint** symbol is displayed.

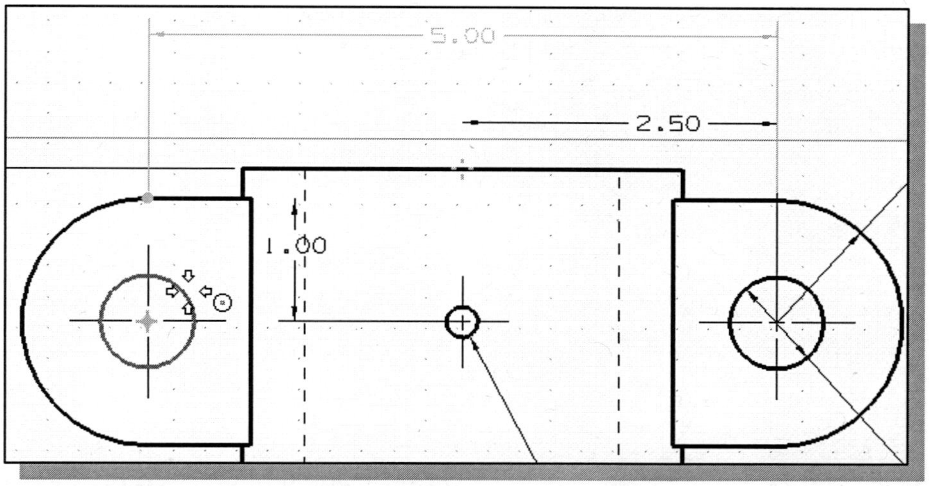

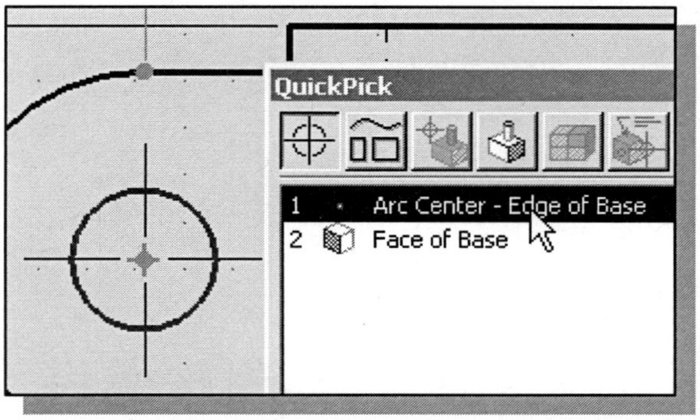

9. Choose **Arc Center** in the *QuickPick* dialog box if necessary.

10. On your own, repeat the above steps and add/modify/hide/delete the necessary dimensions as shown in the figure below.

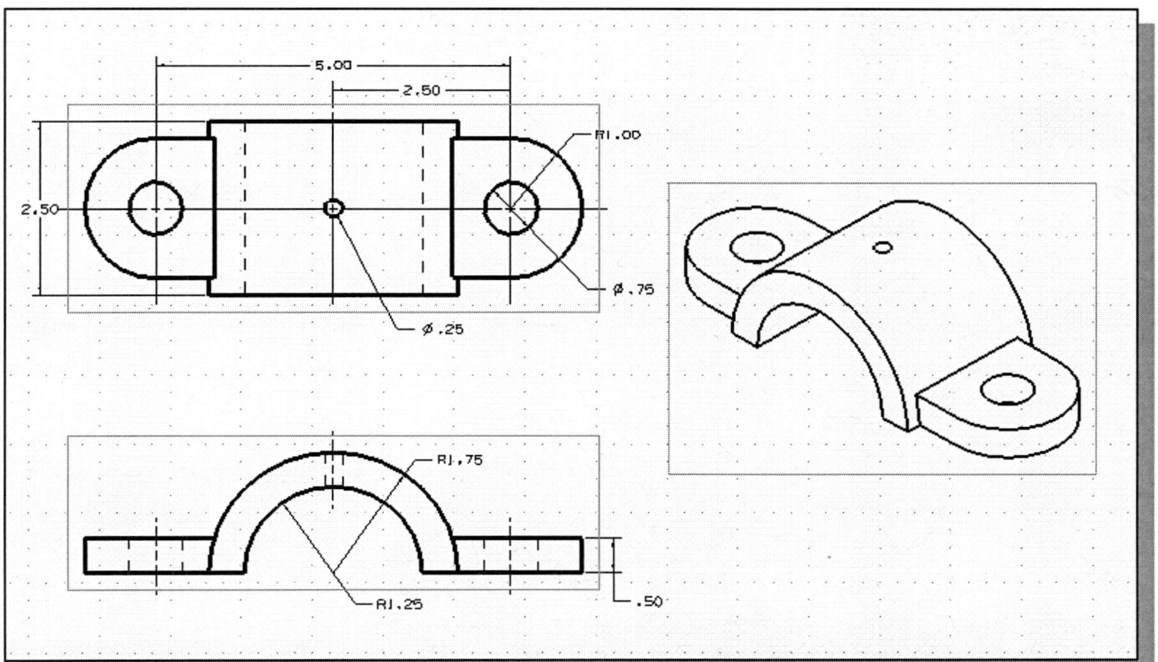

Associative Functionality – Modifying Feature Dimensions

- *UGS NX's associative functionality* allows us to change the design at any level, and the system reflects the changes at all levels automatically.

1. Select the **Start** icon with a single click of the left-mouse-button (MB1) in the *Standard* toolbar.

2. Pick **Modeling** in the pull-down list as shown in the figure to switch to the *Part Modeling* mode.

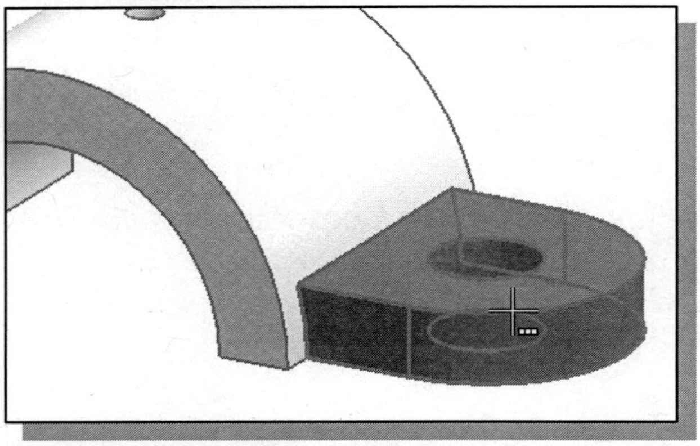

3. Double-click, with the left-mouse-button (MB1), on the *base* feature to enter the ***Edit*** mode.

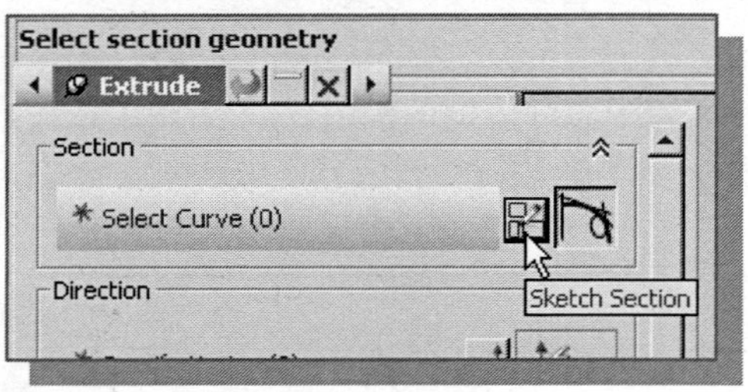

4. Select **Sketch Section** in the *Extrude* window to enter the *2D Sketcher*.

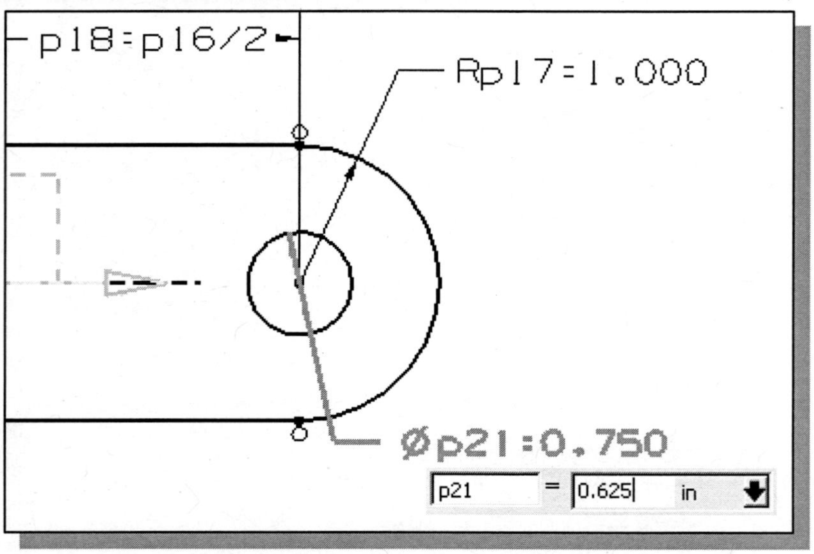

5. Double-click on the diameter ***0.750*** dimension of the *base* feature as shown in the figure.

6. In the *Edit Dimension* dialog box, enter **0.625** as the new diameter dimension.

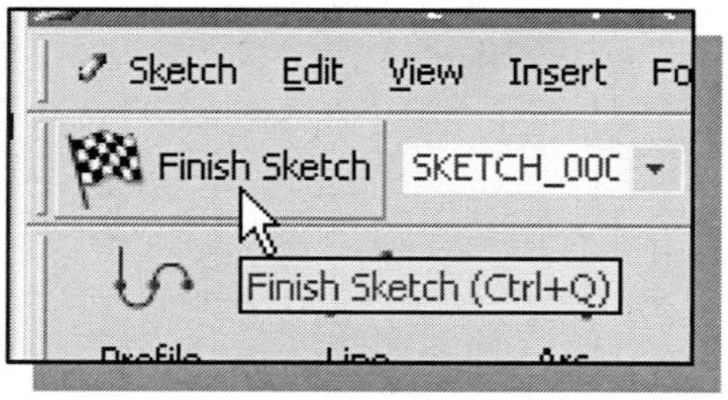

7. Click **Finish Sketch** to exit the *NX Sketcher* mode and return to the *Feature* option dialog window.

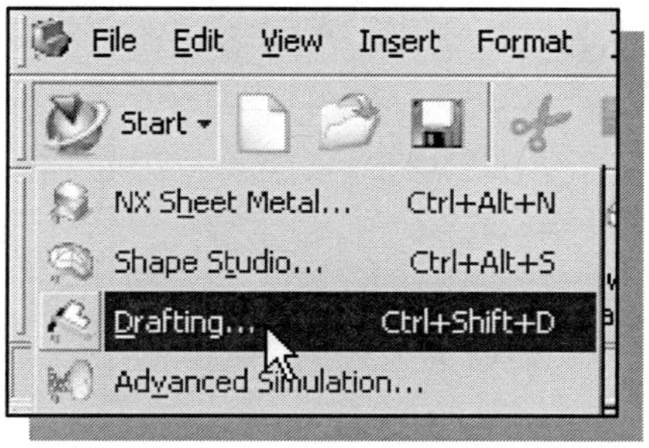

8. Click on the **Start** icon in the *Standard* toolbar area to display the available options.

9. Select **Drafting** from the option list.

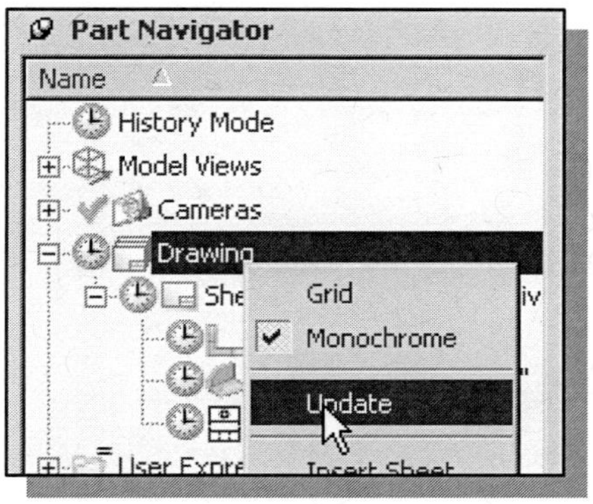

➢ Near the bottom left corner, *UGS NX* indicates the drawing needs to be updated. The little clock symbol in the *Part Navigator* also implies an update is needed.

10. Right-mouse click on the ***Drawing*** item to bring up the option menu and choose **Update** as shown.

➢ Notice the diameter dimension in the top view is updated to **0.625**. (On your own, adjust the display to display 3 digits.)

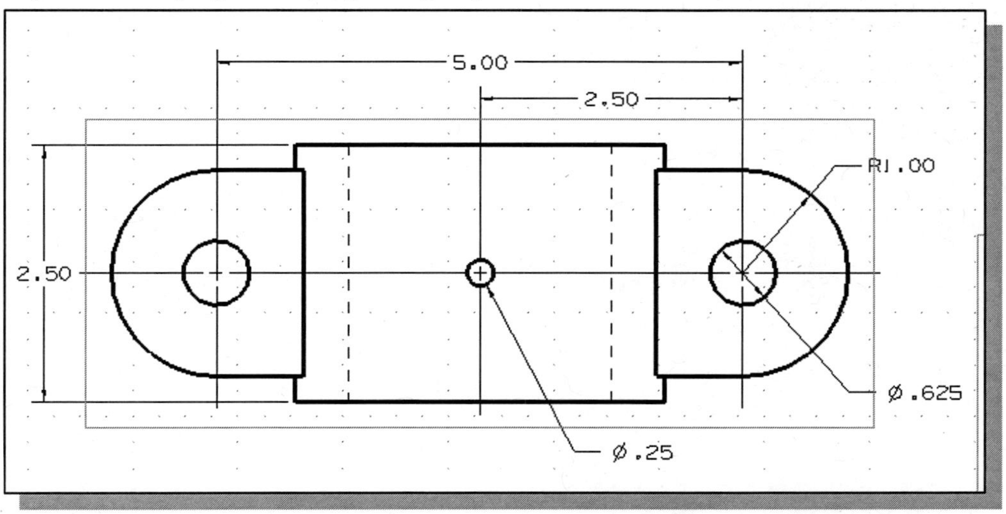

❖ One of the great advantages of *parametric modeling* is the ease of making modifications to designs. The *associative functionality* is an impressive and important feature of *parametric modeling*.

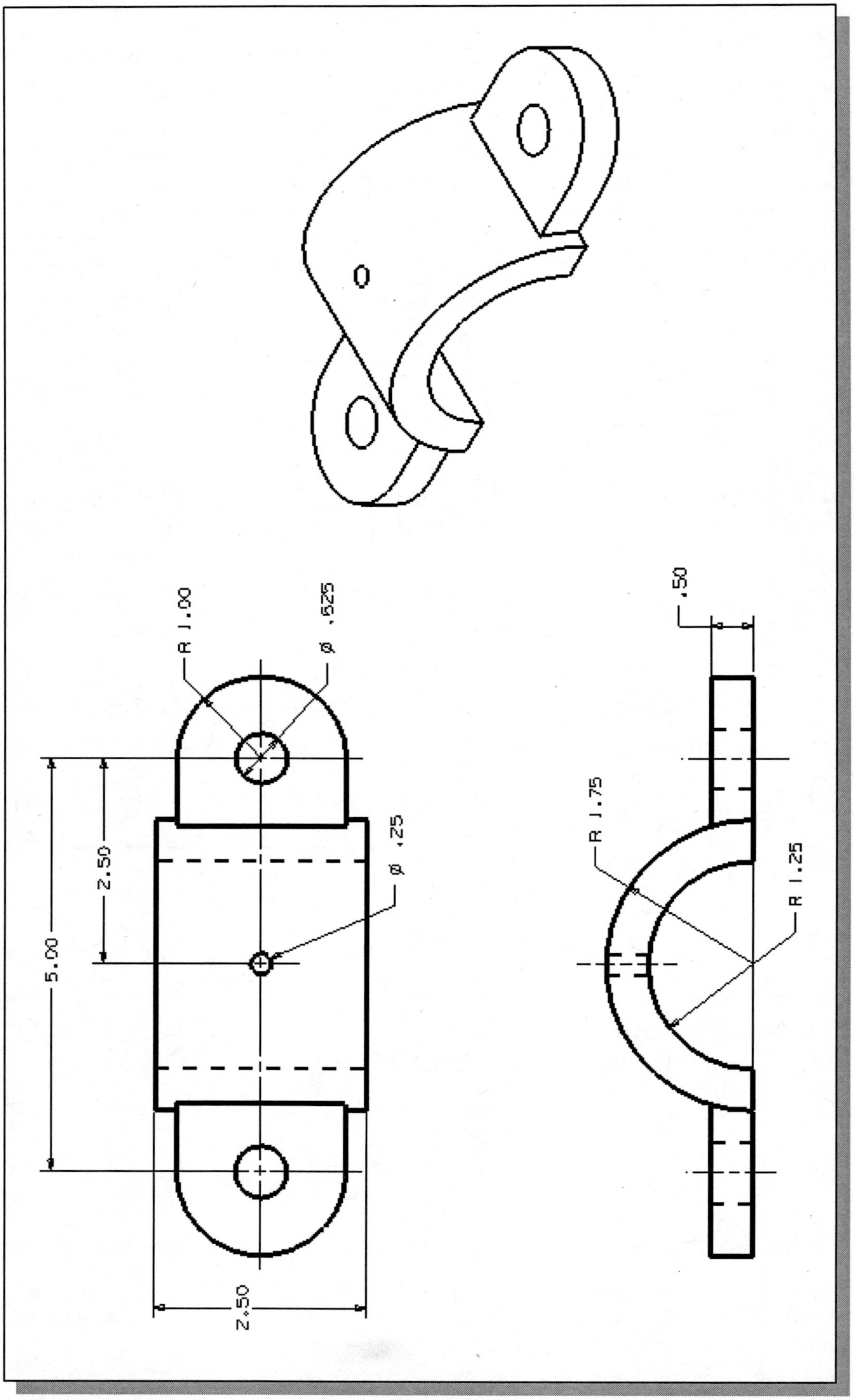
R 1.00
Ø .625
Ø .25
2.50
5.00
2.50
.50
R 1.75
R 1.25

Questions:

1. What does *UGS NX*'s *associative functionality* allow us to do?
2. How do we reposition a view in a drawing?
3. How do we display feature/model dimensions in the *Drafting* mode?
4. What is the difference between a *feature dimension* and a *reference dimension*?
5. How do we reposition dimensions?
6. What is a *base* view?
7. Describe the general usage of the **Hide** command.
8. Create sketches showing the steps you plan to use to create the model shown on the next page:

Exercises: (Create the Solid models and the associated 2D drawings.)

1. Dimensions are in inches.

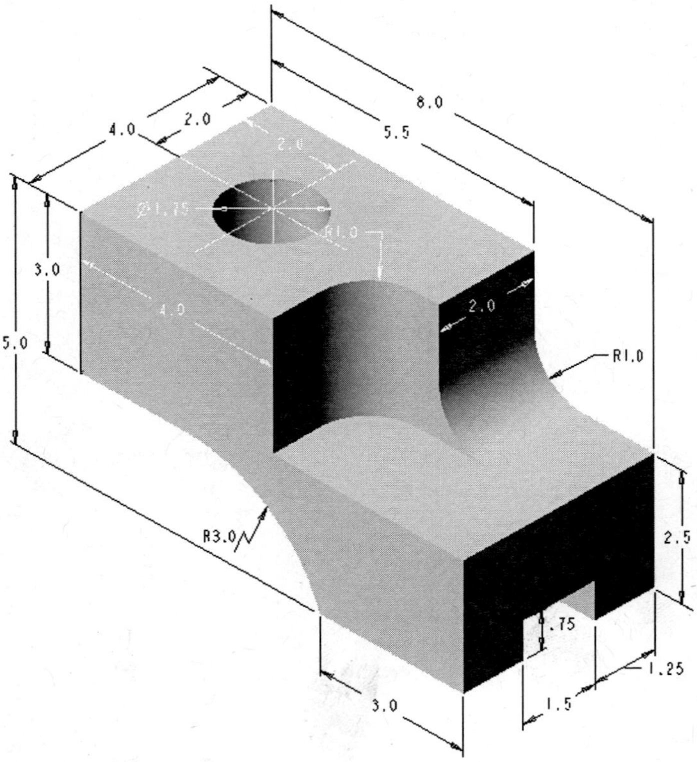

2. Dimensions are in inches.

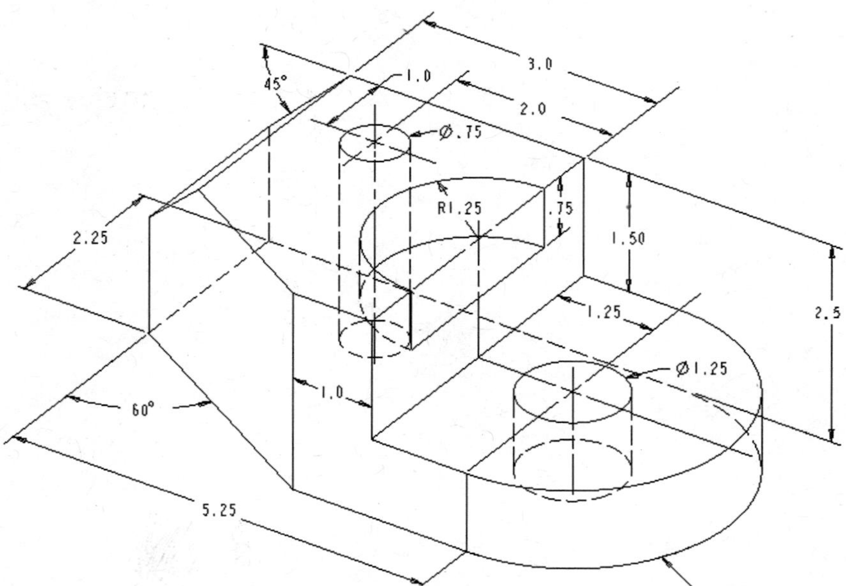

Chapter 9
Datum Features and Auxiliary Views

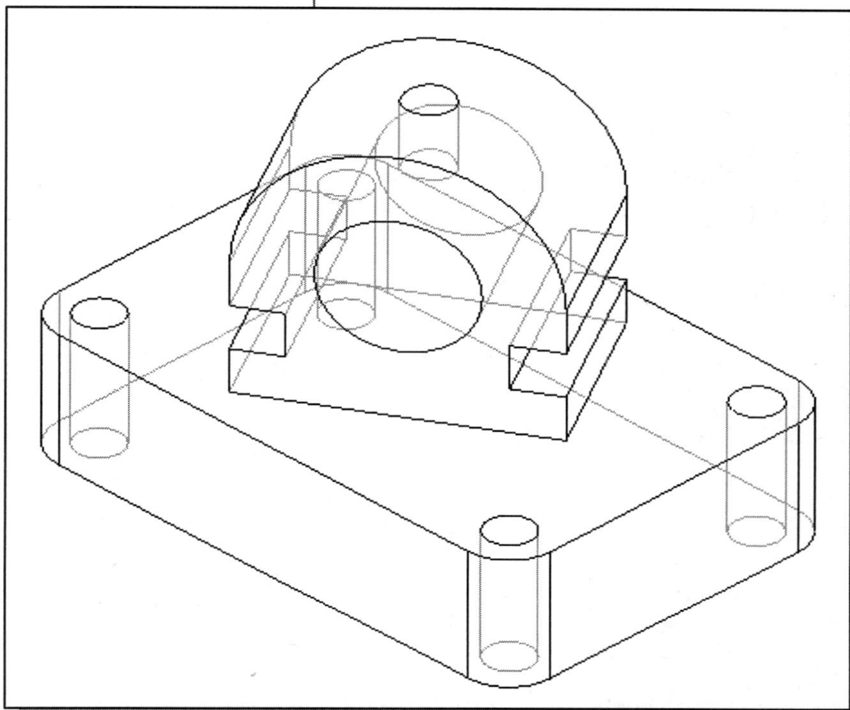

Learning Objectives

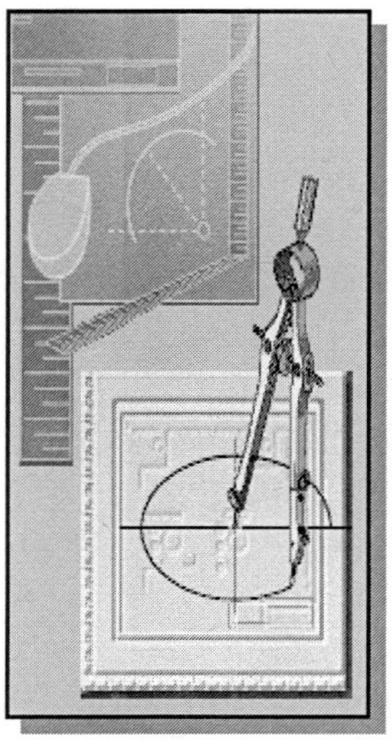

- ♦ Understand the Concepts and Use of Datum Features
- ♦ Use the Different Options to Create Datum Features
- ♦ Create Auxiliary Views in 2D Drawing Mode
- ♦ Create and Adjust Centerlines
- ♦ Create a New Border and Title Block
- ♦ Create and Use a Template File in 2D Drawing mode

Datum Features

Feature-based parametric modeling is a cumulative process. The relationships that we define between features determine how a feature reacts when other features are changed. Because of this interaction, certain features must, by necessity, precede others. A new feature can use previously defined features to define information such as size, shape, location and orientation. *UGS NX* provides several tools to automate this process. *Datum features* can be thought of as user-definable datum, which are updated with the part geometry. We can create *datum planes*, *axes*, or *points* that do not already exist. *Datum features* can also be used to align features or to orient parts in an assembly. In this chapter, the use of the **Offset** option and the **Angled** option to create new *datum planes*, surfaces that do not already exist, are illustrated. By creating parametric *datum features*, the established feature interactions in the CAD database assure the capturing of the design intent. The default *datum features*, which are aligned to the origin of the coordinate system, can be used to assist the construction of the more complex geometric features.

Auxiliary Views in 2D Drawings

An important rule concerning multiview drawings is to draw enough views to accurately describe the design. This usually requires two or three of the regular views, such as a *front* view, a *top* view and/or a *side* view. However, many designs have features located on inclined surfaces that are not parallel to the regular planes of projection. To truly describe the feature, the true shape of the feature must be shown using an ***auxiliary*** **view**. An *auxiliary* view has a line of sight that is perpendicular to the inclined surface, as viewed looking directly at the inclined surface. An *auxiliary* view is a supplementary view that can be constructed from any of the regular views. Using the solid model as the starting point for a design, *auxiliary* views can easily be created in 2D drawings. In this chapter, the general procedure of creating *auxiliary* views in 2D drawings from solid models is illustrated.

The *Rod-Guide* Design

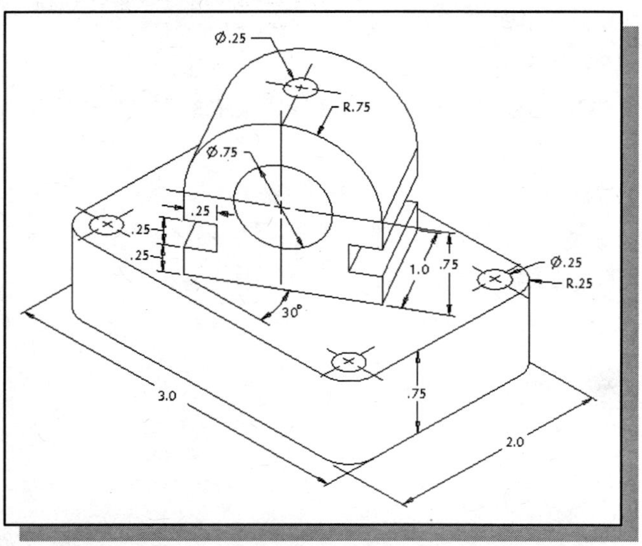

❖ Based on your knowledge of *UGS NX* so far, how would you create this design? What are the more difficult features involved in the design? Take a few minutes to consider a modeling strategy and do preliminary planning by sketching on a piece of paper. You are also encouraged to create the design on your own prior to following through the tutorial.

Modeling Strategy

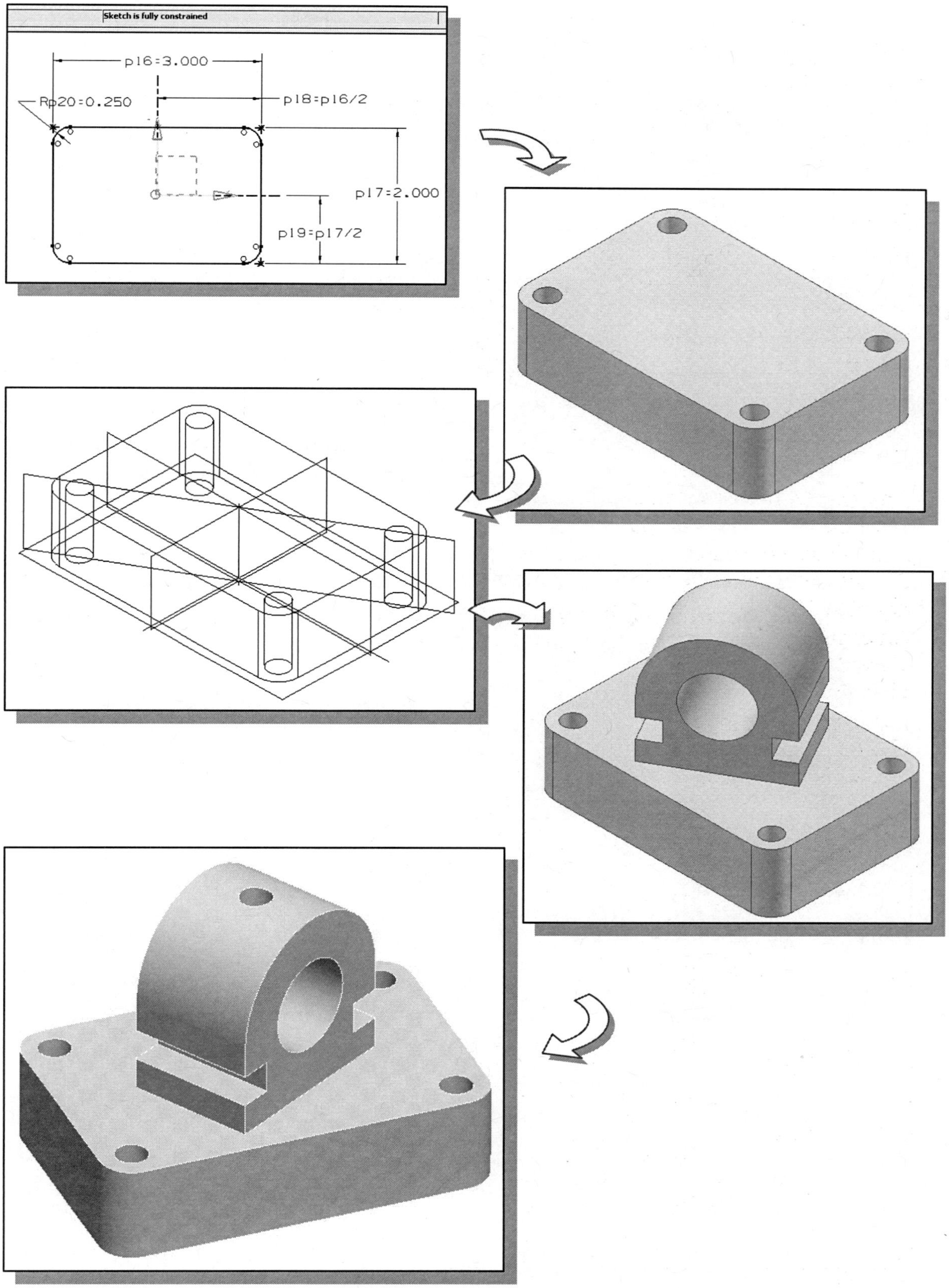

Starting *UGS NX*

1. Select the *UGS NX* option on the *Start* menu or select the *UGS NX* icon on the desktop to start *UGS NX*. The *UGS NX* main window will appear on the screen.

2. Select the **New** icon with a single click of the left-mouse-button (MB1) in the *Standard* toolbar area.

3. Select the **Inches** *Units* as shown in the figure below.

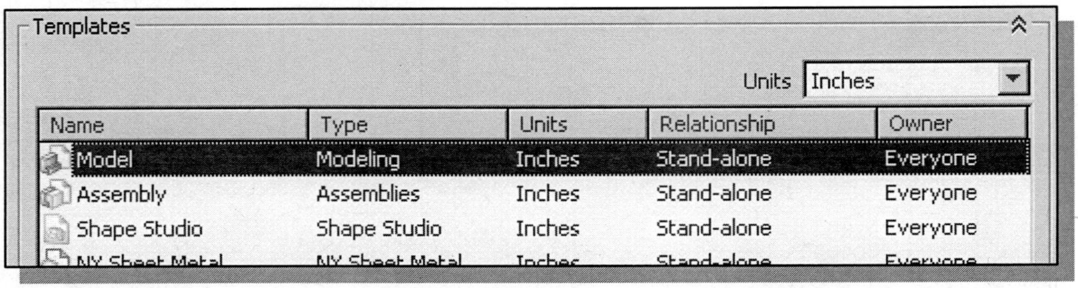

4. Select **Model** in the *Templates* list. Note that the *Model* template will allow us to switch directly into the ***Modeling*** task as indicated in the *Templates* list.

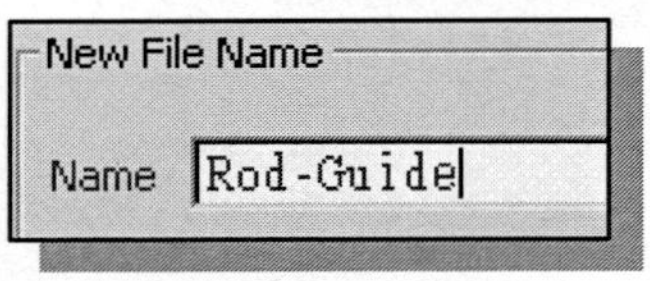

5. In the *New File Name* section, enter **Rod-Guide** as the file *Name*.

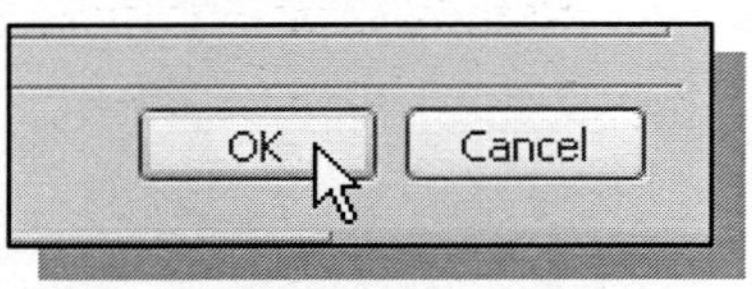

6. Click **OK** to proceed with the New File command.

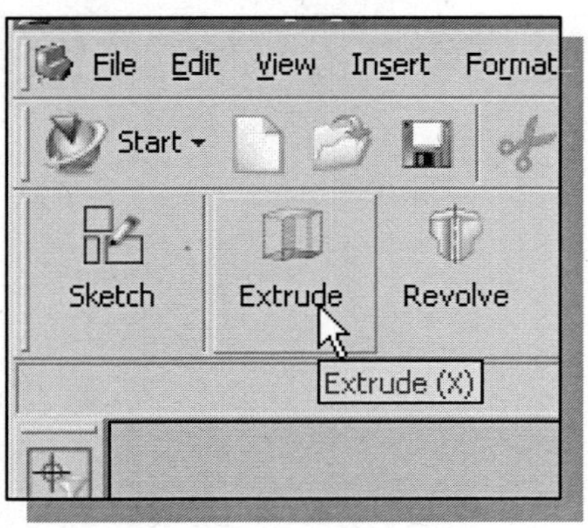

7. In the ***Feature*** toolbars (toolbars aligned to the right edge of the main window), select the **Extrude** icon as shown.

Creating the Base Feature

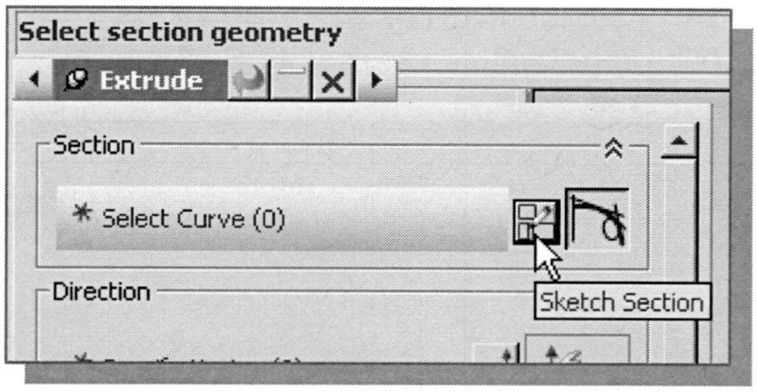

1. Click the **Sketch Section** button to enter the *2D Sketcher* mode and begin to create a new *2D sketch.*

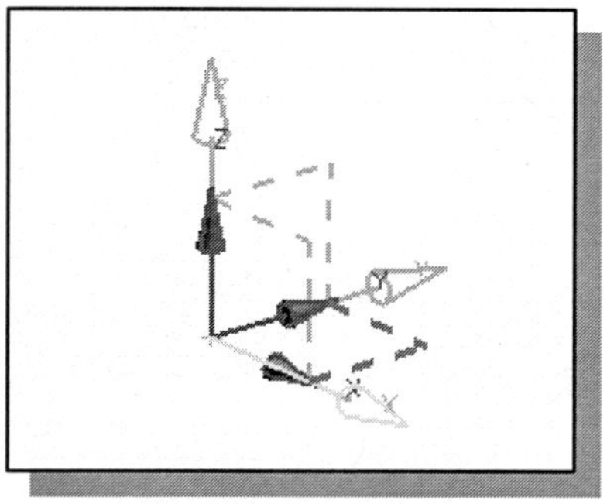

❖ Note the default *sketch plane* is aligned to the *X-Y* plane of the displayed work coordinate system.

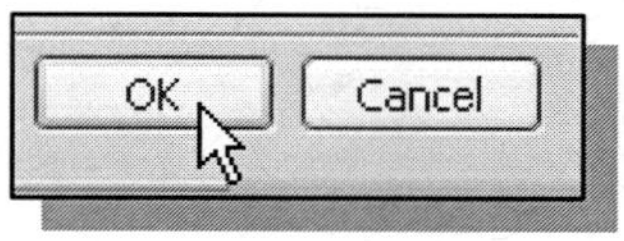

2. Click **OK** to accept the default setting of the *sketch plane*.

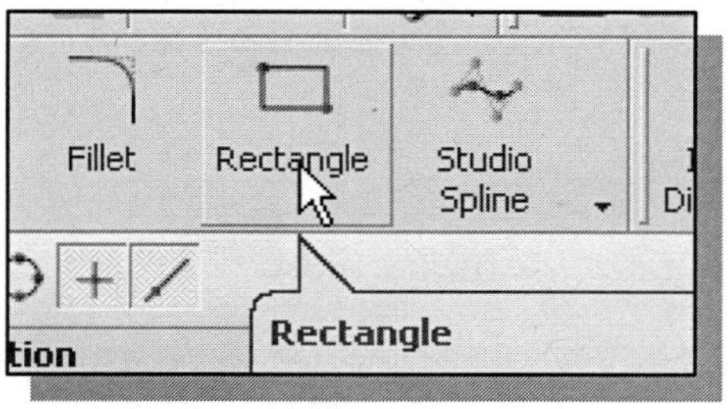

3. Select the **Rectangle** command by clicking once with the left-mouse-button on the icon in the *Sketch Curve* toolbar.

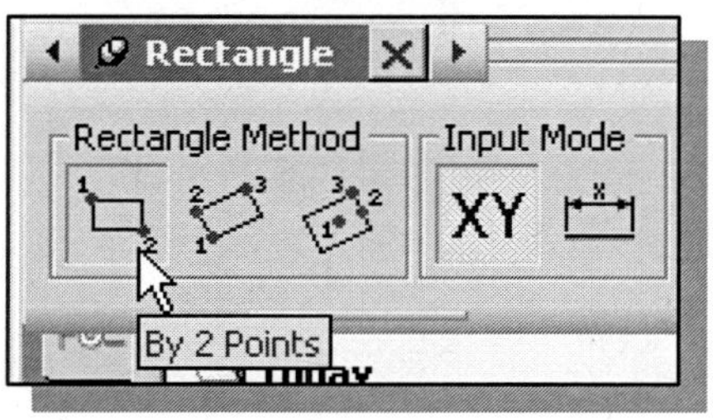

4. Notice the different options available for creating rectangles; confirm the **By 2 Points** option is activated as shown.

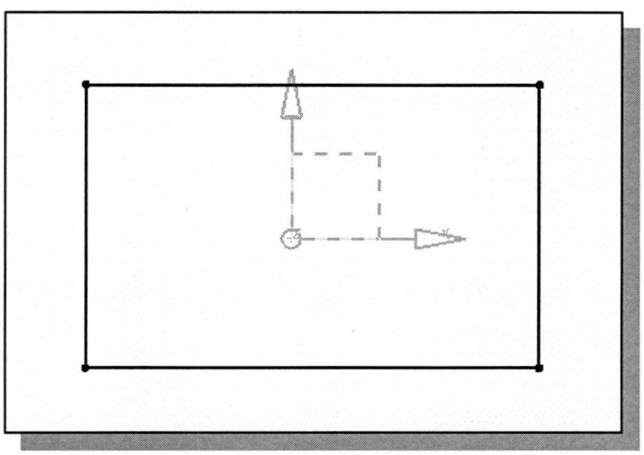

5. Create a rectangle of arbitrary size with the datum coordinate system near the center of the rectangle as shown.

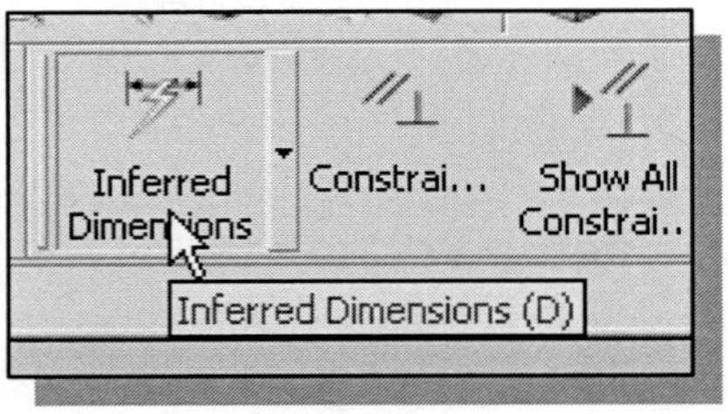

6. On your own, use the **Inferred Dimensions** command to create and adjust the 2D sketch as shown in the figure below.

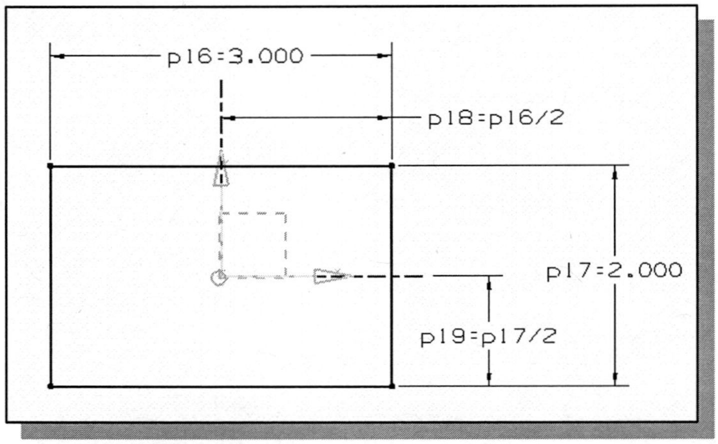

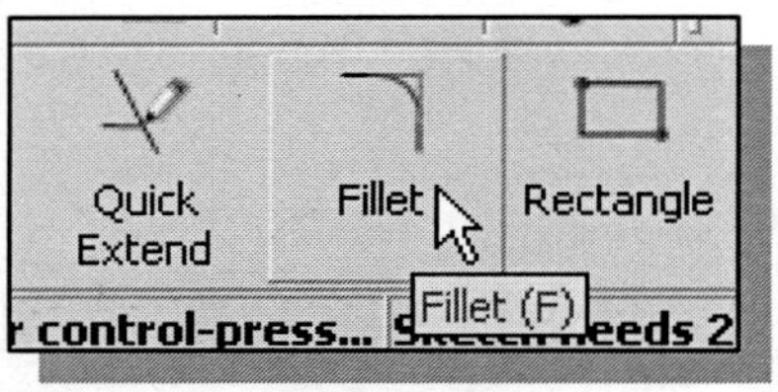

7. Select the **Fillet** command by clicking once with the left-mouse-button (MB1) on the icon in the *Sketch Curve* toolbar.

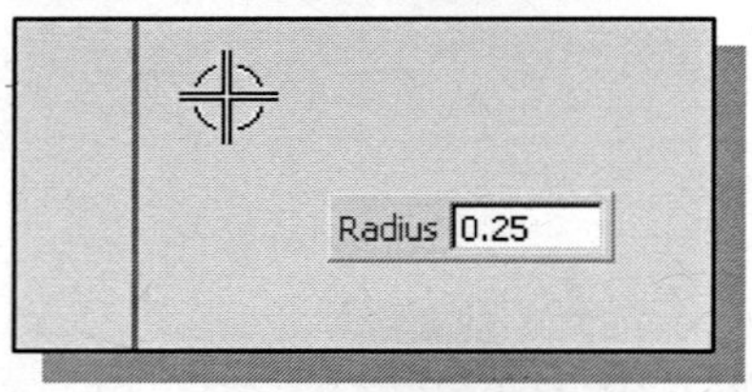

8. Enter **0.25** as the new *Radius* of the fillet.

9. Create the four rounded corners and apply the proper constraints to make the sketch fully constrained, as shown in the figure below.

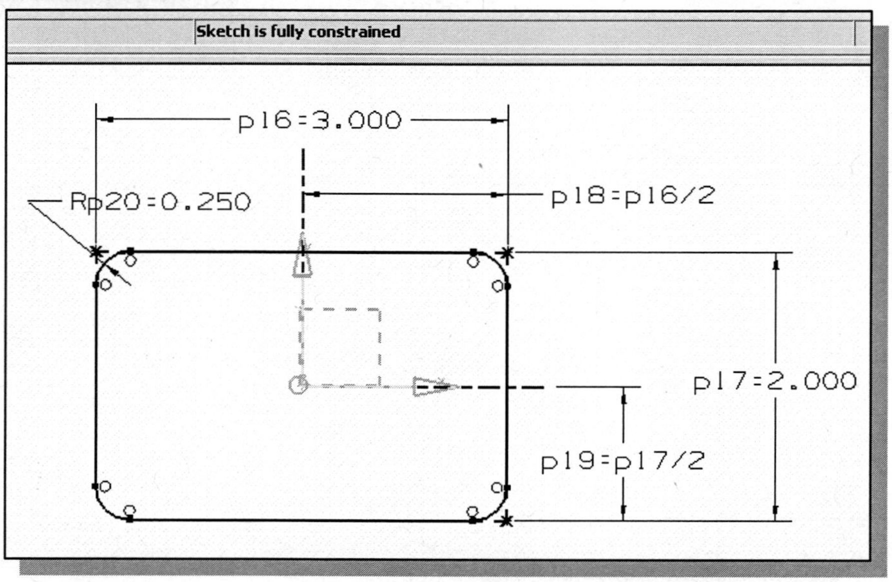

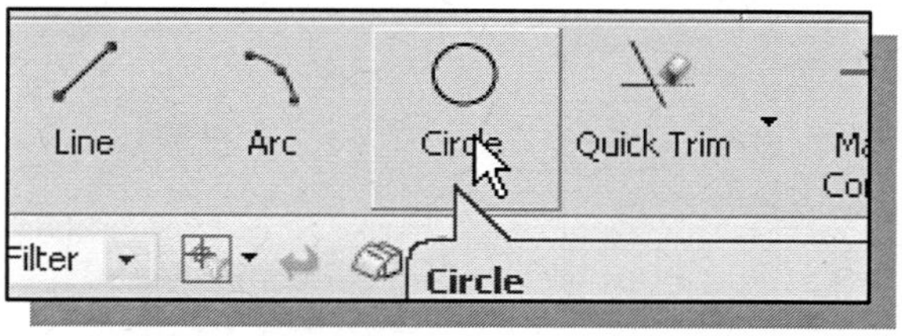

10. Select the **Circle** command by clicking once with the left-mouse-button (MB1) on the icon in the *Sketch Curve* toolbar.

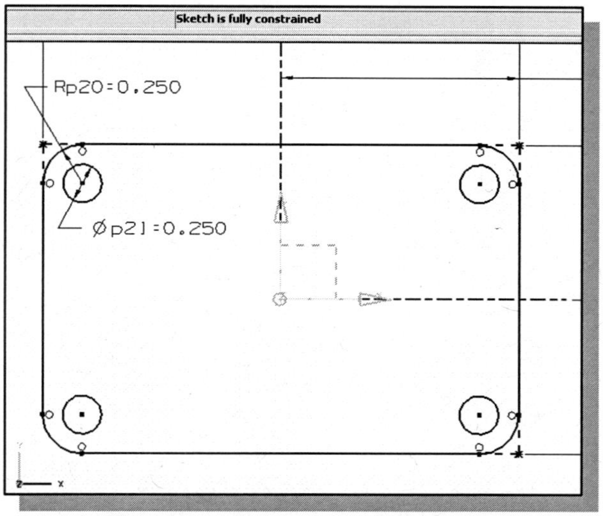

11. Create four circles aligned to the centers of the four arcs as shown.

❖ The design intent can be maintained by applying the proper dimensions and constraints as the sketches are constructed.

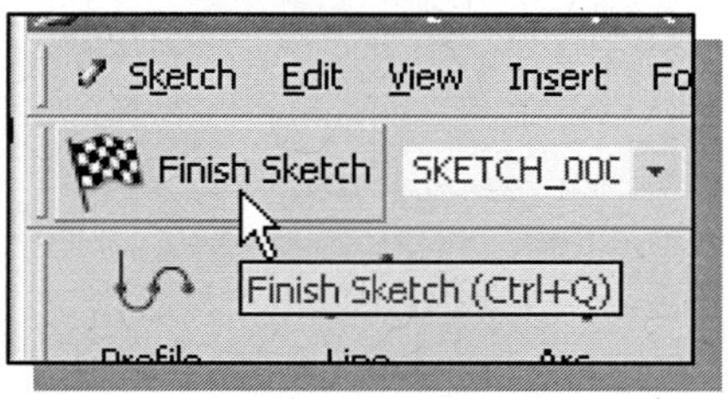

12. Click **Finish Sketch** to exit the *NX Sketcher* mode and return to the *Feature* option dialog window.

13. In the *Extrude* popup window, enter **0.75** as the extrusion *Distance*.

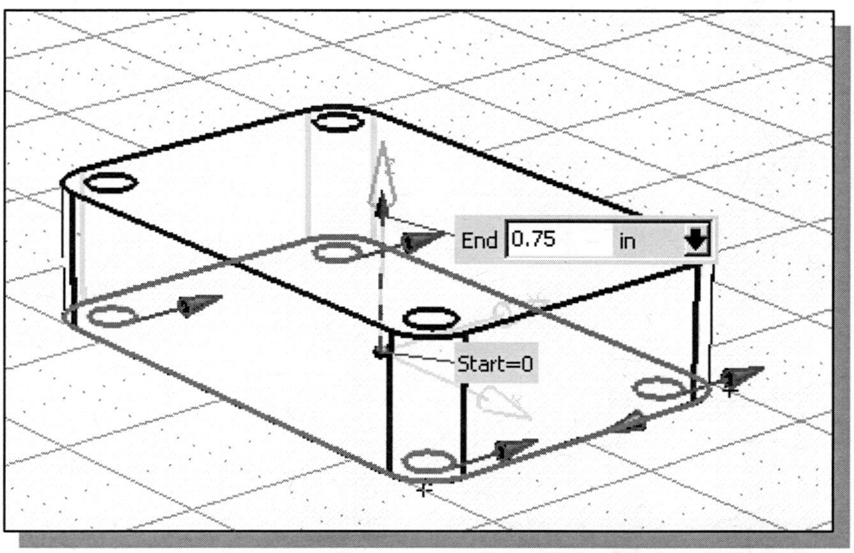

14. Click the **OK** button to proceed with creating the feature.

Creating an Angled Datum Plane

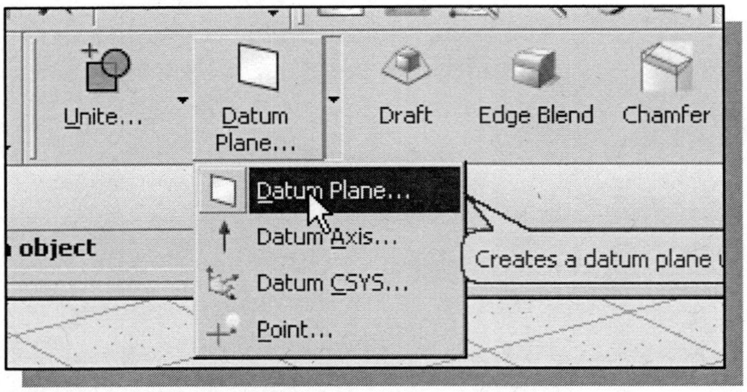

1. In the *Part Features* toolbar, select the **Datum Plane** command by left-clicking the icon.

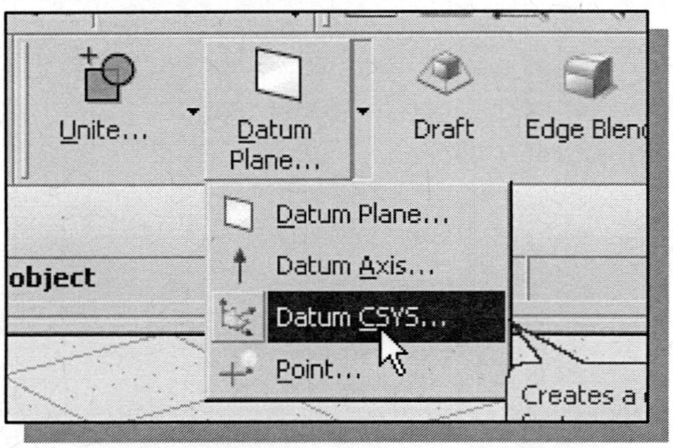

❖ Note that all the template files we have used so far contain a datum coordinate system that was created through the **Datum CSYS** command.

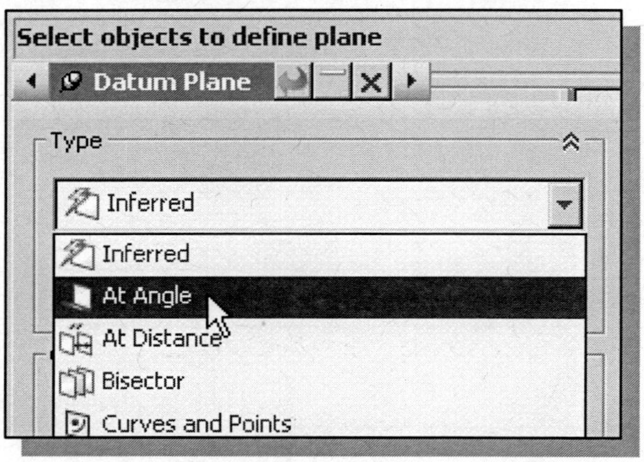

❖ In the *Datum Plane* dialog box, different options are available to create datum planes. Note that different components are needed for each option.

2. Select the **At Angle** option by clicking the corresponding icon as shown in the figure.

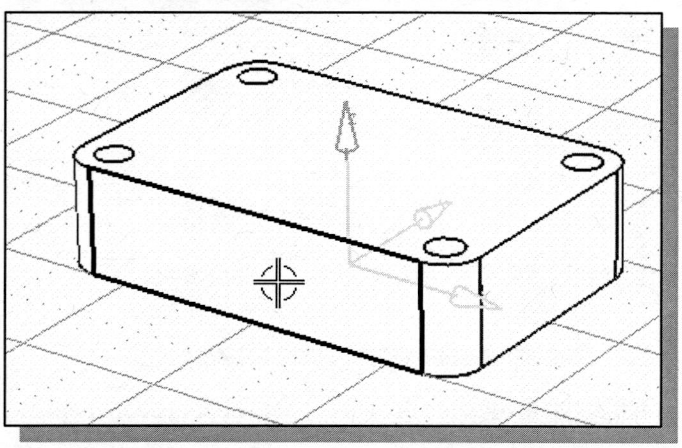

3. Inside the graphics window, select the ***front*** **face** of the *base* feature as the first reference of the new *datum plane*.

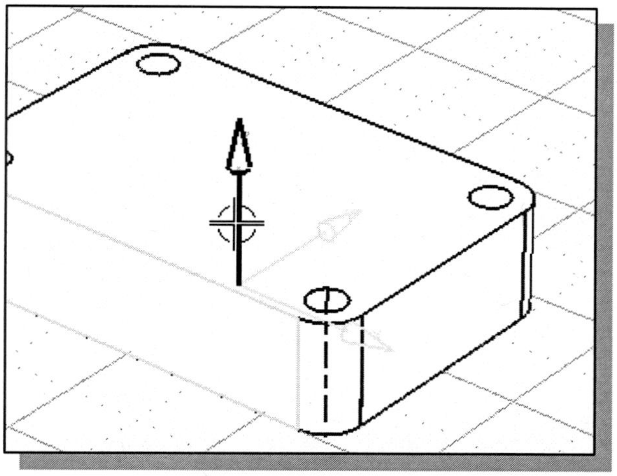

4. Inside the graphics window, left-click once to select the ***Z* axis** as the second reference of the new *datum plane*.

5. In the *Angle* popup window, enter **-30** as the rotation *Angle* for the new *datum plane* as shown in the figure below.

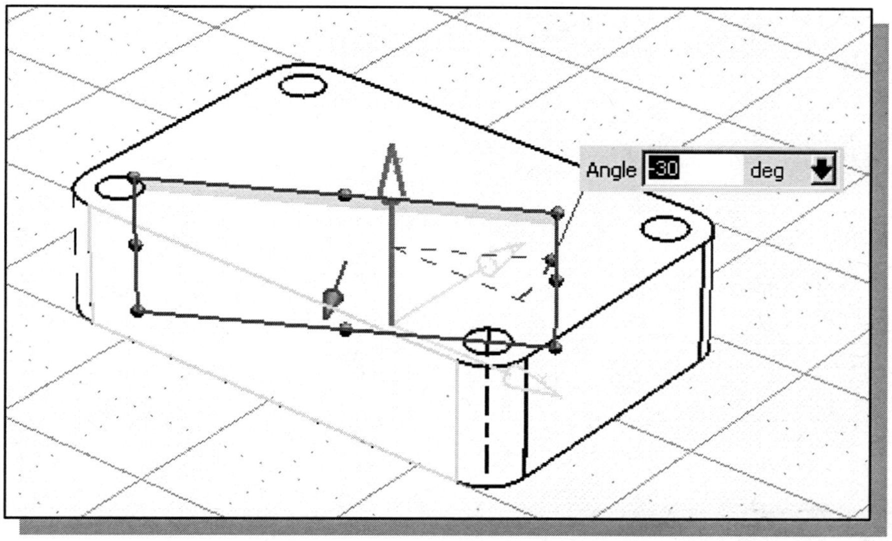

❖ Note that the *angle* is measured relative to the selected reference plane.

6. On your own, examine the other settings for the *datum plane*, such as the ***Plane Orientation*** option.

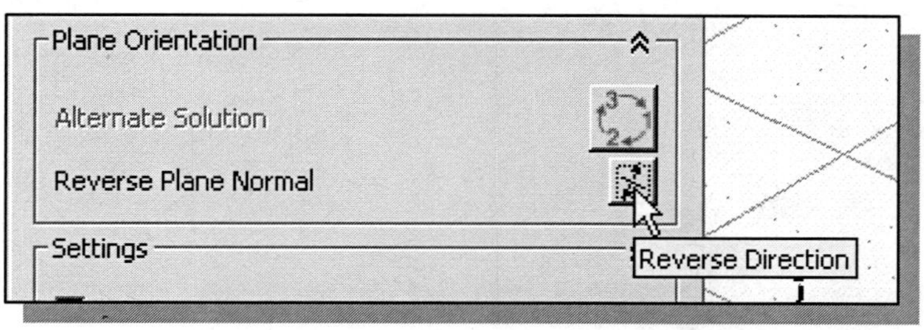

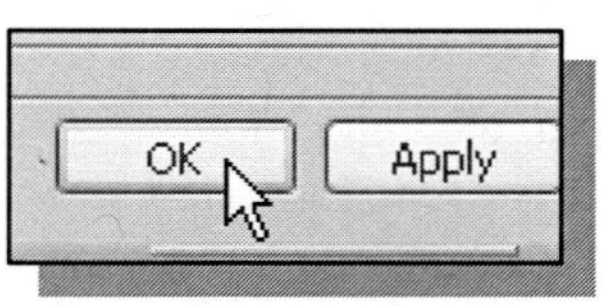

7. Click the **OK** button to accept the settings and create the angled *datum plane*.

Creating an Extruded Feature using the Datum Plane

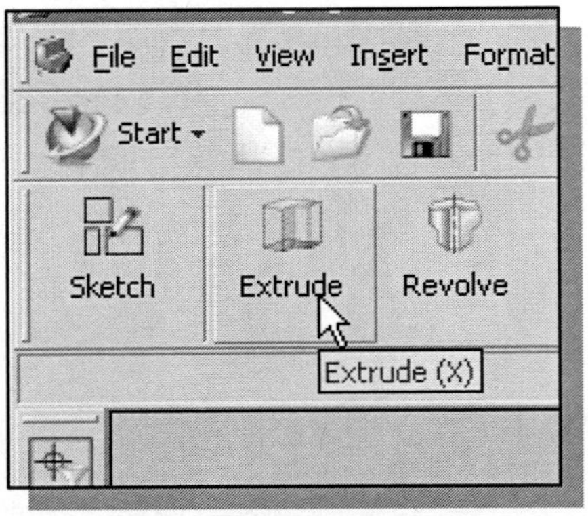

1. In the ***Feature*** toolbars (toolbars aligned to the right edge of the main window), select the **Extrude** icon as shown.

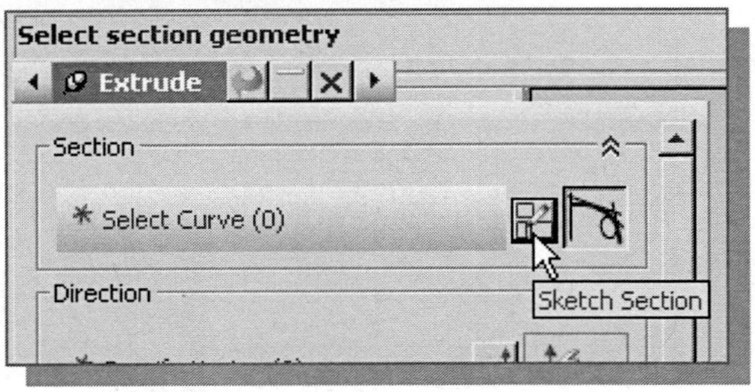

2. Click the **Sketch Section** button to enter the *2D Sketcher* mode and begin to create a new *2D sketch.*

3. Select the newly created datum plane as shown.

4. Click **OK** to accept the selection.

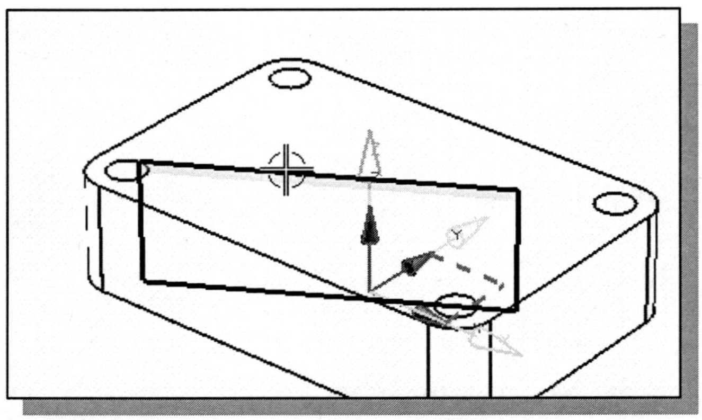

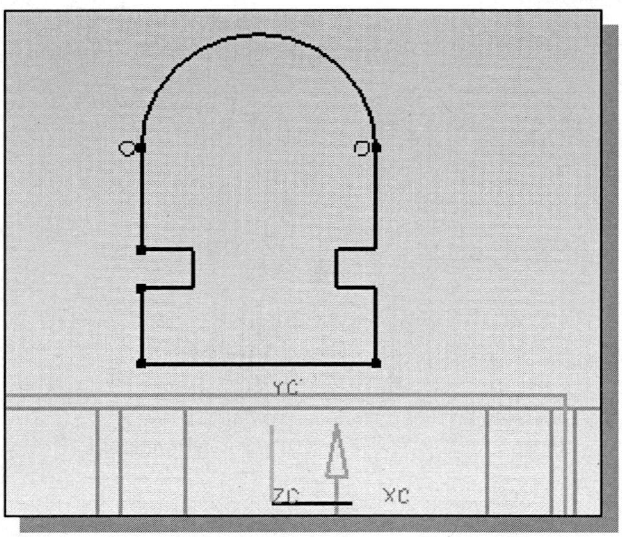

5. On your own, create a rough 2D sketch, above the base feature as shown in the figure, by using the **Profile** command. Note the line segments are aligned to each other and the arc is tangent to the adjacent vertical edges.

❖ We will position the sketch by adding proper constraints in the next section.

Apply Proper Constraints

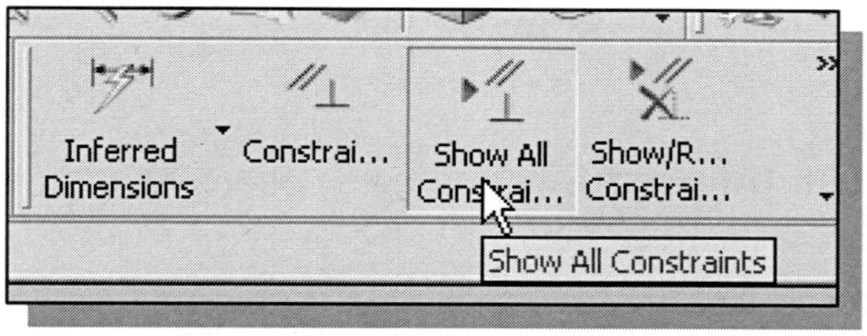

1. Select the **Show All Constraints** command in the *Sketch Constraints* toolbar.

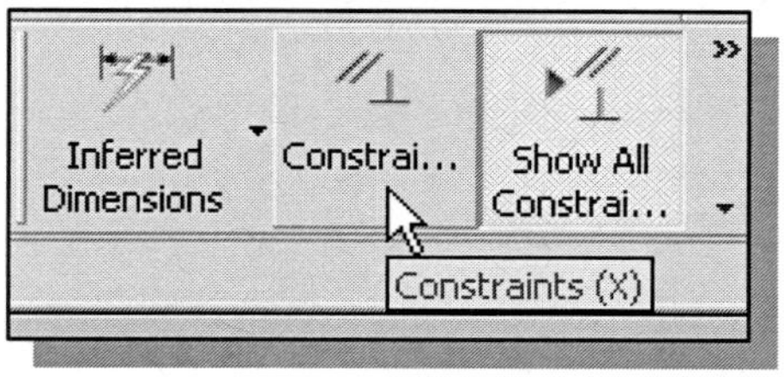

2. Select the **Constraints** command in the *Sketch Constraints* toolbar.

3. On your own, apply the **Equal Length** constraint to match the shorter line segments on both sides of the 2D sketch as shown.

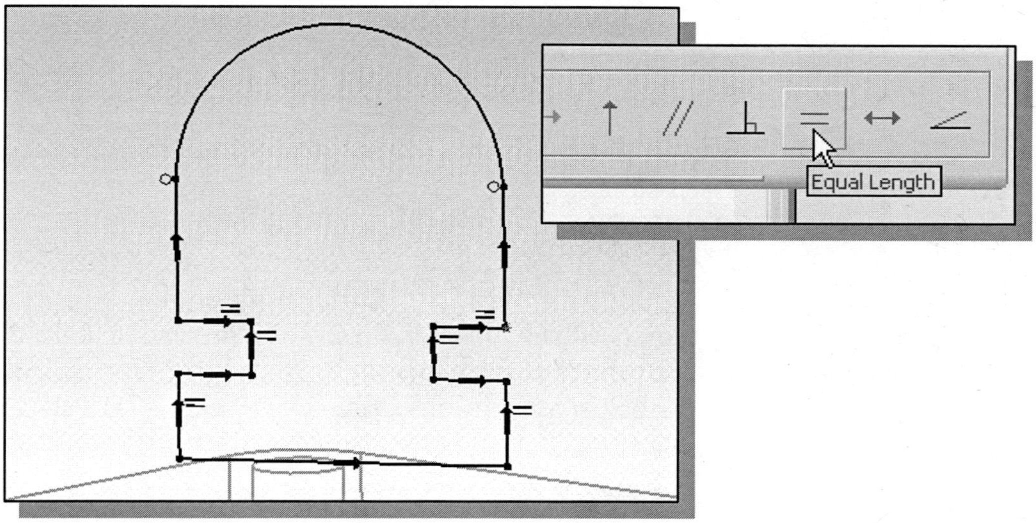

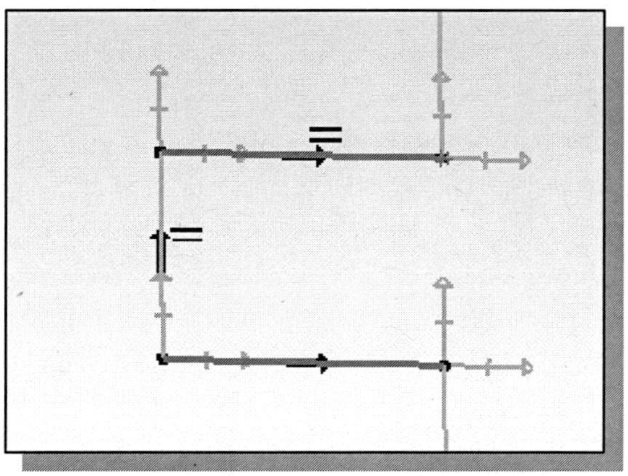

4. Select the two horizontal segments and apply another **Equal Length** constraint as shown.

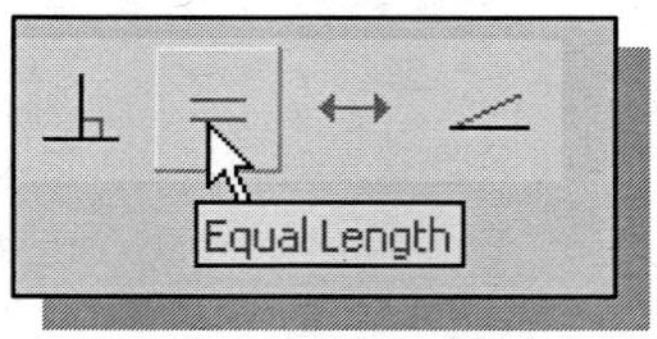

5. Repeat the same process and apply another **Equal Length** constraint on the other side. Also add two **Colinear** constraints to align the outside edges.

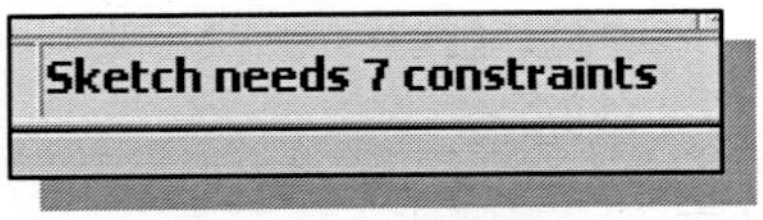

❖ Notice the message "*Sketch needs 7 constraints*" is displayed. Can you identify the three constraints needed to fully constrain the sketch?

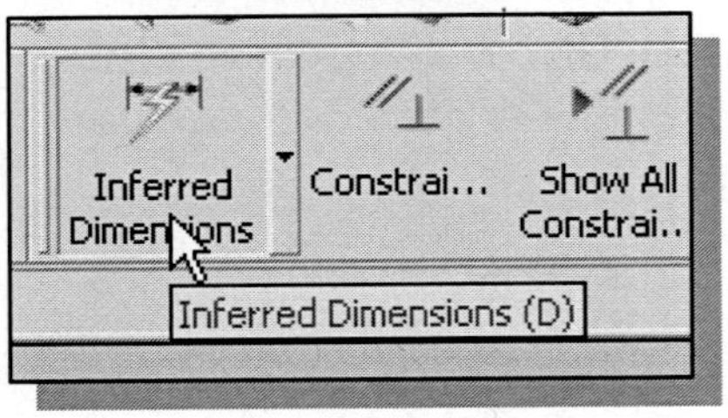

6. Select the **Inferred Dimensions** command in the *Sketch Constraints* toolbar as shown.

7. On your own, create the five dimensions as shown in the figure below.

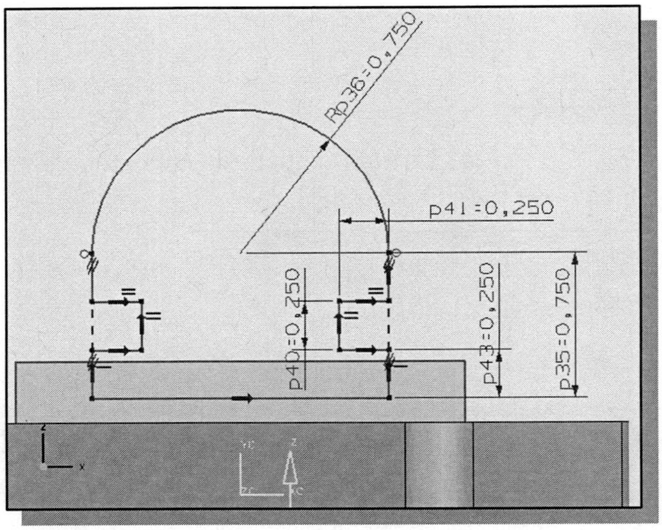

8. The last two dimensions are needed to position the 2D sketch relative to the 3D environment, for which we can reference either the *base* feature or the *datum axes*. On your own, create the two dimensions (page 44 and page 47) as shown in the figure below.

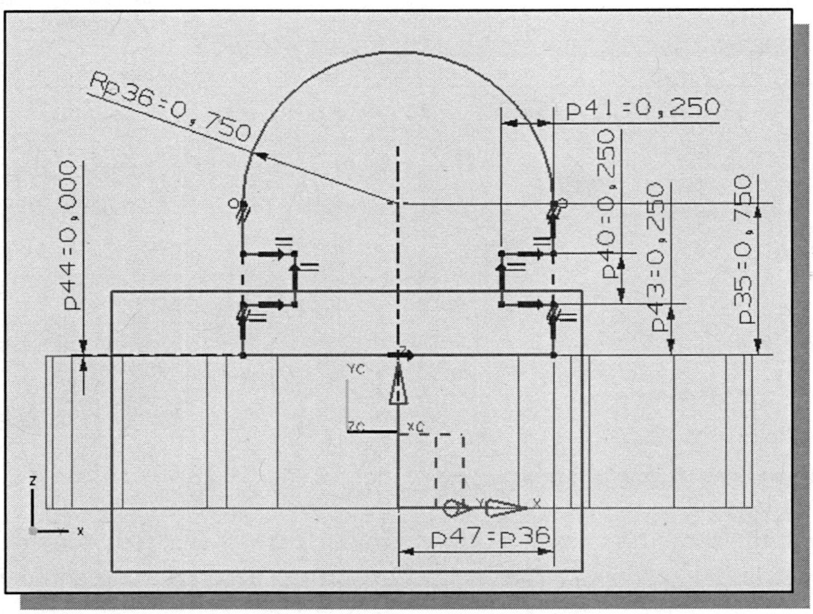

9. On your own, add a **0.75** circle and complete the 2D sketch as shown in the figure.

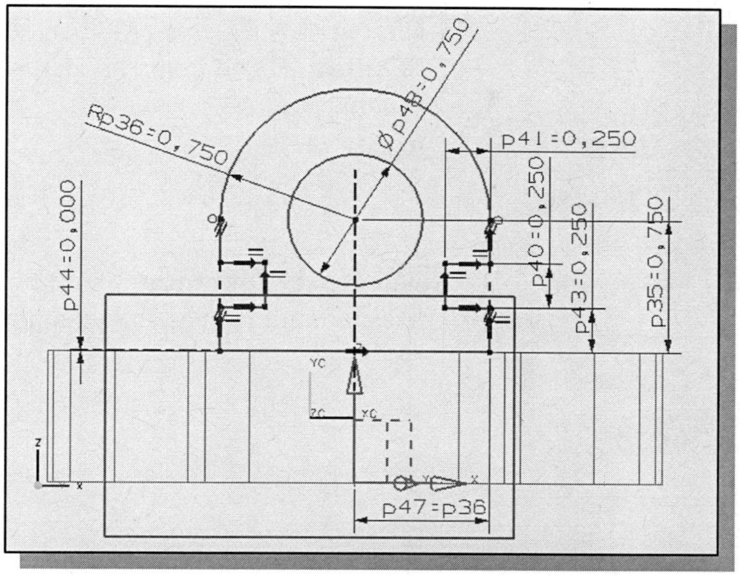

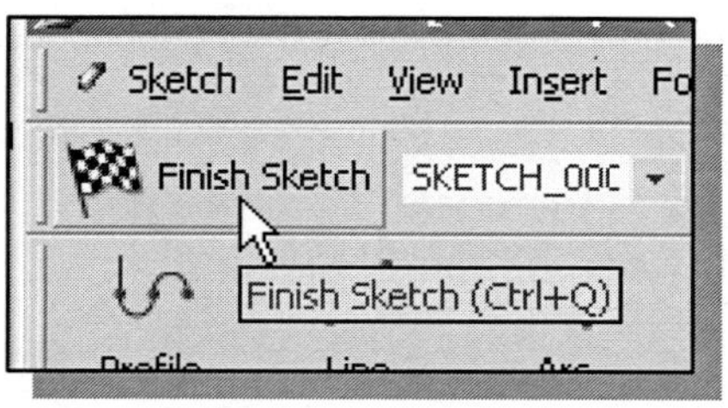

10. Click **Finish Sketch** to exit the *NX Sketcher* mode and return to the *Feature* option dialog window.

11. In the *Extrude* popup window, set the *Boolean* option is set to **Unite** as shown.

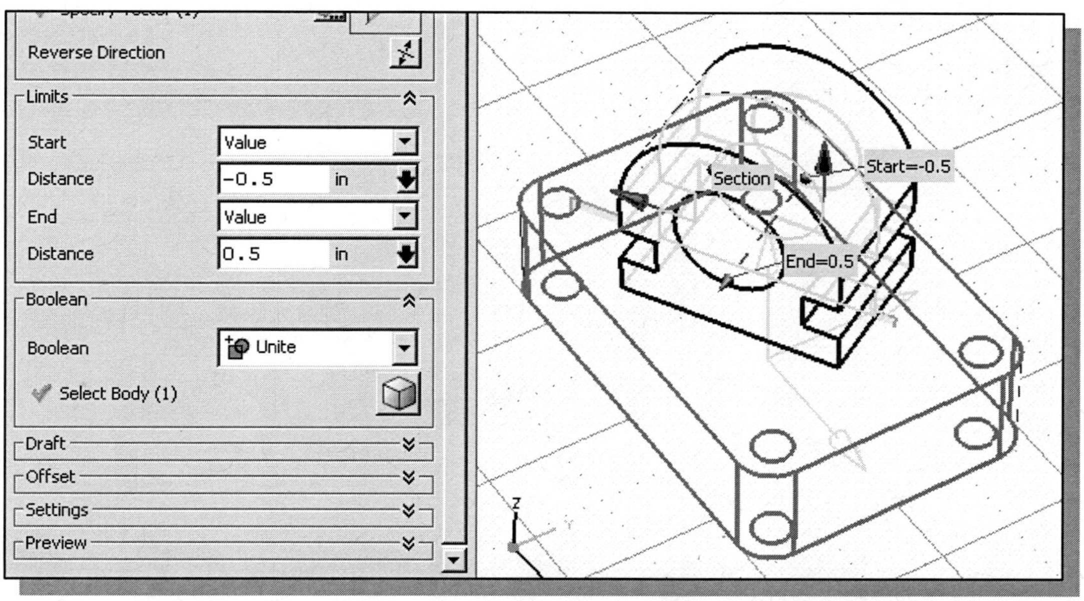

12. In the *Extrude* popup window, enter **-0.5** and **0.5** as the extrusion *Start* and *End Limits*. Click **OK** to create the extrusion feature.

Creating an Offset Datum Plane

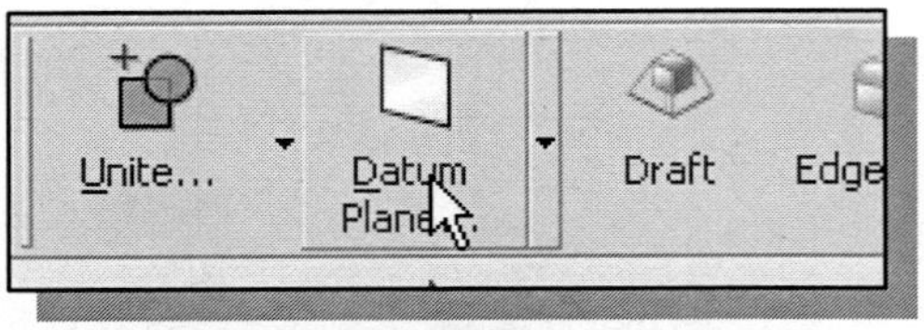

1. In the *Part Features* toolbar, select the **Datum Plane** command by left-clicking the icon.

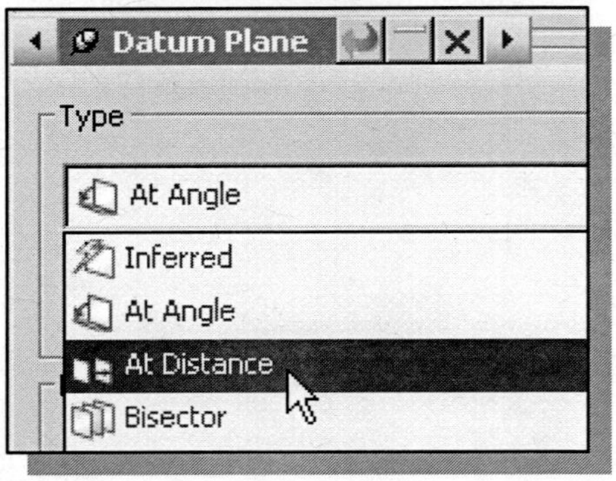

2. Select the **At Distance** option by clicking the corresponding icon as shown in the figure.

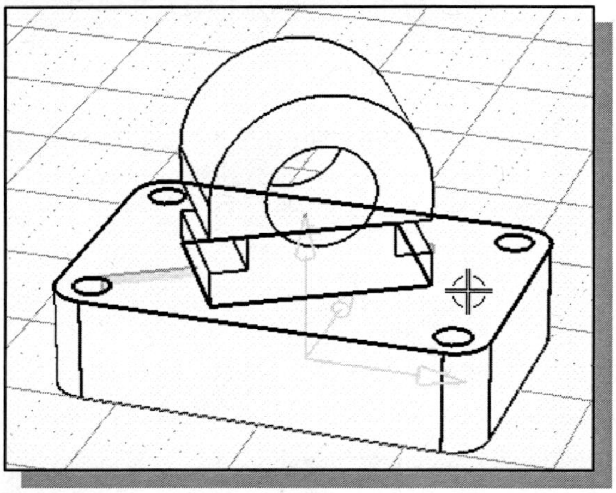

3. Inside the graphics window, select the ***top* face** of the *base* feature as the reference of the new *datum plane*.

4. Enter **0.75** as the *Offset Distance* and create only **one** *datum plane* as shown.

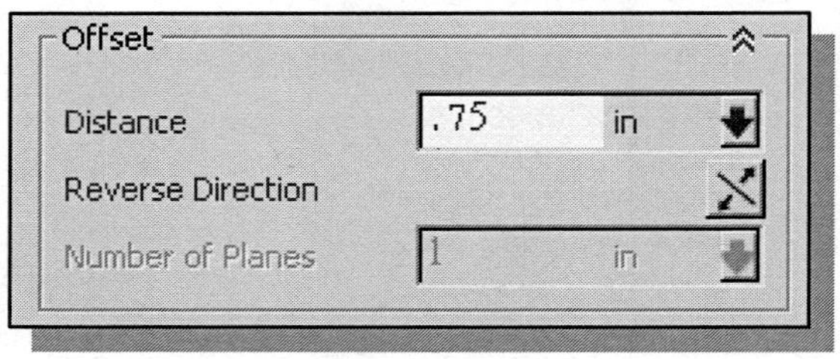

5. Click **OK** to create the offset *datum plane*.

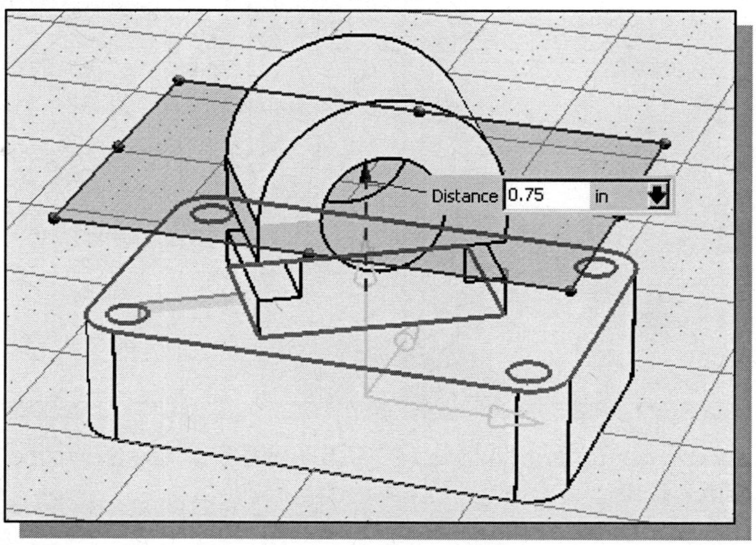

Creating a Hole Feature using the new Datum Plane

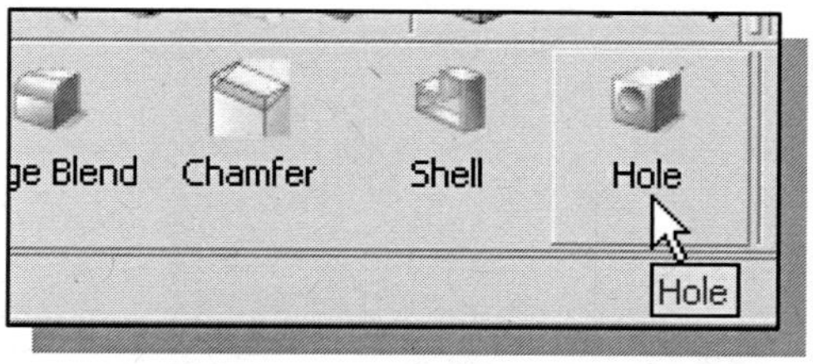

1. In the *Feature Operation* toolbar (the toolbar that is located to the right side of the *Form Feature* toolbar), select the **Hole** command by releasing the left-mouse-button on the icon.

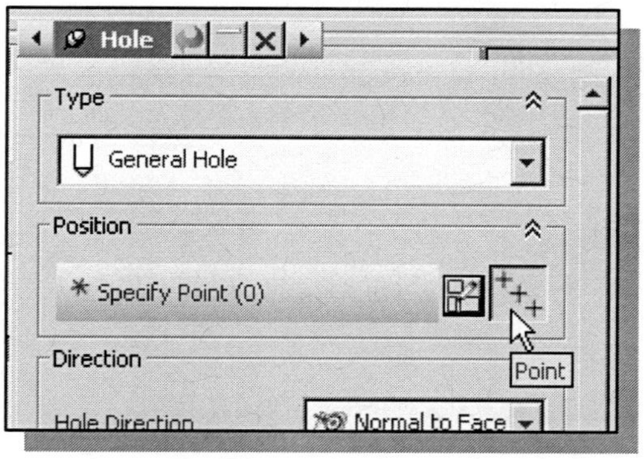

2. In the *Hole* window, notice the default hole *Type* is set to **General Hole** as shown.

❖ Note that by default, the *Position* of the hole is specified using the **Point** command.

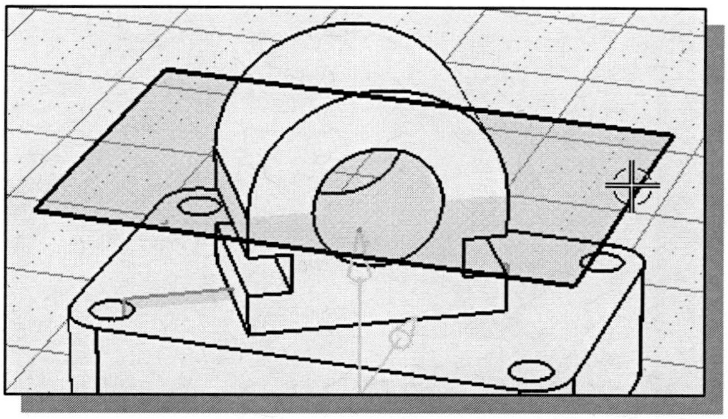

3. Pick the new *datum plane* as shown.

4. Click **OK** to accept the current inferred point, which is aligned to the origin of the coordinate system.

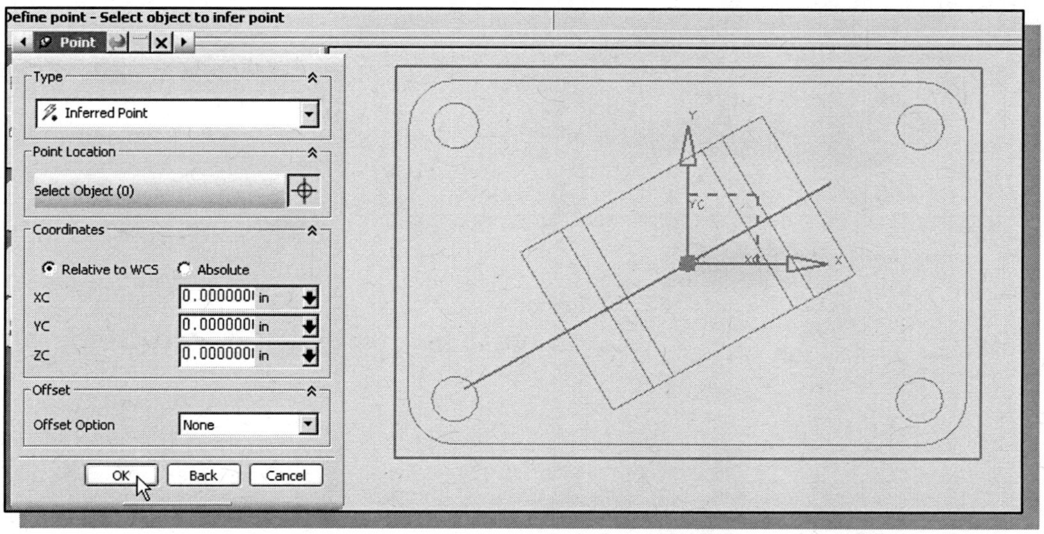

5. Set the hole *Direction* to **Along Vector** and set direction to align with the ***Z-C*** axis

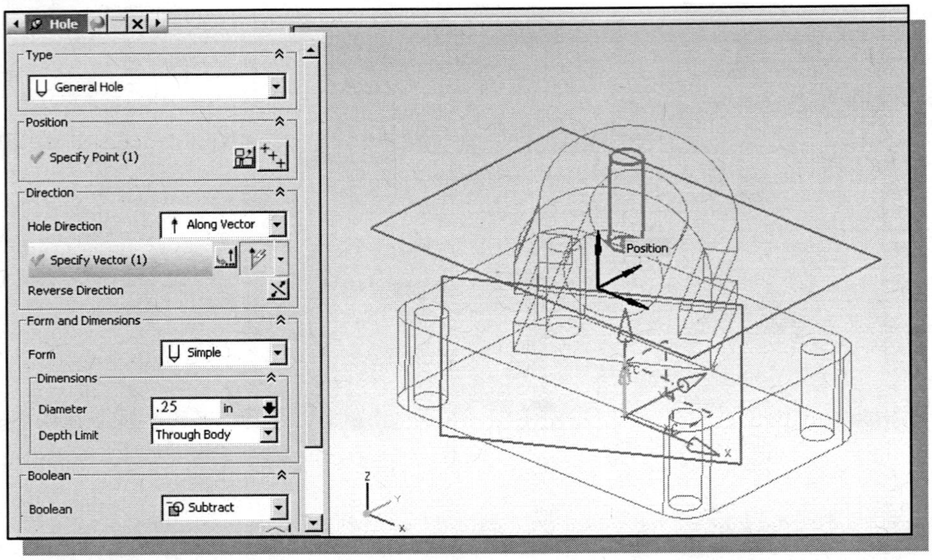

6. Enter **0.25** as the diameter of the hole.

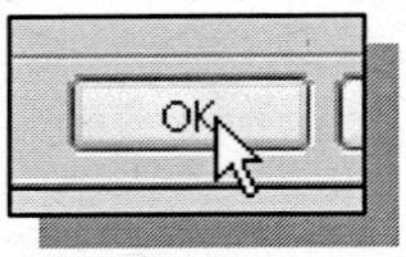

7. Click **OK** to create the *hole* feature.

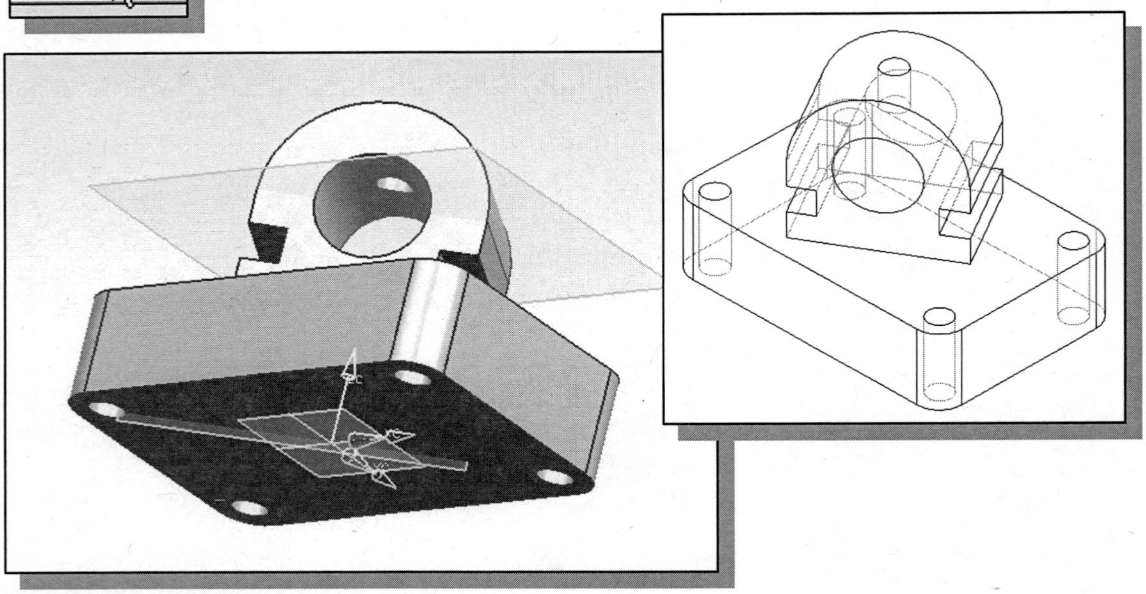

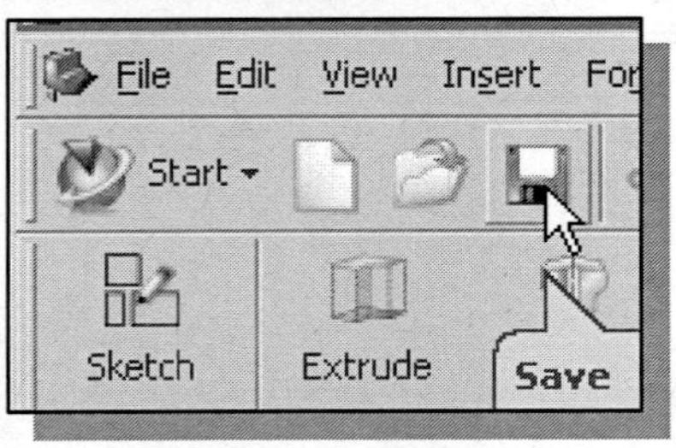

8. Click **Save** to save the design as ***Rod-Guide.prt***.

Creating a Title Block Template

❖ Several options are available in *UGS NX* to create drawing templates. In this section, we will examine the use of **Export/Import** commands to create drawing templates.

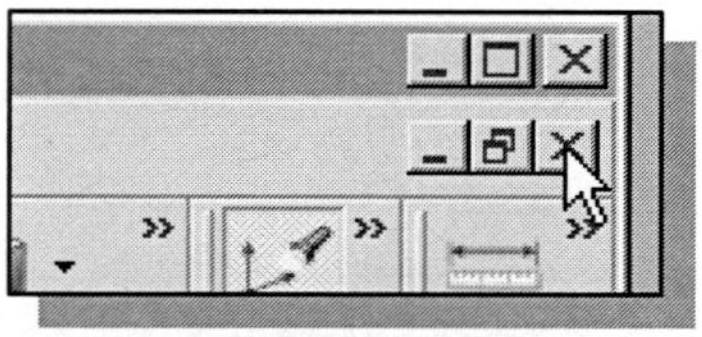

1. Close the *Rod-Guide* model by clicking on the lower [**X**] near the upper right corner of the *NX* main window as shown.

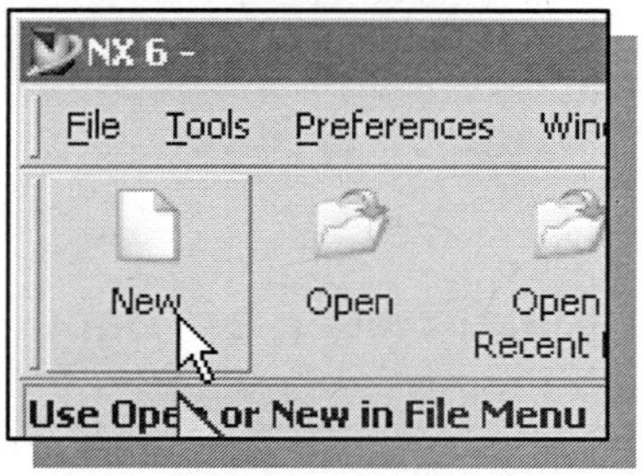

2. Start a new file by clicking the **New** icon with the left-mouse-button (MB1) in the *Standard* toolbar area.

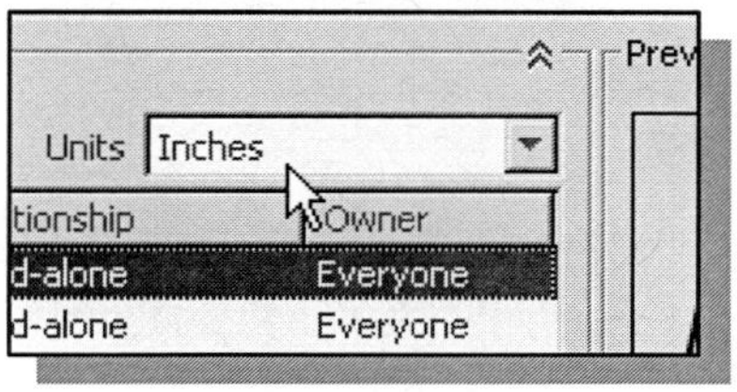

3. In the *New Part File* window, set the *Units* to **Inches** as shown.

4. Select **Blank** in the *Templates* list. Note that the *Blank* template contains no pre-defined settings.

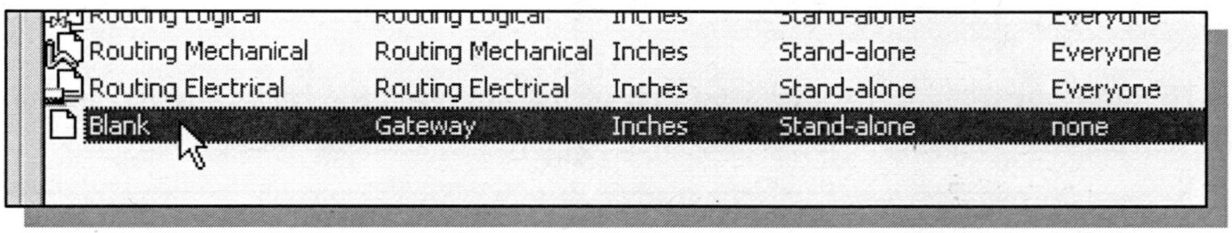

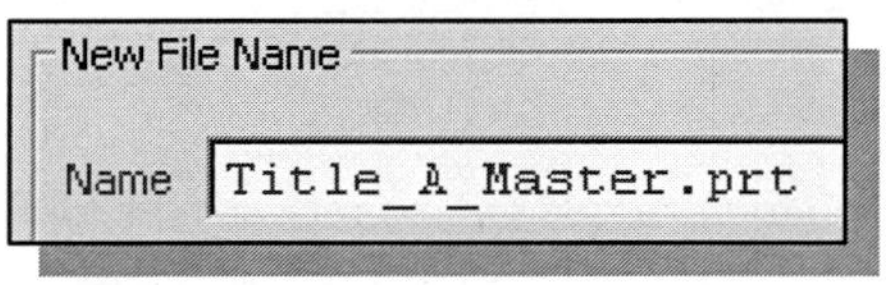

5. In the *New File Name* section, enter **Title_A_Master** as the file *Name*.

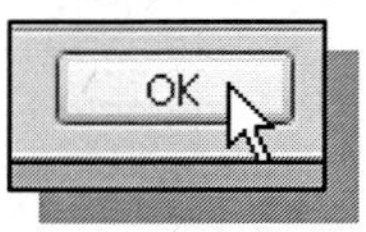

6. Click **OK** to proceed with the New Part File command.

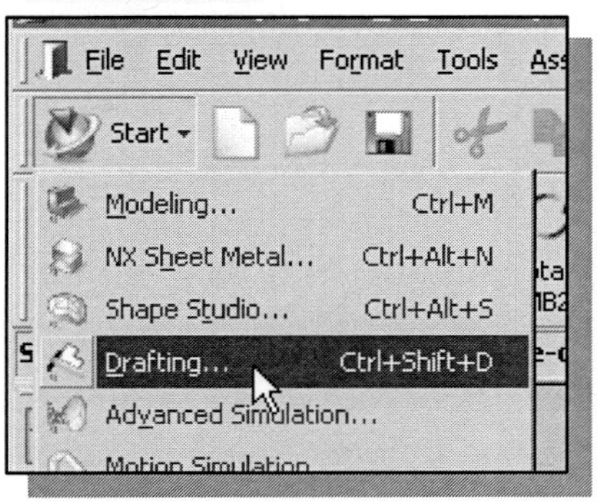

7. Select the **Start** icon with a single click of the left-mouse-button (MB1) in the *Standard* toolbar.

8. Pick **Drafting** in the pull-down list as shown in the figure.

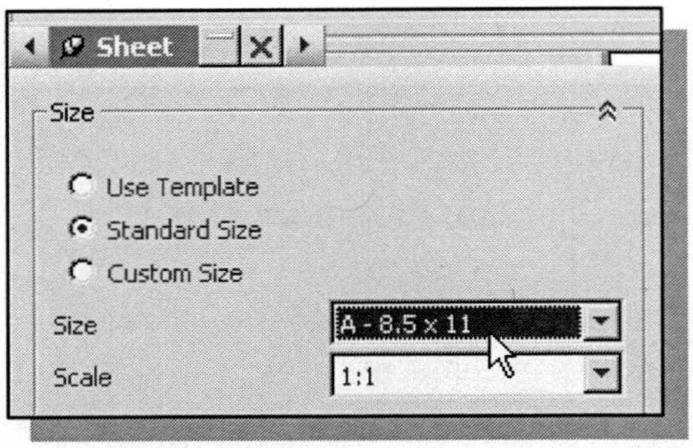

9. Select **A-8.5X11** from the sheet ***Size*** list.

10. Confirm the ***Scale*** is set to **1:1**, which is ***full scale***.

❖ Note that ***Sh1*** is the default drawing sheet name that is displayed above the sheet *Size* list.

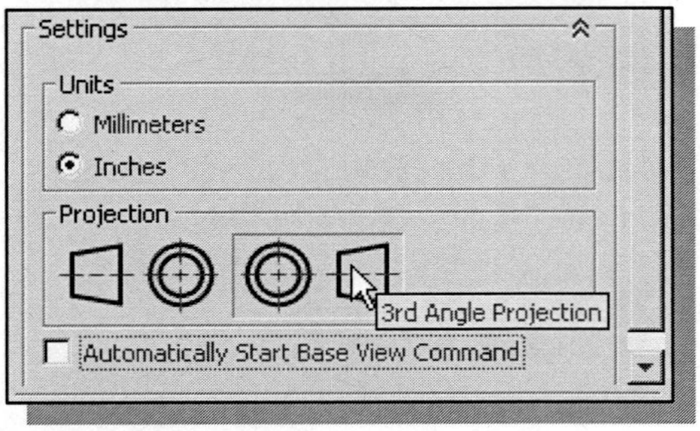

11. In the settings area, confirm the *Projection* type is set to **3rd Angle Projection** as shown.

12. **Uncheck** the **Automatically Start Base View Command** option as shown.

13. Click **OK** to accept the settings and proceed with the creation of the drawing sheet.

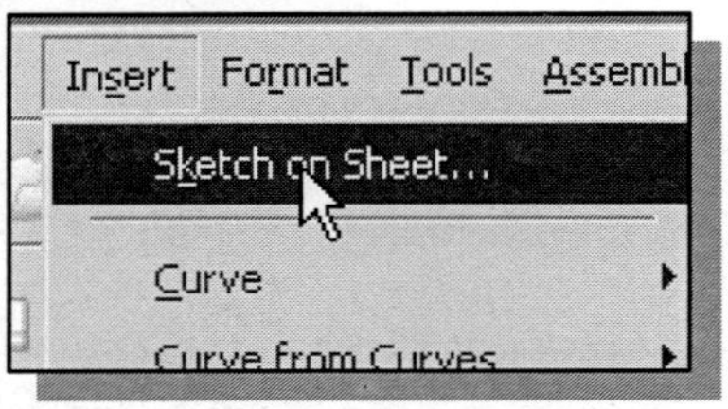

14. Select the **Sketch on Sheet** in the *Insert* pull-down menu as shown in the figure.

15. Create a rectangle and adjust the size of the rectangle to **10.25 x 7.75** as shown in the figure below.

16. On your own, click and drag one of the edges of the rectangle to reposition the rectangle so that it is roughly at the center of the drawing sheet.

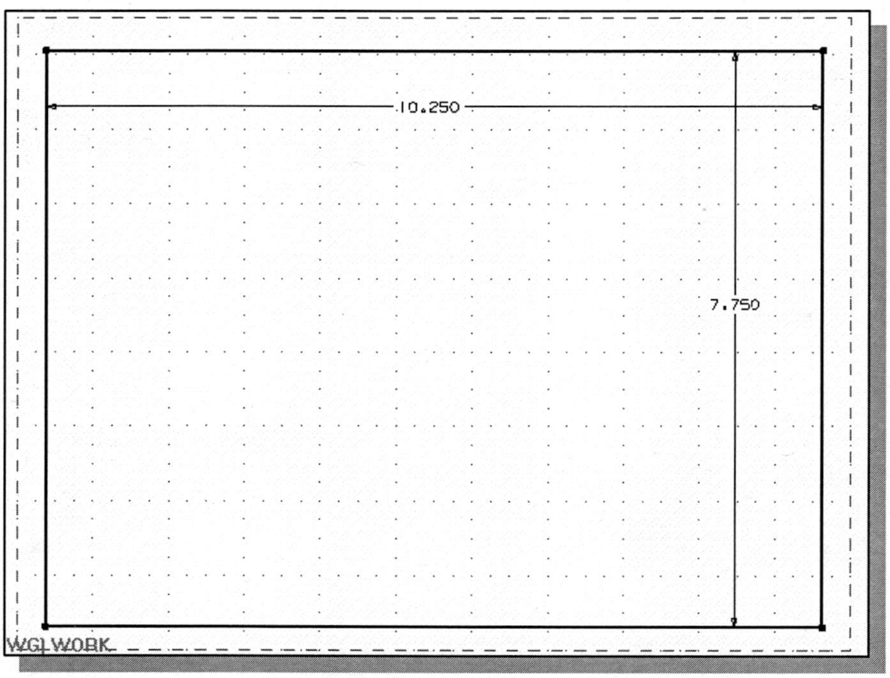

❖ Note that any sketches created in *Drafting* mode are still parametric sketches, which means we can apply different types of constraints to assure the proper geometric properties of the 2D sketches.

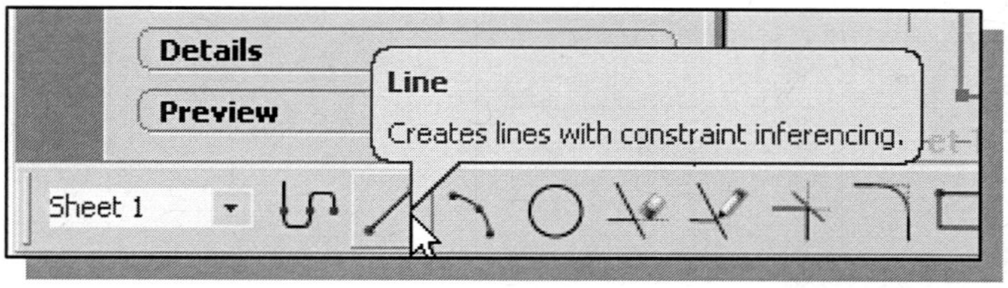

17. Select the **Line** command by clicking once with the left-mouse-button as shown.

18. On your own, create and adjust the horizontal and vertical lines with the dimensions as shown. (Hint: Apply proper constraints first.)

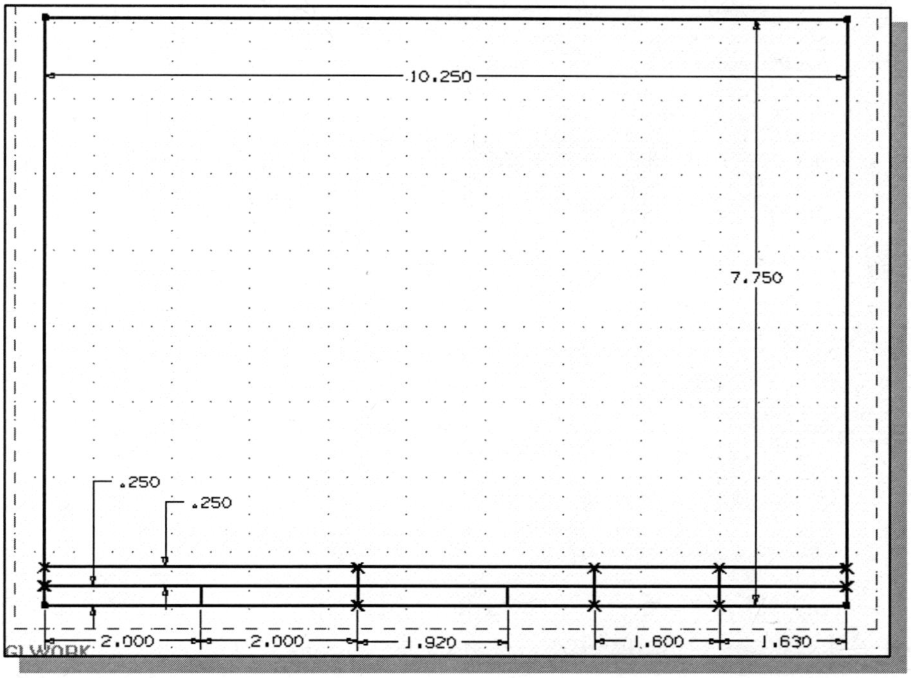

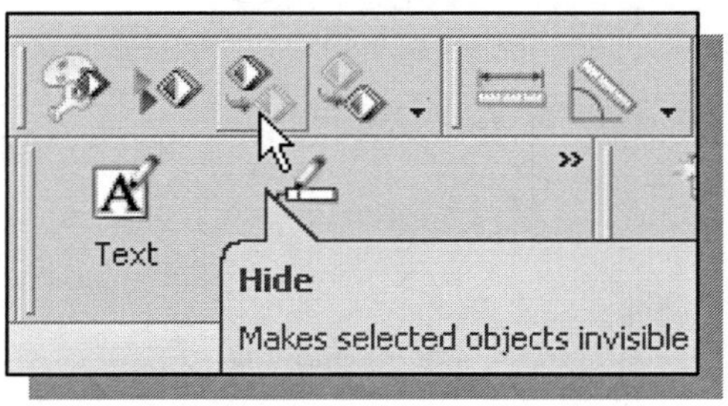

19. Select the **Hide** command in the *Utility* toolbar as shown.

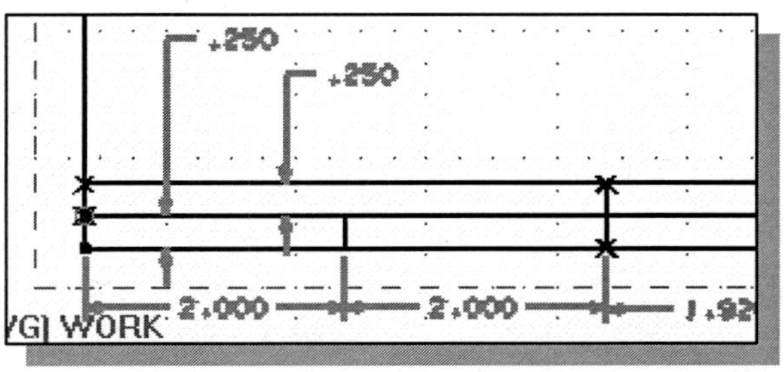

20. Select all the dimensions by clicking with the left-mouse-button on the dimension text as shown.

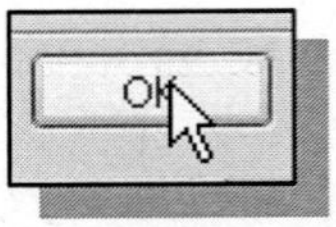

21. Click **OK** to accept the selection and proceed to hide the selected items.

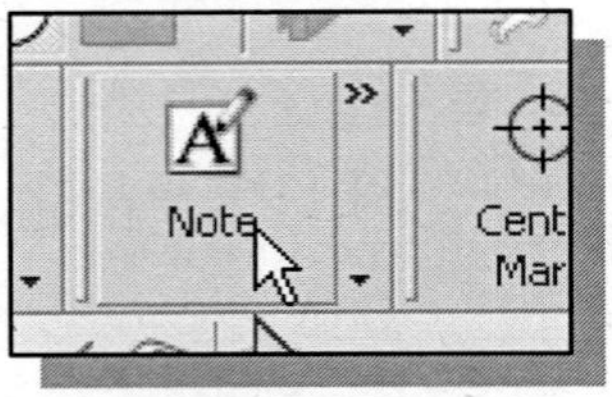

22. Click **Note** in the toolbar as shown.

23. Pick the **Annotation Style** option in the *Settings* area as shown.

24. Enter **0.125** as the *Character Size* and **0.75** as the new *Aspect Ratio*.

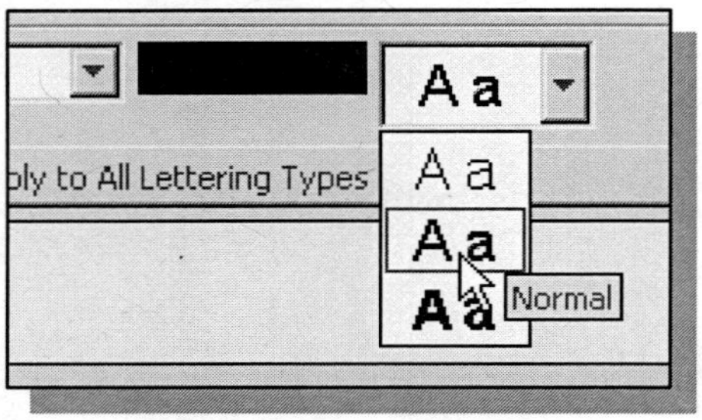

25. Set the *Color* to **black**.

26. Choose **Normal** to set the *Linewidth* for the selected font *Style*.

27. Click **OK** to accept the settings.

28. Enter your school name, or company name, in the *Annotation Editor* box and place the text in the title block as shown.

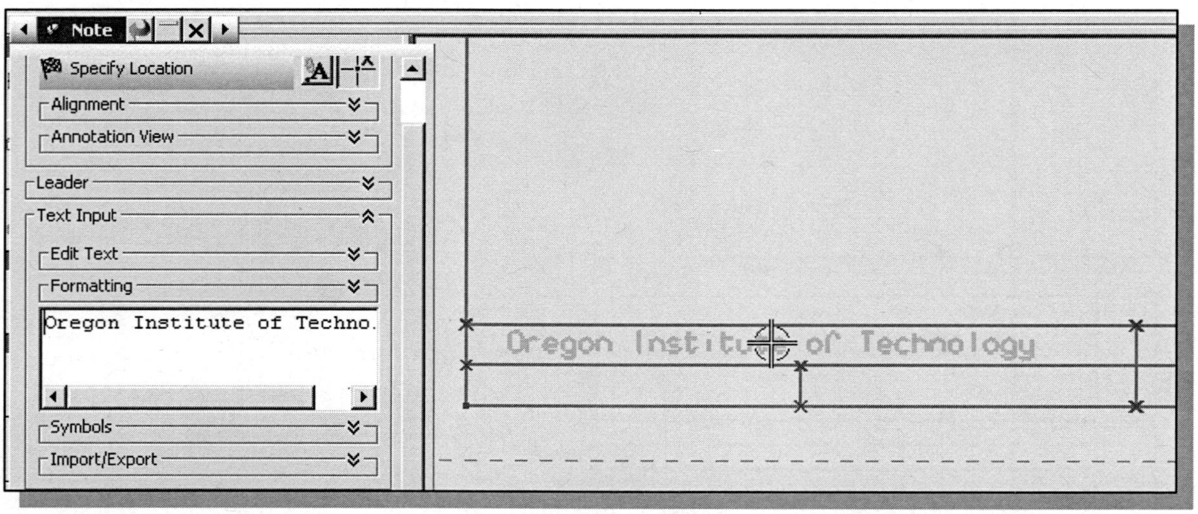

29. On your own, repeat the above steps and enter the text as shown in the figure below.

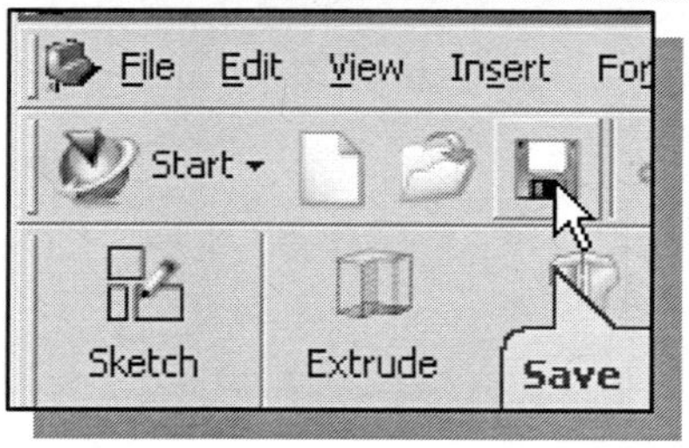

30. Save the title block design by clicking **Save** in the *Standard* toolbar as shown.

❖ Note that this is our master file; we can make modifications and generate a new template if necessary.

Using the Export File command

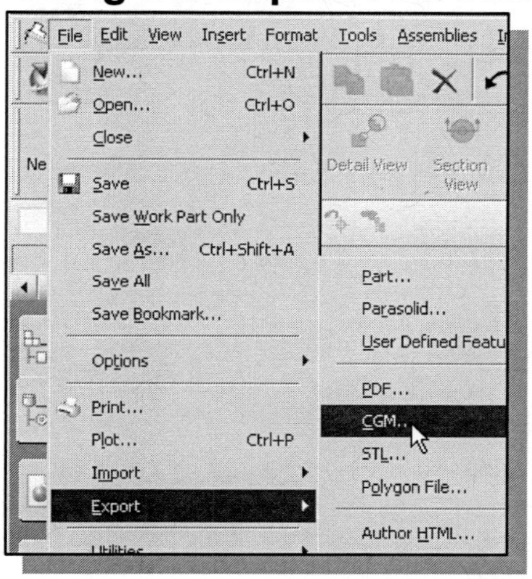

1. Select the **Export CGM** command through the *File* pull-down menu:

   [File] → [Export] → [CGM]

❖ Note the different options available, such as Bitmap, JPEG, STL, IGES and DXF/DWG. You are encouraged to try using some of these formats.

2. Set the *Files of Type* option to **CGM** and enter the *File name* **Title_A_Master_sheet1**. Click **OK** to save the file.

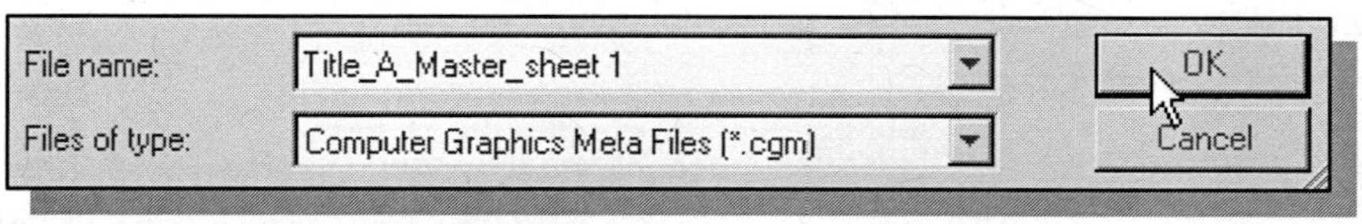

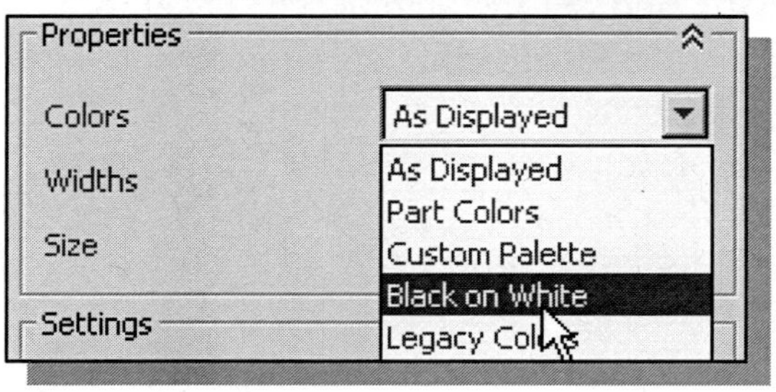

3. Under the *Properties* options, set the *Colors* option to **Black on White** as shown in the figure.

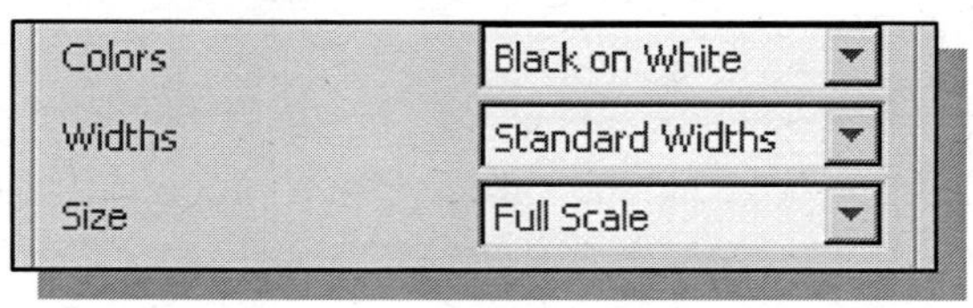

4. Confirm the *Scale factor* is set to **1.0**.

5. Click **OK** to accept the settings and save the CGM file.

Reopen the *Rod-Guide* Design

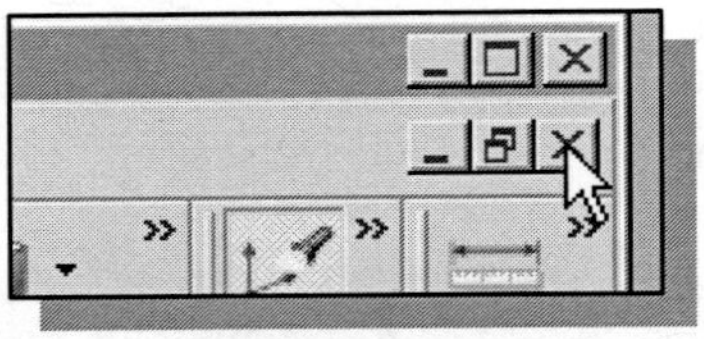

1. Close the *Title_A_Master* file by clicking on the lower **[X]** near the upper right corner of the *NX* main window as shown.

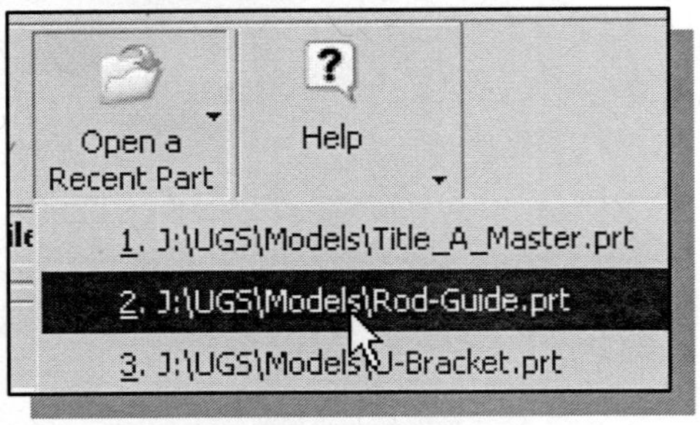

2. Reopen the ***Rod-Guide*** design through the **Open a Recent Part** icon as shown.

3. Click on the **Start** icon in the *Standard* toolbar area to display the available options.

4. Select **Drafting** from the option list.

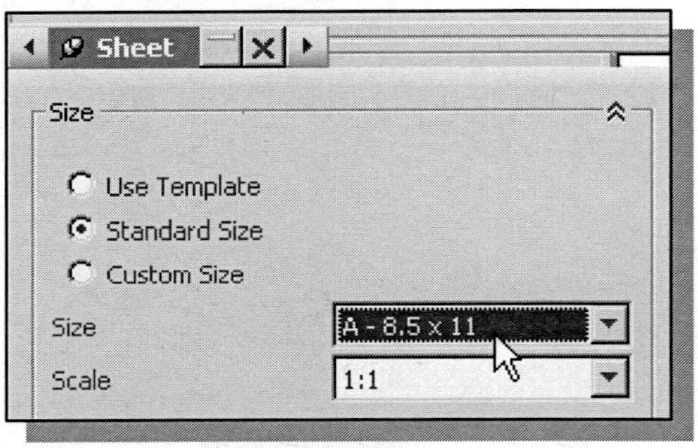

5. Select **A-8.5x11** from the sheet *Size* list.

6. Confirm the *Scale* is set to **1:1**, which is ***full scale***.

➢ Note that ***Sheet 1*** is the default drawing sheet name that is displayed in the *Drawing Sheet Name* area.

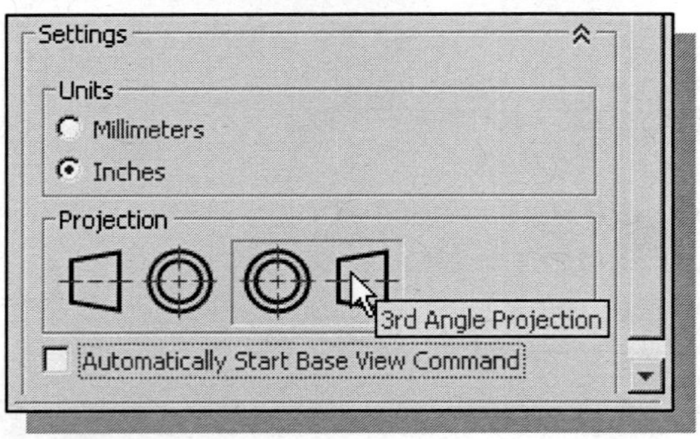

7. In the settings area, confirm *Units* are set to **Inches** and the *Projection* type is set to **3rd Angle Projection** as shown.

8. **Uncheck** the **Automatically Start Base View Command** option as shown.

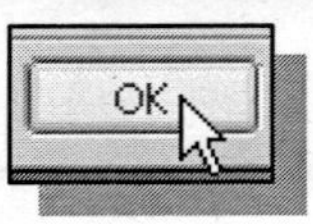

9. Click **OK** to accept the settings and proceed with the creation of the drawing sheet.

Importing the Title Block

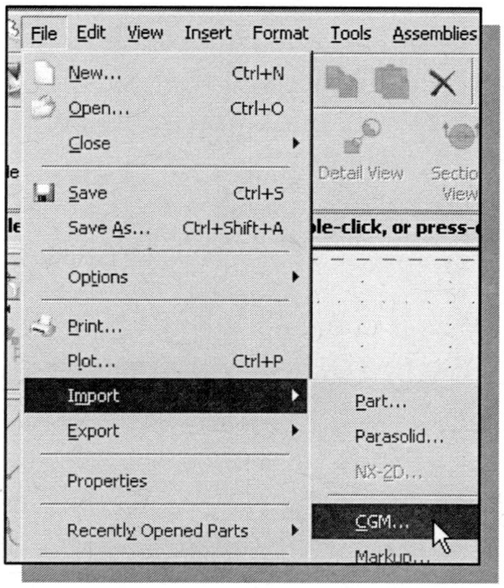

1. Select the **Import CGM** command through the *File* pull-down menu:

   [File] → [Import] → [CGM]

2. Enter or select **Title_A_Master_sheet 1.cgm** in the *Import CGM* window as shown.

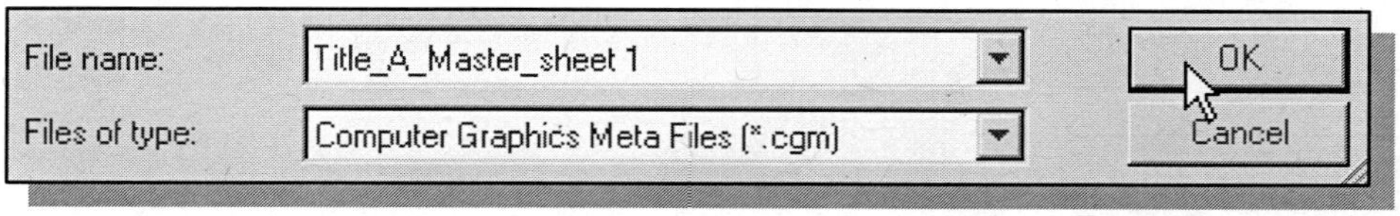

3. Click **OK** to proceed with importing the selected CGM file.

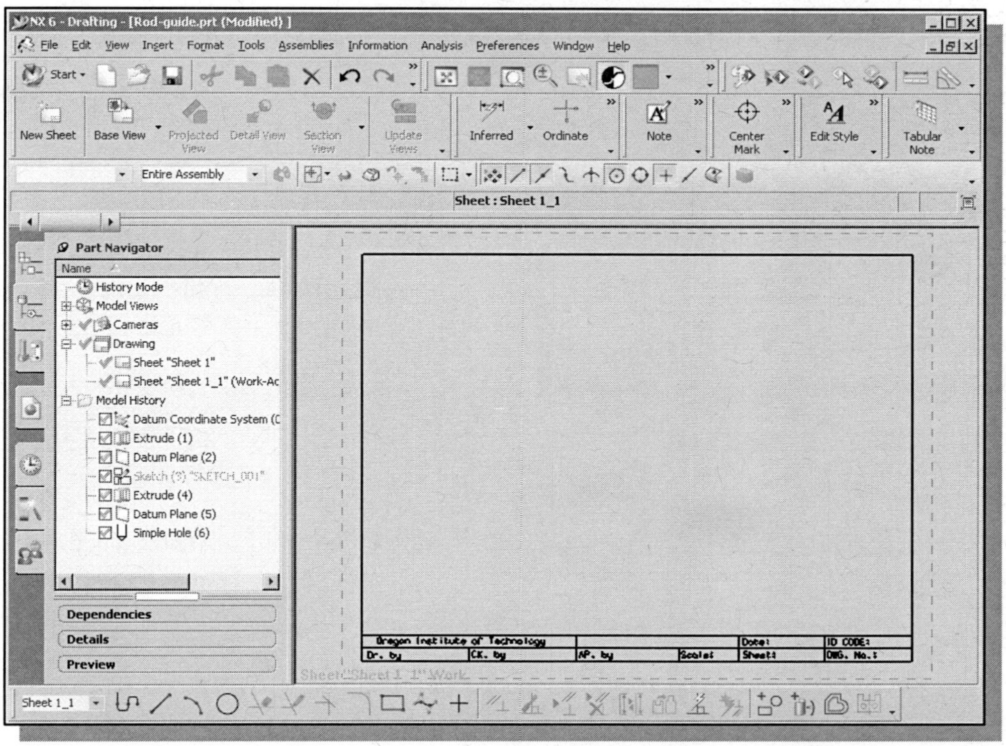

❖ The Import/Export commands provide a fairly flexible way to reuse title blocks and borders. You are encouraged to try the other file formats.

Adding a Base View

❖ In *UGS NX Drawing* mode, the first drawing view we create is called a ***base* view**. A *base* view is the primary view in a drawing; other views can be derived from this view. When creating a *base* view, *UGS NX* allows us to specify one of the principal views to be shown. By default, *UGS NX* will treat the *X-Z* plane as the *front* view of the solid model. Note that there can be more than one *base* view in a drawing.

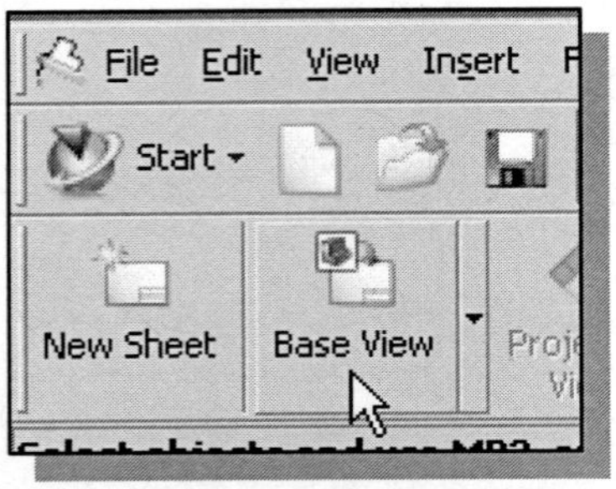

1. Click on the **Base View** icon in the *Drawing Layout* toolbar to create a new base view.

2. In the *Base View* option toolbar, set the view option to **TOP** as shown.

3. In the *Settings* option list, click the **View Style** icon as shown.

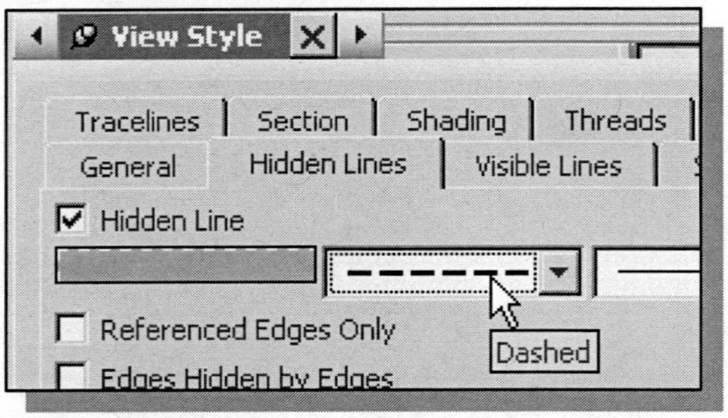

4. In the *View Style* window, click the **Hidden Lines** tab as shown.

5. Choose **Dashed** as the linetype to be used for hidden lines in the *base* view.

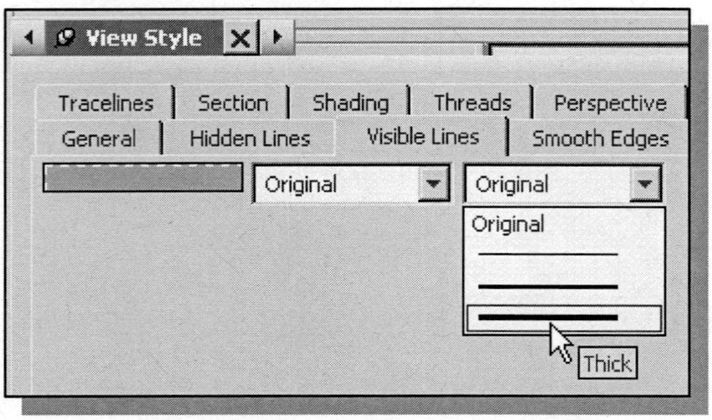

6. Click on the **Visible Lines** tab and select **Thick** as the linetype for the *base* view.

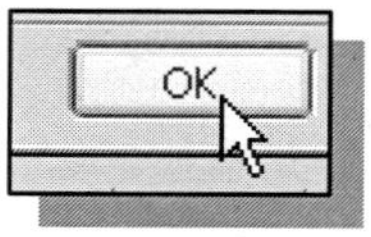

7. Click **OK** to accept the settings and exit the **View Style** command.

8. Place the ***base* view**, the *top* view of the ***Rod-Guide*** model, near the upper left corner of the drawing sheet as shown.

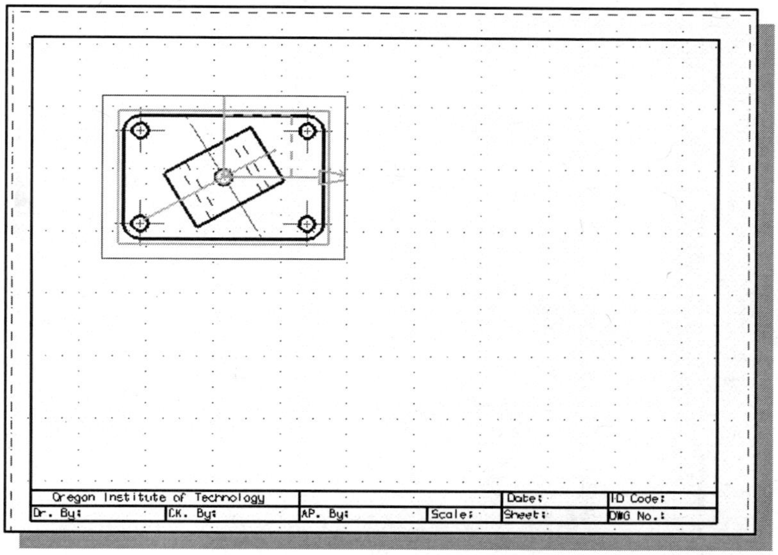

Creating an Auxiliary View

❖ In *UGS NX Drawing* mode, the **Projected View** command is used to create standard views such as the *top* view and *front* view. For non-standard views, the **Auxiliary View** command is used. *Auxiliary* views are created using orthographic projections. Orthographic projections are aligned to the *base* view and inherit the *base* view's scale and display settings.

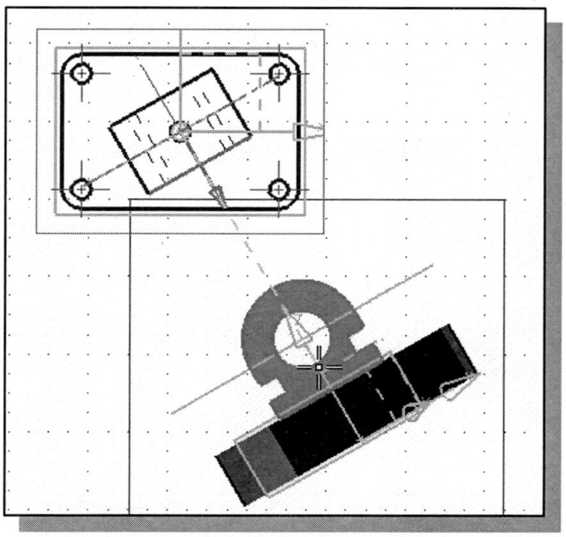

1. Activate the **Associative** option as shown.

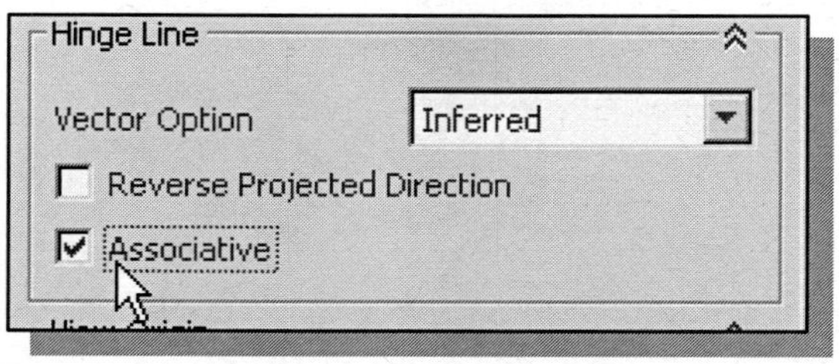

2. Move the cursor below the *top* view and watch the display of the *projected* view. Click the left-mouse-button when the front edge of the upper section of the 3D model is **highlighted**.

❖ In *UGS NX*, creating an *auxiliary* view is very similar to creating a *standard* view.

3. Use the middle-mouse-button (MB2) or click **Close** to end the command.

Turning Off the Datum Planes and DCS

➢ The display of the datum planes and datum coordinate system can be turned off in *Drafting* mode.

1. Select the **Hide** command through the *Edit* pull-down menu:

   [Edit] → [Show and Hide] → [Hide]

➢ The Hide command can be used to temporarily turn off the display of objects.

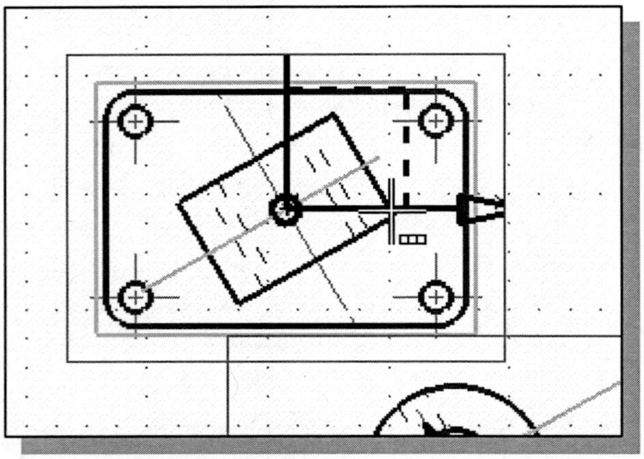

2. Select the datum coordinate system near the center of the *top* view as shown.

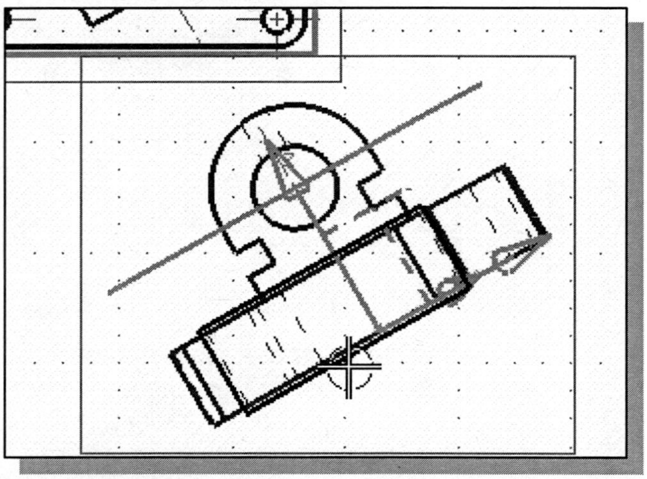

3. Select the two datum planes in the *auxiliary* view as shown.

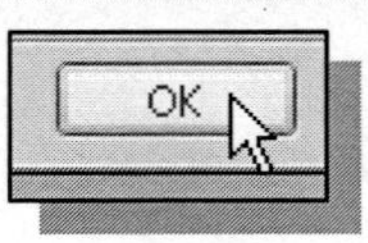

4. Click **OK** to accept the selections and proceed to hide the selected objects.

Turning Off the Display Borders option

❖ The display of the borders around the 2D views can be turned off by setting the drafting preferences.

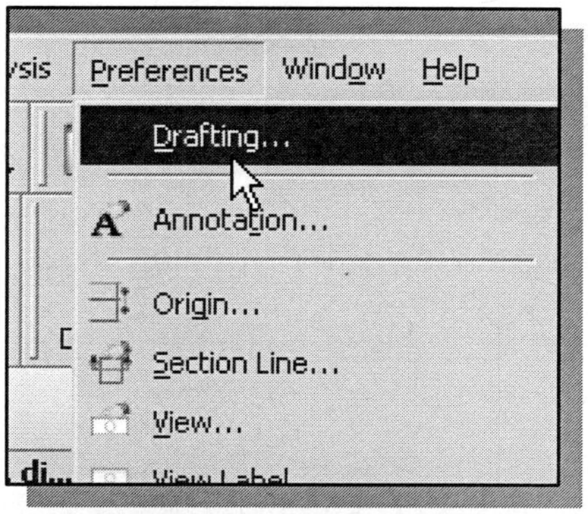

1. Select **Drafting** in the *Preferences* pull-down menu as shown.

2. Turn off the **Display Borders** option under the **View** tab as shown.

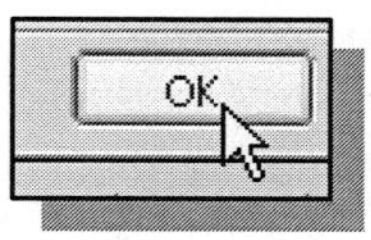

3. Click **OK** to accept the settings and exit the **View Style** command.

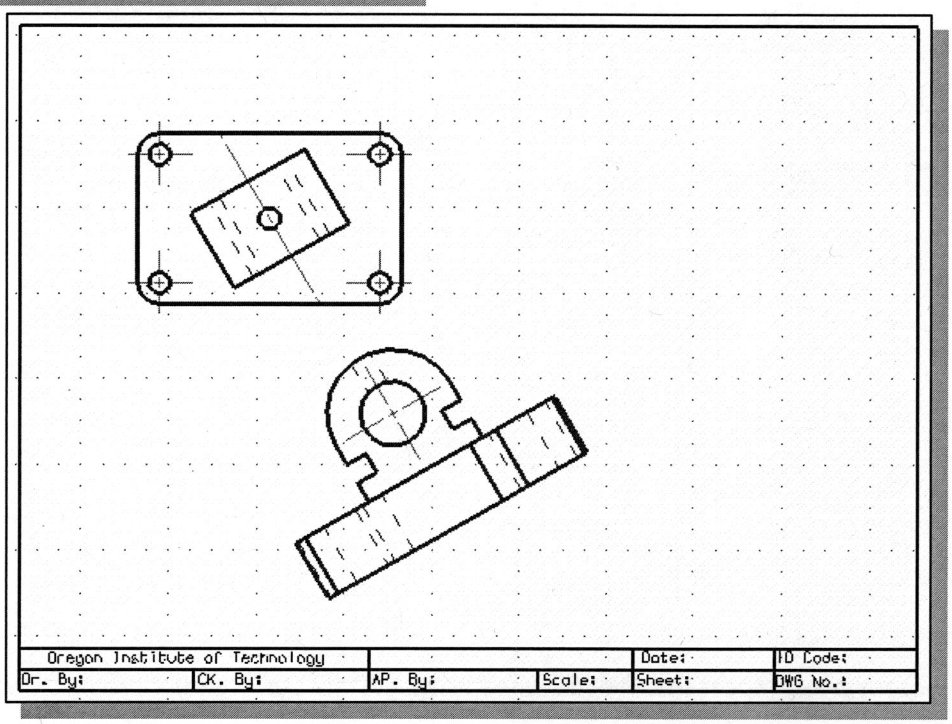

Creating another Base View

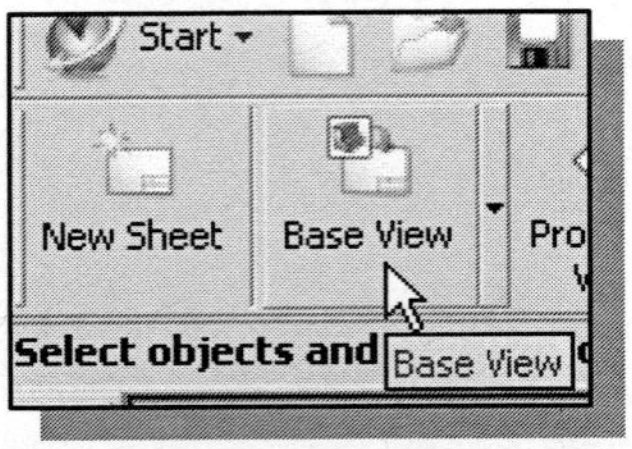

1. Click on the **Base View** in the *Drawing Layout* toolbar to create a new *base* view.

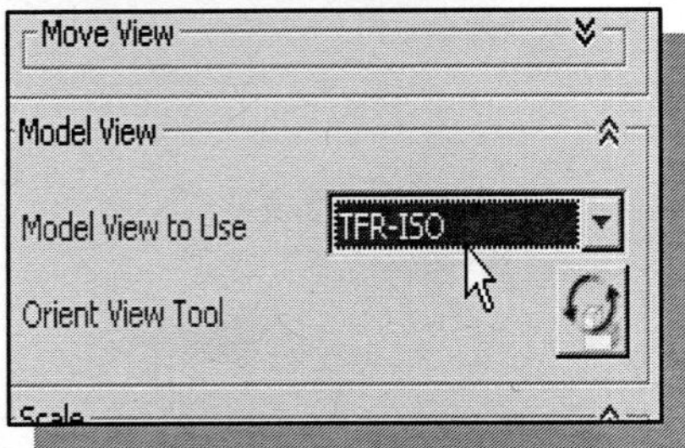

2. Select **TFR-ISO** in the view list, and place an *isometric* view at the right side of the drawing sheet as shown.

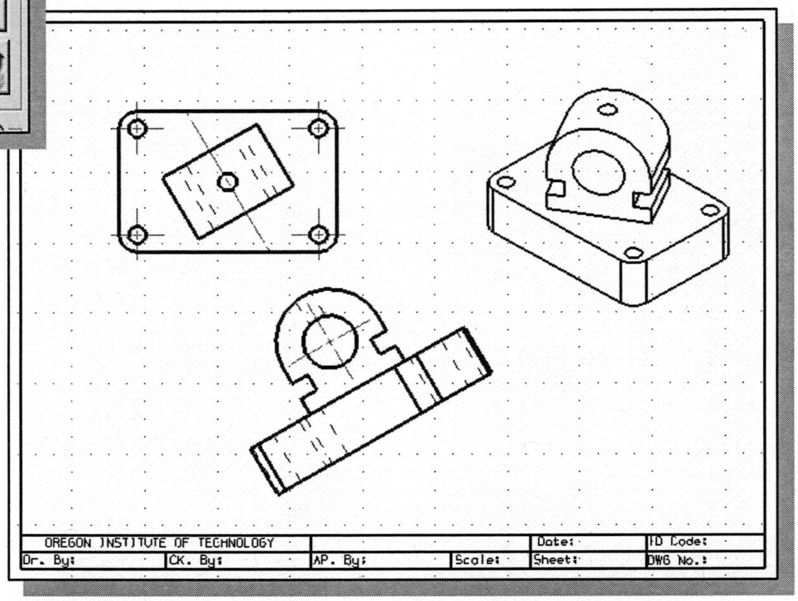

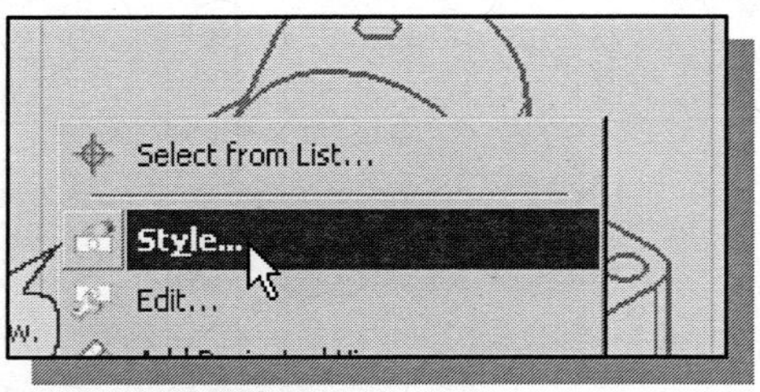

3. Right-mouse-click once on the *isometric* view to bring up the option list.

4. Select the **Style** option as shown.

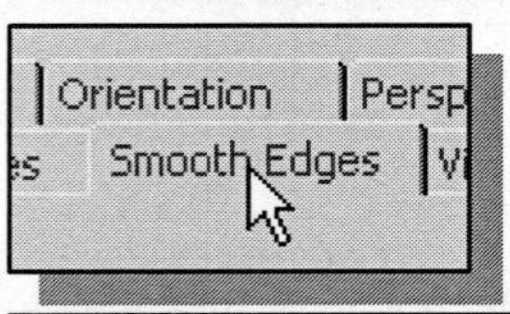

5. Left-mouse-click (MB1) the **Smooth Edges** tab as shown.

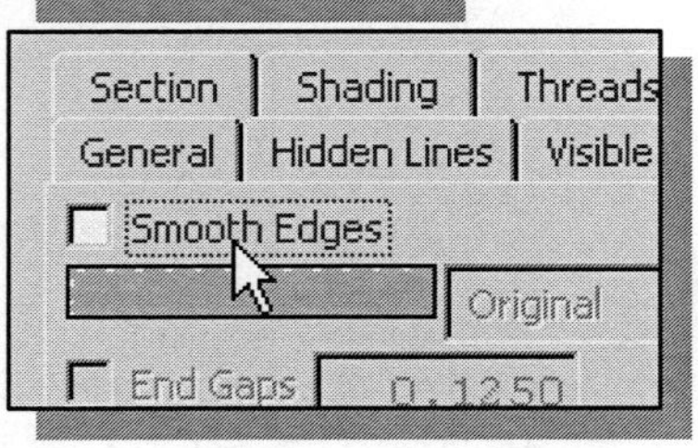

6. Turn *OFF* the **Smooth Edges** option as shown.

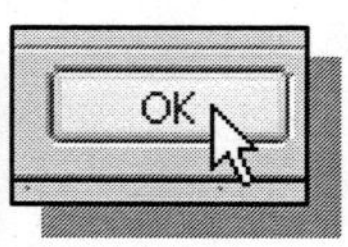

7. Click **OK** to accept the settings.

8. On your own, repeat the above steps to turn off the edges in the *auxiliary* view.

Drawing Display Option

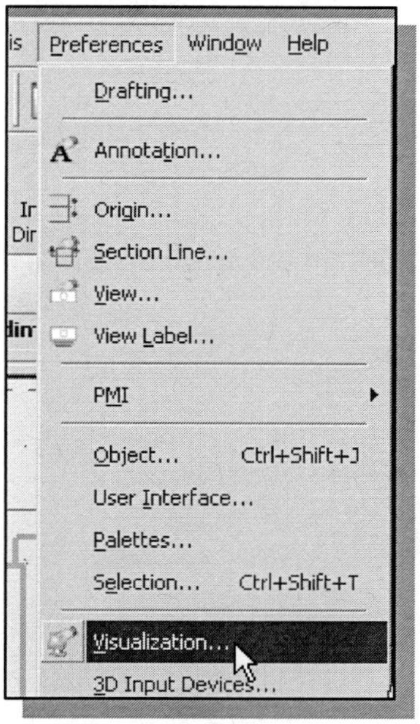

1. Select **Visualization** in the *Preferences* pull-down menu as shown.

2. Click on the **Color Settings** tab as shown.

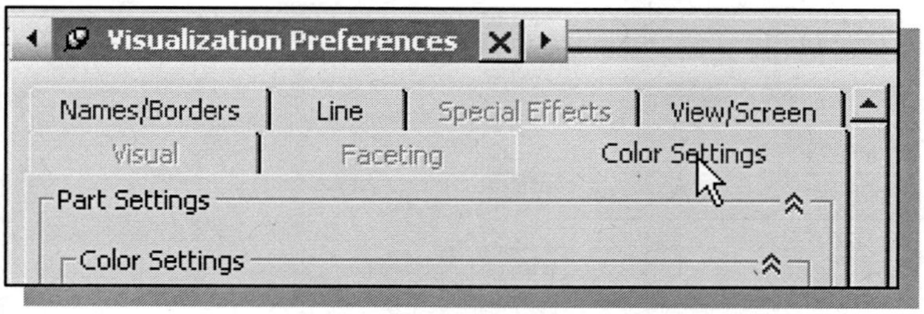

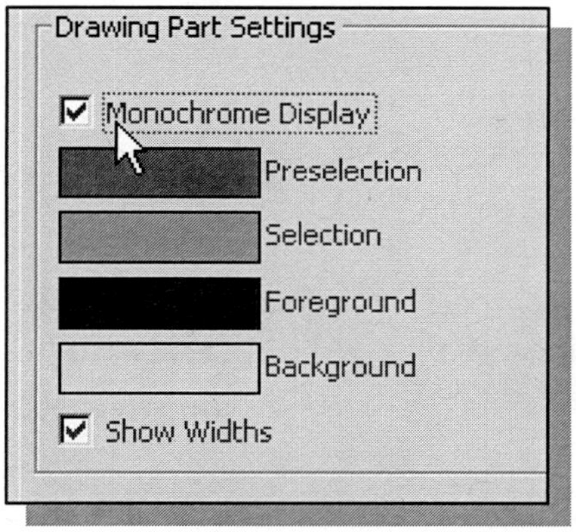

3. Activate the **Monochrome Display** and the **Show Widths** options as shown.

4. On your own, set the ***Background*** color to **white**.

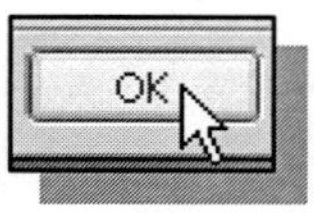

5. Click **OK** to accept the settings and exit the *Visualization Preferences* window.

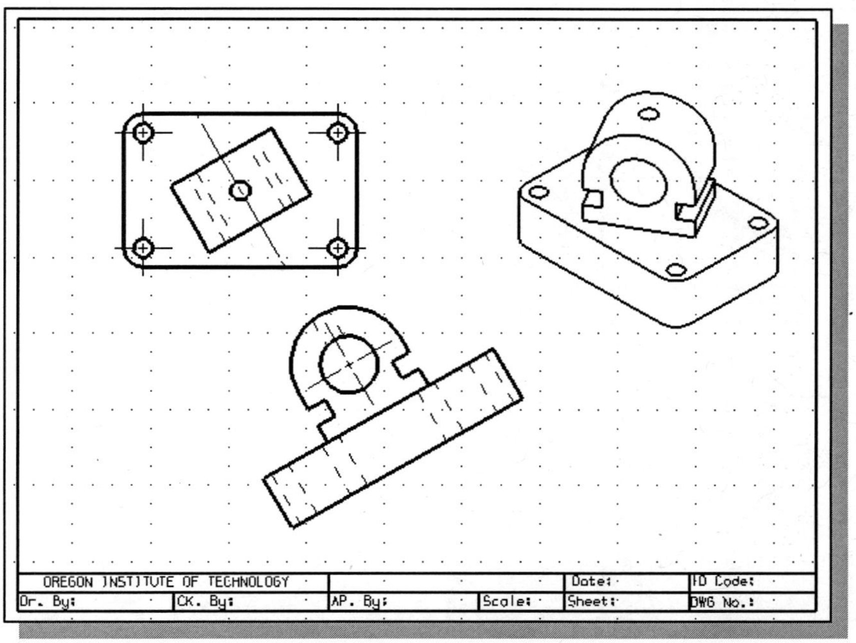

Displaying Feature Dimensions

- By default, feature dimensions are not displayed in 2D views in *UGS NX*.

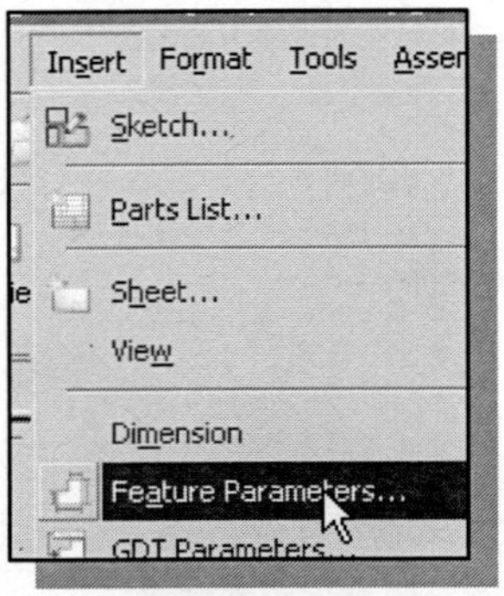

1. Select **Feature Parameters** in the *Insert* pull-down list as shown.

2. In the *Feature Parameters* window, notice the **ansi** standard is used for the dimension settings.

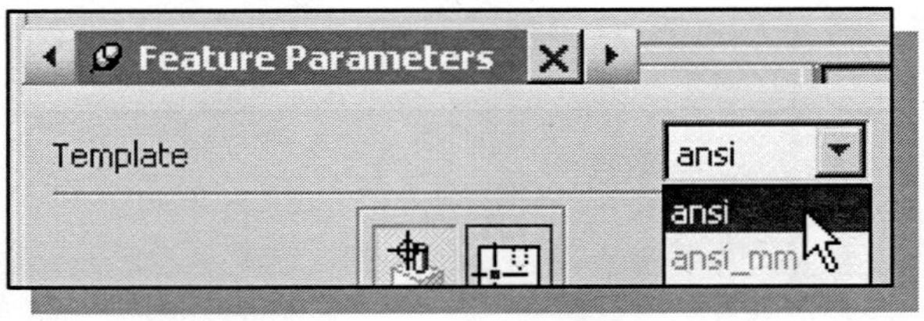

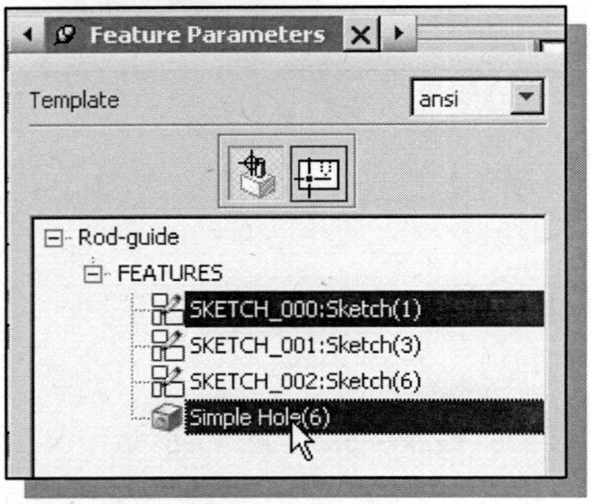

❖ Two steps are required; (1) select the feature used and (2) select the view to place the dimensions.

3. Expand the *FEATURES* list and choose the ***base*** feature *Sketch(1)* and the ***hole*** feature *Hole(6)* as shown.

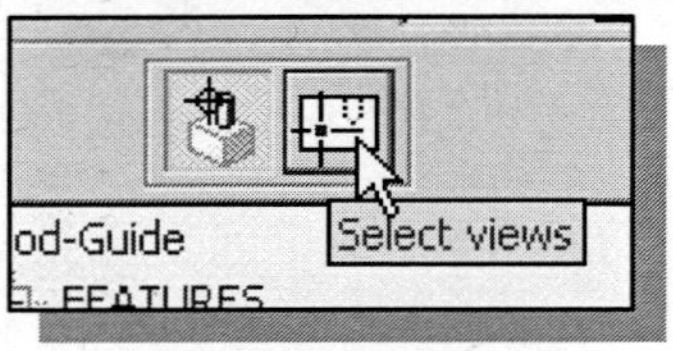

4. Click the **Select Views** icon to proceed to the next step.

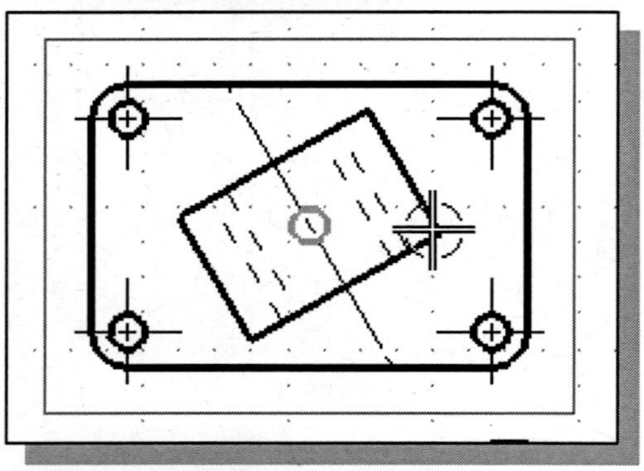

5. Inside the graphics window, select the ***top*** view by clicking once with the left-mouse-button (MB1) as shown.

❖ Note that the corresponding view name is highlighted as soon as we click on a view in the graphics window.

6. Click **Apply** to accept the settings.

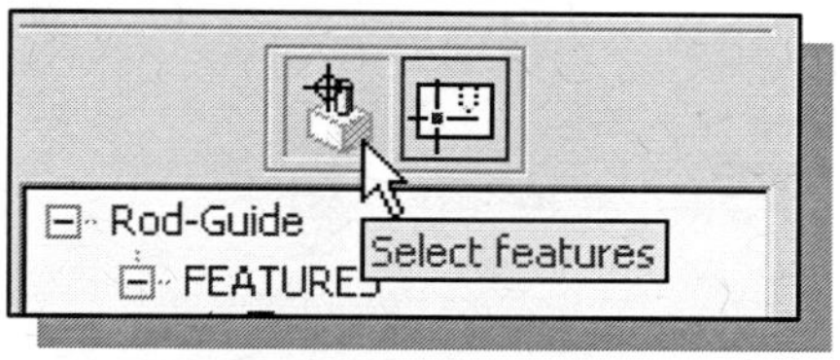

7. Left-mouse-click on the **Select features** button as shown.

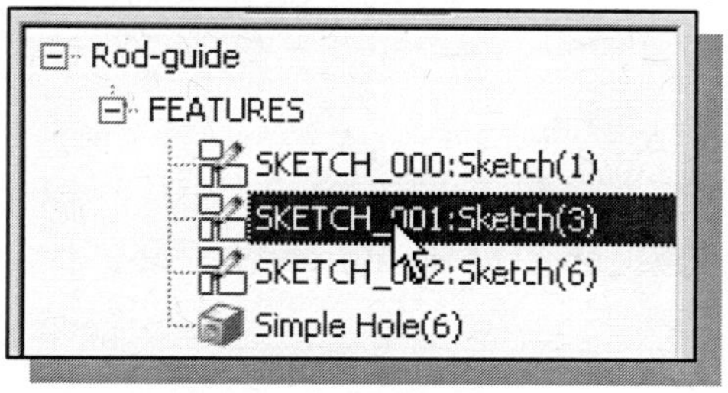

8. Select the ***second extrude feature*** by left-clicking once in the *FEATURES* list.

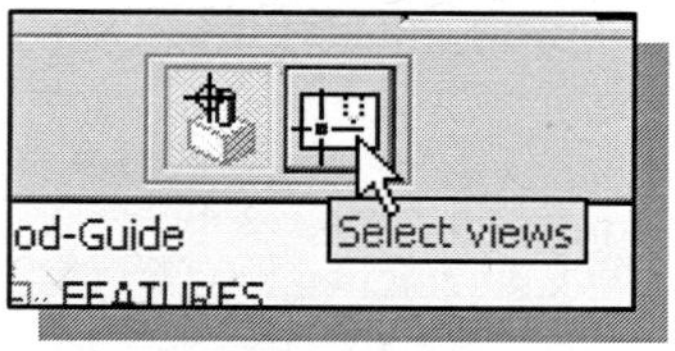

9. Click the **Select Views** icon to proceed to the next step.

10. Inside the *Feature Parameters* window, select the **Aux View** by clicking once with the left-mouse-button (MB1) as shown.

11. Click **OK** to accept the settings and exit the *Feature Parameters* window.

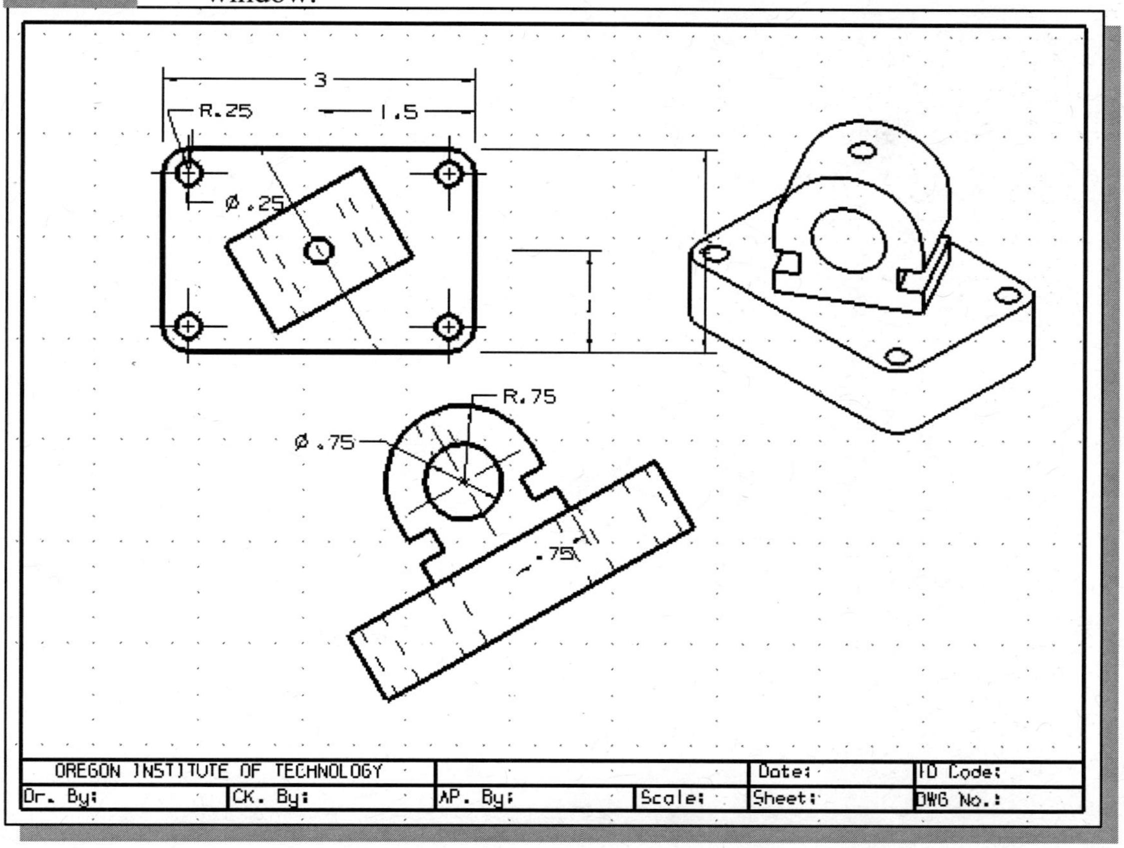

Delete and Adding Dimensions

❖ We will use the **Delete** command to remove the unwanted feature dimensions.

1. Select the **Delete** command through the *Edit* pull-down menu:
[Edit] → [Delete]

➢ The **Delete** command can also be activated using the key combination [**Ctrl+D**].

2. On your own, select the **dimensions** that are not needed in the *top* view.

3. Click **OK** to accept the selections.

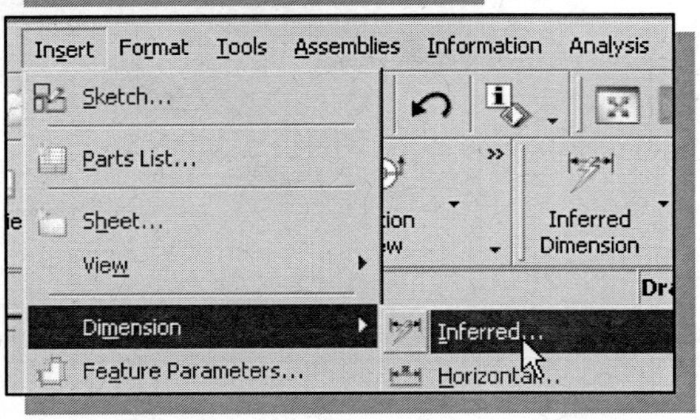

4. Select **Inferred Dimension** in the toolbar or select the command through the *Insert* pull-down menu:
[Insert] → [Dimension] → [Inferred]

5. On your own, create the necessary dimensions in the *auxiliary* view as shown in the figure below.

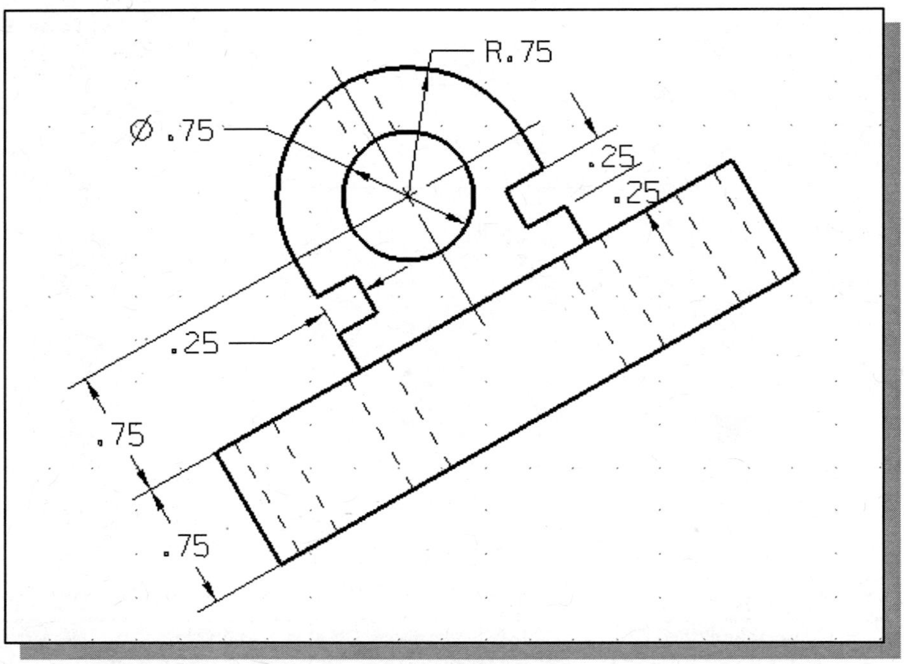

6. On your own, create the necessary dimensions and center line to complete the *Rod-Guide* drawing as shown in the figure below.

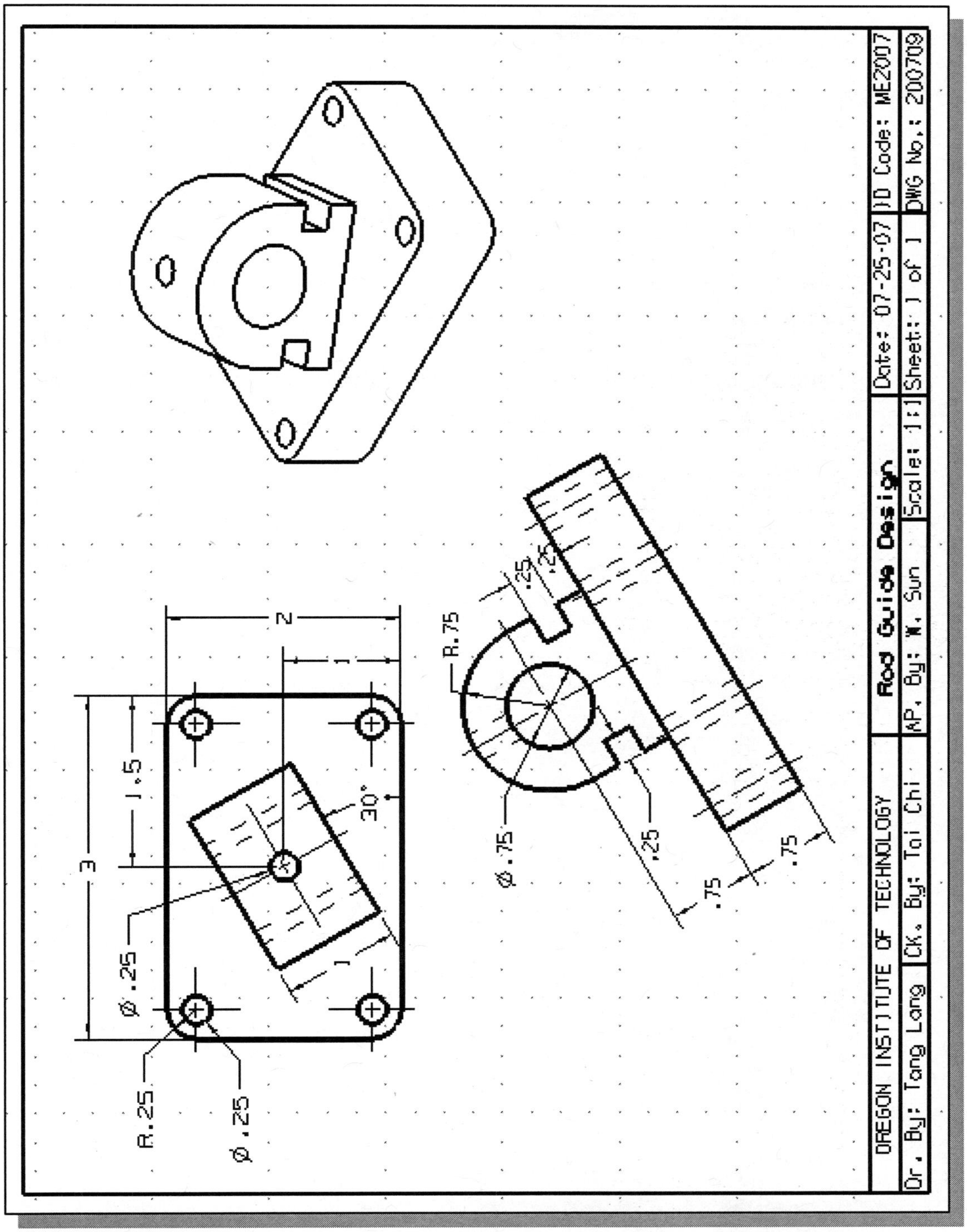

Questions:

1. What are the different types of *datum features* available in *UGS NX*?

2. Why are *datum features* important in parametric modeling?

3. Describe the purpose of *auxiliary* views in 2D drawings?

4. What are the required elements in order to create an *auxiliary* view?

5. What are the advantages of using a *template* file?

6. Describe the differences between the *1st angle projection* and *3rd angle projection* used in drafting standards.

7. Describe the general procedure to display feature dimensions in the *Drafting* mode of *UGS NX6*.

Exercises: (Create the Solid models and the associated 2D drawings.)

1. Dimensions are in inches.

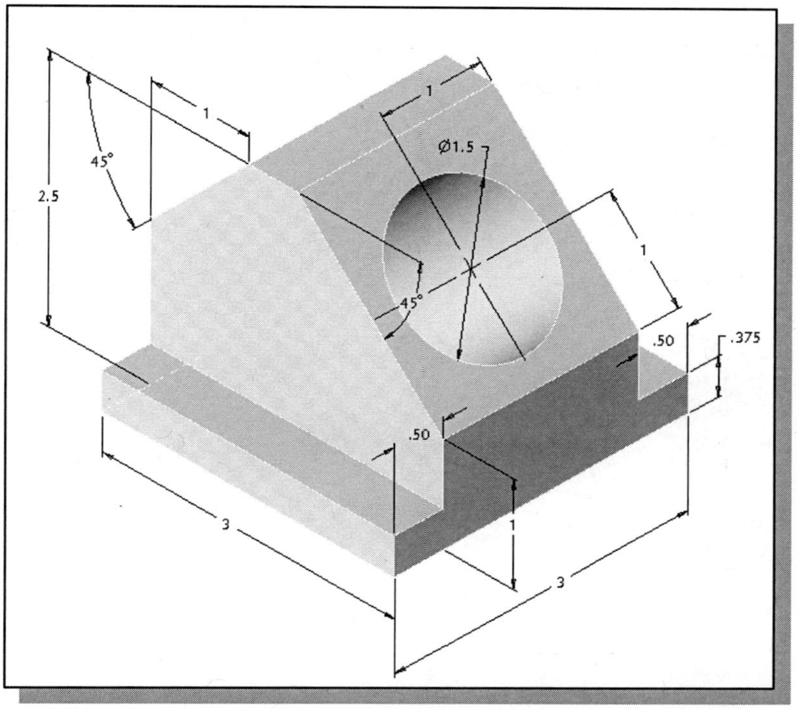

2. Dimensions are in millimeters.

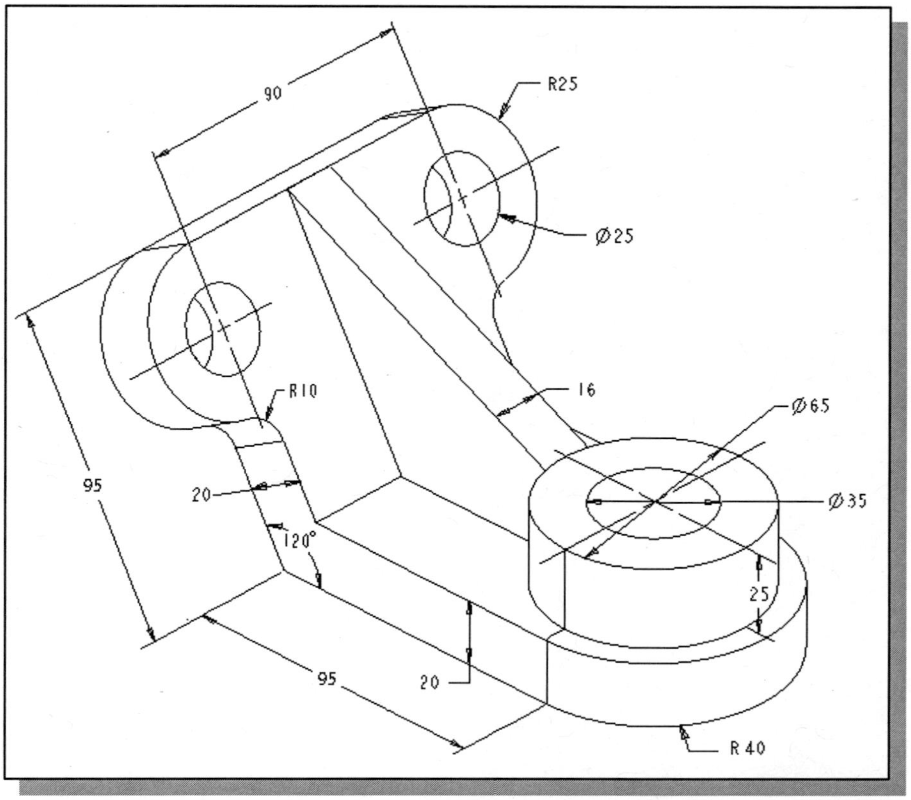

Notes:

Chapter 10
Symmetrical Features in Designs

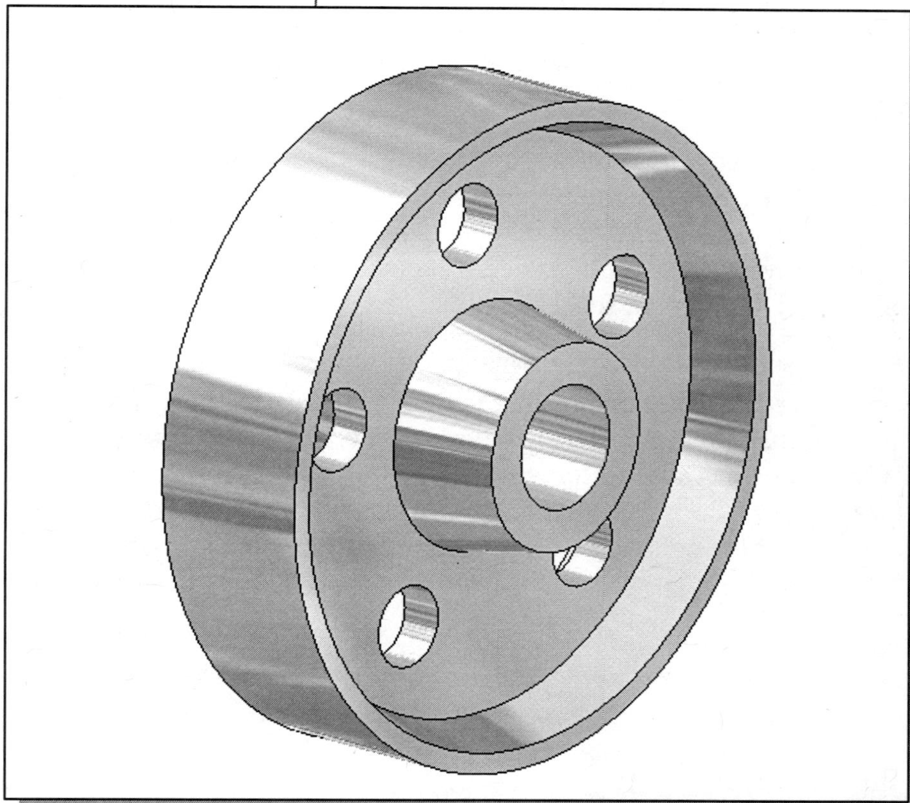

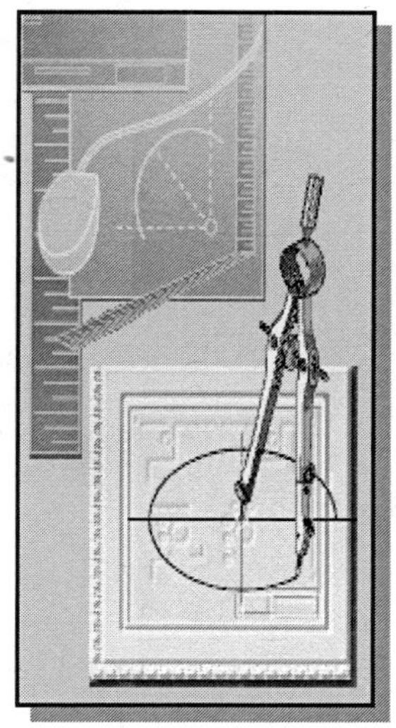

Learning Objectives

- ♦ Create Revolved Features
- ♦ Use the Mirror Feature Command
- ♦ Import a pre-made Border and Title Block
- ♦ Create Circular Patterns
- ♦ Use UGS NX's Associative Functionality
- ♦ Use the Basic Tools to create Symmetrical Features

Introduction

In parametric modeling, it is important to identify and determine the features that exist in the design. *Feature-based parametric modeling* enables us to build complex designs by working on smaller and simpler units. This approach simplifies the modeling process and allows us to concentrate on the characteristics of the design. Symmetry is an important characteristic that is often seen in designs. Symmetrical features can be easily accomplished by the assortment of tools that are available in feature-based modeling systems, such as *UGS NX.*

The modeling technique of extruding two-dimensional sketches along a straight line to form three-dimensional features, as illustrated in the previous chapters, is an effective way to construct solid models. For designs that involve cylindrical shapes, shapes that are symmetrical about an axis, revolving two-dimensional sketches about an axis can form the needed three-dimensional features. In solid modeling, this type of feature is called a ***revolved feature***.

In *UGS NX*, besides using the **Revolve** command to create revolved features, several options are also available to handle symmetrical features. For example, we can create multiple identical copies of symmetrical features with the **Feature Pattern** command, or create mirror images of models using the **Mirror Feature** command. We can also use *construction geometry* to assist the construction of more complex features. In this lesson, the construction and modeling techniques of these more advanced options are illustrated.

A Revolved Design: *Pulley*

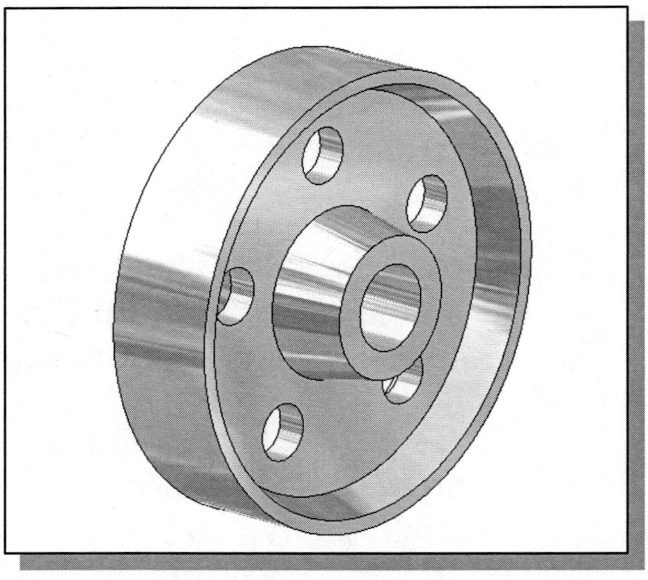

- ❖ Based on your knowledge of *UGS NX*, how many features would you use to create the design? Which feature would you choose as the **base feature** of the model? Identify the symmetrical features in the design and consider other possibilities in creating the design. You are encouraged to create the model on your own prior to following through the tutorial.

Modeling Strategy – A Revolved Design

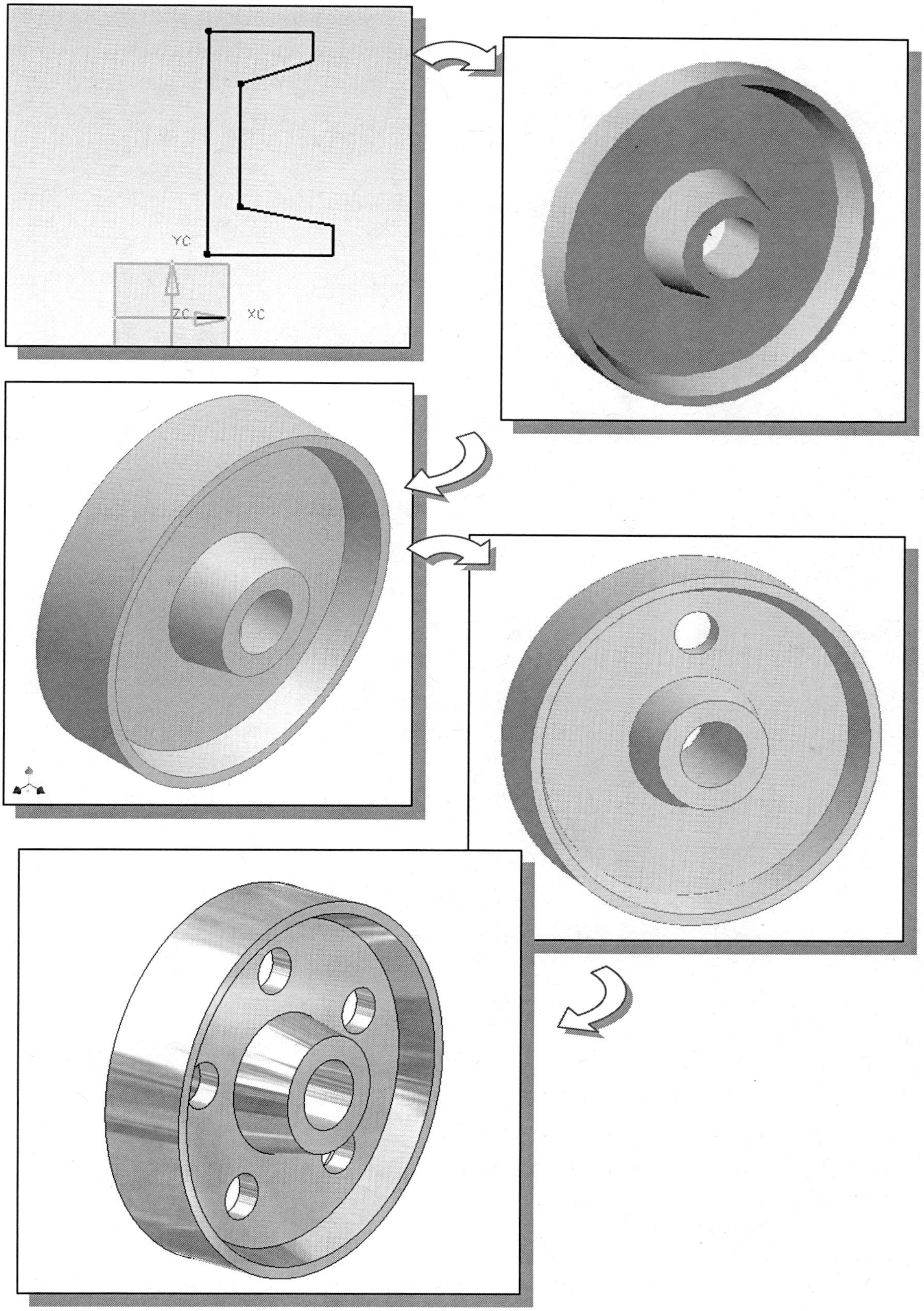

Starting *UGS NX*

1. Select the **UGS NX** option on the *Start* menu or select the **UGS NX** icon on the desktop to start *UGS NX*. The *UGS NX* main window will appear on the screen.

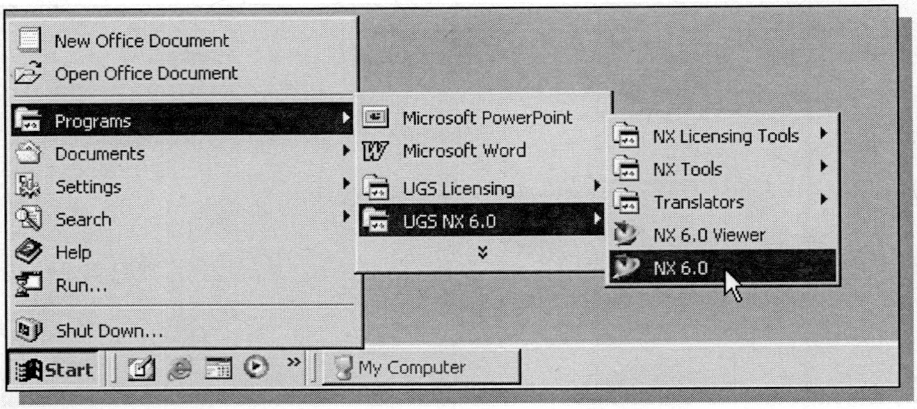

2. Select the **New** icon with a single click of the left-mouse-button (MB1) in the *Standard* toolbar area.

3. Confirm the *Units* are set to **Inches** as shown in the figure below.

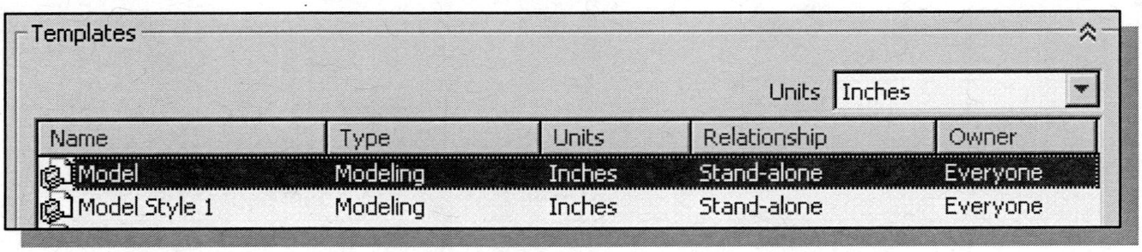

4. Select **Model** in the *Templates* list. Note that the *Model* template will allow us to switch directly into the *Modeling* task as indicated in the *Templates* list.

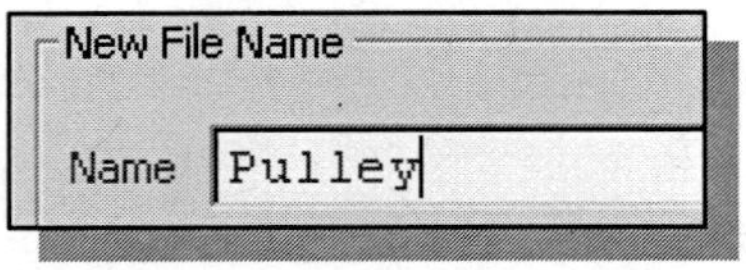

5. In the *New File Name* area, enter **Pulley** as the file *Name*.

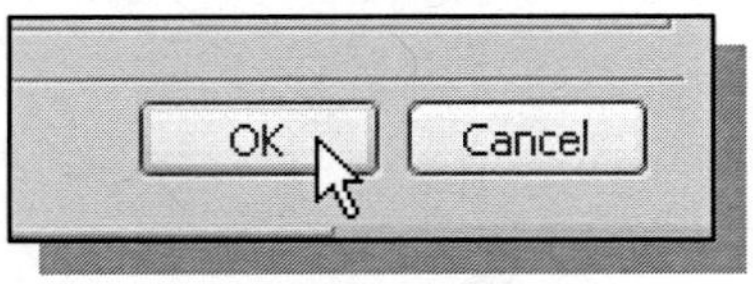

6. Click **OK** to proceed with the New File command.

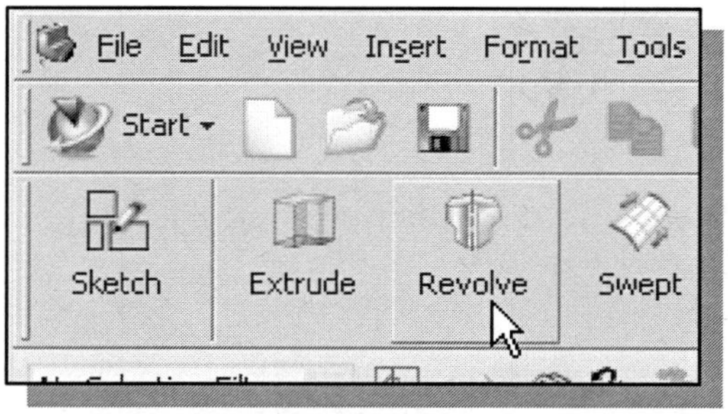

7. In the ***Feature*** toolbars select the **Revolve** icon as shown.

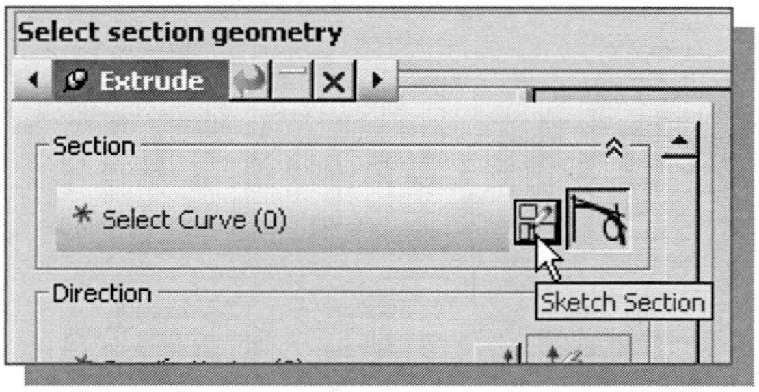

8. Click the **Sketch Section** button to enter the *2D Sketcher* mode and begin creatIng a new *2D sketch.*

❖ The procedure required for the revolved feature is very similar to that of the **Extrude** command. Both use 2D sketches, but one pulls in a straight line where the other one pulls in a circular direction.

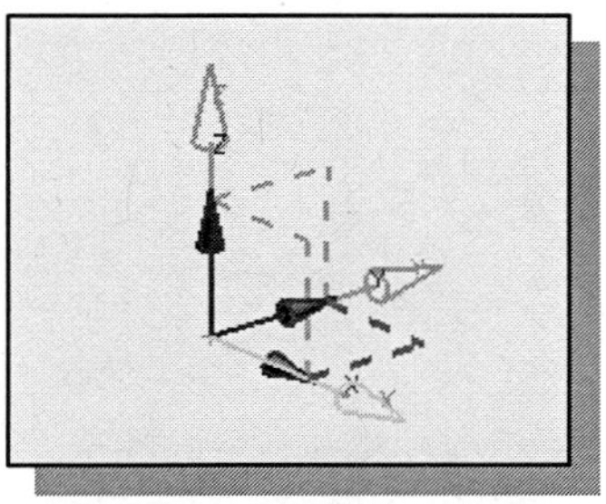

❖ Note the default *sketch plane* is aligned to the ***X-Y*** plane of the displayed datum coordinate system.

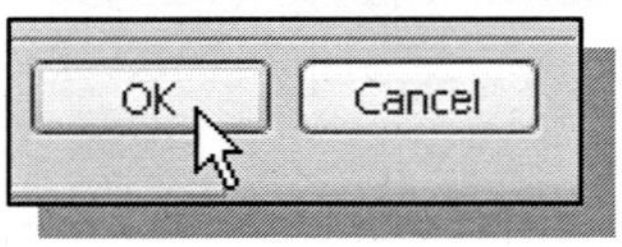

9. Click **OK** to accept the default setting of the *sketch plane.*

10. Create a closed-region sketch as shown below. (Note that the *Pulley* design is symmetrical about a horizontal axis as well as a vertical axis, which allows us to simplify the 2D sketch as shown below.)

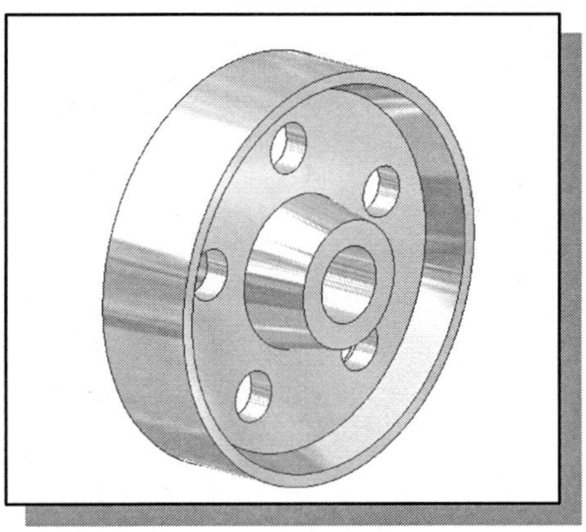

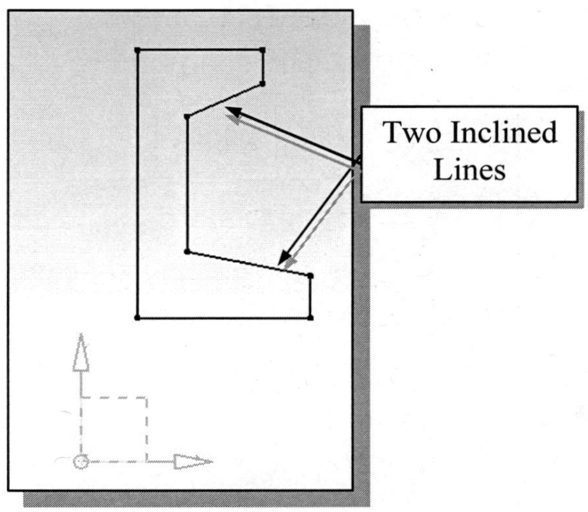

Completing the Sketch and Create the Feature

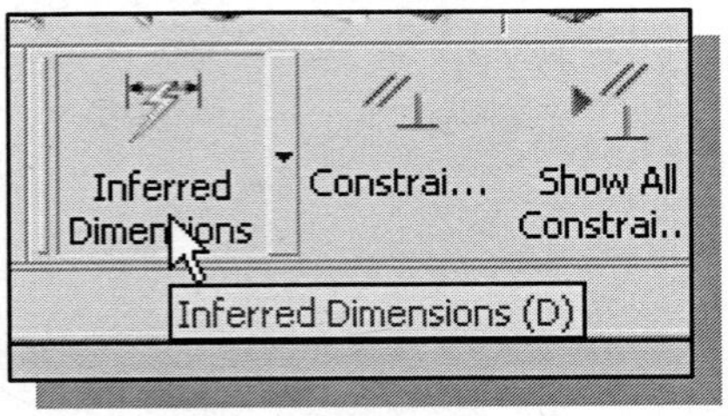

1. Select the **Inferred Dimensions** command in the *Sketch Constraints* toolbar as shown.

2. On your own, create and adjust the dimensions as shown below. (Hint: Modify the smaller numbers first.)

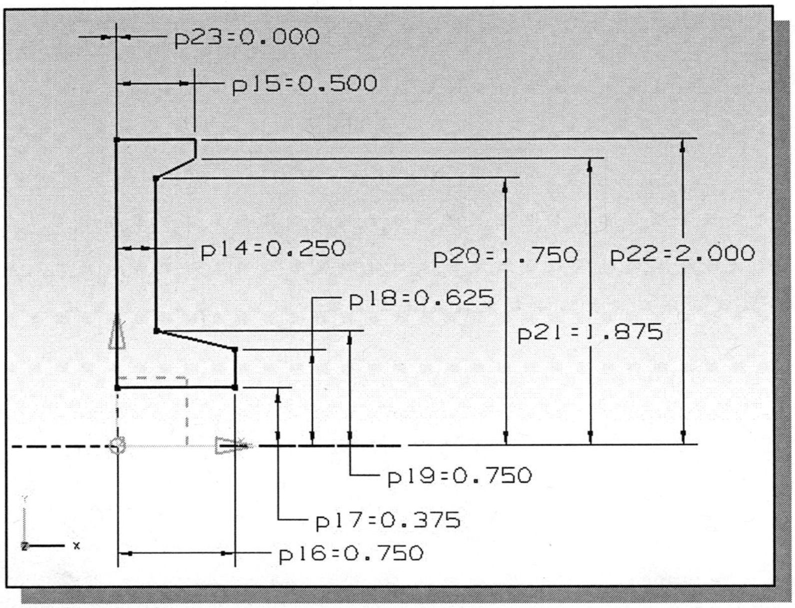

3. Click **Finish Sketch** to exit the *NX Sketcher* mode and return to the *Feature* option dialog window.

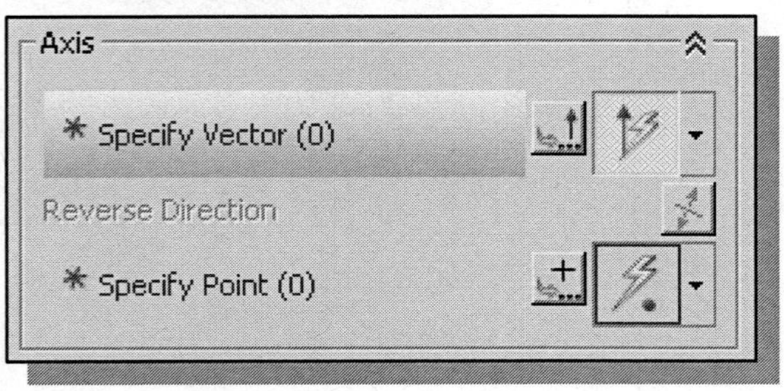

4. In the ***Revolve*** feature dialog box, the ***Specify Vector*** option is activated. *UGS NX* expects the definition of a rotational axis.

❖ For a revolved feature, there are two required elements: a 2D sketch and an axis of rotation.

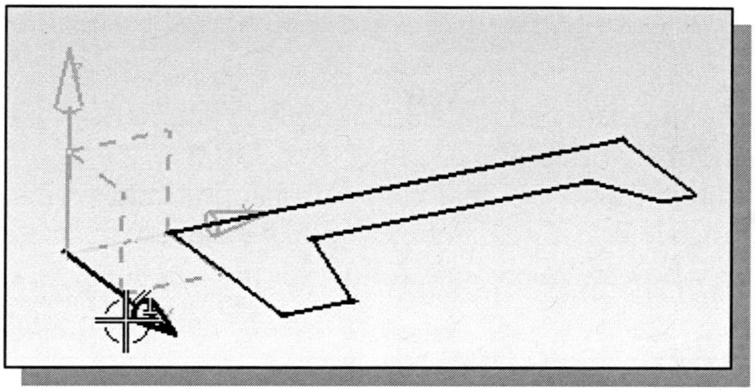

5. Select the ***X* axis** of the DCS/WCS to set the rotation vector.

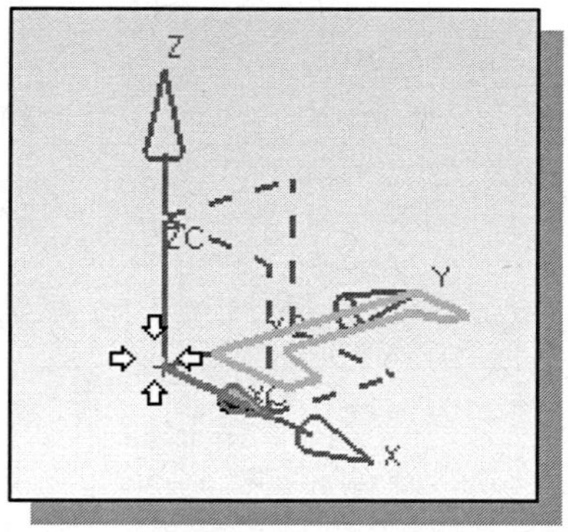

6. Select the **origin** of the DCS/WCS to set the rotation axis point.

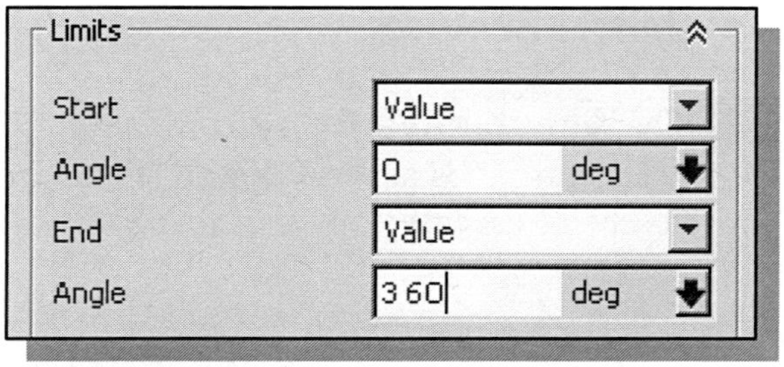

7. Confirm the *Start Angle* is set at **0** and the *End Angle* is set at **360**, in the angular *Limits* area as shown.

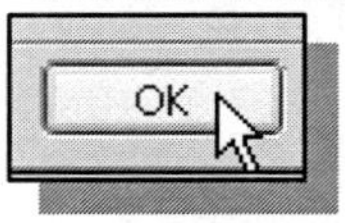

8. Click **OK** to create the revolved feature.

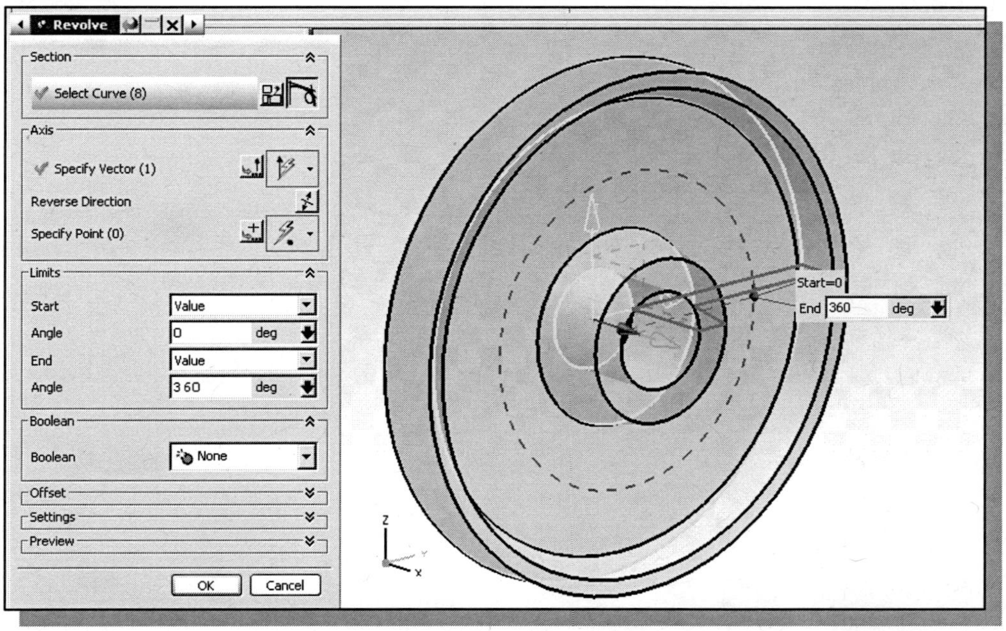

❖ Note that it is possible to create the above revolved feature using the **Extrude** command, but the tapered shape will take several extra steps to complete. It is quite important for a designer to recognize the symmetrical features in the design and use the most effective options to create them.

Mirroring Features

- In *UGS NX*, features can be mirrored to create and maintain complex symmetrical features. We can mirror a feature about a work plane or a specified surface. We can create a mirrored feature while maintaining the original parametric definitions, which can be quite useful in creating symmetrical features. For example, we can create one quadrant of a feature, and then mirror it twice to create a solid with four identical quadrants.

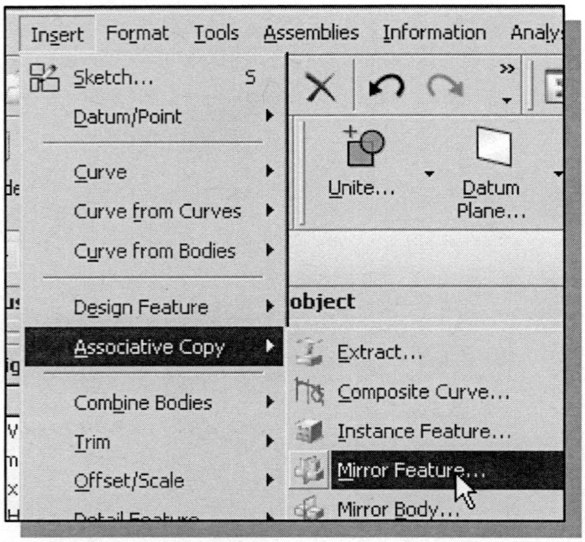

1. Select the **Associative Copy** command through the *Insert* pull-down menu:
   [Insert] → [Associative Copy] → [Mirror Feature]

➢ The **Associative Copy** command group provides several options that can be used to create copies of features.

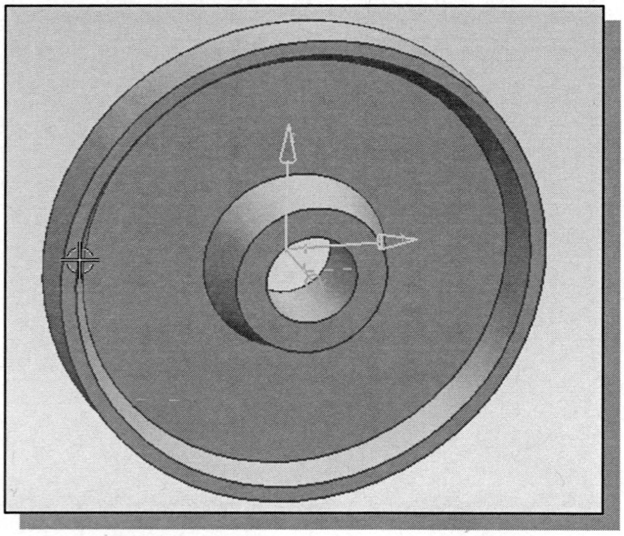

2. Select the ***revolved* feature** in the graphics window as shown.

3. Use the middle-mouse-button (MB2), or click **OK** to proceed with the Mirror command.

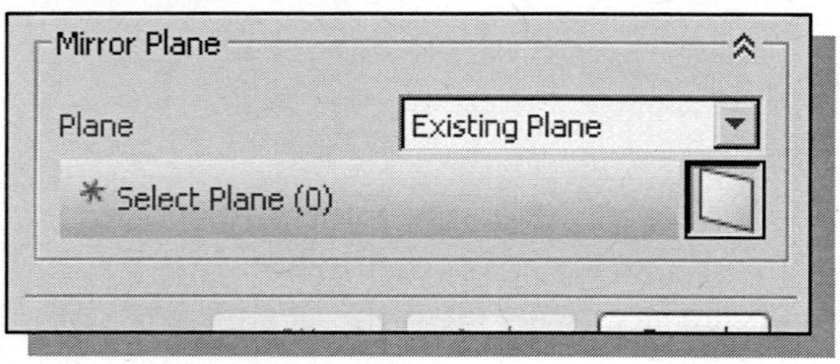

4. Note that the ***Mirror Plane*** selection option is activated as shown. In the message area, the message "*Select mirror plane*" is displayed.

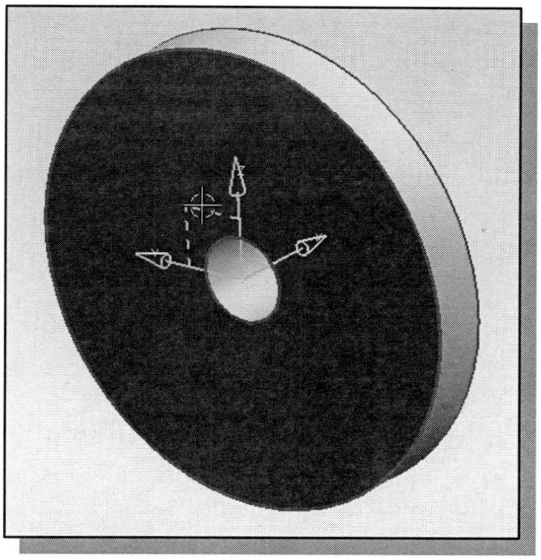

5. On your own, dynamically rotate the solid model so that we are viewing the back surface as shown.

6. Select the back surface as the planar surface about which to mirror.

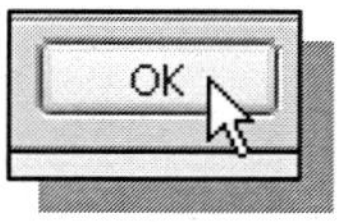

7. Click on the **OK** button to accept the settings and create a mirrored feature.

8. Select **Wireframe with Dim Edges** in the *Display* toolbar to adjust the display of the model on the screen.

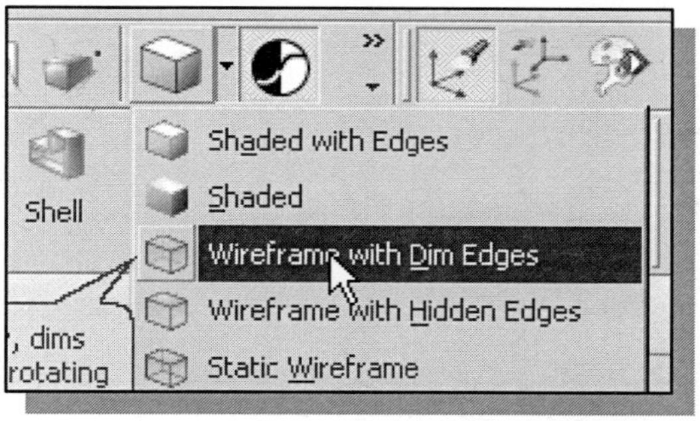

❖ Note the Mirror Feature command has created a separate feature.

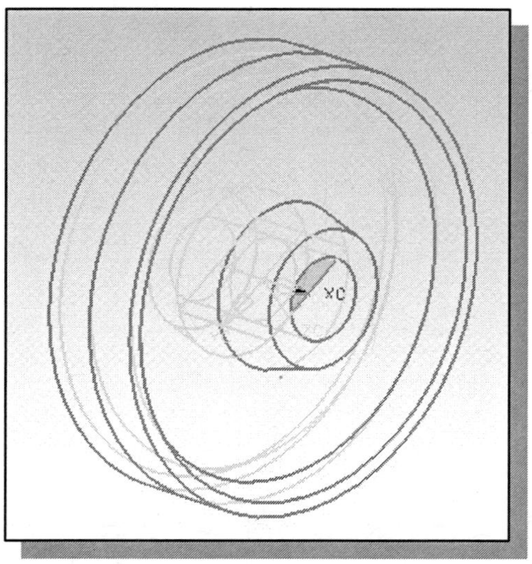

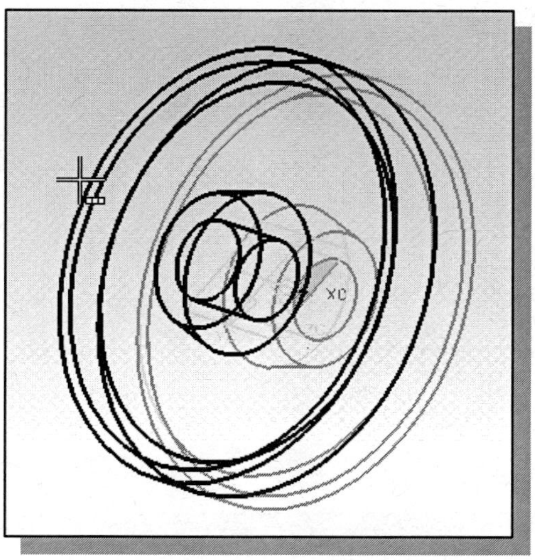

Joining the Two Solid Features

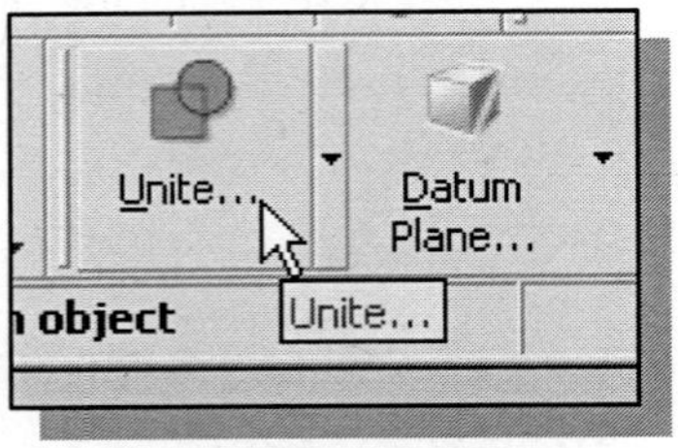

1. Activate the **Unite** command by clicking the left-mouse-button on the icon as shown.

❖ The Unite command can be used to join two separate bodies into one object.

❖ Note the first selection option, *Target Body*, is activated as shown.

2. On your own, select the original revolved feature as the *Target Body*.

❖ Note the second selection option, *Tool Body*, is activated as shown.

3. On your own, select the mirrored feature as the *Tool Body*.

4. Do not activate any of the other options listed under *Settings* as we want to create one solid model

5. Click on the **OK** button to accept the settings and create a mirrored feature.

6. On your own, use the 3D-Rotate command to dynamically rotate the solid model and view the resulting solid.

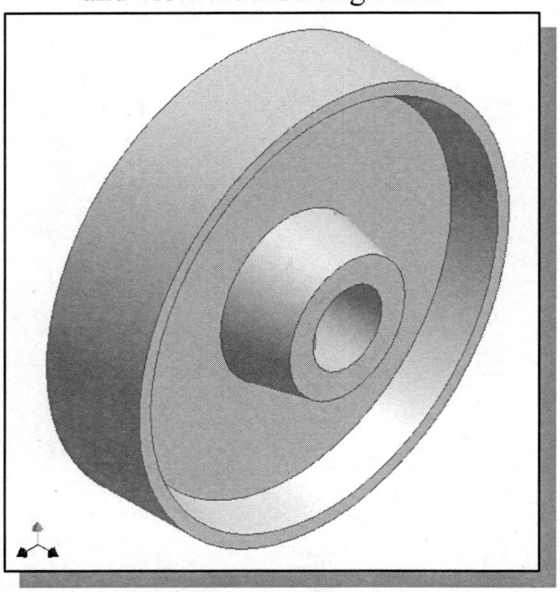

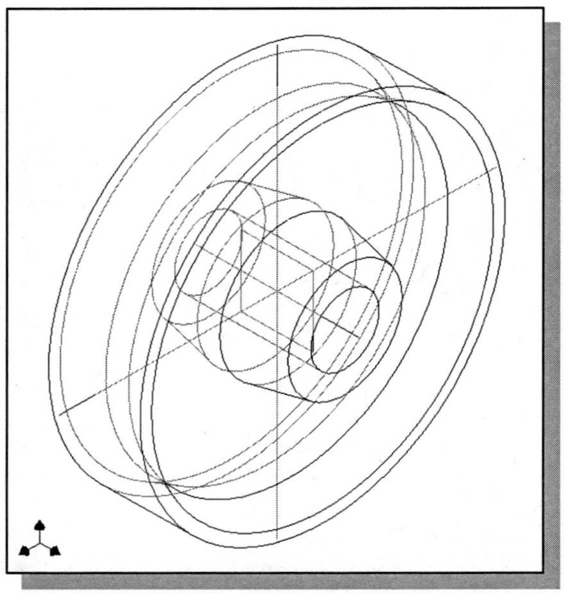

Creating a Pattern Leader

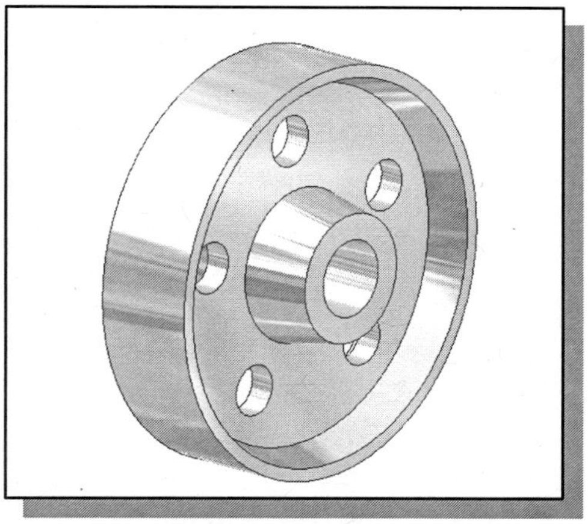

- The *Pulley* design requires the placement of five identical holes on the base solid. Instead of creating the five holes one at a time, we can simplify the creation of these holes by using the **Circular Array** command, which allows us to create duplicate features. Prior to using the Circular Array command, we will first create a ***pattern leader***, which is a regular extruded feature.

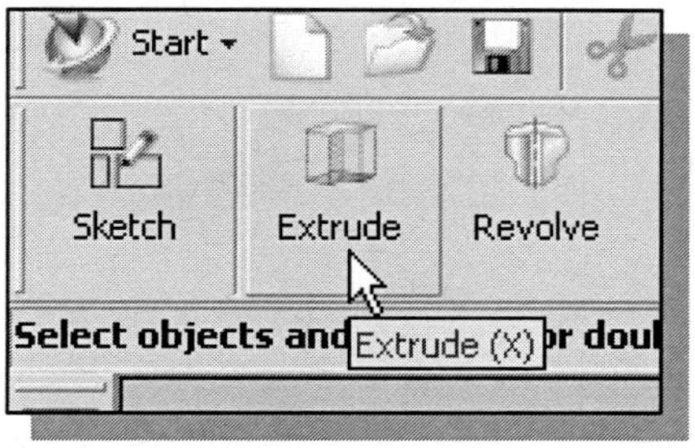

1. In the *Form Feature* toolbars (toolbars aligned to the right edge of the main window), select the Extrude icon as shown.

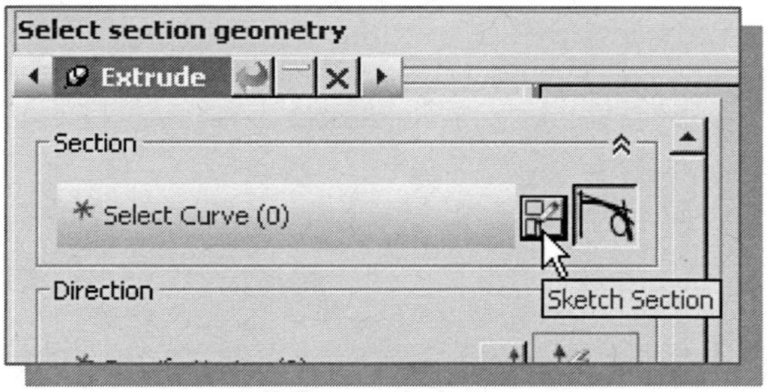

2. Click the **Sketch Section** button to begin creating a new *2D sketch.*

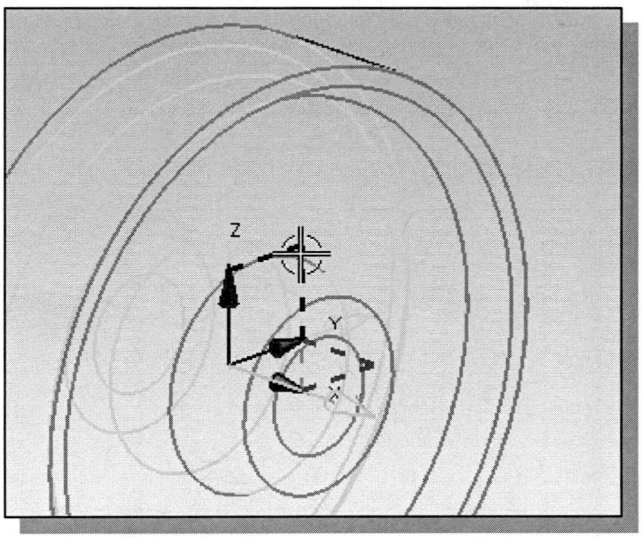

3. Select the vertical plane that is through the center of the model as the *sketch plane* as shown.

4. Click **OK** to accept the selection of the *sketch plane.*

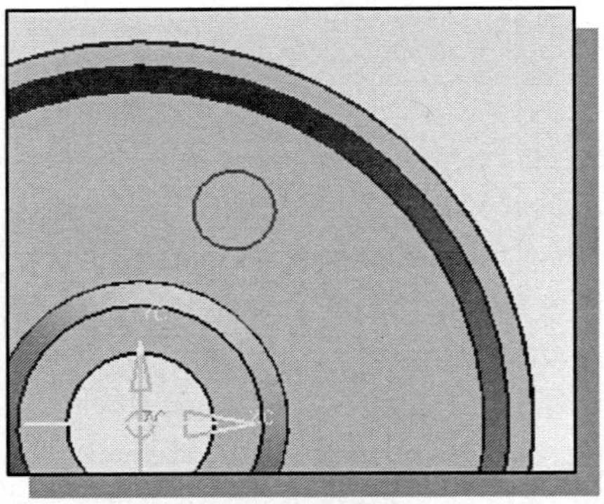

5. Create a circle, near the upper right corner as shown in the figure.

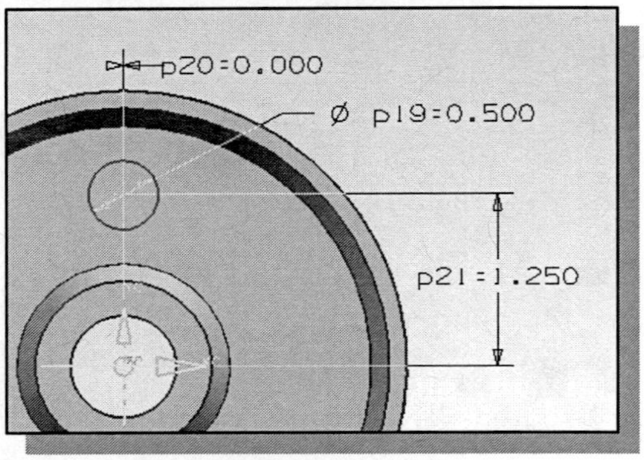

6. On your own, create the three dimensions as shown.

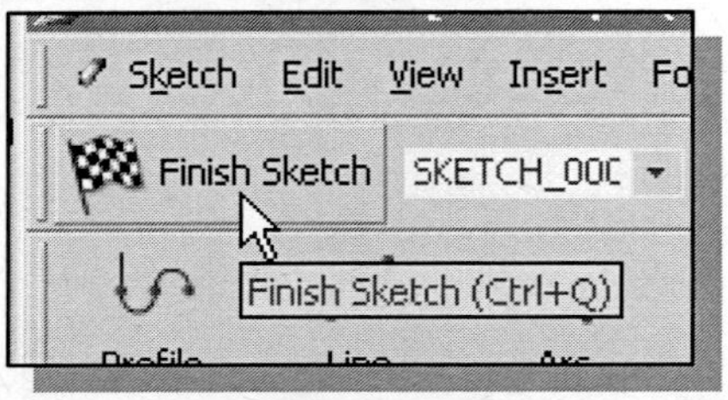

7. Click **Finish Sketch** to exit the *NX Sketcher* mode and return to the *Feature* option dialog window.

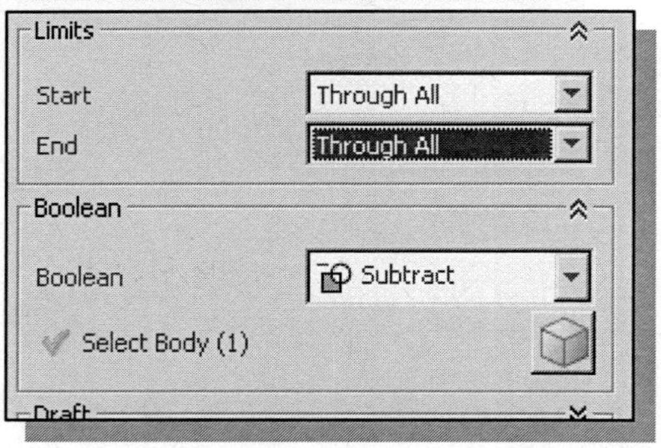

8. Inside the *Extrude* dialog box, select the **Subtract** operation, and set both *Limits* to **Through All** as shown.

9. Click on the **OK** button to accept the settings and create the subtract feature.

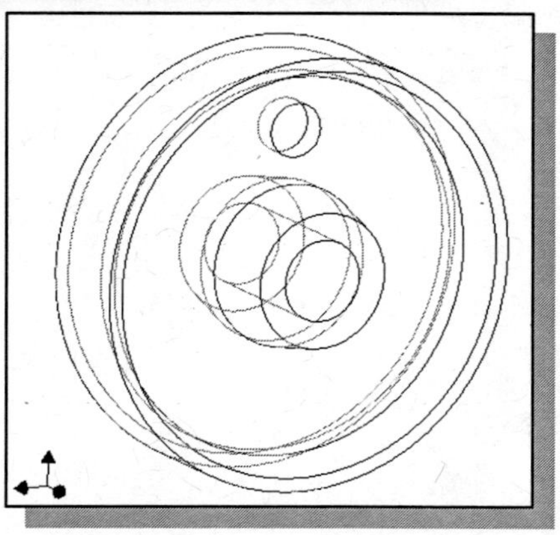

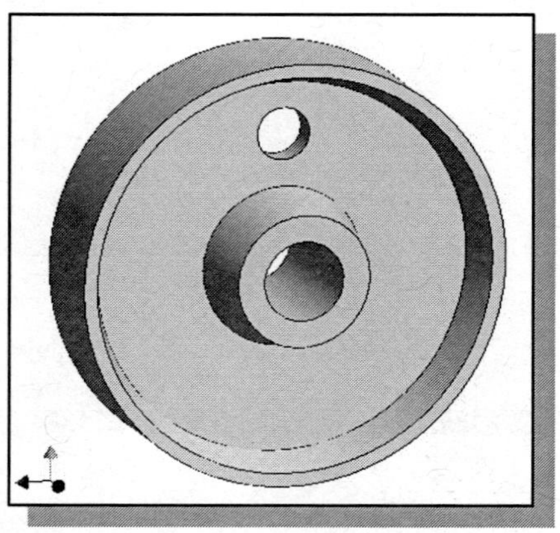

Circular Array

In *UGS NX*, existing features can be easily duplicated with the two array commands, **Rectangular Array** and **Circular Array**. The arrayed features can be parametrically linked to the original feature, which means any modifications to the original feature are also reflected in the arrayed features. Three elements are needed for creating a circular array: (1) the rotation axis about which the instances are generated, (2) the total number of instances in the array (including the original feature), and (3) the angle between the instances.

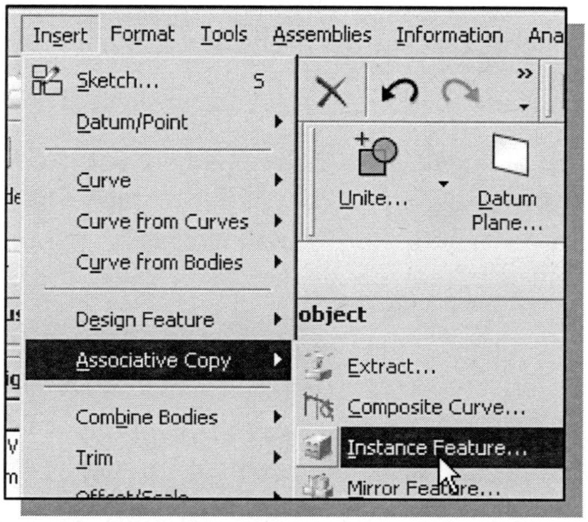

1. Select the **Associative Copy** command through the *Insert* pull-down menu: **[Insert] → [Associative Copy] → [Instance Feature]**

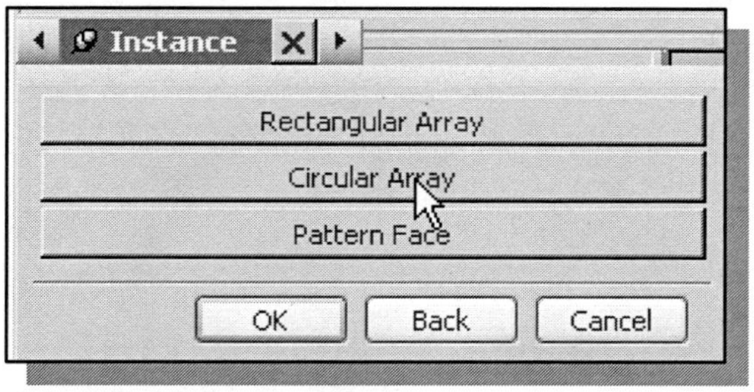

2. In the *Instance* window, select the **Circular Array** command by clicking the left-mouse-button on the icon.

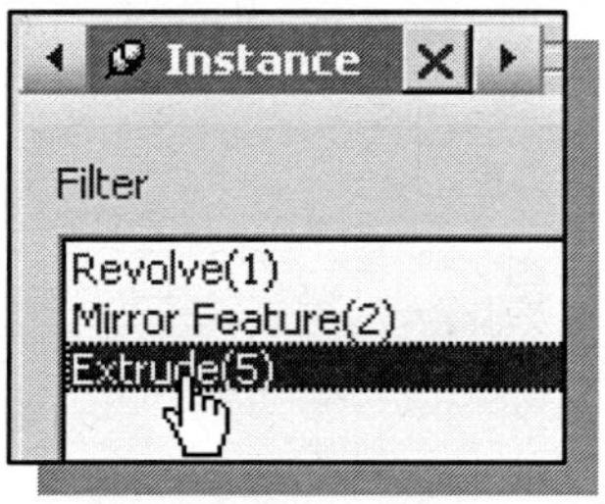

3. Choose the last feature, the *Extrude* feature, in the *Instance* window as shown.

4. Click **OK** to proceed to the next step.

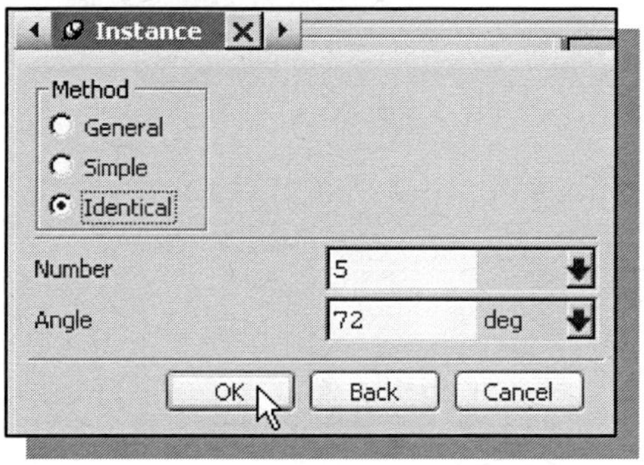

5. Select the **Identical** *Method*, enter **5** as the total *Number* of instances, and **72** degrees as the *Angle* in between the instances as shown.

6. Click **OK** to proceed to the next step of the **Circular Array** command.

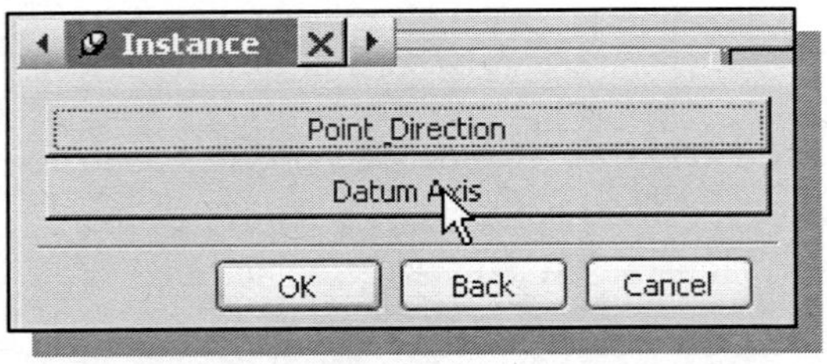

7. Select **Datum Axis** in the option list to proceed with the **Circular Array** command.

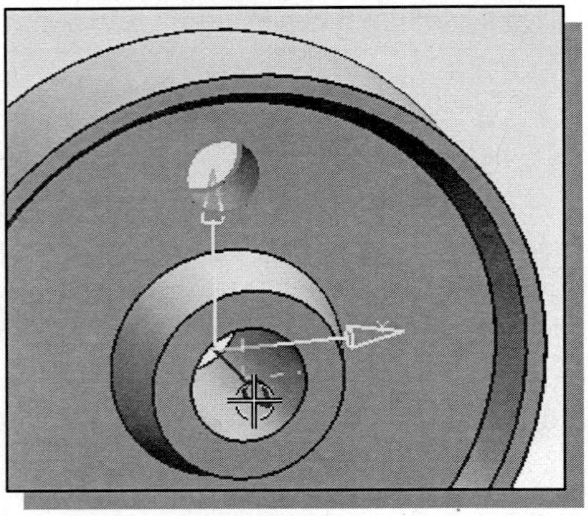

8. Select the ***X* axis** as the datum axis, the axis of rotation, as shown in the figure.

❖ Once the necessary parameters are set, *UGS NX* will show a preview of the feature. On your own, confirm the instances are constructed correctly.

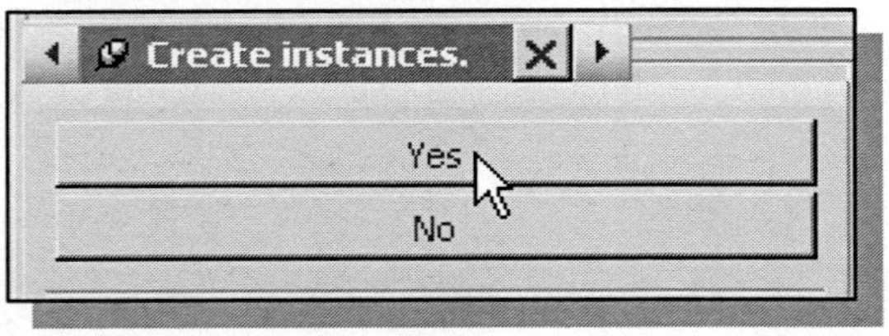

9. Click on the **Yes** button to accept the settings and create the *circular array.*

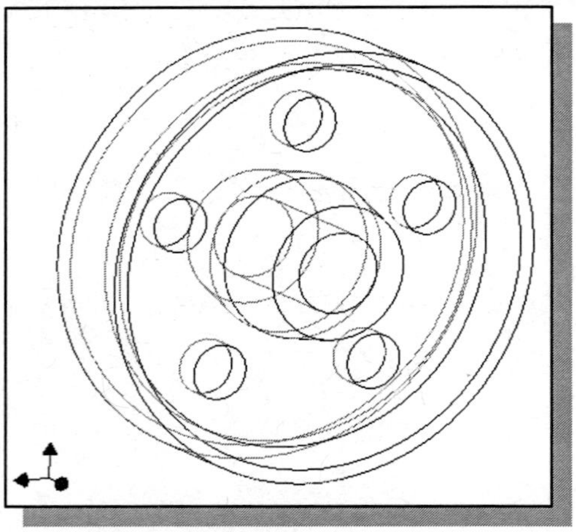

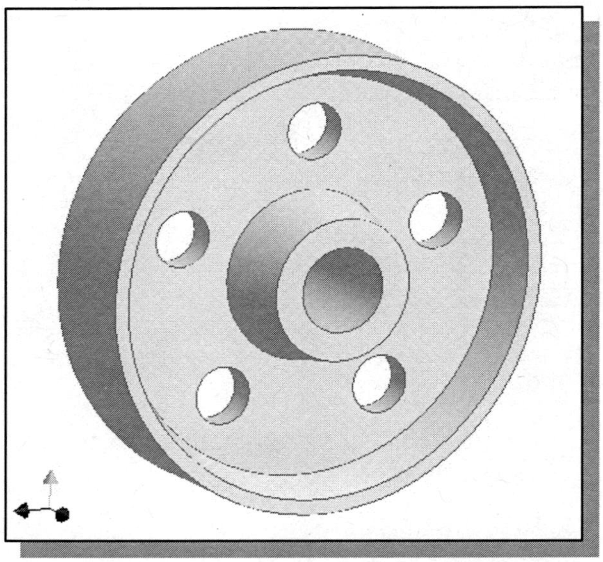

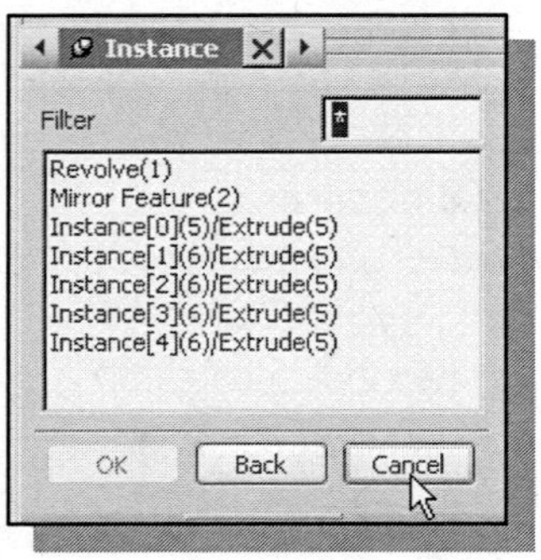

10. Notice the generated instances are now listed in the *FEATURES* list. Click **Cancel** to exit the **Associative Copy** command.

Create a New Drawing in the Drafting Mode

1. Click on the **Start** icon in the *Standard* toolbar area to display the available options.

2. Select **Drafting** from the option list.

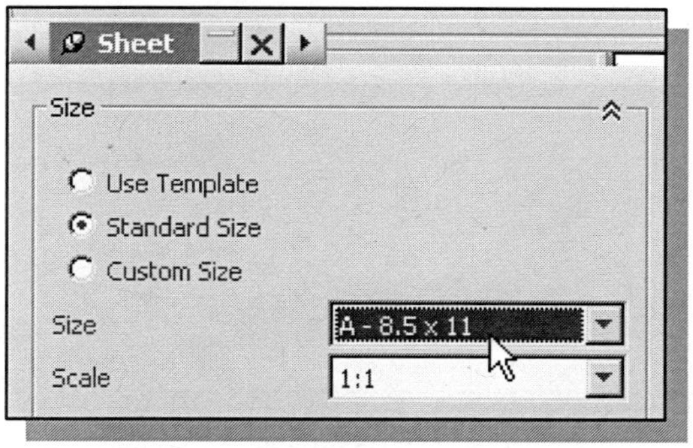

3. Select **A-8.5x11** from the sheet *Size* list.

4. Confirm the *Scale* is set to **1:1**, which is ***full scale***.

➢ Note that ***Sheet 1*** is the default drawing sheet name that is displayed in the *Drawing Sheet Name* area.

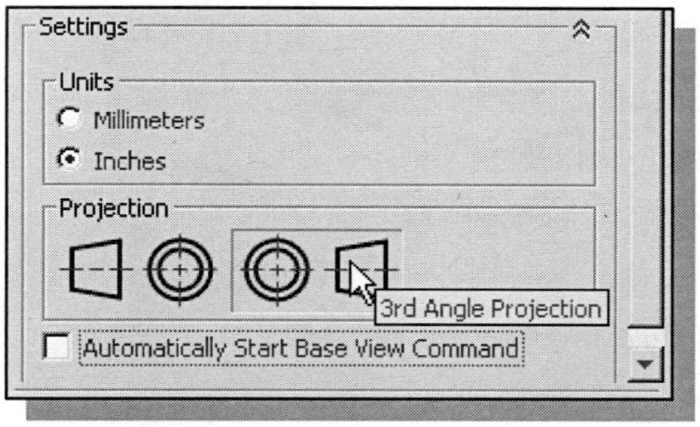

5. In the settings area, confirm the *Units* are set to **Inches** and the *Projection* type is set to **3rd Angle Projection** as shown.

6. **Uncheck** the **Automatically Start Base View Command** option as shown.

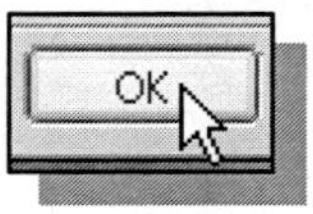

7. Click **OK** to accept the settings and proceed with the creation of the drawing sheet.

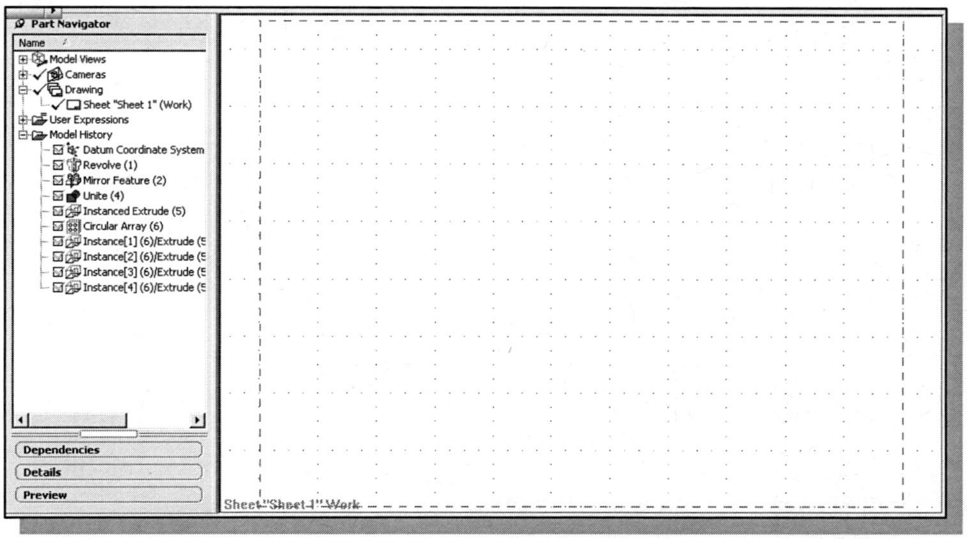

Importing the Title Block

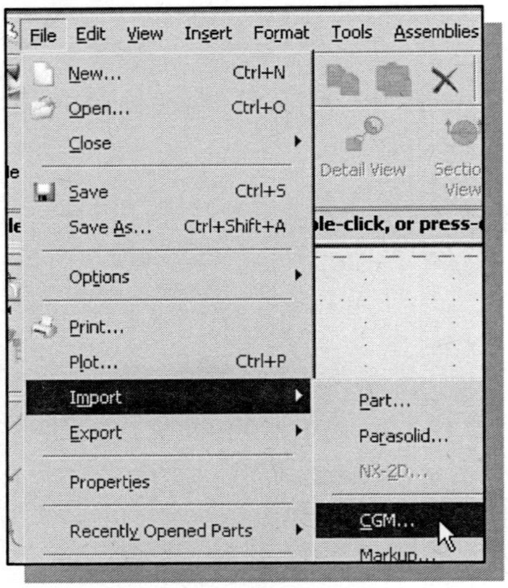

1. Select the **Import CGM** command through the *File* pull-down menu:

   [File] → [Import] → [CGM]

2. Enter or select **Title_A_Master_sheet 1.cgm** in the *Import CGM* window as shown.

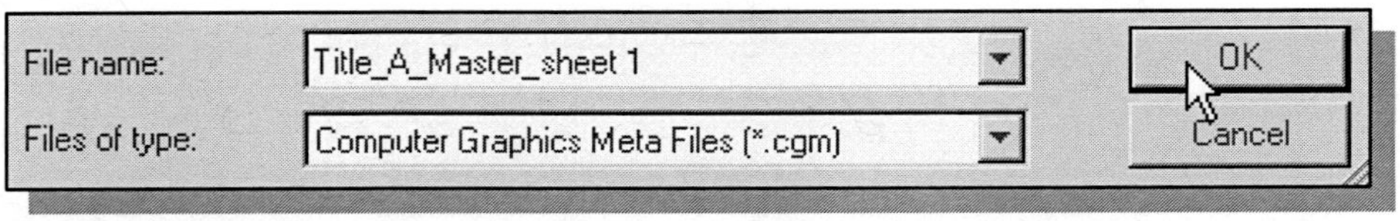

3. Click **OK** to proceed with importing the selected CGM file.

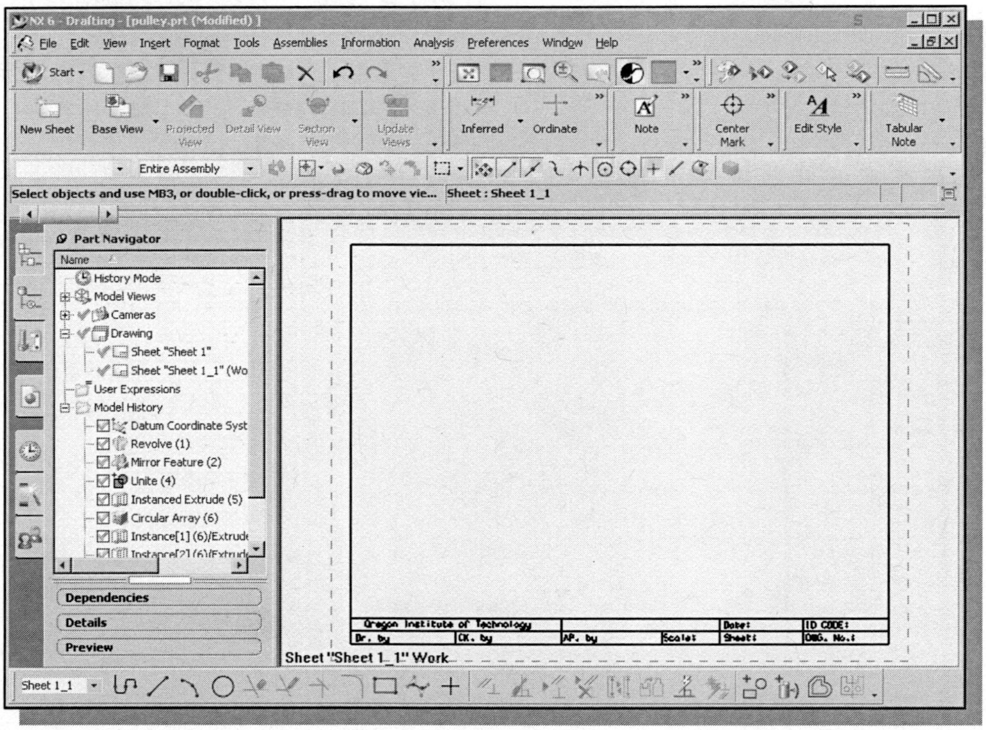

❖ The Import/Export commands provide a fairly flexible way to reuse titleblocks and borders. You are encouraged to try the other file formats.

Creating 2D Views

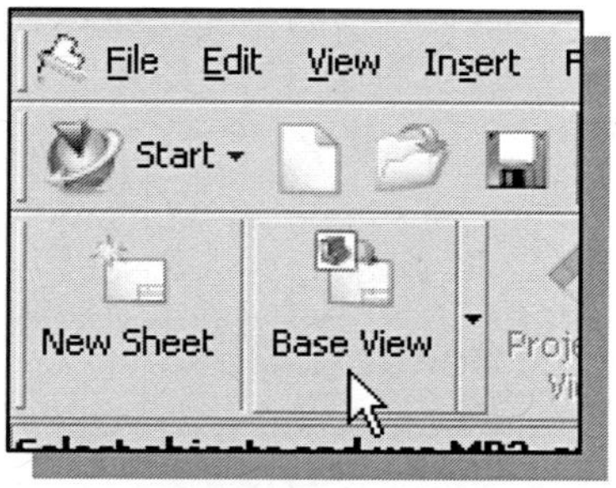

1. Click on the **Base View** icon in the *Drawing Layout* toolbar to create a new base view.

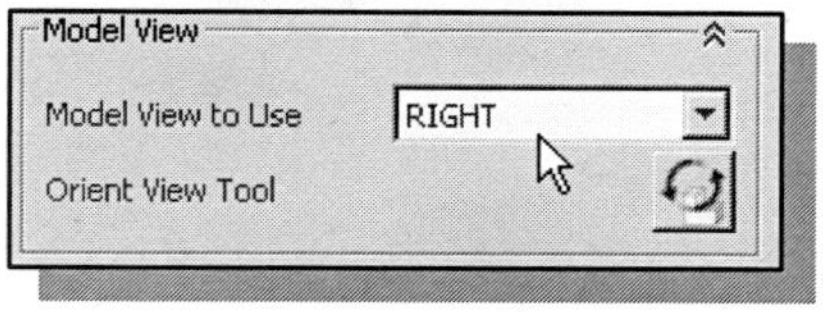

2. In the *Base View* option toolbar, set the view option to **Right** as shown.

3. Place the ***base* view**, the *right* view of the *Pulley* model, on the left side of the drawing sheet as shown.

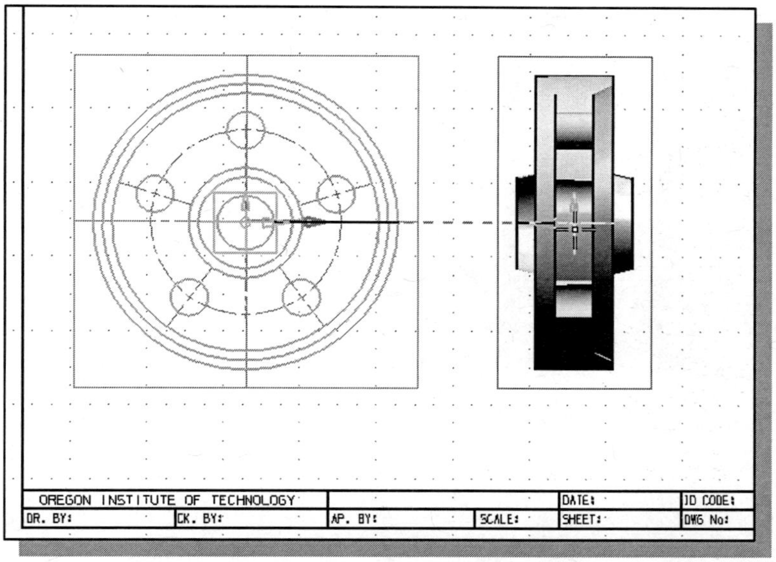

4. On your own, create a *side* view as shown in the figure above.

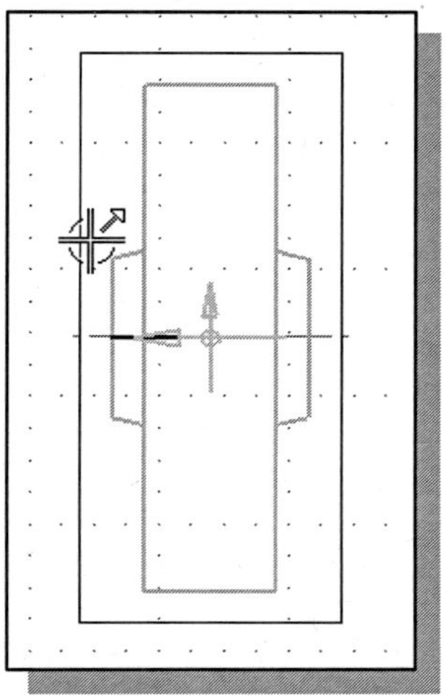

❖ Note the default display of views does not show any hidden lines. And as we realize a section view is more suitable for our design, we will delete this *projected* view and create a *section* view.

5. Select the ***projected* view** by clicking with the left-mouse-button (MB1) on the view border as shown.

6. Hit the [**Delete**] key, on the keypad, once to erase the view completely.

Adding a Section View

❖ Two elements are needed when creating a section view: (1) the parent view, from which the projection is derived, and (2) a cutting plane line identifying where the virtual cut is to occur.

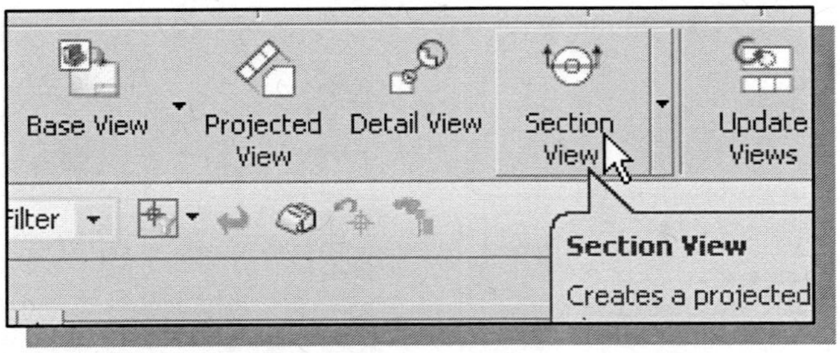

1. Select the **Section View** command through the *Drawing Layout* toolbar as shown.

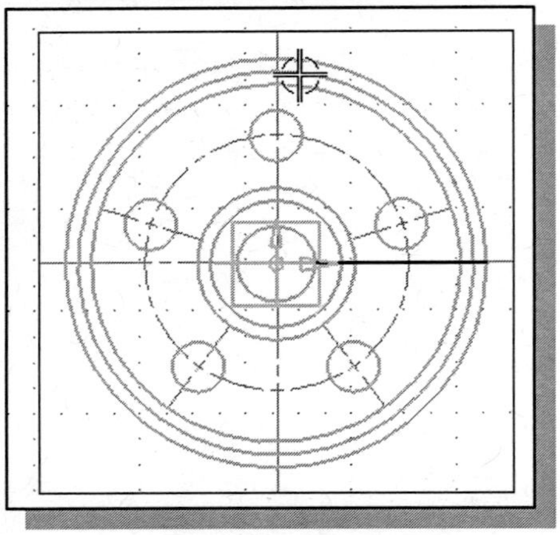

2. Click on the ***base* view** to set the view as the *parent* view of the new view.

3. Select the **Section Line Style** option in the option toolbar as shown.

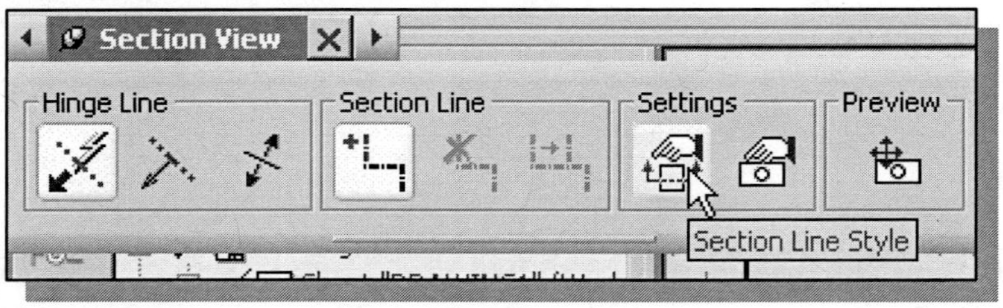

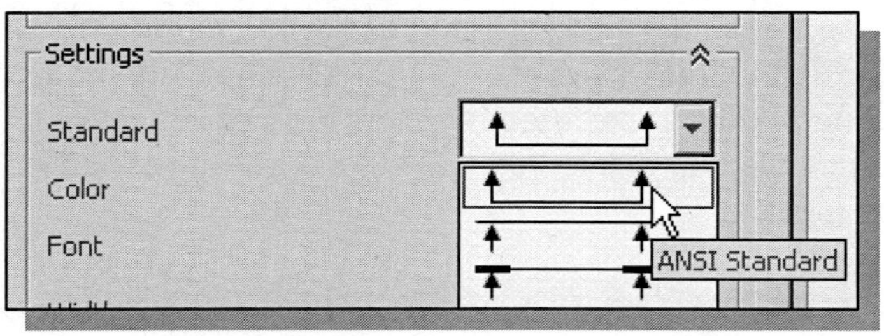

4. Set the *Standard* option to use the **ANSI Standard** for the cutting plane line.

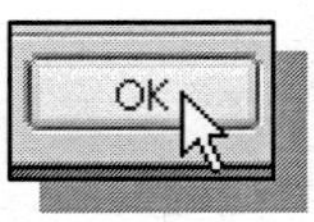

5. Click **OK** to accept the settings and proceed with the creation of the cutting plane line.

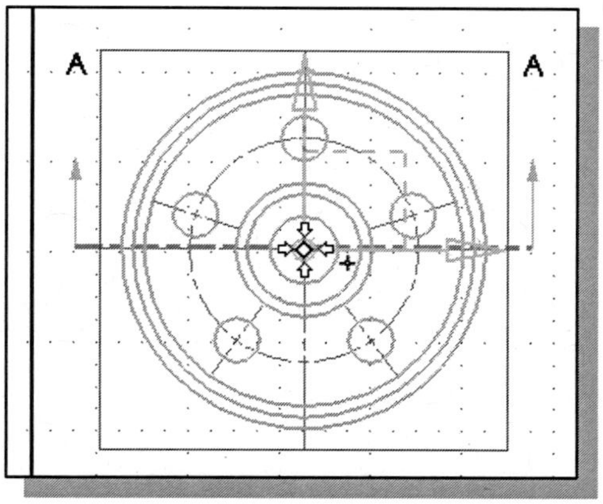

6. Inside the graphics window, select the **center** of the *base* view to align the center of the cutting plane line as shown.

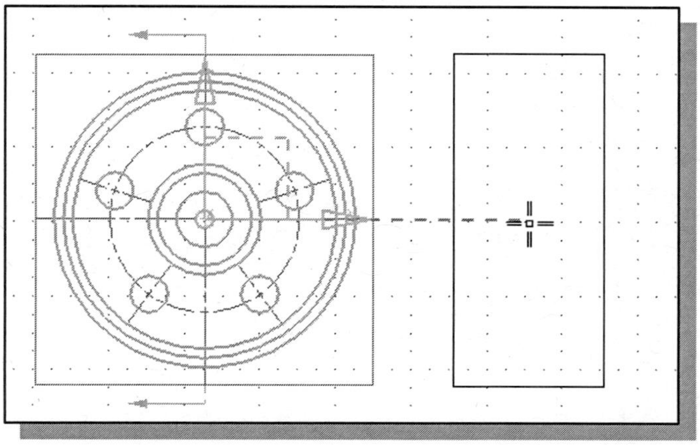

7. Rotate the cutting plane line until it is vertical by moving the cursor to the right of the *base* view.

8. Position the *section* view to the right side of the *base* view as shown.

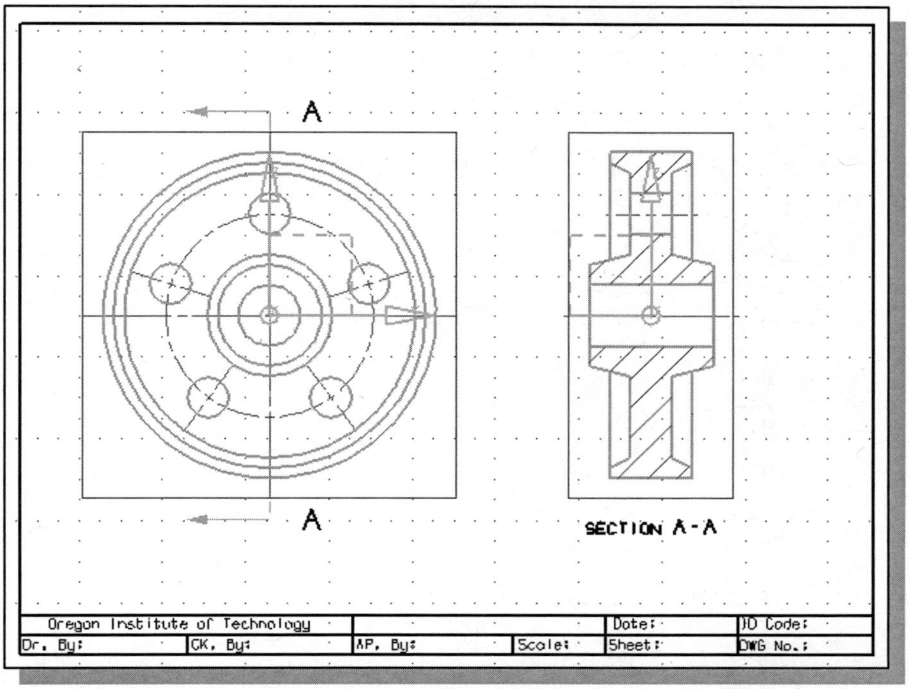

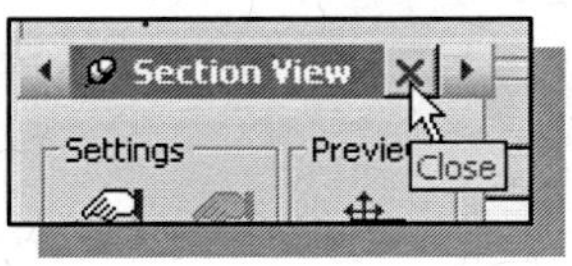

9. Click the [**X**] icon to close the *Section View* option menu.

Turning Off the Datum Features

➢ The display of the datum planes and WCS can be turned off in *Drafting* mode or in *Modeling* mode.

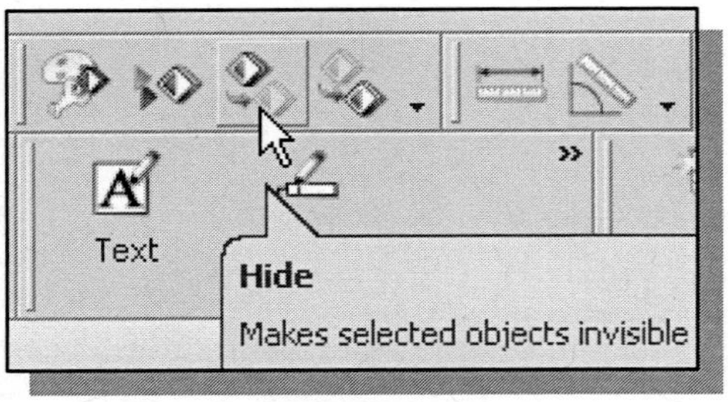

1. Select the **Hide** command in the *Utility* toolbar as shown.

2. On your own, select the two datum axes near the center of the *base* view as shown.

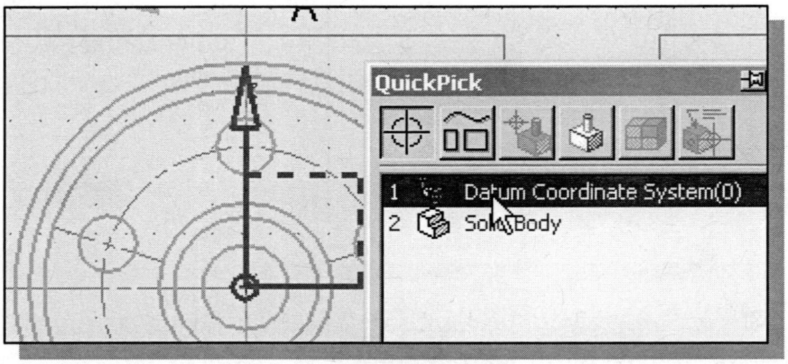

❖ Hint: Pick **Datum Coordinate System** in the *QuickPick* window if necessary.

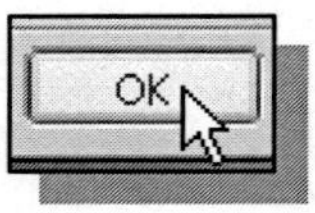

3. Click **OK** to accept the selection. Your drawing should appear as shown in the figure.

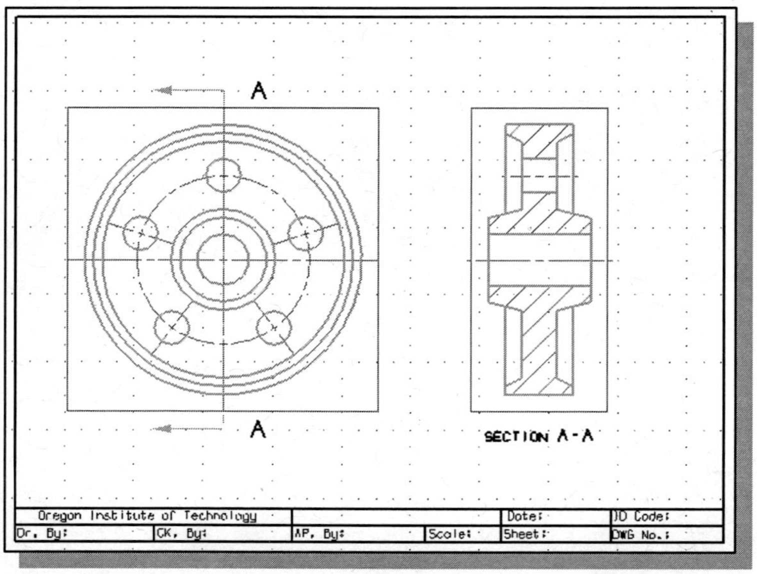

Adding Dimensions

❖ One main advantage of *parametric modeling* over traditional CAD systems is its flexibility and multiple options available for different situations. For example, for the *Pulley* design; instead of using many of the feature dimensions, we will use reference dimensions in the 2D drawing. All of the 2D drawing views are still associated with the 3D model, and any changes to the solid model will be reflected in the 2D drawing instantly.

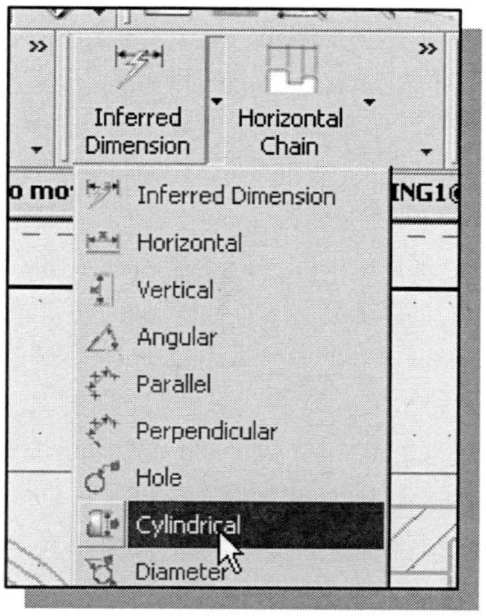

1. Select the **Cylindrical Dimension** command by selecting the corresponding icon in the *Standard* toolbar area as shown.

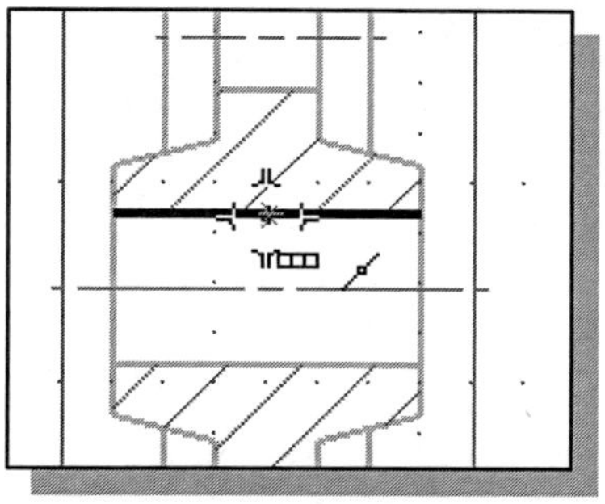

2. Select the horizontal line that is above the centerline as shown.

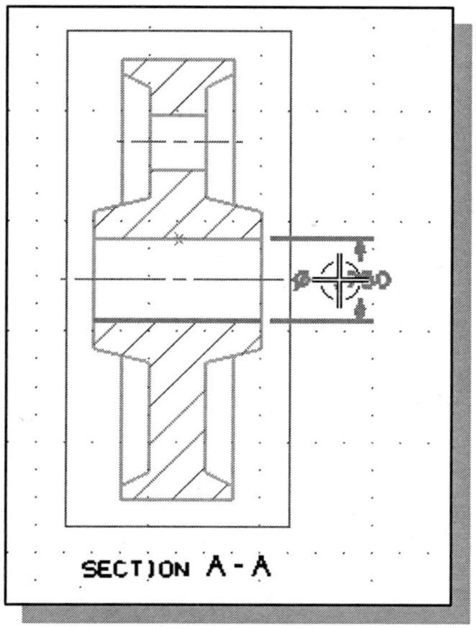

3. Select the horizontal line that is below the centerline as shown.

4. Place the dimension to the right side of the section view.

❖ The **Cylindrical Dimension** command automatically adds the diameter symbol in front of the dimension value.

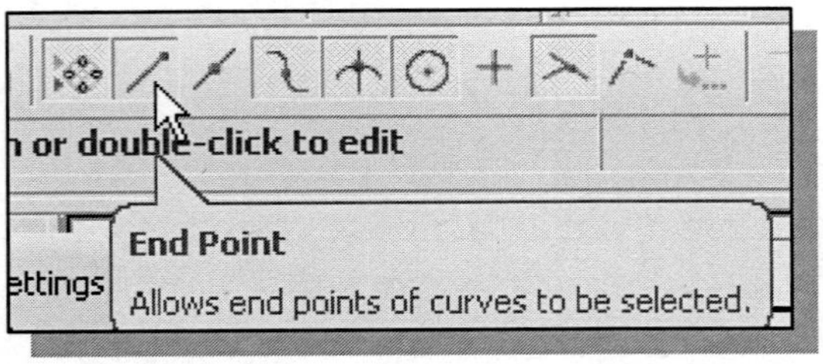

5. Activate the snap to **End Point** option in the *Snap* option toolbar as shown.

❖ Also note the different snap options available in the toolbar.

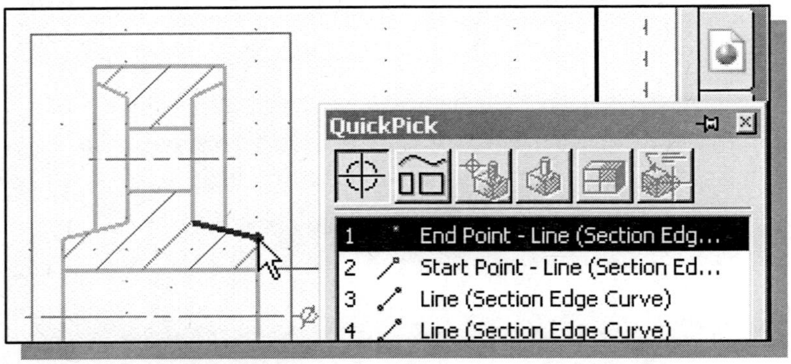

6. Select the endpoint of the inclined line as shown.

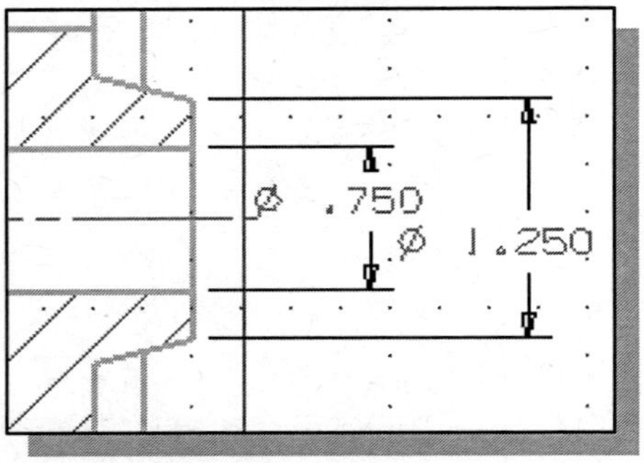

7. Select the corresponding point and place the dimension to the right side as shown.

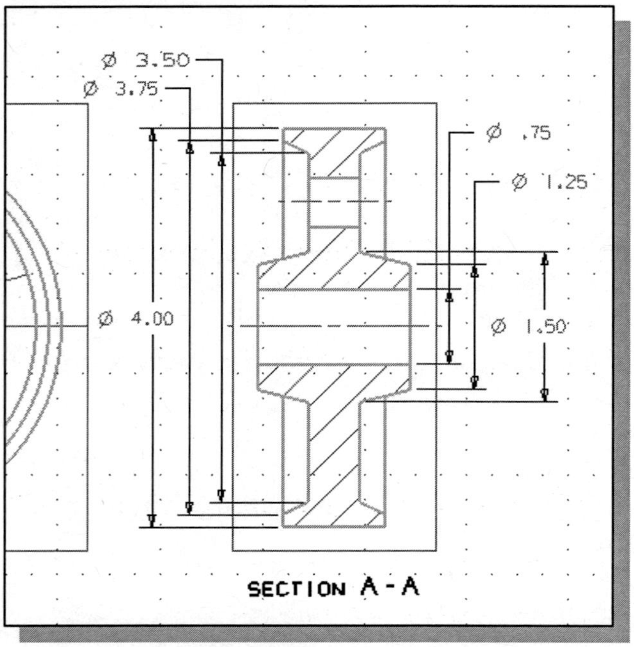

8. On your own, repeat the above steps and create the cylindrical dimensions in the section view as shown.

❖ Hint: Use the drag and drop option to reposition the dimensions.

Adjusting the Display of the Views

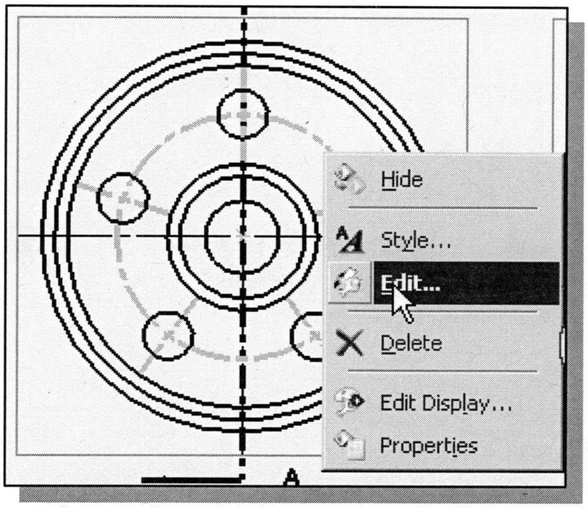

1. Select the **centerline** of the hole pattern by clicking once with the left-mouse-button.

2. Inside the graphics window, click once with the right-mouse-button to bring up the option list and choose **Edit** as shown.

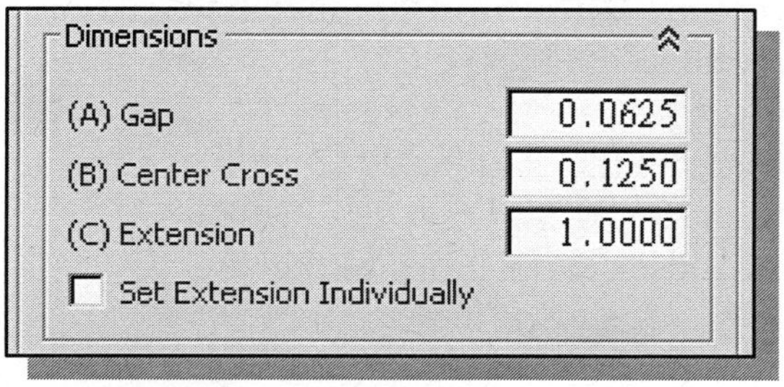

3. Enter **1.0** as the new *Extension* distance for the centerline as shown.

4. Select **Drafting Preferences** through the pull-down menu as shown.

5. Turn ***OFF*** the **Display Borders** option as shown.

6. Click **OK** to exit the Drafting Preferences command.

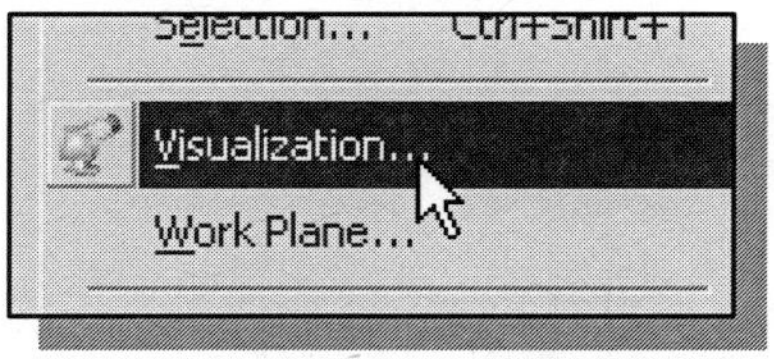

7. Select **Visualization Preferences** through the pull-down menu as shown.

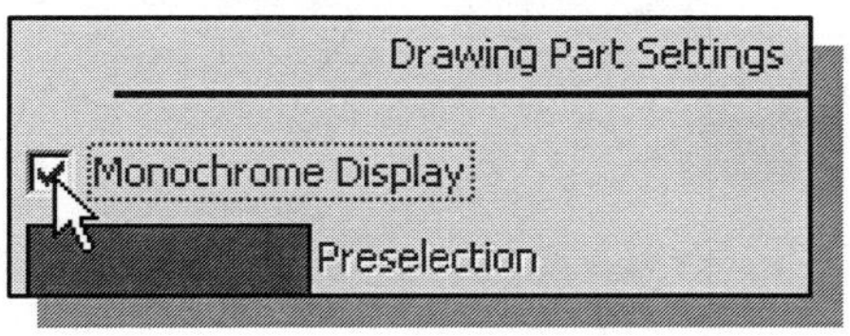

8. Turn ***ON*** the **Monochrome Display** option as shown.

9. Click **OK** to exit the Visualization Preferences command.

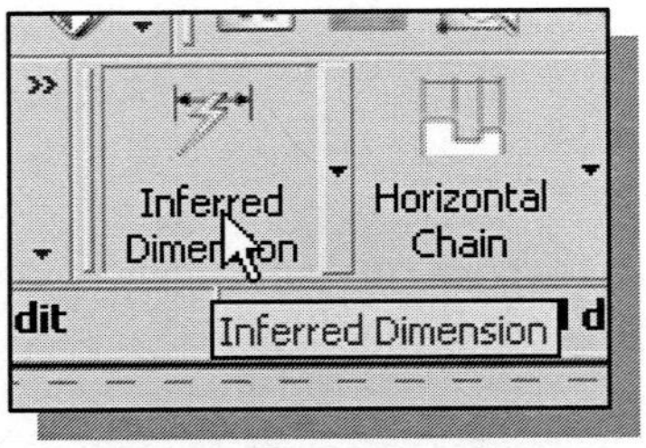

10. Select the **Inferred Dimension** command as shown.

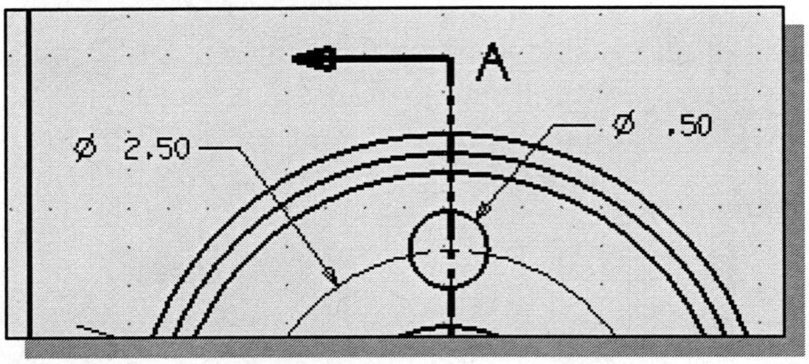

11. Create the two diameter dimensions as shown.

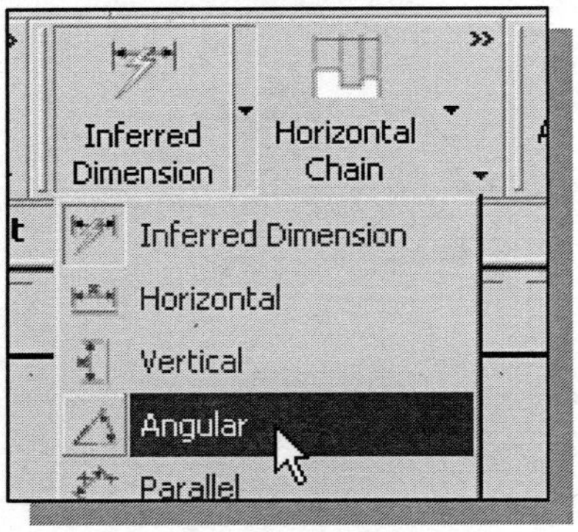

12. Select the **Angular Dimension** command through the *Standard* toolbar as shown.

13. On your own, create the angular dimension as shown.

14. On your own, adjust the positions of the dimensions/views as shown in the figure.

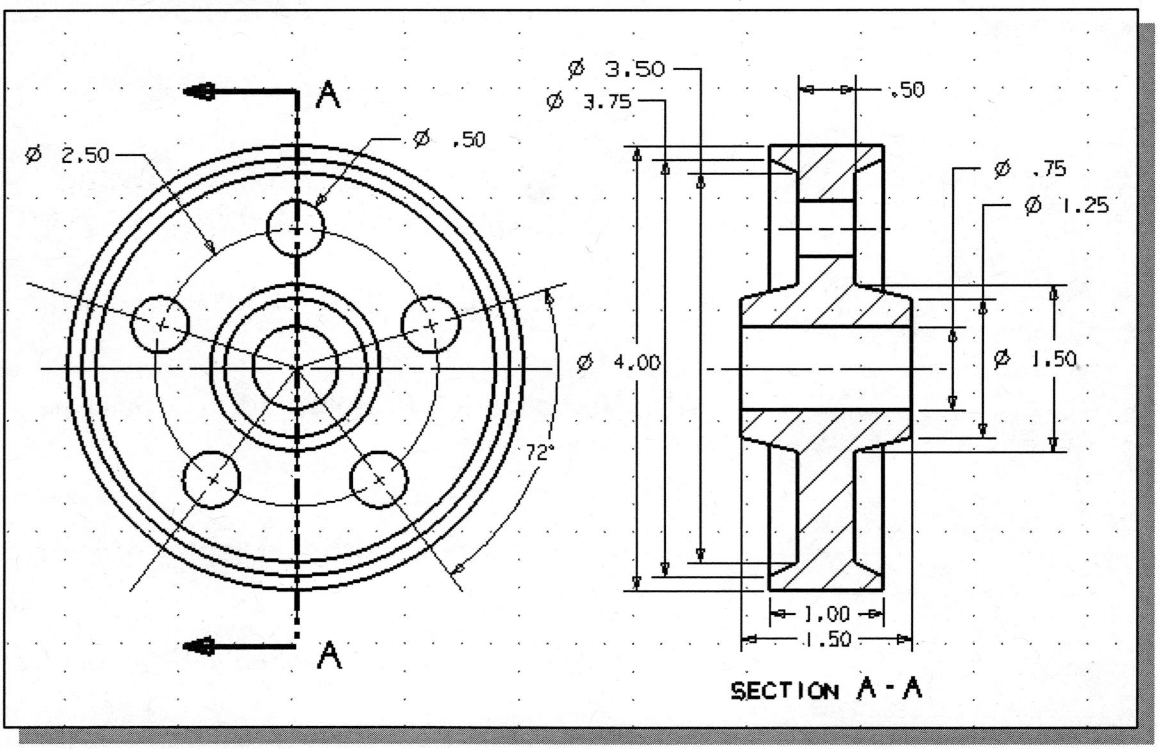

Associative Functionality – A Design Change

- *UGS NX's associative functionality* allows us to change the design quickly, and the system reflects the changes at all levels automatically. We will illustrate the associative functionality by changing the circular pattern from five holes to six holes.

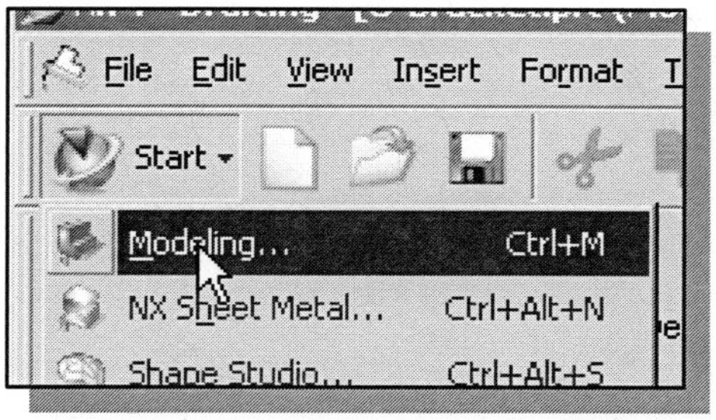

1. Switch back to the *Modeling* module by selecting **Modeling** in the *Start* list as shown.

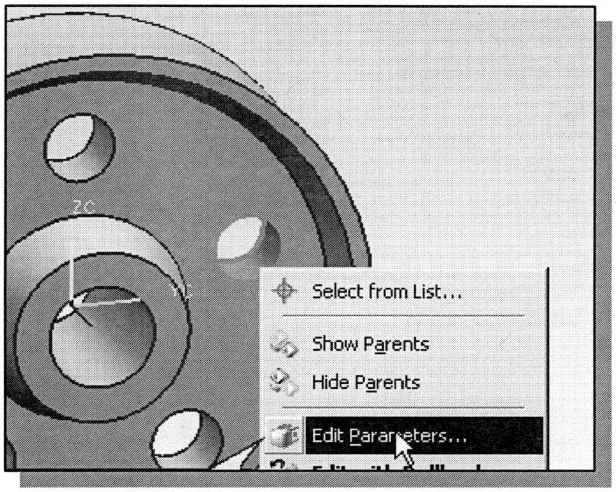

2. Right-click on one of the arrayed features to bring up the option menu.

3. Select **Edit Parameters...** in the popup menu to switch to *Edit* mode.

4. Select the **Instance Array Dialog** option to edit the associated parameters.

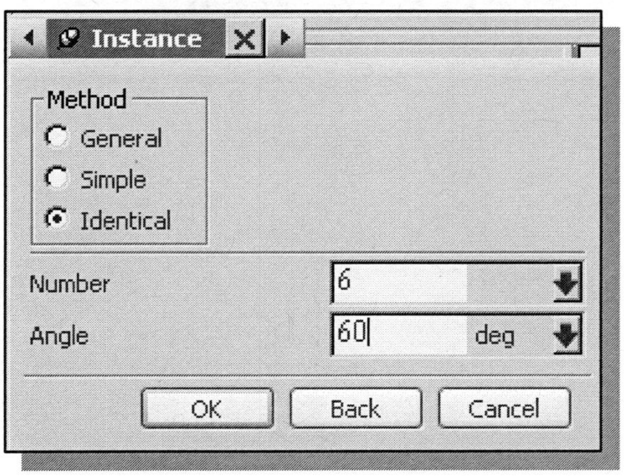

5. Adjust the *Number* option to **6** and the *Angle* option to **60** as shown in the figure.

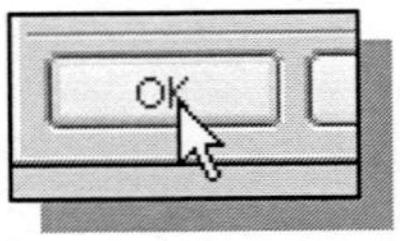

6. Click **OK** to accept the settings and proceed with the updating of the solid model.

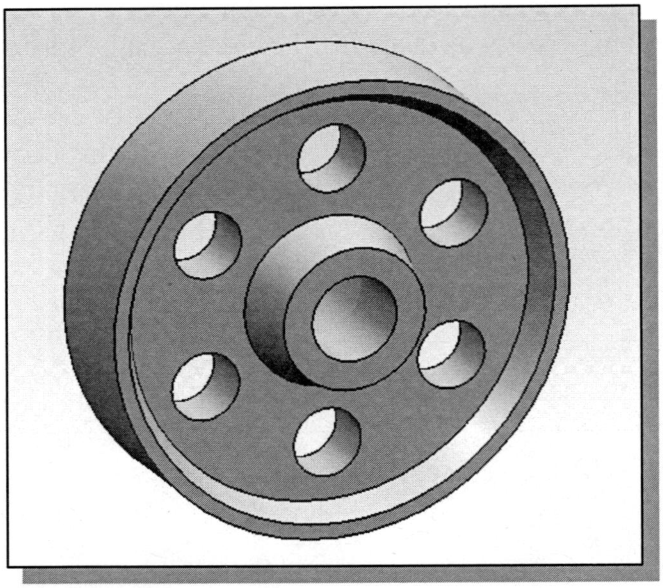

7. On your own, switch back to the *Drafting* mode.

8. Notice the **clock** icon in front of the *Drawing* item. By default, the drawing will not be updated automatically; the clock icon simply means an update is needed.

9. Right-mouse-click on ***Drawing*** and select **Update** in the popup menu as shown.

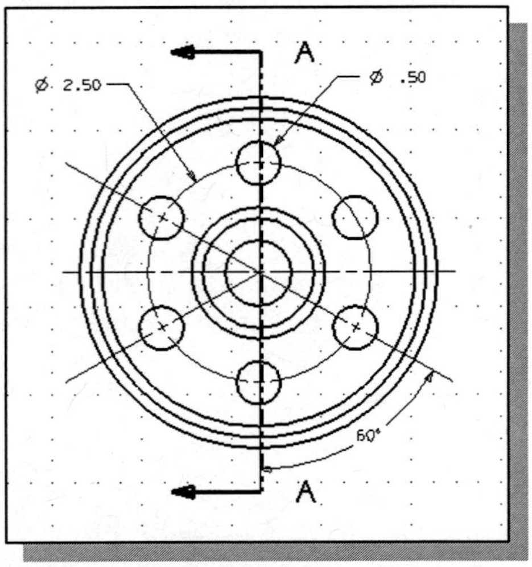

❖ Note that even though the views are updated correctly, we are missing some of the centerlines.

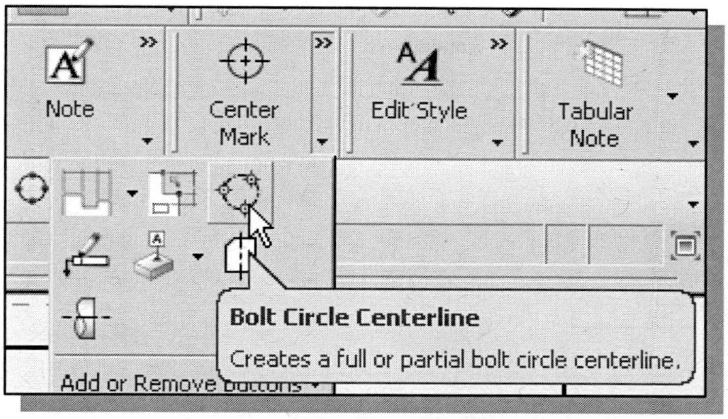

10. Select the **Partial Bolt Circle Centerline** command as shown.

❖ We will only add in the missing centerline for the hole on the upper right side.

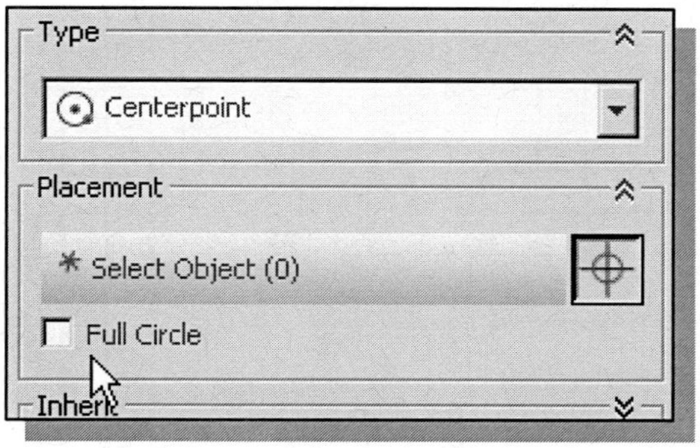

11. Set the *Type* option to **Centerpoint** as shown in the figure.

12. Turn *OFF* the **Full Circle** option.

13. Set the dimension *Extension* to **1.0.**

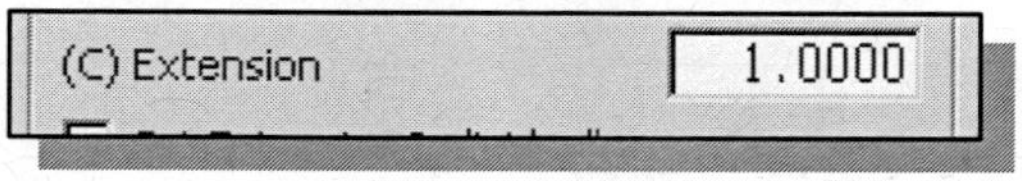

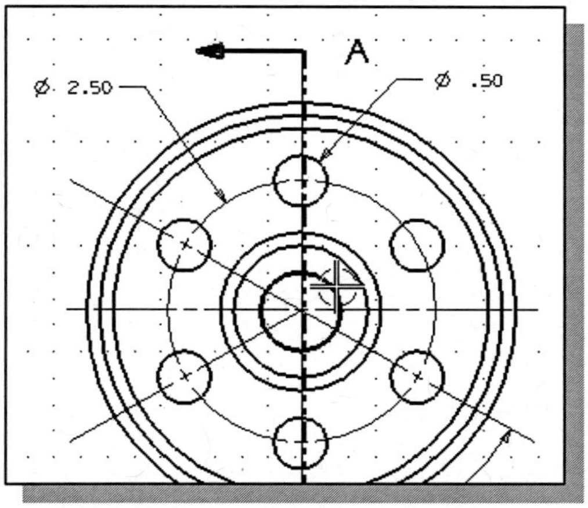

14. Click on the circle near the center of the model as the center location of the new centerline.

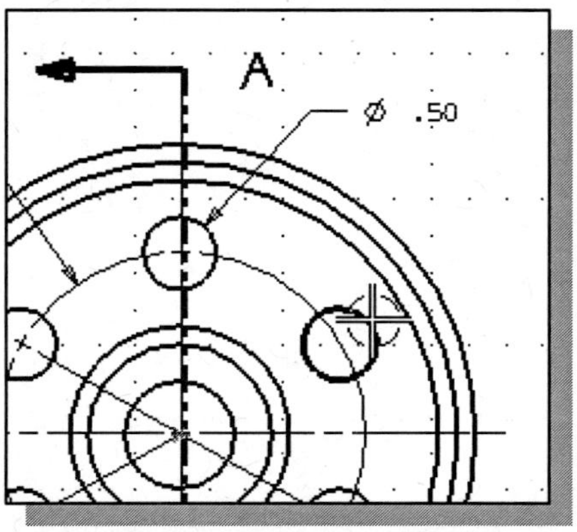

15. Click on the small circle that is missing the centerline.

16. Click **Apply** to create the missing centerline.

17. On your own, complete the drawing as shown.

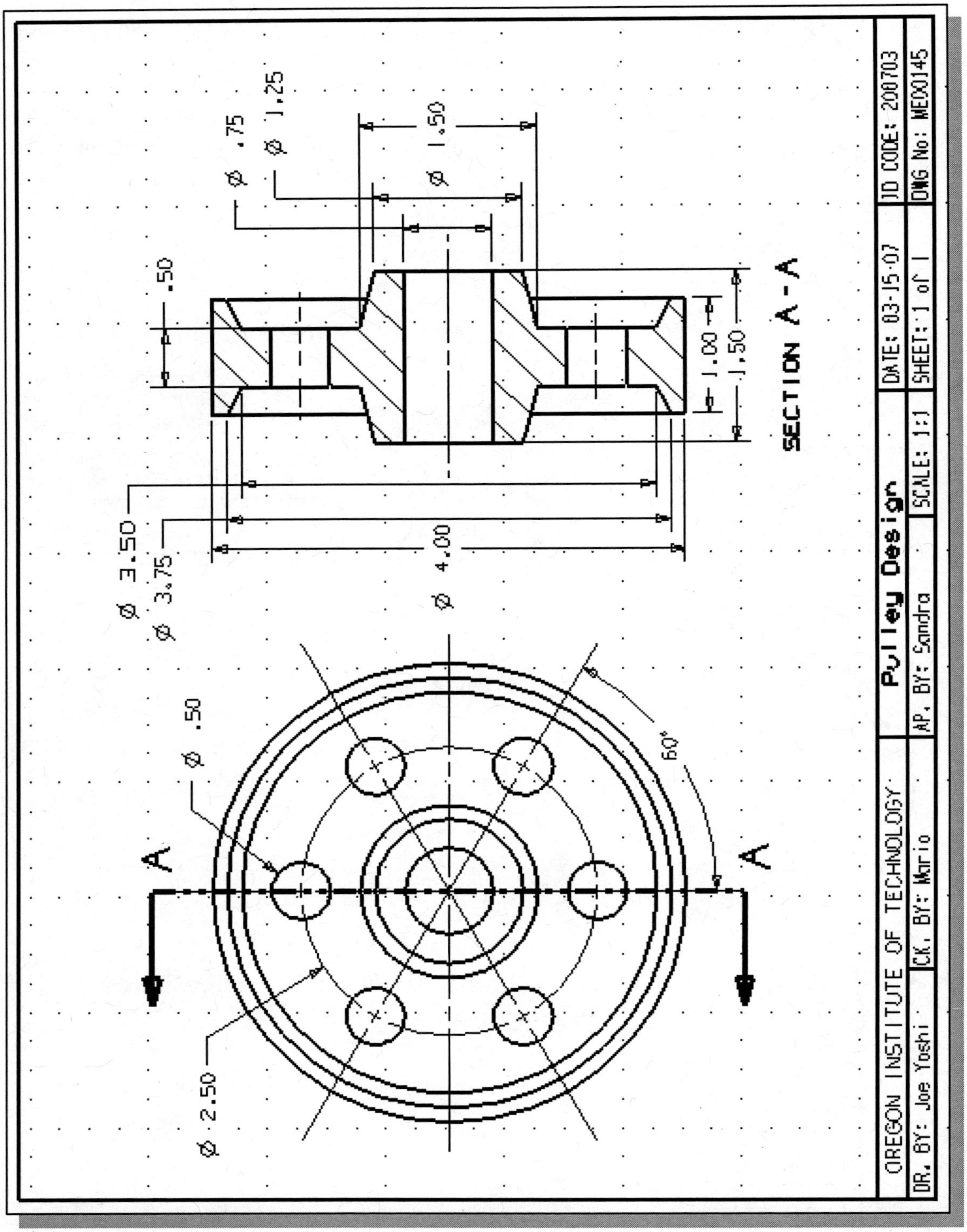

Questions:

1. List the different symmetrical features created in the *Pulley* design.

2. Why is it important to identify symmetrical features in designs?

3. Describe the steps required in using the **Mirror Feature** command.

4. When and why should we use the **Array** option?

5. What are the required elements in order to generate a *section* view?

6. How do you reuse a predefined title block in *Drafting* mode?

7. What are the general steps required to create a section view in *UGS NX6*?

8. Describe the different options available in *UGS NX6* to create centerlines in the *Drafting* mode.

9. Create sketches showing the steps you plan to use to create the model shown on the next page:

Exercises: (All dimensions are in inches.)

1.

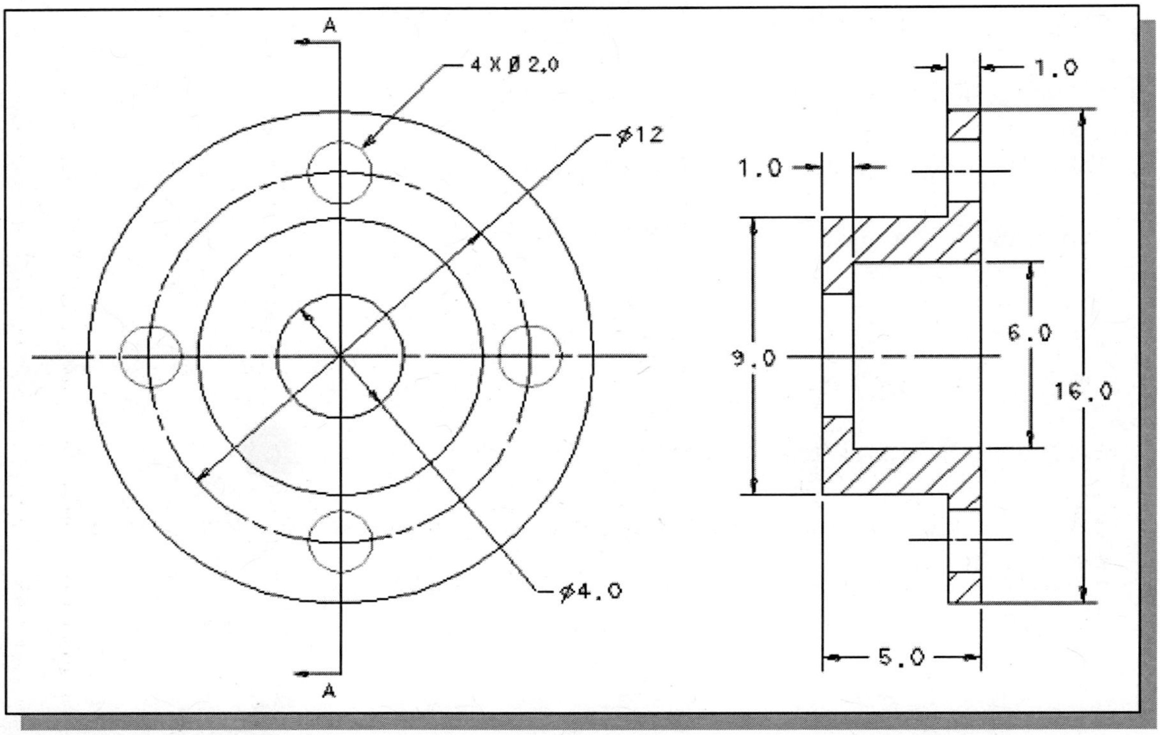

2. Plate thickness: 0.125 inch

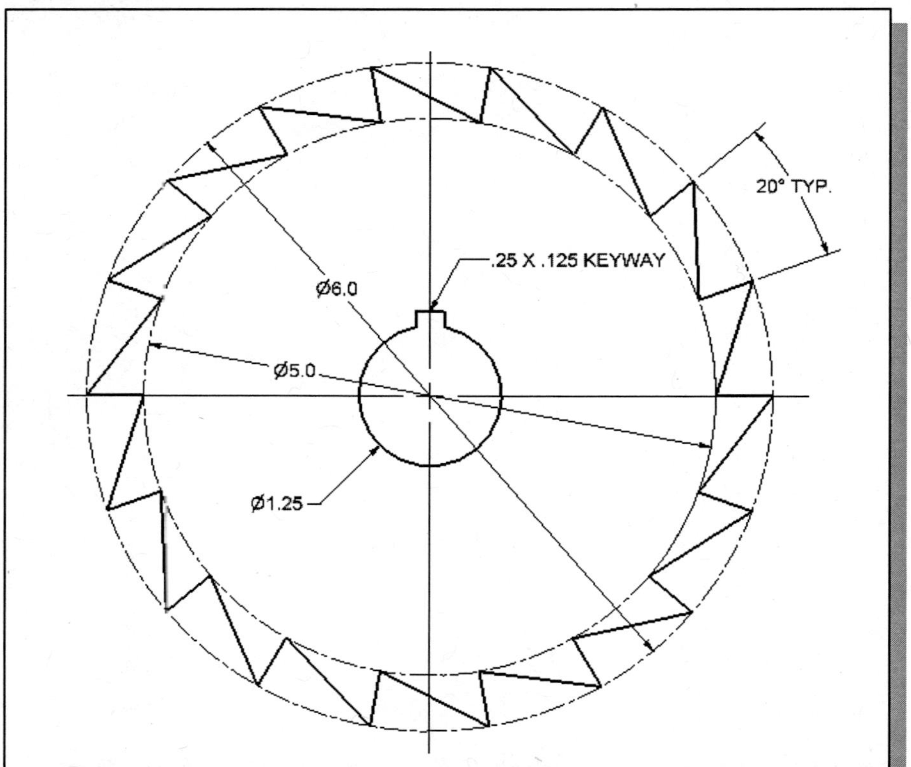

3.

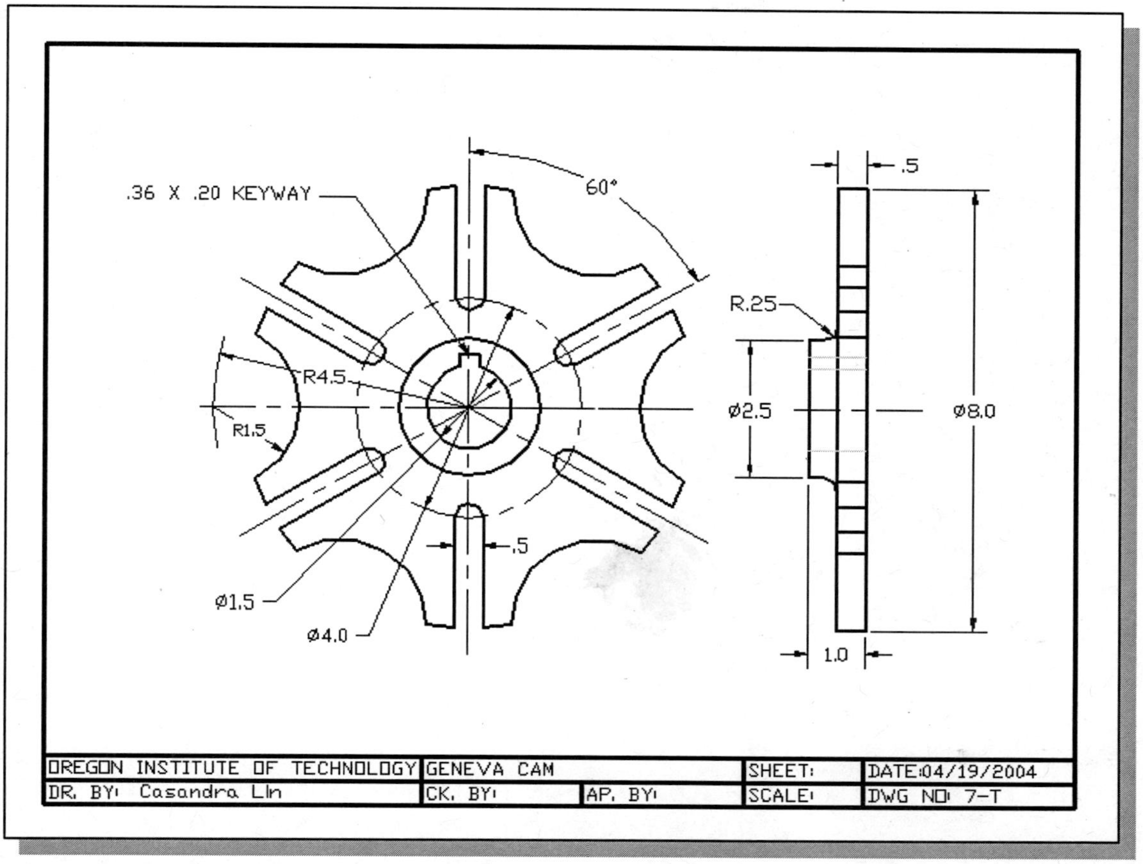
.36 X .20 KEYWAY
60°
R4.5
R1.5
.5
Ø1.5
Ø4.0
.5
R.25
Ø2.5
Ø8.0
1.0
OREGON INSTITUTE OF TECHNOLOGY
GENEVA CAM
SHEET:
DATE:04/19/2004
DR. BY: Casandra Lin
CK. BY:
AP. BY:
SCALE:
DWG NO: 7-T

Notes:

Chapter 11
Advanced 3D Construction Tools

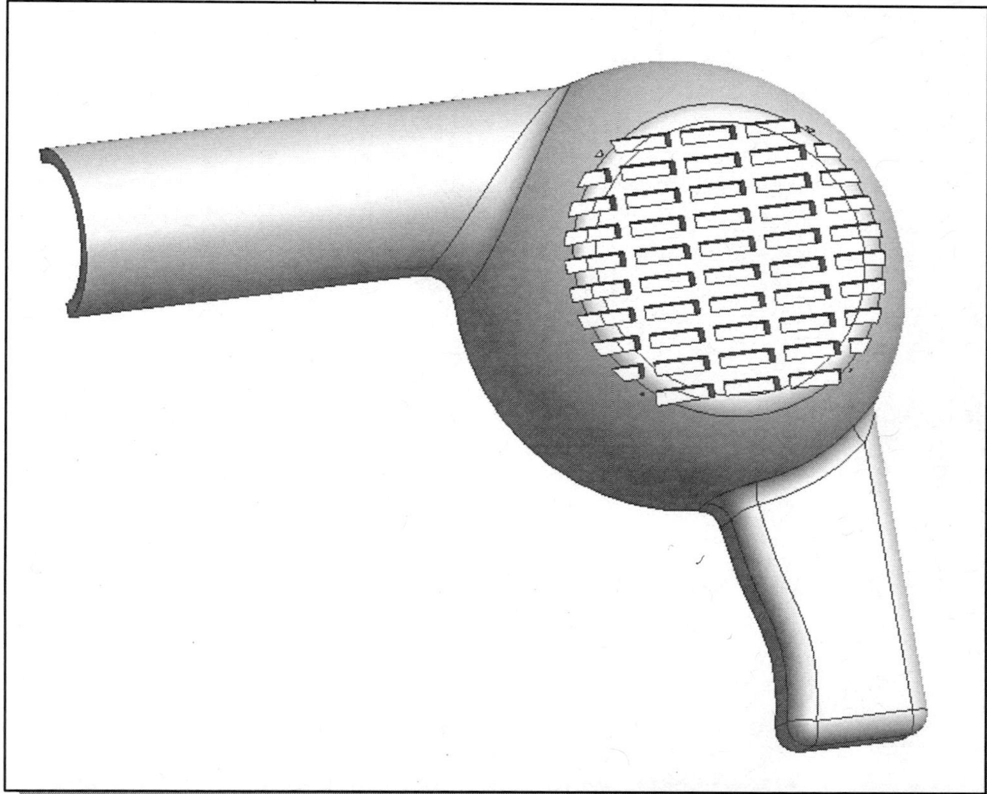

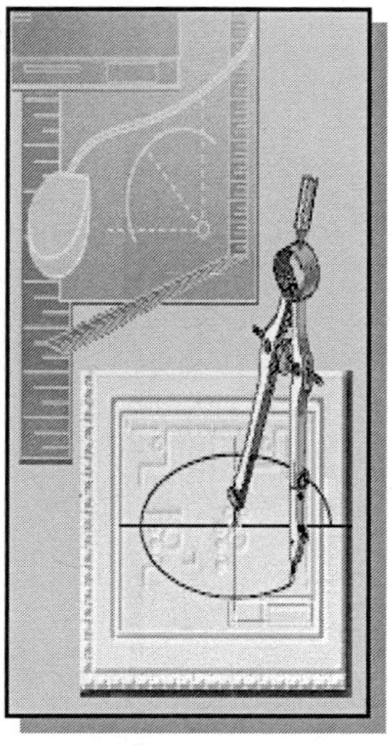

Learning Objectives

- ♦ Understand the uses of the available 3D Construction Tools
- ♦ Set up Multiple Datum Planes
- ♦ Create Swept Features
- ♦ Use the Rectangular Array command
- ♦ Use the Shell Command
- ♦ Create 3D Rounds & Fillets

Introduction

UGS NX provides an assortment of three-dimensional construction tools to make the creation of solid models easier and more efficient. As demonstrated in the previous lessons, creating **extruded** features and **revolved** features are the two most common methods used to create 3D models. In this next example, we will examine the procedures for using the **Sweep** command, the **Shell** command, the **Rectangular Array** command, and also for creating **3D rounds** and **fillets** along the edges of a solid model. These types of features are common characteristics of molded parts.

The **Sweep** option is defined as moving a cross-section through a path in space to form a three-dimensional object. To define a sweep in *UGS NX*, we define two sections: the trajectory and the cross-section.

The **Shell** option is defined as hollowing out the inside of a solid, leaving a shell of specified wall thickness.

The **Edge Blend** command allows us to create 3D rounds and fillets along the edges of a solid model. The Edge Blend command is one of the placed feature commands available in *UGS NX*.

A Thin-Walled Design: *Dryer Housing*

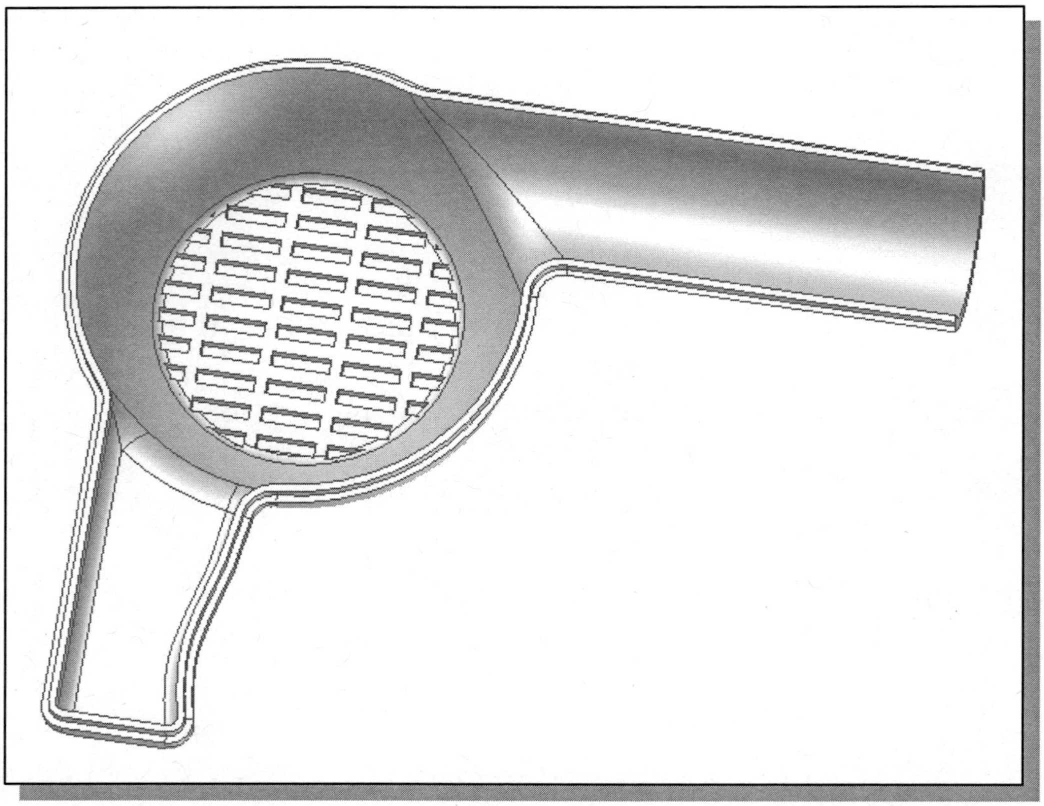

Modeling Strategy

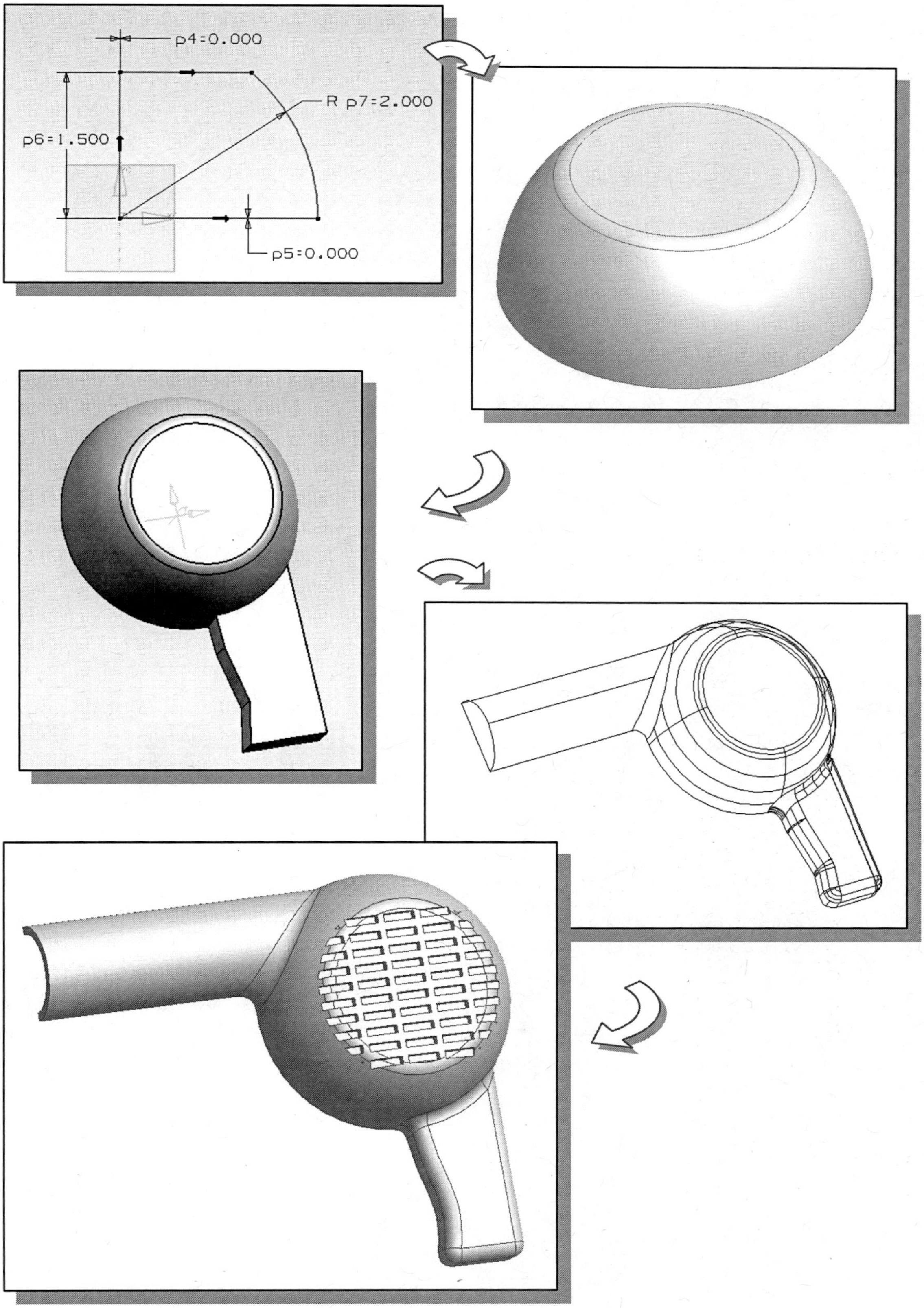

Starting *UGS NX*

1. Select the **UGS NX** option on the *Start* menu or select the **UGS NX** icon on the desktop to start *UGS NX*. The *UGS NX* main window will appear on the screen.

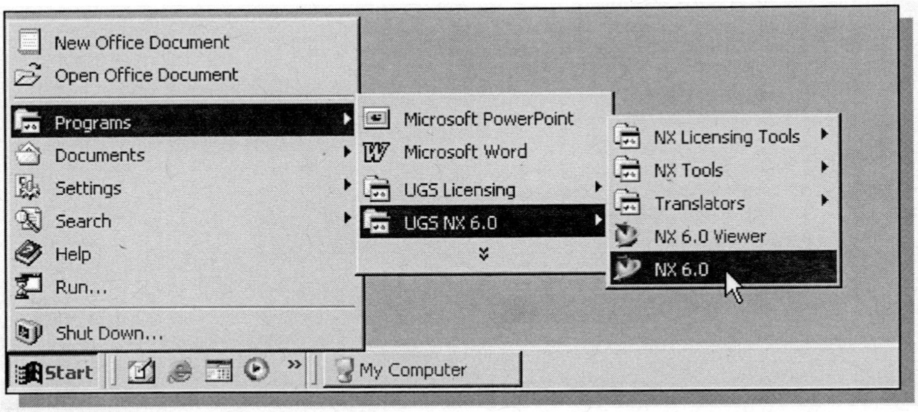

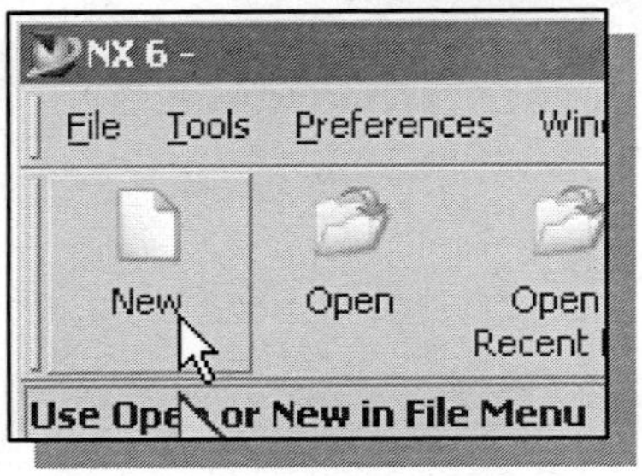

2. Select the **New** icon with a single click of the left-mouse-button (MB1) in the *Standard* toolbar area.

3. Select **Inches** for the *Units* as shown in the figure below.

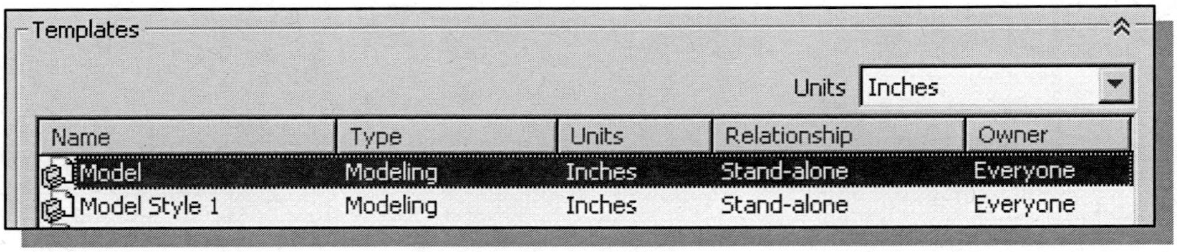

4. Select **Model** in the *Templates* list. Note that the *Model* template will allow us to switch directly into the *Modeling* task as indicated in the *Templates* list.

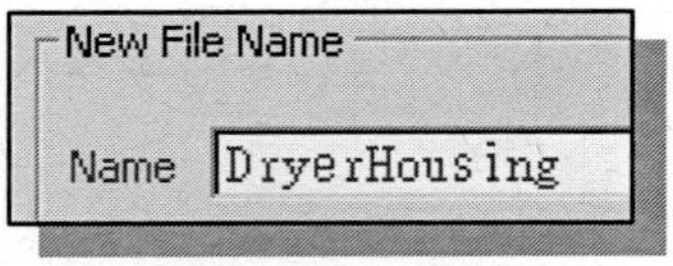

5. In the *New File Name* area, enter **DryerHousing** as the file *Name*.

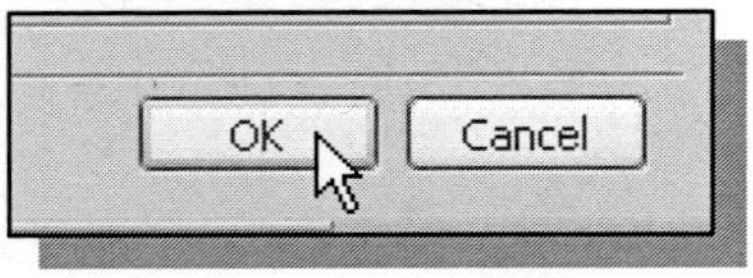

6. Click **OK** to proceed with the **New File** command.

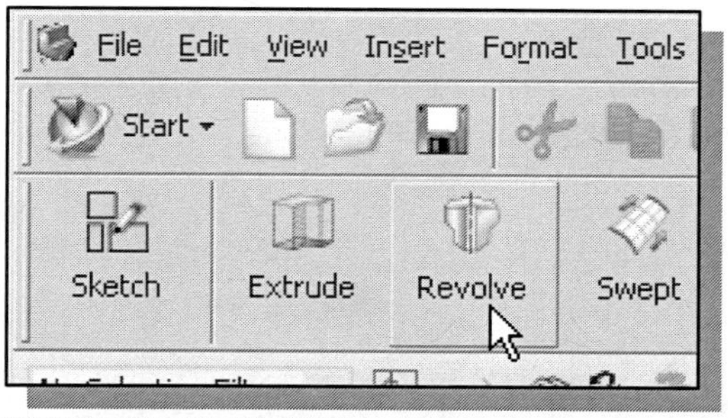

7. In the ***Feature*** toolbars, select the **Revolve** icon as shown.

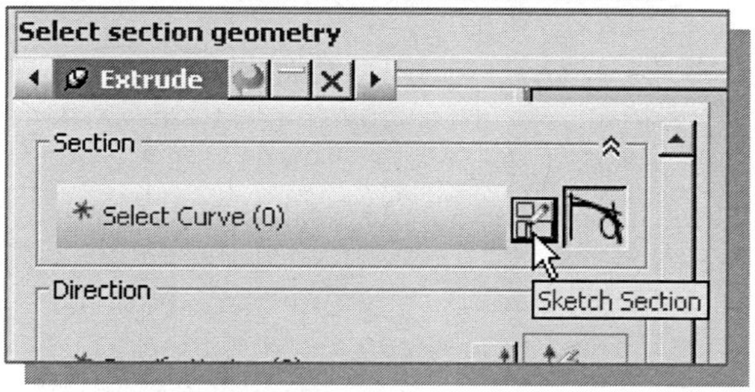

8. Click the **Sketch Section** button to enter the *2D Sketcher* mode and begin creating a new *2D sketch*.

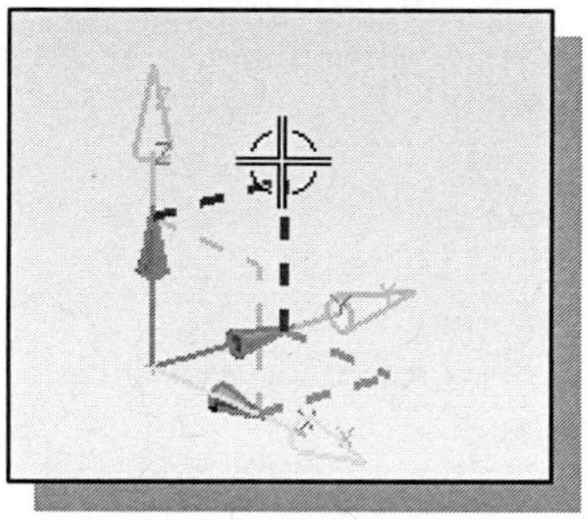

9. Set the *sketch plane* to the ***Y-Z*** plane of the displayed datum coordinate system.

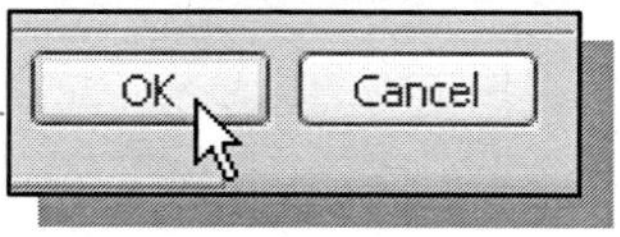

10. Click **OK** to accept the setting of the *sketch plane*.

Creating the 2D Sketch for the Base Feature

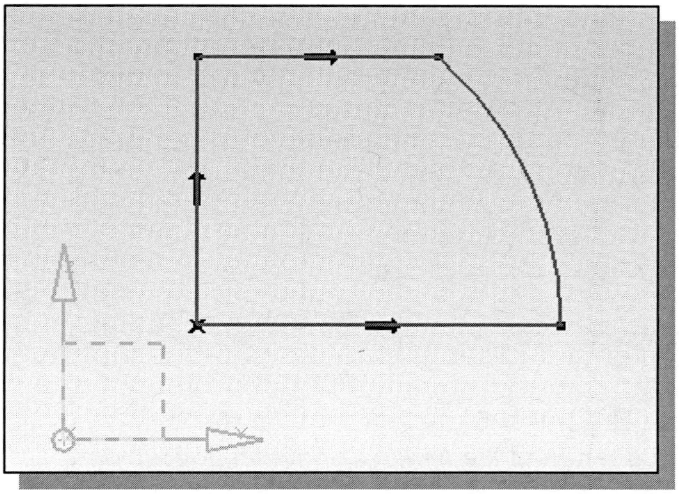

1. On your own, using the **Line** and **Arc** commands, create the 2D sketch as shown. Note that all line segments are either horizontal or vertical, and the arc center is aligned to the lower left corner of the sketch.

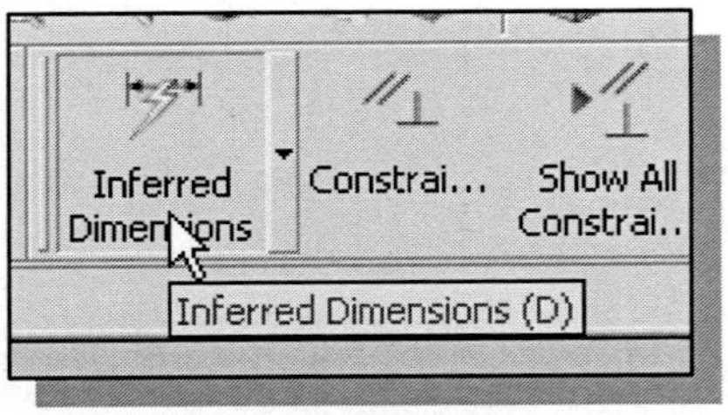

2. Select the **Inferred Dimensions** command in the *Sketch Constraints* toolbar as shown.

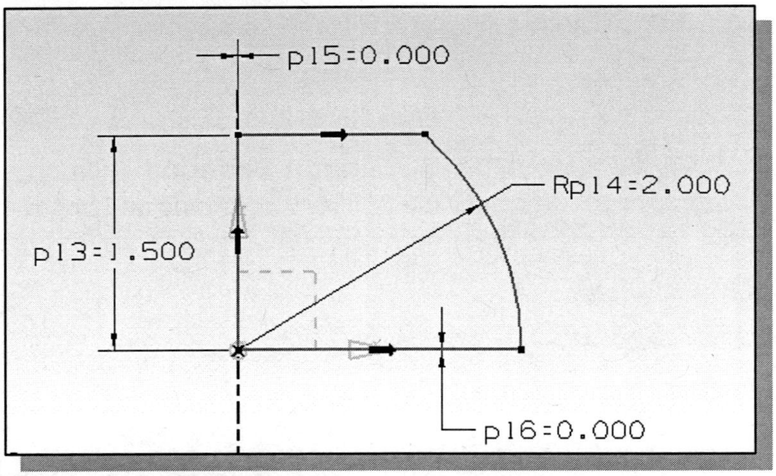

3. On your own, create the four dimensions as shown. (Hint: Two of the dimensions are used to position the sketch relative to the datum coordinate system. This can also be done by applying geometric constraints.)

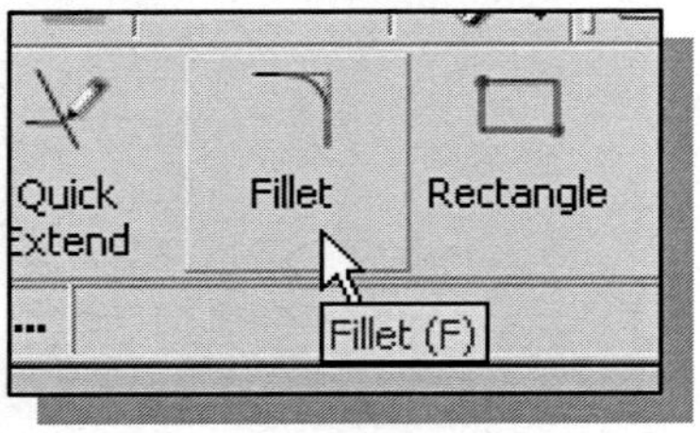

4. Click on the **Fillet** icon in the *2D Sketch Curve* toolbar.

5. Select the top horizontal line and the arc to create a rounded corner as shown.

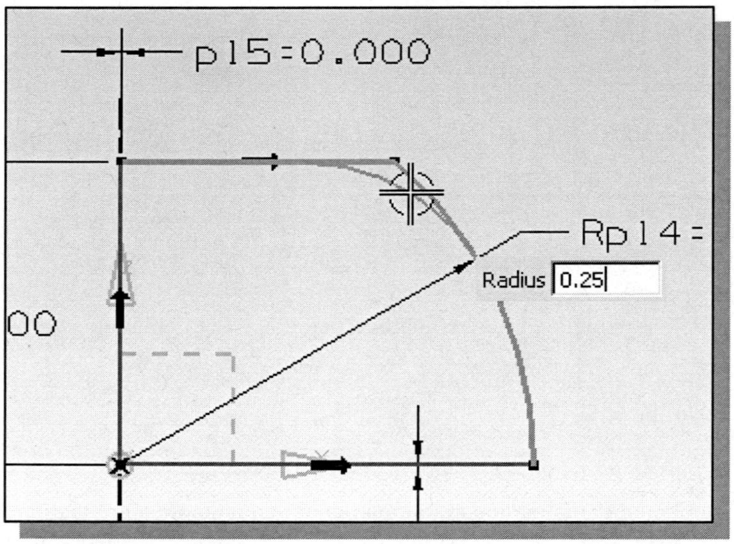

6. In the *Radius* box, set the ***radius*** to **0.25**.

7. On your own, add the fillet radius dimension to fully constrain the 2D sketch.

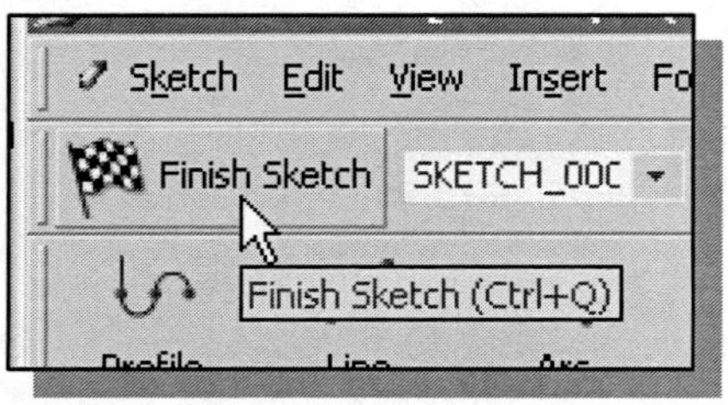

8. Click **Finish Sketch** to exit the *NX Sketcher* mode and return to the *Feature* option dialog window.

Create a Revolved Feature

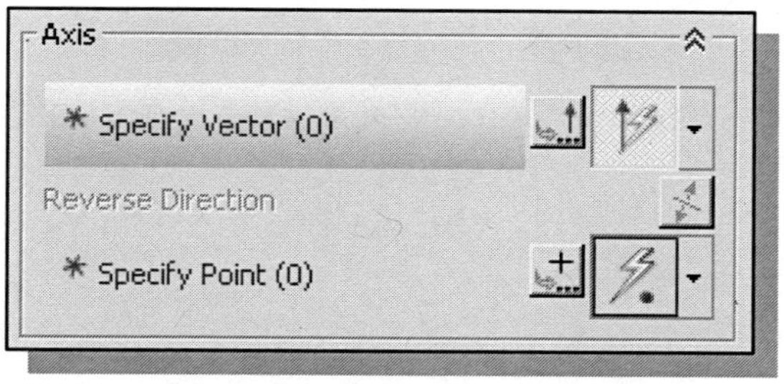

1. In the *Revolve* dialog box, the **Specify Vector** option is activated as shown.

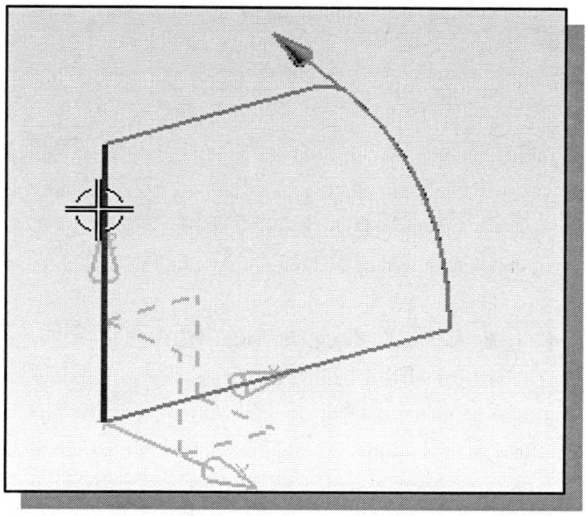

2. Select the **vertical edge** or the ***Z* datum axis** as the axis of rotation as shown.

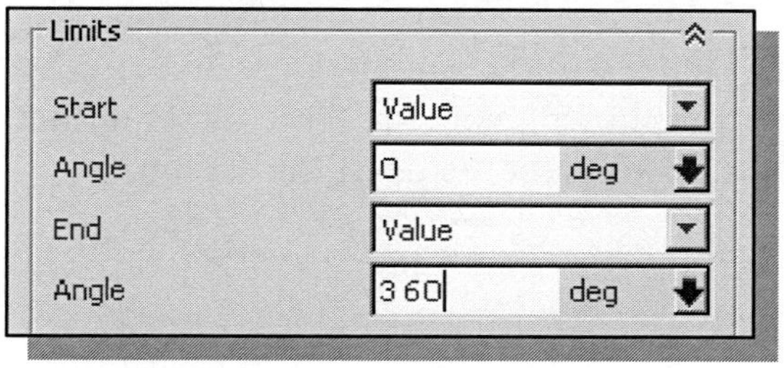

3. Confirm the *Start Angle* is set at **0** and the *End Angle* at **360**, in the angular *Limits* area as shown.

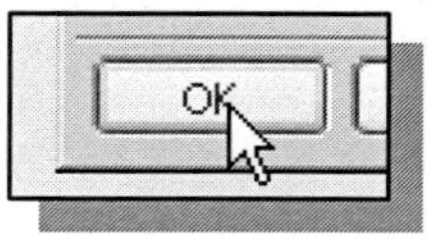

4. Click on the **OK** button to accept the settings and create the revolved feature.

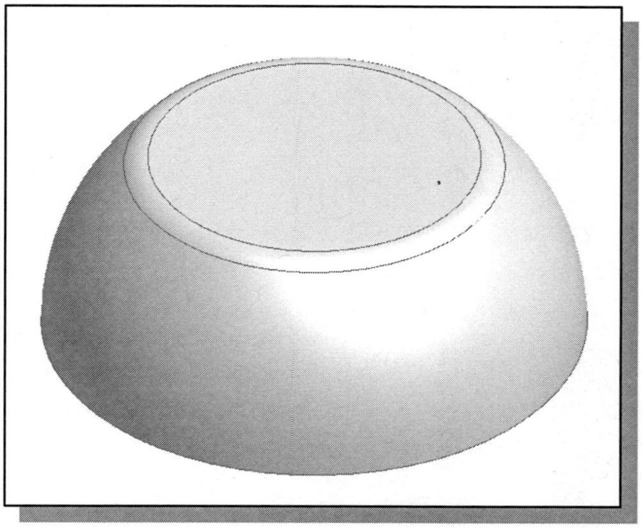

Creating the Dryer Handle

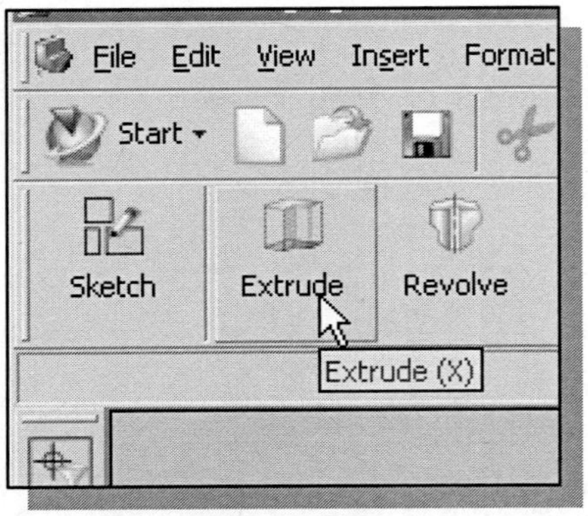

1. In the *Form Feature* toolbars, select the **Extrude** icon as shown.

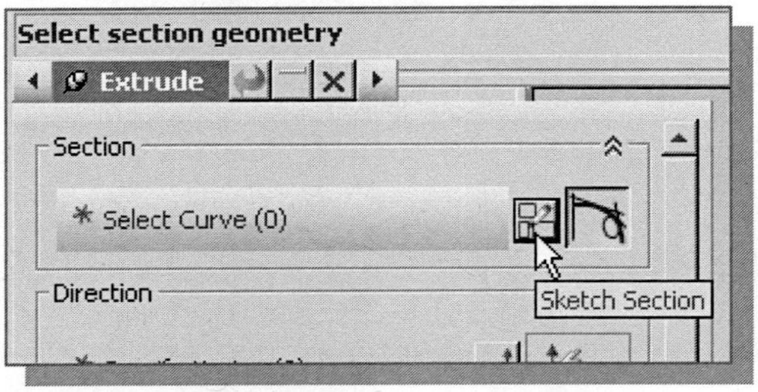

2. Click the **Sketch Section** button to begin creating a new *2D sketch.*

3. Click **OK** to accept the default *X-Y* plane as the *sketch plane.*

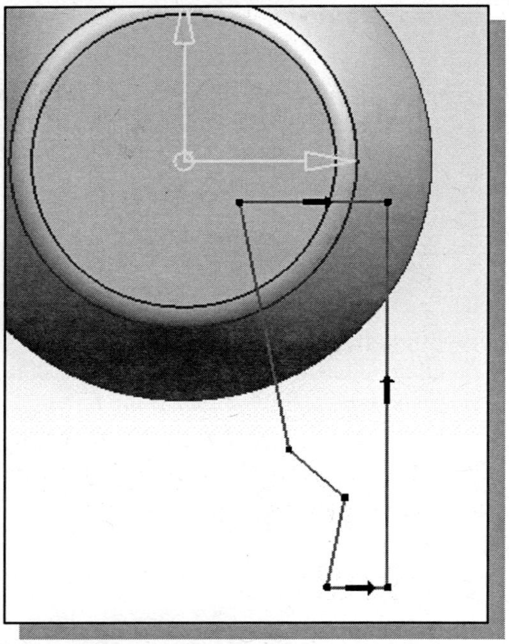

4. Using the **Profile** command, create the 2D sketch as shown. Note the three inclined line segments on the left side of the sketch.

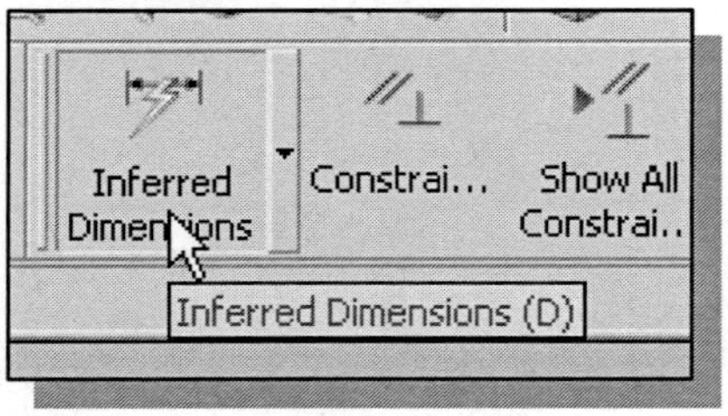

5. Select the **Inferred Dimensions** command in the *Sketch Constraints* toolbar as shown.

6. On your own, create the seven dimensions as shown in the figure.

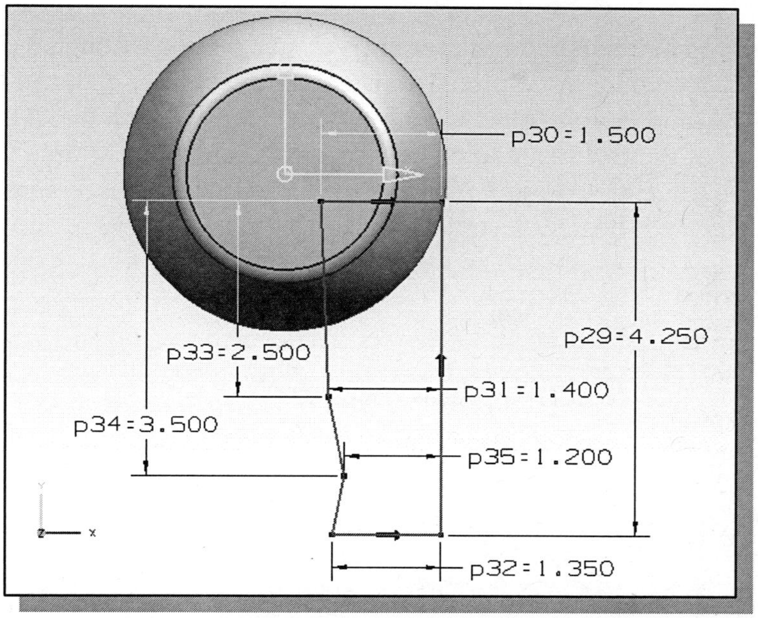

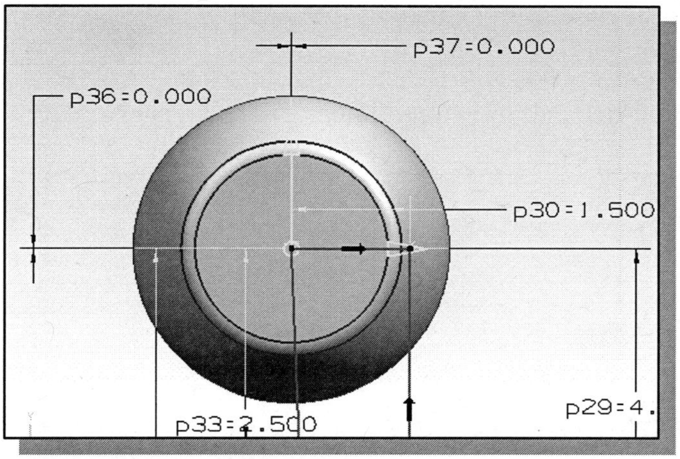

7. On your own, create the two locational dimensions to align the upper left corner of the 2D sketch to the origin of the DCS as shown.

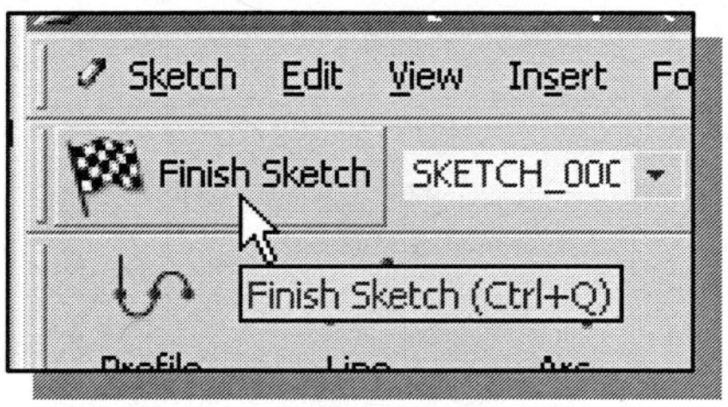

9. Click **Finish Sketch** to exit the *NX Sketcher* mode and return to the *Feature* option dialog window.

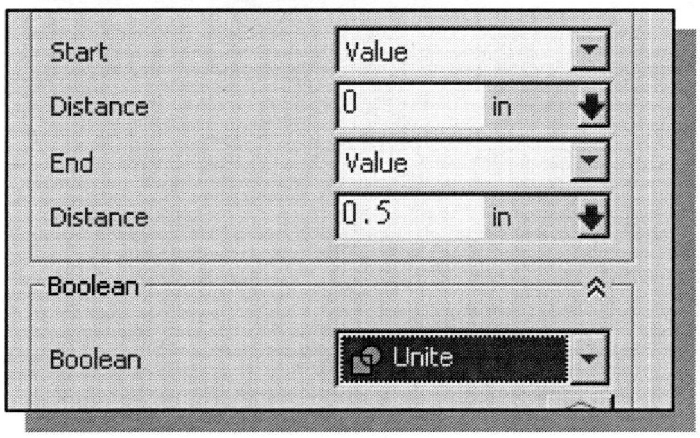

10. In the *Extrude* dialog box, set the *Boolean* option to **Unite** and the *End Distance* to **0.5** as shown.

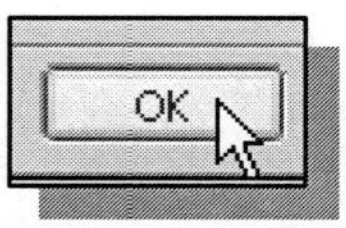

11. Click **OK** to create the extrude feature.

Creating a Swept Feature

- The **Sweep** command is defined as moving a planar section through a planar (2D) or 3D path in space to form a three-dimensional solid object. The path can be an open curve or a closed loop, but must be on an intersecting plane with the 2D section. To illustrate the use of the **Sweep** command, we will begin with a simple feature, which can be done with the **Extrude** command as well. Another swept feature, using existing geometry, will be demonstrated as the last feature of the design.

➢ The Swept Path

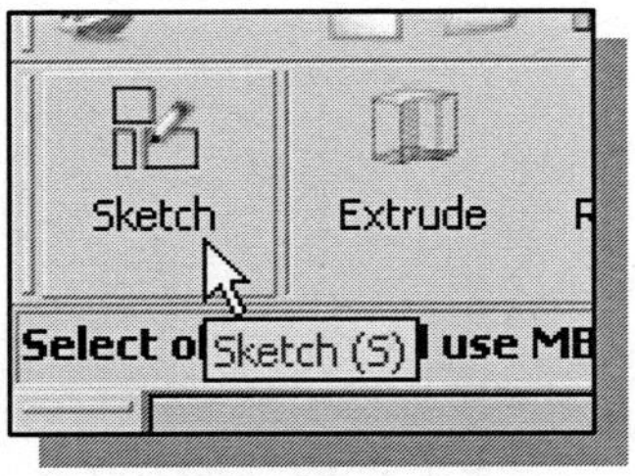

1. In the *Form Feature* toolbar's *Standard* toolbar, select the **Sketch** command by left-clicking once on the icon.

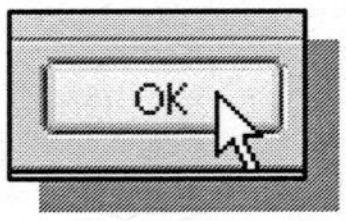

2. Click **OK** to accept the default *X-Y* plane as the *sketch plane.*

3. On your own, create a horizontal line and the three dimensions to constrain it as shown in the figure below.

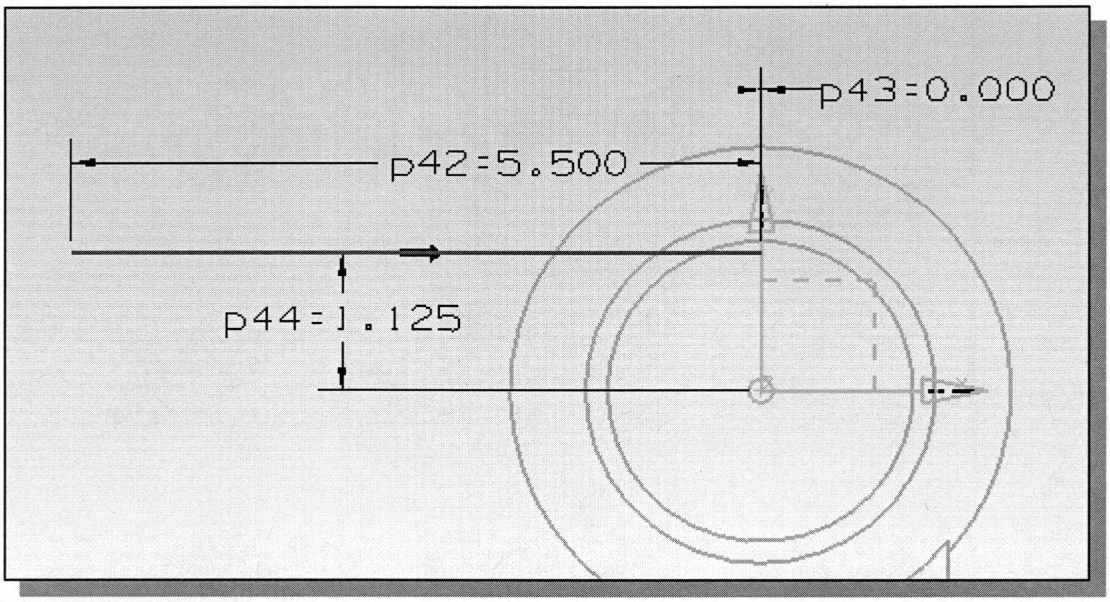

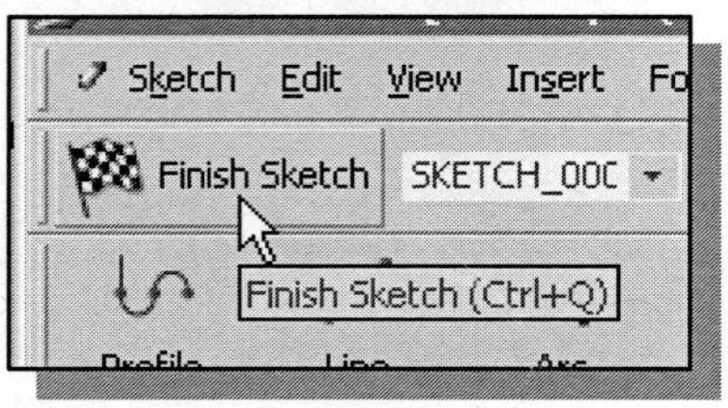

4. Click **Finish Sketch** to exit the *NX Sketcher* mode and end the *Sketch* option.

➢ **The 2D section:** The 2D section needs to be created in a plane that is not parallel to the path. We will use the *YC-ZC* plane as the *sketch plane.*

5. In the *Form Feature* toolbar's *Standard* toolbar, select the **Sketch** command by left-clicking once on the icon.

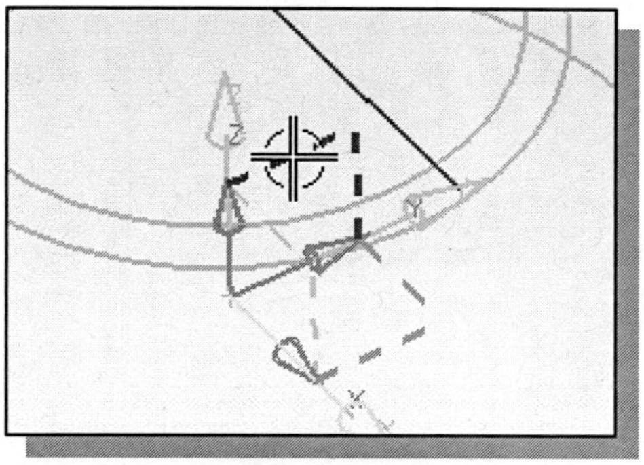

6. Select the ***Y-Z*** plane to align the *sketch plane* as shown. (Hint: Set the display to wireframe display to aid the selection.)

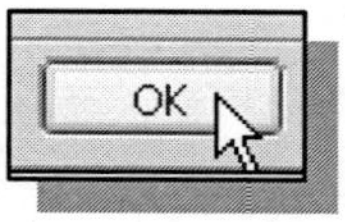

7. Click **OK** to accept the selection of the *sketch plane*.

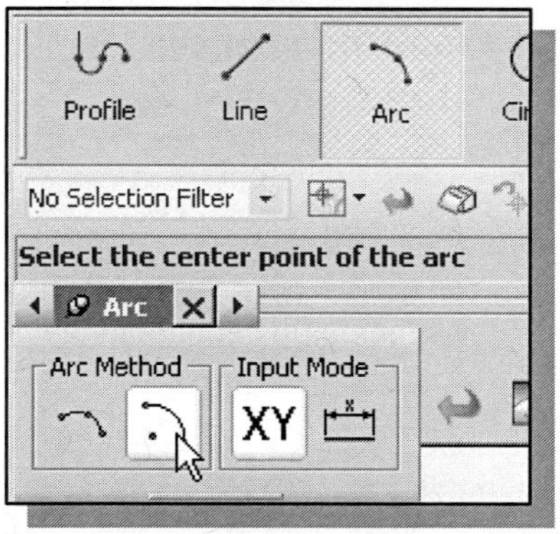

8. Activate the **Arc** command and choose the **Arc by Center and Endpoints** option as shown.

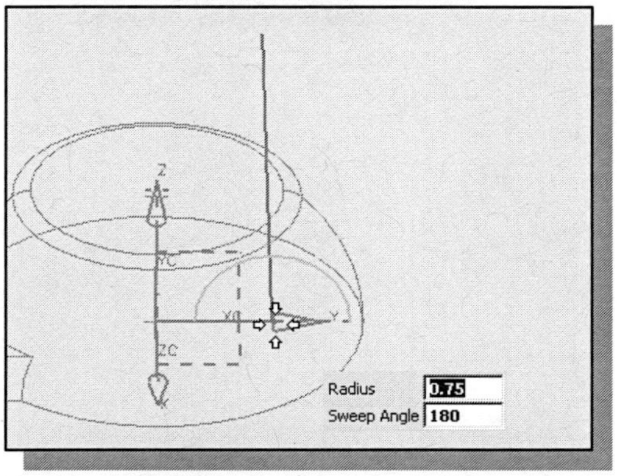

9. Align the arc center to the endpoint of the line segment we just created.

10. Set the arc *Radius* to **0.75** and *Sweep Angle* to **180** as shown.

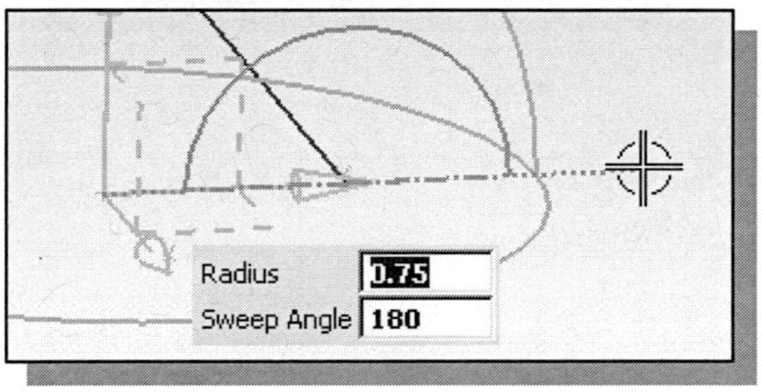

11. Click at a location that is toward the right side of the arc to set the arc direction as shown.

12. Click once with the middle-mouse-button to end the **Arc** command.

13. On your own, create a **line segment** connecting the two endpoints of the arc we just created.

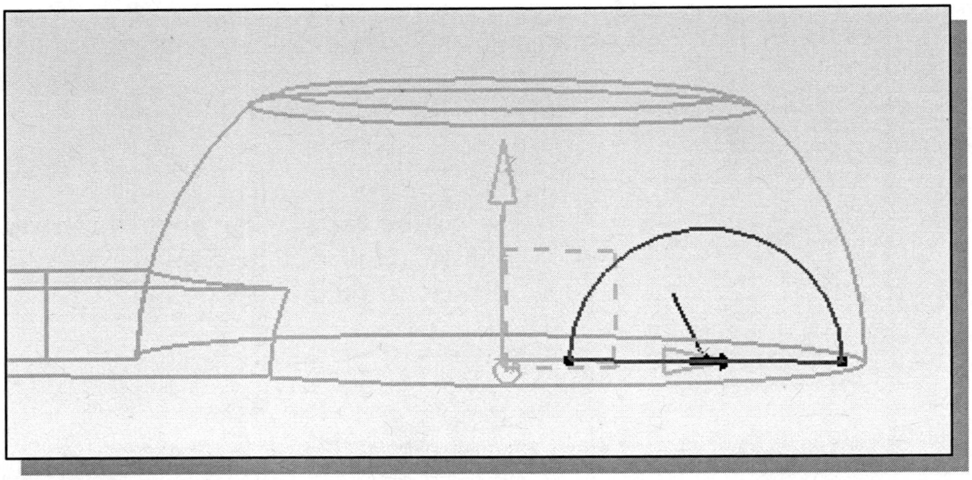

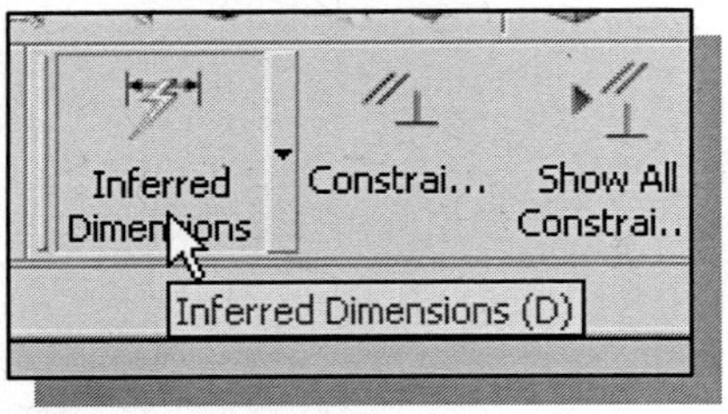

14. Select the **Inferred Dimensions** command in the *Sketch Constraints* toolbar as shown.

15. Create the two dimensions to fully constrain the 2D sketch as shown in the figure below.

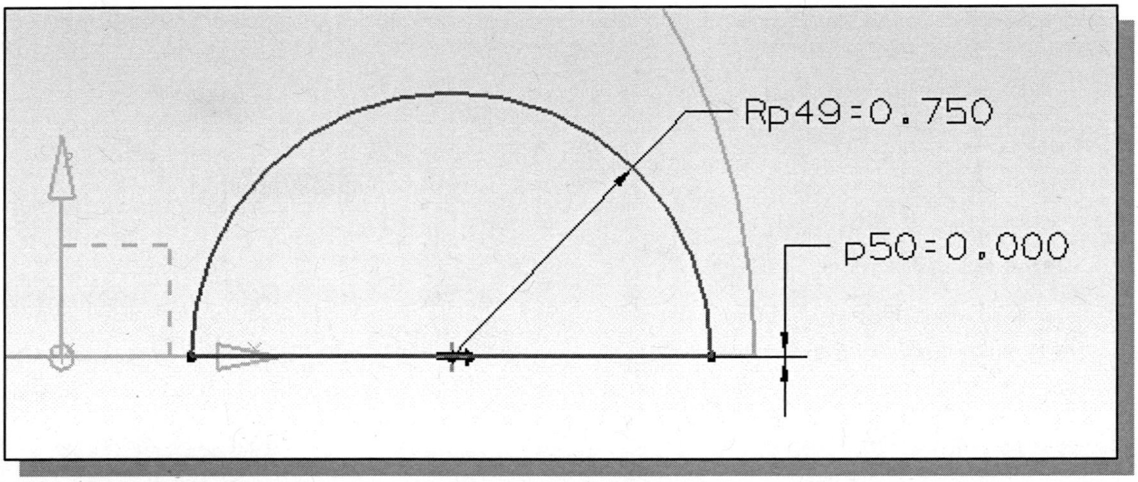

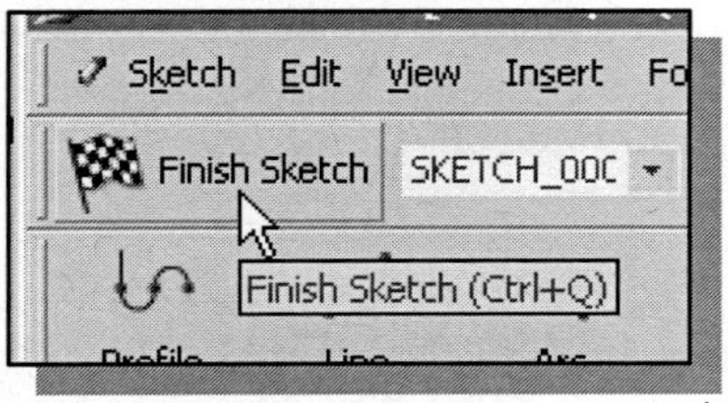

16. Click **Finish Sketch** to exit the *NX Sketcher* mode and end the *Sketch* option.

➢ Create the Swept feature

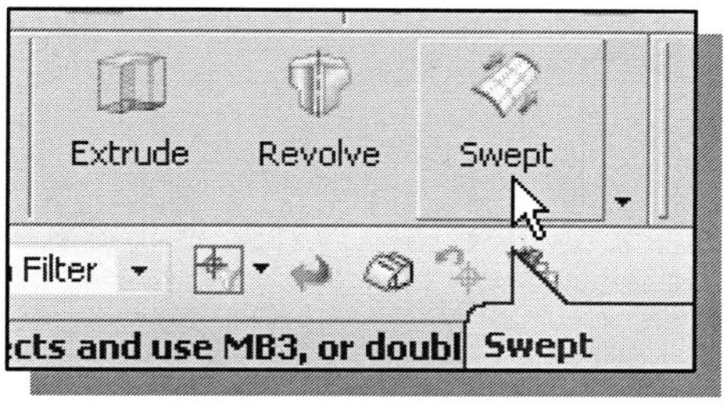

1. Select the **Swept** command in the *2D Sketch Panel* as shown.

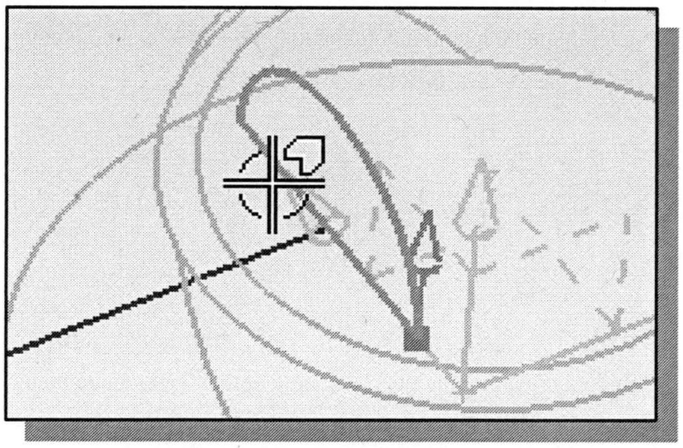

2. Select both the **arc** and the connecting **line segment** as the *section curves* as shown.

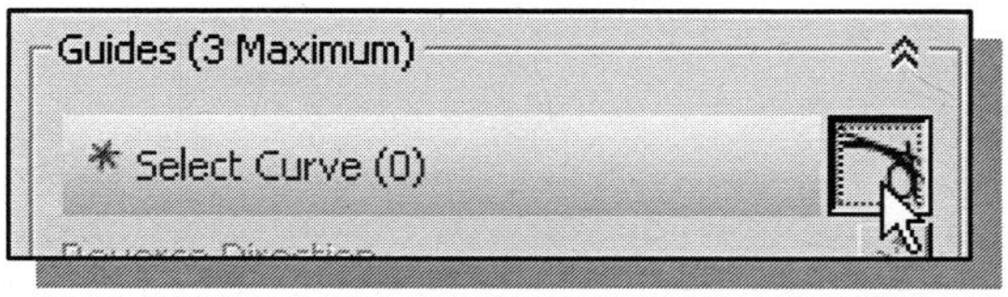

3. Click on the **Guides** icon to activate the *Guide Selection* option.

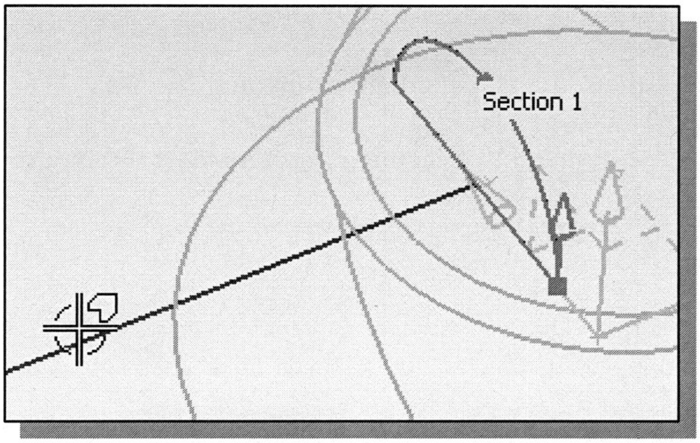

4. Select the **perpendicular line segment** as the *Guide* as shown.

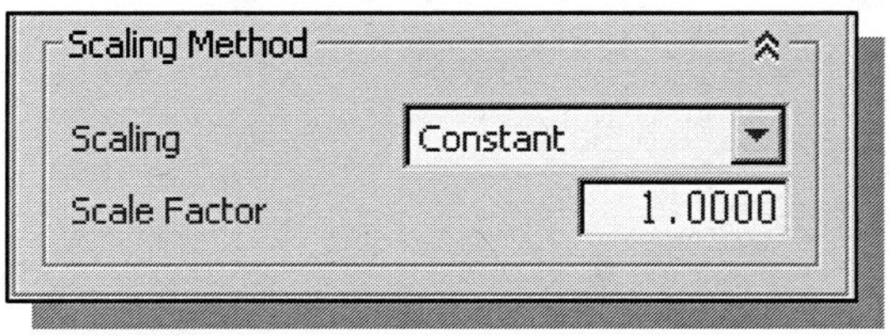

5. Confirm the *Scaling* method is set to **Constant** and **1.00** is the *Scale Factor*.

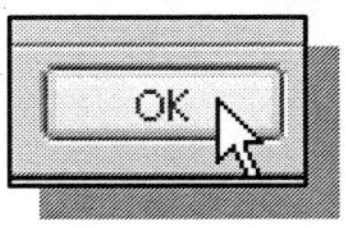

6. Click **OK** to accept the selections and create the swept feature.

Joining the Two Solid Features

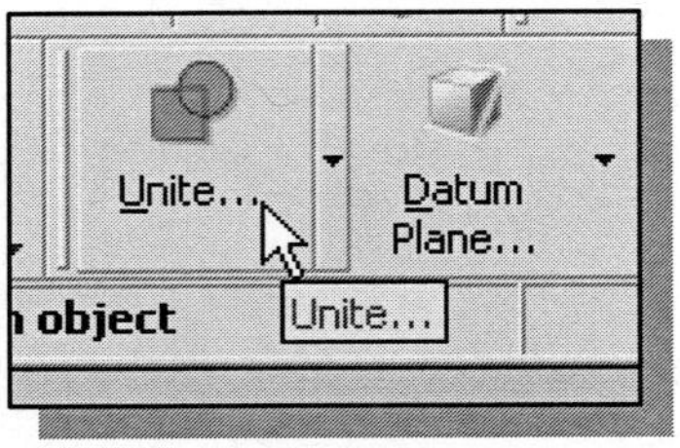

1. Activate the **Unite** command by clicking the left-mouse-button on the icon as shown.

❖ The Unite command can be used to join two separate bodies into one object.

❖ Note the first selection option, *Target Body*, is activated as shown.

2. On your own, select the original revolved feature as the *Target Body*.

❖ Note the second selection option, *Tool Body*, is activated as shown.

3. On your own, select the swept feature as the *Tool Body*.

4. Do not activate any of the other options listed under *Settings* as we want to create one solid model

5. Click on the **OK** button to accept the settings and create a mirrored feature.

6. On your own, use the 3D-Rotate command to dynamically rotate the solid model and view the resulting solid.

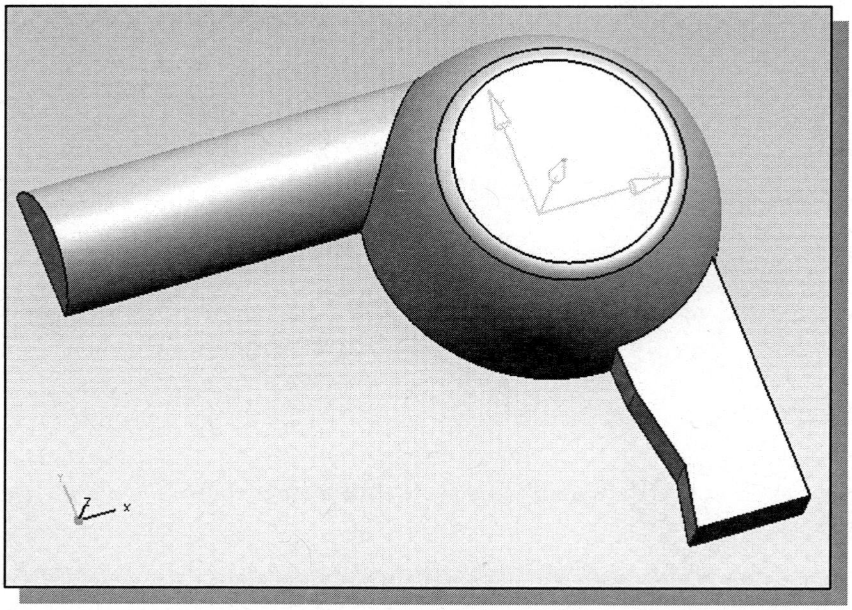

Hiding the 2D sketches

➤ Note the two sketches used to create the swept feature were built separately and therefore they are available for other features.

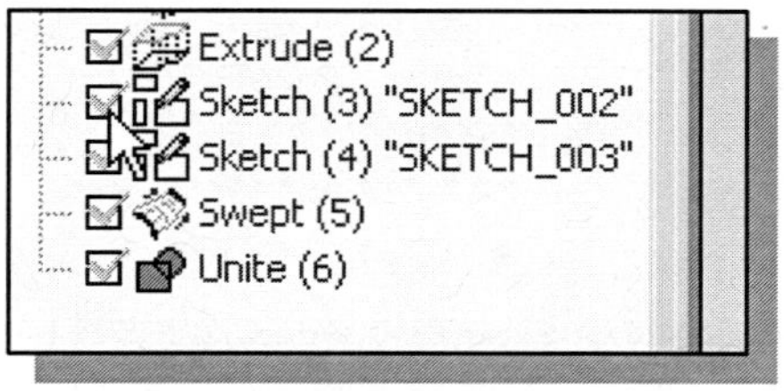

1. On your own, uncheck *Sketch (3)* and notice the entire swept feature will be suppressed.

2. Click **Undo** to reverse the last step, the suppression of the sketch and swept feature.

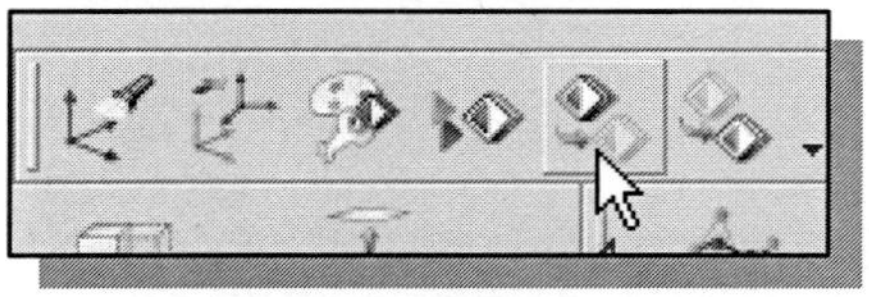

3. Click **Hide** in the *Utility* toolbar as shown.

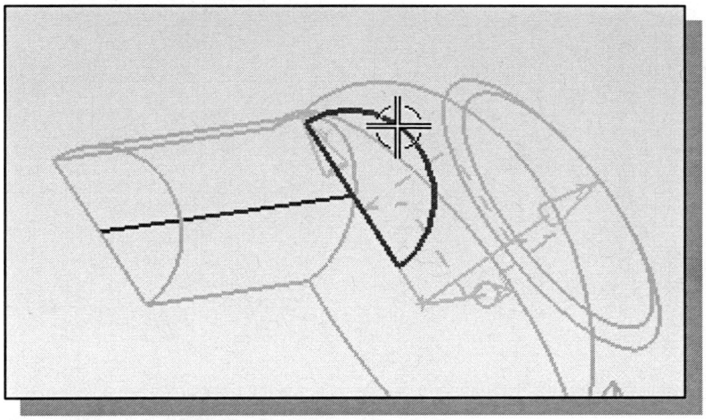

4. Click on the arc and notice the entire sketch is selected.

5. Click **OK** to accept the selection.

➤ Notice the sketch remains active, although it is not shown.

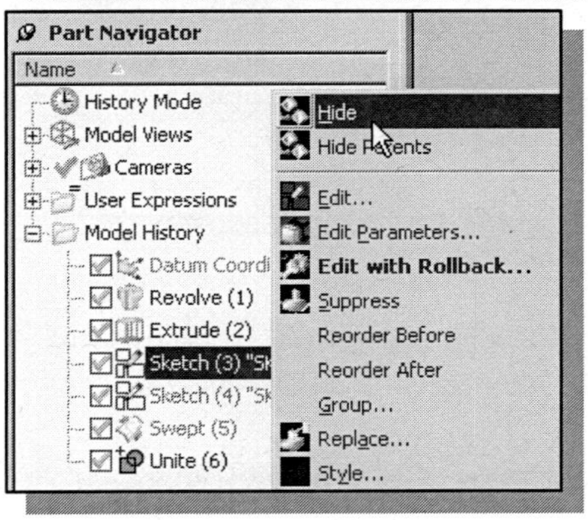

6. Right-mouse click on the other sketch and pick **Hide** to achieve the same result.

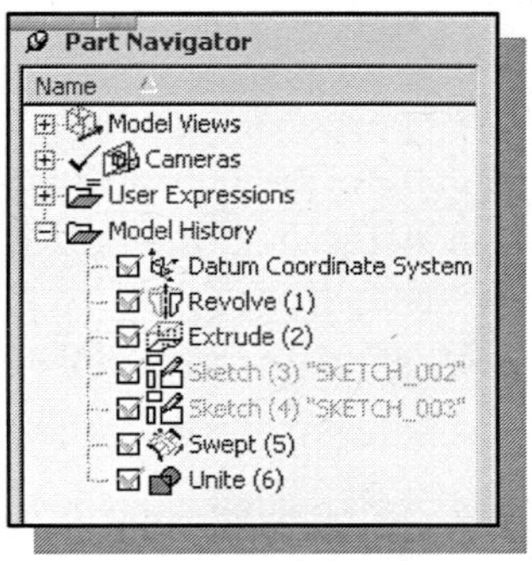

➤ The gray color of the two sketches indicates both sketches have been turned *OFF*.

Create 3D Rounds and Fillets

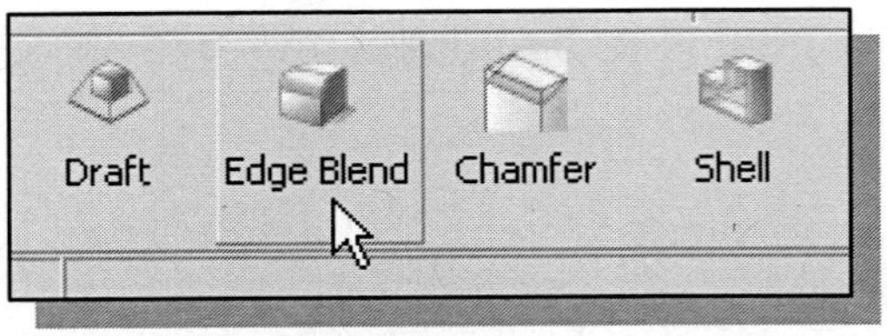

1. In the *Feature Operations* toolbar, select the **Edge Blend** command by left-clicking once on the icon.

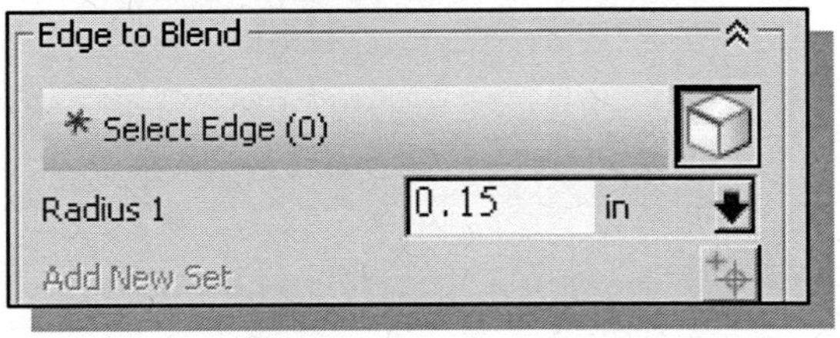

2. Note the Select Edge option is activated, also the default edge blend option is set to ***Constant Radius***.

3. Set the ***Radius 1*** option to **0.15** as shown in the figure above.

4. Select the **five edges** as shown in the figure; note that the four straight edges are on the handle section.

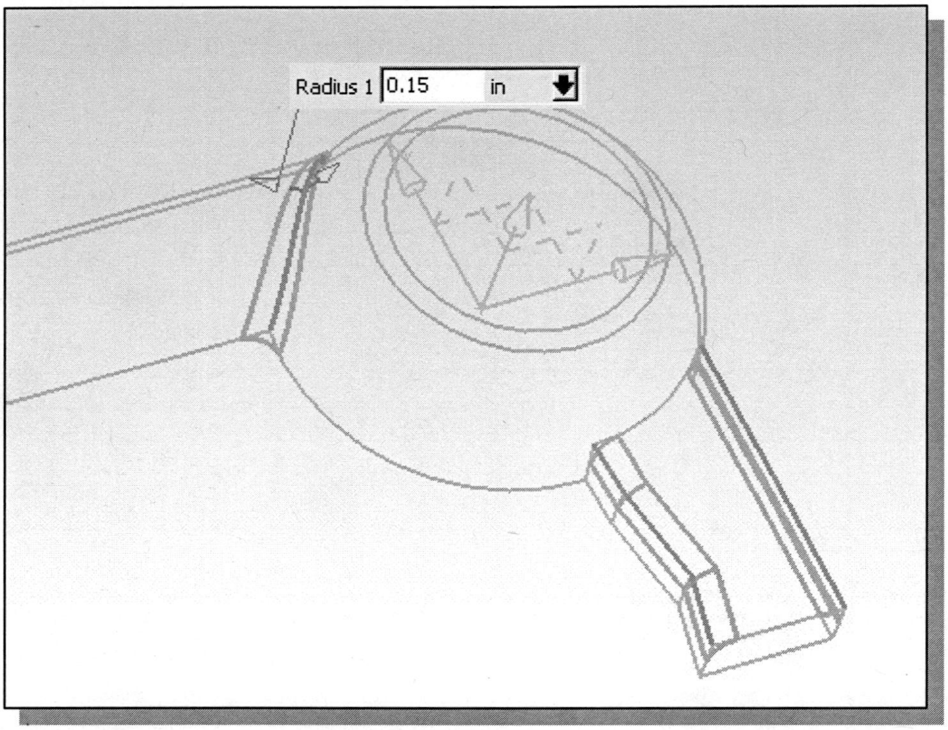

5. Click **Apply** to accept the selections and proceed to create the first set of 3D rounds and fillets for our model.

➢ Note that by selecting Apply, the Edge Blend command remains active.

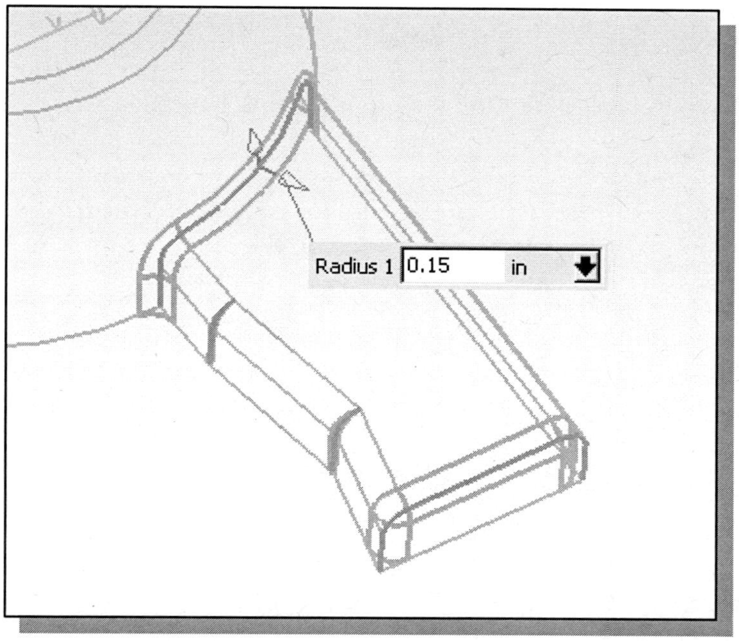

6. Select the four edges as shown in the figure.

7. Maintain the same *Radius* of **0.15** as shown in the figure.

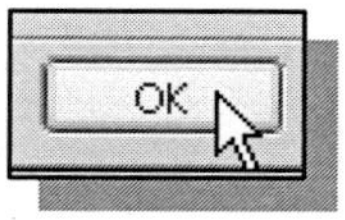

8. Click **OK** to accept the selections and proceed to create the second set of 3D rounds and fillets for our model.

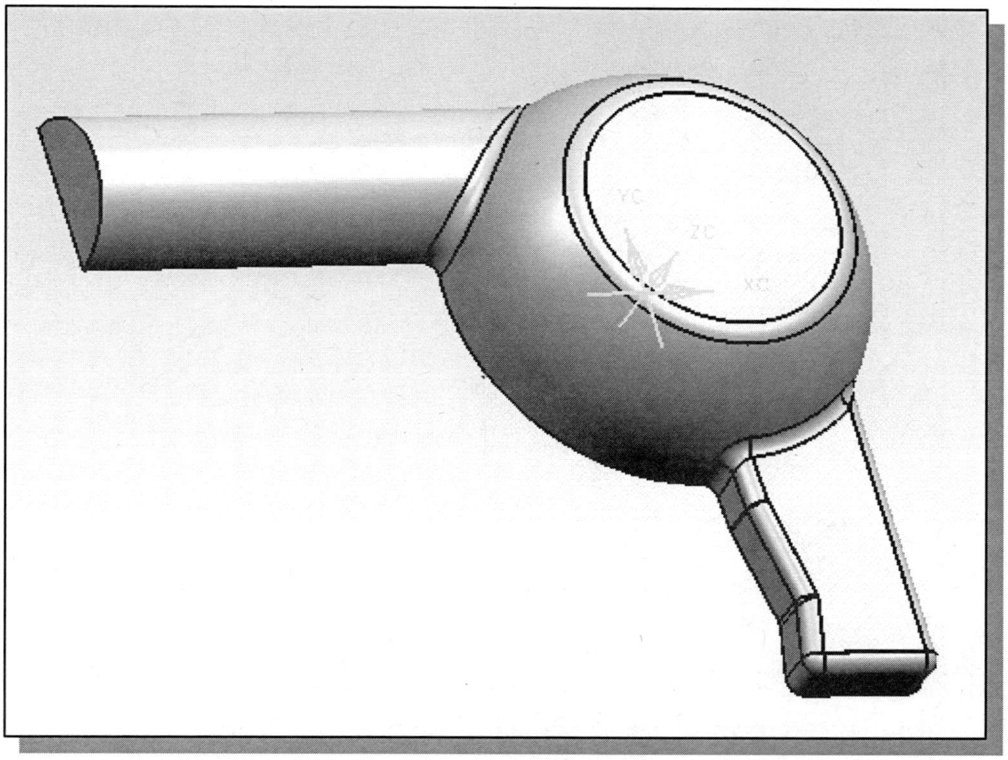

Creating a Shell Feature

- The **Shell** command can be used to hollow out the inside of a solid, leaving a shell of specified wall thickness.

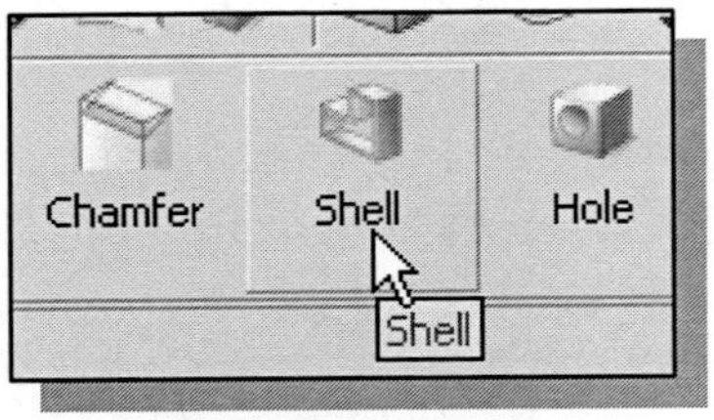

1. In the *Feature Operations* toolbar, select the **Shell** command by left-clicking once on the icon.

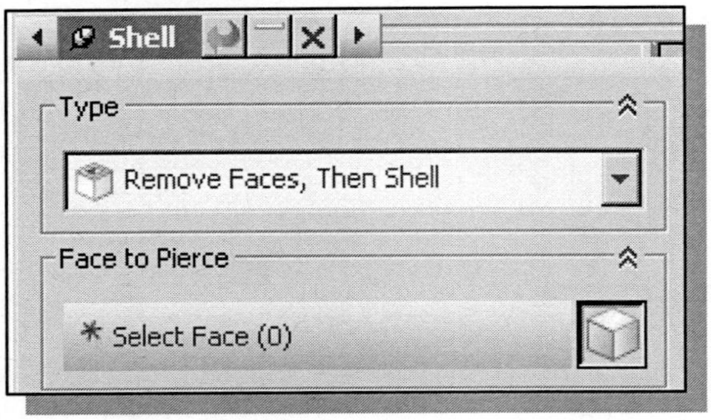

➢ Note that the **Remove Faces** option is activated by default.

2. On your own, use the **3D Rotation** option to display the back faces of the model as shown below.

3. Select the two faces as shown below.

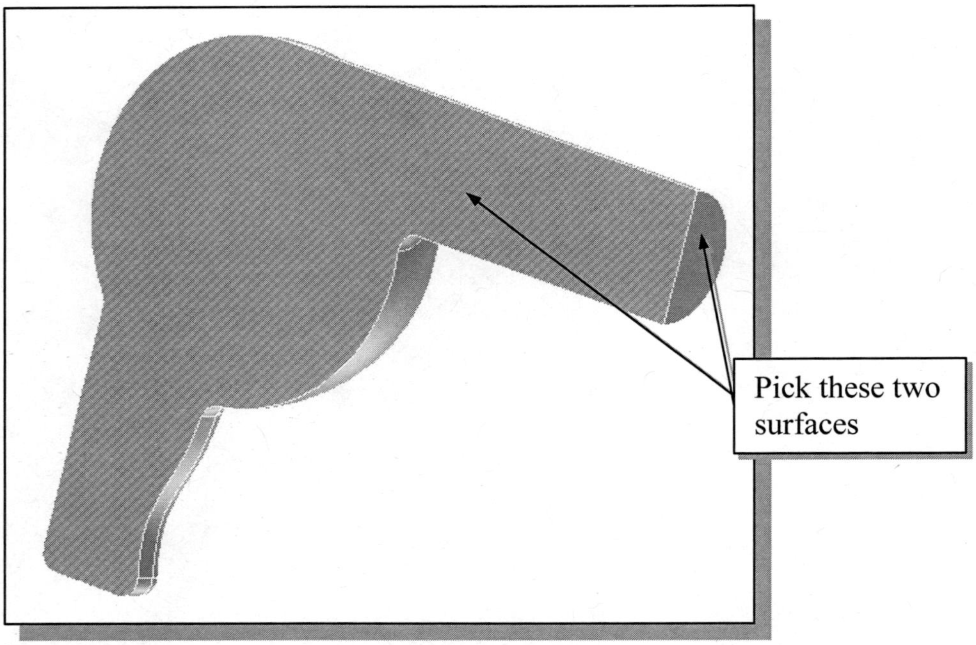

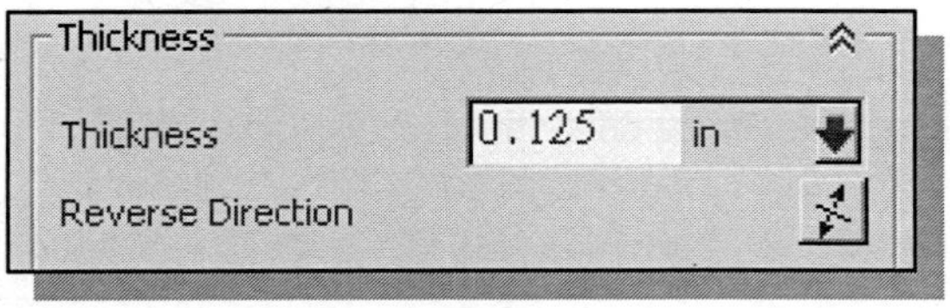

4. In the *Shell* dialog box, set the ***Thickness*** option to a value of **0.125** as shown.

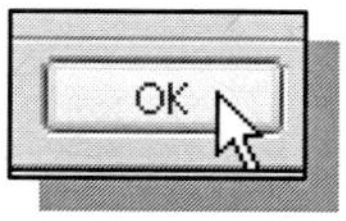

5. In the *Shell* dialog box, click on the **OK** button to accept the settings and create the shell feature.

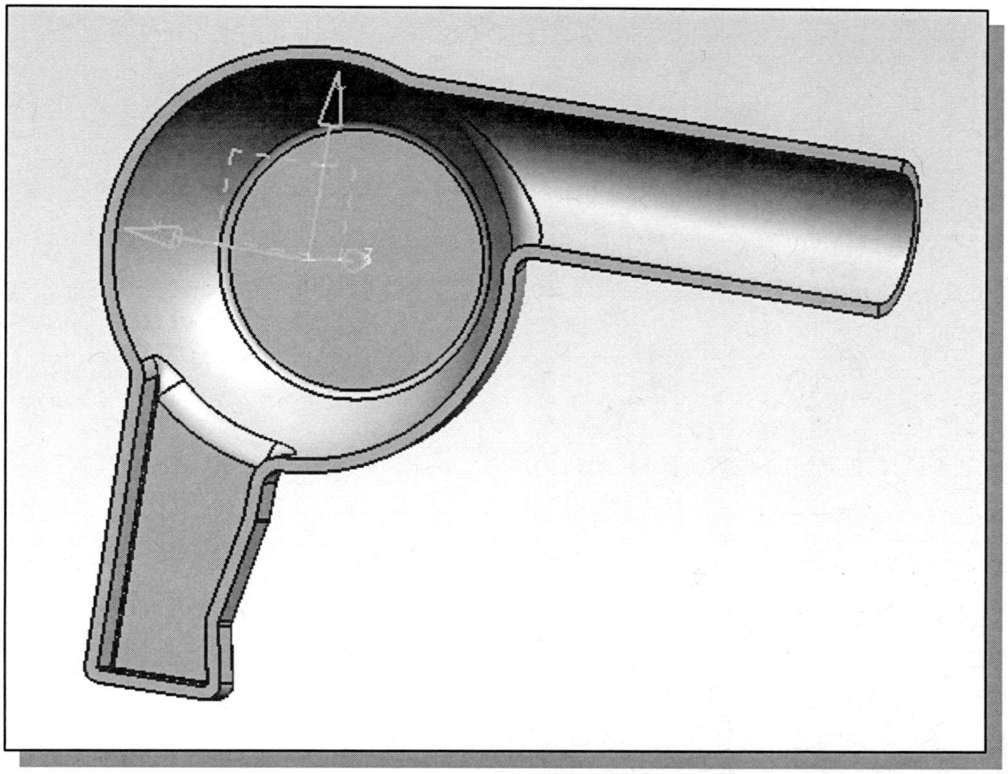

Create a Pattern Leader

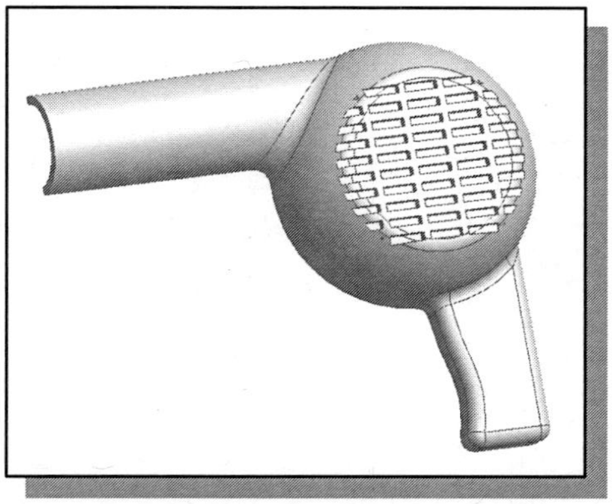

- The *Dryer Housing* design requires the placement of identical holes on the top face of the solid. Instead of creating the holes one at a time, we can simplify the creation of these holes by using the **Rectangular Array** command to create duplicate features. Prior to using the command, we will first create a ***pattern leader***, which is a regular extrude feature.

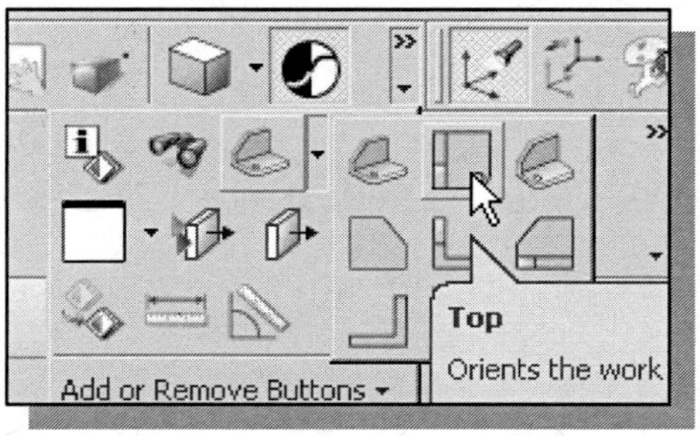

1. Select **Top** view in the *Standard* toolbar to adjust the display of the model on the screen.

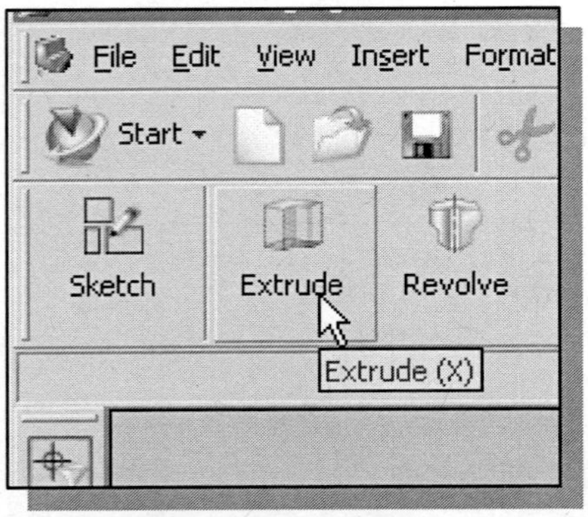

2. In the *Form Feature* toolbars, select the **Extrude** icon as shown.

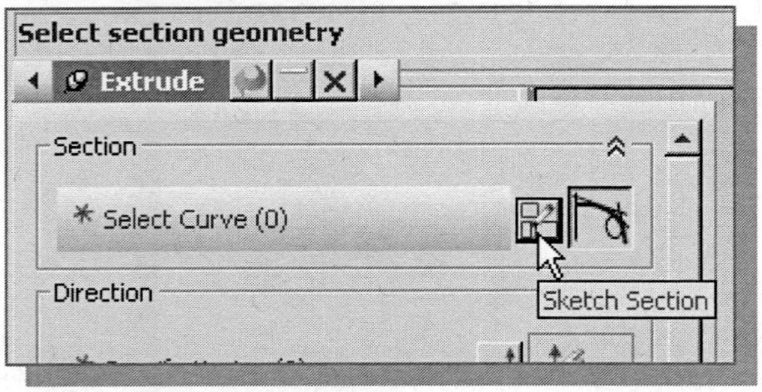

3. Click the **Sketch Section** button to begin creating a new *2D sketch.*

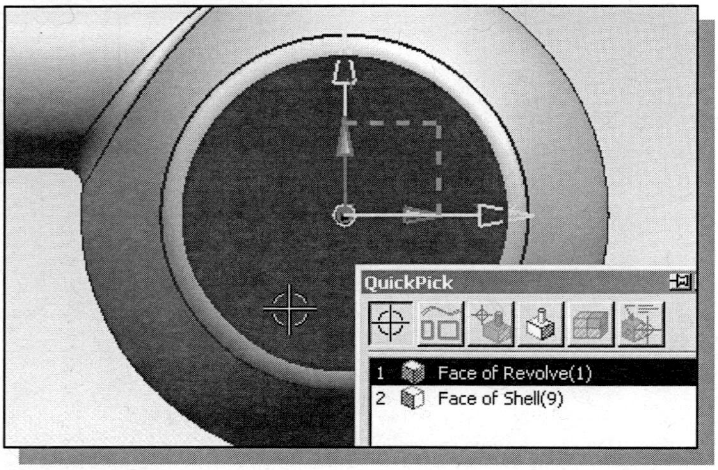

4. Pick the top face of the *base* feature. Choose **Face of Revolve** in the *QuickPick* box, as shown.

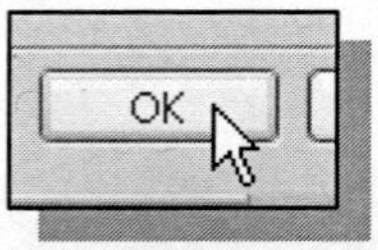

5. Click **OK** to accept the selection of the *sketch plane.*

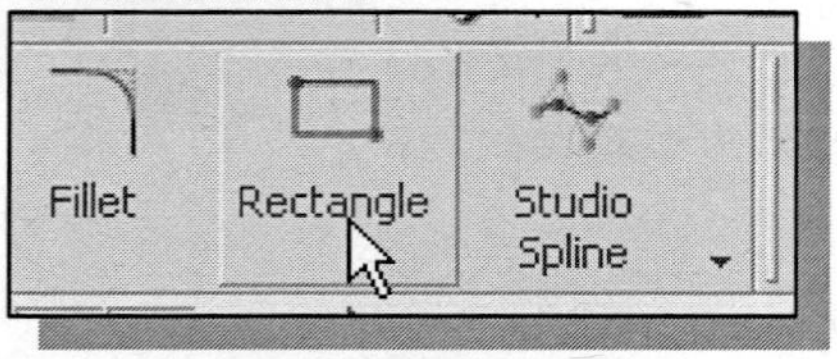

6. Activate the **Rectangle** command by clicking the corresponding icon as shown.

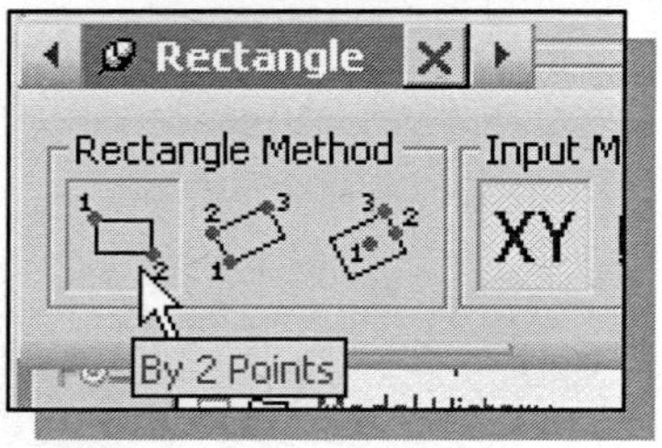

7. Confirm the **By 2 Points** option is activated.

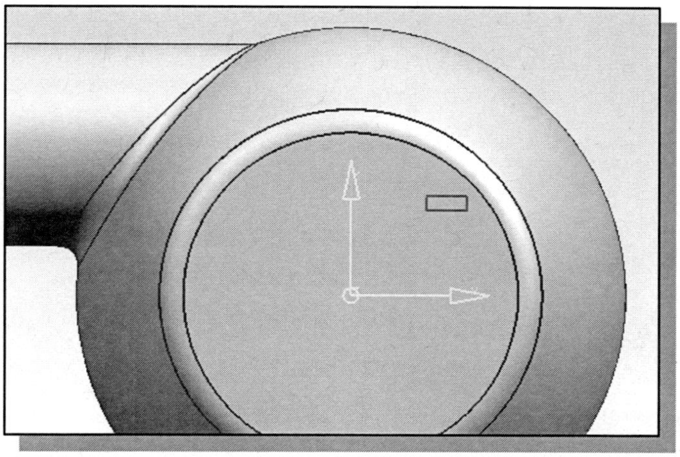

8. Create a rectangle of arbitrary size that is toward the right side of the graphics window as shown.

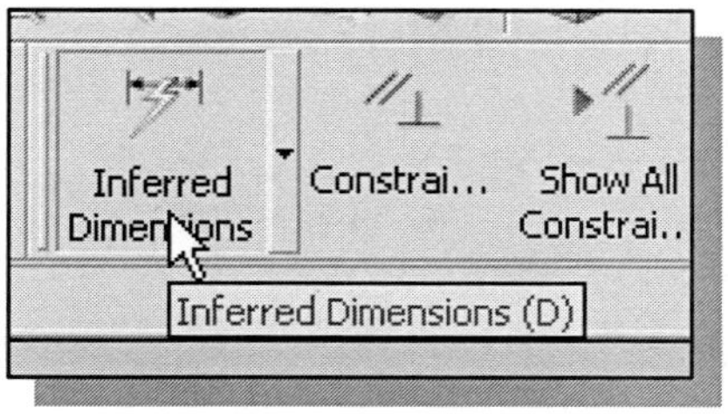

9. Select the **Inferred Dimensions** command in the *Sketch Constraints* toolbar as shown.

10. On your own, create and modify the dimensions as shown in the figure below.

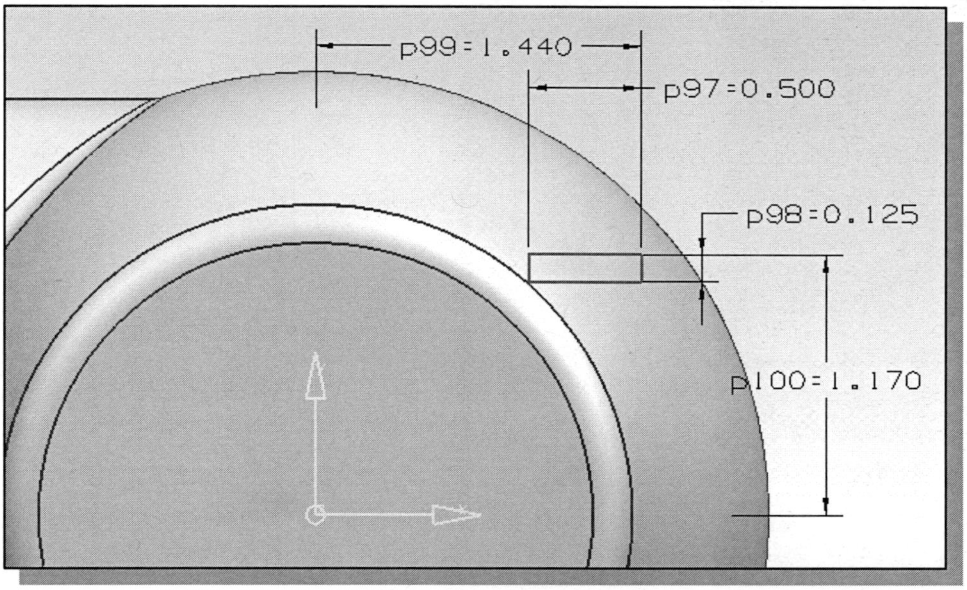

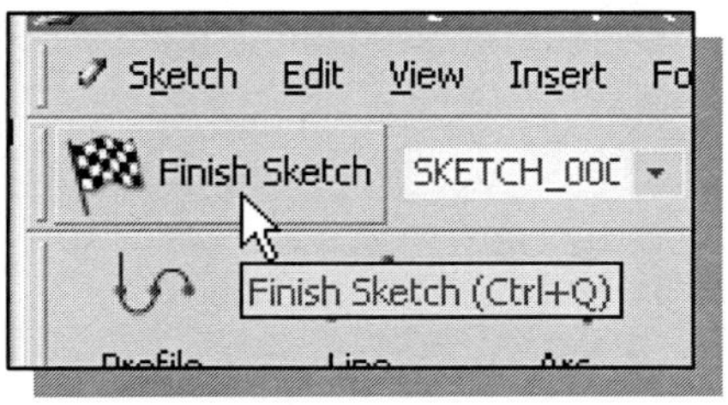

11. Click **Finish Sketch** to exit the *NX Sketcher* mode and return to the *Feature* option dialog window.

12. In the *Extrude* dialog box, set the *Boolean* option to **Subtract** as shown.

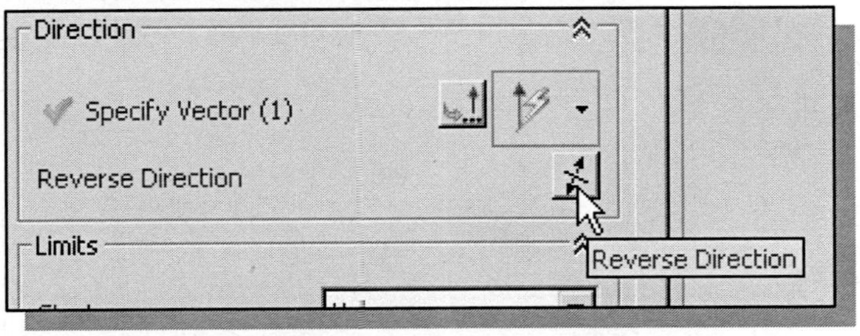

13. Click the **Reverse Direction** icon to make the cut into the solid model.

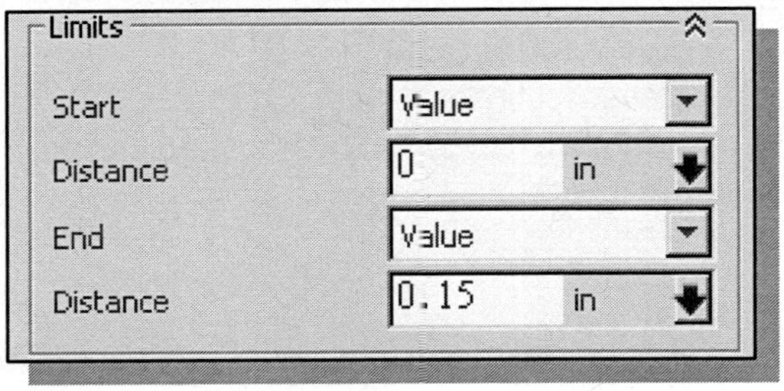

14. Set the *End* limit to **0.15** as shown.

15. In the *Extrude* dialog box, click **OK** to proceed with creating the subtract feature.

- Note that the pattern leader created is a fairly small cut on the solid model.

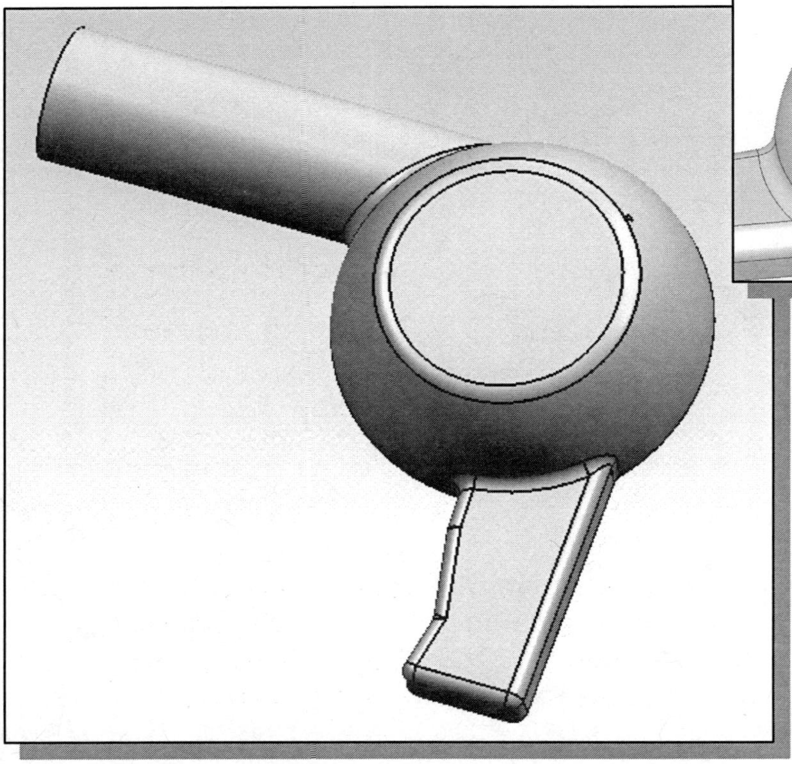

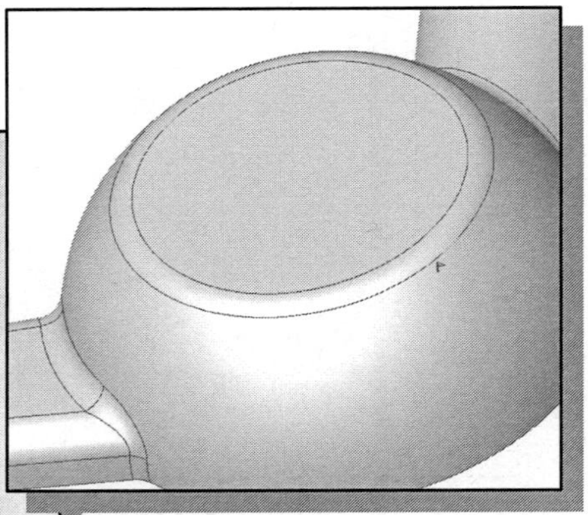

Creating a Rectangular Array

- In *UGS NX*, existing features can be easily duplicated. The **Array** commands allow us to create both rectangular and circular arrays of features. The arrayed features are parametrically linked to the original feature; any modifications to the original feature are also reflected on the arrayed features.

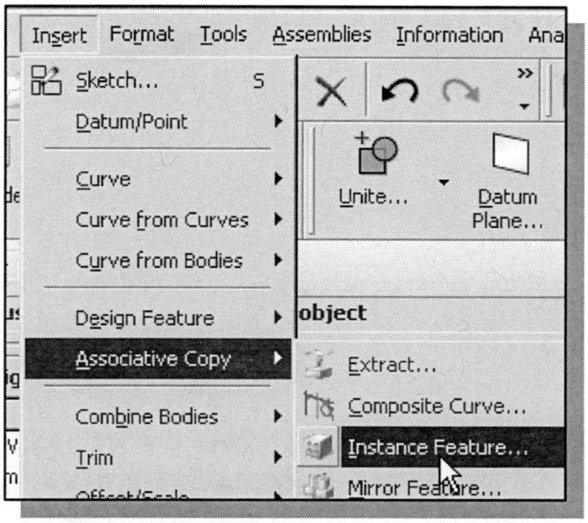

1. Select the **Associative Copy** command through the *Insert* pull-down menu:

   [Insert] → [Associative Copy] → [Instance Feature]

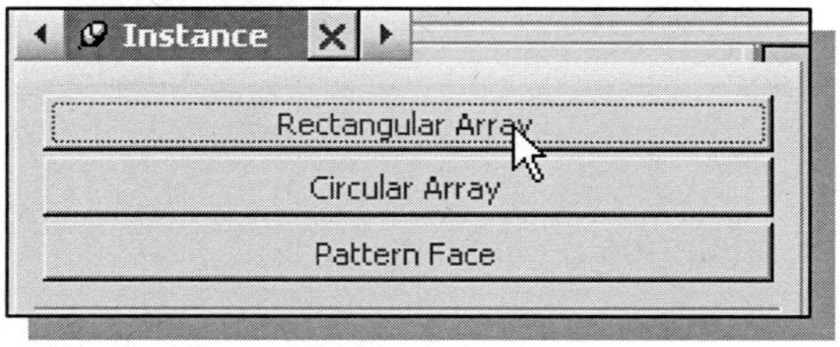

2. In the *Instance* window, select the **Rectangular Array** command by clicking the left-mouse-button on the icon.

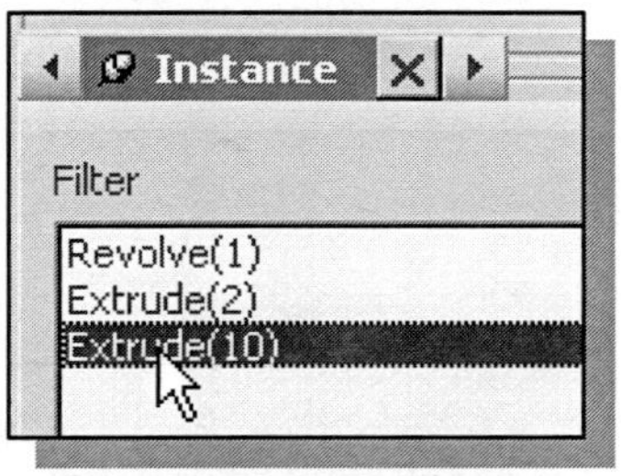

3. Choose the last feature, the *Extrude* feature, in the *Instance* window as shown.

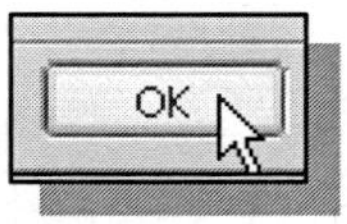

4. Click **OK** to proceed to the next step.

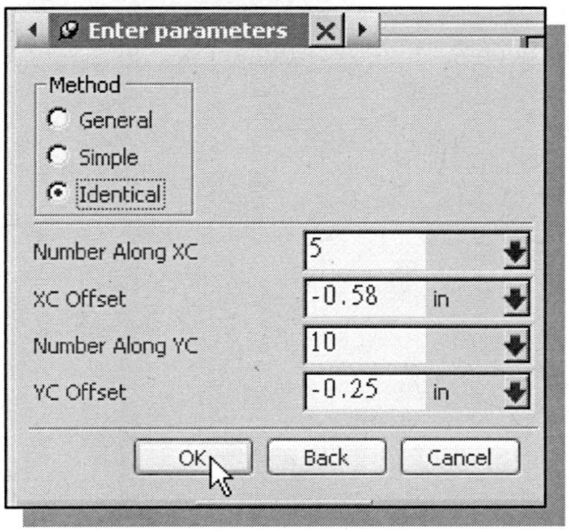

5. In the *Enter Parameters* dialog box, set the *Method* option to **Identical** as shown.

6. Enter **5** in the *Number Along XC* box and **-0.6** in the *XC Offset* box as shown.

7. Enter **10** in the *Number Along YC* box, and enter **-0.25** in the *YC Offset* box as shown.

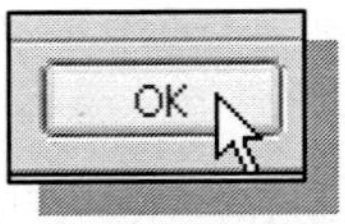

8. Click **OK** in the option to proceed with the Rectangular Array command.

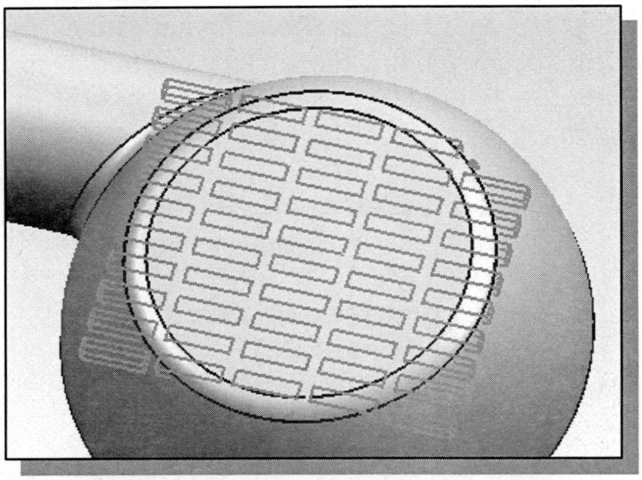

➤ On the screen, a preview of the rectangular array is displayed as shown.

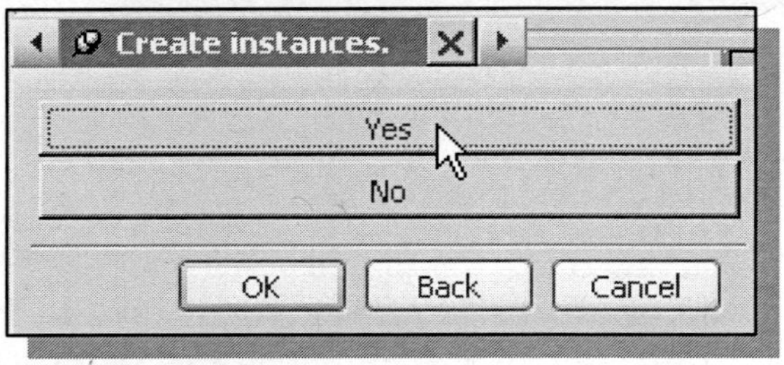

9. Click **Yes** in the option to proceed with the creation of the ***rectangular array***.

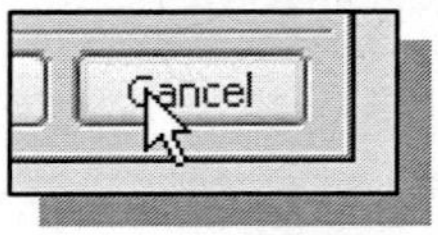

10. Click **Cancel** to exit the Instance command.

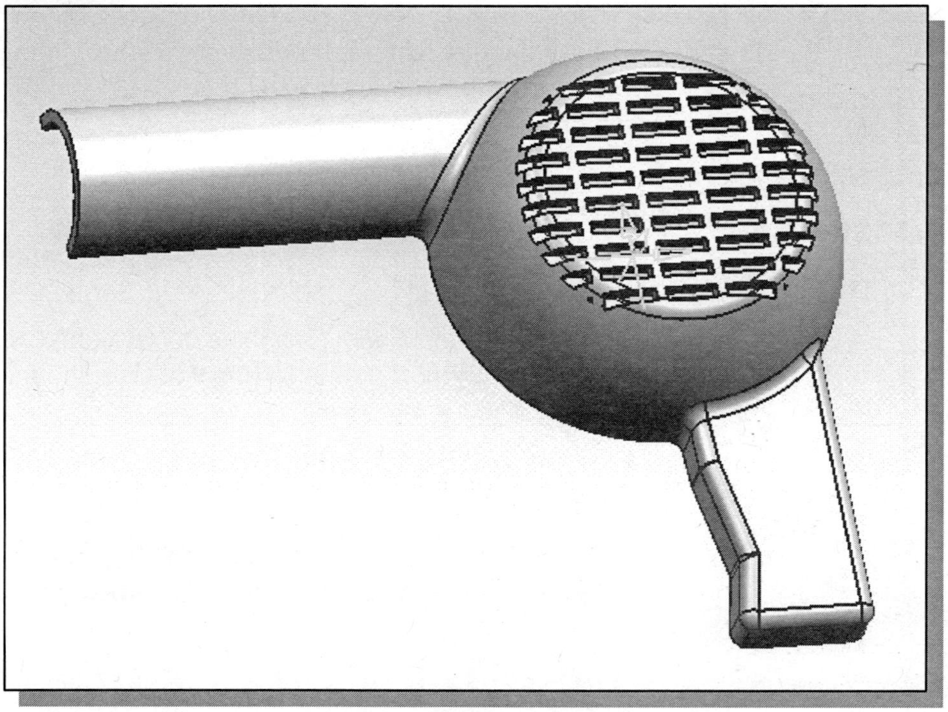

Creating a Swept Cut Feature

❖ The **Sweep** operation is defined as moving a planar section through a planar(2D) or 3D path in space to form a three-dimensional solid object. The path can be an open curve or a closed loop, but must be on an intersecting plane with the section. The **Extrude** operation, which we have used in the previous lessons, is a specific type of sweep. The **Extrude** operation is also known as a ***linear sweep*** operation, in which the sweep control path is always a line perpendicular to the two-dimensional section. Linear sweeps of unchanging shape result in what are generally called ***prismatic solids*** which means solids with a constant cross-section from end to end. In *UGS NX*, we create a ***swept feature*** by defining a path and then a 2D sketch of a cross section. The sketched profile is then swept along the planar path. The Sweep along Guide operation is used for objects that have uniform shapes along a trajectory.

➢ Define the Sweep Section

1. In the *Form Feature* toolbar's *Standard* toolbar, select the **Sketch** command by left-clicking once on the icon.

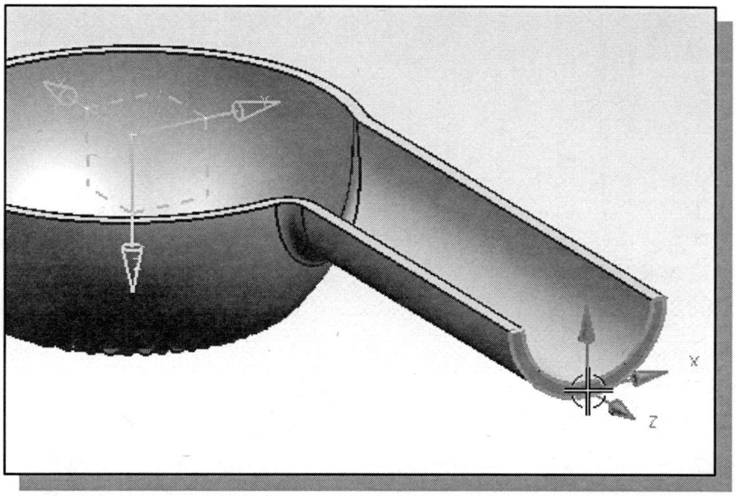

2. Select the plane on the **circular end** of the model to align the *sketch plane* as shown.

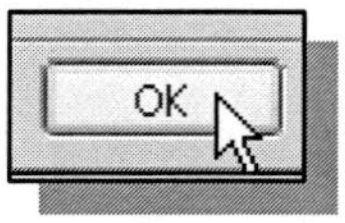

3. Click **OK** to accept the selection of the *sketch plane.*

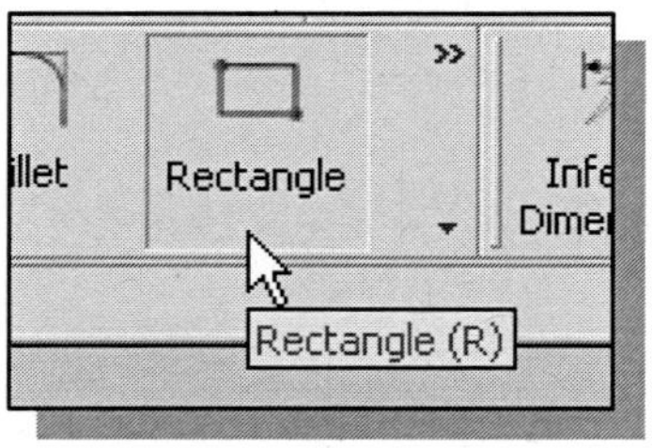

4. Activate the **Rectangle** command and choose the **By 2 Points** option.

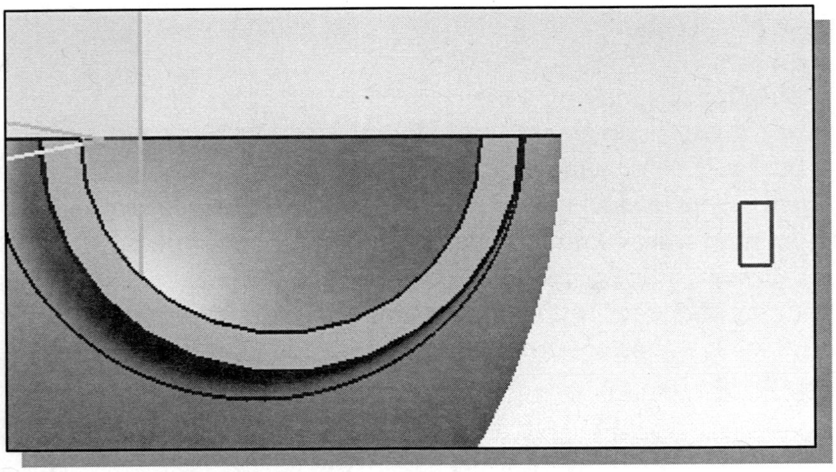

5. On your own, create a rectangle that is toward the right side of the model as shown.

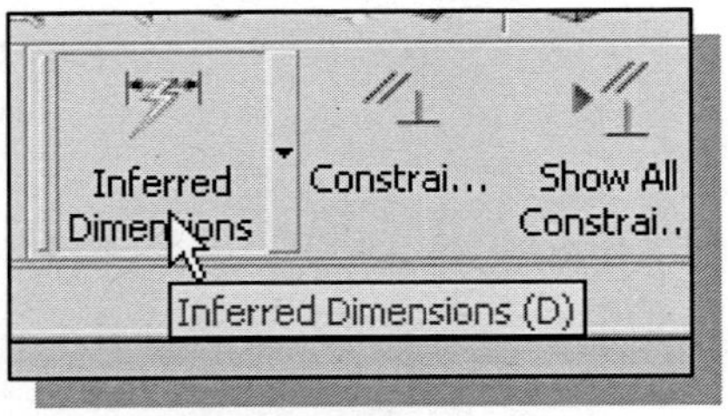

6. Select the **Inferred Dimensions** command in the *Sketch Constraints* toolbar as shown.

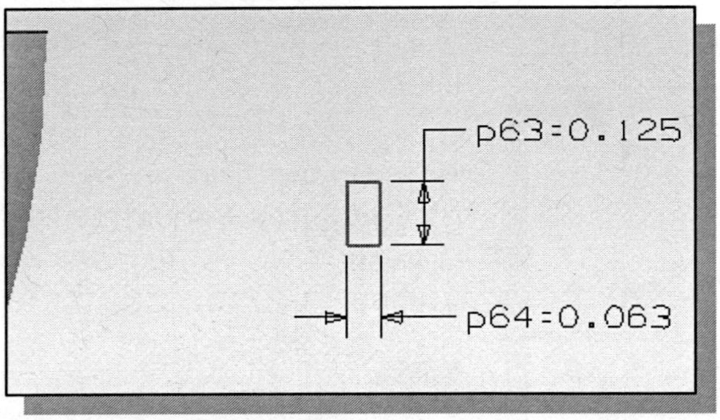

7. Create the two size dimensions of the rectangle as shown in the figure.

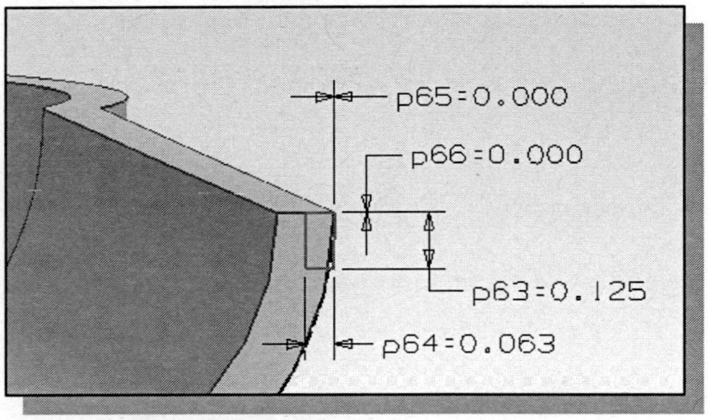

8. Using the endpoint of the larger arc as reference, create the two location dimensions to fully constrain the sketch as shown in the figure.

9. Click **Finish Sketch** to exit the *NX Sketcher* mode and end the *Sketch* option.

➢ Create the Swept feature

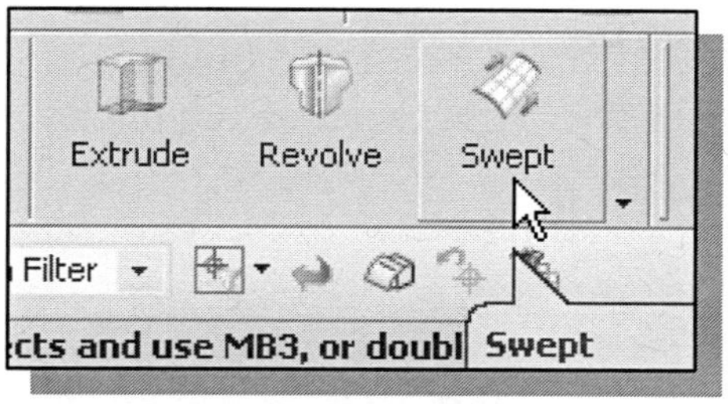

1. Select the **Swept** command in the *2D Sketch Panel* as shown.

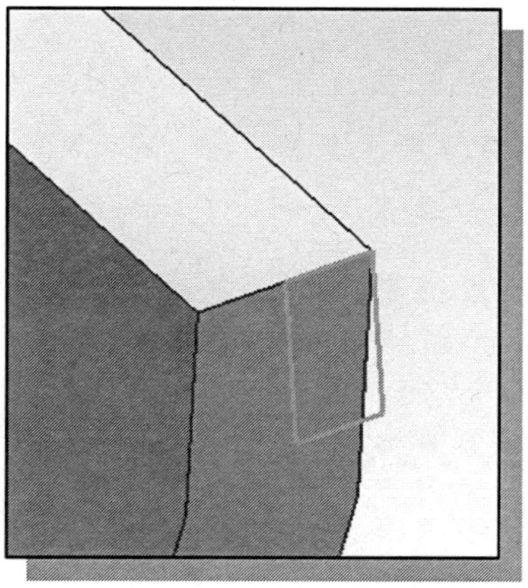

2. Select the four segments of the **rectangle** as the *section string* as shown. (Hint: Use the dynamic zoom function to assist the selection.)

3. Click on the **Guide** icon to activate the *Guide Selection* option.

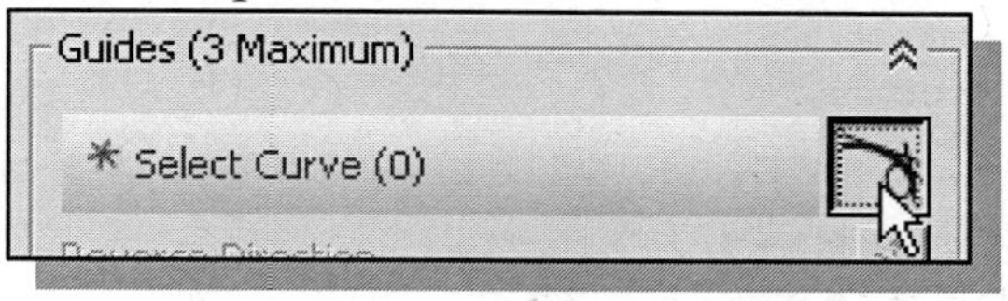

4. Select the adjacent straight line connected to the top corner of the rectangle.

5. Continue to select all of the outer edges as shown.

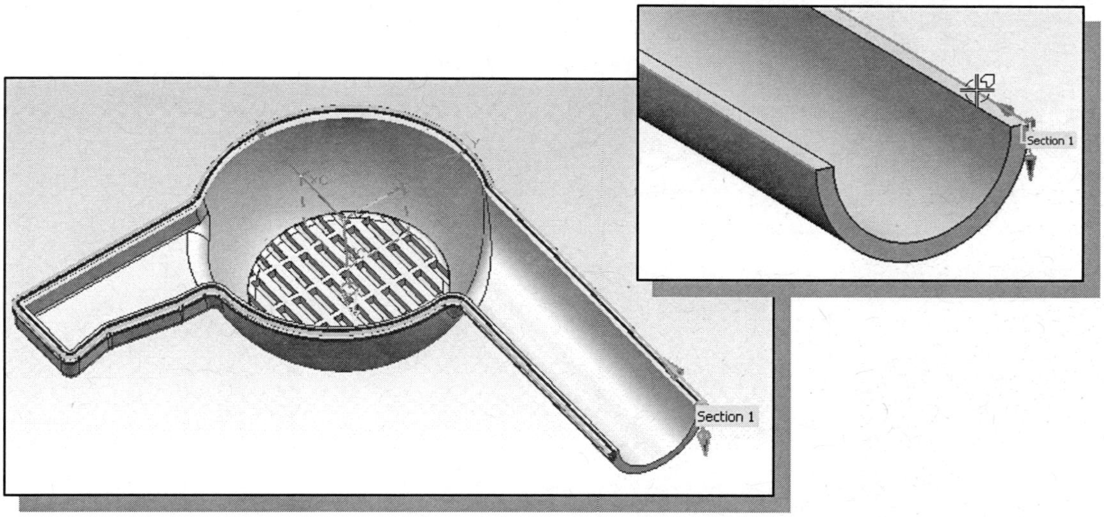

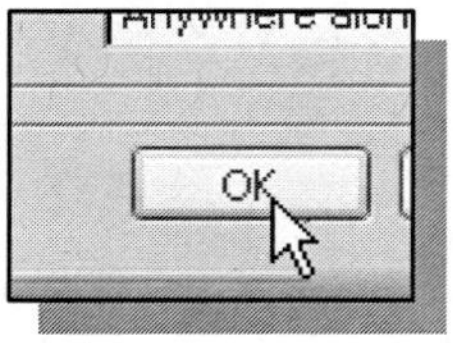

6. Click **OK** to accept the selections and create the swept feature.

➢ Note the swept feature is a separate solid from the dryer housing, a Boolean subtract is needed to combine the two solids.

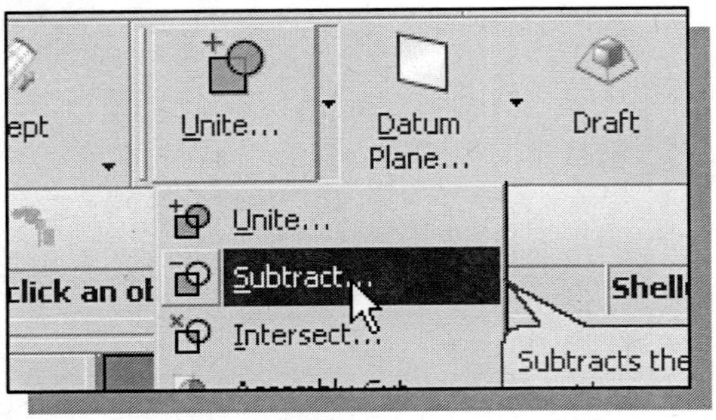

7. Click the **Subtract** icon to perform the cut operation of the swept feature from the existing model.

8. Select the **main body** of the *Dryer Housing* model as the *Target body.*

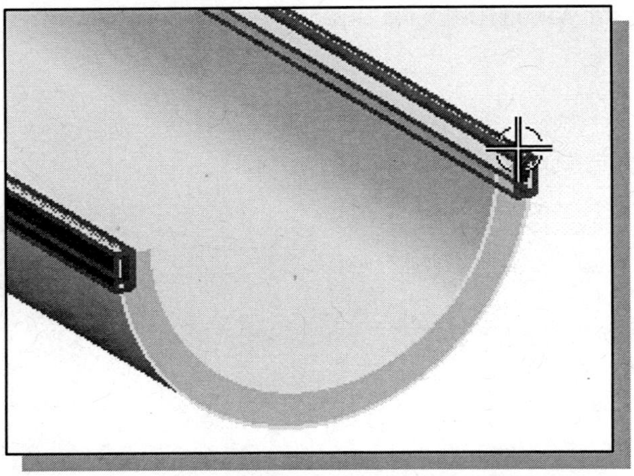

9. Select the **swept feature** as the *Tool body.*

10. In the *Subtract* dialog box, click **OK** to proceed with the operation and complete the model.

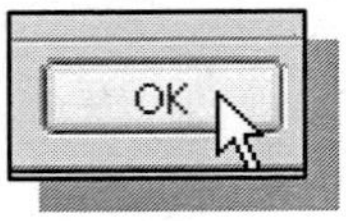

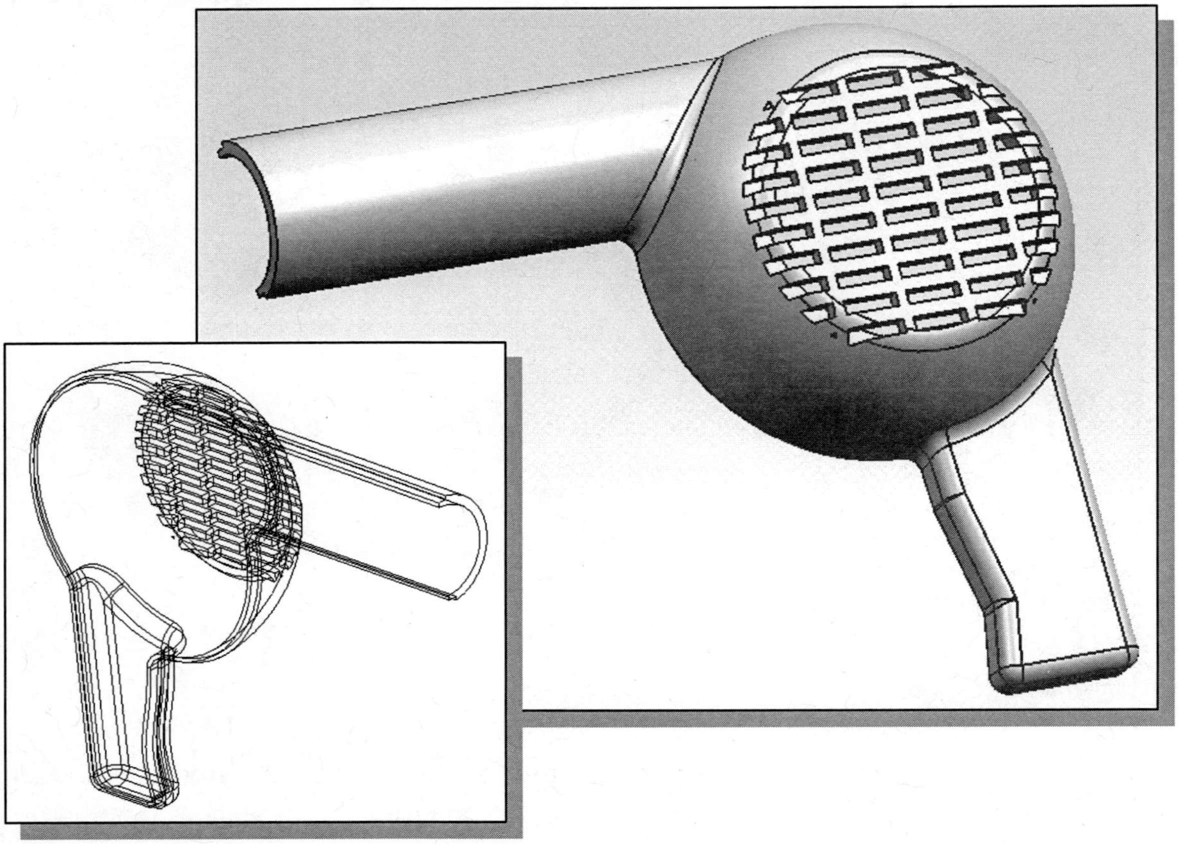

Questions:

1. Keeping the *History Tree* in mind, what is the difference between *subtract with a pattern* and *subtract each one individually*?

2. What is the difference between **Sweep** and **Extrude**?

3. What are the advantages and disadvantages of creating fillets using the **3D Fillets** command and creating fillets in the 2D profiles?

4. Describe the steps used to create the *Shell* feature in the lesson.

5. How do we modify the *Array* parameters after the model is built?

6. Describe the elements required in creating a *Swept* feature.

7. Create sketches showing the steps you plan to use to create the model shown on the next page:

Exercises:

1. Dimensions are in inches.

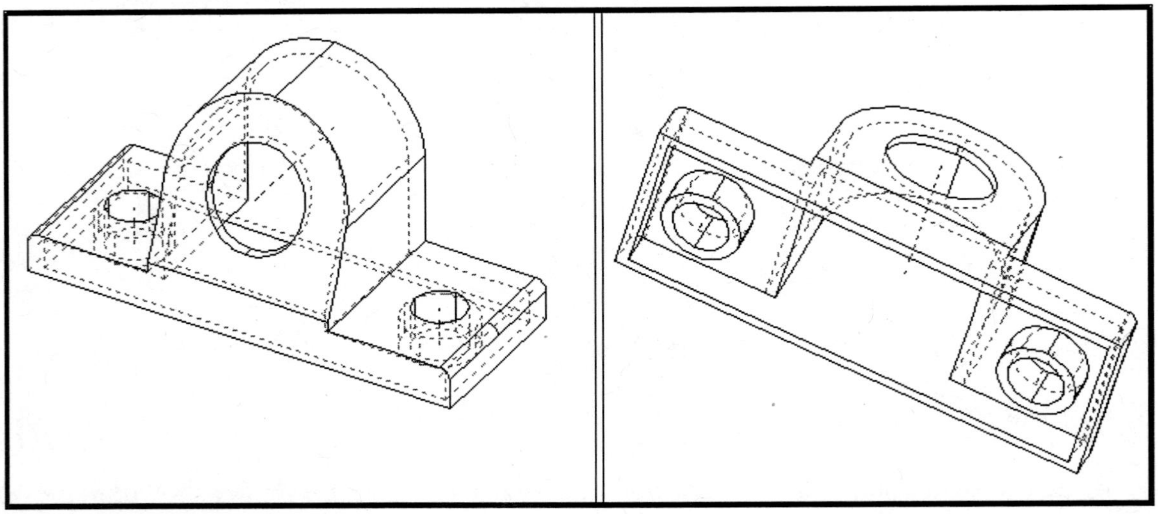

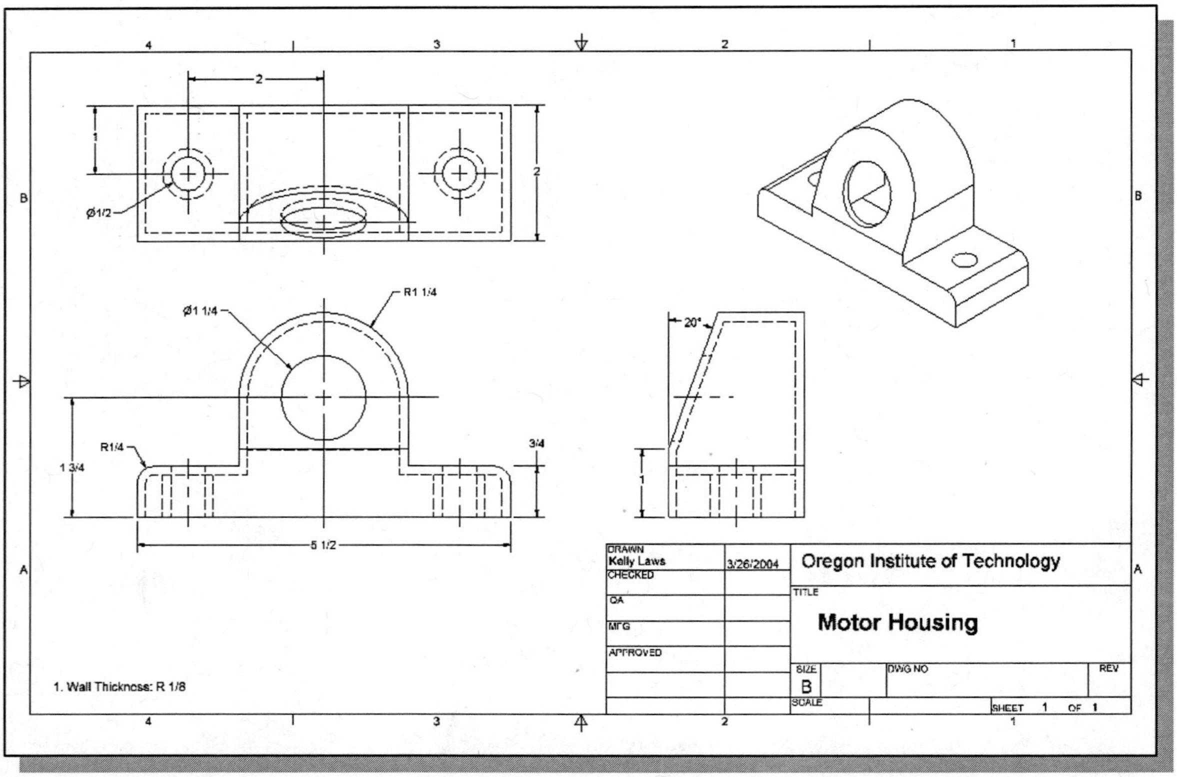

2. Using the same dimensions given in the tutorial, construct the other half of the dryer housing. Plan ahead, and consider how you would create the matching half of the design? (Save both parts so that you can create an assembly model once you have completed chapter 12.)

3. Dimensions are in inches.

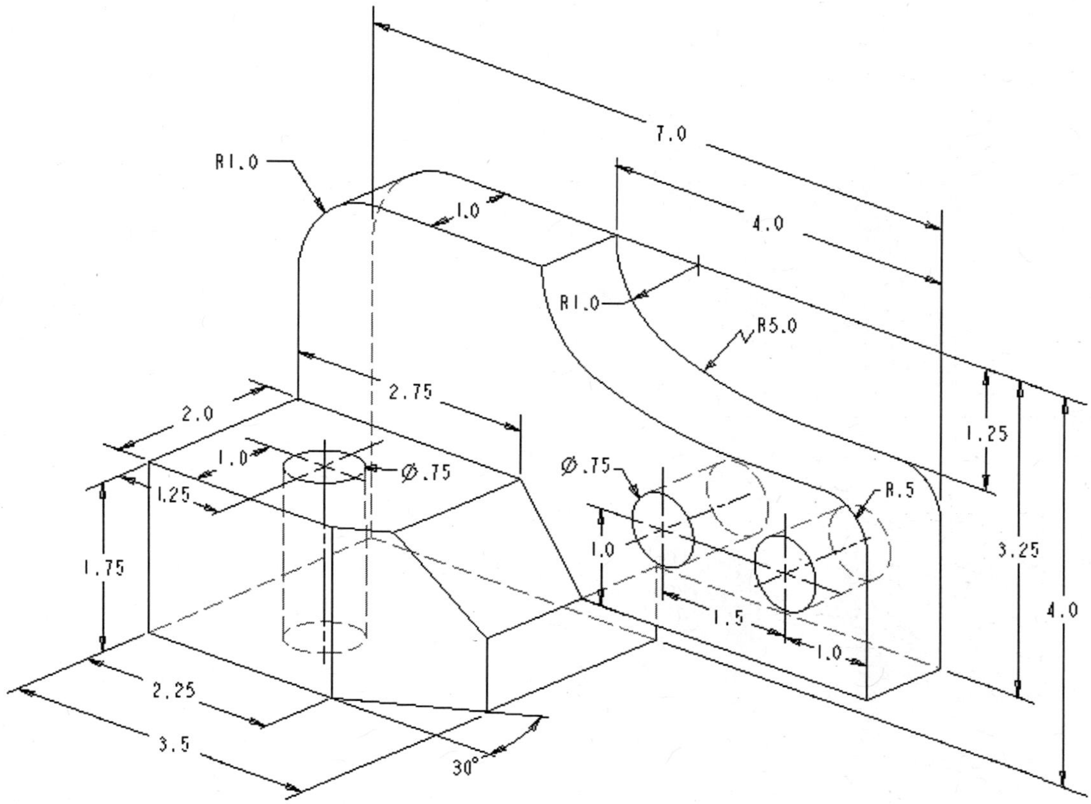

Notes:

Chapter 12
Assembly Modeling – Putting It All Together

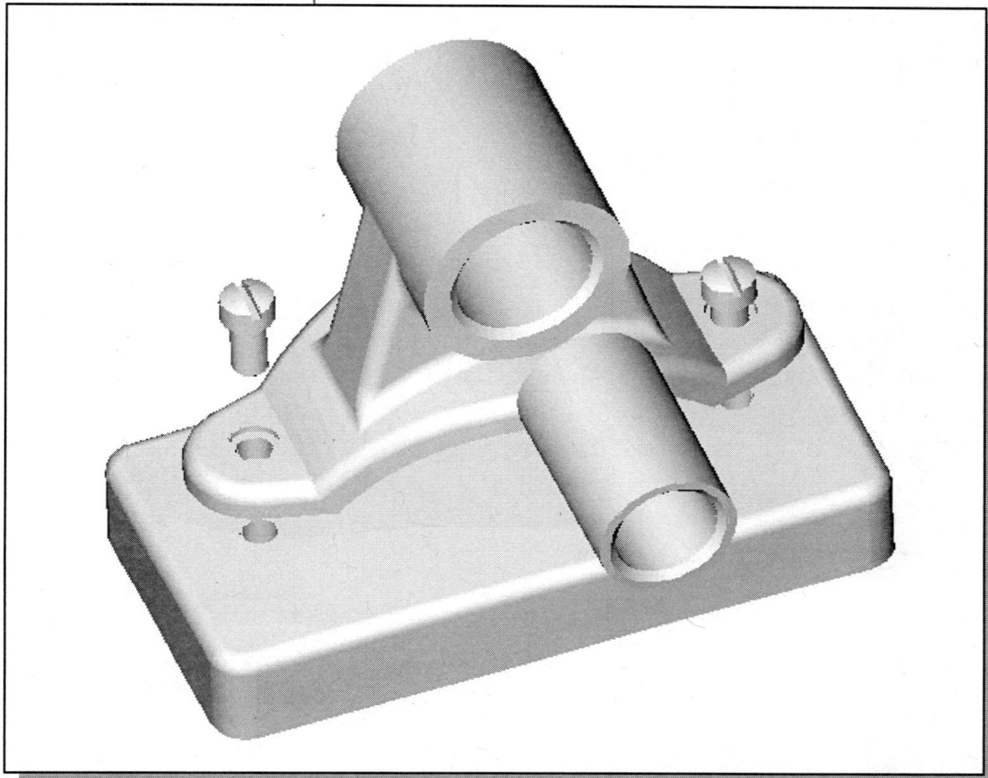

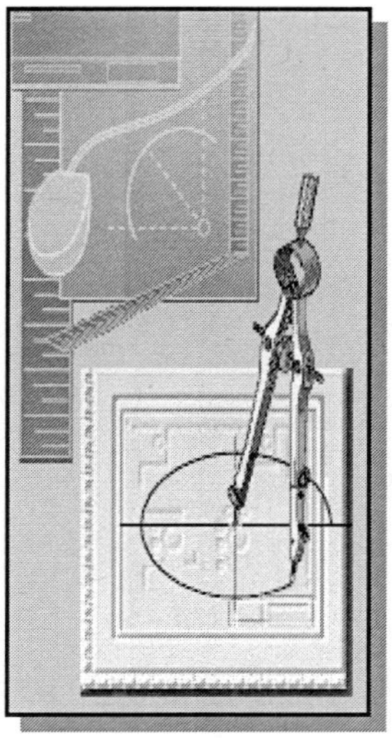

Learning Objectives

- Understand the Assembly Modeling Methodology
- Add Existing Parts in the Assembly Modeler Mode
- Understand and Utilize Assembly Constraints
- Understand the Degrees of Freedom concept
- Create Exploded Assemblies
- Create an Assembly Drawing from the Solid Model

Introduction

In the previous lessons, we have gone over the fundamentals of creating basic parts and drawings. In this lesson, we will examine the assembly modeling functionality of *UGS NX*. We will start with a demonstration on how to create and modify assembly models. The main task in creating an assembly is establishing the assembly relationships between parts. To assemble parts into an assembly, we will need to consider the assembly relationships between parts. It is a good practice to assemble parts based on the way they would be assembled in the actual manufacturing process. We should also consider breaking down the assembly into smaller subassemblies, which helps the management of parts. In *UGS NX*, a subassembly is treated the same way as a single part during assembly. Many parallels exist between assembly modeling and part modeling in parametric modeling software such as *UGS NX*.

UGS NX provides full associative functionality in all design modules, including assemblies. When we change a part model, *UGS NX* will automatically reflect the changes in all assemblies that use the part. We can also modify a part in an assembly. **Full associative functionality** is the main feature of parametric solid modeling software that allows us to increase productivity by reducing design cycle time.

The *Shaft-Support* Assembly

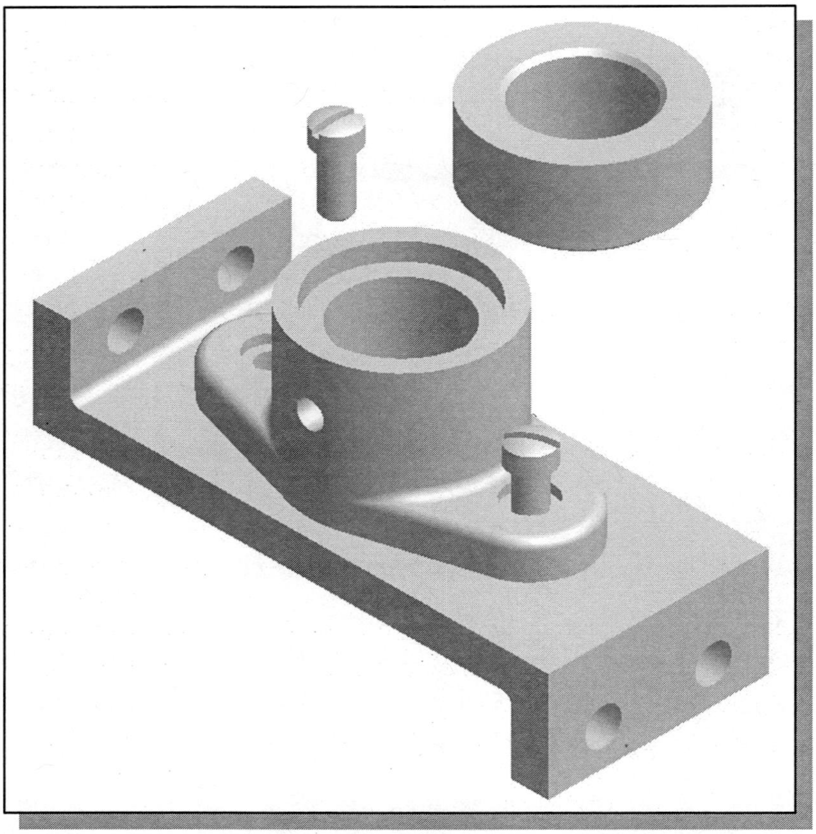

Assembly Modeling Methodology

The *UGS NX* assembly modeler provides tools and functions that allow us to create 3D parametric assembly models. An assembly model is a 3D model with any combination of multiple part models. *Parametric assembly constraints* can be used to control relationships between parts in an assembly model.

UGS NX can work with any of the assembly modeling methodologies:

The Bottom Up approach

The first step in the *bottom up* assembly modeling approach is to create the individual parts. The parts are then pulled together into an assembly. This approach is typically used for smaller projects with very few team members.

The Top Down approach

The first step in the *top down* assembly modeling approach is to create the assembly model of the project. Initially, individual parts are represented by names or symbolically. The details of the individual parts are added as the project gets further along. This approach is typically used for larger projects or during the conceptual design stage. Members of the project team can then concentrate on the particular section of the project to which he/she is assigned.

The Middle Out approach

The *middle out* assembly modeling approach is a mixture of the bottom-up and top-down methods. This type of assembly model is usually constructed with most of the parts already created and additional parts are designed and created using the assembly for construction information. Some requirements are known and some standard components are used, but new designs must also be produced to meet specific objectives. This combined strategy is a very flexible approach for creating assembly models.

The different assembly modeling approaches described above can be used as guidelines to manage design projects. Keep in mind that we can start modeling our assembly using one approach and then switch to a different approach without any problems.

In this lesson, the *bottom up* assembly modeling approach is illustrated. All of the parts (components) required to form the assembly are created first. *UGS NX's* assembly modeling tools allow us to create complex assemblies by using components that are created in part files or are placed in assembly files. A component can be a subassembly or a single part, where features and parts can be modified at any time. The sketches and profiles used to build part features can be fully or partially constrained. Partially constrained features may be adaptive, which means the size or shape of the associated parts are adjusted in an assembly when the parts are constrained to other parts. The basic concept and procedure of using the adaptive assembly approach is demonstrated in the tutorial.

Additional Parts

- Four parts are required for the assembly: (1) ***Collar***, (2) ***Bearing***, (3) ***Base-Plate*** and (4) ***Cap-Screw***. Create the four parts as shown below, then save the models as separate part files: *Collar*, *Bearing*, *Base-Plate*, and *Cap-Screw*. (Close all part files or exit *UGS NX* after you have created the parts.)

(1) ***Collar***

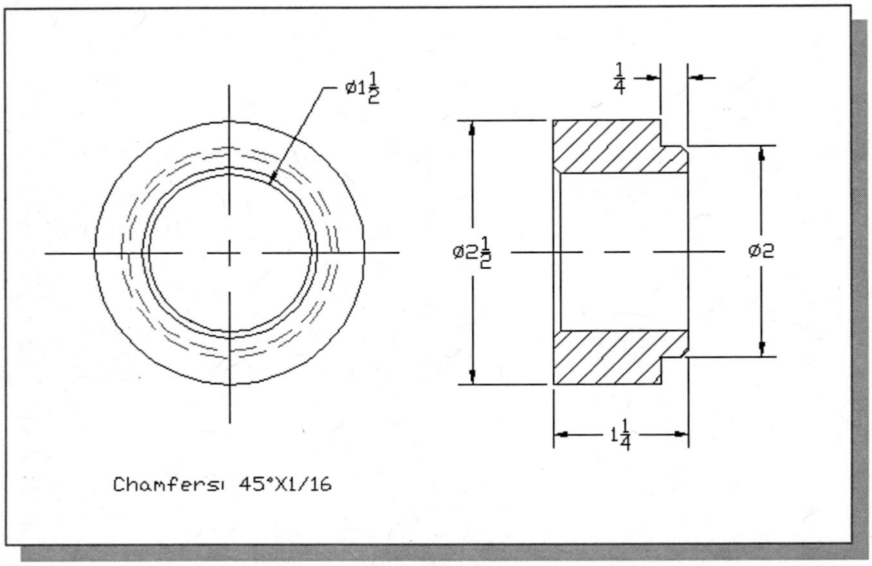

(2) ***Bearing*** (Construct the part with the datum origin aligned to the bottom center.)

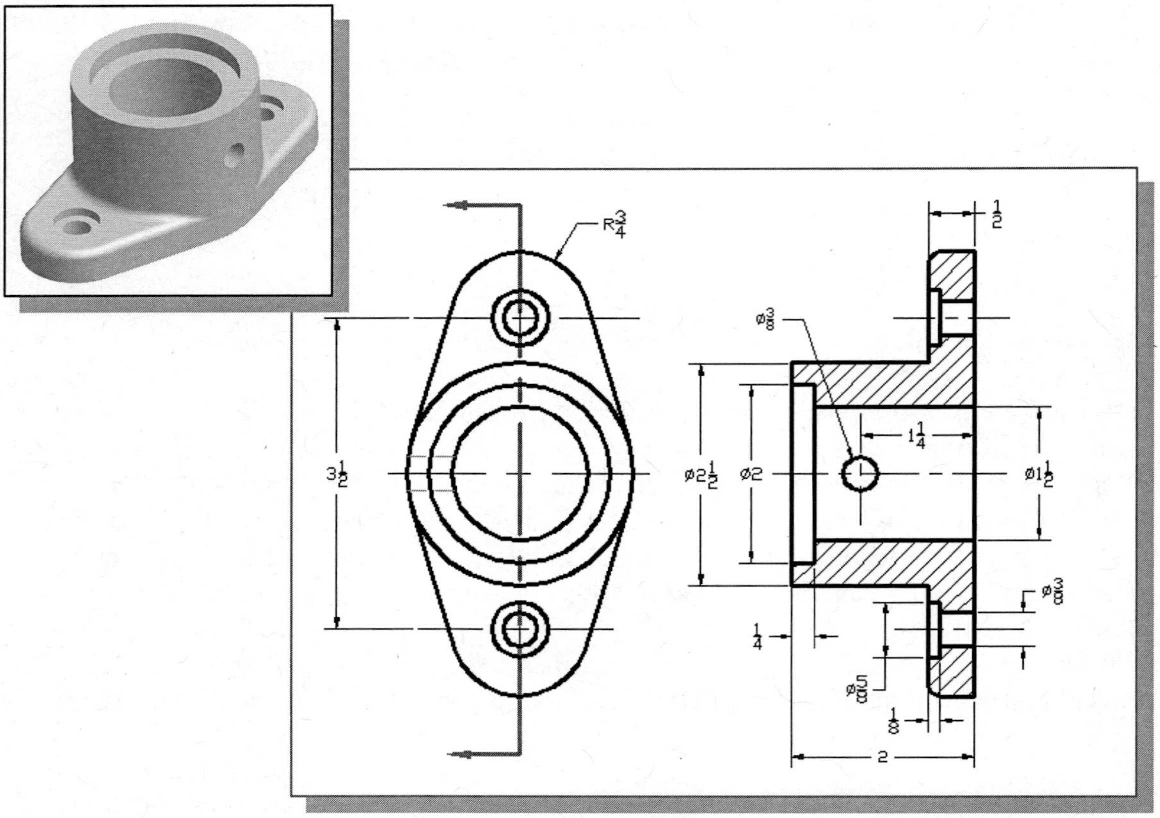

(3) ***Base-Plate*** (Construct the part with the datum origin aligned to the bottom center.)

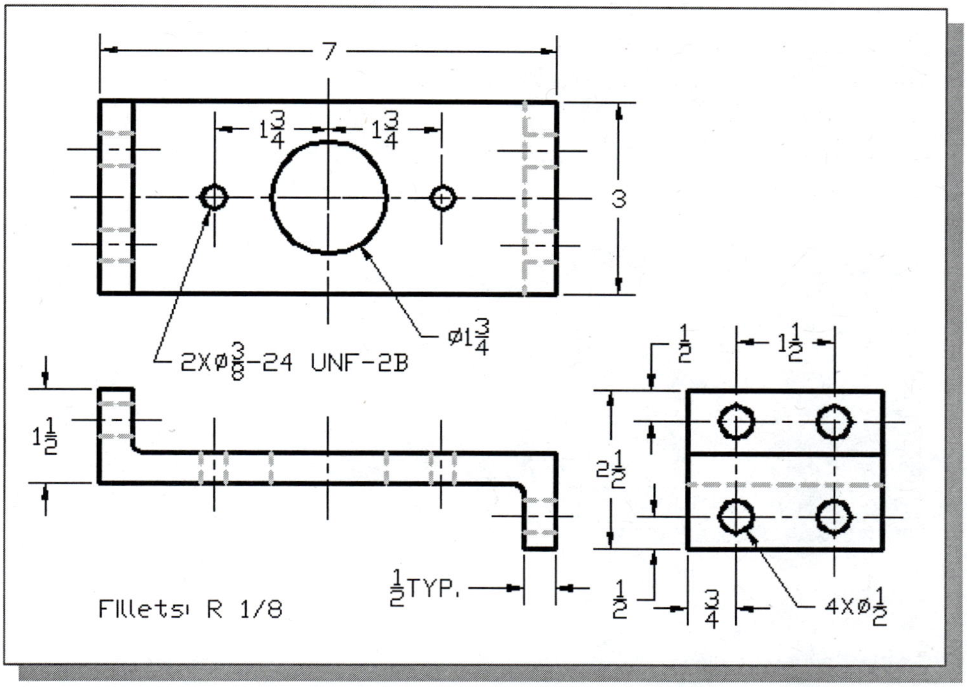

(4) ***Cap-Screw***

➢ We will omit the threads in this model. Threads contain complex three-dimensional curves and surfaces; it will slow down the display considerably. Hint: create a revolved feature using the profile shown below.

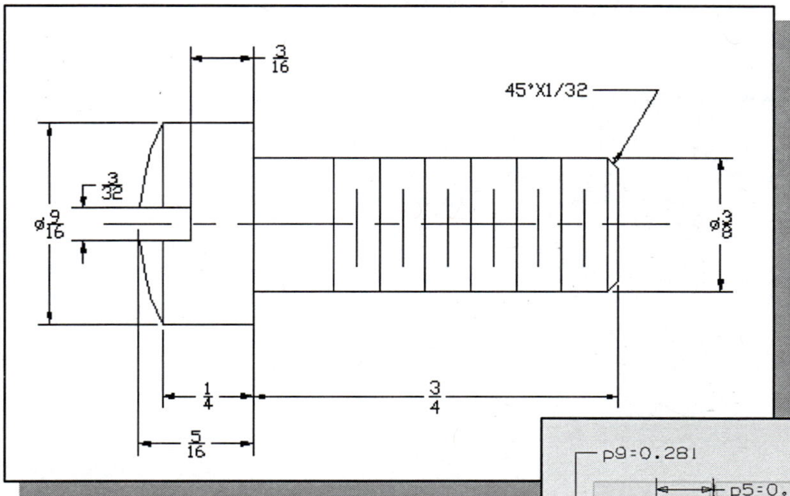

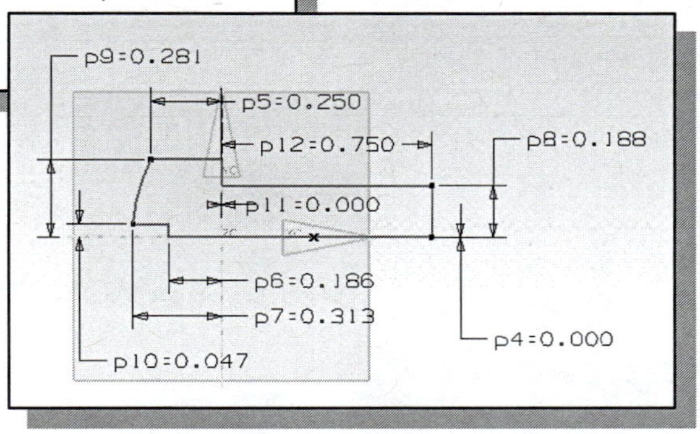

Starting *UGS NX*

1. Select the **UGS NX** option on the *Start* menu or select the **UGS NX** icon on the desktop to start *UGS NX*. The *UGS NX* main window will appear on the screen.

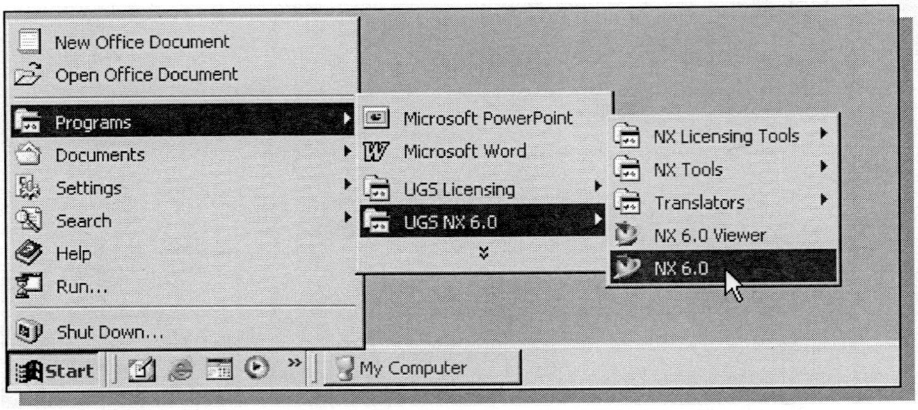

2. Select the **New** icon with a single click of the left-mouse-button (MB1) in the *Standard* toolbar area.

3. Select **Inches** for the *Units* as shown in the figure below.

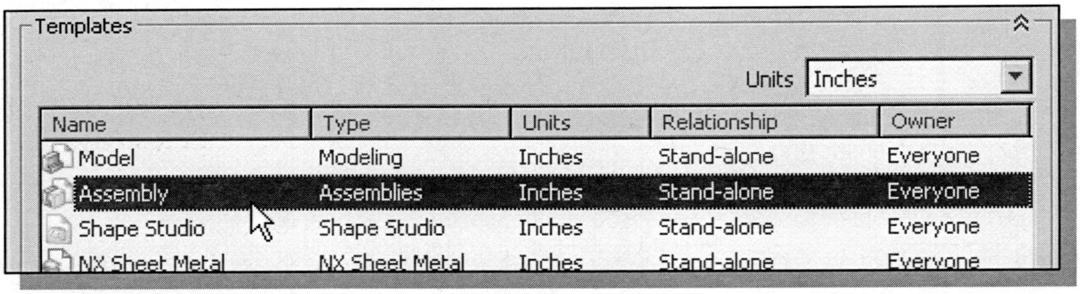

4. Select **Assembly** in the *Templates* list. Note that the *Assembly* template will allow us to switch directly into the *Assemblies* task with settings related to creating assembly models.

5. In the *New File Name* area, enter **Shaft-Support** as the file *Name*.

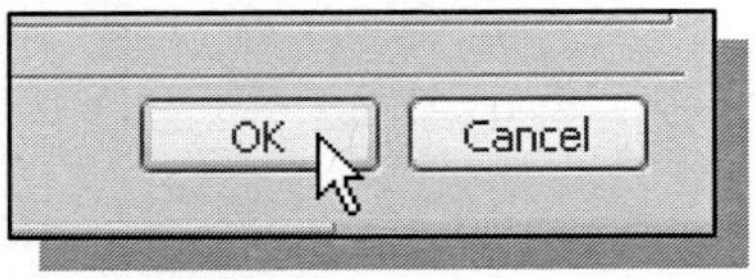

6. Click **OK** to proceed with the New File command.

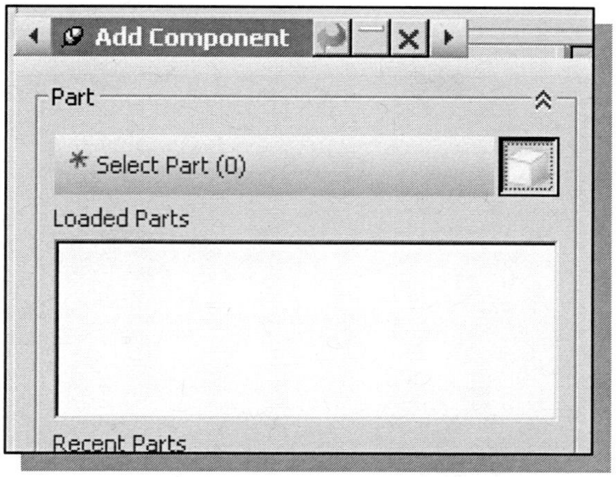

➢ Notice the **Add Component** command is automatically activated. Currently there are no loaded parts, as indicated in the ***Loaded Parts*** area shown in the figure.

Loading and Placing the First Component

- The first component placed in an assembly should be a fundamental part or subassembly. The first component in an assembly file sets the orientation of all subsequent parts and subassemblies. The origin of the first component is aligned to the origin of the assembly coordinates and the part is grounded (all degrees of freedom are removed). The rest of the assembly is built on the first component, the ***base component***. In most cases, this *base component* should be one that is **not likely to be removed** and **preferably a non-moving part** in the design. Note that there is no distinction in an assembly between components; the first component we place is usually considered as the *base component* because it is usually a fundamental component to which others are constrained. For our project, we will use the ***Base-Plate*** as the base component in the assembly.

1. In the ***Add Component*** window, click **Open** to load an existing part.

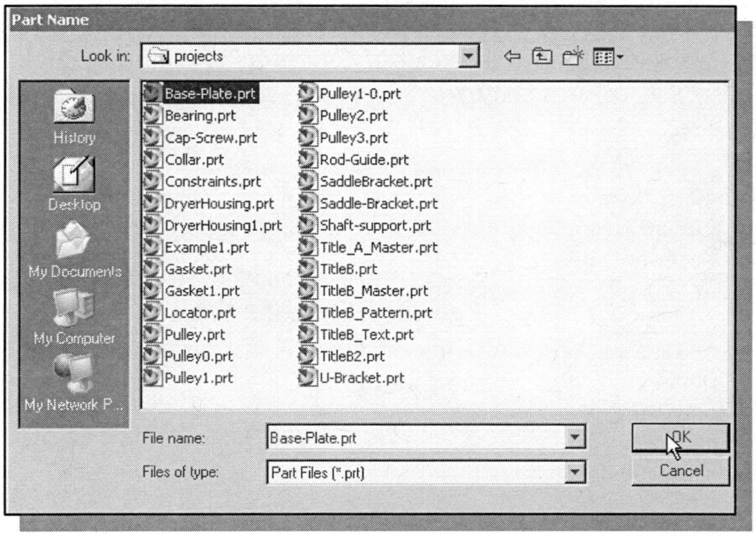

2. Select the ***Base-Plate*** (part file: ***Base-Plate.prt***) in the list window.

3. Click **OK** to accept the selection.

➢ By default, the selected component is displayed in a separate preview window. Notice that we can also place multiple copies of the same component.

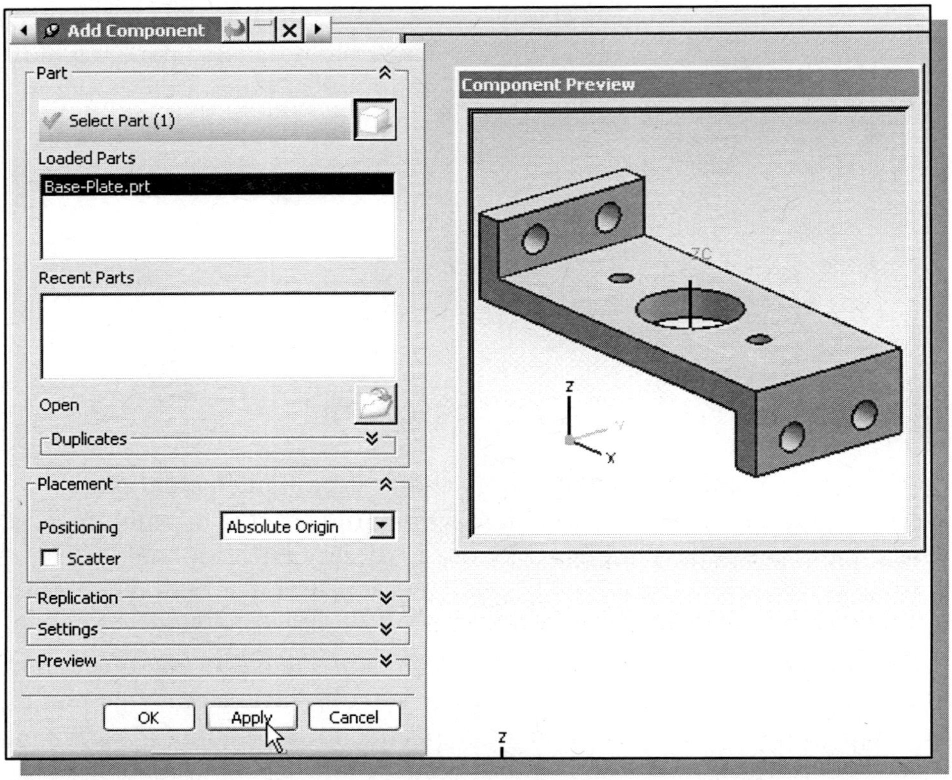

4. Set the *Placement* option to the **Absolute Origin** of the default assembly coordinate system as shown.

5. Click **OK** to accept the settings and place the part.

Placing the Second Component

➢ We will retrieve the *Bearing* part as the second component of the assembly model.

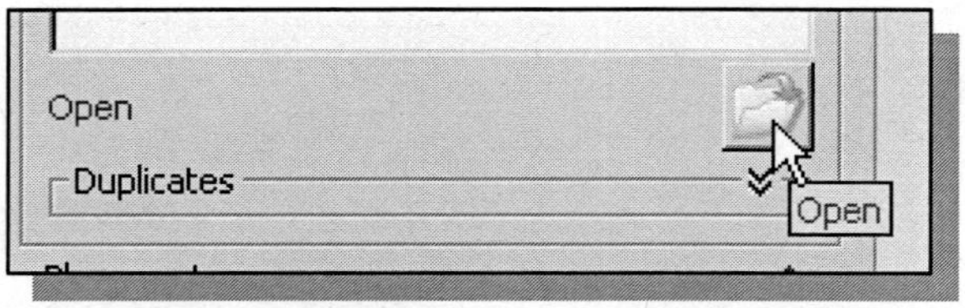

1. In the ***Add Component*** window, click **Open** to load an existing part.

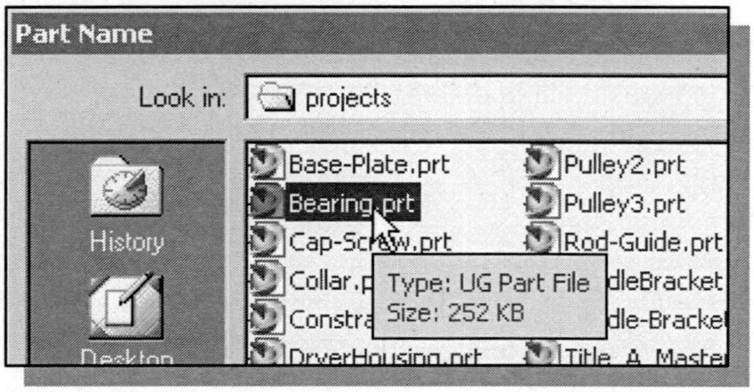

2. Select the ***Bearing*** design (part file: ***Bearing.prt***) in the list window. Click on the **OK** button to retrieve the model.

3. Set the *Placement* method is set to **By Constraints** as shown in the figure.

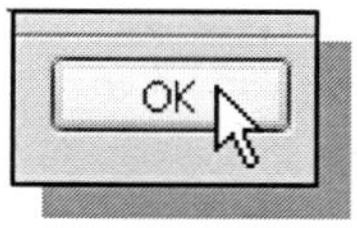

4. Click **OK** to accept the selection and proceed to load the ***Bearing*** file.

Degrees of Freedom and Assembly Constraints

- Each component in an assembly has six **degrees of freedom (DOF)**, or ways in which rigid 3D bodies can move: movement along the *X*, *Y*, and *Z* axes (translational freedom), plus rotation around the *X*, *Y*, and *Z* axes (rotational freedom). *Linear DOF*s allow the part to move in the direction of the specified vector. *Rotational DOF*s allow the part to turn about the specified axis.

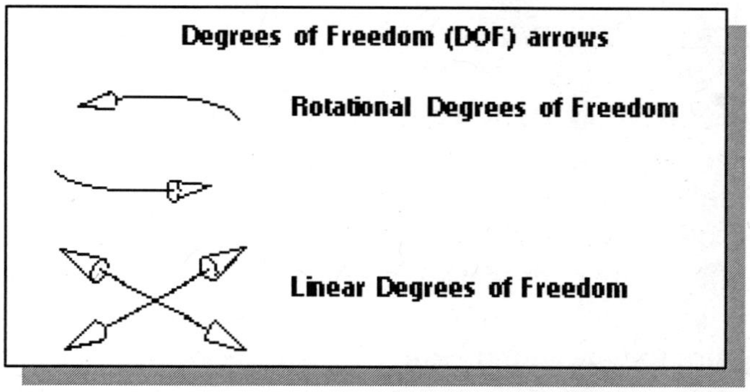

- In parametric modeling, the degrees-of-freedom symbol generally shows the remaining degrees of freedom (both translational and rotational) for one or more components of the active assembly. When a component is fully constrained in an assembly, the component cannot move in any direction. The position of the component is fixed relative to other assembly components. All of its degrees of freedom are removed. When we place an assembly constraint between two selected components, they are positioned relative to one another. Movement is still possible in the unconstrained directions.

➢ It is usually a good idea to fully constrain components so that their behavior is predictable as changes are made to the assembly. Leaving some degrees of freedom open can sometimes help retain design flexibility. As a general rule, we should use only enough constraints to ensure predictable assembly behavior and avoid unnecessary complexity.

- We are now ready to assemble the components together. We will start by placing assembly constraints on the ***Bearing*** and the ***Base-Plate***.

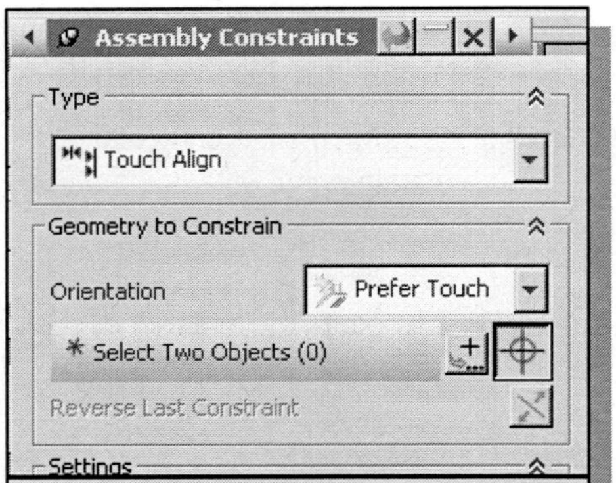

➤ Notice the ***Add Constraints*** window appears on the screen. The **assembly constraints** are used to define the relations between mating parts.

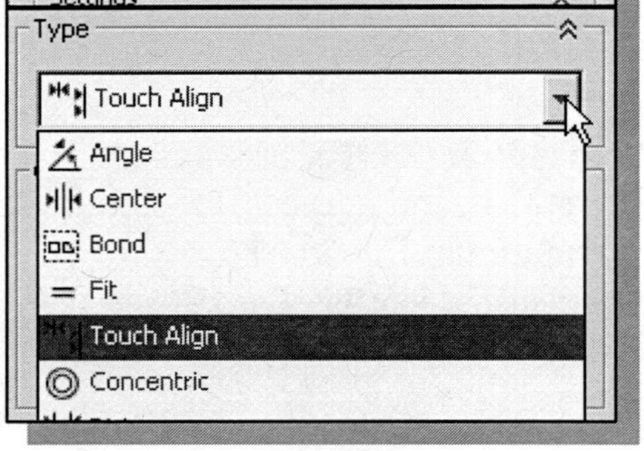

5. Click on the down-arrow to display the different types of assembly constraints that are available

To assemble components into an assembly, we need to establish the assembly relationships between components. It is a good practice to assemble components the way they would be assembled in the actual manufacturing process. **Assembly constraints** create a parent/child relationship that allows us to capture the design intent of the assembly. Because the component that we are placing actually becomes a child to the already assembled components, we must use caution when choosing constraint types and references to make sure they reflect the intent.

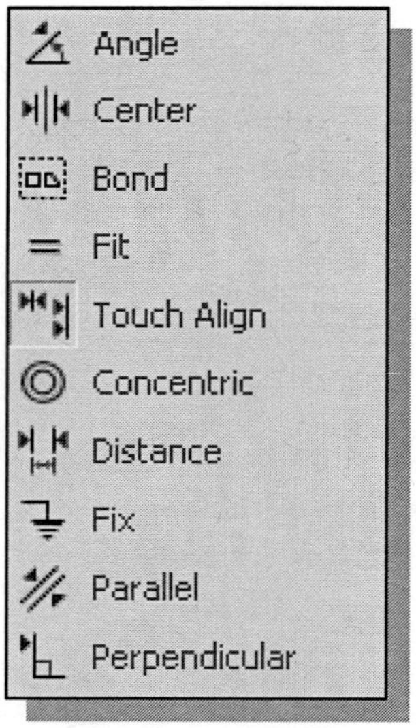

- In *UGS NX*, ten different assembly constraints are available.

- Assembly models are created by applying proper *assembly constraints* to the individual components. The constraints are used to restrict the movement between parts. Constraints eliminate rigid body degrees of freedom (**DOF**). A 3D part has *six degrees of freedom* since the part can rotate and translate relative to the three coordinate axes. Each time we add a constraint between two parts, one or more DOF is eliminated. The movement of a fully constrained part is restricted in all directions. Six basic types of assembly constraints are available in *UGS NX*: Align, Mate, Angle, Parallel, Perpendicular and Insert. Each type of constraint removes different combinations of rigid body degrees of freedom. Note that it is possible to apply different constraints and achieve the same results.

- **Touch (Mate)** – Constraint positions components face-to-face, or adjacent to one another, with faces flush. Removes one degree of linear translation and two degrees of angular rotation between planar surfaces. Selected surfaces point in opposite directions. The Touch constraint positions selected faces normal to one another, with faces coincident.

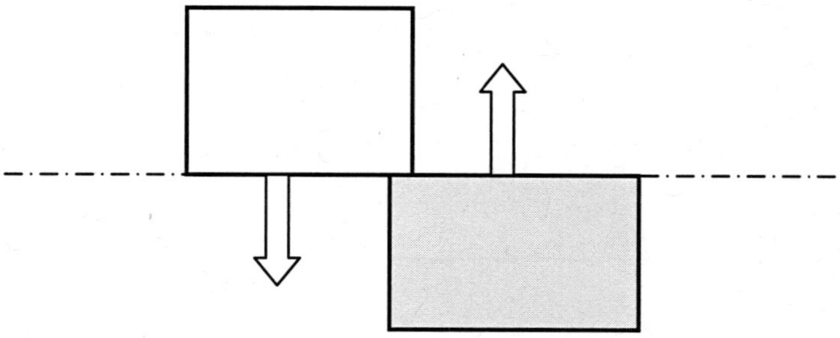

- **Align** – Makes two planes coplanar with their faces aligned in the same direction. Selected surfaces point in the same direction. The Align constraint aligns components adjacent to one another with faces aligned. For axisymmetric objects, Align can be used to align two circles or cylindrical surfaces, including their center axes and planes. Selected circular surfaces can become co-axial or tangent to each other.

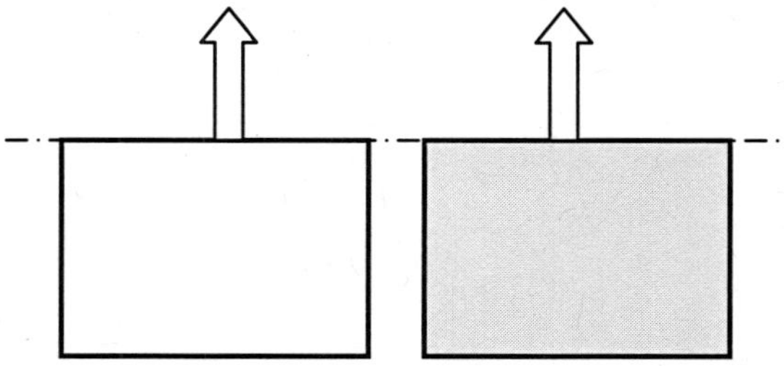

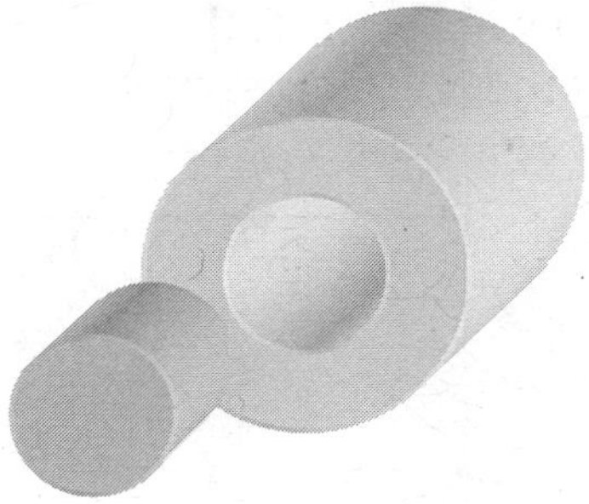

- **Angle** – Creates an angular assembly constraint between parts, subassemblies, or assemblies. Selected surfaces point in the direction specified by the angle.

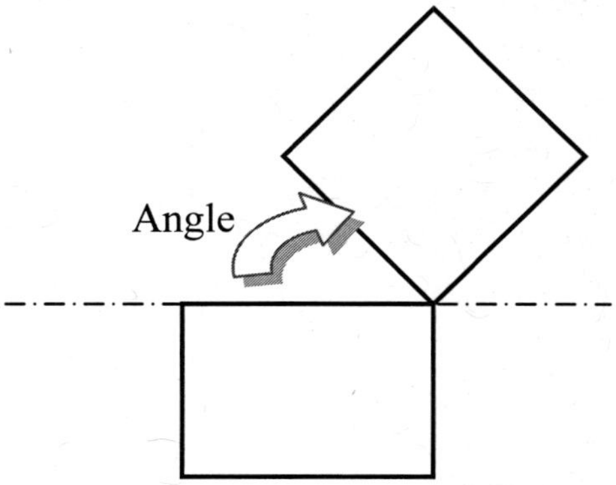

- **Parallel** – Constrains the surfaces or direction vectors of two selected objects as parallel to each other.

➢ **Perpendicular** – Constrains the surfaces or direction vectors of two objects as perpendicular to each other.

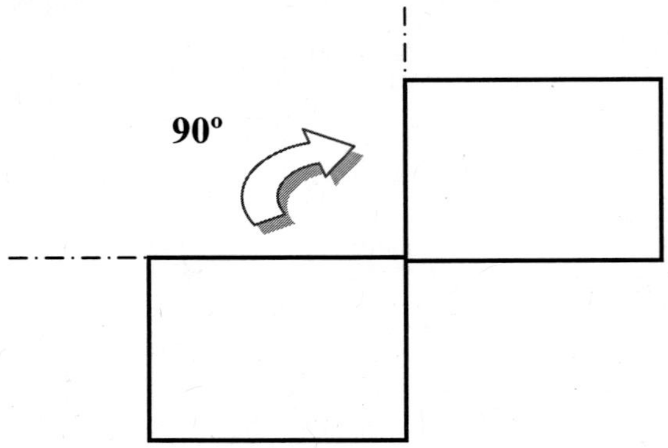

➢ **Concentric** – Lets you center one object to the center of the other of object.

➢ **Center** – Lets you center one object anywhere along the center of another object, or center one or two objects between a pair of objects.

➢ **Distance** – Constraint positions components face-to-face, and can be offset by a specified **distance**. Specifies the minimum 3D distance between two objects. You can control on which side of the surface the solution should be by using positive or negative values. The Distance constraint is similar to the Touch constraint, which also positions selected faces normal to one another, with faces coincident.

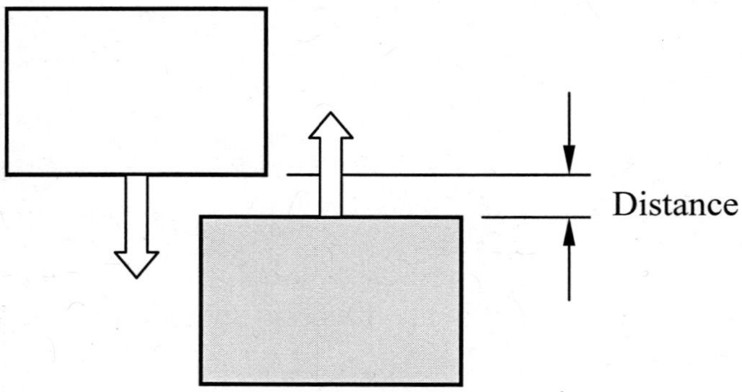

➢ **Align/Tangent** – Aligns selected faces, planes, cylinders, spheres, and cones to contact at the point of tangency. Tangency may be on the inside or outside of a curve, depending on the selection of the direction of the surface normal. A Tangent constraint removes one degree of translational freedom.

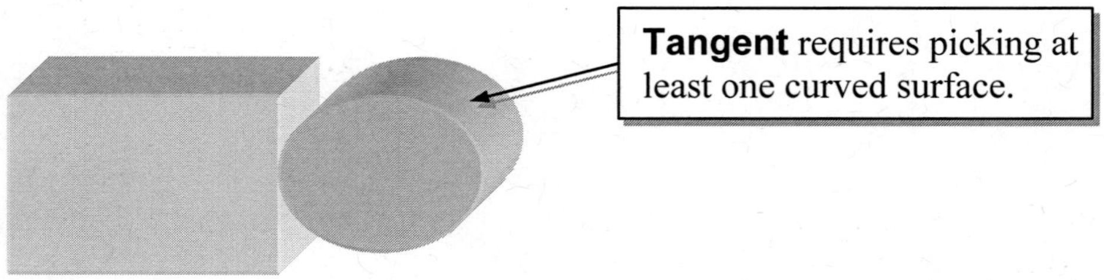

Apply the First Assembly Constraint

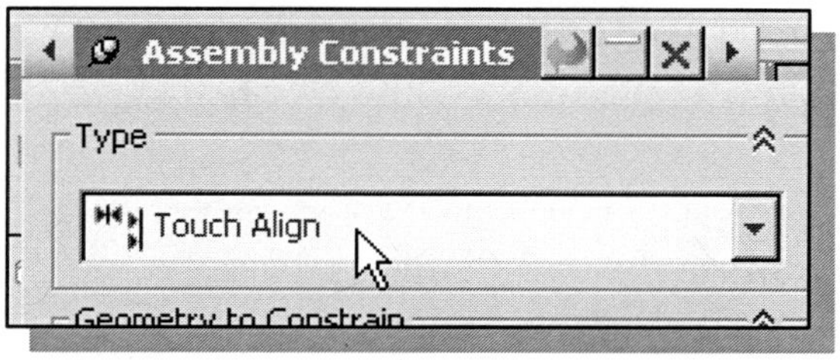

1. In the *Assembly Constraints* dialog box, confirm the constraint *Type* is set to **Touch Align**.

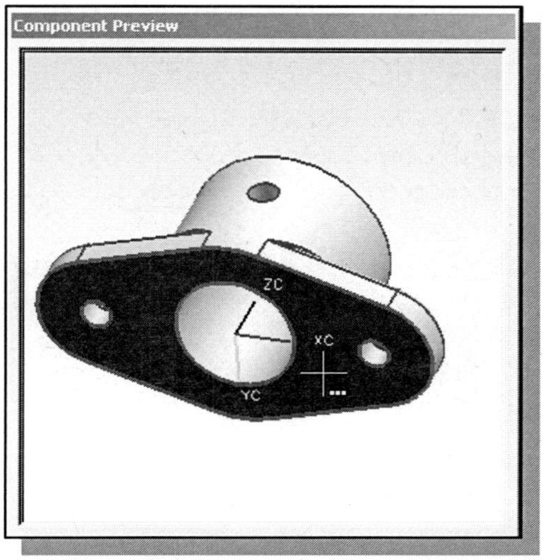

2. On your own, use the middle-mouse-button (MB2) to dynamically rotate the displayed model to view the bottom of the *Bearing* part, as shown in the figure.

3. Click on the bottom face of the *Bearing* part as the first selection to apply the constraint, as shown in the figure above. If necessary, select the corresponding surface in the *QuickPick* window.

4. Select the top horizontal surface of the base part as the second selection for the Mate alignment command. Note the Mate constraint requires the selection of opposite directions of the surface normals.

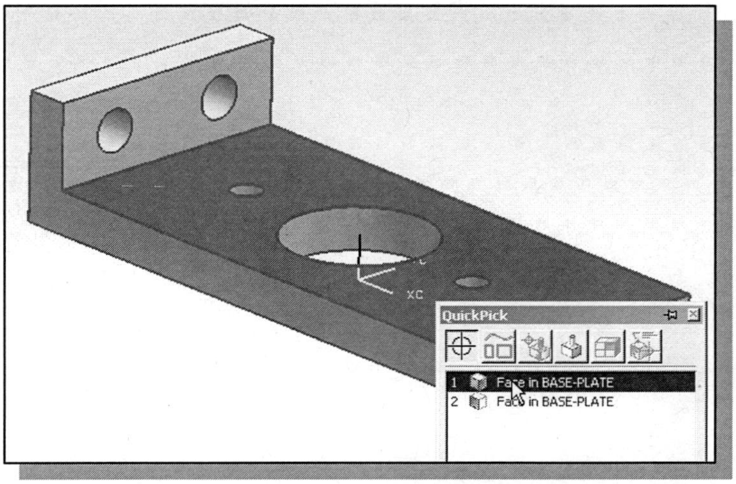

➢ Do not click on the **OK** button yet; we will apply additional constraints to place the *Bearing* part.

Apply another Align Constraint

❖ In *UGS NX*, the **Touch Align** constraint can be viewed as the general all purpose constraining tool. Besides aligning flat surfaces, the **Align** constraint can also be used to align axes of cylindrical features.

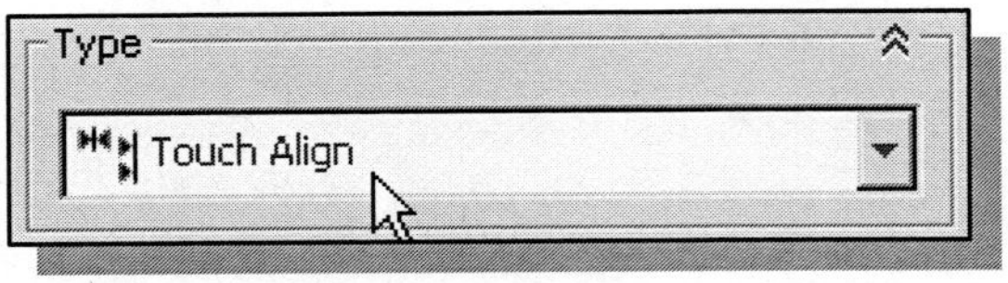

1. Confirm the constraint *Type* is set to **Touch Align** as shown.

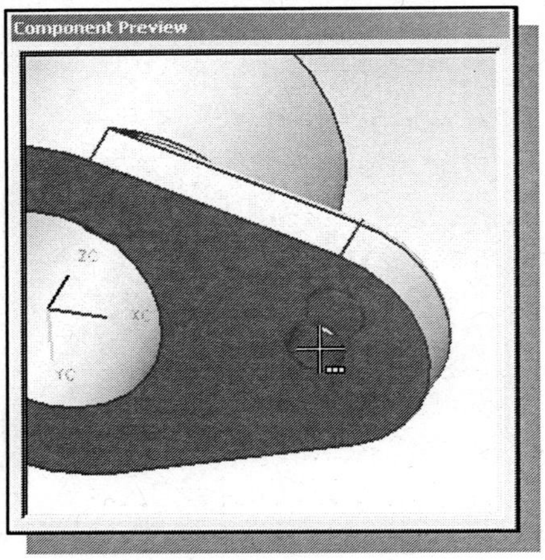

2. Select the **center axis** of the right counter bore hole of the *Bearing* part as shown. (Hint: Use the *Dynamic Viewing* option to assist the selection.)

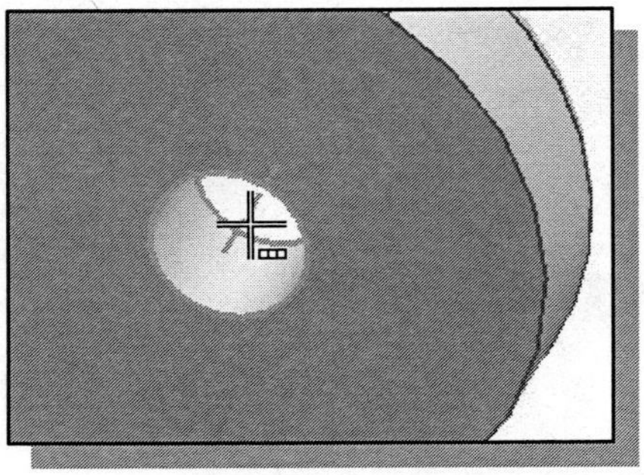

3. Select the **center axis** of the right small hole on the *Base-Plate* part as shown.

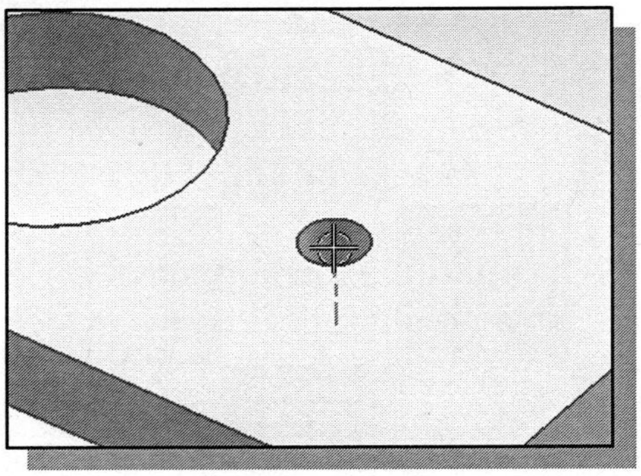

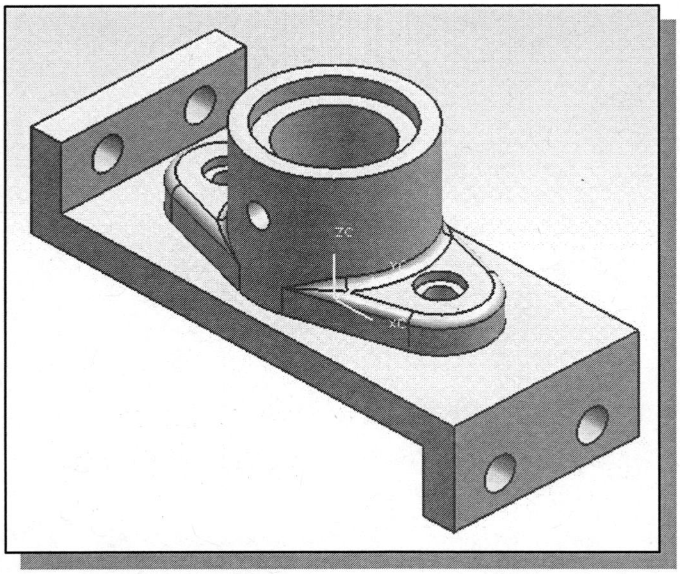

4. Click **OK** to exit the **Assembly Constraints** command.

➢ Inside the graphics window, the applied constraints are represented by the associated symbols.

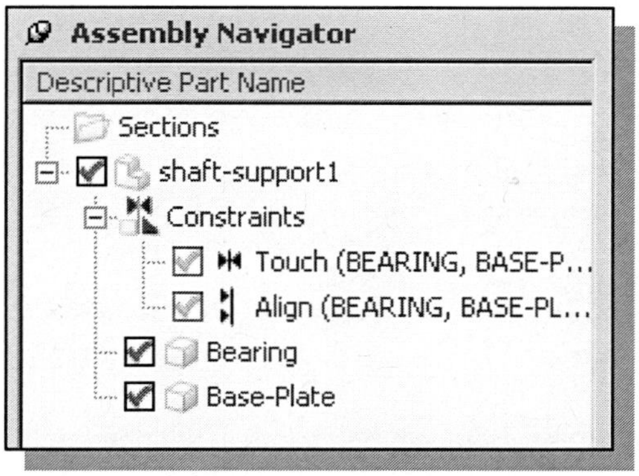

5. Inside the *Assembly Navigator*, click on the plus sign in front of the ***Constraints*** item to expand the list and note all of the applied constraints are displayed

➢ The *Assembly Navigator* can be used to manage the existing constraints. Also, note that Touch and Align are identified as two separate types of constraints.

➢ The *Bearing* part may appear to be placed and constrained correctly, but it can still rotate about the aligned vertical axis.

Constrained Move

❖ To see how well a component is constrained, we can also perform a constrained move. A constrained move is done by using the **Move Component** command, which allows us to drag the component in the graphics window with the left-mouse-button. A constrained move will honor previously applied assembly constraints. That is, the selected component and parts constrained to the component move together in their constrained positions.

1. In the *Assembly Panel*, select the **Move Component** command by left-mouse-clicking the icon.

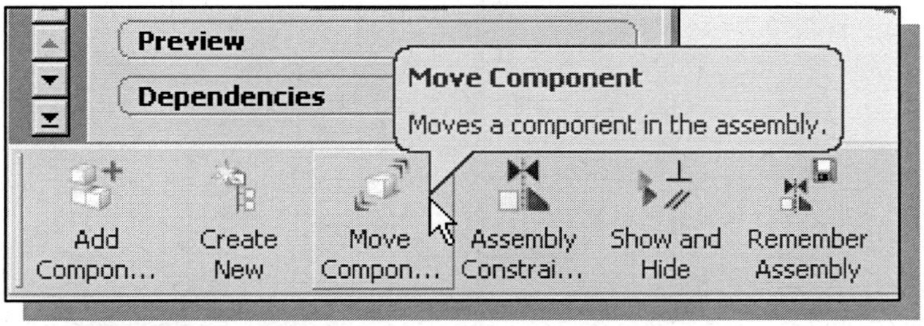

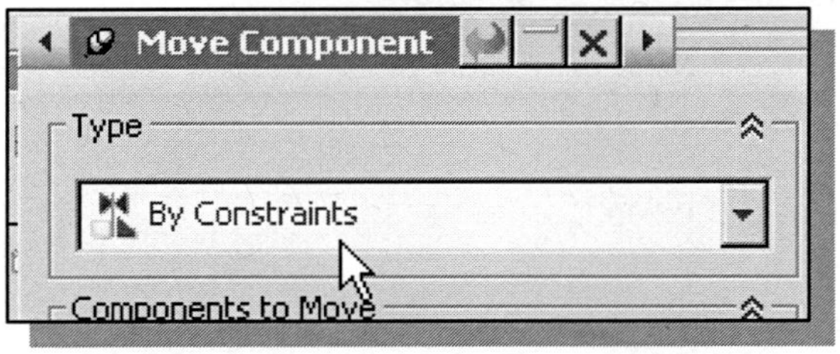

2. Set the *Type* option to **By Constraints**, as shown in the figure.

3. Switch ***ON*** the Move Selected Components Only option as shown.

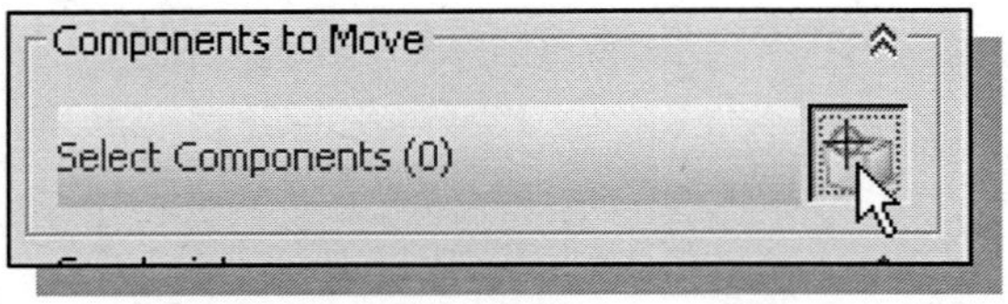

4. Activate the **Select Components** option as shown.

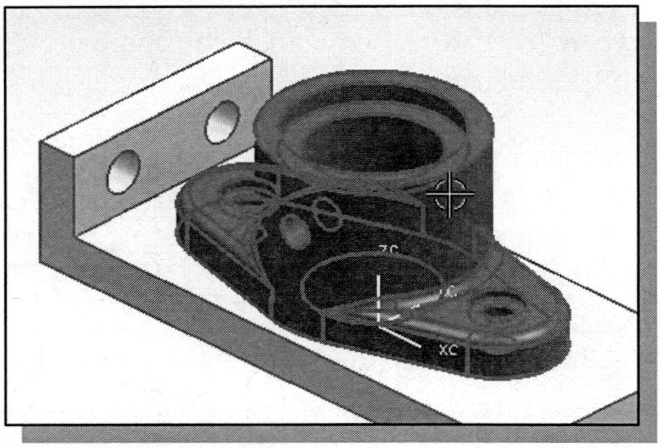

5. Inside the graphics window, select the *Bearing* part as shown in the figure.

6. Click once with the middle-mouse-button (**MB2**) to accept the selection.

7. Press and hold down the left-mouse-button and drag the *Bearing* part downward.

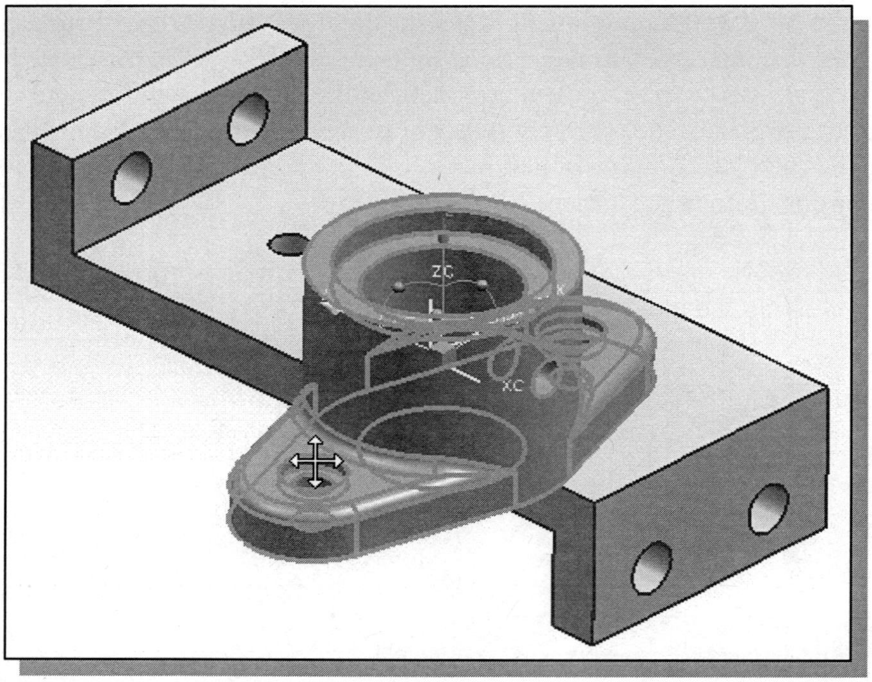

❖ The *Bearing* part can freely rotate about the constrained axis.

8. On your own, dynamically rotate and view the alignment of the *Bearing* part.

9. Adjust the display as shown in the figure above and **Exit** the **Reposition Component** command.

Apply another Assembly Constraint

- Besides selecting the surfaces of solid models to apply constraints, we can also select the individual geometry, such as edges or points, to apply the assembly constraints. For the *Bearing* part, we will apply another **Align** constraint to two center points and eliminate the last rotational DOF.

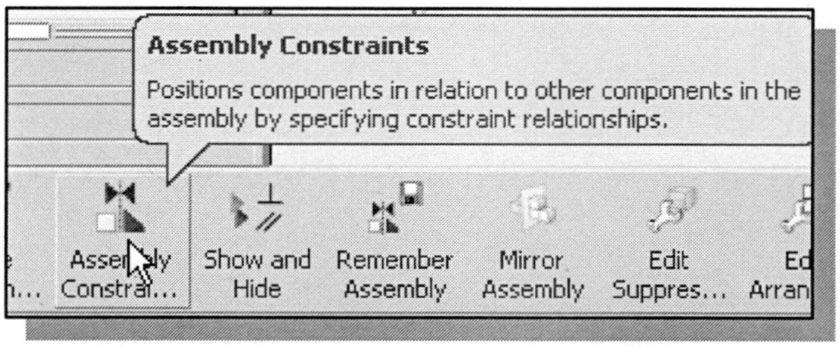

1. In the *Assembly Panel* (the toolbar that is located to the bottom side of the graphics window), select the **Assembly Constraints** command by left-mouse-clicking the icon.

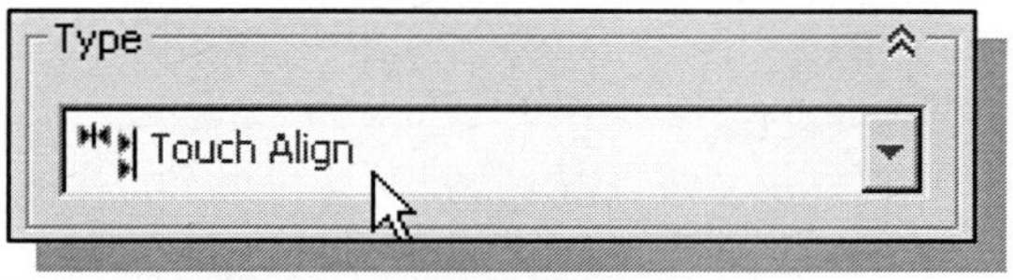

2. In the constraint *Type* option panel, set the constraint *Type* to **Touch Align** as shown.

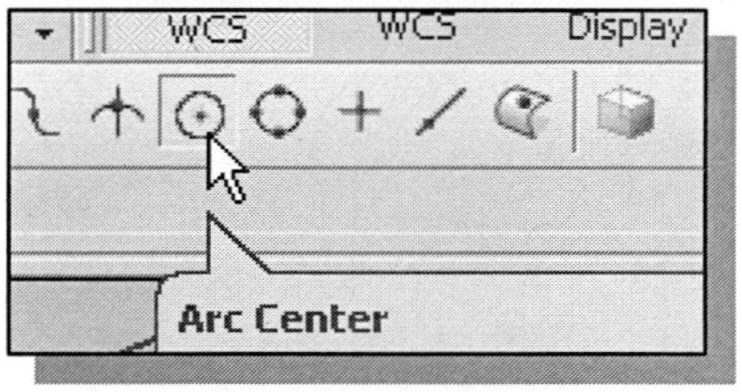

3. Switch the *Snap* option to **Arc Center** as shown.

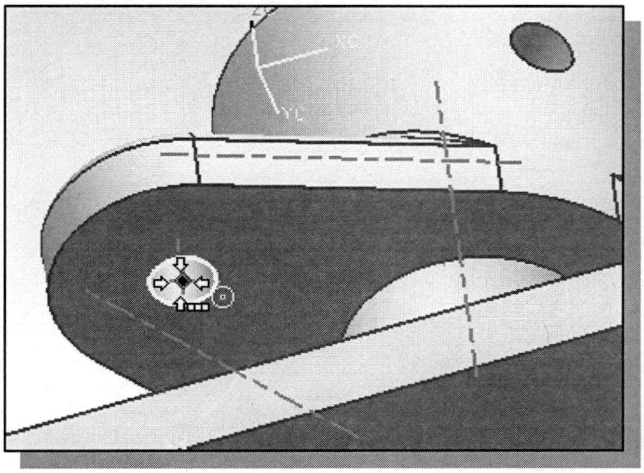

4. Rotate and select the bottom center point of small hole of the *Bearing* part as the first part for the **Align** constraint.

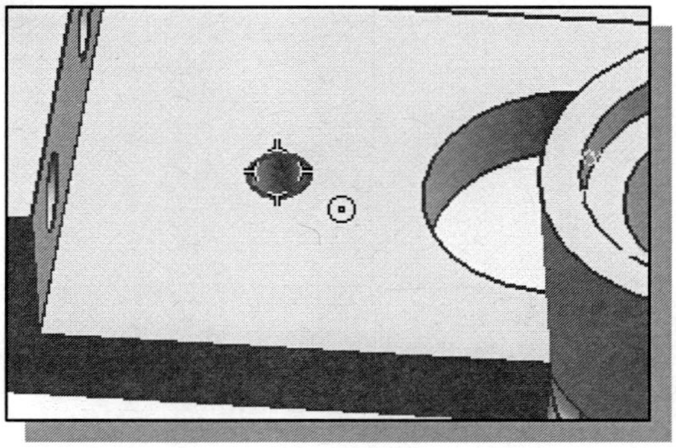

5. Select the center point of the drill hole on the *Base-Plate* part as the second item for the **Align** constraint.

➢ Note that we can also *align* the two center axes.

6. Click on the **OK** button to exit the Assembly Constraints command.

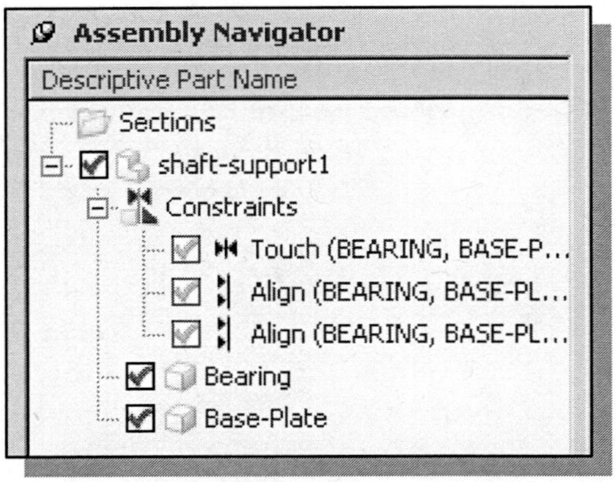

➢ Notice the new constraint is also added in the *Assembly Navigator*.

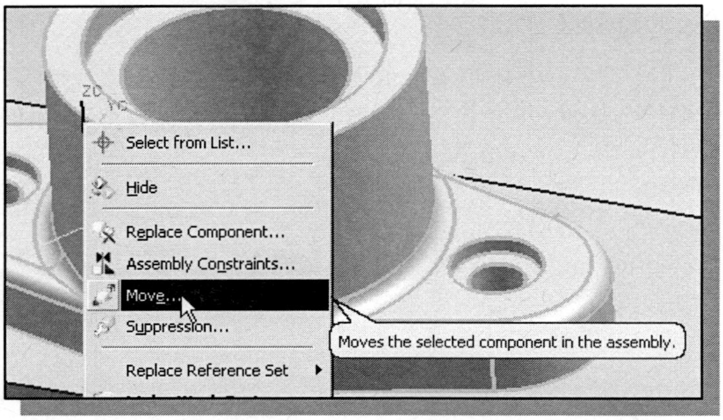

7. Inside the graphics window, right-mouse-click on the *Bearing* part to bring up the option menu.

8. Select the **Move...** command as shown.

9. On your own, try to perform a constrained move.

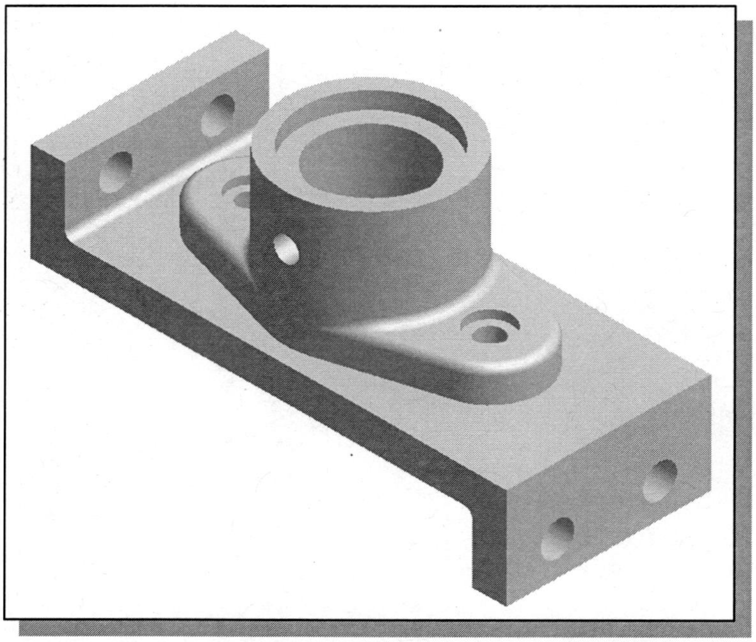

❖ Note the *Bearing* part is now **fully constrained,** and therefore a *constrained move* cannot be done.

Placing the Third Component

➢ We will retrieve the *Collar* part as the third component of the assembly model.

1. In the *Assembly Panel* (the toolbar that is located to the bottom of the graphics window), select the **Add Component** command by left-mouse-clicking the icon.

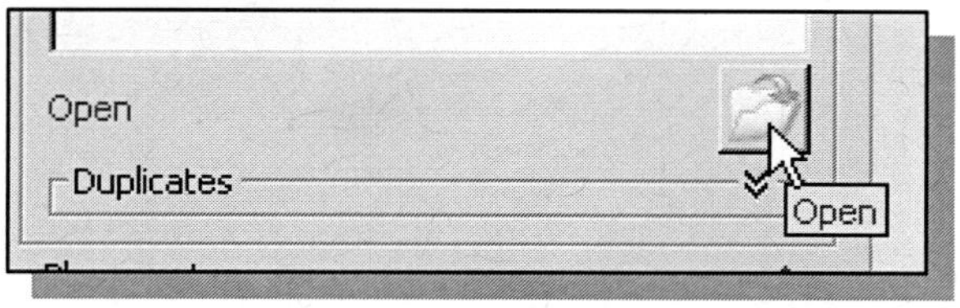

2. In the ***Add Component*** window, click **Open** to load an existing part.

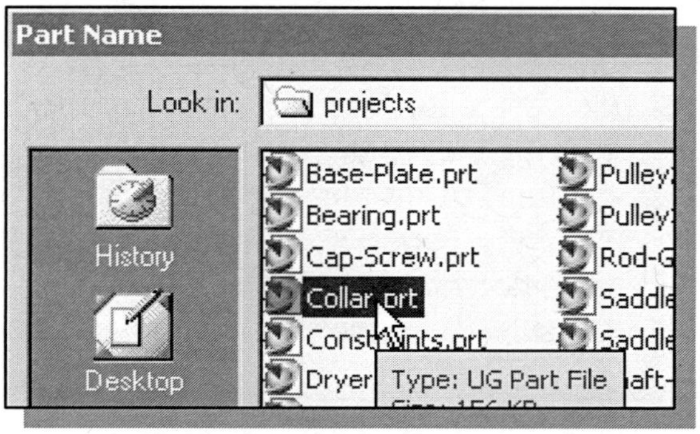

3. Select the ***Collar*** design (part file: ***Collar.prt***) in the list window. Click on the **OK** button to retrieve the model.

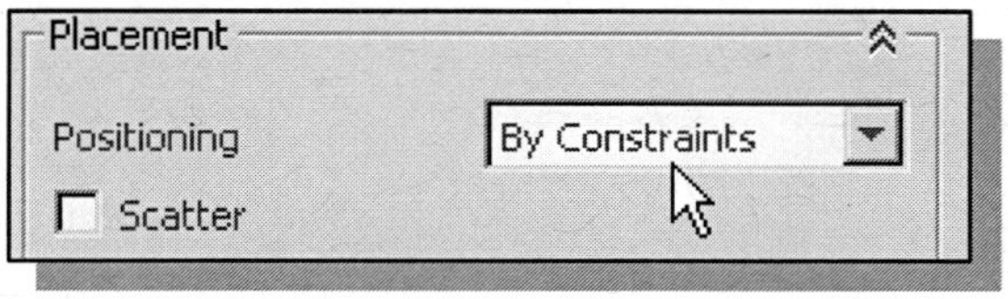

4. Confirm the *Positioning* method is set to **By Constraints** as shown in the figure.

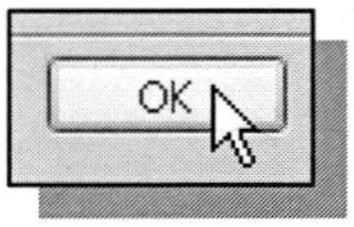

5. Click **OK** to accept the selection and proceed to load the file.

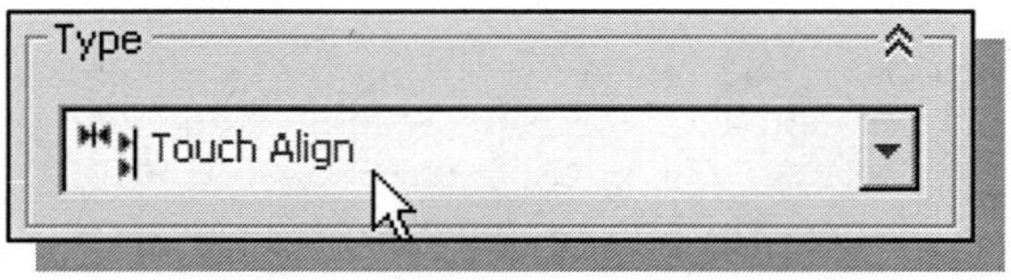

6. In the mating *Type* option panel, confirm the constraint type is set to **Touch Align** as shown.

7. Switch *OFF* the *Snap* to **Arc Center** option, by clicking on the icon as shown.

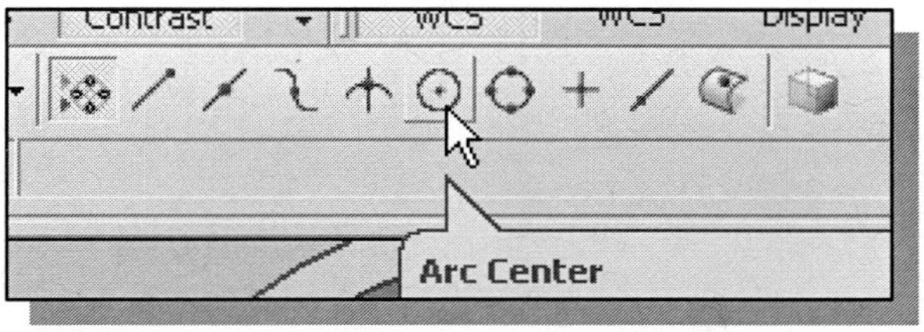

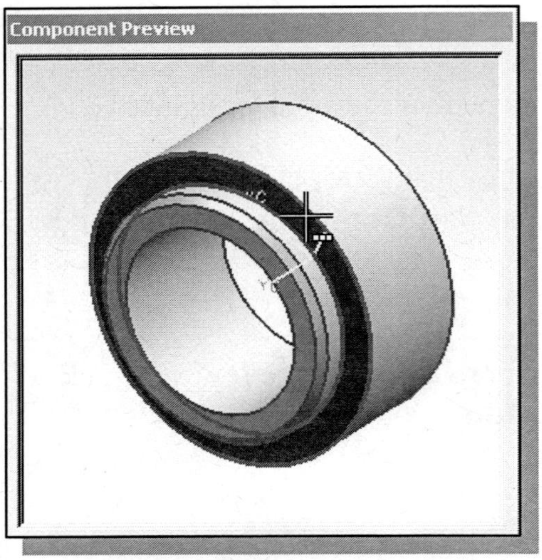

8. Click on the outer circular face at the bottom of the *Collar* part as the first selection to apply the **Mate** constraint, as shown in the figure.

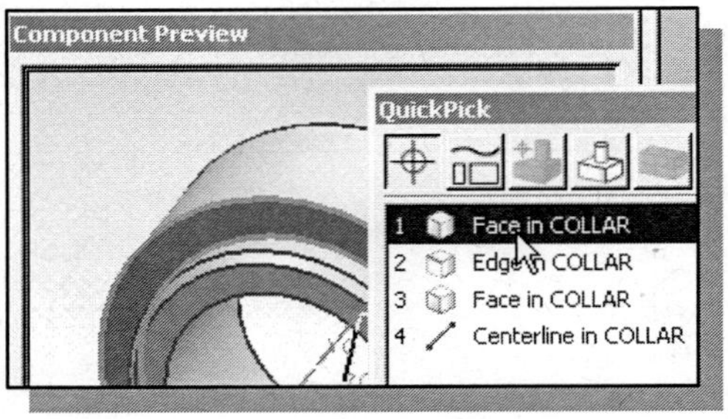

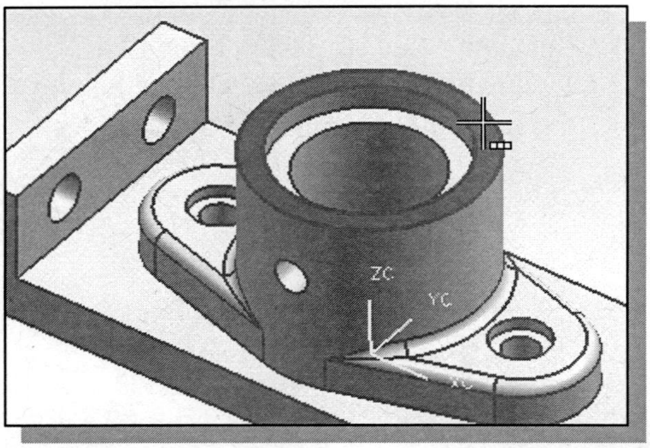

9. Select the top circular surface of the bearing part as the second selection for the **Touch** alignment command. Note the **Touch** constraint requires the selection of opposite directions of the surface normals.

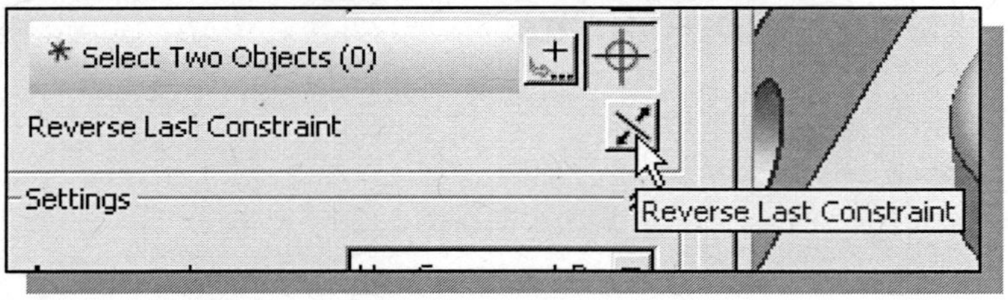

10. Click the **Reverse Last Constraint** button to reverse the direction of the aligned surfaces.

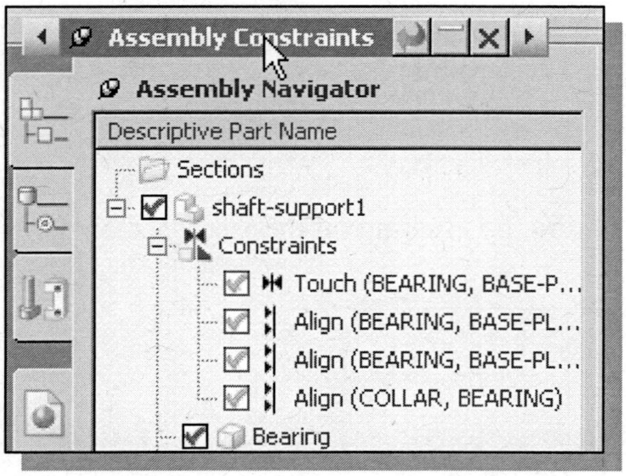

➢ Click on the title area of the ***Assembly Constraints*** dialog box to switch to viewing the ***Assembly Navigator*** and notice the new constraint has been added.

➢ Is **Align** the intended constraint?

➢ Click on the title area again to switch back to the **Assembly Constraints** command.

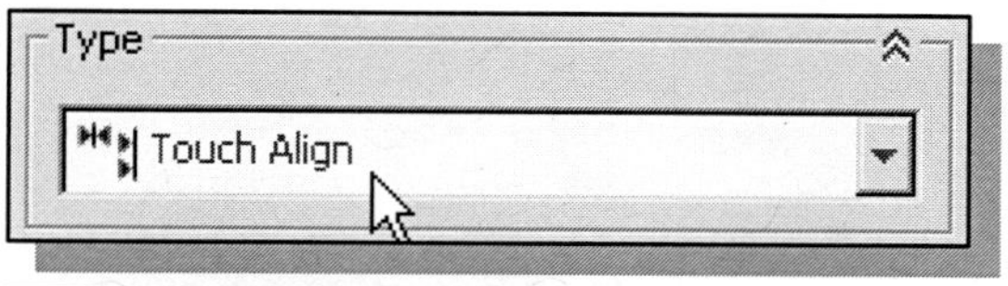

11. Confirm the *Positioning* method is still set to **Touch Align** as shown in the figure.

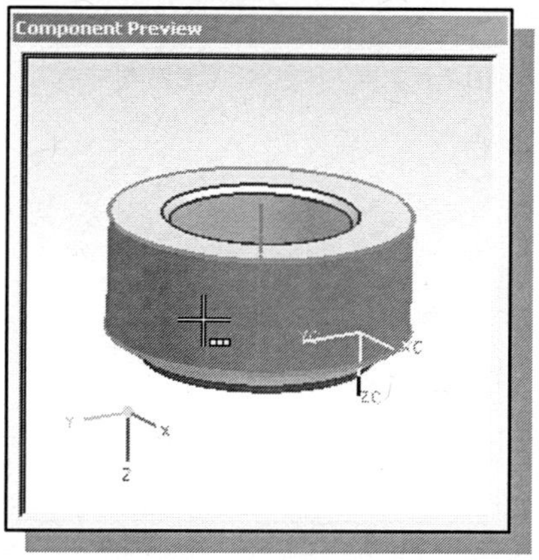

12. Select the outer cylindrical surface of the *Collar* part as shown.

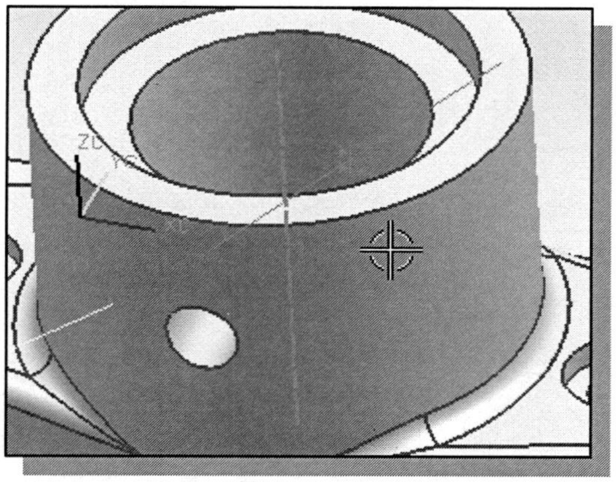

13. Select the outer cylindrical surface of the *Bearing* part as shown. If necessary, select the corresponding surface in the *QuickPick* window.

14. Click on the **OK** button to exit the Assembly Constraints command.

➢ Notice the resulting assembly is not quite what we intended.

Quick Editing of Applied Constraints

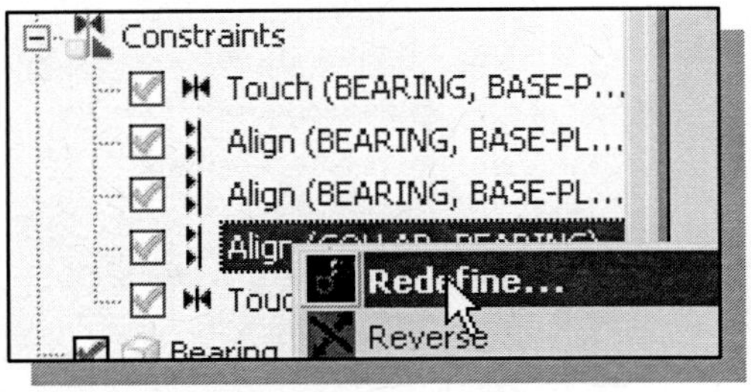

1. Inside the *Assembly Navigator* window, right-mouse-click on the fourth constraint to bring up the option menu and select **Redefine** as shown.

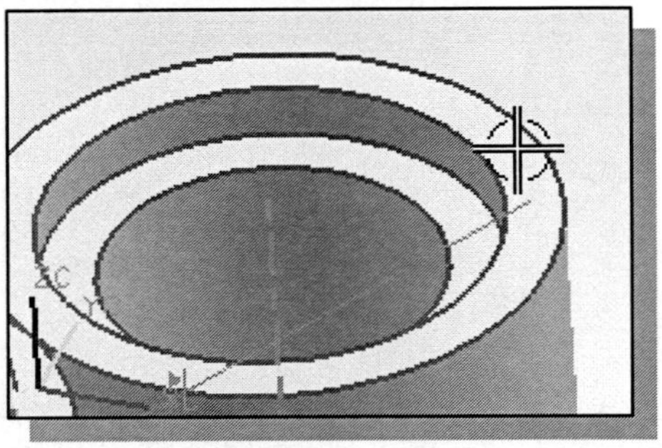

2. Hold down the [**Shift**] key and select the highlighted top surface of the *Bearing* part to de-select the surface.

3. Click at the same location to select the same surface again.

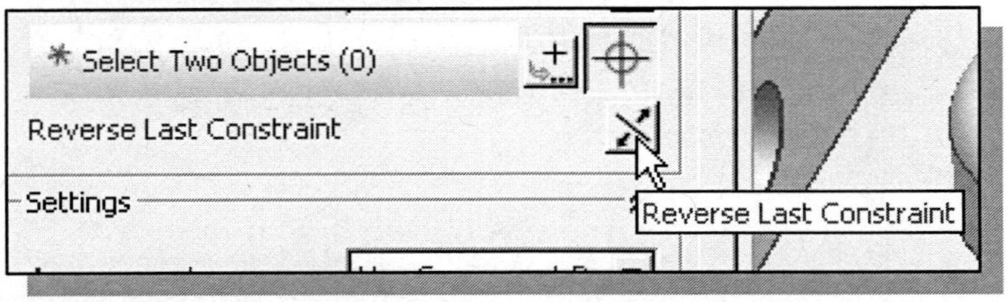

4. Click the **Reverse Last Constraint** button to reverse the direction of the aligned surfaces.

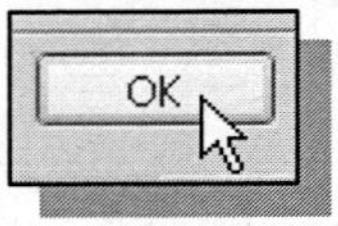

5. Click **OK** to exit the **Assembly Constraints** command.

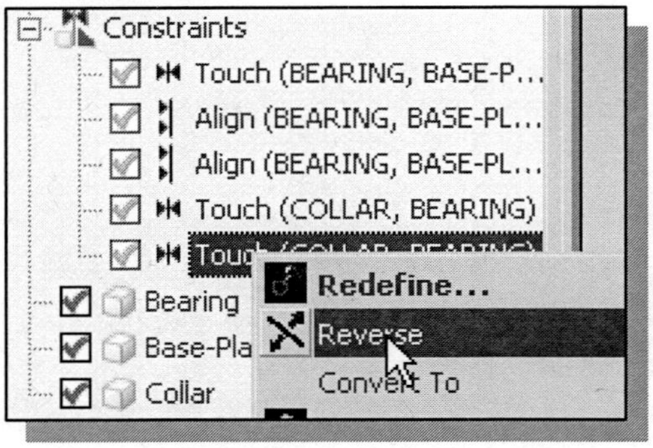

- ➢ There is another approach to quickly reverse the directions of aligned surfaces, which is still done through the option menu.

6. Inside the *Assembly Navigator* window, right-mouse-click on the fourth constraint to bring up the option menu and select **Reverse** as shown.

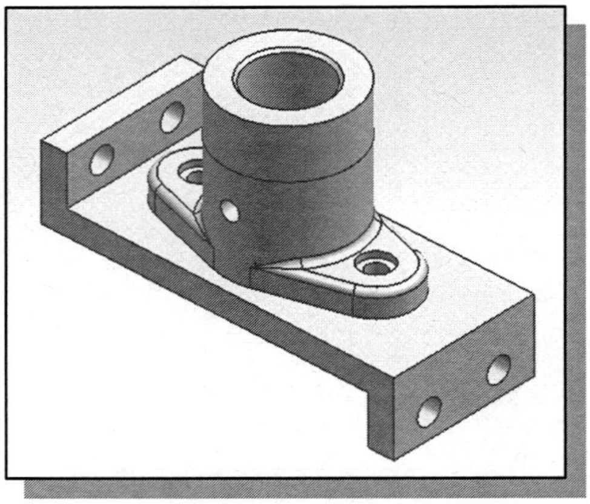

- ➢ Note that one rotational degree of freedom remains open; the *Collar* part can still freely rotate about the vertical axis through the center of the part.

Assemble the First Cap-Screw

➤ Two *Cap-Screw* parts are needed to complete the assembly model.

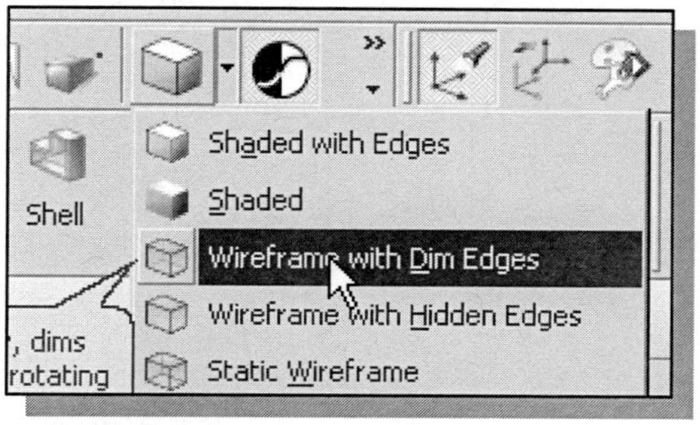

1. Set the display option to **Wireframe with Dim Edges** by clicking on the corresponding icon as shown in the figure.

2. In the *Assembly Panel* (the toolbar that is located to the bottom of the graphics window), select the **Add Component** command by left-mouse-clicking the icon.

3. In the *Add Component* window, click **Open** to load an existing part.

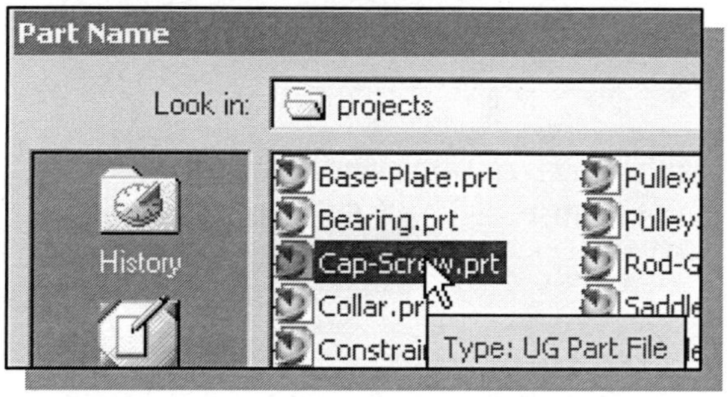

4. Select the ***Cap-Screw*** design (part file: ***Cap-Screw.prt***) in the list window. And click on the **OK** button to retrieve the model.

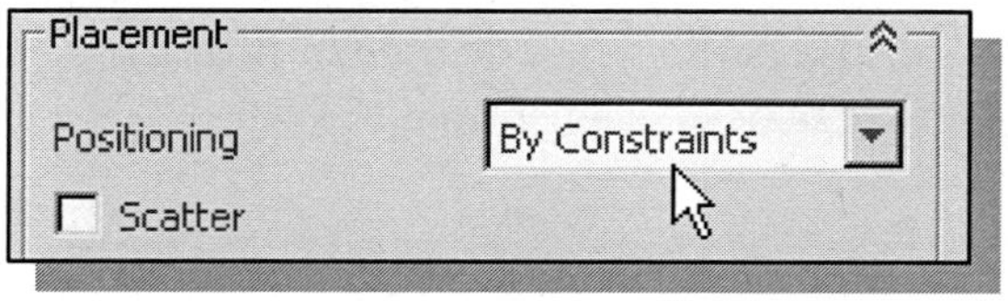

5. Confirm the *Positioning* method is set to **By constraints** as shown in the figure.

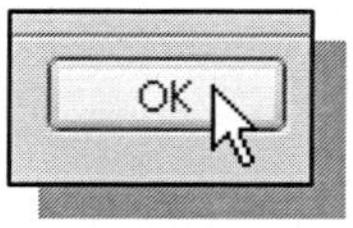

6. Click **OK** to accept the selection and proceed to load the file.

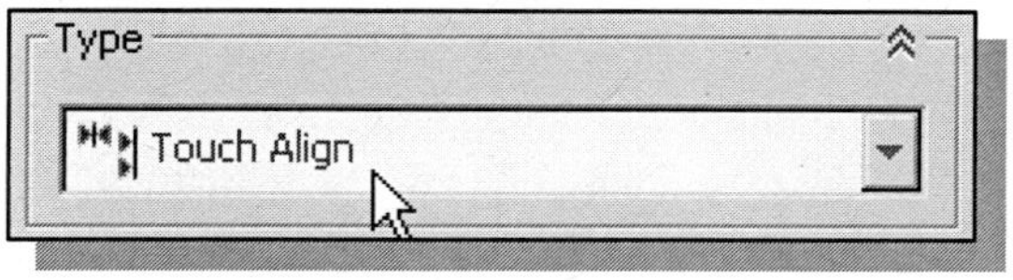

7. In the *Type* option panel, confirm the constraint type is set to **Touch Align** as shown.

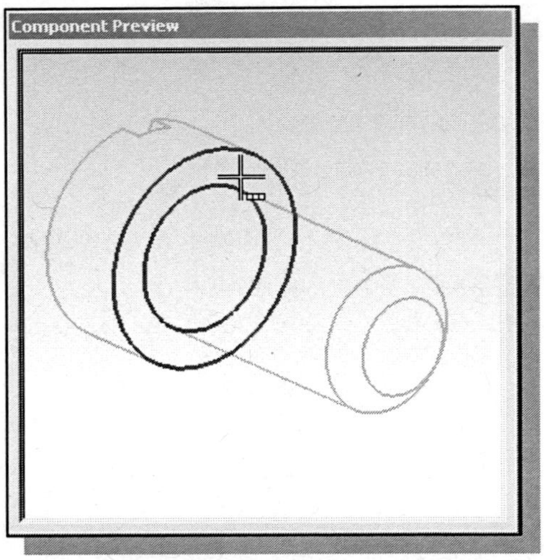

8. Select the circular surface on the bottom of the head of the *Cap-Screw* part as shown.

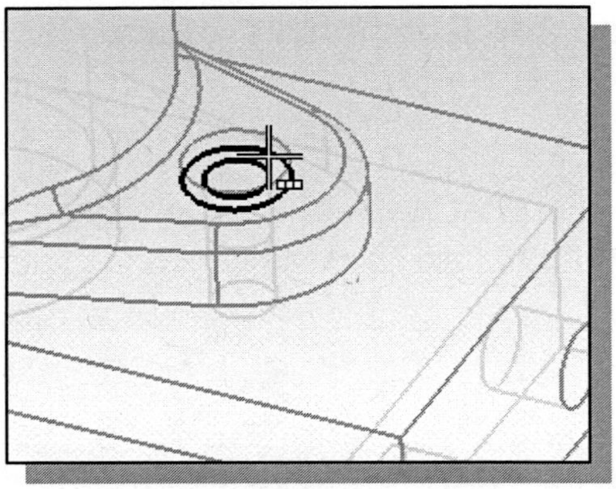

9. Select the circular surface of the counterbore of the *Bearing* part as shown.

➢ We will continue to add additional constraints to the assembly model.

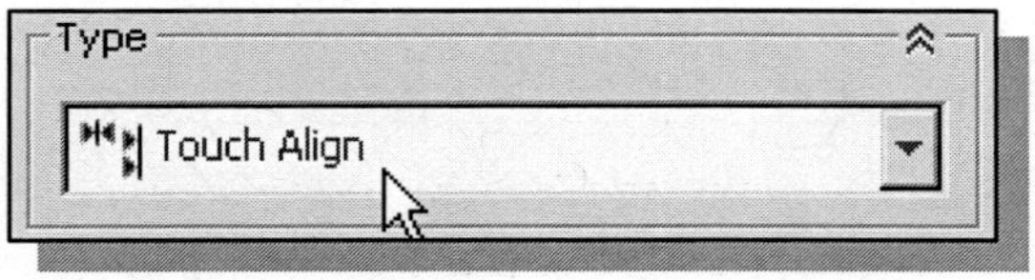

10. In the *Type* option panel, confirm the constraint type is set to **Touch Align** as shown.

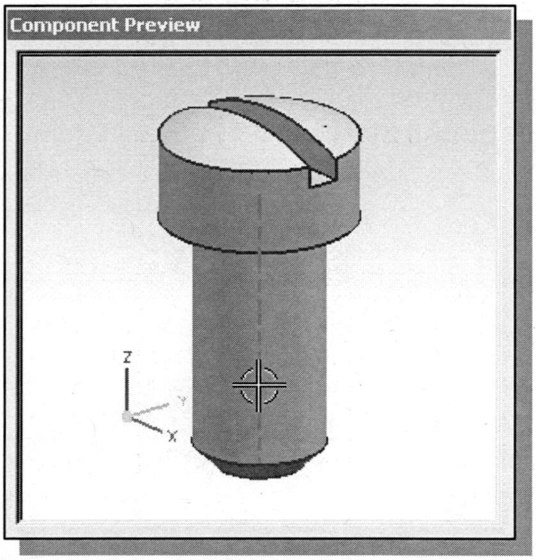

11. Select the center axis of the shaft of the *Cap-Screw* part as shown.

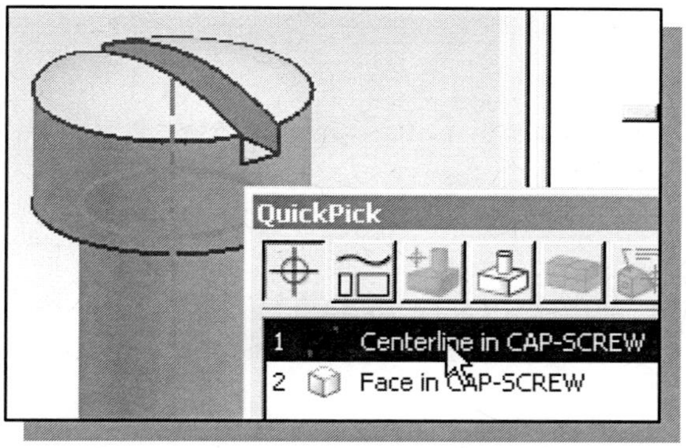

12. Select **Centerline in CAP-SCREW** in the *QuickPick* dialog box if necessary.

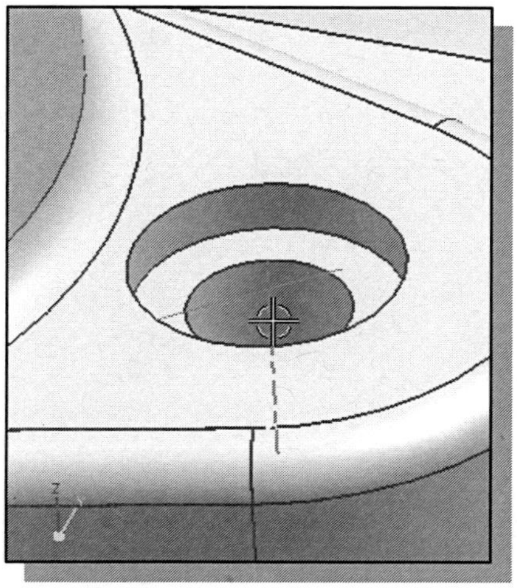

13. Select the center axis of the counterbore surface on the *Bearing* part as shown.

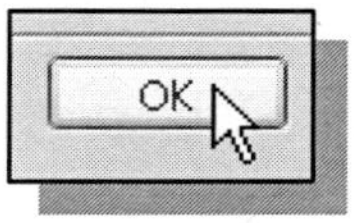

14. Click **OK** to accept the selection and proceed to load the file.

➢ The *Cap-Screw* part is moved into the existing assembly.

➢ Note that one rotational degree of freedom remains open; the *Cap-Screw* part can still freely rotate about the vertical axis through the center of the part.

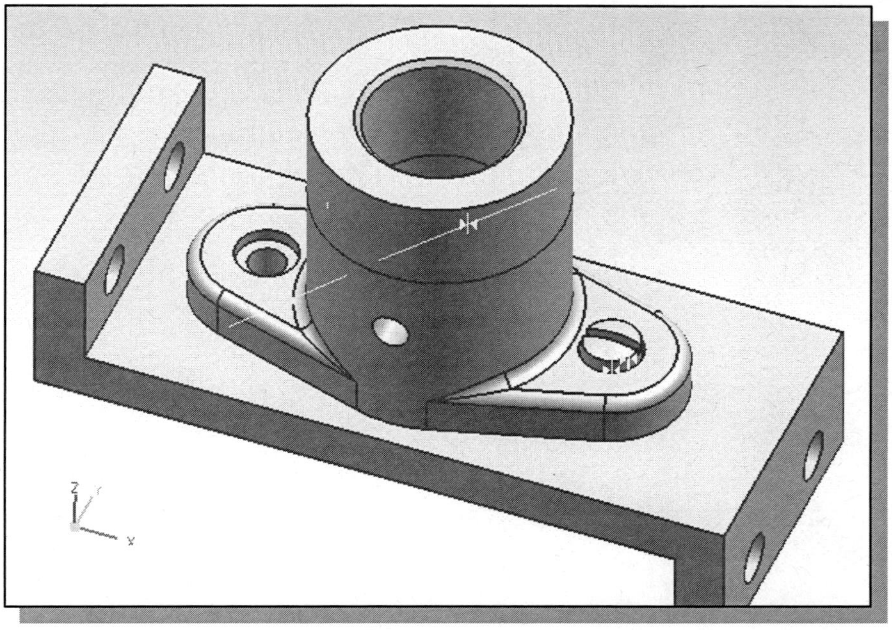

Placing the second Cap-Screw part

- For the ***Shaft-Support*** assembly, we need two copies of the ***Cap-screw*** part. The second *Cap-Screw* will be a separate copy of the original part, each with its own assembly constraints.

1. In the *Assembly Panel* (the toolbar that is located to the bottom of the graphics window), select the **Add Component** command by left-mouse-clicking the icon.

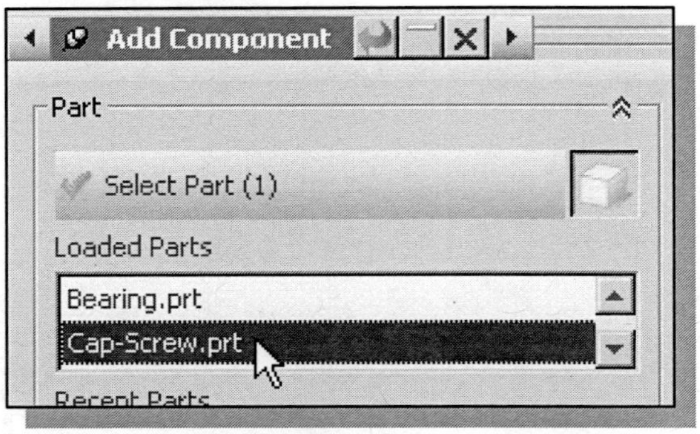

2. In the *Loaded Parts* list, click ***Cap-Screw.prt*** to re-use the already loaded part.

3. Confirm the *Positioning* method is set to **By constraints** as shown in the figure.

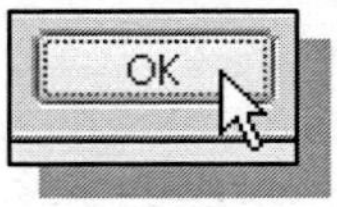

4. Click on the **OK** button to accept the selection of the part.

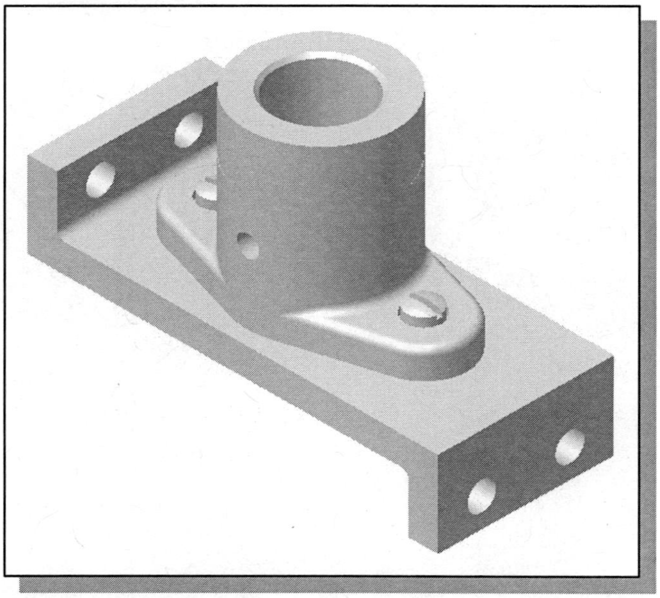

➢ On your own, use the proper constraints and assemble the second *Cap-Screw* in place as shown in the figure.

Exploded View of the Assembly

- Exploded assemblies are often used in design presentations, catalogs, sales literature, and in the shop to show all of the parts of an assembly and how they fit together. In *UGS NX*, an exploded assembly can be created by two methods: (1) using the **Auto-explode** command, which provides a very simple and quick method to create an exploded view, and (2) using the **Edit Explosion** command to arrange the individual components. For our example, we will create an exploded assembly by using the Auto-explode command.

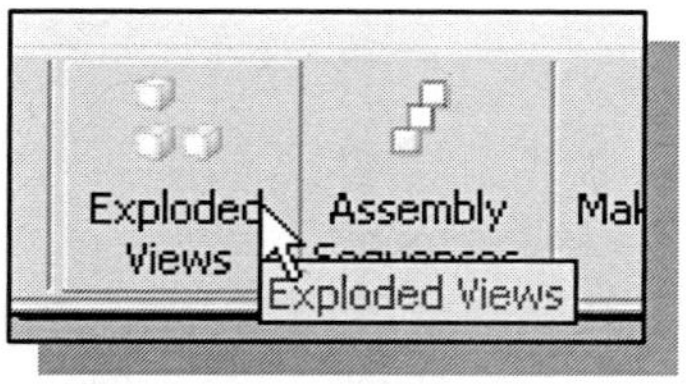

1. In the *Assembly Panel,* select the **Exploded Views** command by left-mouse-clicking once on the icon.

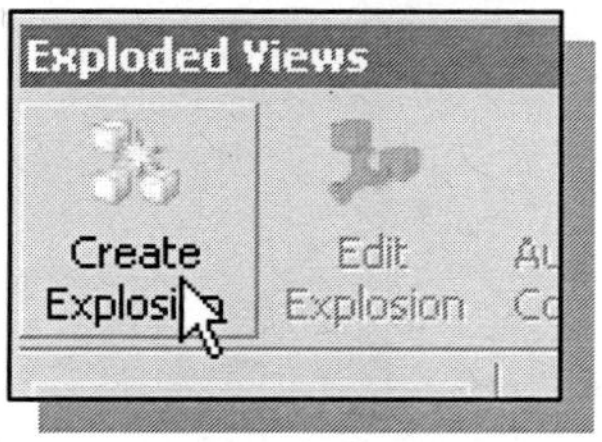

2. In the *Exploded Views* panel, select the **Create Explosion** command.

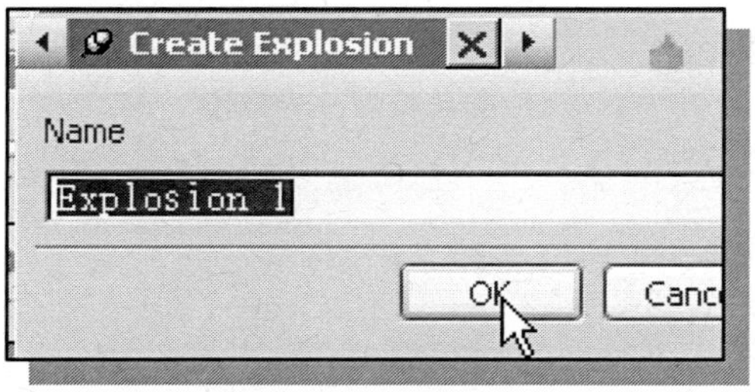

3. Click **OK** to accept the default explosion name, *Explosion 1.*

- Note that in *UGS NX*, multiple exploded views can be set up within the same assembly model.

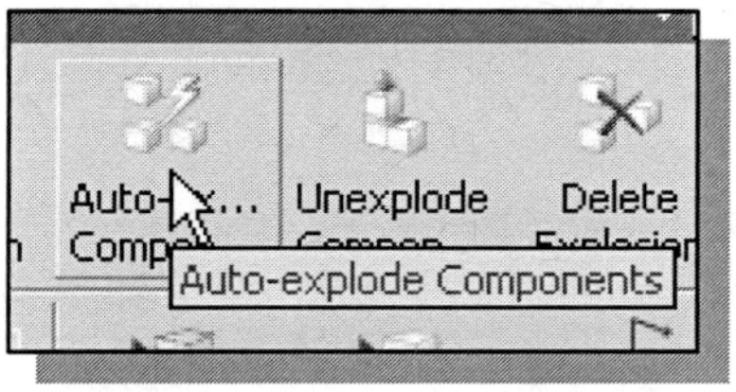

4. In the *Exploded Views* panel, select the **Auto-explode Components** command.

5. Select the ***Collar*** part as shown.

6. Click **OK** to accept the selection.

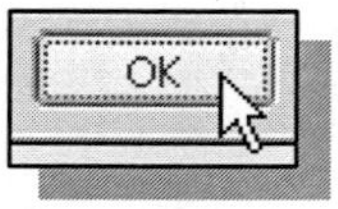

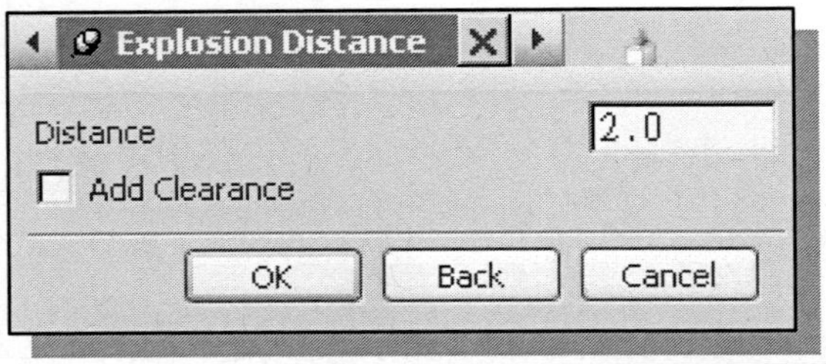

7. Enter **2.0** in the *Distance* option box.

8. Click **OK** to accept the setting.

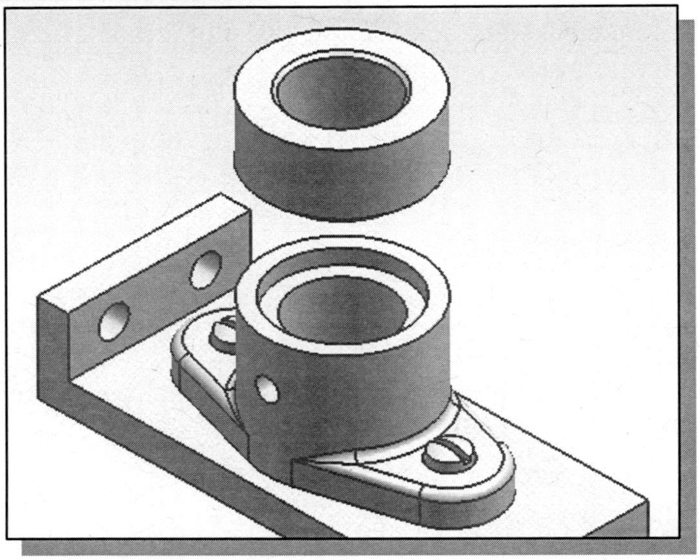

9. In the *Exploded Views* panel, select the **Auto-explode Components** command.

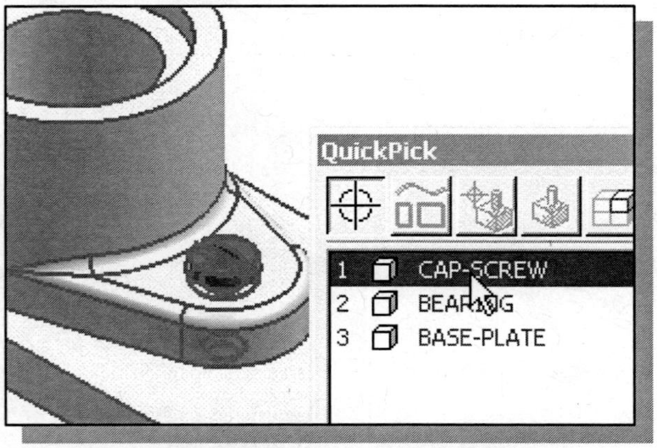

10. Inside the graphics window, select the ***Cap-Screw*** part as shown.

11. Click **OK** to accept the selection.

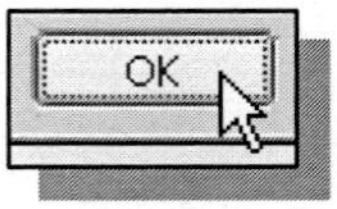

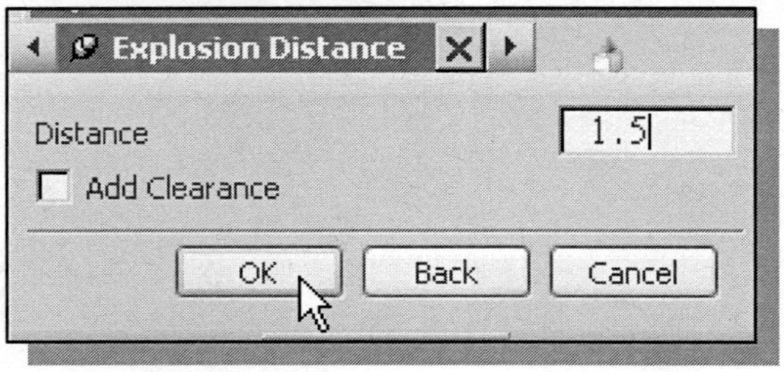

12. Enter **1.5** in the *Distance* option box.

13. Click **OK** to accept the setting.

14. On your own, repeat the above steps and complete the exploded assembly by repositioning the components as shown in the figure below.

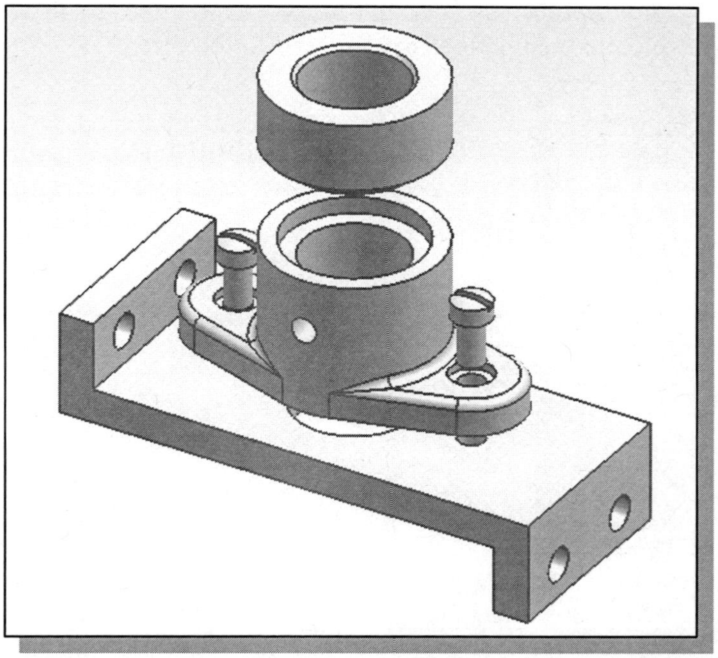

Switching the Exploded/Unexploded Views

- *UGS NX* allows us to store as many exploded views as desired and we can also switch to any of the exploded views by choosing the from the *Exploded Views* list box.

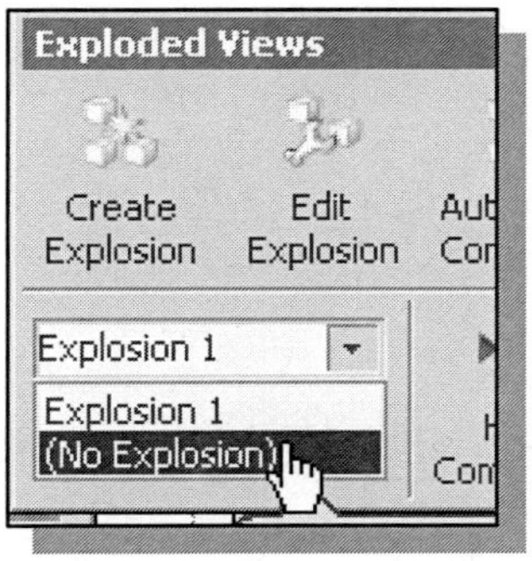

1. Inside the *Exploded Views* dialog box, select **(No Explosion)** to switch to the unexploded view of the assembly model.

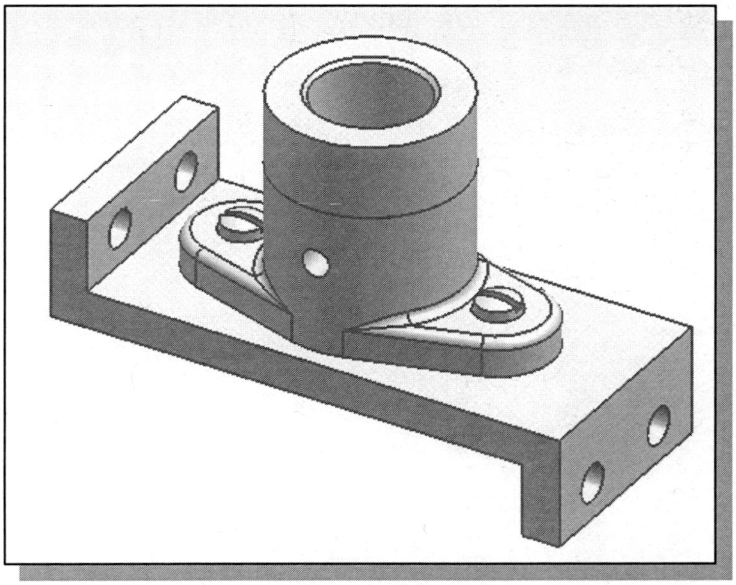

Editing the Components

- The *associative functionality* of *UGS NX* allows us to change the design at any level, and the system reflects the changes at all levels automatically.

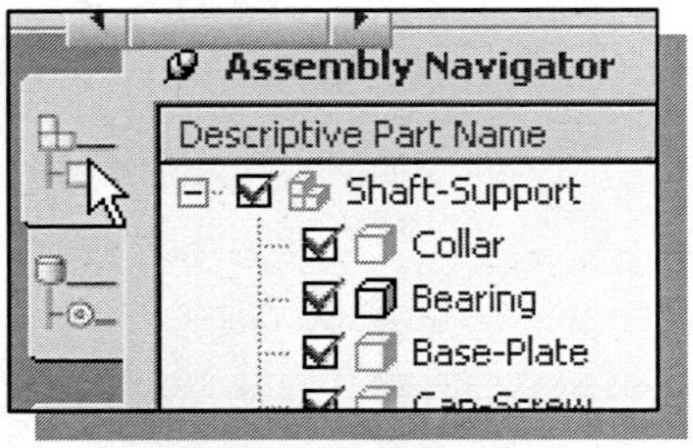

1. Click on the **Assembly Navigator** tab, if it is not activated already, to the left of the graphics window.

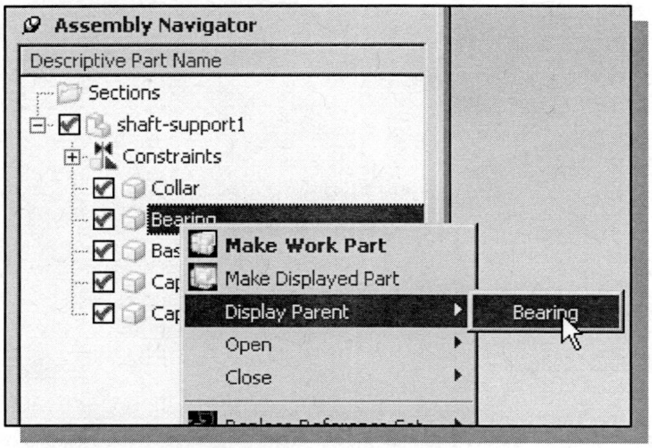

2. Right-mouse-click once on the ***Bearing*** part to bring up the option menu and select **Display Parent – Bearing** in the option list as shown.

❖ Note that we are opening up the *Bearing* part in the *NX Gateway* mode. We will need to switch to the *Part Editing* mode to edit the design.

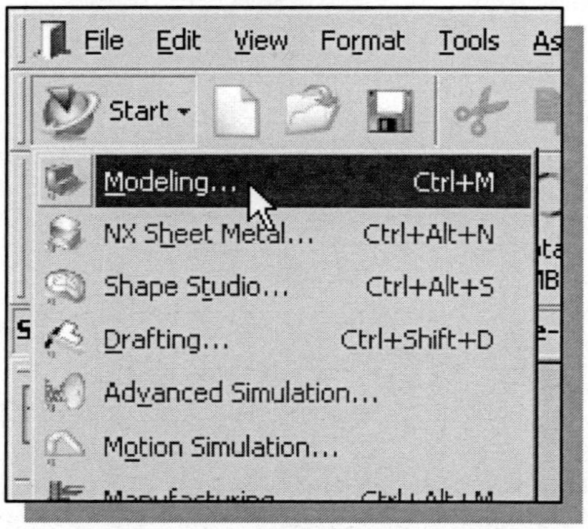

3. Select the **Start** icon with a single click of the left-mouse-button (MB1) in the *Standard* toolbar.

4. Pick **Modeling** in the pull-down list as shown in the figure.

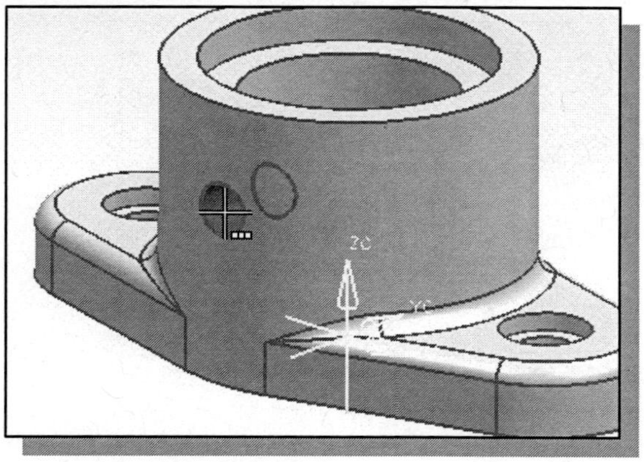

5. Double-click the left-mouse-button on the **small hole feature** to enter *Editing* mode.

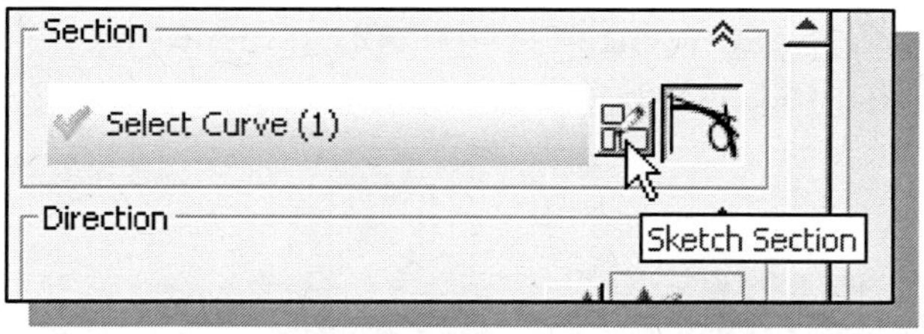

6. Click on the **Sketch Section** button to enter *2D Sketcher* mode.

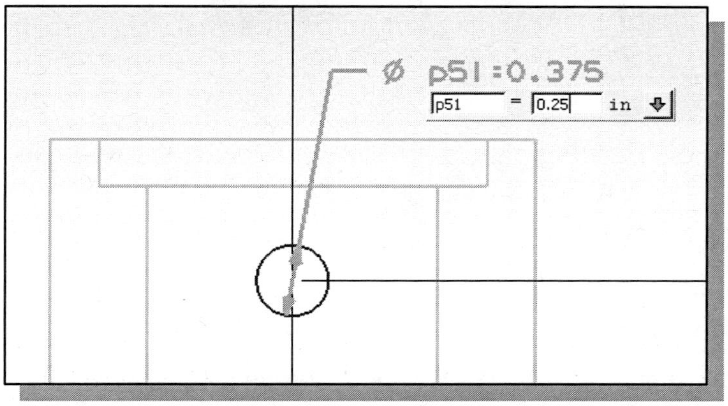

7. On your own, adjust the diameter of the **small drill hole** to **0.25** as shown.

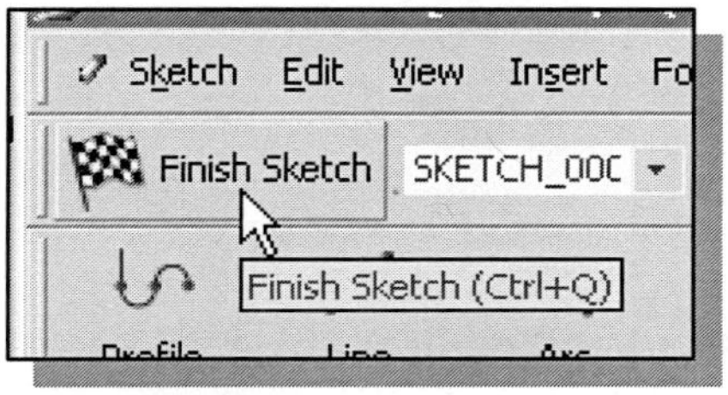

8. Click **Finish Sketch** to exit the *NX Sketcher* mode and return to the *Feature* option dialog window.

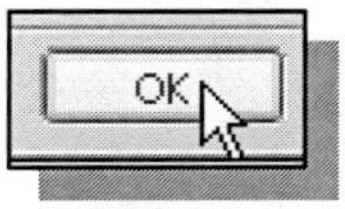

9. Click **OK** to proceed with updating the model.

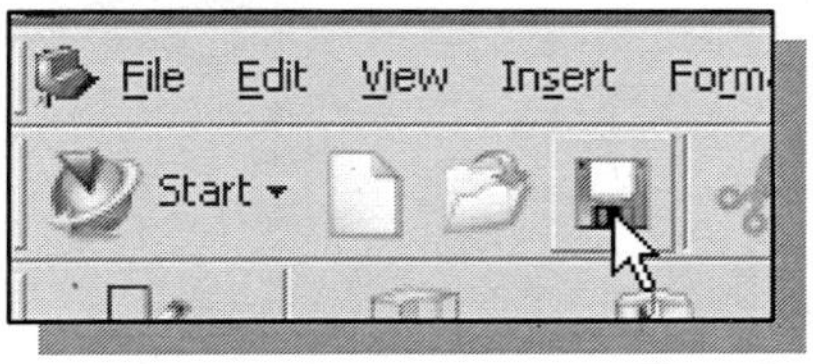

10. Click the **Save** button to save the modification of the *Bearing* part.

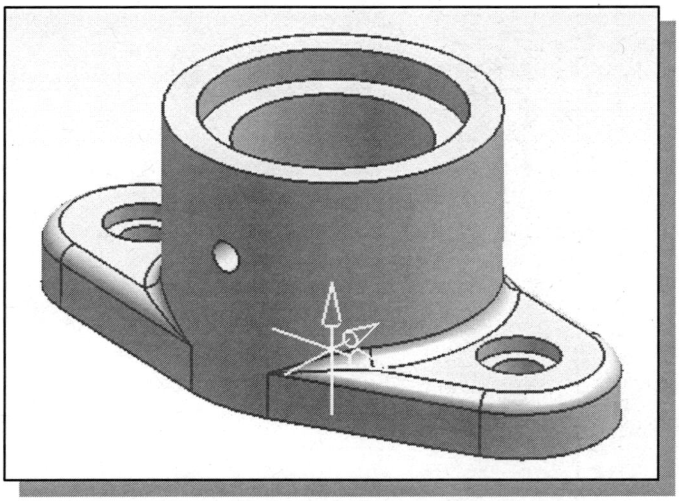

11. Right-mouse-click once on the ***Bearing*** part to bring up the option menu and select **Display Parent – Shaft-Support** in the option list as shown.

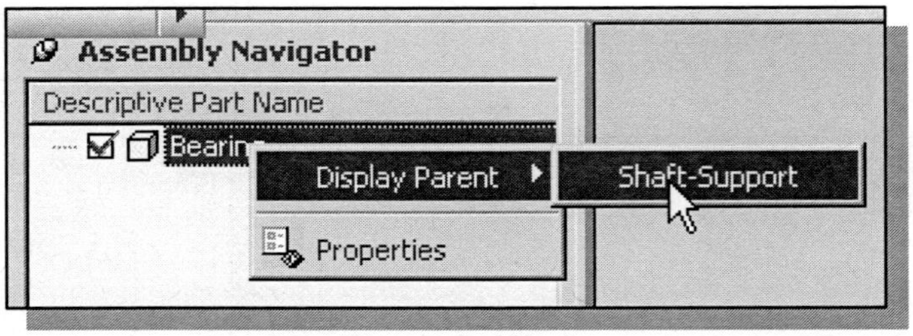

❖ Note that we are opening up the *Bearing* part in *NX Gateway* mode. We will need to switch to the *Part Editing* mode to edit the design.

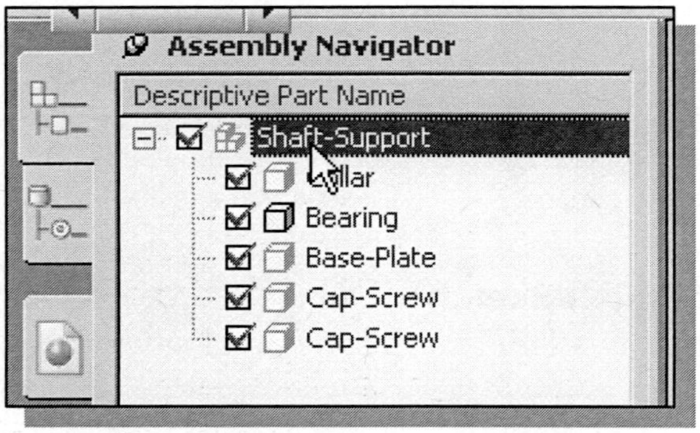

12. Double-click with the left-mouse-button on the *Shaft-Support* name to reactivate the assembly model.

➢ *UGS NX* has updated the *Bearing* part in all levels, including the current *Assembly* mode.

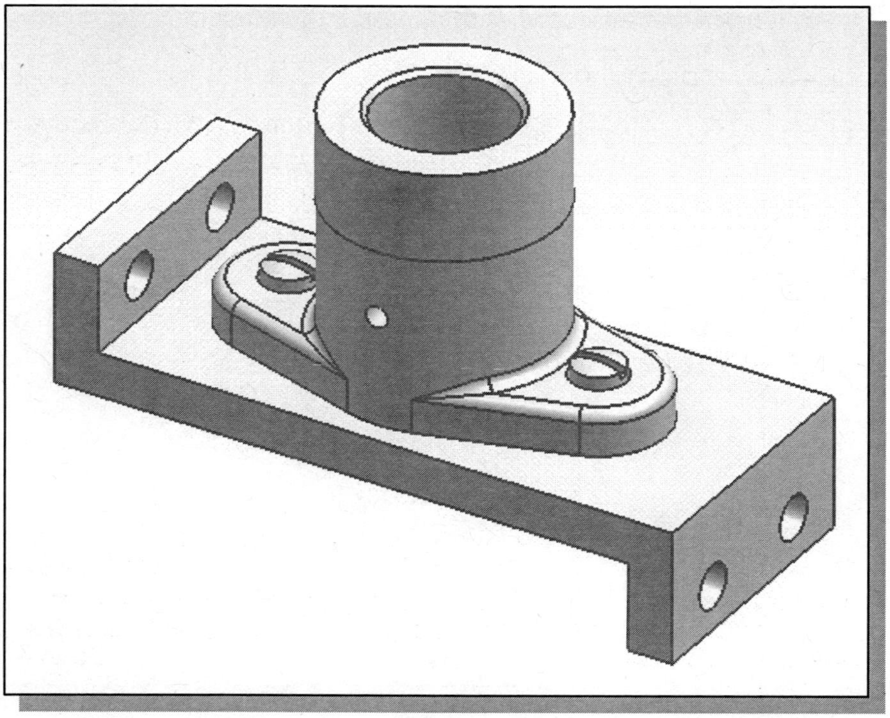

Set up a Drawing of the Assembly Model

1. Click on the **Start** icon in the *Standard* toolbar area to display the available options.

2. Select **Drafting** from the option list.

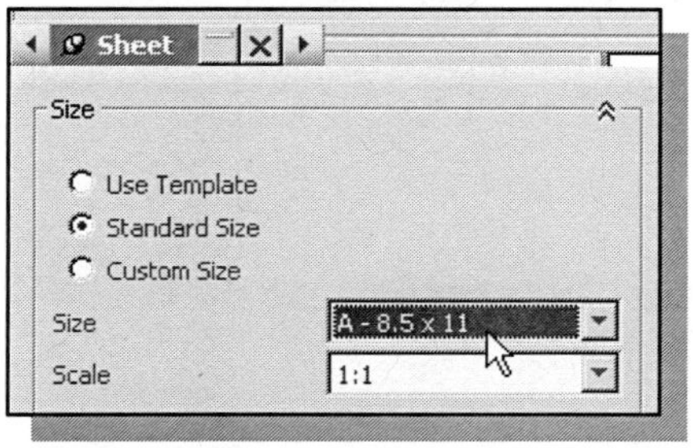

3. Select **A-8.5x11** from the sheet *Size* list. Confirm the *Scale* is set to **1:1**, which is *full scale*.

4. Confirm the *Projection* type is set to **3rd Angle Projection** and uncheck the **Automatically Start Base View Command** option.

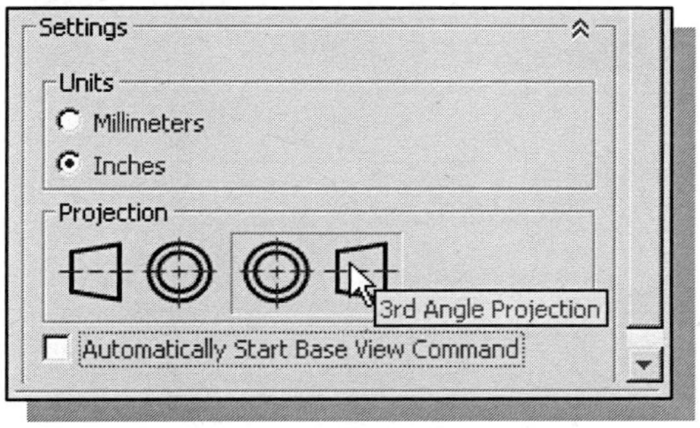

5. Click **OK** to accept the settings and proceed with the creation of the drawing sheet.

➢ Note that a new graphics window appears on the screen. The dashed rectangle indicates the size of the current active drawing sheet.

Importing the Title Block

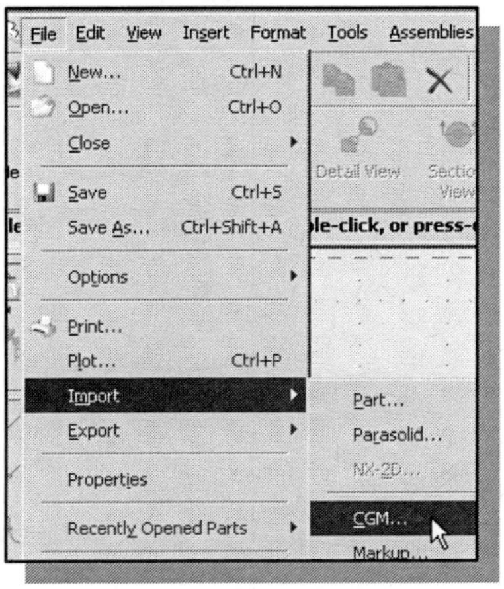

1. Select the **Import CGM** command through the *File* pull-down menu:

   [File] → [Import] → [CGM]

2. Enter or select **Title_A_Master_sheet 1.cgm** in the *Import CGM* window and click **OK** to proceed with importing the selected CGM file as shown.

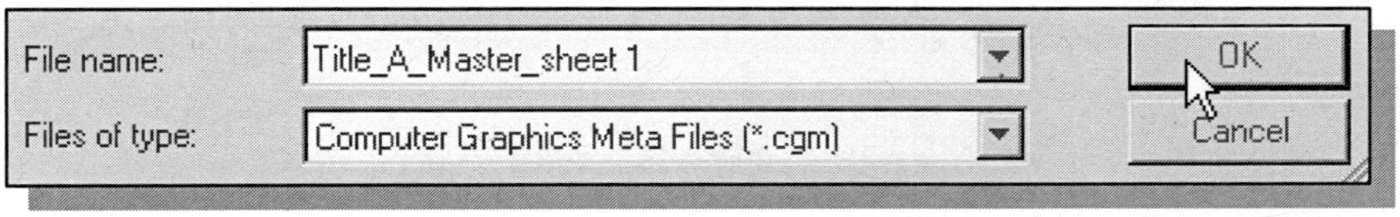

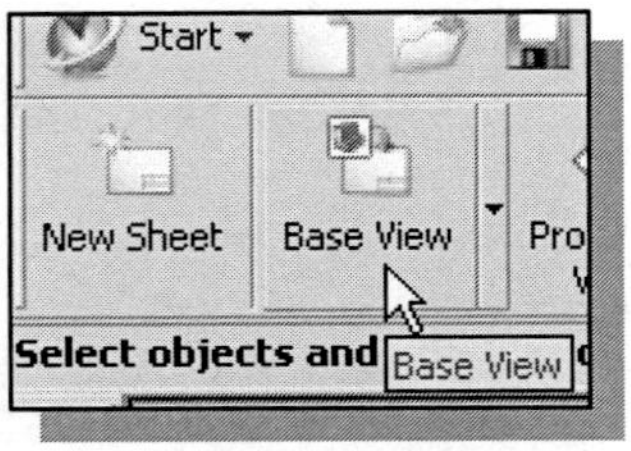

3. Click on **Base View** in the *Drawing Layout* toolbar to create a new base view.

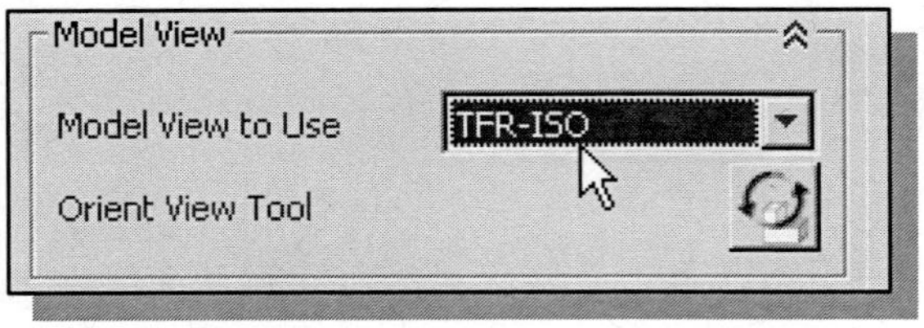

4. Select **TFR-ISO** in the view list, and place an isometric view to the right side of the drawing sheet as shown.

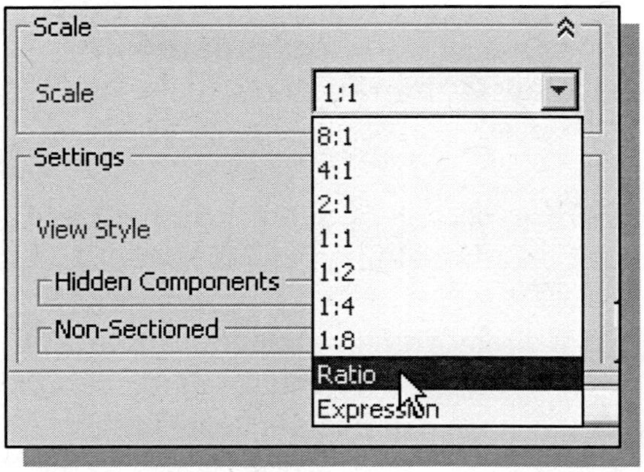

5. Click on the *Scale* option and choose **Ratio** as shown.

6. Set the *Scale* factor to **3.0:4.0** in the input box as shown (0.75 scale).

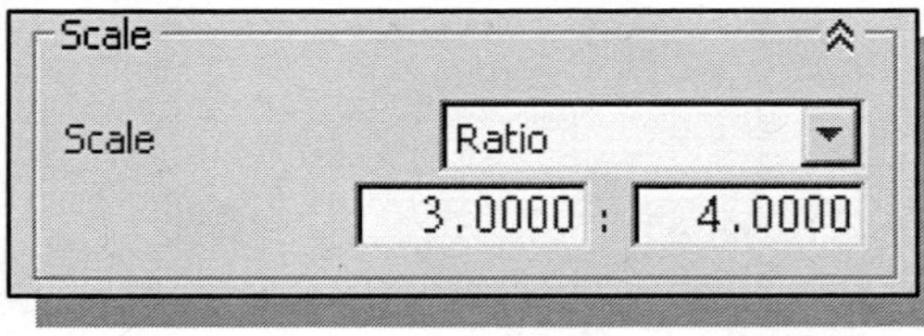

7. Move the cursor inside the graphics window and place the ***base*** view near the left side of the border as shown.

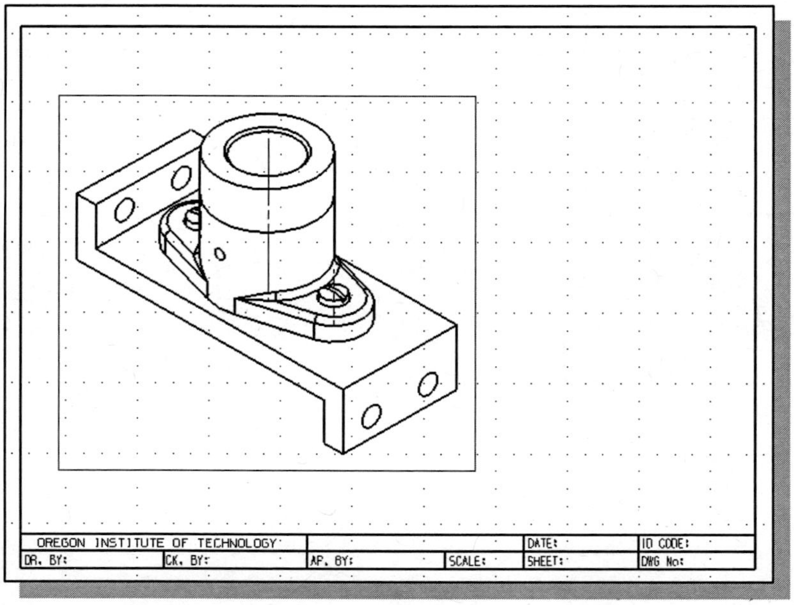

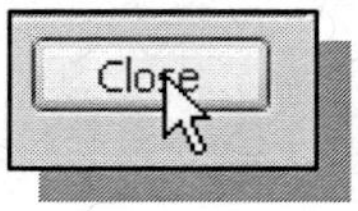

8. Click **Close** to exit the Base View option.

Creating a Parts List

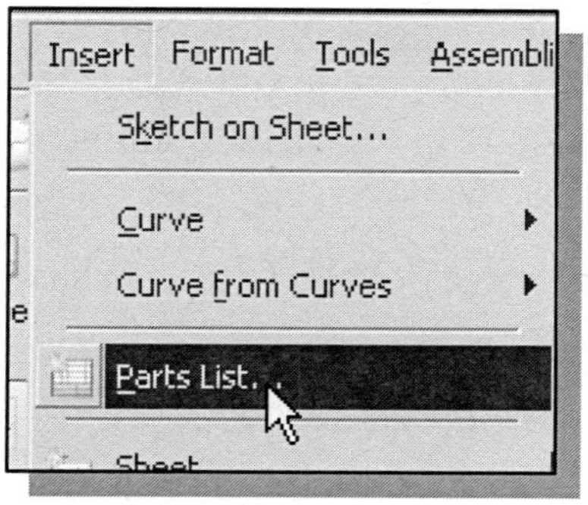

1. Select the **Parts List** command through the *Insert* pull-down menu:

   [Insert] → [Parts List]

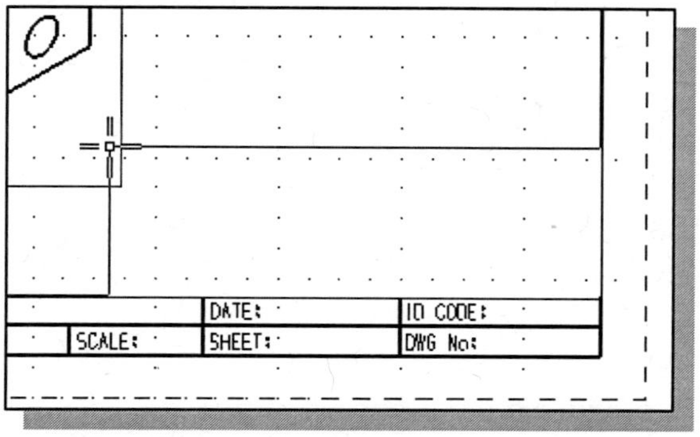

2. A rectangle representing a *Parts List* appears on the screen. Move the box so that it aligns with the upper right corner of the title block as shown.

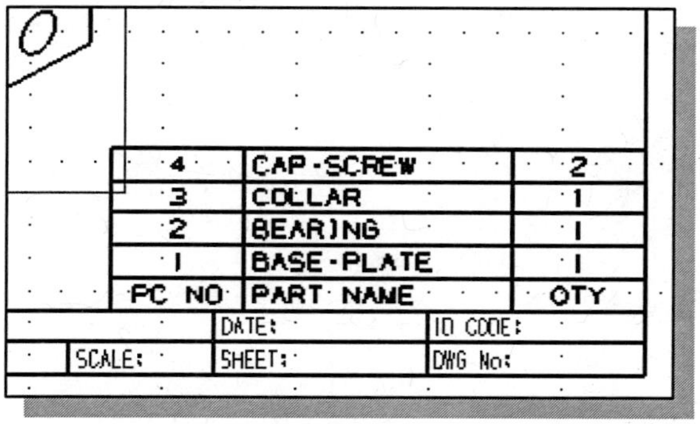

3. Click once with the left-mouse-button to place the ***parts list*** as shown.

- Note that *UGS NX* automatically fills in the parts list contents.

Completing the Assembly Drawing

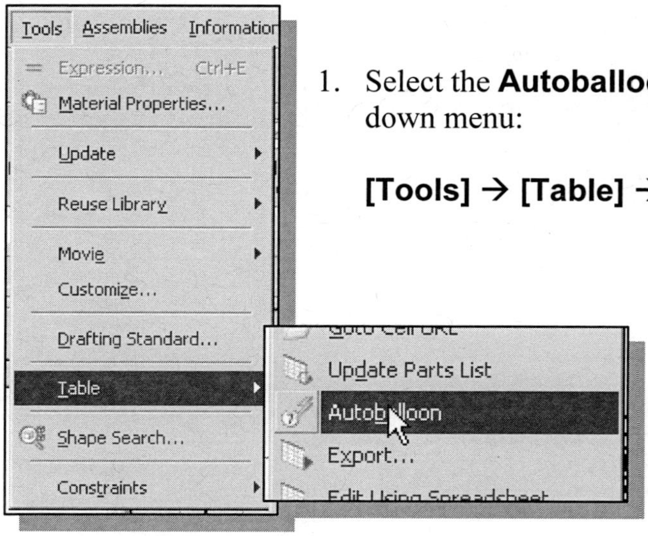

1. Select the **Autoballoon** command through the *Tools* pull-down menu:

   [Tools] → [Table] → [Autoballoon]

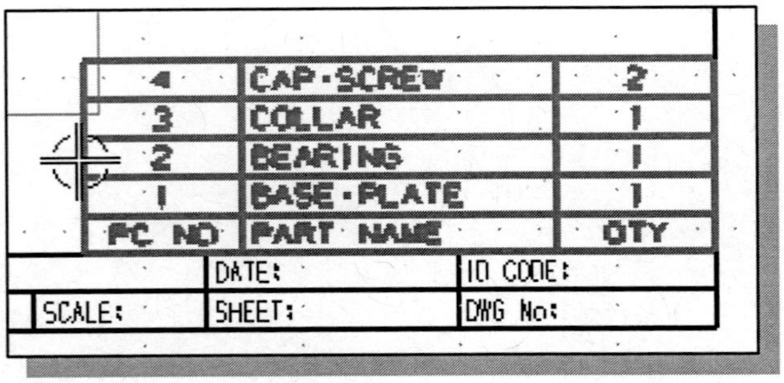

2. Select the parts list by clicking once with the left-mouse-button.

3. Click once with the middle-mouse-button to accept the selection.

- Note that *UGS NX* automatically creates the corresponding balloons based on the contents of the parts list.

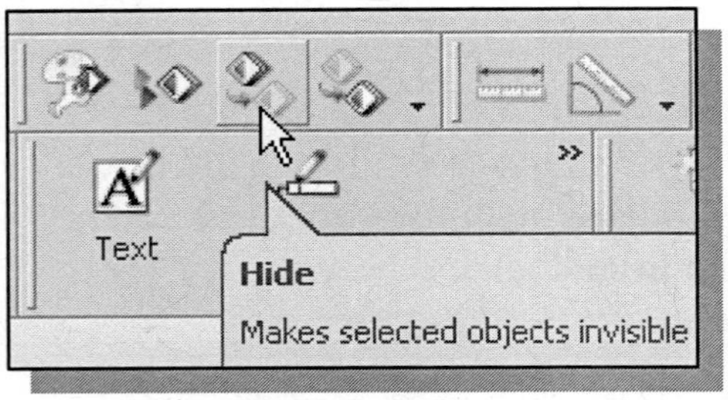

4. On your own, reposition the view and the balloons, and remove the center lines using the Hide command. (Hint: Use the Edit Associativity option to re-attach balloons, if necessary.)

5. On your own, fill in the title block and complete the drawing as shown.

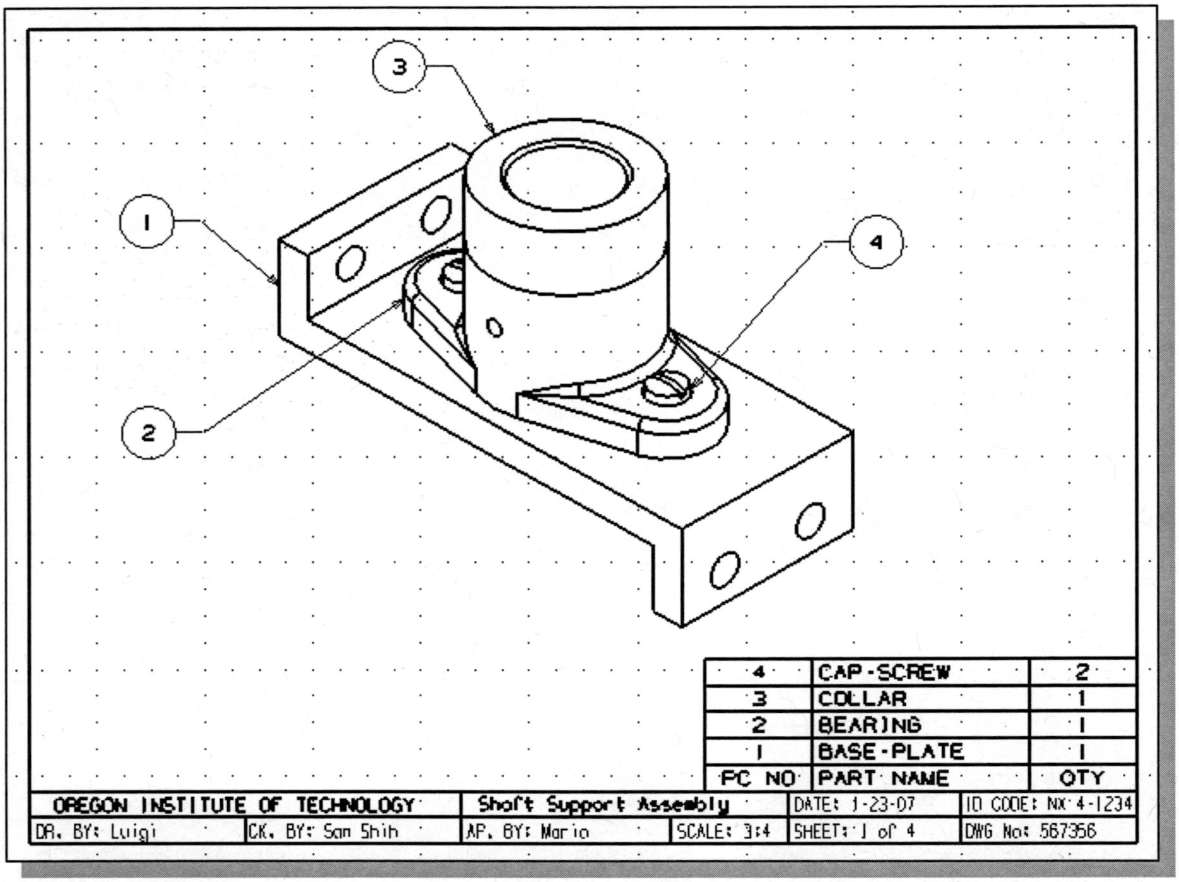

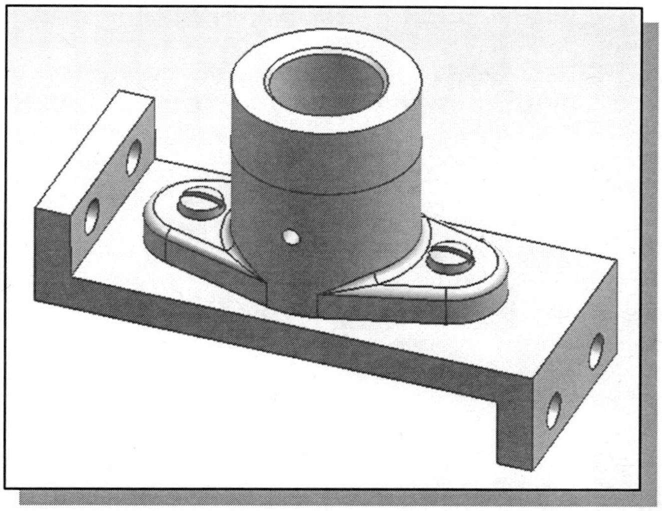

Conclusion

Design includes all activities involved from the original concept to the finished product. Design is the process by which products are created and modified. For many years designers sought ways to describe and analyze three-dimensional designs without building physical models. With advancements in computer technology, the creation of parametric models on computers offers a wide range of benefits. Parametric models are easier to interpret and can be easily altered. Parametric models can be analyzed using finite element analysis software, and simulation of real-life loads can be applied to the models and the results graphically displayed.

Throughout this text, various modeling techniques have been presented. Mastering these techniques will enable you to create intelligent and flexible solid models. The goal is to make use of the tools provided by *UGS NX* and to successfully capture the **DESIGN INTENT** of the product. In many instances, only a single approach to the modeling tasks was presented; you are encouraged to repeat all of the lessons and develop different ways of thinking in accomplishing the same tasks. We have only scratched the surface of *UGS NX*'s functionality. The more time you spend using the system, the easier it will be to perform parametric modeling with *UGS NX.*

Summary of Modeling Considerations

- **Design Intent** – Determine the functionality of the design; select features that are central to the design.
- **Order of Features** – Consider the parent/child relationships necessary for all features.
- **Dimensional and Geometric Constraints** – The way in which the constraints are applied determines how the components are updated.
- **Relations** – Consider the orientation and parametric relationships required between features and in an assembly.

Questions:

1. What is the purpose of using ***assembly constraints***?

2. List three of the commonly used ***assembly constraints***.

3. Describe the difference between the **Touch** constraint and the **Align** constraint.

4. In an assembly, can we place more than one copy of a part? How is it done?

5. How should we determine the assembly order of different parts in an assembly model?

6. How do we adjust the information listed in the **parts list** of an assembly drawing?

7. In *UGS NX*, describe the procedure to create **balloon callouts**?

8. Create sketches showing the steps you plan to use to create the four parts required for the assembly shown on the next page:

Ex.1)

Ex.2)

Ex.3)

Ex.4)

Exercises:

1. **Wheel Assembly** (Create a set of detail and assembly drawings. All dimensions are in mm.)

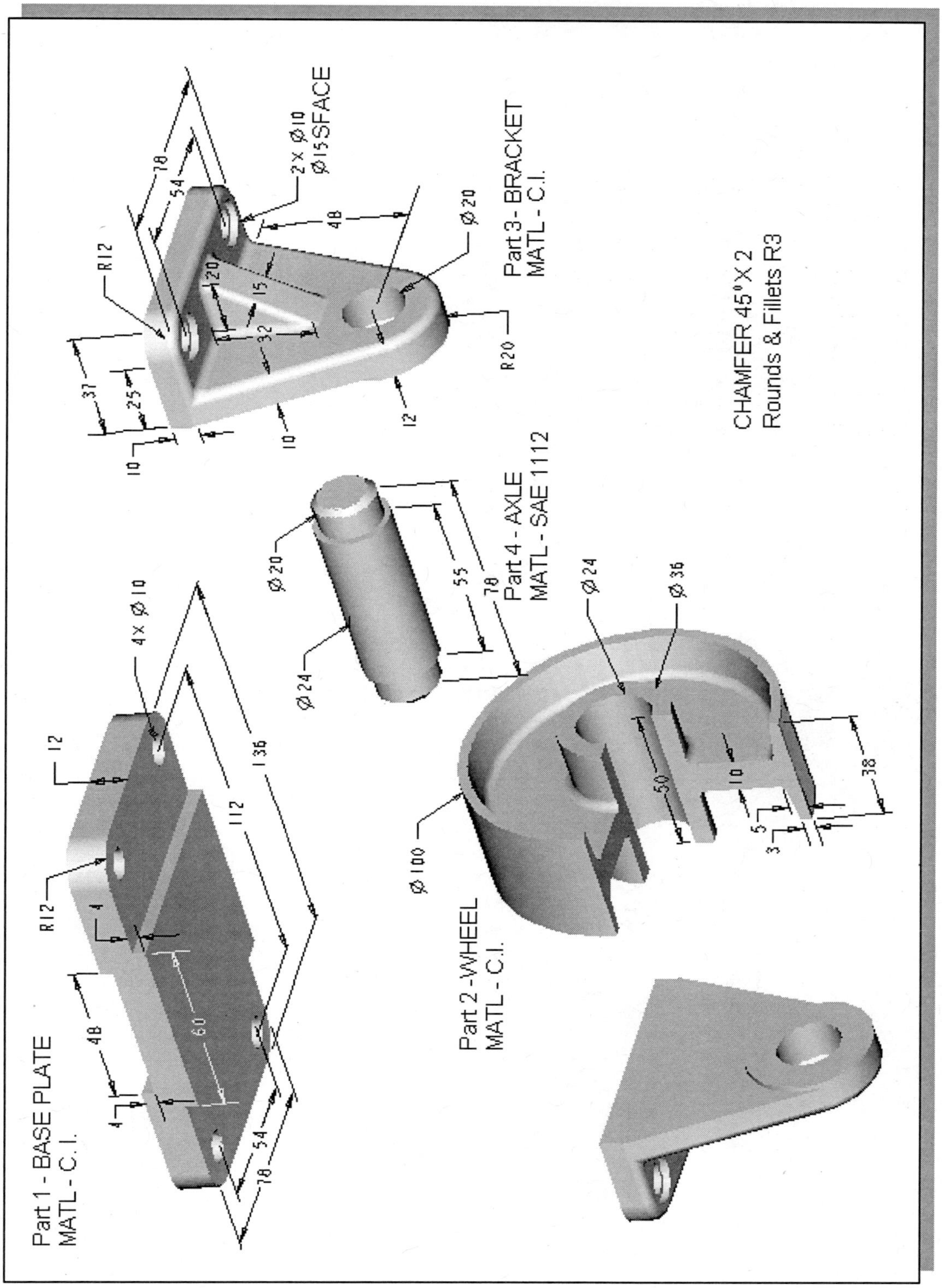

2. **Leveling Assembly** (Create a set of detail and assembly drawings. All dimensions are in mm.)

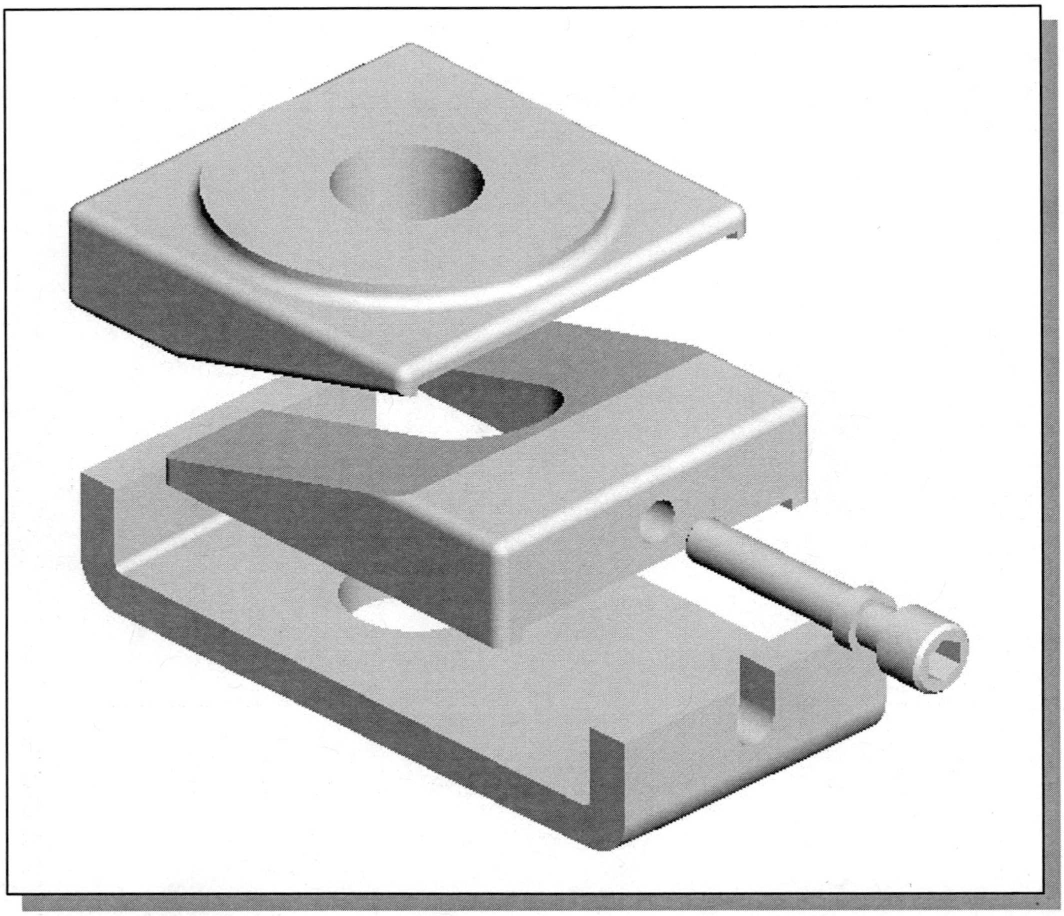

(a) **Base Plate**

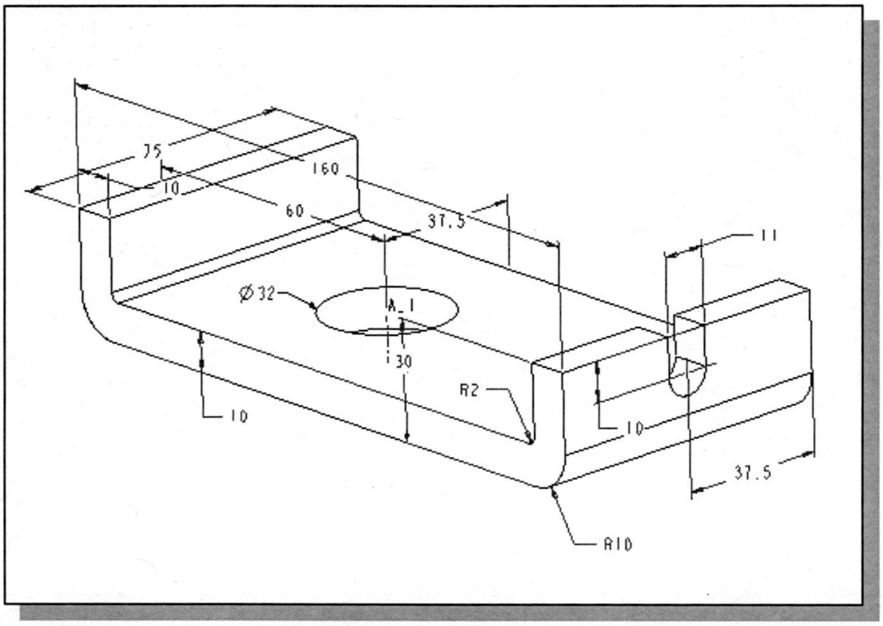

(b) **Sliding Block** (Rounds & Fillets: R3)

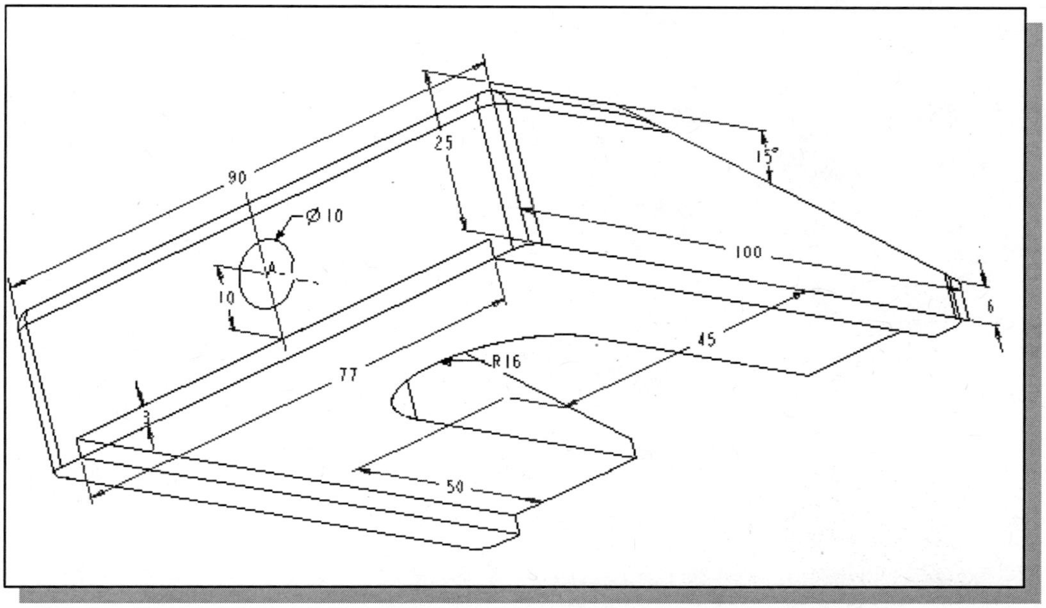

(c) **Lifting Block** (Rounds & Fillets: R3)

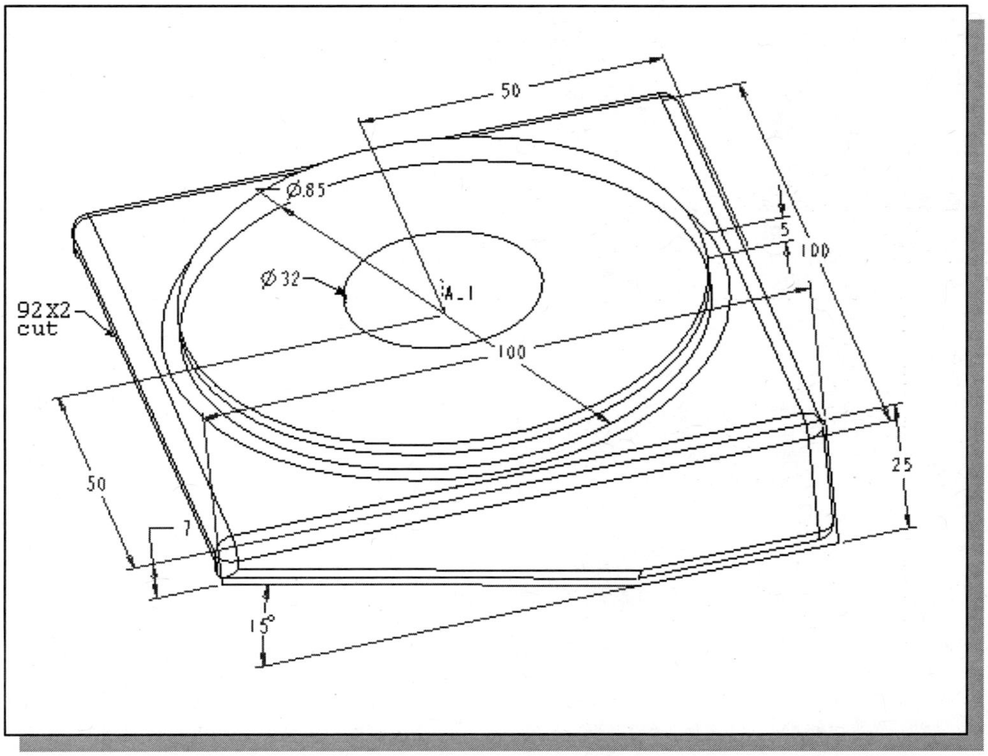

(d) **Adjusting Screw** (M10 × 1.5)

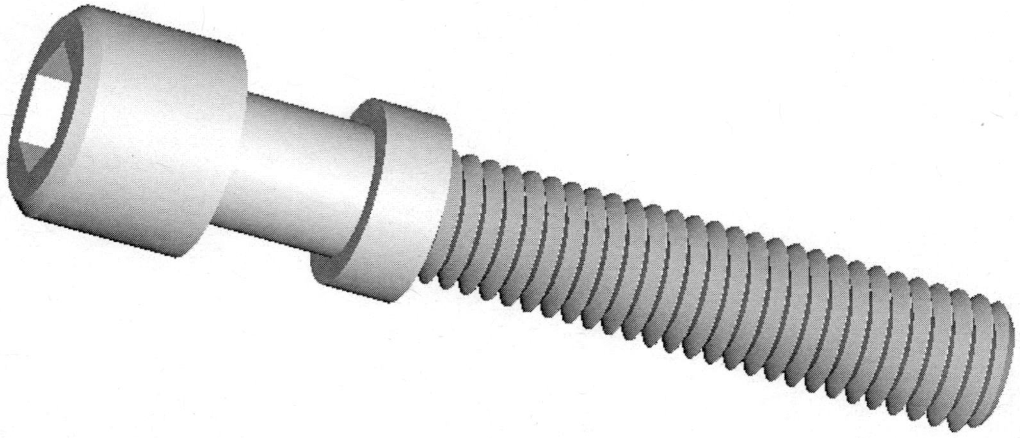

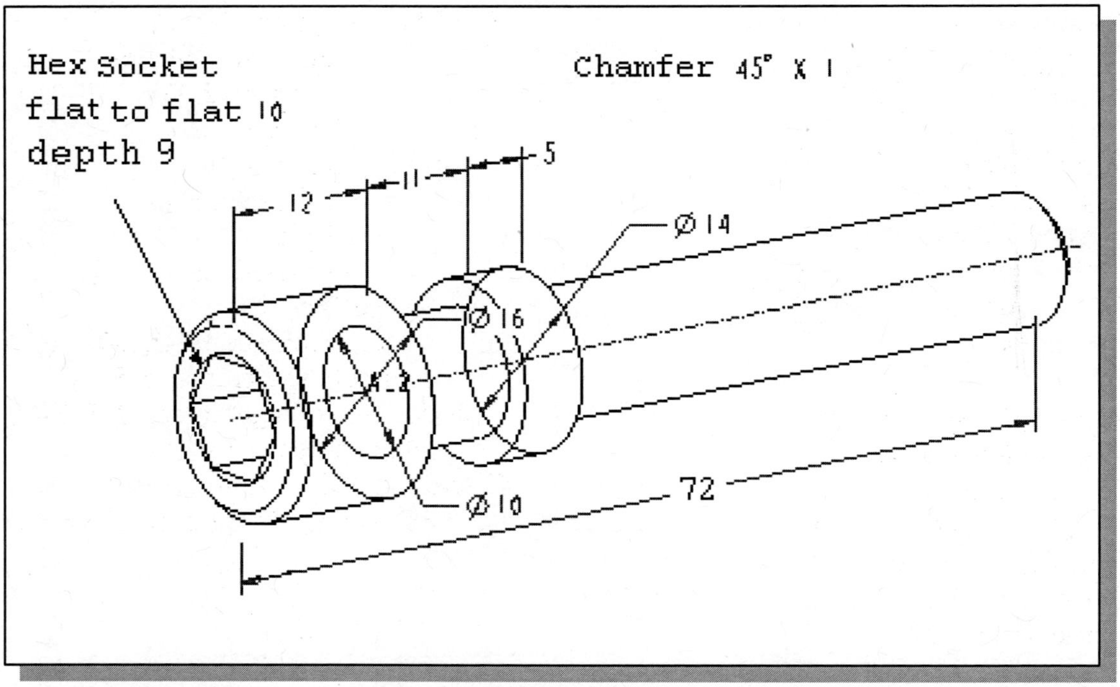

INDEX